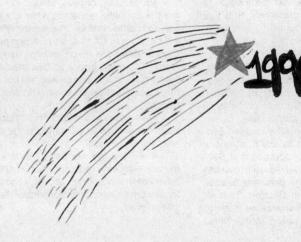

1999

Honda Accord L̶X̶
Automotive Repair Manual

by Jay Storer, Robert Maddox and John H Haynes

Member of the Guild of Motoring Writers

Models covered:

All Honda Accord models
1998 through 2002

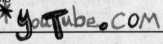
YouTube.COM

(42014 - 10V10)

ABCDE
FGHIJ
KLM

2

Haynes Publishing Group
Sparkford Nr Yeovil
Somerset BA22 7JJ England

Haynes North America, Inc
859 Lawrence Drive
Newbury Park
California 91320 USA
www.haynes.com

About this manual

Its purpose

The purpose of this manual is to help you get the best value from your vehicle. It can do so in several ways. It can help you decide what work must be done, even if you choose to have it done by a dealer service department or a repair shop; it provides information and procedures for routine maintenance and servicing; and it offers diagnostic and repair procedures to follow when trouble occurs.

We hope you use the manual to tackle the work yourself. For many simpler jobs, doing it yourself may be quicker than arranging an appointment to get the vehicle into a shop and making the trips to leave it and pick it up. More importantly, a lot of money can be saved by avoiding the expense the shop must pass on to you to cover its labor and overhead costs. An added benefit is the sense of satisfaction and accomplishment that you feel after doing the job yourself.

Using the manual

The manual is divided into Chapters. Each Chapter is divided into numbered Sections, which are headed in bold type between horizontal lines. Each Section consists of consecutively numbered paragraphs.

At the beginning of each numbered Section you will be referred to any illustrations which apply to the procedures in that Section. The reference numbers used in illustration captions pinpoint the pertinent Section and the Step within that Section. That is, illustration 3.2 means the illustration refers to Section 3 and Step (or paragraph) 2 within that Section.

Procedures, once described in the text, are not normally repeated. When it's necessary to refer to another Chapter, the reference will be given as Chapter and Section number. Cross references given without use of the word "Chapter" apply to Sections and/or paragraphs in the same Chapter. For example, "see Section 8" means in the same Chapter.

References to the left or right side of the vehicle assume you are sitting in the driver's seat, facing forward.

Even though we have prepared this manual with extreme care, neither the publisher nor the author can accept responsibility for any errors in, or omissions from, the information given.

NOTE

A **Note** provides information necessary to properly complete a procedure or information which will make the procedure easier to understand.

CAUTION

A **Caution** provides a special procedure or special steps which must be taken while completing the procedure where the Caution is found. Not heeding a Caution can result in damage to the assembly being worked on.

WARNING

A **Warning** provides a special procedure or special steps which must be taken while completing the procedure where the Warning is found. Not heeding a Warning can result in personal injury.

Acknowledgements

Technical writers who contributed to this project include Jeff Kibler. Wiring diagrams originated exclusively for Haynes North America, Inc. by Valley Forge Technical Communications

---

© **Haynes North America, Inc. 1999, 2004**
With permission from J.H. Haynes & Co. Ltd.

A book in the Haynes Automotive Repair Manual Series

Printed in Malaysia

All rights reserved. No part of this book may be reproduced or transmitted in any form or by any means, electronic or mechanical, including photocopying, recording or by any information storage or retrieval system, without permission in writing from the copyright holder.

ISBN-13: 978-1-56392-538-2

ISBN-10: 1-56392-538-9

Library of Congress Catalog Card Number 2004114520

While every attempt is made to ensure that the information in this manual is correct, no liability can be accepted by the authors or publishers for loss, damage or injury caused by any errors in, or omissions from, the information given.

Contents

Haynes photographer, mechanic and author with 1998 Honda Accord

Introduction to the Honda Accord

These models are available in two-door coupe and four-door sedan body styles.

The transversely mounted inline four-cylinder or V6 engines used in these models are equipped with electronic fuel injection.

The engine drives the front wheels through either a five-speed manual or a four-speed automatic transaxle via independent driveaxles.

Independent suspension, featuring coil spring/shock absorber units, is used on all four wheels. The power-assisted rack-and-pinion steering unit is mounted behind the engine.

The brakes are disc at the front and either disc or drum at the rear, with power assist standard. Some models are equipped with Anti-lock Braking Systems (ABS).

Vehicle identification numbers

Modifications are a continuing and unpublicized process in vehicle manufacturing. Since spare parts manuals and lists are compiled on a numerical basis, the individual vehicle numbers are essential to correctly identify the component required.

Vehicle identification number (VIN)

This very important number is stamped on the firewall in the engine compartment and on a plate attached to the dashboard inside the windshield on the driver's side of the vehicle. The VIN also appears on the Vehicle Certificate of Title and Registration. It contains information such as where and when the vehicle was manufactured, the model year and the body style **(see illustration)**.

VIN Engine and model year codes

Two particularly important pieces of information found in the VIN are the engine code and model year code. Counting from the left, the engine code designation is the sixth digit, and the model year code is the first digit after the star symbol at the center of the VIN.

Model year codes

W = 1998   1 = 2001
X = 1999   2 = 2002
Y = 2000

Engine codes

5= F23A1
6= F23A4
8= F23A5
1 or 2 = J30A1

The engine code number is commonly needed when ordering engine parts. Besides being a component of the VIN, this code can also be found near the right (passenger side) end of the engine, near the exhaust manifold on four-cylinder models **(see illustration)** or

The Vehicle Identification Number (VIN) is stamped into a metal plate fastened to the dashboard on the driver's side - it is visible through the windshield

under the starter motor on V6 models **(see illustration)**. The engine code is the first five digits of the number. The engines covered by this manual are:

F23A1........... 2.3L SOHC 16-valve VTEC four-cylinder
F23A4........... 2.3L SOHC 16-valve VTEC four-cylinder
F23A5........... 2.3L SOHC 16-valve four-cylinder
J30A1........... 3.0L SOHC 24-valve V6

Transaxle number

The transaxle number is commonly needed when ordering transaxle parts. On manual transaxles it's located on the bellhousing, near the starter motor. On automatic transaxles, it's located on the front of the transaxle case, above the dipstick **(see illustration)**.

The four-cylinder engine code number (arrow) is located near the exhaust manifold

The V6 engine code (arrow) is located on a pad near the left end of the front cylinder head

The Vehicle Safety Certification label is affixed to the bottom of the driver's door pillar

The transaxle code (V6 shown) is located on a pad near the starter motor - on four-cylinder models, it is located at the top of the transaxle/engine interface

Buying parts

Replacement parts are available from many sources, which generally fall into one of two categories - authorized dealer parts departments and independent retail auto parts stores. Our advice concerning these parts is as follows:

Retail auto parts stores: Good auto parts stores will stock frequently needed components which wear out relatively fast, such as clutch components, exhaust systems, brake parts, tune-up parts, etc. These stores often supply new or reconditioned parts on an exchange basis, which can save a considerable amount of money. Discount auto parts stores are often very good places to buy materials and parts needed for general vehicle maintenance such as oil, grease, filters, spark plugs, belts, touch-up paint, bulbs, etc. They also usually sell tools and general accessories, have convenient hours, charge lower prices and can often be found not far from home.

Authorized dealer parts department: This is the best source for parts which are unique to the vehicle and not generally available elsewhere (such as major engine parts, transmission parts, trim pieces, etc.).

Warranty information: If the vehicle is still covered under warranty, be sure that any replacement parts purchased - regardless of the source - do not invalidate the warranty!

To be sure of obtaining the correct parts, have engine and chassis numbers available and, if possible, take the old parts along for positive identification.

Maintenance techniques, tools and working facilities

Maintenance techniques

There are a number of techniques involved in maintenance and repair that will be referred to throughout this manual. Application of these techniques will enable the home mechanic to be more efficient, better organized and capable of performing the various tasks properly, which will ensure that the repair job is thorough and complete.

Fasteners

Fasteners are nuts, bolts, studs and screws used to hold two or more parts together. There are a few things to keep in mind when working with fasteners. Almost all of them use a locking device of some type, either a lockwasher, locknut, locking tab or thread adhesive. All threaded fasteners should be clean and straight, with undamaged threads and undamaged corners on the hex head where the wrench fits. Develop the habit of replacing all damaged nuts and bolts with new ones. Special locknuts with nylon or fiber inserts can only be used once. If they are removed, they lose their locking ability and must be replaced with new ones.

Rusted nuts and bolts should be treated with a penetrating fluid to ease removal and prevent breakage. Some mechanics use turpentine in a spout-type oil can, which works quite well. After applying the rust penetrant, let it work for a few minutes before trying to loosen the nut or bolt. Badly rusted fasteners may have to be chiseled or sawed off or removed with a special nut breaker, available at tool stores.

If a bolt or stud breaks off in an assembly, it can be drilled and removed with a special tool commonly available for this purpose. Most automotive machine shops can perform this task, as well as other repair procedures, such as the repair of threaded holes that have been stripped out.

Flat washers and lockwashers, when removed from an assembly, should always be replaced exactly as removed. Replace any damaged washers with new ones. Never use a lockwasher on any soft metal surface (such as aluminum), thin sheet metal or plastic.

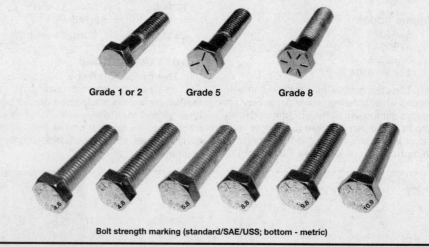

Grade 1 or 2   Grade 5   Grade 8

Bolt strength marking (standard/SAE/USS; bottom - metric)

Grade	Identification	Grade	Identification		
Hex Nut Grade 5	3 Dots	Hex Nut Property Class 9	Arabic 9	Class 10.9	
Hex Nut Grade 8	6 Dots	Hex Nut Property Class 10	Arabic 10	Class 9.8	Class 8.8
Standard hex nut strength markings		Metric hex nut strength markings		Metric stud strength markings	

Fastener sizes

For a number of reasons, automobile manufacturers are making wider and wider use of metric fasteners. Therefore, it is important to be able to tell the difference between standard (sometimes called U.S. or SAE) and metric hardware, since they cannot be interchanged.

All bolts, whether standard or metric, are sized according to diameter, thread pitch and length. For example, a standard 1/2 - 13 x 1 bolt is 1/2 inch in diameter, has 13 threads per inch and is 1 inch long. An M12 - 1.75 x 25 metric bolt is 12 mm in diameter, has a thread pitch of 1.75 mm (the distance between threads) and is 25 mm long. The two bolts are nearly identical, and easily confused, but they are not interchangeable.

In addition to the differences in diameter, thread pitch and length, metric and standard bolts can also be distinguished by examining the bolt heads. To begin with, the distance across the flats on a standard bolt head is measured in inches, while the same dimension on a metric bolt is sized in millimeters (the same is true for nuts). As a result, a standard wrench should not be used on a metric bolt and a metric wrench should not be used on a standard bolt. Also, most standard bolts have slashes radiating out from the center of the head to denote the grade or strength of the bolt, which is an indication of the amount of torque that can be applied to it. The greater the number of slashes, the greater the strength of the bolt. Grades 0 through 5 are commonly used on automobiles. Metric bolts have a property class (grade) number, rather than a slash, molded into their heads to indicate bolt strength. In this case, the higher the number, the stronger the bolt. Property class numbers 8.8, 9.8 and 10.9 are commonly used on automobiles.

Strength markings can also be used to distinguish standard hex nuts from metric hex nuts. Many standard nuts have dots stamped into one side, while metric nuts are marked with a number. The greater the number of dots, or the higher the number, the greater the strength of the nut.

Metric studs are also marked on their ends according to property class (grade). Larger studs are numbered (the same as metric bolts), while smaller studs carry a geometric code to denote grade.

It should be noted that many fasteners, especially Grades 0 through 2, have no distinguishing marks on them. When such is the case, the only way to determine whether it is standard or metric is to measure the thread pitch or compare it to a known fastener of the same size.

Standard fasteners are often referred to as SAE, as opposed to metric. However, it should be noted that SAE technically refers to a non-metric fine thread fastener only. Coarse thread non-metric fasteners are referred to as USS sizes.

Since fasteners of the same size (both standard and metric) may have different

Metric thread sizes	Ft-lbs	Nm
M-6	6 to 9	9 to 12
M-8	14 to 21	19 to 28
M-10	28 to 40	38 to 54
M-12	50 to 71	68 to 96
M-14	80 to 140	109 to 154

Pipe thread sizes		
1/8	5 to 8	7 to 10
1/4	12 to 18	17 to 24
3/8	22 to 33	30 to 44
1/2	25 to 35	34 to 47

U.S. thread sizes		
1/4 - 20	6 to 9	9 to 12
5/16 - 18	12 to 18	17 to 24
5/16 - 24	14 to 20	19 to 27
3/8 - 16	22 to 32	30 to 43
3/8 - 24	27 to 38	37 to 51
7/16 - 14	40 to 55	55 to 74
7/16 - 20	40 to 60	55 to 81
1/2 - 13	55 to 80	75 to 108

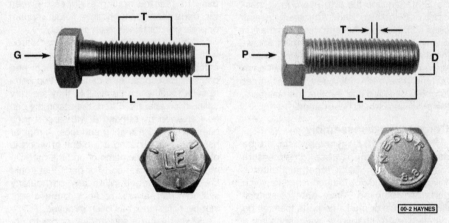

Standard (SAE and USS) bolt dimensions/ grade marks

G   Grade marks (bolt strength)
L   Length (in inches)
T   Thread pitch (number of threads per inch)
D   Nominal diameter (in inches)

Metric bolt dimensions/grade marks

P   Property class (bolt strength)
L   Length (in millimeters)
T   Thread pitch (distance between threads in millimeters)
D   Diameter

strength ratings, be sure to reinstall any bolts, studs or nuts removed from your vehicle in their original locations. Also, when replacing a fastener with a new one, make sure that the new one has a strength rating equal to or greater than the original.

Tightening sequences and procedures

Most threaded fasteners should be tightened to a specific torque value (torque is the twisting force applied to a threaded component such as a nut or bolt). Overtightening the fastener can weaken it and cause it to break, while undertightening can cause it to eventually come loose. Bolts, screws and studs, depending on the material they are made of and their thread diameters, have

specific torque values, many of which are noted in the Specifications at the beginning of each Chapter. Be sure to follow the torque recommendations closely. For fasteners not assigned a specific torque, a general torque value chart is presented here as a guide. These torque values are for dry (unlubricated) fasteners threaded into steel or cast iron (not aluminum). As was previously mentioned, the size and grade of a fastener determine the amount of torque that can safely be applied to it. The figures listed here are approximate for Grade 2 and Grade 3 fasteners. Higher grades can tolerate higher torque values.

Fasteners laid out in a pattern, such as cylinder head bolts, oil pan bolts, differential cover bolts, etc., must be loosened or tightened in sequence to avoid warping the com-

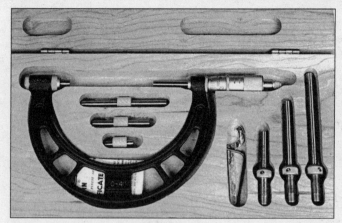

Micrometer set

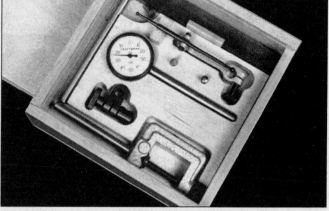

Dial indicator set

ponent. This sequence will normally be shown in the appropriate Chapter. If a specific pattern is not given, the following procedures can be used to prevent warping.

Initially, the bolts or nuts should be assembled finger-tight only. Next, they should be tightened one full turn each, in a criss-cross or diagonal pattern. After each one has been tightened one full turn, return to the first one and tighten them all one-half turn, following the same pattern. Finally, tighten each of them one-quarter turn at a time until each fastener has been tightened to the proper torque. To loosen and remove the fasteners, the procedure would be reversed.

Component disassembly

Component disassembly should be done with care and purpose to help ensure that the parts go back together properly. Always keep track of the sequence in which parts are removed. Make note of special characteristics or marks on parts that can be installed more than one way, such as a grooved thrust washer on a shaft. It is a good idea to lay the disassembled parts out on a clean surface in the order that they were removed. It may also be helpful to make sketches or take instant photos of components before removal.

When removing fasteners from a component, keep track of their locations. Sometimes threading a bolt back in a part, or putting the washers and nut back on a stud, can prevent mix-ups later. If nuts and bolts cannot be returned to their original locations, they should be kept in a compartmented box or a series of small boxes. A cupcake or muffin tin is ideal for this purpose, since each cavity can hold the bolts and nuts from a particular area (i.e. oil pan bolts, valve cover bolts, engine mount bolts, etc.). A pan of this type is especially helpful when working on assemblies with very small parts, such as the carburetor, alternator, valve train or interior dash and trim pieces. The cavities can be marked with paint or tape to identify the contents.

Whenever wiring looms, harnesses or connectors are separated, it is a good idea to

identify the two halves with numbered pieces of masking tape so they can be easily reconnected.

Gasket sealing surfaces

Throughout any vehicle, gaskets are used to seal the mating surfaces between two parts and keep lubricants, fluids, vacuum or pressure contained in an assembly.

Many times these gaskets are coated with a liquid or paste-type gasket sealing compound before assembly. Age, heat and pressure can sometimes cause the two parts to stick together so tightly that they are very difficult to separate. Often, the assembly can be loosened by striking it with a soft-face hammer near the mating surfaces. A regular hammer can be used if a block of wood is placed between the hammer and the part. Do not hammer on cast parts or parts that could be easily damaged. With any particularly stubborn part, always recheck to make sure that every fastener has been removed.

Avoid using a screwdriver or bar to pry apart an assembly, as they can easily mar the gasket sealing surfaces of the parts, which must remain smooth. If prying is absolutely necessary, use an old broom handle, but keep in mind that extra clean up will be necessary if the wood splinters.

After the parts are separated, the old gasket must be carefully scraped off and the gasket surfaces cleaned. Stubborn gasket material can be soaked with rust penetrant or treated with a special chemical to soften it so it can be easily scraped off. A scraper can be fashioned from a piece of copper tubing by flattening and sharpening one end. Copper is recommended because it is usually softer than the surfaces to be scraped, which reduces the chance of gouging the part. Some gaskets can be removed with a wire brush, but regardless of the method used, the mating surfaces must be left clean and smooth. If for some reason the gasket surface is gouged, then a gasket sealer thick enough to fill scratches will have to be used during reassembly of the components. For most applications, a non-drying (or semi-drying) gasket sealer should be used.

Hose removal tips

Warning: *If the vehicle is equipped with air conditioning, do not disconnect any of the A/C hoses without first having the system depressurized by a dealer service department or a service station.*

Hose removal precautions closely parallel gasket removal precautions. Avoid scratching or gouging the surface that the hose mates against or the connection may leak. This is especially true for radiator hoses. Because of various chemical reactions, the rubber in hoses can bond itself to the metal spigot that the hose fits over. To remove a hose, first loosen the hose clamps that secure it to the spigot. Then, with slip-joint pliers, grab the hose at the clamp and rotate it around the spigot. Work it back and forth until it is completely free, then pull it off. Silicone or other lubricants will ease removal if they can be applied between the hose and the outside of the spigot. Apply the same lubricant to the inside of the hose and the outside of the spigot to simplify installation.

As a last resort (and if the hose is to be replaced with a new one anyway), the rubber can be slit with a knife and the hose peeled from the spigot. If this must be done, be careful that the metal connection is not damaged.

If a hose clamp is broken or damaged, do not reuse it. Wire-type clamps usually weaken with age, so it is a good idea to replace them with screw-type clamps whenever a hose is removed.

Tools

A selection of good tools is a basic requirement for anyone who plans to maintain and repair his or her own vehicle. For the owner who has few tools, the initial investment might seem high, but when compared to the spiraling costs of professional auto maintenance and repair, it is a wise one.

To help the owner decide which tools are needed to perform the tasks detailed in this manual, the following tool lists are offered: *Maintenance and minor repair, Repair/overhaul* and *Special.*

The newcomer to practical mechanics

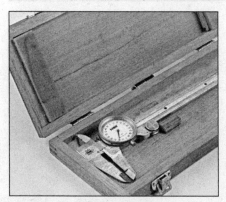

Dial caliper

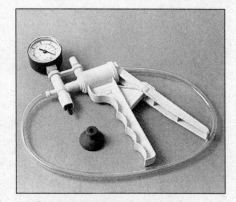

Hand-operated vacuum pump

Timing light

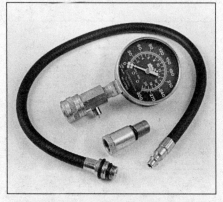

Compression gauge with spark plug
hole adapter

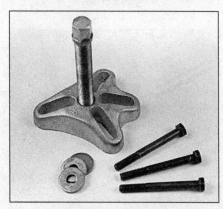

Damper/steering wheel puller

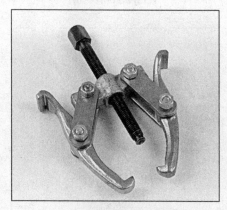

General purpose puller

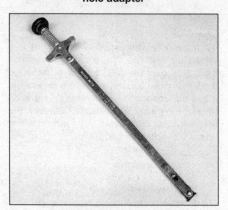

Hydraulic lifter removal tool

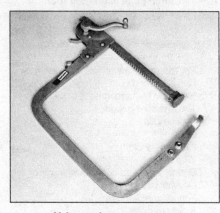

Valve spring compressor

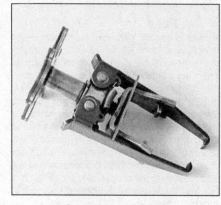

Valve spring compressor

Ridge reamer

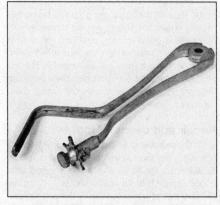

Piston ring groove cleaning tool

Ring removal/installation tool

Ring compressor

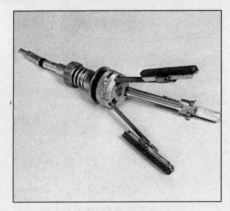

Cylinder hone

Brake hold-down spring tool

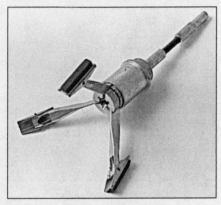

Brake cylinder hone

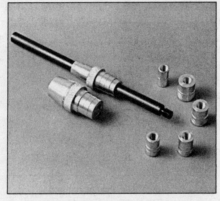

Clutch plate alignment tool

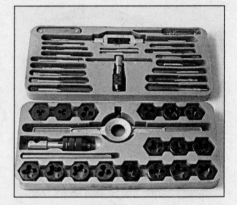

Tap and die set

should start off with the *maintenance and minor repair* tool kit, which is adequate for the simpler jobs performed on a vehicle. Then, as confidence and experience grow, the owner can tackle more difficult tasks, buying additional tools as they are needed. Eventually the basic kit will be expanded into the *repair and overhaul* tool set. Over a period of time, the experienced do-it-yourselfer will assemble a tool set complete enough for most repair and overhaul procedures and will add tools from the special category when it is felt that the expense is justified by the frequency of use.

Maintenance and minor repair tool kit

The tools in this list should be considered the minimum required for performance of routine maintenance, servicing and minor repair work. We recommend the purchase of combination wrenches (box-end and open-end combined in one wrench). While more expensive than open end wrenches, they offer the advantages of both types of wrench.

Combination wrench set (1/4-inch to 1 inch or 6 mm to 19 mm)
Adjustable wrench, 8 inch
Spark plug wrench with rubber insert
Spark plug gap adjusting tool
Feeler gauge set
Brake bleeder wrench

Standard screwdriver (5/16-inch x 6 inch)
Phillips screwdriver (No. 2 x 6 inch)
Combination pliers - 6 inch
Hacksaw and assortment of blades
Tire pressure gauge
Grease gun
Oil can
Fine emery cloth
Wire brush
Battery post and cable cleaning tool
Oil filter wrench
Funnel (medium size)
Safety goggles
Jackstands (2)
Drain pan

Note: *If basic tune-ups are going to be part of routine maintenance, it will be necessary to purchase a good quality stroboscopic timing light and combination tachometer/dwell meter. Although they are included in the list of special tools, it is mentioned here because they are absolutely necessary for tuning most vehicles properly.*

Repair and overhaul tool set

These tools are essential for anyone who plans to perform major repairs and are in addition to those in the maintenance and minor repair tool kit. Included is a comprehensive set of sockets which, though expensive, are invaluable because of their versatil-

ity, especially when various extensions and drives are available. We recommend the 1/2-inch drive over the 3/8-inch drive. Although the larger drive is bulky and more expensive, it has the capacity of accepting a very wide range of large sockets. Ideally, however, the mechanic should have a 3/8-inch drive set and a 1/2-inch drive set.

Socket set(s)
Reversible ratchet
Extension - 10 inch
Universal joint
Torque wrench (same size drive as sockets)
Ball peen hammer - 8 ounce
Soft-face hammer (plastic/rubber)
Standard screwdriver (1/4-inch x 6 inch)
Standard screwdriver (stubby - 5/16-inch)
Phillips screwdriver (No. 3 x 8 inch)
Phillips screwdriver (stubby - No. 2)
Pliers - vise grip
Pliers - lineman's
Pliers - needle nose
Pliers - snap-ring (internal and external)
Cold chisel - 1/2-inch
Scribe
Scraper (made from flattened copper tubing)
Centerpunch
Pin punches (1/16, 1/8, 3/16-inch)
Steel rule/straightedge - 12 inch

*Allen wrench set (1/8 to 3/8-inch or
    4 mm to 10 mm)*
A selection of files
Wire brush (large)
Jackstands (second set)
Jack (scissor or hydraulic type)

Note: *Another tool which is often useful is an electric drill with a chuck capacity of 3/8-inch and a set of good quality drill bits.*

Special tools

The tools in this list include those which are not used regularly, are expensive to buy, or which need to be used in accordance with their manufacturer's instructions. Unless these tools will be used frequently, it is not very economical to purchase many of them. A consideration would be to split the cost and use between yourself and a friend or friends. In addition, most of these tools can be obtained from a tool rental shop on a temporary basis.

This list primarily contains only those tools and instruments widely available to the public, and not those special tools produced by the vehicle manufacturer for distribution to dealer service departments. Occasionally, references to the manufacturer's special tools are included in the text of this manual. Generally, an alternative method of doing the job without the special tool is offered. However, sometimes there is no alternative to their use. Where this is the case, and the tool cannot be purchased or borrowed, the work should be turned over to the dealer service department or an automotive repair shop.

Valve spring compressor
Piston ring groove cleaning tool
Piston ring compressor
Piston ring installation tool
Cylinder compression gauge
Cylinder ridge reamer
Cylinder surfacing hone
Cylinder bore gauge
Micrometers and/or dial calipers
Hydraulic lifter removal tool
Balljoint separator
Universal-type puller
Impact screwdriver
Dial indicator set
*Stroboscopic timing light (inductive
    pick-up)*
Hand operated vacuum/pressure pump
Tachometer/dwell meter
Universal electrical multimeter
Cable hoist
*Brake spring removal and installation
    tools*
Floor jack

Buying tools

For the do-it-yourselfer who is just starting to get involved in vehicle maintenance and repair, there are a number of options available when purchasing tools. If maintenance and minor repair is the extent of the work to be done, the purchase of individual tools is satisfactory. If, on the other hand, extensive work is planned, it would be a good idea to purchase a modest tool set from one of the large retail chain stores. A set can usually be bought at a substantial savings over the individual tool prices, and they often come with a tool box. As additional tools are needed, add-on sets, individual tools and a larger tool box can be purchased to expand the tool selection. Building a tool set gradually allows the cost of the tools to be spread over a longer period of time and gives the mechanic the freedom to choose only those tools that will actually be used.

Tool stores will often be the only source of some of the special tools that are needed, but regardless of where tools are bought, try to avoid cheap ones, especially when buying screwdrivers and sockets, because they won't last very long. The expense involved in replacing cheap tools will eventually be greater than the initial cost of quality tools.

Care and maintenance of tools

Good tools are expensive, so it makes sense to treat them with respect. Keep them clean and in usable condition and store them properly when not in use. Always wipe off any dirt, grease or metal chips before putting them away. Never leave tools lying around in the work area. Upon completion of a job, always check closely under the hood for tools that may have been left there so they won't get lost during a test drive.

Some tools, such as screwdrivers, pliers, wrenches and sockets, can be hung on a panel mounted on the garage or workshop wall, while others should be kept in a tool box or tray. Measuring instruments, gauges, meters, etc. must be carefully stored where they cannot be damaged by weather or impact from other tools.

When tools are used with care and stored properly, they will last a very long time. Even with the best of care, though, tools will wear out if used frequently. When a tool is damaged or worn out, replace it. Subsequent jobs will be safer and more enjoyable if you do.

How to repair damaged threads

Sometimes, the internal threads of a nut or bolt hole can become stripped, usually from overtightening. Stripping threads is an all-too-common occurrence, especially when working with aluminum parts, because aluminum is so soft that it easily strips out.

Usually, external or internal threads are only partially stripped. After they've been cleaned up with a tap or die, they'll still work. Sometimes, however, threads are badly damaged. When this happens, you've got three choices:

1) *Drill and tap the hole to the next suitable oversize and install a larger diameter bolt, screw or stud.*
2) *Drill and tap the hole to accept a threaded plug, then drill and tap the plug to the original screw size. You can also buy a plug already threaded to the original size. Then you simply drill a hole to*
the specified size, then run the threaded plug into the hole with a bolt and jam nut. Once the plug is fully seated, remove the jam nut and bolt.
3) *The third method uses a patented thread repair kit like Heli-Coil or Slimsert. These easy-to-use kits are designed to repair damaged threads in straight-through holes and blind holes. Both are available as kits which can handle a variety of sizes and thread patterns. Drill the hole, then tap it with the special included tap. Install the Heli-Coil and the hole is back to its original diameter and thread pitch.*

Regardless of which method you use, be sure to proceed calmly and carefully. A little impatience or carelessness during one of these relatively simple procedures can ruin your whole day's work and cost you a bundle if you wreck an expensive part.

Working facilities

Not to be overlooked when discussing tools is the workshop. If anything more than routine maintenance is to be carried out, some sort of suitable work area is essential.

It is understood, and appreciated, that many home mechanics do not have a good workshop or garage available, and end up removing an engine or doing major repairs outside. It is recommended, however, that the overhaul or repair be completed under the cover of a roof.

A clean, flat workbench or table of comfortable working height is an absolute necessity. The workbench should be equipped with a vise that has a jaw opening of at least four inches.

As mentioned previously, some clean, dry storage space is also required for tools, as well as the lubricants, fluids, cleaning solvents, etc. which soon become necessary.

Sometimes waste oil and fluids, drained from the engine or cooling system during normal maintenance or repairs, present a disposal problem. To avoid pouring them on the ground or into a sewage system, pour the used fluids into large containers, seal them with caps and take them to an authorized disposal site or recycling center. Plastic jugs, such as old antifreeze containers, are ideal for this purpose.

Always keep a supply of old newspapers and clean rags available. Old towels are excellent for mopping up spills. Many mechanics use rolls of paper towels for most work because they are readily available and disposable. To help keep the area under the vehicle clean, a large cardboard box can be cut open and flattened to protect the garage or shop floor.

Whenever working over a painted surface, such as when leaning over a fender to service something under the hood, always cover it with an old blanket or bedspread to protect the finish. Vinyl covered pads, made especially for this purpose, are available at auto parts stores.

Jacking and towing

Jacking

Warning: *The jack supplied with the vehicle should only be used for changing a tire or placing jackstands under the frame. Never work under the vehicle or start the engine while this jack is being used as the only means of support.*

The vehicle should be on level ground. Place the shift lever in Park, if you have an automatic, or Reverse if you have a manual transaxle. Block the wheel diagonally opposite the wheel being changed. Set the parking brake.

Remove the spare tire and jack from stowage. Remove the wheel cover and trim ring (if so equipped) with the tapered end of the lug nut wrench by inserting and twisting the handle and then prying against the back of the wheel cover. **Caution:** *On some models the wheel cover can't be removed by prying; the wheel nuts must be removed first.* Loosen, but do not remove, the lug nuts (one-half turn is sufficient).

Place the scissors-type jack under the side of the vehicle and adjust the jack height until the slot in the jack head engages with the raised portion of the ridge on the vertical rocker panel flange nearest the wheel to be changed. There is a front and rear jacking point on each side of the vehicle **(see illustration)**.

Turn the jack handle clockwise until the tire clears the ground. Remove the lug nuts and pull the wheel off. Replace it with the spare.

Install the lug nuts with the beveled edges facing in. Tighten them snugly. Don't attempt to tighten them completely until the vehicle is lowered or it could slip off the jack. Turn the jack handle counterclockwise to lower the vehicle. Remove the jack and tighten the lug nuts in a criss-cross pattern.

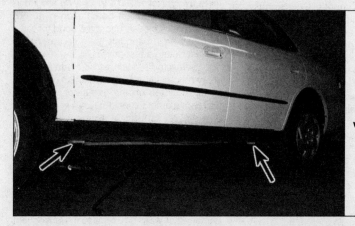

The jacking points are located near the front and rear wheel on each side of the vehicle

Install the cover (and trim ring, if used) and be sure it's snapped into place all the way around.

Stow the tire, jack and wrench. Unblock the wheels.

Towing

As a general rule, the vehicle should be towed with the front (drive) wheels off the ground (the best method is to have the vehicle placed on a flat-bed tow truck). If they can't be raised, place them on a dolly. The ignition key must be in the OFF position, since the steering lock mechanism isn't strong enough to hold the front wheels straight while towing.

Vehicles equipped with an automatic transaxle can be towed from the front with all four wheels on the ground, provided that speeds don't exceed 35 mph and the distance is not over 50 miles. Before towing, check the transmission fluid level (see Chapter 1). If the level is below the HOT line on the dipstick, add fluid or use a towing dolly. Additionally, perform the following steps:

a) Release the parking brake
b) Start the engine
c) Move the transaxle gear selector into D4, then to Neutral
d) Turn off the engine
e) Place the ignition key in the OFF (not the LOCK position).

Caution: *Never tow a vehicle with an automatic transaxle from the rear with the front wheels on the ground.*

When towing a vehicle equipped with a manual transaxle or Continuously Variable Transaxle with all four wheels on the ground, be sure to place the shift lever in neutral and release the parking brake.

Equipment specifically designed for towing should be used. It should be attached to the main structural members of the vehicle, not the bumpers or brackets.

Safety is a major consideration when towing and all applicable state and local laws must be obeyed. A safety chain system must be used at all times. Remember that power steering and power brakes will not work with the engine off.

Anti-theft audio system

1   All EX models were originally equipped with an audio system which includes an anti-theft feature that will render the stereo inoperative. If the power source to the stereo is cut, the stereo will not work until a five-digit code (furnished with the vehicle when it was originally purchased from the dealer) is entered. Even if the power is immediately reconnected, the stereo will not function. If your vehicle is equipped with this anti-theft system, do not disconnect the battery, remove the number 9 (20a) fuse in the under-hood fuse block or remove the stereo unless you have the code number for the stereo.

2   Refer to your vehicle's owner's manual for more complete information on this audio system and it's anti-theft feature.

Unlocking the stereo after a power loss

3   Turn on the radio. The word "CODE" should appear on the display.

4   Using the station reset selector buttons, enter the five-digit code. If you make a mistake when entering the code, continue the five digit sequence anyway - the radio will "beep" after the five digits are entered. **Note:** *You have ten attempts to enter the correct code.*

5   Once the code has been entered correctly, the wore "CODE" should disappear from the display and the radio should play (you'll have to tune in and enter your preset stations, however).

Booster battery (jump) starting

Observe these precautions when using a booster battery to start a vehicle:

 a) *Before connecting the booster battery, make sure the ignition switch is in the Off position.*
 b) *Turn off the lights, heater and other electrical loads.*
 c) *Your eyes should be shielded. Safety goggles are a good idea.*
 d) *Make sure the booster battery is the same voltage as the dead one in the vehicle.*
 e) *The two vehicles MUST NOT TOUCH each other!*
 f) *Make sure the transaxle is in Neutral (manual) or Park (automatic).*
 g) *If the booster battery is not a maintenance-free type, remove the vent caps and lay a cloth over the vent holes.*

Connect the red jumper cable to the positive (+) terminals of each battery **(see illustration)**.

Connect one end of the black jumper cable to the negative (-) terminal of the booster battery. The other end of this cable should be connected to a good ground on the vehicle to be started, such as a bolt or bracket on the body.

Start the engine using the booster battery, then, with the engine running at idle speed, disconnect the jumper cables in the reverse order of connection.

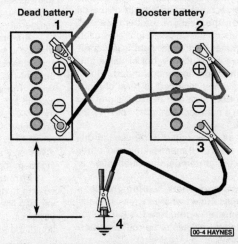

Make the booster battery cable connections in the numerical order shown (note that the negative cable of the booster battery is **NOT** attached to the negative terminal of the dead battery)

Automotive chemicals and lubricants

A number of automotive chemicals and lubricants are available for use during vehicle maintenance and repair. They include a wide variety of products ranging from cleaning solvents and degreasers to lubricants and protective sprays for rubber, plastic and vinyl.

Cleaners

Carburetor cleaner and choke cleaner is a strong solvent for gum, varnish and carbon. Most carburetor cleaners leave a dry-type lubricant film which will not harden or gum up. Because of this film it is not recommended for use on electrical components.

Brake system cleaner is used to remove grease and brake fluid from the brake system, where clean surfaces are absolutely necessary. It leaves no residue and often eliminates brake squeal caused by contaminants.

Electrical cleaner removes oxidation, corrosion and carbon deposits from electrical contacts, restoring full current flow. It can also be used to clean spark plugs, carburetor jets, voltage regulators and other parts where an oil-free surface is desired.

Demoisturants remove water and moisture from electrical components such as alternators, voltage regulators, electrical connectors and fuse blocks. They are non-conductive, non-corrosive and non-flammable.

Degreasers are heavy-duty solvents used to remove grease from the outside of the engine and from chassis components. They can be sprayed or brushed on and, depending on the type, are rinsed off either with water or solvent.

Lubricants

Motor oil is the lubricant formulated for use in engines. It normally contains a wide variety of additives to prevent corrosion and reduce foaming and wear. Motor oil comes in various weights (viscosity ratings) from 5 to 80. The recommended weight of the oil depends on the season, temperature and the demands on the engine. Light oil is used in cold climates and under light load conditions. Heavy oil is used in hot climates and where high loads are encountered. Multi-viscosity oils are designed to have characteristics of both light and heavy oils and are available in a number of weights from 5W-20 to 20W-50.

Gear oil is designed to be used in differentials, manual transmissions and other areas where high-temperature lubrication is required.

Chassis and wheel bearing grease is a heavy grease used where increased loads and friction are encountered, such as for wheel bearings, balljoints, tie-rod ends and universal joints.

High-temperature wheel bearing grease is designed to withstand the extreme temperatures encountered by wheel bearings in disc brake equipped vehicles. It usually contains molybdenum disulfide (moly), which is a dry-type lubricant.

White grease is a heavy grease for metal-to-metal applications where water is a problem. White grease stays soft under both low and high temperatures (usually from -100 to +190-degrees F), and will not wash off or dilute in the presence of water.

Assembly lube is a special extreme pressure lubricant, usually containing moly, used to lubricate high-load parts (such as main and rod bearings and cam lobes) for initial start-up of a new engine. The assembly lube lubricates the parts without being squeezed out or washed away until the engine oiling system begins to function.

Silicone lubricants are used to protect rubber, plastic, vinyl and nylon parts.

Graphite lubricants are used where oils cannot be used due to contamination problems, such as in locks. The dry graphite will lubricate metal parts while remaining uncontaminated by dirt, water, oil or acids. It is electrically conductive and will not foul electrical contacts in locks such as the ignition switch.

Moly penetrants loosen and lubricate frozen, rusted and corroded fasteners and prevent future rusting or freezing.

Heat-sink grease is a special electrically non-conductive grease that is used for mounting electronic ignition modules where it is essential that heat is transferred away from the module.

Sealants

RTV sealant is one of the most widely used gasket compounds. Made from silicone, RTV is air curing, it seals, bonds, waterproofs, fills surface irregularities, remains flexible, doesn't shrink, is relatively easy to remove, and is used as a supplementary sealer with almost all low and medium temperature gaskets.

Anaerobic sealant is much like RTV in that it can be used either to seal gaskets or to form gaskets by itself. It remains flexible, is solvent resistant and fills surface imperfections. The difference between an anaerobic sealant and an RTV-type sealant is in the curing. RTV cures when exposed to air, while an anaerobic sealant cures only in the absence of air. This means that an anaerobic sealant cures only after the assembly of parts, sealing them together.

Thread and pipe sealant is used for sealing hydraulic and pneumatic fittings and vacuum lines. It is usually made from a Teflon compound, and comes in a spray, a paint-on liquid and as a wrap-around tape.

Chemicals

Anti-seize compound prevents seizing, galling, cold welding, rust and corrosion in fasteners. High-temperature ant-seize, usually made with copper and graphite lubricants, is used for exhaust system and exhaust manifold bolts.

Anaerobic locking compounds are used to keep fasteners from vibrating or working loose and cure only after installation, in the absence of air. Medium strength locking compound is used for small nuts, bolts and screws that may be removed later. High-strength locking compound is for large nuts, bolts and studs which aren't removed on a regular basis.

Oil additives range from viscosity index improvers to chemical treatments that claim to reduce internal engine friction. It should be noted that most oil manufacturers caution against using additives with their oils.

Gas additives perform several functions, depending on their chemical makeup. They usually contain solvents that help dissolve gum and varnish that build up on carburetor, fuel injection and intake parts. They also serve to break down carbon deposits that form on the inside surfaces of the combustion chambers. Some additives contain upper cylinder lubricants for valves and piston rings, and others contain chemicals to remove condensation from the gas tank.

Miscellaneous

Brake fluid is specially formulated hydraulic fluid that can withstand the heat and pressure encountered in brake systems. Care must be taken so this fluid does not come in contact with painted surfaces or plastics. An opened container should always be resealed to prevent contamination by water or dirt.

Weatherstrip adhesive is used to bond weatherstripping around doors, windows and trunk lids. It is sometimes used to attach trim pieces.

Undercoating is a petroleum-based, tar-like substance that is designed to protect metal surfaces on the underside of the vehicle from corrosion. It also acts as a sound-deadening agent by insulating the bottom of the vehicle.

Waxes and polishes are used to help protect painted and plated surfaces from the weather. Different types of paint may require the use of different types of wax and polish. Some polishes utilize a chemical or abrasive cleaner to help remove the top layer of oxidized (dull) paint on older vehicles. In recent years many non-wax polishes that contain a wide variety of chemicals such as polymers and silicones have been introduced. These non-wax polishes are usually easier to apply and last longer than conventional waxes and polishes.

Conversion factors

Length (distance)

Inches (in)	X	25.4	= Millimetres (mm)	X 0.0394	= Inches (in)
Feet (ft)	X	0.305	= Metres (m)	X 3.281	= Feet (ft)
Miles	X	1.609	= Kilometres (km)	X 0.621	= Miles

Volume (capacity)

Cubic inches (cu in; in^3)	X	16.387	= Cubic centimetres (cc; cm^3)	X 0.061	= Cubic inches (cu in; in^3)
Imperial pints (Imp pt)	X	0.568	= Litres (l)	X 1.76	= Imperial pints (Imp pt)
Imperial quarts (Imp qt)	X	1.137	= Litres (l)	X 0.88	= Imperial quarts (Imp qt)
Imperial quarts (Imp qt)	X	1.201	= US quarts (US qt)	X 0.833	= Imperial quarts (Imp qt)
US quarts (US qt)	X	0.946	= Litres (l)	X 1.057	= US quarts (US qt)
Imperial gallons (Imp gal)	X	4.546	= Litres (l)	X 0.22	= Imperial gallons (Imp gal)
Imperial gallons (Imp gal)	X	1.201	= US gallons (US gal)	X 0.833	= Imperial gallons (Imp gal)
US gallons (US gal)	X	3.785	= Litres (l)	X 0.264	= US gallons (US gal)

Mass (weight)

Ounces (oz)	X	28.35	= Grams (g)	X 0.035	= Ounces (oz)
Pounds (lb)	X	0.454	= Kilograms (kg)	X 2.205	= Pounds (lb)

Force

Ounces-force (ozf; oz)	X	0.278	= Newtons (N)	X 3.6	= Ounces-force (ozf; oz)
Pounds-force (lbf; lb)	X	4.448	= Newtons (N)	X 0.225	= Pounds-force (lbf; lb)
Newtons (N)	X	0.1	= Kilograms-force (kgf; kg)	X 9.81	= Newtons (N)

Pressure

Pounds-force per square inch (psi; lbf/in^2; lb/in^2)	X	0.070	= Kilograms-force per square centimetre (kgf/cm^2; kg/cm^2)	X 14.223	= Pounds-force per square inch (psi; lbf/in^2; lb/in^2)
Pounds-force per square inch (psi; lbf/in^2; lb/in^2)	X	0.068	= Atmospheres (atm)	X 14.696	= Pounds-force per square inch (psi; lbf/in^2; lb/in^2)
Pounds-force per square inch (psi; lbf/in^2; lb/in^2)	X	0.069	= Bars	X 14.5	= Pounds-force per square inch (psi; lbf/in^2; lb/in^2)
Pounds-force per square inch (psi; lbf/in^2; lb/in^2)	X	6.895	= Kilopascals (kPa)	X 0.145	= Pounds-force per square inch (psi; lbf/in^2; lb/in^2)
Kilopascals (kPa)	X	0.01	= Kilograms-force per square centimetre (kgf/cm^2; kg/cm^2)	X 98.1	= Kilopascals (kPa)

Torque (moment of force)

Pounds-force inches (lbf in; lb in)	X	1.152	= Kilograms-force centimetre (kgf cm; kg cm)	X 0.868	= Pounds-force inches (lbf in; lb in)
Pounds-force inches (lbf in; lb in)	X	0.113	= Newton metres (Nm)	X 8.85	= Pounds-force inches (lbf in; lb in)
Pounds-force inches (lbf in; lb in)	X	0.083	= Pounds-force feet (lbf ft; lb ft)	X 12	= Pounds-force inches (lbf in; lb in)
Pounds-force feet (lbf ft; lb ft)	X	0.138	= Kilograms-force metres (kgf m; kg m)	X 7.233	= Pounds-force feet (lbf ft; lb ft)
Pounds-force feet (lbf ft; lb ft)	X	1.356	= Newton metres (Nm)	X 0.738	= Pounds-force feet (lbf ft; lb ft)
Newton metres (Nm)	X	0.102	= Kilograms-force metres (kgf m; kg m)	X 9.804	= Newton metres (Nm)

Vacuum

Inches mercury (in. Hg)	X	3.377	= Kilopascals (kPa)	X 0.2961	= Inches mercury
Inches mercury (in. Hg)	X	25.4	= Millimeters mercury (mm Hg)	X 0.0394	= Inches mercury

Power

Horsepower (hp)	X	745.7	= Watts (W)	X 0.0013	= Horsepower (hp)

Velocity (speed)

Miles per hour (miles/hr; mph)	X	1.609	= Kilometres per hour (km/hr; kph)	X 0.621	= Miles per hour (miles/hr; mph)

Fuel consumption*

Miles per gallon, Imperial (mpg)	X	0.354	= Kilometres per litre (km/l)	X 2.825	= Miles per gallon, Imperial (mpg)
Miles per gallon, US (mpg)	X	0.425	= Kilometres per litre (km/l)	X 2.352	= Miles per gallon, US (mpg)

Temperature

Degrees Fahrenheit = ($°C \times 1.8$) + 32

Degrees Celsius (Degrees Centigrade; °C) = ($°F - 32$) x 0.56

*It is common practice to convert from miles per gallon (mpg) to litres/100 kilometres (l/100km), where mpg (Imperial) x l/100 km = 282 and mpg (US) x l/100 km = 235

Safety first!

Regardless of how enthusiastic you may be about getting on with the job at hand, take the time to ensure that your safety is not jeopardized. A moment's lack of attention can result in an accident, as can failure to observe certain simple safety precautions. The possibility of an accident will always exist, and the following points should not be considered a comprehensive list of all dangers. Rather, they are intended to make you aware of the risks and to encourage a safety conscious approach to all work you carry out on your vehicle.

Essential DOs and DON'Ts

DON'T rely on a jack when working under the vehicle. Always use approved jackstands to support the weight of the vehicle and place them under the recommended lift or support points.

DON'T attempt to loosen extremely tight fasteners (i.e. wheel lug nuts) while the vehicle is on a jack - it may fall.

DON'T start the engine without first making sure that the transmission is in Neutral (or Park where applicable) and the parking brake is set.

DON'T remove the radiator cap from a hot cooling system - let it cool or cover it with a cloth and release the pressure gradually.

DON'T attempt to drain the engine oil until you are sure it has cooled to the point that it will not burn you.

DON'T touch any part of the engine or exhaust system until it has cooled sufficiently to avoid burns.

DON'T siphon toxic liquids such as gasoline, antifreeze and brake fluid by mouth, or allow them to remain on your skin.

DON'T inhale brake lining dust - it is potentially hazardous (see *Asbestos* below).

DON'T allow spilled oil or grease to remain on the floor - wipe it up before someone slips on it.

DON'T use loose fitting wrenches or other tools which may slip and cause injury.

DON'T push on wrenches when loosening or tightening nuts or bolts. Always try to pull the wrench toward you. If the situation calls for pushing the wrench away, push with an open hand to avoid scraped knuckles if the wrench should slip.

DON'T attempt to lift a heavy component alone - get someone to help you.

DON'T rush or take unsafe shortcuts to finish a job.

DON'T allow children or animals in or around the vehicle while you are working on it.

DO wear eye protection when using power tools such as a drill, sander, bench grinder, etc. and when working under a vehicle.

DO keep loose clothing and long hair well out of the way of moving parts.

DO make sure that any hoist used has a safe working load rating adequate for the job.

DO get someone to check on you periodically when working alone on a vehicle.

DO carry out work in a logical sequence and make sure that everything is correctly assembled and tightened.

DO keep chemicals and fluids tightly capped and out of the reach of children and pets.

DO remember that your vehicle's safety affects that of yourself and others. If in doubt on any point, get professional advice.

Asbestos

Certain friction, insulating, sealing, and other products - such as brake linings, brake bands, clutch linings, torque converters, gaskets, etc. - may contain asbestos. Extreme care must be taken to avoid inhalation of dust from such products, since it is hazardous to health. If in doubt, assume that they do contain asbestos.

Fire

Remember at all times that gasoline is highly flammable. Never smoke or have any kind of open flame around when working on a vehicle. But the risk does not end there. A spark caused by an electrical short circuit, by two metal surfaces contacting each other, or even by static electricity built up in your body under certain conditions, can ignite gasoline vapors, which in a confined space are highly explosive. Do not, under any circumstances, use gasoline for cleaning parts. Use an approved safety solvent.

Always disconnect the battery ground (-) cable at the battery before working on any part of the fuel system or electrical system. Never risk spilling fuel on a hot engine or exhaust component. It is strongly recommended that a fire extinguisher suitable for use on fuel and electrical fires be kept handy in the garage or workshop at all times. Never try to extinguish a fuel or electrical fire with water.

Fumes

Certain fumes are highly toxic and can quickly cause unconsciousness and even death if inhaled to any extent. Gasoline vapor falls into this category, as do the vapors from some cleaning solvents. Any draining or pouring of such volatile fluids should be done in a well ventilated area.

When using cleaning fluids and solvents, read the instructions on the container carefully. Never use materials from unmarked containers.

Never run the engine in an enclosed space, such as a garage. Exhaust fumes contain carbon monoxide, which is extremely poisonous. If you need to run the engine, always do so in the open air, or at least have the rear of the vehicle outside the work area.

If you are fortunate enough to have the use of an inspection pit, never drain or pour gasoline and never run the engine while the vehicle is over the pit. The fumes, being heavier than air, will concentrate in the pit with possibly lethal results.

The battery

Never create a spark or allow a bare light bulb near a battery. They normally give off a certain amount of hydrogen gas, which is highly explosive.

Always disconnect the battery ground (-) cable at the battery before working on the fuel or electrical systems.

If possible, loosen the filler caps or cover when charging the battery from an external source (this does not apply to sealed or maintenance-free batteries). Do not charge at an excessive rate or the battery may burst.

Take care when adding water to a non maintenance-free battery and when carrying a battery. The electrolyte, even when diluted, is very corrosive and should not be allowed to contact clothing or skin.

Always wear eye protection when cleaning the battery to prevent the caustic deposits from entering your eyes.

Household current

When using an electric power tool, inspection light, etc., which operates on household current, always make sure that the tool is correctly connected to its plug and that, where necessary, it is properly grounded. Do not use such items in damp conditions and, again, do not create a spark or apply excessive heat in the vicinity of fuel or fuel vapor.

Secondary ignition system voltage

A severe electric shock can result from touching certain parts of the ignition system (such as the spark plug wires) when the engine is running or being cranked, particularly if components are damp or the insulation is defective. In the case of an electronic ignition system, the secondary system voltage is much higher and could prove fatal.

Troubleshooting

Contents

This section provides an easy reference guide to the more common problems which may occur during the operation of your vehicle. These problems and their possible causes are grouped under headings denoting various components or systems, such as Engine, Cooling system, etc. They also refer you to the chapter and/or section which deals with the problem.

Remember that successful troubleshooting is not a mysterious black art practiced only by professional mechanics. It is simply the result of the right knowledge combined with an intelligent, systematic approach to the problem. Always work by a process of elimination, starting with the simplest solution and working through to the most complex - and never overlook the obvious. Anyone can run the gas tank dry or leave the lights on overnight, so don't assume that you are exempt from such oversights.

Finally, always establish a clear idea of why a problem has occurred and take steps to ensure that it doesn't happen again. If the electrical system fails because of a poor connection, check the other connections in the system to make sure that they don't fail as well. If a particular fuse continues to blow, find out why - don't just replace one fuse after another. Remember, failure of a small component can often be indicative of potential failure or incorrect functioning of a more important component or system.

Engine

1 Engine will not rotate when attempting to start

1 Battery terminal connections loose or corroded (Chapter 1).
2 Battery discharged or faulty (Chapter 1).
3 Automatic transmission not completely engaged in Park (Chapter 7) or clutch not completely depressed (Chapter 8).
4 Broken, loose or disconnected wiring in the starting circuit (Chapters 5 and 12).
5 Starter motor pinion jammed in flywheel ring gear (Chapter 5).
6 Starter solenoid faulty (Chapter 5).
7 Starter motor faulty (Chapter 5).
8 Ignition switch faulty (Chapter 12).
9 Starter pinion or flywheel teeth worn or broken (Chapter 5).

2 Engine rotates but will not start

1 Fuel tank empty.
2 Battery discharged (engine rotates slowly) (Chapter 5).
3 Battery terminal connections loose or corroded (Chapter 1).
4 Leaking fuel injector(s), faulty fuel pump, pressure regulator, etc. (Chapter 4).
5 Fuel not reaching fuel rail (Chapter 4).
6 Ignition components damp or damaged (Chapter 5).
7 Worn, faulty or incorrectly gapped spark plugs (Chapter 1).
8 Broken, loose or disconnected wiring in the starting circuit (Chapter 5).
9 Loose distributor is changing ignition timing (Chapter 5).
10 Broken, loose or disconnected wires at the ignition coil or faulty coil (Chapter 5).
11 Broken or stripped timing belt (Chapter 2).
12 Defective fuel pump relay and/or harness at relay (Chapter 4)

3 Engine hard to start when cold

1 Battery discharged or low (Chapter 1).
2 Malfunctioning fuel system (Chapter 4).

3 Injector(s) leaking (Chapter 4).
4 Distributor rotor carbon tracked (Chapter 5).

4 Engine hard to start when hot

1 Air filter clogged (Chapter 1).
2 Fuel not reaching the fuel injection system (Chapter 4).
3 Corroded battery connections, especially ground (Chapter 1).
4 Malfunctioning EVAP system (Chapter 6)

5 Starter motor noisy or excessively rough in engagement

1 Pinion or flywheel gear teeth worn or broken (Chapter 5).
2 Starter motor mounting bolts loose or missing (Chapter 5).

6 Engine starts but stops immediately

1 Loose or faulty electrical connections at distributor, coil or alternator (Chapter 5).
2 Insufficient fuel reaching the fuel injector(s) (Chapters 1 and 4).
3 Vacuum leak at the gasket between the intake manifold and throttle body (Chapters 1 and 4).

7 Oil puddle under engine

1 Oil pan gasket and/or oil pan drain bolt washer leaking (Chapter 2).
2 Oil pressure sending unit leaking (Chapter 2).
3 Cylinder head covers leaking (Chapter 2).
4 Engine oil seals leaking (Chapter 2).

8 Engine lopes while idling or idles erratically

1 Vacuum leakage (Chapters 2 and 4).
2 Defective EGR valve (Chapter 6).
3 Air filter clogged (Chapter 1).
4 Fuel pump not delivering sufficient fuel to the fuel injection system (Chapter 4).
5 Fuel pulsation damper faulty (Chapter 4)
6 Leaking head gasket (Chapter 2).
7 Timing belt and/or pulleys worn (Chapter 2).
8 Camshaft lobes worn (Chapter 2).
9 Problem in Engine Mount Control System (Chapter 2).

9 Engine misses at idle speed

1 Spark plugs worn or not gapped properly (Chapter 1).

2 Faulty spark plug wires (Chapter 1).
3 Vacuum leaks (Chapter 1).
4 Incorrect ignition timing (Chapter 1).
5 Uneven or low compression (Chapter 2).

10 Engine misses throughout driving speed range

1 Fuel filter clogged and/or impurities in the fuel system (Chapter 1).
2 Low fuel pressure (Chapter 4).
3 Faulty or incorrectly gapped spark plugs (Chapter 1).
4 Incorrect ignition timing (Chapter 5).
5 Cracked distributor cap, disconnected distributor wires or damaged distributor components (Chapters 1 and 5).
6 Leaking spark plug wires (Chapters 1 or 5).
7 Faulty emission system components (Chapter 6).
8 Low or uneven cylinder compression pressures (Chapter 2).
9 Weak or faulty ignition system (Chapter 5).
10 Vacuum leak in fuel injection system (Chapter 4) , intake manifold (Chapters 2A/2B), fuel injection air control valve (Chapter 6) or vacuum hoses.

11 Engine stumbles on acceleration

1 Spark plugs fouled (Chapter 1).
2 Fuel injection system faulty (Chapter 4).
3 Fuel filter clogged (Chapters 1 and 4).
4 Incorrect ignition timing (Chapter 5).
5 Intake air leak (Chapters 2 and 4).

12 Engine surges while holding accelerator steady

1 Intake air leak (Chapter 4).
2 Fuel pump faulty (Chapter 4).
3 Loose fuel injector wire harness connectors (Chapter 4).
4 Defective ECU or information sensor (Chapter 6).

13 Engine stalls

1 Idle speed incorrect (Chapter 1).
2 Fuel filter clogged and/or water and impurities in the fuel system (Chapters 1 and 4).
3 Distributor components damp or damaged (Chapter 5).
4 Faulty emissions system components (Chapter 6).
5 Faulty or incorrectly gapped spark plugs (Chapter 1).
6 Faulty spark plug wires (Chapter 1).
7 Vacuum leak in the intake manifold or vacuum hoses (Chapters 2 and 4).
8 Valve clearances incorrectly set (Chapter 1).

14 Engine lacks power

1   Incorrect ignition timing (Chapter 5).
2   Excessive play in distributor shaft (Chapter 5).
3   Worn rotor, distributor cap or wires (Chapters 1 and 5).
4   Faulty or incorrectly gapped spark plugs (Chapter 1).
5   Fuel injection system malfunction (Chapter 4).
6   Faulty coil (Chapter 5).
7   Brakes binding (Chapter 9).
8   Automatic transaxle fluid level incorrect (Chapter 1).
9   Clutch slipping (Chapter 8).
10 Fuel filter clogged and/or impurities in the fuel system (Chapters 1 and 4).
11 Emission control system not functioning properly (Chapter 6).
12 Low or uneven cylinder compression pressures (Chapter 2).
13 Obstructed exhaust system (Chapter 4).

15 Engine backfires

1   Emission control system not functioning properly (Chapter 6).
2   Ignition timing incorrect (Chapter 5).
3   Faulty secondary ignition system (cracked spark plug insulator, faulty plug wires, distributor cap and/or rotor) (Chapters 1 and 5).
4   Fuel injection system malfunctioning (Chapter 4).
5   Vacuum leak at fuel injector(s), intake manifold, air control valve or vacuum hoses (Chapters 2 and 4).
6   Valve clearances incorrectly set and/or valves sticking (Chapter 1).

16 Pinging or knocking engine sounds during acceleration or uphill

1   Incorrect grade of fuel.
2   Ignition timing incorrect (Chapter 5).
3   Fuel injection system faulty (Chapter 4).
4   Improper or damaged spark plugs or wires (Chapter 1).
5   Worn or damaged distributor components (Chapter 5).
6   EGR valve not functioning (Chapter 6).
7   Vacuum leak (Chapters 2 and 4).

17 Engine runs with oil pressure light on

1   Low oil level (Chapter 1).
2   Short in wiring circuit (Chapter 12).
3   Faulty oil pressure sender (Chapter 2).
4   Worn engine bearings and/or oil pump (Chapter 2).

18 Engine diesels (continues to run) after switching off

1   Idle speed too high (Chapter 5)
2   Excessive engine operating temperature (Chapter 3).
3   Ignition timing in need of adjustment (Chapter 5).

Engine electrical system

19 Battery will not hold a charge

1   Alternator drivebelt defective or not adjusted properly (Chapter 1).
2   Battery electrolyte level low (Chapter 1).
3   Battery terminals loose or corroded (Chapter 1).
4   Alternator not charging properly (Chapter 5).
5   Loose, broken or faulty wiring in the charging circuit (Chapter 5).
6   Short in vehicle wiring (Chapter 12).
7   Internally defective battery (Chapters 1 and 5).

20 Alternator light fails to go out

1   Faulty alternator or charging circuit (Chapter 5).
2   Alternator drivebelt defective or out of adjustment (Chapter 1).
3   Alternator voltage regulator inoperative (Chapter 5).

21 Alternator light fails to come on when key is turned on

1   Warning light bulb defective (Chapter 5).
2   Fault in the printed circuit, dash wiring or bulb holder (Chapter 12).

Fuel system

22 Excessive fuel consumption

1   Dirty or clogged air filter element (Chapter 1).
2   Incorrectly set ignition timing (Chapter 5).
3   Emissions system not functioning properly (Chapter 6).
4   Fuel injection system malfunctioning (Chapter 4).
5   Low tire pressure or incorrect tire size (Chapter 1).

23 Fuel leakage and/or fuel odor

1   Leaking fuel feed or return line (Chapters 1 and 4).
2   Tank overfilled.
3   Evaporative canister filter clogged (Chapters 1 and 6).

4   Fuel injector internal parts excessively worn (Chapter 4).

Cooling system

24 Overheating

1   Insufficient coolant in system (Chapter 1).
2   Radiator core blocked or grille restricted (Chapter 3).
3   Thermostat faulty (Chapter 3).
4   Electric coolant fan circuit problem (Chapter 3).
5   Radiator cap not maintaining proper pressure (Chapter 3).
6   Ignition timing incorrect (Chapter 5).

25 Overcooling

1   Faulty thermostat (Chapter 3).
2   Inaccurate temperature gauge sending unit (Chapter 3).
3   Electric coolant fan circuit problem (Chapter 3).

26 External coolant leakage

1   Deteriorated/damaged hoses; loose clamps (Chapters 1 and 3).
2   Water pump defective (Chapter 3).
3   Leakage from radiator core or coolant reservoir bottle (Chapter 3).
4   Engine drain or water jacket core plugs leaking (Chapter 2).

27 Internal coolant leakage

1   Leaking cylinder head gasket (Chapter 2).
2   Cracked cylinder bore or cylinder head (Chapter 2).

28 Coolant loss

1   Too much coolant in system (Chapter 1).
2   Coolant boiling away because of overheating (Chapter 3).
3   Internal or external leakage (Chapter 3).
4   Faulty radiator cap (Chapter 3).

29 Poor coolant circulation

1   Inoperative water pump (Chapter 3).
2   Restriction in cooling system (Chapters 1 and 3).
3   Thermostat sticking (Chapter 3).

Clutch

30 Pedal travels to floor - no pressure or very little resistance

1   No fluid in reservoir (Chapter 1).

2   Faulty clutch master cylinder, release cylinder or hydraulic line (Chapter 8).
3   Broken release bearing or fork (Chapter 8).

31 Unable to select gears

1   Faulty transaxle (Chapter 7).
2   Faulty clutch disc (Chapter 8).
3   Release lever and bearing not assembled properly (Chapter 8).
4   Faulty pressure plate (Chapter 8).
5   Pressure plate-to-flywheel bolts loose (Chapter 8).

32 Clutch slips (engine speed increases with no increase in vehicle speed)

1   Clutch plate worn (Chapter 8).
2   Clutch plate is oil soaked by leaking rear main seal (Chapter 8).
3   Clutch plate not seated. It may take 30 or 40 normal starts for a new one to seat.
4   Warped pressure plate or flywheel (Chapter 8).
5   Weak diaphragm spring (Chapter 8).
6   Clutch plate overheated. Allow to cool.

33 Grabbing (chattering) as clutch is engaged

1   Oil on clutch plate lining, burned or glazed facings (Chapter 8).
2   Worn or loose engine or transaxle mounts (Chapters 2 and 7).
3   Worn splines on clutch plate hub (Chapter 8).
4   Warped pressure plate or flywheel (Chapter 8).
5   Burned or smeared resin on flywheel or pressure plate (Chapter 8).

34 Transaxle rattling (clicking)

1   Release lever loose (Chapter 8).
2   Clutch plate damper spring failure (Chapter 8).
3   Low engine idle speed (Chapter 1).

35 Noise in clutch area

1   Fork shaft improperly installed (Chapter 8).
2   Faulty bearing (Chapter 8).

36 Clutch pedal stays on floor

1   Faulty clutch master or release cylinder (Chapter 8).
2   Broken release bearing or fork (Chapter 8).

37 High pedal effort

1   Piston binding in bore of clutch master or release cylinder (Chapter 8).
2   Pressure plate faulty (Chapter 8).

Manual transaxle

38 Knocking noise at low speeds

1   Worn driveaxle constant velocity (CV) joints (Chapter 8).
2   Worn driveaxle bore in differential case (Chapter 7A).*

39 Noise most pronounced when turning

Differential gear noise (Chapter 7A).*

40 Clunk on acceleration or deceleration

1   Loose engine or transaxle mounts (Chapters 2 and 7A).
2   Worn differential pinion shaft in case.*
3   Worn driveaxle bore in differential case (Chapter 7A).*
4   Worn or damaged driveaxle inboard CV joints (Chapter 8).

41 Clicking noise in turns

Worn or damaged outboard CV joint (Chapter 8).

42 Vibration

1   Rough wheel bearing (Chapters 1 and 10).
2   Damaged driveaxle (Chapter 8).
3   Out of round tires (Chapter 1).
4   Tire out of balance (Chapters 1 and 10).
5   Worn CV joint (Chapter 8).

43 Noisy in neutral with engine running

1   Damaged input gear bearing (Chapter 7A).*
2   Damaged clutch release bearing (Chapter 8).

44 Noisy in one particular gear

1   Damaged or worn constant mesh gears (Chapter 7A).*
2   Damaged or worn synchronizers (Chapter 7A).*
3   Bent reverse fork (Chapter 7A).*
4   Damaged fourth speed gear or output gear (Chapter 7A).*

5   Worn or damaged reverse idler gear or idler bushing (Chapter 7A).*

45 Noisy in all gears

1   Insufficient lubricant (Chapter 7A).
2   Damaged or worn bearings (Chapter 7A).*
3   Worn or damaged input gear shaft and/or output gear shaft (Chapter 7A).*

46 Slips out of gear

1   Worn or improperly adjusted linkage (Chapter 7A).
2   Transaxle loose on engine (Chapter 7A).
3   Shift linkage does not work freely, binds (Chapter 7A).
4   Input gear bearing retainer broken or loose (Chapter 7A).*
5   Dirt between clutch cover and engine block (Chapter 7A).
6   Worn shift fork (Chapter 7A).*

47 Leaks lubricant

1   Driveaxle oil seals worn (Chapter 7).
2   Excessive amount of lubricant in transaxle (Chapters 1 and 7A).
3   Loose or broken input gear shaft bearing retainer (Chapter 7A).*
4   Input gear bearing retainer O-ring and/or lip seal damaged (Chapter 7A).*

48 Locked in gear

Lock pin or interlock pin missing (Chapter 7A).*
* Although the corrective action necessary to remedy the symptoms described is beyond the scope of the home mechanic, the above information should be helpful in isolating the cause of the condition so that the owner can communicate clearly with a professional mechanic.

Automatic transaxle

Note: *Due to the complexity of the automatic transaxle, it is difficult for the home mechanic to properly diagnose and service this component. For problems other than the following, the vehicle should be taken to a dealer or transmission shop.*

49 Fluid leakage

1   Automatic transmission fluid is a deep red color. Fluid leaks should not be confused with engine oil, which can easily be blown onto the transaxle by air flow.
2   To pinpoint a leak, first remove all built-up dirt and grime from the transaxle housing with degreasing agents and/or steam cleaning. Then drive the vehicle at low speeds so air flow will not blow the leak far from its source. Raise the vehicle and determine where the

leak is coming from. Common areas of leakage are:

a) *Pan (Chapters 1 and 7)*
b) *Dipstick tube (Chapters 1 and 7)*
c) *Transaxle oil lines (Chapter 7)*
d) *Speed sensor (Chapter 7)*

50 Transaxle fluid brown or has a burned smell

Transaxle fluid burned (Chapter 1).

51 General shift mechanism problems

1 Chapter 7, Part B, deals with checking and adjusting the shift linkage on automatic transaxles. Common problems which may be attributed to poorly adjusted linkage are:

a) *Engine starting in gears other than Park or Neutral.*
b) *Indicator on shifter pointing to a gear other than the one actually being used.*
c) *Vehicle moves when in Park.*

2 Refer to Chapter 7B for the shift linkage adjustment procedure.

52 Transaxle will not downshift with accelerator pedal pressed to the floor

Throttle valve cable out of adjustment (Chapter 7B).

53 Engine will start in gears other than Park or Neutral

Neutral start switch malfunctioning (Chapter 7B).

54 Transaxle slips, shifts roughly, is noisy or has no drive in forward or reverse gears

There are many probable causes for the above problems, but the home mechanic should be concerned with only one possibility - fluid level. Before taking the vehicle to a repair shop, check the level and condition of the fluid as described in Chapter 1. Correct the fluid level as necessary or change the fluid and filter if needed. If the problem persists, have a professional diagnose the cause.

Driveaxles

55 Clicking noise in turns

Worn or damaged outboard CV joint (Chapter 8).

56 Shudder or vibration during acceleration

1 Excessive toe-in (Chapter 10).
2 Incorrect spring heights (Chapter 10).
3 Worn or damaged inboard or outboard CV joints (Chapter 8).
4 Sticking inboard CV joint assembly (Chapter 8).

57 Vibration at highway speeds

1 Out of balance front wheels and/or tires (Chapters 1 and 10).
2 Out of round front tires (Chapters 1 and 10).
3 Worn CV joint(s) (Chapter 8).

Brakes

Note: *Before assuming that a brake problem exists, make sure that:*

a) *The tires are in good condition and properly inflated (Chapter 1).*
b) *The front end alignment is correct (Chapter 10).*
c) *The vehicle is not loaded with weight in an unequal manner.*

58 Vehicle pulls to one side during braking

1 Incorrect tire pressures (Chapter 1).
2 Front end out of line (have the front end aligned).
3 Front, or rear, tires not matched to one another.
4 Restricted brake lines or hoses (Chapter 9).
5 Malfunctioning drum brake or caliper assembly (Chapter 9).
6 Loose suspension parts (Chapter 10).
7 Loose calipers (Chapter 9).
8 Excessive wear of brake shoe or pad material or disc/drum on one side.

59 Noise (high-pitched squeal when the brakes are applied)

Front disc brake pads worn out. The noise comes from the wear sensor rubbing against the disc (does not apply to all vehicles). Replace pads with new ones immediately (Chapter 9).

60 Brake roughness or chatter (pedal pulsates)

1 Excessive lateral runout (Chapter 9).
2 Uneven pad wear (Chapter 9).
3 Defective disc (Chapter 9).

61 Excessive brake pedal effort required to stop vehicle

1 Malfunctioning power brake booster (Chapter 9).
2 Partial system failure (Chapter 9).
3 Excessively worn pads or shoes (Chapter 9).
4 Piston in caliper or wheel cylinder stuck or sluggish (Chapter 9).
5 Brake pads or shoes contaminated with oil or grease (Chapter 9).
6 New pads or shoes installed and not yet seated. It will take a while for the new material to seat against the disc or drum.

62 Excessive brake pedal travel

1 Partial brake system failure (Chapter 9).
2 Insufficient fluid in master cylinder (Chapters 1 and 9).
3 Air trapped in system (Chapters 1 and 9).

63 Dragging brakes

1 Incorrect adjustment of brake light switch (Chapter 9).
2 Master cylinder pistons not returning correctly (Chapter 9).
3 Restricted brakes lines or hoses (Chapters 1 and 9).
4 Incorrect parking brake adjustment (Chapter 9).

64 Grabbing or uneven braking action

1 Malfunction of proportioning valve (Chapter 9).
2 Malfunction of power brake booster unit (Chapter 9).
3 Binding brake pedal mechanism (Chapter 9).

65 Brake pedal feels spongy when depressed

1 Air in hydraulic lines (Chapter 9).
2 Master cylinder mounting bolts loose (Chapter 9).
3 Master cylinder defective (Chapter 9).

66 Brake pedal travels to the floor with little resistance

1 Little or no fluid in the master cylinder reservoir caused by leaking caliper piston(s) (Chapter 9).
2 Loose, damaged or disconnected brake lines (Chapter 9).

67   Parking brake does not hold

Parking brake linkage improperly adjusted (Chapters 1 and 9).

Suspension and steering systems

Note: *Before attempting to diagnose the suspension and steering systems, perform the following preliminary checks:*
a) *Tires for wrong pressure and uneven wear.*
b) *Steering universal joints from the column to the steering gear for loose connectors or wear.*
c) *Front and rear suspension and the steering gear assembly for loose or damaged parts.*
d) *Out-of-round or out-of-balance tires, bent rims and loose and/or rough wheel bearings.*

68   Vehicle pulls to one side

1 Mismatched or uneven tires (Chapter 10).
2 Broken or sagging springs (Chapter 10).
3 Wheel alignment (Chapter 10).
4 Front brake dragging (Chapter 9).

69   Abnormal or excessive tire wear

1 Wheel alignment (Chapter 10).
2 Sagging or broken springs (Chapter 10).
3 Tire out of balance (Chapter 10).
4 Worn shock absorber (Chapter 10).
5 Overloaded vehicle.
6 Tires not rotated regularly.

70   Wheel makes a thumping noise

1 Blister or bump on tire (Chapter 10).
2 Worn shock absorber (Chapter 10).

71   Shimmy, shake or vibration

1 Tire or wheel out-of-balance or out-of-round (Chapter 10).
2 Loose or worn front hub or wheel bearings (Chapters 1, 8 and 10).
3 Worn tie-rod ends (Chapter 10).
4 Worn lower balljoints (Chapters 1 and 10).
5 Excessive wheel runout (Chapter 10).
6 Blister or bump on tire (Chapter 10).

72   Hard steering

1 Lack of lubrication at balljoints and tie-rod ends (Chapters 1 and 10).
2 Front wheel alignment (Chapter 10).
3 Low tire pressure(s) (Chapters 1 and 10).

73   Poor returnability of steering to center

1 Lack of lubrication at balljoints and tie-rod ends (Chapters 1 and 10).
2 Binding in balljoints (Chapter 10).
3 Binding in steering column (Chapter 10).
4 Lack of lubricant in steering gear assembly (Chapter 10).
5 Front wheel alignment (Chapter 10).

74   Abnormal noise at the front end

1 Lack of lubrication at balljoints and tie-rod ends (Chapters 1 and 10).
2 Damaged shock absorber mount (Chapter 10).
3 Worn control arm bushings or tie-rod ends (Chapter 10).
4 Loose stabilizer bar (Chapter 10).
5 Loose wheel nuts (Chapters 1 and 10).
6 Loose suspension bolts (Chapter 10)

75   Wander or poor steering stability

1 Mismatched or uneven tires (Chapter 10).
2 Lack of lubrication at balljoints and tie-rod ends (Chapters 1 and 10).
3 Worn shock absorber/coil spring assemblies (Chapter 10).
4 Loose stabilizer bar (Chapter 10).
5 Broken or sagging springs (Chapter 10).
6 Wheels out of alignment (Chapter 10).

76   Erratic steering when braking

1 Front hub bearings worn (Chapter 10).
2 Broken or sagging springs (Chapter 10).
3 Leaking wheel cylinder or caliper (Chapter 10).
4 Warped discs or drums (Chapter 10).

77   Excessive pitching and/or rolling around corners or during braking

1 Loose stabilizer bar (Chapter 10).
2 Worn shock absorber/coil spring assemblies or mountings (Chapter 10).
3 Broken or sagging springs (Chapter 10).
4 Overloaded vehicle.

78   Suspension bottoms

1 Overloaded vehicle.

2 Worn shock absorber/coil spring assemblies (Chapter 10).
3 Incorrect, broken or sagging springs (Chapter 10).

79   Cupped tires

1 Front wheel or rear wheel alignment (Chapter 10).
2 Worn shock absorber/coil spring assemblies (Chapter 10).
3 Wheel bearings worn (Chapter 10).
4 Excessive tire or wheel runout (Chapter 10).
5 Worn balljoints (Chapter 10).

80   Excessive tire wear on outside edge

1 Inflation pressures incorrect (Chapter 1).
2 Excessive speed in turns.
3 Front end alignment incorrect (excessive toe-in). Have professionally aligned.
4 Suspension arm bent or twisted (Chapter 10).

81   Excessive tire wear on inside edge

1 Inflation pressures incorrect (Chapter 1).
2 Front end alignment incorrect (toe-out). Have professionally aligned.
3 Loose or damaged steering or suspension components (Chapter 10).

82   Tire tread worn in one place

1 Tires out of balance.
2 Damaged or buckled wheel. Inspect and replace if necessary.
3 Defective tire (Chapter 1).

83   Excessive play or looseness in steering system

1 Front hub bearing(s) worn (Chapter 10).
2 Tie-rod end loose (Chapter 10).
3 Steering gear loose or worn (Chapter 10).
4 Worn or loose steering intermediate shaft (Chapter 10).

84   Rattling or clicking noise in steering gear

1 Steering gear loose (Chapter 10).
2 Steering gear defective.

Chapter 1
Tune-up and routine maintenance

Contents

Specifications

Recommended lubricants and fluids

Note: *The fluids and lubricants listed here are those recommended by the manufacturer at the time this manual was printed. Vehicle manufacturers occasionally upgrade their fluid and lubricant specifications. Check with your local auto parts store for the most current fluid and lubricant recommendations for your vehicle.*

Engine oil	
Type	API grade SJ multigrade fuel efficient oil
Viscosity	See accompanying chart
Automatic transmission fluid	Honda Premium Formula automatic transmission fluid or equivalent
Manual transaxle lubricant	Honda Genuine Manual Transmission Fluid (MTF) or equivalent
Brake fluid type	DOT 3 brake fluid
Power steering system fluid	Honda power steering fluid or equivalent
Fuel type	Unleaded gasoline, 87 octane or higher

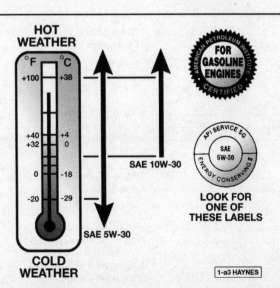

Engine oil viscosity chart

HOT WEATHER

FOR GASOLINE ENGINES
AMERICAN PETROLEUM INSTITUTE · CERTIFIED

API SERVICE SG
SAE 5W-30
ENERGY CONSERVING

LOOK FOR ONE OF THESE LABELS

°F °C
+100 +38
+40 +4
+32 0
0 -18
-20 -29

SAE 10W-30

SAE 5W-30

COLD WEATHER

1-a3 HAYNES

Capacities*

Engine oil (including oil filter)
   V6 engine .... 4.6 quarts
   Four-cylinder engine .... 4.5 quarts
Automatic transaxle (drain and refill)
   V6 engine .... 3.1 quarts
   Four-cylinder engine .... 2.6 quarts
Manual transaxle .... 2 quarts
Coolant
   V6 engine .... 5.9 quarts
   Four-cylinder engine
      Automatic transaxle .... 5.7 quarts
      Manual transaxle .... 5.8 quarts

All capacities approximate. Add as necessary to bring to appropriate level.

Ignition system

Spark plug type and gap
   Type
      1998 and 1999 four-cylinder engine .... NGK ZFR5F-11 or equivalent
      V6 engine and 2000 and later four-cylinder engine ...... NGK PZFR5F-11 or equivalent
   Gap .... 0.039 to 0.043-inch
Spark plug wire resistance .... Less than 25,000 ohms
Engine firing order
   Four-cylinder engine 1-3-4-2
   V6 engine 1-4-2-5-3-6

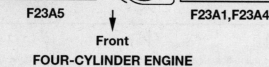

Note: *On 2000 and later V6 engines, a coil-over-plug ignition system is used. There's no distributor.*

Cylinder location and distributor rotation
The blackened terminal shown on the distributor cap indicates the Number One spark plug wire position

Idle Speed

Four-cylinder engine .... 650 to 750 rpm
V6 engine .... 630 to 730 rpm

Cooling system

Thermostat rating
   Starts to open .... 173-degrees F
   Fully open .... 194-degrees F

Accessory drivebelt deflection

V6 engine
   Power steering pump
      New belt .... 5/16 to 7/16-inch
      Old belt .... 1/2 to 5/8-inch
   Alternator .... see tension indicator on vehicle
Four-cylinder engine
   Power steering pump
      New belt .... 7/16 to 1/2-inch
      Old belt .... 1/2 to 5/8-inch
   Alternator
      Without air-conditioning
         New belt .... 5/16 to 3/8-inch
         Old belt .... 7/16 to 1/2-inch
      With air-conditioning
         New belt .... 3/16 to 1/4-inch
         Old belt .... 5/16 to 3/8-inch

Brakes

Disc brake pad lining thickness (minimum) 1/16-inch
Drum brake shoe lining thickness (minimum).. 3/32-inch
Parking brake adjustment
    Drum rear brake .... 4 to 7 clicks
    Disc rear brake .... 6 to 9 clicks

Valve clearance (engine cold)

Intake
    Four cylinder engine.. 0.009 to 0.011-inch
    V6 engine .... 0.008 to 0.009-inch
Exhaust .... 0.011 to 0.013-inch

Torque specifications

Ft-lbs (unless otherwise indicated)

Note: *One foot-pound (ft-lb) of torque is equivalent to 12 inch-pounds (in-lbs) of torque. Torque values below approximately 15 ft-lbs are expressed in inch-pounds, since most foot-pound torque wrenches are not accurate at these smaller values.*

Automatic transaxle
    Drain plug... 36
    Filler plug (V6 only) 33
Manual transaxle
    Drain plug... 29
    Filler plug 33
Spark plugs... 156 in-lbs
Wheel lug nuts 80

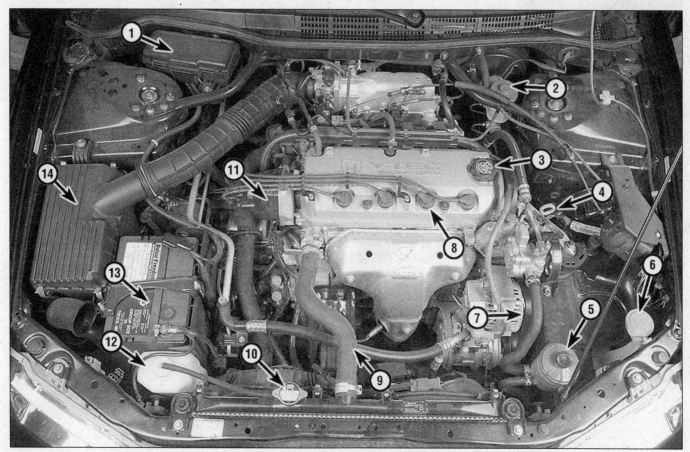

Typical four-cylinder engine compartment layout

1	Fuse/relay panel	6	Windshield washer fluid reservoir	11	Distributor cap
2	Brake master cylinder reservoir	7	Alternator drivebelt	12	Engine coolant reservoir
3	Engine oil filler cap	8	Spark plug and wire boot	13	Battery
4	Engine oil dipstick	9	Radiator hose	14	Air filter housing
5	Power steering fluid reservoir	10	Radiator cap		

Typical V6 engine compartment layout

1	Fuse/relay panel	6	Distributor cap	11	Engine oil dipstick
2	Brake master cylinder reservoir	7	Radiator cap	12	Power steering fluid reservoir
3	Air filter housing	8	Radiator hose	13	Windshield washer fluid reservoir
4	Battery	9	Spark plug and wire boot	14	Anti-lock Brake System (ABS) unit
5	Engine coolant reservoir	10	Engine oil filler cap	15	ABS fuse block

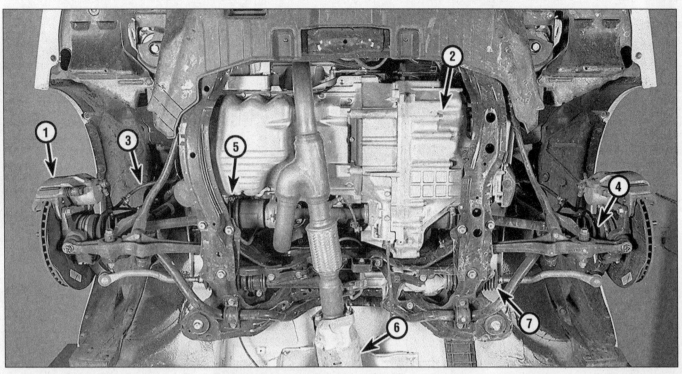

Typical engine compartment underside components

1	Front brake caliper	4	Outer driveaxle boot	6	Exhaust system
2	Transaxle drain plug (automatic)	5	Engine oil drain plug	7	Steering gear boot
3	Brake line				

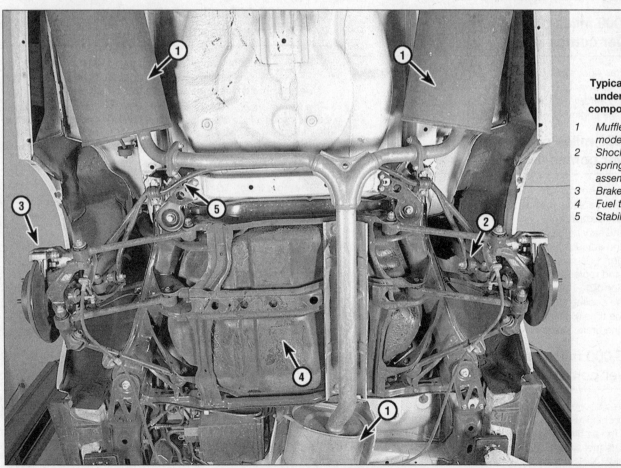

Typical rear underside components

1 Muffler (V6 model shown)
2 Shock and spring assembly
3 Brake caliper
4 Fuel tank
5 Stabilizer bar

1 Honda Accord Maintenance schedule

The maintenance intervals in this manual are provided with the assumption that you, not the dealer, will be doing the work. These are the minimum maintenance intervals recommended by the factory for vehicles that are driven daily. If you wish to keep your vehicle in peak condition at all times, you may wish to perform some of these procedures even more often. Because frequent maintenance enhances the efficiency, performance and resale value of your car, we encourage you to do so. If you drive in dusty areas, tow a trailer, idle or drive at low speeds for extended periods or drive for short distances (less than four miles) in below freezing temperatures, shorter intervals are also recommended.

When your vehicle is new, follow the maintenance schedule to the letter, record the maintenance performed in your owners manual and keep all receipts to protect the new vehicle warranty. In many cases, the initial maintenance check is done at no cost to the owner.

Every 250 miles or weekly, whichever comes first

Check the engine oil level (Section 4)
Check the engine coolant level (Section 4)
Check the windshield washer fluid level (Section 4)
Check the brake and clutch fluid level (Section 4)
Check the tires and tire pressures (Section 5)

Every 3000 miles or 3 months, whichever comes first

All items listed above plus:
Check the power steering fluid level (Section 6)
Check the automatic transaxle fluid level (Section 7)
Change the engine oil and oil filter (Section 8)

Every 7500 miles or 6 months, whichever comes first

All items listed above plus:
Inspect and replace, if necessary, the windshield wiper
    blades (Section 9)
Check and service the battery (Section 10)
Check and adjust, if necessary, the engine drivebelts
    (Section 11)
Inspect and replace, if necessary, all underhood hoses
    (Section 12)
Check the cooling system (Section 13)
Rotate the tires (Section 14)
Inspect the brake system (Section 15)*

Every 15,000 miles or 12 months, whichever comes first

All items listed above plus:
Seat belt check (Section 16)
Replace the air filter (Section 17)*
Inspect the fuel system (Section 18)

Check the manual transaxle lubricant level (Section 19)*
Inspect the suspension, steering components and driveaxle
    boots (Section 20)*
Exhaust system check (Section 21)

Every 30,000 miles or 24 months, whichever comes first

All items listed above plus:
Replace the spark plugs, 1998 and 1999 four-cylinder models
    (Section 22)
Inspect and replace, if necessary, the spark plug wires,
    distributor cap and rotor (Section 23)
Check and, if necessary, replace the PCV valve (Section 24)
Check and adjust, if necessary, the engine idle speed
    (Section 25)
Service the cooling system (drain, flush and refill) (Section 26)
Replace the brake fluid (Section 27)
Change the automatic transaxle fluid (Section 28)**
Change the manual transaxle lubricant (Section 29)
Replace the air-conditioning filter (Section 30)**
Check and adjust if necessary, the valve clearance (Section 31)

Every 105,000 miles or 72 months, whichever comes first

Replace the spark plugs, 2000 and later four-cylinder and V6
    models (see Section 22)
Replace the timing and balance shaft belts (Chapter 2)***

*This item is affected by "severe" operating conditions as described below. If your vehicle is operated under "severe" conditions, perform all maintenance indicated with a * at 7500 mile/6 month intervals. Severe conditions are indicated if you mainly operate your vehicle under one or more of the following conditions:

Operating in dusty areas
Towing a trailer
Idling for extended periods and/or low speed operation
Operating when outside temperatures remain below freezing
    and when most trips are less than five miles

**If operated under one or more of the following conditions, change the automatic transaxle fluid every 15,000 miles:

In heavy city traffic where the outside temperature regularly
    reaches 90-degrees F (32-degrees C) or higher
In hilly or mountainous terrain

***This item is affected by "severe" operating conditions as described below. If operated under one or more of the following conditions, replace the timing and balance shaft belts every 60,000 miles:

Operating in dusty areas
Towing a trailer
Idling for extended periods and/or low speed operation
Operating when outside temperatures remain below freezing
    and when most trips are less than five miles
In heavy city traffic or where the outside temperature
    regularly reaches 90-degrees F (32-degrees C) or higher

2 Introduction

This Chapter is designed to help the home mechanic maintain his/her car for peak performance, economy, safety and long life.

The following Sections deal specifically with each item on the maintenance schedule. Visual checks, adjustments, component replacement and other helpful items are included. Refer to the accompanying photos of the engine compartment and the underside of the vehicle for the location of various components.

Servicing your vehicle in accordance with the mileage/time maintenance schedule and the following Sections will provide it with a planned maintenance program that should result in a long and reliable service life. This is a comprehensive plan, so maintaining some items but not others at the specified service intervals will not produce the same results.

As you service your car, you will discover that many of the procedures can - and should - be grouped together because of the nature of the particular procedure you're performing or because of the close proximity of two otherwise unrelated components to one another. For example, if the vehicle is raised for chassis lubrication, you should inspect the exhaust, suspension, steering and fuel systems while you're under the vehicle. When you're rotating the tires, it makes good sense to check the brakes and wheel bearings since the wheels are already removed.

Finally, let's suppose you have to borrow or rent a torque wrench. Even if you only need to tighten the spark plugs, you might as well check the torque of as many critical fasteners as time allows.

The first step of this maintenance program is to prepare yourself before the actual work begins. Read through all Sections pertinent to the procedures you're planning to do, then make a list of and gather together all the parts and tools you will need to do the job. If it looks as if you might run into problems during a particular segment of some procedure, seek advice from your local parts man or dealer service department.

3 Tune-up general information

The term tune-up is used in this manual to represent a combination of individual operations rather than one specific procedure.

If, from the time the vehicle is new, the routine maintenance schedule is followed closely and frequent checks are made of fluid levels and high wear items, as suggested throughout this manual, the engine will be kept in relatively good running condition and the need for additional work will be minimized.

More likely than not, however, there will be times when the engine is running poorly due to lack of regular maintenance. This is even more likely if a used vehicle, which has not received regular and frequent maintenance checks, is purchased. In such cases, an engine tune-up will be needed outside of the regular routine maintenance intervals.

The first step in any tune-up or engine diagnosis to help correct a poor running engine would be a cylinder compression check. A check of the engine compression (see Chapter 2 Part C) will give valuable information regarding the overall performance of many internal components and should be used as a basis for tune-up and repair procedures. If, for instance, a compression check indicates serious internal engine wear, a conventional tune-up will not help the running condition of the engine and would be a waste of time and money. Because of its importance, compression checking should be performed by someone with the proper compression testing gauge and the knowledge to use it properly.

The following series of operations are those most often needed to bring a generally poor running engine back into a proper state of tune.

Minor tune-up

Check all engine related fluids (Section 4)
Clean, inspect and test the battery (Section 10)
Check and adjust the drivebelts (Section 11)
Check all underhood hoses (Section 12)
Check the cooling system (Section 13)
Check the air filter (Section 17)
Inspect the spark plug wires, distributor cap and rotor (Section 23)

Major tune-up

All items listed under minor tune-up, plus . . .
Replace the spark plugs (Section 22)
Check the idle speed (Section 25)
Replace the air filter (Section 17)
Replace the distributor cap and rotor (Section 23)
Replace the spark plug wires (Section 23)
Check the fuel system (Section 18)

4 Fluid level checks (every 250 miles or weekly)

1   Fluids are an essential part of the lubrication, cooling, brake, clutch and other systems. Because these fluids gradually become depleted and/or contaminated during normal operation of the vehicle, they must be periodically replenished. See *Recommended lubricants, fluids and capacities* at the beginning of this Chapter before adding fluid to any of the following components. **Note:** *The vehicle must be on level ground before fluid levels can be checked.*

Engine oil

Refer to illustrations 4.4 and 4.6

2   The engine oil level is checked with a dipstick located at the front side of the engine **(see engine compartment layout illustrations)**. The dipstick extends through a metal tube from which it protrudes down into the engine oil pan.

3   The oil level should be checked before the vehicle has been driven, or about 15 minutes after the engine has been shut off. If the oil is checked immediately after driving the vehicle, some of the oil will remain in the upper engine components, producing an inaccurate reading on the dipstick.

4   Pull the dipstick from the tube and wipe all the oil from the end with a clean rag or paper towel. Insert the clean dipstick all the way back into its metal tube and pull it out again. Observe the oil at the end of the dipstick. At its highest point, the level should be between the upper and lower holes **(see illustration)**.

5   It takes one quart of oil to raise the level from the lower hole to the upper hole on the dipstick. Do not allow the level to drop below the lower hole or oil starvation may cause engine damage. Conversely, overfilling the engine (adding oil above the upper hole) may cause oil fouled spark plugs, oil leaks or oil seal failures.

6   Remove the threaded cap from the valve cover to add oil **(see illustration)**. Use

4.4 The oil level should be between the two holes in the dipstick - if it isn't, add enough oil to bring the level to or near the upper hole (it takes one quart to raise the level from the lower hole to the upper hole)

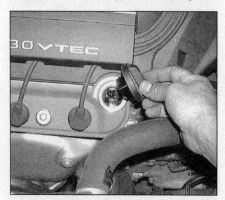

4.6 The threaded oil filler cap is located on the valve cover - to prevent dirt from contaminating the engine, always make sure the area around this opening is clean before unscrewing the cap

an oil can spout or funnel to prevent spills. After adding the oil, install the filler cap hand tight. Start the engine and look carefully for any small leaks around the oil filter or drain plug. Stop the engine and check the oil level again after it has had sufficient time to drain from the upper block and cylinder head galleys.

7   Checking the oil level is an important preventive maintenance step. A continually dropping oil level indicates oil leakage through damaged seals, from loose connections, or past worn rings or valve guides. If the oil looks milky in color or has water droplets in it, a cylinder head gasket may be blown or the oil cooler could be leaking. The engine should be checked immediately. The condition of the oil should also be checked. Each time you check the oil level, slide your thumb and index finger up the dipstick before wiping off the oil. If you see small dirt or metal particles clinging to the dipstick, the oil should be changed (see Section 8).

Engine coolant

Refer to illustration 4.9

Warning: *Do not allow antifreeze to come in contact with your skin or painted surfaces of the vehicle. Rinse off spills immediately with plenty of water. Antifreeze is highly toxic if ingested. Never leave antifreeze lying around in an open container or in puddles on the floor; children and pets are attracted by it's sweet smell and may drink it. Check with local authorities about disposing of used antifreeze. Many communities have collection centers which will see that antifreeze is disposed of safely.*

Note: *Non-toxic antifreeze is now manufactured and available at local auto parts stores, but even this type should be disposed of properly.*

8   All vehicles covered by this manual are equipped with a pressurized coolant-recovery system. A coolant reservoir located on the right side of the engine compartment is connected by a hose to the base of the radiator filler neck. If the coolant heats up during engine operation, coolant can escape through the pressurized filler cap, then through the connecting hose into the reservoir. As the engine cools, the coolant is automatically drawn back into the cooling system to maintain the correct level.

9   The coolant level in the reservoir should be checked regularly. It must be between the MAX and MIN lines on the tank. The level will vary with the temperature of the engine. When the engine is cold, the coolant level should be at or slightly above the MIN mark on the tank. Once the engine has warmed up, the level should be at or near the MAX mark. If it isn't, allow the fluid in the tank to cool, then remove the cap from the reservoir **(see illustration)** and add coolant to bring the level up to the MAX line. **Caution:** *Use only ethylene glycol type coolant and water in the mixture ratio recommended by your owner's manual. Do not use supplemental inhibitors or additives. If only a small amount of coolant is required to bring the system up to the*

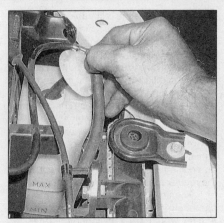

4.9 Make sure the coolant level is between the MAX and MIN lines on the coolant reservoir - if it's below the MIN line, unscrew the cap and add a sufficient quantity of the specified mixture of antifreeze and water

proper level, water can be used. However, repeated additions of water will dilute the recommended antifreeze and water solution. In order to maintain the proper ratio of antifreeze and water, it is advisable to top up the coolant level with the correct mixture. Refer to your owner's manual for the recommended ratio.

10   If the coolant level drops within a short time after replenishment, there may be a leak in the system. Inspect the radiator, hoses, engine coolant filler cap, drain plugs, air bleeder bolt and water pump. If no leak is evident, have the radiator cap pressure tested.

Warning: *Never remove the radiator cap or the coolant recovery reservoir cap when the engine is running or has just been shut down, because the cooling system is hot. Escaping steam and scalding liquid could cause serious injury.*

11   If it is necessary to open the radiator cap, wait until the system has cooled completely, then wrap a thick cloth around the cap and turn it to the first stop. If any steam escapes, wait until the system has cooled further, then remove the cap.

12   When checking the coolant level, always note its condition. It should be relatively clear. If it is brown or rust colored, the system should be drained, flushed and refilled. Even if the coolant appears to be normal, the corrosion inhibitors wear out with use, so it must be replaced at the specified intervals.

13   Do not allow antifreeze to come in contact with your skin or painted surfaces of the vehicle. Flush contacted areas immediately with plenty of water.

Windshield washer fluid

Refer to illustration 4.14

14   Fluid for the windshield washer system is stored in a plastic reservoir which is located at the left (four-cylinder models) or right (V6 models) front corner of the engine compartment **(see illustration)**. Check the fluid level on four-cylinder models by detach-

4.14 The windshield washer fluid reservoir is located at the left (four-cylinder models) or right (V6 models, shown) front corner of the engine compartment - fluid can be added after removing up the cap

ing the cap and pulling up the dipstick while on V6 models the level markings are on the filler neck. In milder climates, plain water can be used to top up the reservoir, but the reservoir should be kept no more than 2/3 full to allow for expansion should the water freeze. In colder climates, the use of a specially designed windshield washer fluid, available at your dealer and any auto parts store, will help lower the freezing point of the fluid. Mix the solution with water in accordance with the manufacturer's directions on the container. Do not use regular antifreeze. It will damage the vehicle's paint.

Brake and clutch fluid

Refer to illustration 4.16

15   The brake master cylinder is mounted on the front of the power booster unit and the clutch master cylinder next to it on the firewall within the engine compartment. Models with an Anti-lock Brake System (ABS) also have a reservoir for the ABS modulator located on the right side of the engine compartment. ABS-equipped vehicles should be driven for a few minutes to equalize the fluid in the system before checking the fluid level in the reservoirs. If the level rises significantly above the MAX mark, have the system checked by a dealer because this could indicate a malfunction in the ABS system.

16   To check the fluid level of the brake or clutch master cylinder, simply look at the MAX and MIN marks on the reservoir **(see illustration)**. The level should be between the two marks. If the vehicle is equipped with an Anti-lock Brake System (ABS), the fluid level in the ABS unit reservoir must also be checked. It's located on the right (passenger) side of the engine compartment.

17   If the level is low, wipe the top of the reservoir cover with a clean rag to prevent contamination of the brake system before lifting the cap.

18   Add only the specified brake fluid to the brake, clutch or ABS reservoir (refer to *Rec-*

4.16 The brake fluid should be kept between the MIN and MAX marks on the reservoir - turn and lift up the cap to add fluid

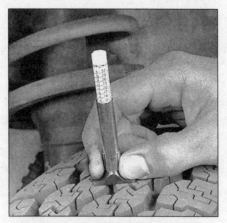

5.2 Use a tire tread depth gauge to monitor tire wear they are available at auto parts stores and service stations and cost very little

ommended lubricants and fluids at the front of this Chapter or to your owner's manual). Mixing different types of brake fluid can damage the system. Fill the brake master cylinder reservoir only to about 3/4-inch below the MAX line - this brings the fluid to the correct level when you put the cap back on. **Warning:** *Use caution when filling the reservoir - brake fluid can harm your eyes and damage painted surfaces. Do not use brake fluid that has been opened for more than one year or has been left open. Brake fluid absorbs moisture from the air. Excess moisture can cause a dangerous loss of braking.*

19   While the reservoir cap is removed, inspect the master cylinder reservoir for contamination. If deposits, dirt particles or water droplets are present, the system should be drained and refilled (see Chapters 8 or 9).
20   After filling the reservoir to the proper level, make sure the lid is properly seated to prevent fluid leakage and/or system pressure loss.
21   The brake fluid in the master cylinder will drop slightly as the brake pads at each wheel wear down during normal operation. If the master cylinder requires repeated replenishing to keep it at the proper level,

this is an indication of leakage in the brake system, which should be corrected immediately. Check all brake lines and connections, along with the wheel cylinders and booster (see Section 15 for more information). A drop in the clutch reservoir level indicates a leak in the clutch hydraulic system (see Chapter 8).
22   If, upon checking the brake master cylinder fluid level, you discover an empty or nearly empty reservoir, the brake system should be bled (see Chapter 9).

5   Tire and tire pressure checks (every 250 miles or weekly)

Refer to illustrations 5.2, 5.3, 5.4a, 5.4b and 5.8

1   Periodic inspection of the tires may spare you from the inconvenience of being stranded with a flat tire. It can also provide you with vital information regarding possible problems in the steering and suspension systems before major damage occurs.
2   Normal tread wear can be monitored with a simple, inexpensive device known as a tread depth indicator **(see illustration)**. When the tread depth reaches the specified minimum, replace the tire(s).
3   Note any abnormal tread wear **(see illustration)**. Tread pattern irregularities such as cupping, flat spots and more wear on one side than the other are indications of front end alignment and/or balance problems. If

UNDERINFLATION

INCORRECT TOE-IN OR EXTREME CAMBER

CUPPING

Cupping may be caused by:
- Underinflation and/or mechanical irregularities such as out-of-balance condition of wheel and/or tire, and bent or damaged wheel.
- Loose or worn steering tie-rod or steering idler arm.
- Loose, damaged or worn front suspension parts.

OVERINFLATION

FEATHERING DUE TO MISALIGNMENT

5.3 This chart will help you determine the condition of the tires, the probable cause(s) of abnormal wear and the corrective action necessary

5.4a If a tire looses air on a steady basis, check the valve core first to make sure it's snug (special inexpensive wrenches are commonly available at auto parts stores)

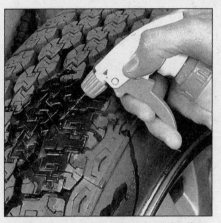

5.4b If the valve core is tight, raise the corner of the vehicle with the low tire and spray a soapy water solution onto the tread as the tire is turned slowly - leaks will cause small bubbles to appear

5.8 To extend the life of the tires, check the air pressure at least once a week with an accurate gauge (don't forget the spare)

any of these conditions are noted, take the vehicle to a tire shop or service station to correct the problem.

4   Look closely for cuts, punctures and embedded nails or tacks. Sometimes a tire will hold its air pressure for a short time or leak down very slowly even after a nail has embedded itself into the tread. If a slow leak persists, check the valve core to make sure it is tight **(see illustration)**. Examine the tread for an object that may have embedded itself into the tire or for a "plug" that may have begun to leak (radial tire punctures are repaired with a plug that is installed in a puncture). If a puncture is suspected, it can be easily verified by spraying a solution of soapy water onto the puncture area **(see illustration)**. The soapy solution will bubble if there is a leak. Unless the puncture is inordinately large, a tire shop or gas station can usually repair the punctured tire.

5   Carefully inspect the inner side of each tire for evidence of brake fluid leakage. If you see any, inspect the brakes immediately.

6   Correct tire air pressure adds miles to the lifespan of the tires, improves mileage and enhances overall ride quality. Tire pressure cannot be accurately estimated by looking at a tire, particularly if it is a radial. A tire pressure gauge is therefore essential. Keep an accurate gauge in the glovebox. The pressure gauges fitted to the nozzles of air hoses at gas stations are often inaccurate.

7   Always check tire pressure when the tires are cold. "Cold," in this case, means the vehicle has not been driven over a mile in the three hours preceding a tire pressure check. A pressure rise of four to eight pounds is not uncommon once the tires are warm.

8   Unscrew the valve cap protruding from the wheel or hubcap and push the gauge firmly onto the valve **(see illustration)**. Note the reading on the gauge and compare this figure to the recommended tire pressure shown on the tire placard on the left door jamb. Be sure to reinstall the valve cap to keep dirt and moisture out of the valve stem mechanism. Check all four tires and, if neces-

6.4 The power steering fluid reservoir is translucent so the fluid level can be checked without removing the cap keep the fluid between the two lines

sary, add enough air to bring them up to the recommended pressure levels.

9   Don't forget to keep the spare tire inflated to the specified pressure (consult your owner's manual). Note that the air pressure specified for the compact spare is significantly higher than the pressure of the regular tires.

---

6   Power steering fluid level check (every 3000 miles or 3 months)

Refer to illustration 6.4

1   The power steering system relies on fluid which may, over a period of time, require replenishing.

2   The fluid reservoir for the power steering pump is located on the inner fender panel near the left front of the engine compartment on four-cylinder models, and at the right front on V6 models.

3   For the check, the front wheels should be pointed straight ahead and the engine should be off. The fluid should be cold when

7.5 The automatic transaxle fluid level should be in the cross-hatched area on the dipstick

checking the level.

4   On all models, the reservoir is translucent plastic and the fluid level can be checked visually **(see illustration)**.

5   If additional fluid is required, pour the specified type directly into the reservoir, using a funnel to prevent spills.

6   If the reservoir requires frequent fluid additions, all power steering hoses, hose connections, the power steering pump and the steering gear should be carefully checked for leaks.

---

7   Automatic transaxle fluid level check (every 3000 miles or 3 months)

Refer to illustration 7.5

1   The level of the automatic transaxle fluid should be carefully maintained. Low fluid level can lead to slipping or loss of drive, while overfilling can cause foaming, loss of fluid and transaxle damage.

2   The transaxle fluid level should only be checked on level ground within one minute of the engine being shut off.

3   Remove the dipstick with the yellow loop handle - it's located down low on the front of the transaxle in the passenger's side of the engine compartment on four-cylinder

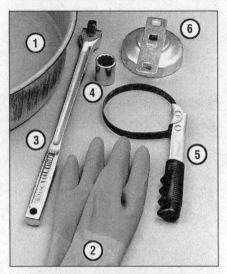

8.2 These tools are required when changing the engine oil and filter

1   **Drain pan** - It should be fairly shallow in depth, but wide to prevent spills
2   **Rubber gloves** - When removing the drain plug and filter, you will get oil on your hands (the gloves will prevent burns)
3   **Breaker bar** - Sometimes the oil drain plug is tight, and a long breaker bar is needed to loosen it
4   **Socket** - To be used with the breaker bar or a ratchet (must be the correct size to fit the drain plug)
5   **Filter wrench** - This is a metal band-type wrench, which requires clearance around the filter to be effective
6   **Filter wrench** - This type fits on the bottom of the filter and can be turned with a ratchet or breaker bar (different-size wrenches are available for different types of filters)

models and on the driver's side on V6 models. Check the level of the fluid on the dipstick and note its condition.
4   Wipe the fluid from the dipstick with a clean rag and reinsert it.
5   Pull the dipstick out again and note the fluid level **(see illustration)**. The level should be between the upper and lower marks on the dipstick. If the level is low, add the specified automatic transmission fluid. On four-cylinder models, add the fluid through the dipstick opening with a funnel. On V6 models, remove the filler plug and add the fluid through the filler hole with a funnel.
6   Add just enough of the specified fluid to fill the transaxle to the proper level. It takes about one pint to raise the level from the lower mark to the upper mark, so add the fluid a little at a time and keep checking the level until it is correct.
7   The condition of the fluid should also be checked along with the level. If the fluid at the end of the dipstick is black or a dark reddish brown color, or if it emits a burned smell, the fluid should be changed (see Section 26). If you are in doubt about the condition of the

8.7 Use the proper size box-end wrench or socket to remove the oil drain plug without rounding off the corners

fluid, purchase some new fluid and compare the two for color and smell.

8   Engine oil and oil filter change (every 3000 miles or 3 months)

Refer to illustrations 8.2, 8.7, 8.12 and 8.14

1   Frequent oil changes are the best preventive maintenance the home mechanic can give the engine, because aging oil becomes diluted and contaminated, which leads to premature engine wear.
2   Make sure you have all the necessary tools before you begin this procedure **(see illustration)**. You should also have plenty of rags or newspapers handy for mopping up any spills.
3   Access to the underside of the vehicle is greatly improved if the vehicle can be lifted on a hoist, driven onto ramps or supported by jackstands. **Warning:** *Do not work under a vehicle which is supported only by a bumper, hydraulic or scissors-type jack.*
4   If this is your first oil change, get under the vehicle and familiarize yourself with the locations of the oil drain plug and the oil filter. The engine and exhaust components will be warm during the actual work, so try to anticipate any potential problems before the engine and accessories are hot.
5   Park the vehicle on a level spot. Start the engine and allow it to reach its normal operating temperature. Warm oil and sludge will flow out more easily. Turn off the engine when it's warmed up. Remove the filler cap from the valve cover.
6   Raise the vehicle and support it securely on jackstands. **Warning:** *Never get beneath the vehicle when it is supported only by a jack. The jack provided with your vehicle is designed solely for raising the vehicle to remove and replace the wheels. Always use jackstands to support the vehicle when it becomes necessary to place your body underneath the vehicle.*
7   Being careful not to touch the hot exhaust components, place the drain pan under the drain plug in the bottom of the pan and remove the plug **(see illustration)**. You

8.12 The oil filter is usually on very tight and will require a special wrench for removal - DO NOT use the wrench to tighten the new filter

may want to wear gloves while unscrewing the plug the final few turns if the engine is hot.
8   Allow the old oil to drain into the pan. It may be necessary to move the pan farther under the engine as the oil flow slows to a trickle. Inspect the old oil for the presence of metal shavings and chips.
9   After all the oil has drained, wipe off the drain plug with a clean rag. Even minute metal particles clinging to the plug would immediately contaminate the new oil.
10   Clean the area around the drain plug opening, reinstall the plug and tighten it securely, but do not strip the threads.
11   Move the drain pan into position under the oil filter.
12   Loosen the oil filter **(see illustration)** by turning it counterclockwise with an oil filter wrench. Once the filter is loose, use your hands to unscrew it from the block. Just as the filter is detached from the block, immediately tilt the open end up to prevent the oil inside the filter from spilling out. **Warning:** *The exhaust system may still be hot, so be careful.*
13   With a clean rag, wipe off the mounting surface on the block. If a residue of old oil is allowed to remain, it will smoke when the block is heated up. Also make sure that none of the old gasket remains stuck to the mounting surface. It can be removed with a scraper if necessary.

8.14 Lubricate the oil filter gasket with clean engine oil before installing the filter on the engine

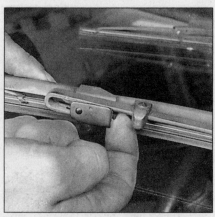

9.6 Press in on the tab and push the blade assembly out of the hook at the end to remove it

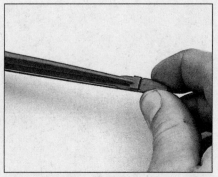

9.7 Squeeze the blade element tabs, then pull the element out of the metal frame and remove it

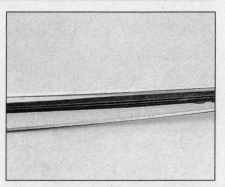

9.8 The metal retainers must be inserted into the slots in the rubber before installation

14   Compare the old filter with the new one to make sure they are the same type. Smear some clean engine oil on the rubber gasket of the new filter and screw it into place **(see illustration)**. Because overtightening the filter will damage the gasket, do not use a filter wrench to tighten the filter. Tighten it by hand until the gasket contacts the seating surface. Then seat the filter by giving it an additional 3/4-turn.

15   Remove all tools, rags, etc. from under the vehicle, being careful not to spill the oil in the drain pan, then lower the vehicle.

16   Add new oil to the engine through the oil filler cap in the valve cover. Use a funnel, if necessary, to prevent oil from spilling onto the top of the engine. Pour three quarts of fresh oil into the engine. Wait a few minutes to allow the oil to drain into the pan, then check the level on the oil dipstick (see Section 4 if necessary). If the oil level is at or near the upper hole on the dipstick, install the filler cap hand tight, start the engine and allow the new oil to circulate.

17   Allow the engine to run for about a minute. While the engine is running, look under the vehicle and check for leaks at the oil pan drain plug and around the oil filter. If either is leaking, stop the engine and tighten the plug or filter.

18   Wait a few minutes to allow the oil to trickle down into the pan, then recheck the level on the dipstick and, if necessary, add enough oil to bring the level to the upper hole.

19   During the first few trips after an oil change, make it a point to check frequently for leaks and proper oil level.

20   Used motor oil cannot be re-used in its present state and should be recycled. Oil reclamation centers, auto repair shops and gas stations will normally accept the oil, which can be refined and used again. After the oil has cooled, it can be drained into a suitable container (capped plastic jugs, topped bottles, milk cartons, etc.) for transport to one of these recycling sites. New or used oil should never be allowed to go into street drains or into the ground.

9   Windshield wiper blade inspection and replacement (every 7500 miles or 6 months)

Refer to illustrations 9.6, 9.7 and 9.8

1   The windshield wiper and blade assembly should be inspected periodically for damage, loose components and cracked or worn blade elements.

2   Road film can build up on the wiper blades and affect their efficiency, so they should be washed regularly with a mild detergent solution.

3   The action of the wiping mechanism can loosen bolts, nuts and fasteners, so they should be checked and tightened, as necessary, at the same time the wiper blades are checked.

4   If the wiper blade elements are cracked, worn or warped, or no longer clean adequately, they should be replaced with new ones.

5   Lift the arm assembly away from the glass for clearance.

6   Press in on the lock tab and push the blade assembly down the wiper arm, out of the hook at the end **(see illustration)**.

7   Squeeze the blade element tabs tightly and pull the element out of the metal frame **(see illustration)**.

8   Remove the metal retainers from the element and install them in the new element **(see illustration)**.

9   Insert the element into the frame and push it until the element tabs lock.

10   Place the metal arm assembly in the hook on the wiper arm and press it into place until the lock tab snaps into place.

10   Battery check, maintenance and charging (every 7500 miles or 6 months)

Warning: *Certain precautions must be followed when checking and servicing the battery. Hydrogen gas, which is highly flammable, is always present in the battery cells, so keep lighted tobacco and all other open*

10.1 Tools and materials required for battery maintenance

1   *Face shield/safety goggles* - When removing corrosion with a brush, the acidic particles can easily fly up into your eyes

2   *Baking soda* - A solution of baking soda and water can be used to neutralize corrosion

3   *Petroleum jelly* - A layer of this on the battery posts will help prevent corrosion

4   *Battery post/cable cleaner* - This wire brush cleaning tool will remove all traces of corrosion from the battery posts and cable clamps

5   *Treated felt washers* - Placing one of these on each post, directly under the cable clamps, will help prevent corrosion

6   *Puller* - Sometimes the cable clamps are very difficult to pull off the posts, even after the nut/bolt has been completely loosened. This tool pulls the clamp straight up and off the post without damage

7   *Battery post/cable cleaner* - Here is another cleaning tool which is a slightly different version of Number 4 above, but it does the same thing

8   *Rubber gloves* - Another safety item to consider when servicing the battery; remember that's acid inside the battery!

10.6 Compare the color showing in your battery's indicator window (arrow) with the color chart decal on the battery

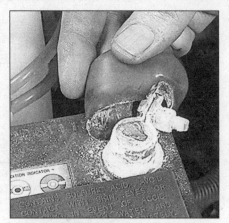

10.7a Battery terminal corrosion usually appears as light, fluffy powder

10.7b Removing the cable from a battery post with a wrench - sometimes special battery pliers are required for this procedure if corrosion has caused deterioration of the nut hex (always remove the ground cable first and hook it up last!)

10.8a When cleaning the cable clamps, all corrosion must be removed (the inside of the clamp is tapered to match the taper on the post, so don't remove too much material)

10.8b Regardless of the type of tool used on the battery posts, a clean, shiny surface should be the result

Maintenance

Refer to illustrations 10.7a, 10.7b, 10.8a and 10.8b

7   If corrosion, which looks like white, fluffy deposits **(see illustration)** is evident, particularly around the terminals, the battery should be removed for cleaning. Loosen the cable clamp bolts with a wrench, being careful to remove the ground cable first, and slide them off the terminals **(see illustration)**. Then disconnect the hold-down clamp bolt and nut, remove the clamp and lift the battery from the engine compartment.

8   Clean the cable clamps thoroughly with a battery brush or a terminal cleaner and a solution of warm water and baking soda **(see illustration)**. Wash the terminals and the top of the battery case with the same solution but make sure that the solution doesn't get into the battery. When cleaning the cables, terminals and battery top, wear safety goggles and rubber gloves to prevent any solution from coming in contact with your eyes or hands. Wear old clothes too - even diluted, sulfuric acid splashed onto clothes will burn holes in them. If the terminals have been extensively corroded, clean them up with a terminal cleaner **(see illustration)**. Thoroughly wash all cleaned areas with plain water.

9   Whenever the battery is removed for cleaning or charging, inspect the battery carrier before reinstalling the battery in the engine compartment. If the carrier is dirty or covered with corrosion, clean it in the same solution of warm water and baking soda. Inspect the metal brackets which support the carrier to make sure that they are not covered with corrosion. If they are, wash them off. If corrosion is extensive, sand the brackets down to bare metal and spray them with a zinc-based primer (available in spray cans at auto paint and body supply stores).

10   Reinstall the battery back into the engine compartment. Make sure that no

flames and sparks away from the battery. The electrolyte inside the battery is actually dilute sulfuric acid, which will cause injury if splashed on your skin or in your eyes. It will also ruin clothes and painted surfaces. When removing the battery cables, always detach the negative cable first and hook it up last!

Check

Refer to illustrations 10.1 and 10.6

1   A routine preventive maintenance program for the battery in your vehicle is the only way to ensure quick and reliable starts. But before performing any battery maintenance, make sure that you have the proper equipment necessary to work safely around the battery **(see illustration)**.

2   There are also several precautions that should be taken whenever battery maintenance is performed. Before servicing the battery, always turn the engine and all accessories off and disconnect the cable from the negative terminal of the battery.

3   The battery produces hydrogen gas, which is both flammable and explosive. Never create a spark, smoke or light a match

around the battery. Always charge the battery in a ventilated area.

4   Electrolyte contains poisonous and corrosive sulfuric acid. Do not allow it to get in your eyes, on your skin on your clothes. Never ingest it. Wear protective safety glasses when working near the battery. Keep children away from the battery.

5   Note the external condition of the battery. If the positive terminal and cable clamp on your vehicle's battery is equipped with a rubber protector, make sure that it's not torn or damaged. It should completely cover the terminal. Look for any corroded or loose connections, cracks in the case or cover or loose hold-down clamps. Also check the entire length of each cable for cracks and frayed conductors.

6   Some models with sealed batteries have a battery condition indicator on top of the battery **(see illustration)**. Compare the color showing in the window to the condition color chart on the battery. You may catch a low-charge battery condition before it strands you on the roadside. If the color indicate a low state of charge, charge the battery and examine the charging system (see Chapter 5 and this Section).

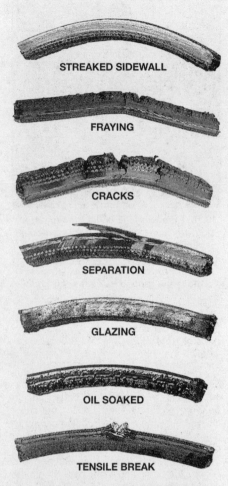

STREAKED SIDEWALL

FRAYING

CRACKS

SEPARATION

GLAZING

OIL SOAKED

TENSILE BREAK

11.3a Here are some of the more common problems associated with V-belts (check the belts very carefully to prevent an untimely breakdown)

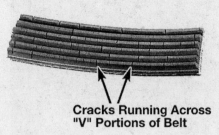

ACCEPTABLE

Cracks Running Across "V" Portions of Belt

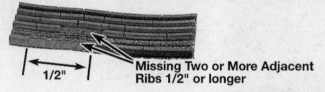

1/2"   Missing Two or More Adjacent Ribs 1/2" or longer

UNACCEPTABLE

11.3b Check ribbed (serpentine) belts for signs of wear like these - if the belt looks worn, replace it

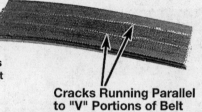

Cracks Running Parallel to "V" Portions of Belt

parts or wires are laying on the carrier during installation of the battery. Information on removing and installing the battery can be found in Chapter 5. Information on jump starting can be found at the front of this manual. For more detailed battery checking procedures, refer to the *Haynes Automotive Electrical Manual*.

11   Install a pair of specially-treated felt washers around the terminals (available at auto parts stores), then coat the terminals and the cable clamps with petroleum jelly or grease to prevent further corrosion. Install the cable clamps and tighten the nuts, being careful to install the negative cable last.

12   Install the hold-down clamp and nuts. Tighten the nuts only enough to hold the battery firmly in place. Overtightening these nuts can crack the battery case.

13   Make sure that the battery tray is in good condition and the hold-down clamp bolts are tight. If the battery is removed from the tray, make sure no parts remain in the bottom of the tray when the battery is reinstalled. When reinstalling the hold-down clamp bolts, do not overtighten them.

Charging

Warning: *When batteries are being charged, hydrogen gas, which is very explosive and flammable, is produced. Do not smoke or allow open flames near a charging or a recently charged battery. Wear eye protection when near the battery during charging. Also, make sure the charger is unplugged before connecting or disconnecting the battery from the charger.*

14   Slow-rate charging is the best way to restore a battery that's discharged to the point where it will not start the engine. It's also a good way to maintain the battery charge in a vehicle that's only driven a few miles between starts. Maintaining the battery charge is particularly important in the winter when the battery must work harder to start the engine and electrical accessories that drain the battery are in greater use.

15   It's best to use a one or two-amp battery charger (sometimes called a "trickle" charger). They are the safest and put the least strain on the battery. They are also the least expensive. For a faster charge, you can use a higher amperage charger, but don't use one rated more than 1/10th the amp/hour rating of the battery. Rapid boost charges that claim to restore the power of the battery in one to two hours are hardest on the battery and can damage batteries not in good condition. This type of charging should only be used in emergency situations.

16   The average time necessary to charge a battery should be listed in the instructions that come with the charger. As a general rule, a trickle charger will charge a battery in 12 to 16 hours.

11   Drivebelt check, adjustment and replacement (every 7500 miles or 6 months)

Check

Refer to illustrations 11.3a, 11.3b, 11.4 and 11.5

1   The drivebelts, or V-belts as they are sometimes called, are located at the front of the engine and play an important role in the overall operation of the vehicle and its components. Due to their function and material make-up, the belts are prone to failure after a period of time and should be inspected and adjusted periodically to prevent major engine damage.

2   The number of belts used on a particular vehicle depends on the accessories installed. Drivebelts are used to turn the alternator, power steering pump, water pump and air conditioning compressor. Depending on the pulley arrangement, more than one of these components may be driven by a single belt.

3   With the engine off, open the hood and locate the various belts at the front of the engine. Using your fingers (and a flashlight, if necessary), move along the belts checking for cracks and separation of the belt plies. Also check for fraying and glazing, which gives the belt a shiny appearance **(see illustrations)**. Both sides of each belt should be inspected, which means you will have to twist the belt to check the underside.

4   The tension of each belt is checked by pushing on the belt at a distance halfway between the pulleys. Push firmly with your

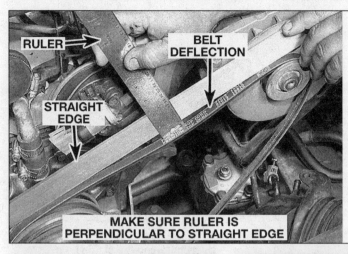

RULER

BELT DEFLECTION

STRAIGHT EDGE

MAKE SURE RULER IS PERPENDICULAR TO STRAIGHT EDGE

11.4 Measuring drivebelt deflection with a straightedge and ruler

11.5 Belt wear indicator on the V6 models (arrow) - when the belt reaches the maximum wear mark it must be replaced

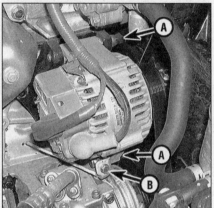

11.7a To adjust the alternator belt on four-cylinder models, loosen the pivot bolt (A) and the lower mounting nut , then turn the adjustment bolt (B) clockwise to tighten the belt, or counterclockwise to loosen the belt

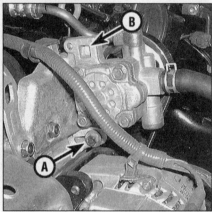

11.7b To adjust the power steering belt on four-cylinder models, loosen the mounting bolts (A indicates one at the rear, another is in front), insert the square drive-end of a 1/2-inch drive breaker bar in the hole (B) to tighten or loosen the belt, then tighten the mounting bolts

thumb and see how much the belt moves (deflects) **(see illustration)**. As rule of thumb, if the distance from pulley center-to-pulley center is between 7 and 11 inches, the belt should deflect 1/4-inch. If the belt travels between pulleys spaced 12 to 16 inches apart, the belt should deflect 1/2-inch for a V-belt or 1/4-inch for a serpentine belt.

5   V6 models are quipped with an automatic tensioner for the alternator/compressor belt. The automatic tensioner is equipped with an indicator on the tensioner indicating the belt wear range. When the belt is stretched beyond its useful life, the alignment of the indicator marks will show this condition **(see illustration)**.

Adjustment

Refer to illustrations 11.7a and 11.7b

6   On V6 models, the alternator/compressor belt is equipped with an automatic-tensioner, it is not possible to adjust belt tension. All other belts are manually-adjusted, it is necessary to adjust the belt tension by moving the belt-driven accessory on its bracket.

7   The alternator on four-cylinder models and the power steering pump on V6 models are adjusted by loosening the mounting bolts and turning the adjusting bolt counterclockwise to loosen the belt and clockwise to tighten the belt. The power steering pump on four cylinder models is adjusted by loosening the mounting bolts and adjusting the belt tension with a 1/2-inch drive breaker bar **(see illustrations)**.

8   After the belts have been adjusted, measure the belt tension in accordance with one of the above methods. Repeat the adjustment procedure until the drivebelt is tensioned properly.

Replacement

9   To replace the alternator belt on V6 models, place the appropriate-size long han-dled wrench on the center bolt of the ten-sioner pulley, rotate the tensioner counter-clockwise and remove the belt. On all other models, follow the above adjustment proce-dures to loosen the belt, slip the belt off the pulleys tund remove it. Since belts tend to

wear out more or less at the same time, it's a good idea to replace all of them at the same time. Mark each belt and the corresponding pulley grooves so the replacement belts can be installed properly. Models with a number of accessories driven by the same serpentine belt usually have a belt-routing diagram on a decal in the engine compartment or on the underside of the hood.

10   Take the old belts with you when pur-chasing new ones in order to make a direct comparison for length, width and design. Keep in mind that your old belt may have stretched, and the correct new belt may be slightly shorter. When installing a new ribbed belt, make sure it is centered on its drive pulley.

11   Install the belt by reversing the removal procedures. When installing a ribbed belt, make sure it is centered on the pulleys, it must not overlap either edge of the pulleys. Adjust the belt as described earlier in this Section.

12   Underhood hose check and replacement (every 7500 miles or 6 months)

Caution: *Replacement of air conditioning hoses must be left to a dealer service depart-ment or air conditioning shop that has the equipment to evacuate the system safely. Never remove air conditioning components or hoses until the system has been evacuated and the refrigerant recovered by an air condi-tioning shop.*

General

1   High temperatures in the engine com-partment can cause the deterioration of the rubber and plastic hoses used for engine, accessory and emission systems operation. Periodic inspection should be made for cracks, loose clamps, material hardening and leaks.

2   Information specific to the cooling sys-tem hoses can be found in Section 13.

3   Some, but not all, hoses are secured to the fittings with clamps. Where clamps are used, check to be sure they haven't lost their tension, allowing the hose to leak. If clamps aren't used, make sure the hose has not expanded and/or hardened where it slips over the fitting, allowing it to leak.

Vacuum hoses

4   It's quite common for vacuum hoses, especially those in the emissions system, to be color coded or identified by colored stripes molded into them. Various systems require hoses with different wall thickness, collapse resistance and temperature resistance. When replacing hoses, be sure the new ones are made of the same material.

5   Often the only effective way to check a hose is to remove it completely from the vehicle. If more than one hose is removed, be sure to label the hoses and fittings to ensure correct installation.

6   When checking vacuum hoses, be sure to include any plastic T-fittings in the check. Inspect the fittings for cracks and the hose where it fits over the fitting for distortion, which could cause leakage.

7   A small piece of vacuum hose (1/4-inch inside diameter) can be used as a stethoscope to detect vacuum leaks. Hold one end of the hose to your ear and probe around vacuum hoses and fittings, listening for the "hissing" sound characteristic of a vacuum leak. **Warning:** *When probing with the vacuum hose stethoscope, be very careful not to come into contact with moving engine components such as the drivebelts, cooling fan, etc.*

Fuel hose

Warning: *Gasoline is extremely flammable, so take extra precautions when you work on any part of the fuel system. Don't smoke or allow open flames or bare light bulbs near the work area, and don't work in a garage where a natural gas-type appliance (such as a water heater or clothes dryer) with a pilot light is present. Since gasoline is carcinogenic, wear latex gloves when there's a possibility of being exposed to fuel, and, if you spill any fuel on your skin, rinse it off immediately with soap and water. Mop up any spills immediately and do not store fuel-soaked rags where they could ignite. The fuel system is under constant pressure, so, if any fuel lines are to be disconnected, the fuel pressure in the system must be relieved first (see Chapter 4 for more information). When you perform any kind of work on the fuel system, wear safety glasses and have a Class B type fire extinguisher on hand.*

8   Check all rubber fuel lines for deterioration and chafing. Check especially for cracks in areas where the hose bends and just before fittings, such as where a hose attaches to the fuel filter.

9   When replacing hose, use only hose that is specifically designed for your fuel injection system.

Metal lines

10   Sections of metal line are often used for fuel line between the fuel pump and fuel injection system. Check carefully to be sure the line has not been bent or crimped and that cracks have not started in the line.

11   If a section of metal fuel line must be replaced, only seamless steel tubing should be used, since copper and aluminum tubing don't have the strength necessary to withstand normal engine vibration.

12   Check the metal brake lines where they enter the master cylinder and brake proportioning unit (if used) for cracks in the lines or loose fittings. Any sign of brake fluid leakage calls for an immediate, thorough inspection of the brake system.

---

13   Cooling system check (every 7500 miles or 6 months)

Refer to illustration 13.4

1   Many major engine failures can be attributed to a faulty cooling system. If the vehicle is equipped with an automatic transaxle, the cooling system also cools the transmission fluid and thus plays an important role in prolonging transaxle life.

2   The cooling system should be checked with the engine cold. Do this before the vehicle is driven for the day or after the engine has been shut off for at least three hours.

3   Remove the radiator cap by turning it to the left until it reaches a stop. If you hear a hissing sound (indicating there is still pressure in the system), wait until it stops. Now press down on the cap with the palm of your hand and continue turning to the left until the cap can be removed. Thoroughly clean the cap, inside and out, with clean water. Also clean the filler neck on the radiator. All traces of corrosion should be removed. The coolant inside the radiator should be relatively transparent. If it's rust colored, the system should be drained and refilled (see Section 26). If the coolant level isn't up to the top, add additional antifreeze/coolant mixture (see Section 4).

4   Carefully check the large upper and lower radiator hoses along with the smaller diameter heater hoses which run from the engine to the firewall. Inspect each hose along its entire length, replacing any hose which is cracked, swollen or shows signs of deterioration. Cracks may become more apparent if the hose is squeezed **(see illustration)**. Regardless of condition, it's a good idea to replace hoses with new ones every two years.

5   Make sure that all hose connections are tight. A leak in the cooling system will usually show up as white or rust colored deposits on the areas adjoining the leak. If wire-type clamps are used at the ends of the hoses, it may be a good idea to replace them with more secure screw-type clamps.

6   Use compressed air or a soft brush to remove bugs, leaves, etc. from the front of the radiator or air conditioning condenser. Be

Check for a chafed area that could fail prematurely.

Check for a soft area indicating the hose has deteriorated inside.

Overtightening the clamp on a hardened hose will damage the hose and cause a leak.

Check each hose for swelling and oil-soaked ends. Cracks and breaks can be located by squeezing the hose.

13.4 Hoses, like drivebelts, have a habit of failing at the worst possible time - to prevent the inconvenience of a blown radiator or heater hose, inspect them carefully as shown here

---

careful not to damage the delicate cooling fins or cut yourself on them.

7   Every other inspection, or at the first indication of cooling system problems, have the cap and system pressure tested. If you don't have a pressure tester, most gas stations and repair shops will do this for a minimal charge.

---

14   Tire rotation (every 7500 miles or 6 months)

Refer to illustrations 14.2a and 14.2b

1   The tires should be rotated at the specified intervals and whenever uneven wear is noticed. Since the vehicle will be raised and the tires removed anyway, check the brakes (see Section 15) at this time.

2   Radial tires must be rotated in a specific pattern **(see illustrations)**. Most models are

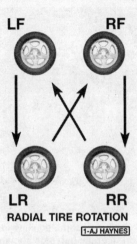

RADIAL TIRE ROTATION
1-AJ HAYNES

14.2a Recommended radial tire rotation pattern for models with NON-DIRECTIONAL tires

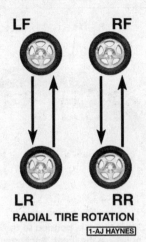

RADIAL TIRE ROTATION
1-AJ HAYNES

14.2b Recommended radial tire rotation pattern for models with DIRECTIONAL tires

15.7a You will find an inspection window (arrow) in each caliper - the inner brake pad lining thickness can be determined by looking through this window

15.7b To inspect the outer pad thickness (arrow), look at the end of the pad

equipped with non-directional tires, but some models have directional tires, which have a different rotation pattern. When choosing replacement tires, examine the sidewalls. Directional tires have arrows on the sidewall that indicate the direction they must turn, and a set of these tires includes two left-side tires and two right-side tires. The left and right side tires must not be rotated to the other side.

3   Refer to the information in *Jacking and towing* at the front of this manual for the proper procedures to follow when raising the vehicle and changing a tire. If the brakes are to be checked, do not apply the parking brake as stated. Make sure the tires are blocked to prevent the vehicle from rolling.

4   Preferably, the entire vehicle should be raised at the same time. This can be done on a hoist or by jacking up each corner and then lowering the vehicle onto jackstands placed under the frame rails. Always use four jackstands and make sure the vehicle is firmly supported.

5   After rotation, check and adjust the tire pressures as necessary and be sure to check the lug nut tightness. Ideally, lug nuts should be torqued to Specifications with a torque wrench, and rechecked after 25 miles of driving.

6   For further information on the wheels and tires, refer to Chapter 10.

15   Brake system check (every 7500 miles or 6 months)

Warning : *The dust created by the brake system may contain asbestos, which is harmful to your health. Never blow it out with compressed air and don't inhale any of it. An approved filtering mask should be worn when working on the brakes. Do not, under any circumstances, use petroleum-based solvents to clean brake parts. Use brake system cleaner only! Try to use non-asbestos replacement parts whenever possible.*
Note: *For detailed photographs of the brake*

system, refer to Chapter 9.

1   In addition to the specified intervals, the brakes should be inspected every time the wheels are removed or whenever a defect is suspected.

2   Any of the following symptoms could indicate a potential brake system defect: The vehicle pulls to one side when the brake pedal is depressed; the brakes make squealing or dragging noises when applied; brake pedal travel is excessive; the pedal pulsates; or brake fluid leaks, usually onto the inside of the tire or wheel.

3   Loosen the wheel lug nuts.

4   Raise the vehicle and place it securely on jackstands.

5   Remove the wheels (see *Jacking and towing* at the front of this book, or your owner's manual, if necessary).

Disc brakes

Refer to illustrations 15.7a, 15.7b, 15.9 and 15.11

6   There are two pads (an outer and an inner) in each caliper. The pads are visible with the wheels removed.

7   Check the pad thickness by looking at each end of the caliper and through the inspection window in the caliper body **(see illustrations)**. If the lining material is less than the thickness listed in this Chapter's Specifi-

cations, replace the pads. **Note:** *Keep in mind that the lining material is riveted or bonded to a metal backing plate and the metal portion is not included in this measurement.*

8   If it is difficult to determine the exact thickness of the remaining pad material by the above method, or if you are at all concerned about the condition of the pads, remove the caliper(s), then remove the pads from the calipers for further inspection (refer to Chapter 9).

9   Once the pads are removed from the calipers, clean them with brake cleaner and re-measure them with a ruler or a vernier

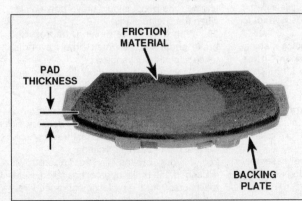

15.9 If a more precise measurement of pad thickness is necessary, remove the pads and measure the remaining friction material

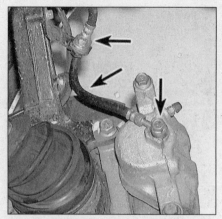

15.11 Check along the brake hoses and at each fitting (arrow) for deterioration and cracks

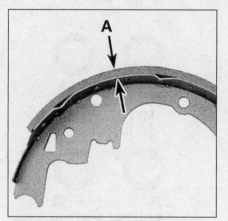

15.15 If the lining is bonded to the brake shoe, measure the lining thickness from the outer surface to the metal shoe, as shown here; if the lining is riveted to the shoe, measure from the lining outer surface to the rivet head

15.16 Typical assembled view of a rear drum brake (left side shown)

15.17 Check the wheel cylinder boots for leaking fluid indicating that the cylinder must be replaced or rebuilt

caliper **(see illustration)**.

10   Measure the disc thickness with a micrometer to make sure that it still has service life remaining. If any disc is thinner than the specified minimum thickness, replace it (refer to Chapter 9). Even if the disc has service life remaining, check its condition. Look for scoring, gouging and burned spots. If these conditions exist, remove the disc and have it resurfaced (see Chapter 9).

11   Before installing the wheels, check all brake lines and hoses for damage, wear, deformation, cracks, corrosion, leakage, bends and twists, particularly in the vicinity of the rubber hoses at the calipers **(see illustration)**. Check the clamps for tightness and the connections for leakage. Make sure that all hoses and lines are clear of sharp edges, moving parts and the exhaust system. If any of the above conditions are noted, repair, reroute or replace the lines and/or fittings as necessary (see Chapter 9).

Drum brakes

Refer to illustrations 15.15, 15.16 and 15.17

12   On models with rear drum brakes, make sure the parking brake is off then tap on the outside of the drum with a rubber mallet to loosen it.

13   Remove the brake drums.

14   With the drums removed, carefully clean the brake assembly with brake system cleaner. **Warning:** *Don't blow the dust out with compressed air and don't inhale any of it (it may contain asbestos, which is harmful to your health).*

15   Note the thickness of the lining material on both front and rear brake shoes. If the material has worn away to within 1/16-inch of the recessed rivets or 1/8-inch of the metal backing on bonded type shoes, the shoes should be replaced **(see illustration)**. The shoes should also be replaced if they're cracked, glazed (shiny areas), or covered with brake fluid.

16   Make sure all the brake assembly springs are connected and in good condition **(see illustration)**.

17   Check the brake components for signs of fluid leakage. With your finger or a small screwdriver, carefully pry back the rubber cups on the wheel cylinder located at the top of the brake shoes **(see illustration)**. Any leakage here is an indication that the wheel cylinders should be replaced immediately (see Chapter 9). Also, check all hoses and connections for signs of leakage.

18   Wipe the inside of the drum with a clean rag and denatured alcohol or brake cleaner. Again, be careful not to breathe the dangerous asbestos dust.

19   Check the inside of the drum for cracks, score marks, deep scratches and "hard spots" which will appear as small discolored areas. If imperfections cannot be removed with fine emery cloth, the drum must be taken to an automotive machine shop for resurfacing.

20   Repeat the procedure for the remaining wheel. If the inspection reveals that all parts are in good condition, reinstall the brake drums, install the wheels and lower the vehicle to the ground.

Brake booster check

21   Sit in the driver's seat and perform the following sequence of tests.

22   With the brake fully depressed, start the engine - the pedal should move down a little when the engine starts.

23   With the engine running, depress the brake pedal several times - the travel distance should not change.

24   Depress the brake, stop the engine and hold the pedal in for about 30 seconds - the pedal should neither sink nor rise.

25   Restart the engine, run it for about a minute and turn it off. Then firmly depress the brake several times - the pedal travel should decrease with each application.

26   If your brakes do not operate as described, the brake booster has failed. Refer to Chapter 9 for the replacement procedure.

Parking brake

27   Slowly pull up on the parking brake and count the number of clicks you hear until the handle is up as far as it will go. The adjustment is correct if you hear the specified number of clicks (see this Chapter's Specifications). If you hear more or fewer clicks, it's time to adjust the parking brake (see Chapter 9).

28   An alternative method of checking the parking brake is to park the vehicle on a steep hill with the parking brake set and the transmission in Neutral. If the parking brake cannot prevent the vehicle from rolling, it is in need of adjustment (see Chapter 9).

16   Seat belt check (every 15,000 miles or 12 months)

1   Check seat belts, buckles, latch plates and guide loops for obvious damage and signs of wear.

2   See if the seat belt reminder light comes on when the key is turned to the Run or Start position. A chime should also sound. On passive restraint systems, the shoulder belt should move into position in the A-pillar.

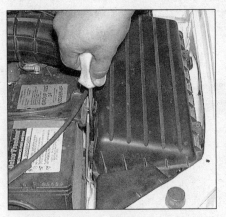

17.2 Loosen the air cleaner cover screws

17.4 Move the cover aside and remove the filter element

18.6 Inspect fuel filler hoses for cracks and make sure the clamps (arrows) are tight

3   The seat belts are designed to lock up during a sudden stop or impact, yet allow free movement during normal driving. Make sure the retractors return the belt against your chest while driving and rewind the belt fully when the buckle is unlatched.

4   If any of the above checks reveal problems with the seat belt system, replace parts as necessary.

17 Air filter replacement (every 15,000 miles or 12 months)

Refer to illustrations 17.2 and 17.4

1   At the specified intervals, the air filter should be replaced with a new one.

2   Loosen the air cleaner cover screws **(see illustration)**.

3   Lift the cover up.

4   Lift the air filter element out of the housing and wipe out the inside of the air cleaner housing with a clean rag **(see illustration)**.

5   While the air cleaner cover is off, be careful not to drop anything down into the air cleaner assembly.

6   Place the new filter in the air cleaner housing. Make sure it seats properly in the lower half of the housing.

7   Install the air cleaner cover and tighten the screws securely.

18 Fuel system check (every 15,000 miles or 12 months)

Refer to illustration 18.6, 18.7 and 18.9
Warning: *Gasoline is extremely flammable, so take extra precautions when you work on any part of the fuel system. Don't smoke or allow open flames or bare light bulbs near the work area, and don't work in a garage where a natural gas-type appliance (such as a water heater or clothes dryer) with a pilot light is present. Since gasoline is carcinogenic, wear latex gloves when there's a possibility of being exposed to fuel, and, if you spill any fuel on your skin, rinse it off immediately with soap and water. Mop up any spills immediately and do not store fuel-soaked rags where*

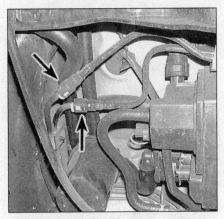

18.7 Carefully inspect fuel line fittings (arrows) for damage

they could ignite. When you perform any kind of work on the fuel system, wear safety glasses and have a Class B type fire extinguisher on hand. The fuel system is under constant pressure, so, before any lines are disconnected, the fuel system pressure must be relieved (see Chapter 4).

1   If you smell gasoline while driving or after the vehicle has been sitting in the sun, inspect the fuel system immediately.

2   Remove the gas filler cap and inspect if for damage and corrosion. The gasket should have an unbroken sealing imprint. If the gasket is damaged or corroded, install a new cap.

3   Inspect the fuel feed and return lines for cracks. Make sure that the connections between the fuel lines and the fuel injection system and between the fuel lines and the in-line fuel filter are tight. **Warning:** *Your vehicle is fuel injected, so you must relieve the fuel system pressure before servicing fuel system components. The fuel system pressure-relief procedure is outlined in Chapter 4.*

4   If the fuel injectors are visible, look for signs of fuel leakage (wet spots) around any of the injectors, they may need new O-rings (see Chapter 4).

5   Since some components of the fuel system - the fuel tank and part of the fuel feed and return lines, for example - are underneath the vehicle, they can be inspected

18.9 The charcoal canister (arrow) is located underneath the rear of the vehicle

more easily with the vehicle raised on a hoist. If that's not possible, raise the vehicle and support it on jackstands.

6   With the vehicle raised and safely supported, inspect the gas tank and filler neck for punctures, cracks and other damage. The connection between the filler neck and the tank is particularly critical. Sometimes a rubber filler neck will leak because of loose clamps or deteriorated rubber **(see illustration)**. Inspect all fuel tank mounting brackets and straps to be sure that the tank is securely attached to the vehicle. **Warning:** *Do not, under any circumstances, try to repair a fuel tank (except rubber components). A welding torch or any open flame can easily cause fuel vapors inside the tank to explode.*

7   Carefully check all rubber hoses and metal lines leading away from the fuel tank **(see illustration)**. Check for loose connections, deteriorated hoses, crimped lines and other damage. Repair or replace damaged sections as necessary (see Chapter 4).

8   The evaporative emissions control system can also be a source of fuel odors. The function of the system is to store fuel vapors from the fuel tank in a charcoal canister until they can be routed to the intake manifold where they mix with incoming air before being burned in the combustion chambers.

9   The most common symptom of a faulty

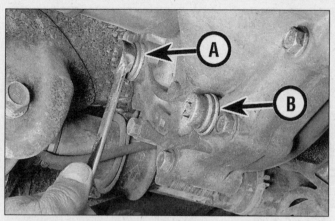

19.1 The manual transaxle fill plug (A) and drain plug (B) are located on the side of the transaxle

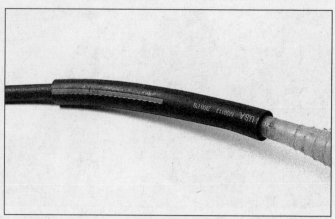

19.2a Use two different size pieces of hose to make an adapter on the funnel . . .

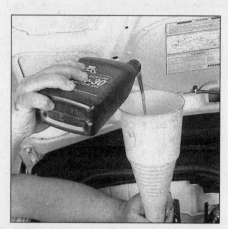

19.2b . . . so you can easily add lubricant to the transaxle from above

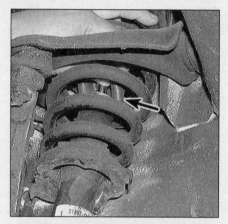

20.6 Check the front and rear struts for leakage where the rod enters the tube (arrow)

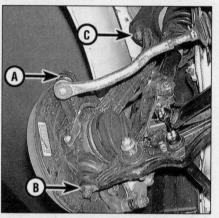

20.9a Inspect the tie rod ends (A) and the balljoints (B is the lower, C is the upper) for torn grease seals

evaporative emissions system is a strong odor of fuel in the engine compartment. If a fuel odor has been detected, and you have already checked the areas described above, check the charcoal canister, located under the rear of the vehicle, and the hoses connected to it **(see illustration)**.

19   Manual transaxle lubricant level check (every 15,000 miles or 12 months)

Refer to illustrations 19.1, 19.2a and 19.2b

1   The manual transaxle does not have a dipstick. To check the fluid level, raise the vehicle and support it securely on jackstands. The check/fill and drain plugs are on the side of the transaxle housing **(see illustration)**. Remove the check/fill plug. If the lubricant level is correct, it should be up to the lower edge of the hole.

2   If the transaxle needs more lubricant (if the level is not up to the hole), use a funnel to add more **(see illustrations)**. Stop filling the transaxle when the lubricant begins to run out the hole.

3   Install the plug and tighten it securely. Drive the vehicle a short distance, then check for leaks.

20   Suspension, steering and driveaxle boot check (every 15,000 miles or 12 months)

Note: The steering linkage and suspension components should be checked periodically. Worn or damaged suspension and steering linkage components can result in excessive and abnormal tire wear, poor ride quality and vehicle handling and reduced fuel economy. For detailed illustrations of the steering and suspension components, refer to Chapter 10.

Shock absorber check

Refer to illustration 20.6

1   Park the vehicle on level ground, turn the engine off and set the parking brake. Check the tire pressures.

2   Push down at one corner of the vehicle, then release it while noting the movement of the body. It should stop moving and come to rest in a level position within one or two bounces.

3   If the vehicle continues to move up-and-down or if it fails to return to its original position, a worn or weak shock absorber is probably the reason.

4   Repeat the above check at each of the three remaining corners of the vehicle.

5   Raise the vehicle and support it securely on jackstands.

6   Check the shock absorbers for evidence of fluid leakage **(see illustration)**. A light film of fluid is no cause for concern. Make sure that any fluid noted is from the shocks and not from some other source. If leakage is noted, replace the shocks as a set.

7   Check the shocks to be sure that they are securely mounted and undamaged. Check the upper mounts for damage and wear. If damage or wear is noted, replace the shocks as a set (front or rear).

8   If the shocks must be replaced, refer to Chapter 10 for the procedure.

Steering and suspension check

Refer to illustrations 20.9a, 20.9b, 20.9c, 20.9d and 20.11

9   Visually inspect the steering and suspension components (front and rear) for damage and distortion. Look for damaged seals, boots and bushings and leaks of any kind Examine the bushings where the lower control arm meets the chassis, and on models

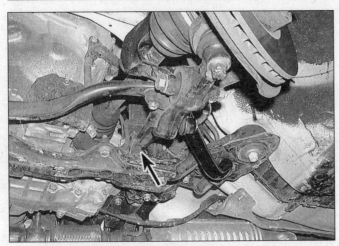

20.9b Inspect the lower control arm bushings (arrow)

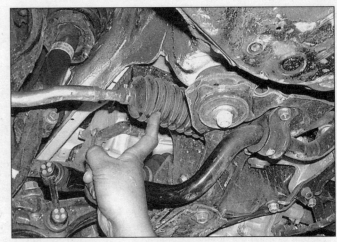

20.9c Check the steering gear boots for cracks and leaking steering fluid

20.9d Check the stabilizer bar bushings (arrows) for deterioration at the front and rear of the vehicle

20.11 With the steering wheel in the lock position and the vehicle raised, grasp the front tire as shown and try to move it back-and-forth - if any play is noted, check the steering gear mounts and tie rod ends for looseness

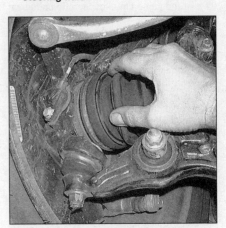

20.14 Flex the inner and outer driveaxle boots by hand to check for cracks and/or leaking grease

that have strut rods, where the strut rod is bushed, either at the lower control arm or the chassis end (see illustrations).

10   Clean the lower end of the steering knuckle. Have an assistant grasp the lower edge of the tire and move the wheel in-and-out while you look for movement at the steering knuckle-to-control arm balljoint. If there is any movement the suspension balljoint(s) must be replaced.

11   Grasp each front tire at the front and rear edges, push in at the front, pull out at the rear and feel for play in the steering system components If any freeplay is noted, check the idler arm and the tie-rod ends for looseness (see illustration).

12   Additional steering and suspension system information and illustrations can be found in Chapter 10.

Driveaxle boot check

Refer to illustration 20.14

13   The driveaxle boots are very important because they prevent dirt, water and foreign material from entering and damaging the constant velocity (CV) joints. Oil and grease can cause the boot material to deteriorate

prematurely, so it's a good idea to wash the boots with soap and water. Because it constantly pivots back and forth following the steering action of the front hub, the outer CV boot wears out sooner and should be inspected regularly.

14   Inspect the boots for tears and cracks as well as loose clamps (see illustration). If there is any evidence of cracks or leaking lubricant, they must be replaced as described in Chapter 8.

21   Exhaust system check (every 15,000 miles or 12 months)

Refer to illustrations 21.2a, 21.2b and 21.2c

1   With the engine cold (at least three hours after the vehicle has been driven), check the complete exhaust system from the engine to the end of the tailpipe. Ideally, the inspection should be done with the vehicle on a hoist to permit unrestricted access. If a

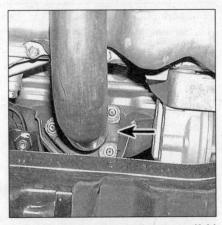

21.2a Check the exhaust pipe-to manifold flange (arrow) for signs of leakage

hoist isn't available, raise the vehicle and support it securely on jackstands.

2   Check the exhaust pipes and connections for evidence of leaks, severe corrosion and damage. Make sure that all brackets and hangers are in good condition and tight (see illustrations).

21.2b Check all of the flanged and slip-jointed exhaust connections - look for stains that indicate exhaust leakage

21.2c Check the exhaust system hangers (arrow indicates one) for damage and cracks

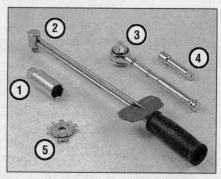

22.2 Tools required for changing spark plugs

1 *Spark plug socket* - *This will have special padding inside to protect the spark plug's porcelain insulator*
2 *Torque wrench* - *Although not mandatory, using this tool is the best way to ensure the plugs are tightened properly*
3 *Ratchet* - *Standard hand tool to fit the spark plug socket*
4 *Extension* - *Depending on model and accessories, you may need special extensions and universal joints to reach one or more of the plugs*
5 *Spark plug gap gauge* - *This gauge for checking the gap comes in a variety of styles. Make sure the gap for your engine is included*

3   At the same time, inspect the underside of the body for holes, corrosion, open seams, etc. which may allow exhaust gases to enter the passenger compartment. Seal all body openings with silicone or body putty.

4   Rattles and other noises can often be traced to the exhaust system, especially the mounts and hangers. Try to move the pipes, muffler and catalytic converter. If the components can come in contact with the body or suspension parts, secure the exhaust system with new mounts.

5   Check the running condition of the engine by inspecting inside the end of the tailpipe. The exhaust deposits here are an indication of engine state-of-tune. If the pipe is black and sooty or coated with white deposits, the engine may need a tune-up, including a thorough fuel system inspection and adjustment.

22 Spark plug check and replacement (see maintenance schedule)

Refer to illustrations 22.2, 22.5a, 22.5b, 22.8, 22.9 and 22.10

1   The spark plug wires should be checked whenever new spark plugs are installed (see the next Section). The 2000 through 2002 V6 model does not have spark plug wires or a distributor. This distributorless system consists of an individual ignition coil/Ignition Control Module (ICM) mounted above each spark plug. So, for this model, disregard any following steps for removing and checking spark plug wires.

2   In most cases, the tools necessary for spark plug replacement include a spark plug socket which fits onto a ratchet (spark plug sockets are padded inside to prevent damage to the porcelain insulators on the new plugs), various extensions and a gap gauge to check and adjust the gap on the new plugs **(see illustration)**. A special plug wire removal tool is available for separating the wire boots from the spark plugs, and is a good idea on these models because the boots fit very

tightly. A torque wrench should be used to tighten the new plugs. It is a good idea to allow the engine to cool before removing or installing the spark plugs.

3   The best approach when replacing the spark plugs is to purchase the new ones in advance, adjust them to the proper gap and replace the plugs one at a time. When buying the new spark plugs, be sure to obtain the correct plug type for your particular engine. The plug type can be found in the Specifications at the front of this Chapter and on the Emission Control Information label located under the hood. If these two sources list different plug types, consider the emission control label correct.

4   Allow the engine to cool completely before attempting to remove any of the plugs. While you are waiting for the engine to cool, check the new plugs for defects and adjust the gap.

5   Check the gap by inserting the proper thickness gauge between the electrodes at the tip of the plug **(see illustration)**. The gap between the electrodes should be the same as the one specified on the Emissions Control Information label or in Chapter 5. The wire

should slide between the electrodes with a slight amount of drag. If the gap is incorrect, use the adjuster on the gauge body to bend the curved side electrode slightly until the proper gap is obtained **(see illustration)**. If the side electrode is not exactly over the center electrode, bend it with the adjuster until it is. Check for cracks in the porcelain insulator (if any are found, the plug should not be used).

6   With the engine cool, remove the spark plug wire as described in the next Section from one spark plug. Pull only on the boot at the end of the wire - do not pull on the wire. A plug wire removal tool should be used if avail-

22.5a Spark plug manufacturers recommend using a wire-type gauge when checking the gap - if the wire does not slide between the electrodes with a slight drag, adjustment is required

22.5b To change the gap, bend the side electrode only, as indicated by the arrows, and be very careful not to crack or chip the porcelain insulator surrounding the center electrode

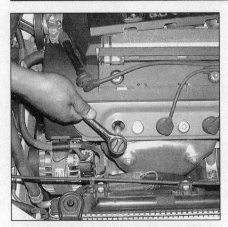

22.8 Because they are deeply recessed, an extension will be required when removing or installing the spark plugs

22.9 A light coat of anti-seize compound applied to the threads of the spark plugs will keep the threads in the cylinder head from being damaged the next time the plugs are removed

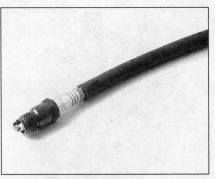

22.10 A piece of rubber hose will aid in getting the spark plug started in the hole

able. On the 2000 and later V6 models, remove an ignition coil to access a spark plug one at a time (see Chapter 5, Section 7, *2000 and later V6 engine Ignition Coil Replacement*). After removing a coil, follow steps 7 through 10 here, to check and replace the spark plug. Repeat for each cylinder.

7 If compressed air is available, use it to blow any dirt or foreign material away from the spark plug hole. A common bicycle pump will also work. The idea here is to eliminate the possibility of debris falling into the cylinder as the spark plug is removed.

8 The spark plugs on some models are difficult to reach so a spark plug socket incorporating a universal joint will be useful. On other models, an extension is needed to reach into deep spark plug recesses. Place the spark plug socket over the plug and remove it from the engine by turning it in a counterclockwise direction **(see illustration)**.

9 Compare the spark plug with the chart shown on the inside back cover of this manual to get an indication of the general running condition of the engine. Before installing the new plugs, it is a good idea to apply a thin coat of anti-seize compound to the threads **(see illustration)**.

10 Thread one of the new plugs into the hole until you can no longer turn it with your

fingers, then tighten it with a torque wrench (if available) or the ratchet. It's a good idea to slip a short length of rubber hose over the end of the plug to use as a tool to thread it into place **(see illustration)**. The hose will grip the plug well enough to turn it, but will start to slip if the plug begins to cross-thread in the hole - this will prevent damaged threads and the accompanying repair costs.

11 Before pushing the spark plug wire onto the end of the plug, inspect the wire following the procedures outlined in the next Section.

12 Attach the plug wire to the new spark plug, again using a twisting motion on the boot until it's seated on the spark plug.

13 Repeat the procedure for the remaining spark plugs, replacing them one at a time to prevent mixing up the spark plug wires.

23 Spark plug wire, distributor cap and rotor check and replacement (every 30,000 miles or 24 months)

Refer to illustrations 23.4, 23.11a, 23.11b, 23.11c, 23.12a and 23.12b

1 The spark plug wires should be checked whenever new spark plugs are installed.

2 Begin this procedure by making a visual check of the spark plug wires while the engine is running. In a darkened garage (make sure there is adequate ventilation) start the engine and observe each plug wire. Be careful not to come into contact with any moving engine parts. If there is a break in the wire, you will see arcing or a small spark at the damaged area. If arcing is noticed, make a note to obtain new wires, then allow the engine to cool and check the distributor cap and rotor.

3 The spark plug wires should be inspected one at a time to prevent mixing up the order, which is essential for proper engine operation. Each original plug wire should be numbered to help identify its location. If the number is illegible, a piece of tape can be marked with the correct number and wrapped around the plug wire.

4 Disconnect the plug wire from the spark plug. A removal tool can be used for this purpose or you can grasp the rubber boot, twist the boot half a turn and pull the boot free **(see illustration)**. Do not pull on the wire itself.

5 Check inside the boot for corrosion, which will look like a white crusty powder.

6 Push the wire and boot back onto the end of the spark plug. It should fit tightly onto the end of the plug. If it doesn't, remove the wire and use pliers to carefully crimp the metal connector inside the wire boot until the fit is snug.

7 Using a clean rag, wipe the entire length of the wire to remove built-up dirt and grease. Once the wire is clean, check for burns, cracks and other damage. Do not bend the wire sharply, because the conductor might break.

8 Remove the rubber boot around the distributor (if equipped) and disconnect the wire from the distributor. Again, pull only on the rubber boot. Check for corrosion and a tight fit. Replace the wire in the distributor.

9 Inspect the remaining spark plug wires, making sure that each one is securely fastened at the distributor and spark plug when the check is complete.

10 If new spark plug wires are required, purchase a set for your specific engine model. Remove and replace the wires one at a time to avoid mix-ups in the firing order.

11 Detach the distributor cap by loosening the cap retaining screws. Check the distributor cap for cracks, carbon tracks and worn, burned or loose contacts **(see illustrations)**.

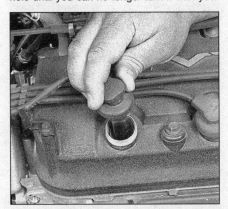

23.4 When removing the spark plug wires, pull only on the boot using a twisting/pulling motion

23.11a Remove the distributor cap retaining bolts (arrow indicates one bolt on 1998 and 1999 V6 models)

23.11b Check the outside of the distributor cap for cracks, a broken tower or carbon tracks

23.11c Check the inside of the distributor cap for carbon tracks, charred or eroded terminals or a damaged rotor button (in center) - if in doubt about its condition, replace it

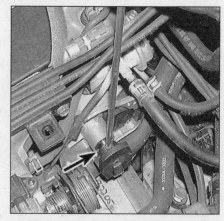

23.12a Remove the rotor retaining screw (arrow), then pull off the rotor and inspect it thoroughly

12   Loosen the retaining screw and pull the rotor off the distributor shaft and examine it for cracks and carbon tracks **(see illustrations)**. Replace the cap and rotor if any damage or defects are noted.

13   It is common practice to install a new cap and rotor whenever new spark plug wires are installed, but if you wish to continue using the old cap, check the resistance between the spark plug wires and the cap first. If the indicated resistance is more than the maximum value listed in this Chapter's Specifications, replace the cap and/or wires.

14   When installing a new cap, remove the wires from the old cap one at a time and attach them to the new cap in the exact same location **Note:** *If an accidental mix-up occurs, refer to the firing order Specifications at the beginning of this Chapter. On most models, the location of the number one plug wire tower is marked on the distributor cap.*

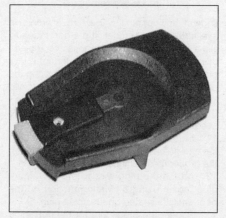

23.12b Check the distributor rotor for cracks, a corroded rotor tip and insufficient spring tension (if in doubt about its condition, buy a new one)

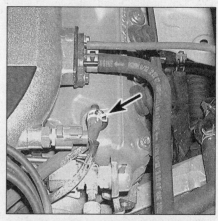

24.2a PCV valve location (arrow) - V6 models

24   Positive Crankcase Ventilation (PCV) valve check and replacement (every 30,000 miles or 24 months)

Refer to illustration 24.2a, 24.2b and 24.4

1   The Positive Crankcase Ventilation (PCV) system directs blowby gases from the crankcase through the PCV valve and hose back into the intake manifold so they can be burned in the engine. The system consists of a hose leading from the valve cover to the intake manifold and a fresh air hose between the air cleaner assembly and the rocker arm cover.

2   The PCV valve and hose is located in the valve cover **(see illustrations)**.

3   With the engine idling at normal operating temperature, pull the valve (with hose attached) from the valve cover.

4   Place your finger over the valve opening or hose **(see illustration)**. If there's no vacuum, check for a plugged hose, manifold port, or the valve itself. Replace any plugged or deteriorated hoses.

5   Turn off the engine and shake the PCV valve, listening for a rattle. If the valve doesn't rattle, replace it with a new one.

6   To replace the valve, pull it from the end of the hose, noting its installed position.

7   When purchasing a replacement PCV valve, make sure it's for your particular vehi-

cle and engine size. Compare the old valve with the new one to make sure they're the same.

8   Push the valve into the end of the hose until it's seated.

9   Inspect all rubber hoses and grommets for damage and hardening. Replace them, if necessary.

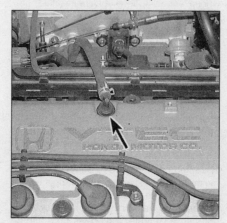

24.2b PCV valve location (arrow) - four-cylinder models

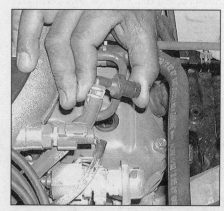

24.4 With the engine running at idle, remove the PCV valve and verify that vacuum can be felt at the end of the valve

25.4 Before checking or adjusting the idle, disconnect the EVAP purge control solenoid (arrow) (V6 model shown)

25.9 The idle speed screw is located on the throttle body, remove the plug (arrow) and use a screwdriver to turn the adjusting screw until the idle speed is correct

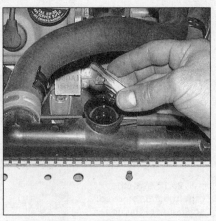

26.5 Push down on the radiator cap and rotate it counterclockwise - never remove it when the engine is hot!

26.6 The radiator drain plug (arrow) is located at the bottom of the radiator, on the right side on V6 models (shown) or on the left side on four-cylinder models - remove the plastic door in the splash panel for access

10   Press the PCV valve and hose securely into position. For further information on the PCV system refer to Chapter 6.

25   Idle speed check and adjustment (30,000 miles or 24 months)

Check

Refer to illustration 25.4

1   Engine idle speed is the speed at which the engine operates when no accelerator pedal pressure is applied, as when stopped at a traffic light. The speed is critical to the performance of the engine itself, as well as many subsystems.

2   Set the parking brake firmly and block the wheels to prevent the vehicle from rolling. Place the transaxle in Neutral (manual transaxle) or Park (automatic transaxle).

3   Connect a hand-held tachometer in accordance with the tool manufacturer's instructions.

4   Disconnect the two-pin electrical connector from the EVAP purge control solenoid **(see illustration)**.

5   Start the engine and run it at 3000 rpm until it warms up to normal operating temperature (the cooling fan comes on).

6   Slowly release the accelerator until the idle drops to normal speed. Make sure all accessories are turned off and the transaxle is in Neutral (manual transaxle) or Park (automatic transaxle).

7   Note the idle speed on the tachometer and compare it to that listed on the VECI label or in this Chapter's Specifications. **Note:** *If the idle speed listed on the VECI label is different than that listed in this Chapter's Specifications, use the specification shown on the VECI label.*

Adjustment

Refer to illustration 25.9

8   Before adjusting the idle speed, make sure the engine cooling fan is off.

9   If the idle speed is too low or too high,

remove the plug and turn the idle speed adjusting screw to obtain the specified idle speed **(see illustration)**. Make changes only in quarter-turn increments. Allow the idle to stabilize for one minute and recheck the idle speed.

10   Turn off the engine and disconnect the tachometer. Reconnect the EVAP solenoid.

26   Cooling system servicing (draining, flushing and refilling) (every 30,000 miles or 24 months)

Warning : *Do not allow antifreeze to come in contact with your skin or painted surfaces of the vehicle. Rinse off spills immediately with plenty of water. Antifreeze is highly toxic if ingested. Never leave antifreeze lying around in an open container or in puddles on the floor; children and pets are attracted by it's sweet smell and may drink it. Check with local authorities about disposing of used antifreeze. Many communities have collection centers which will see that antifreeze is disposed of safely.*

1   Periodically, the cooling system should be drained, flushed and refilled to replenish the antifreeze mixture and prevent formation of rust and corrosion, which can impair the performance of the cooling system and cause engine damage.

2   At the same time the cooling system is serviced, all hoses and the radiator cap should be inspected and replaced if defective (see Section 13).

3   Since antifreeze is a corrosive and poisonous solution, be careful not to spill any of the coolant mixture on the vehicle's paint or your skin. If this happens, rinse it off immediately with plenty of clean water. Consult local authorities about where to recycle or dispose of antifreeze before draining the cooling system. In many areas, reclamation centers have been set up to collect automobile oil and drained antifreeze/water mixtures, rather than

allowing them to be added to the sewage system.

Draining

Refer to illustrations 26.5 and 26.6

4   Apply the parking brake and block the wheels. If the vehicle has just been driven, wait several hours to allow the engine to cool down before beginning this procedure.

5   Once the engine is completely cool, remove the radiator cap and the reservoir cap **(see illustration)**.

6   Drain the radiator by opening the drain plug at the bottom of the radiator **(see illustration)**. If the drain plug is corroded and can't be turned easily, or if the radiator isn't equipped with a plug, disconnect the lower radiator hose to allow the coolant to drain. Be careful not to get antifreeze on your skin or in your eyes.

7   After the coolant stops flowing out of the radiator, remove the lower radiator hose and allow the remaining fluid in the upper half of the engine block to drain.

8   While the coolant is draining from the

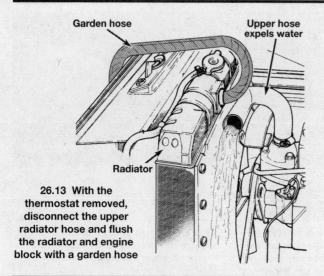

26.13 With the thermostat removed, disconnect the upper radiator hose and flush the radiator and engine block with a garden hose

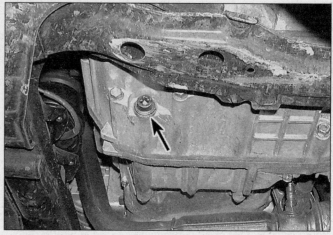

28.7 Use a 3/8-inch ratchet and extension to remove the automatic transaxle drain plug (arrow)

engine block, disconnect the hose from the coolant reservoir and remove the reservoir (see Chapter 3 if necessary). Flush the reservoir out with water until it's clean, and if necessary, wash the inside with soapy water and a brush to make reading the fluid level easier.

9   While the coolant is draining, check the condition of the radiator hoses, heater hoses and clamps (refer to Section 13 if necessary).

10   Replace any damaged clamps or hoses (refer to Chapter 3 for detailed replacement procedures).

Flushing

Refer to illustration 26.13

11   Once the system is completely drained, remove the thermostat from the engine (see Chapter 3). Then reinstall the thermostat housing without the thermostat. This will allow the system to be thoroughly flushed.

12   Reinstall the lower radiator hose and tighten the radiator drain plug. Turn your heating system controls to Hot, so that the heater core will be flushed at the same time as the rest of the cooling system.

13   Disconnect the upper radiator hose, then place a garden hose in the upper radiator inlet and flush the system until the water runs clear at the upper radiator hose **(see illustration)**.

14   In severe cases of contamination or clogging of the radiator, remove the radiator (see Chapter 3) and have a radiator repair facility clean and repair it if necessary.

15   Many deposits can be removed by the chemical action of a cleaner available at auto parts stores. Follow the procedure outlined in the manufacturer's instructions. **Note:** *When the coolant is regularly drained and the system refilled with the correct antifreeze/water mixture, there should be no need to use chemical cleaners or descalers.*

Refilling

16   To refill the system, install the thermostat, reconnect any radiator hoses and install the reservoir and the overflow hose.

17   Place the heater temperature control in the maximum heat position.

18   Make sure to use the proper coolant listed in this Chapter's Specifications. Slowly fill the radiator with the recommended mixture of antifreeze and water to the base of the filler neck. Then add coolant to the reservoir until it reaches the FULL COLD mark. Wait five minutes and recheck the coolant level in the radiator, adding if necessary.

19   Leave the radiator cap off and run the engine in a well-ventilated area until the thermostat opens (coolant will begin flowing through the radiator and the upper radiator hose will become hot).

20   Turn the engine off and let it cool. Add more coolant mixture to bring the level back up to the base of the filler neck.

21   Squeeze the upper radiator hose to expel air, then add more coolant mixture if necessary. Replace the radiator cap.

22   Place the heater temperature control and the blower motor speed control to their maximum setting.

23   Start the engine, allow it to reach normal operating temperature and check for leaks.

27   Brake fluid change (every 30,000 miles or 24 months)

Warning: *Brake fluid can harm your eyes and damage painted surfaces, so use extreme caution when handling or pouring it. Do not use brake fluid that has been standing open or is more than one year old. Brake fluid absorbs moisture from the air. Excess moisture can cause a dangerous loss of braking effectiveness.*

1   At the specified intervals, the brake fluid should be drained and replaced. Since the brake fluid may drip or splash when pouring it, place plenty of rags around the master cylinder to protect any surrounding painted surfaces.

2   Before beginning work, purchase the specified brake fluid (see *Recommended*

lubricants and fluids at the beginning of this Chapter).

3   Remove the cap from the master cylinder reservoir.

4   Using a hand suction pump or similar device, withdraw the fluid from the master cylinder reservoir.

5   Add new fluid to the master cylinder until it rises to the base of the filler neck.

6   Bleed the brake system as described in Chapter 9 at all four brakes until new and uncontaminated fluid is expelled from the bleeder screw. Be sure to maintain the fluid level in the master cylinder as you perform the bleeding process. If you allow the master cylinder to run dry, air will enter the system.

7   Refill the master cylinder with fluid and check the operation of the brakes. The pedal should feel solid when depressed, with no sponginess. **Warning:** *Do not operate the vehicle if you are in doubt about the effectiveness of the brake system.*

28   Automatic transaxle fluid change (every 30,000 miles or 24 months)

Refer to illustration 28.7

1   At the specified time intervals, the automatic transaxle fluid should be drained and replaced.

2   Before beginning work, purchase the specified transmission fluid (*see Recommended lubricants and fluids* at the front of this Chapter).

3   Other tools necessary for this job include jackstands to support the vehicle in a raised position, a 3/8-inch drive ratchet and extension, a drain pan capable of holding at least eight pints, newspapers and clean rags.

4   The fluid should be drained immediately after the vehicle has been driven. Hot fluid is more effective than cold fluid at removing built-up sediment. **Warning:** *Fluid temperature can exceed 350-degrees F in a hot transaxle. Wear protective gloves.*

5   After the vehicle has been driven to

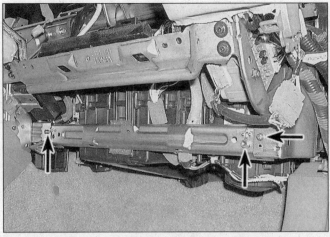

30.3 Remove the screws (arrows) and the glove box
reinforcement panel

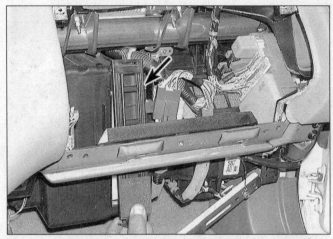

30.4 Release the snap at the bottom, then remove the
filter lid (arrow)

warm up the fluid, raise it and place it on jackstands for access to the transaxle drain plug.

6   Move the necessary equipment under the vehicle, being careful not to touch any of the hot exhaust components.

7   Place the drain pan under the transaxle drain plug and remove the drain plug. It's located near the bottom of the transaxle on the right side on four-cylinder models or the left side on V6 models (see illustration). Be sure the drain pan is in position, as fluid will come out with some force. Once the fluid is drained, clean the drain plug and reinstall it securely.

8   Lower the vehicle.

9   Pull out the dipstick (four-cylinder models) or remove the filler bolt (marked ATF on V6 models), and add new fluid to the transaxle through the dipstick or bolt hole (see Recommended lubricants and fluids for the recommended fluid type and capacity). Use a funnel to prevent spills (see illustrations 19.2a and 19.2b). It is best to add a little fluid at a time, continually checking the level with the dipstick (see Section 7). Allow the fluid time to drain into the pan.

10   Install the dipstick or filler bolt.

11   Start the engine and shift the selector into all positions from P through 2, then shift into P and apply the parking brake.

12   Turn off the engine and check the fluid level. Add fluid to bring the level into the cross-hatched area on the dipstick.

29   Manual transaxle lubricant change (every 30,000 miles or 24 months)

1   At the specified time intervals, the manual transaxle lubricant should be drained and replaced.

2   Before beginning work, purchase the specified transaxle lubricant (see Recommended lubricants and fluids and Capacities at the beginning of this Chapter).

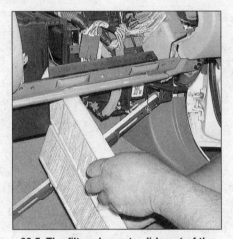

30.5 The filter elements slide out of the evaporator housing - removing the bottom filter first allows room to remove the upper filter

3   Other tools necessary for this job include jackstands to support the vehicle in a raised position, 3/8-inch drive ratchet, a drain pan capable of holding at least four quarts, newspapers and clean rags.

4   After the vehicle has been driven to warm up the fluid, raise it and place it on jackstands for access to the transaxle drain plug. Place the drain pan under the transaxle, remove the drain plug (see illustration 19.1) and allow the old oil to drain into the pan.

5   Reinstall the drain plug securely.

6   Add new fluid through the filler hole until it begins to run out of the filler hole (see Section 19). Install the check/fill plug and tighten it securely.

30   Air conditioning filter replacement (every 30,000 miles or 24 months)

Refer to illustrations 30.3, 30.4, 30.5 and 30.6
Warning: The models covered by this manual are equipped with a Supplemental Restraint

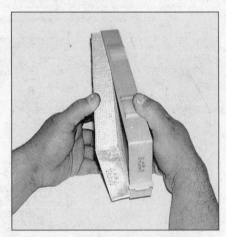

30.6 Install the new filters in the filter carriers

System (SRS), more commonly known as airbags. Always disable the airbag system before working in the vicinity of the impact sensors, steering column or instrument panel to avoid the possibility of accidental deployment of the airbag, which could cause personal injury (see Chapter 12).

1   These models are equipped with two air filtering elements in the air conditioning system, located in a housing next to the evaporator, under the right side of the instrument panel.

2   Refer to Chapter 11 for removal of the glove compartment assembly.

3   Remove the three screws and the glove box reinforcement panel (see illustration).

4   Release the snap at the bottom and remove the air conditioning filter lid (see illustration).

5   Slide the lower and upper filter assemblies out of the evaporator housing (see illustration).

6   Remove the old filters from the filter carriers, clean the carriers and insert the new filters (see illustration).

7   Installation is the reverse of the removal procedure.

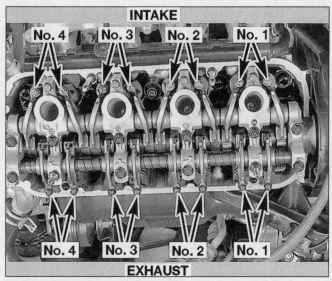

31.6 Valve layout - four-cylinder engine

31.7 Insert a feeler gauge between the valve stem and rocker arm, loosen the lock-nut with a box-end wrench and adjust the clearance with a screwdriver

31.14 Rotate the crankshaft clockwise until the TDC mark for number 1 cylinder (A) on the camshaft sprocket aligns with the mark (B) on the rear cover - there are stamped marks for each cylinder number on the sprocket

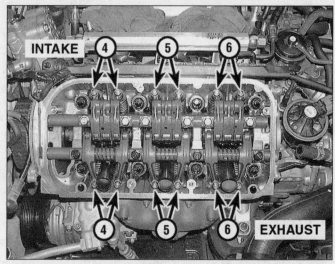

31.15a Valve layout for V6 models - front cylinder bank

31 Valve clearance check and adjustment (as required)

Check

1   The valve clearance generally does not need adjustment unless valvetrain components have been replaced, or a valve job has been performed.

2   The simplest check for proper valve adjustment is to listen carefully to the engine running with the hood open. If the valvetrain is noisy, adjustment is necessary.

3   The valve clearance must be checked and adjusted with the engine cold.

Adjustment

Four-cylinder models

Refer to illustrations 31.6 and 31.7

4   Remove the valve cover and the timing belt upper cover (see Chapter 2A).

5   Place the number one piston (closest to

the drivebelt end of the engine) at Top Dead Center (TDC) on the compression stroke. This is accomplished by rotating the crankshaft pulley counterclockwise until the "UP" mark on the camshaft sprocket is at the 12 o'clock position (see Chapter 2A).

6   With the engine in this position, the number one cylinder valve adjustment can be checked and adjusted **(see illustration)**.

7   Starting with the intake valve. Insert a feeler gauge of the correct thickness (see this Chapter's Specifications) between the valve stem and the rocker arm **(see illustration)**. Withdraw it; you should feel a slight drag. If there's no drag or a heavy drag, loosen the adjuster nut and back off the adjuster screw. Carefully tighten the adjuster screw until you can feel a slight drag on the feeler gauge as you withdraw it.

8   Hold the adjuster screw with a screwdriver (to keep it from turning) and tighten the locknut. Recheck the clearance to make sure it hasn't changed. Repeat the procedure in this Step and the previous Step on the other

intake valve, then on the two exhaust valves.

9   Rotate the crankshaft pulley 180-degrees counterclockwise (the camshaft sprocket will turn 90-degrees) until the number three cylinder is at TDC. With the number three cylinder at TDC, the UP mark on the camshaft sprocket should be at the exhaust side (nine O'clock position). Check and adjust the number three cylinder valves.

10   Rotate the crankshaft pulley 180-degrees counterclockwise until the number four cylinder is at TDC. With the number four cylinder at TDC, the UP mark on the camshaft sprocket should be pointed straight down. Check and adjust the number four cylinder valves.

11   Rotate the crankshaft pulley 180-degrees counterclockwise to bring the number two cylinder to TDC. The UP mark on the camshaft sprocket should be on the intake side (three o'clock position). Check and adjust the number two cylinder valves.

12   Install the valve cover and the timing belt upper cover.

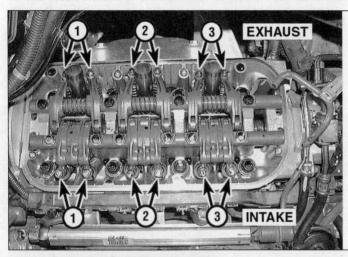

31.15b Valve layout for V6 models - rear cylinder bank

16 Rotate the crankshaft pulley clockwise until the number four mark on the camshaft sprocket aligns with the mark on the rear cover, and check and adjust the valves for cylinder number four. Repeat this procedure following the firing order, with number two being next, then five, three and finally six. In each case, rotate the crankshaft clockwise in sequence until the number on the camshaft sprocket aligns with the mark on the rear cover for the cylinder you are adjusting.
17 Refer to Chapter 2B and install the valve covers, timing belt upper cover and upper intake manifold plenum.

32 Maintenance Required Indicator resetting

Refer to illustration 32.2

1 The Maintenance Required Indicator will glow after your vehicle has gone 6000 miles since the last service. It will light for two seconds when starting the vehicle, then go out after about ten seconds, to warn you that service is due soon. If you exceed 7,500 miles between service, it will stay on all the time.
2 After performing the required maintenance (see the maintenance schedule), reset the Maintenance Required Indicator. With the key Off, hold the Select/Reset button on the instrument panel while the ignition key is turned to On (engine not running). Hold the button down for 10 seconds or more until the Maintenance indicator goes out **(see illustration)**.

32.2 The Select/Reset button (arrow) is used to reset the Maintenance Required indicator light

V6 models

Refer to illustrations 31.14, 31.15a and 31.15b

13 Refer to Chapter 2B for removal of the upper intake manifold plenum, the timing belt upper cover from the front cylinder bank and valve covers.
14 Rotate the crankshaft clockwise and position the number one piston at TDC (see Chapter 2B). When positioned correctly at TDC, the number one mark on the front-bank camshaft sprocket will align with the mark on the rear cover **(see illustration)**.
15 In this position, adjust the valves for cylinder number one **(see illustrations)**. There are four valves for each cylinder. Check and adjust the valve clearance as described in Steps 7 and 8 above.

Notes

Chapter 2 Part A
Four-cylinder engine

Contents

Specifications

General

Firing order	1-3-4-2
Cylinder numbers (front-to-rear)	1-2-3-4
Direction of crankshaft rotation	Counterclockwise
Bore	3.39 inches
Stroke	3.82 inches
Displacement	138 cubic inches (2.3 liters)
Intake/exhaust manifold warpage limit	0.006 inch

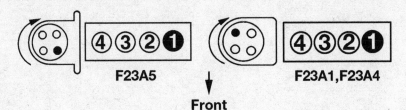

F23A5   **Front**   F23A1, F23A4

Cylinder location and distributor rotation

The blackened terminal shown on the distributor cap indicates the Number One spark plug wire position

Camshaft

Endplay	
Standard	0.002 to 0.006 inch
Maximum	0.020 inch
Runout	0.002 inch (maximum)
Journal oil clearance	
Standard	0.002 to 0.0035 inch
Maximum	0.006 inch
Camshaft lobe height	
VTEC	
Intake	
primary	1.4872 inches
mid	1.5640 inches
secondary	1.3575 inches
Exhaust	1.5105 inches
Non-VTEC	
Intake	1.5094 inches
Exhaust	1.4849 inches

Oil pump

Inner-to-outer rotor tip clearance
    Standard .... 0.001 to 0.006 inch
    Service limit .... 0.008 inch
Outer rotor-to-pump body clearance
    Standard .... 0.004 to 0.007 inch
    Service limit .... 0.008 inch
Pump housing-to-rotor axial clearance
    Standard .... 0.001 to 0.003 inch
    Service limit... 0.005 inch

Torque specifications

Ft-lbs (unless otherwise indicated)

Note: *One foot-pound (ft-lb) of torque is equivalent to 12 inch-pounds (in-lbs) of torque. Torque values below approximately 15 ft-lbs are expressed in inch-pounds, since most foot-pound torque wrenches are not accurate at these smaller values.*

Air intake plenum bolts	16
Camshaft bearing cap bolts	
6.0 x 1.0 mm	108 in-lbs
8.0 x 1.25 mm	16
Valve cover bolts	86 in-lbs
Balance shaft/timing belt tensioner nut	33
Camshaft sprocket bolt	43
Crankshaft pulley bolt	181
Cylinder head bolts	
Step 1	22
Step 2	Tighten an additional 90-degrees
Step 3	Tighten an additional 90-degrees
Step 4 (new bolts only)	Tighten an additional 90-degrees
Flywheel-to-crankshaft bolts	76
Driveplate-to-crankshaft bolts	54
Intake manifold nuts	16
Exhaust manifold nuts	23
Balance shaft (front) sprocket bolt	22
Balance shaft (rear) sprocket bolt	18
Oil pan-to-engine bolts	120 in-lbs
Oil pressure relief valve plug	29
Oil pump pick-up tube bolts/nuts	104 in-lbs
Oil pump housing bolts	104 in-lbs
Rear main oil seal housing bolts	104 in-lbs
Timing belt cover bolts (upper and lower)	104 in-lbs
Water pump bolts	See Chapter 3
Front engine mount	
Bracket-to-chassis bolts	28
Bracket-to-engine bolts	28
Through-bolt	47
Rear engine mount	
Mount-to-chassis bolts	28
Bracket-to-engine bolts	40
Nut for mount stud	40
Left engine mount	
Bracket-to-engine bolt/nuts	40
Mount-to-chassis bolts	28
Right engine mount	
Through-bolt	40
Bracket-to-transaxle nuts	28
Mount-to-chassis bolts	28

1   General information

This Part of Chapter 2 is devoted to in-vehicle repair procedures for the 2.3L engine. All information concerning engine removal and installation and engine block and cylinder head overhaul can be found in Chapter 2, Part C.

There are two basic versions of the 2.3L engine in the models covered by this manual. The F23A5 is the base engine, and the F23A1 and F23A4 are virtually the same engine with the addition of the VTEC valve train (see Section 6).

The following repair procedures are based on the assumption that the engine is installed in the vehicle. If the engine has been removed from the vehicle and mounted on a stand, many of the steps outlined in this Part of Chapter 2 will not apply.

The Specifications included in this Part of Chapter 2 apply only to the procedures contained in this chapter. Chapter 2C con-tains the Specifications necessary for cylinder head and engine block rebuilding.

The four-cylinder models covered by this manual are equipped with a 2.3L fuel-injected, four-cylinder engine with a single overhead camshaft that controls four valves per cylinder (total 16-valves). It is a compact and light-weight engine with an aluminum engine block and cylinder head. The engine is also equipped with two balance shafts that help smooth out vibration created by the opposing force of the pistons and crankshaft.

The crankshaft is supported by the main bearing caps, which are tied into a unit by the main cap "bridge", with the number four bearing (the thrust bearing) assigned the additional task of controlling crankshaft endplay.

The pistons have two compression rings and one oil control ring. The semi-floating piston pins are press fitted into the small end of the connecting rod. The connecting rod big ends are also equipped with renewable insert-type plain bearings.

The engine is liquid-cooled, utilizing a centrifugal impeller-type pump, driven by a toothed belt, to circulate coolant around the cylinders and combustion chambers and through the intake manifold.

Lubrication is handled by a rotor-type oil pump mounted on the front of the engine under the timing belt cover. It's inner rotor is driven by two flats on the front of the crankshaft. The oil is filtered continuously by a cartridge-type filter mounted on the firewall side of the engine.

2 Repair operations possible with the engine in the vehicle

Clean the engine compartment and the exterior of the engine with some type of degreaser before any work is done. It will make the job easier and help keep dirt out of the internal areas of the engine.

Depending on the components involved, it may be helpful to remove the hood to improve access to the engine as repairs are performed (refer to Chapter 11 if necessary). Cover the fenders to prevent damage to the paint. Special pads are available, but an old bedspread or blanket will also work.

If vacuum, exhaust, oil or coolant leaks develop, indicating a need for gasket or seal replacement, the repairs can generally be made with the engine in the vehicle. The intake and exhaust manifold gaskets, oil pan gasket, crankshaft oil seals and cylinder head gasket are all accessible with the engine in place.

Exterior engine components, such as the intake and exhaust manifolds, the oil pan, the water pump, the starter motor, the alternator, the distributor and the fuel system components can be removed for repair with the engine in place.

Since the cylinder head can be removed without pulling the engine, camshaft and valve component servicing can also be accomplished with the engine in the vehicle. Replacement of the timing or balance shaft belts and sprockets is also possible with the engine in the vehicle.

In extreme cases caused by a lack of necessary equipment, repair or replacement of piston rings, pistons, connecting rods and rod bearings is possible with the engine in the vehicle. However, this practice is not recommended because of the cleaning and preparation work that must be done to the components involved.

3.7 Mark the distributor housing directly beneath the number one spark plug wire terminal (arrow; double-check the distributor cap to verify that the rotor points to the number 1 spark plug wire)

3 Top Dead Center (TDC) for number one piston - locating

Refer to illustrations 3.7 and 3.8
Note: *The following procedure is based on the assumption that the spark plug wires and distributor are correctly installed. If you are trying to locate TDC to install the distributor correctly, piston position must be determined by feeling for compression at the number one spark plug hole, then aligning the ignition timing marks as described in Step 8.*

1   Top Dead Center (TDC) is the highest point in the cylinder that each piston reaches as it travels up-and-down when the crankshaft turns. Each piston reaches TDC on the compression stroke and again on the exhaust stroke, but TDC generally refers to piston position on the compression stroke.

2   Positioning the piston(s) at TDC is an essential part of many procedures such as camshaft and timing belt/sprocket removal and distributor removal.

3   Before beginning this procedure, be sure to place the transaxle in Neutral and apply the parking brake or block the rear wheels. Also, disable the ignition system by detaching the primary (low voltage) electrical connectors from the ignition coil. Remove the spark plugs (see Chapter 1).

4   In order to bring any piston to TDC, the crankshaft must be turned using one of the methods outlined below. When looking at the front of the engine, normal crankshaft rotation is counterclockwise.

   a) *The preferred method is to turn the crankshaft with a socket and ratchet attached to the bolt threaded into the front of the crankshaft.*

   b) *A remote starter switch, which may save some time, can also be used. Follow the instructions included with the switch. Once the piston is close to TDC, use a socket and ratchet as described in the previous paragraph.*

3.8 Align the white mark on the crankshaft pulley with the notch in the pointer then check to see if the distributor rotor is pointing to the number 1 cylinder (if not, the crankshaft will have to be rotated 360-degrees) - the second mark (arrow) is usually red and is for ignition timing

   c) *If an assistant is available to turn the ignition switch to the Start position in short bursts, you can get the piston close to TDC without a remote starter switch. Make sure your assistant is out of the vehicle, away from the ignition switch, then use a socket and ratchet as described in Paragraph a) to complete the procedure.*

5   Note the position of the terminal for the number one spark plug wire on the distributor cap. If the terminal isn't marked, follow the plug wire from the number one cylinder spark plug to the cap. On original caps, the number one terminal is marked A1 (VTEC engines) or A (non-VTEC models).

6   Detach the cap from the distributor and set it aside (see Chapter 1 if necessary).

7   Mark the distributor cover directly under the rotor terminal **(see illustration)** for the number 1 cylinder.

8   Turn the crankshaft counterclockwise until the TDC mark (white mark) on the crankshaft pulley is aligned with the groove in the pointer **(see illustration)**.

9   Look at the distributor rotor - it should be pointing directly at the mark you made on the distributor body (cover). If the rotor is pointing at the mark, go to Step 12. If it isn't, go to Step 10.

10   If the rotor is 180-degrees off, the number one piston is at TDC on the exhaust stroke.

11   To get the piston to TDC on the compression stroke, turn the crankshaft one complete turn (360-degrees) counterclockwise. The rotor should now be pointing at the mark on the distributor. When the rotor is pointing at the number one spark plug wire terminal in the distributor cap and the crankshaft pulley timing marks are aligned, the number one piston is at TDC on the compression stroke.

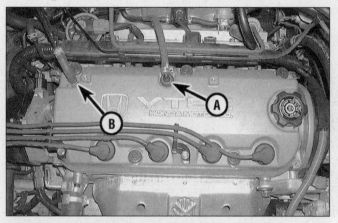

4.4 Pull out the PCV valve (A) and loosen the clamp to remove the breather hose (B)

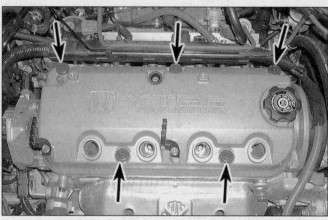

4.7 Remove the valve cover bolts (arrows)

12   After the number one piston has been positioned at TDC on the compression stroke, TDC for any of the remaining pistons can be located by turning the crankshaft and following the firing order. Mark the remaining spark plug wire terminal locations on the distributor body just like you did for the number one terminal, then number the marks to correspond with the cylinder numbers. As you turn the crankshaft, the rotor will also turn. When it's pointing directly at one of the marks on the distributor, the piston for that particular cylinder is at TDC on the compression stroke.

4   Valve cover - removal and installation

Removal

Refer to illustrations 4.4 and 4.7

1   Detach the cable from the negative battery terminal. **Caution:** *The radio in your vehicle is equipped with an anti-theft system. Make sure you have the correct activation code before disconnecting the battery.*

2   Pull the spark plug wires from their plugs (see Chapter 1). Be sure to mark each wire for correct installation.

3   Mark and detach any hoses or wires that will interfere with the removal of the valve cover.

4   Remove the PCV valve and disconnect the breather hose from the valve cover **(see illustration)**.

5   Wipe off the valve cover thoroughly to prevent debris from falling onto the exposed cylinder head or camshaft/valve train assembly.

6   Remove the bolt holding the ground strap at the timing belt end of the cover.

7   Remove the valve cover bolts and their sealing washers **(see illustration)**.

8   Carefully lift off the valve cover and gasket. If the gasket is stuck to the cylinder head, tap it with a rubber mallet to break the seal. Do not pry between the cover and cylinder head or you'll damage the gasket mating surfaces.

Installation

9   The one-piece valve cover gasket can be re-used if it isn't damaged. Peel the gasket carefully out of the groove in the cover and clean the mating surfaces of the cylinder head and the valve cover with a rag soaked in lacquer thinner or acetone.

10   Install a new rubber gasket into the valve cover. Install the molded rubber gasket onto the cover by pushing it into the slot that circles the valve cover perimeter. Apply RTV to the four corners where the cover goes over the front and rear camshaft caps. Install the valve cover, sealing grommets, washers and bolts and tighten them to the torque listed in this Chapter's Specifications. **Note:** *Make sure the RTV sealant has slightly hardened before installing the valve cover, but do not allow more than 10 minutes to elapse before installing the cover. If the weather is damp and cold, the sealant will take some extra time to harden. The valve cover bolt sealing washers can be lubricated with soapy water for easy installation.*

12   On VTEC models, check the condition of the spark plug sealing washers before installing the valve cover.

13   The remainder of installation is the reverse of removal.

5   VTEC system - description and component checks

1   The VTEC system is Honda's design for Variable Valve Timing and Lift Electronic Control. Engines equipped with this system are identified by the VTEC lettering cast into the valve cover, and the designation F23A1 or F23A4 on the radiator side of the engine block.

2   The differences between the base engine and the VTEC counterpart is strictly in the components and operation of the valve train. The engine short block, oiling and cooling systems are identical, as are all attached components.

3   The engine management computer has the ability to physically change which cam-

shaft intake lobes are being used to operate the intake valves. The computer turns the system ON or OFF, depending on sensor input.

4   The following are used to determine VTEC operation:

a) *Engine speed (rpm)*
b) *Vehicle speed (mph)*
c) *Throttle position*
d) *Engine load (measured by Manifold Absolute Pressure (MAP) sensor)*
e) *Coolant temperature*

5   The camshaft has three different intake valve lobe profiles (lift and duration specifications).

6   At low speeds, the secondary intake valve operates on its own camshaft lobe, which has very low lift and duration (compared to the primary valve). The opening is intended to be just enough to keep atomized fuel from building up, "puddling", at the valve head. This limited valve operation is designed to provide good low end torque and responsiveness, by inducing swirl in the combustion chamber from the primary intake valve, which operates with a normal profile.

7   When performance is needed, the primary and secondary rocker arms are locked together through the use of an electrically controlled hydraulic system. Hydraulically operated synchronizing pistons lock all three rocker arms together. When activated, both intake valves open to the higher lift and duration of the middle rocker arm, which has its own camshaft lobe. **Note:** *The secondary rocker arm no longer contacts its own camshaft lobe, until the system is disengaged.*

Component checks

Note: *Some checks and inspections of the VTEC components requires removal of the rocker arm assembly (see Section 6).*

VTEC lock-up control solenoid valve

Refer to illustrations 5.8, 5.9, 5.10, 5.13 and 5.14

Note 1: *A problem in the VTEC solenoid valve circuit will set a diagnostic **trouble code** and*

5.8 The VTEC lock-up solenoid (arrow) and pressure switch are located at the right rear of the cylinder head

5.9 There should be continuity between the solenoid valve connector and chassis ground

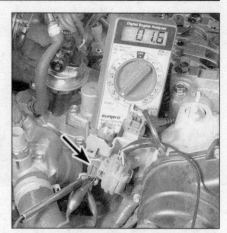

5.10 Check for continuity between the two terminals of the VTEC oil pressure switch (arrow)

5.13 With your finger, check for free movement of the solenoid plunger (arrow)

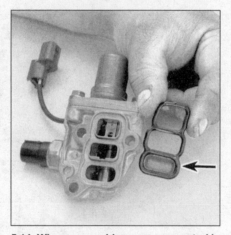

5.14 Whenever problems are suspected in the VTEC system, check the O-ring and filter (arrow) behind the VTEC solenoid

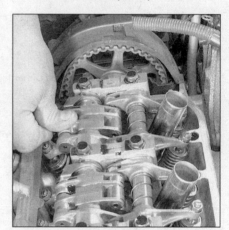

5.16 Push down on the mid-rocker of cylinder number 1 to check the action of the VTEC rocker assembly - it should move independently of the primary and secondary intake rockers

turn on the Check Engine light on the dash. Refer to Chapter 6 for accessing trouble codes.

Note 2: *Most problems in the VTEC system are with the solenoid valve and its filter. Regular engine oil and filter changes are necessary trouble-free operation of the valve.*

8   The lock-up VTEC solenoid valve **(see illustration)** is located on the right rear of the cylinder head (firewall side of head).

9   Check for continuity between VTEC solenoid valve connector and body ground **(see illustration)**. There should be 14 to 30 ohms; if not, replace the VTEC solenoid valve.

10   With the ignition off, pull the harness plug from the pressure switch and check for continuity between the two oil pressure switch terminals on the VTEC solenoid **(see illustration)**. There should be continuity. If not, replace the oil pressure switch.

11   Turn the ignition on and check for voltage between oil pressure switch harness blue/black wire and ground. There should be approximately 12 volts. If not, inspect for an open or short to ground in the blue/black wire between the connector and the PCM.

12   With the ignition still in the ON position, measure the voltage across the terminals of the oil pressure switch harness. There should be approximately 12 volts. If not, repair the open in the brown/black wire.

13   Remove the solenoid and push the plunger to check for free movement **(see illustration)**. Use a new O-ring when reinstalling the solenoid.

14   Remove the complete solenoid assembly from the cylinder head and check the filter/O-ring for clogging **(see illustration)**. Clean and reinstall with a new O-ring. A clogged filter screen is often the cause of system problems.

Rocker arms

Refer to illustration 5.16

15   Position the number one piston at Top Dead Center (see Section 3). Remove the valve cover (see Section 4).

16   Push on the mid-intake rocker arm for cylinder number 1 to see that it moves independently of the primary and secondary intake rockers **(see illustration)**. Check the rocker arms for the other cylinders at their own TDC positions.

Lost motion assembly

17   The four lost motion assemblies sit in pockets in the cylinder head.

18   Remove the individual lost motion assemblies from the cylinder head **(see illustration 6.7)**.

19   Test each lost motion assembly by pushing the plunger with your finger. A light pressure should move the plunger slightly, and firmer pressure will move it further. If the assembly doesn't move smoothly, replace it.

Synchronizing assembly

Refer to illustration 5.22

20   Once the rocker arm assemblies have been removed and disassembled (see Section 6), separate the rocker arms and synchronizing components.

VTEC components:

a) *Primary rocker arm*
b) *Secondary rocker arm*
c) *Mid rocker arm*
d) *Synchronizing piston A*
e) *Synchronizing piston B*
f) *Timing piston*

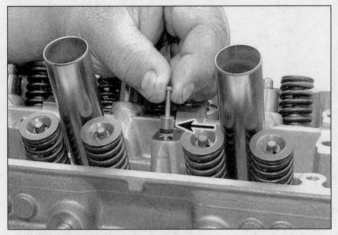

5.22 To remove the oil control orifice for cleaning, thread a machine screw into the top and pull up on the orifice (arrow)

6.4 Leave the camshaft bearing cap bolts in place as you remove the rocker arm assembly

6.5 Rocker arm assembly components - VTEC engines

A   *Number 5 camshaft holder*
B   *Exhaust rocker arm B*
C   *Exhaust shaft spring*
D   *Secondary intake rocker arm*
E   *Mid intake rocker arm*
F   *Pistons*
G   *Primary intake rocker arm*
H   *Timing plate*
I   *Intake rocker spring*
J   *Number 1 camshaft holder*

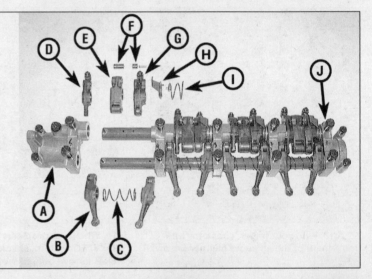

21   Inspect the timing spring, making sure it's not broken or collapsed. Replace it if necessary.

22   Inspect all other parts (rocker arms and synchronizing pistons) for wear, galling, scoring or signs of overheating (bluish in color). Replace any parts necessary. Remove the oil control orifice from the number 3 camshaft holder **(see illustration)**, clean and reinstall it (non-VTEC engines).

23   Reassembly is the reverse of removal. **Note:** *Reassemble and hold together (rubber bands work well) each cylinder's components before trying to assemble on the rocker shaft (see Section 6).*

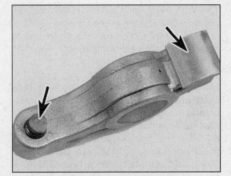

6.6 Check the contact face and adjuster tip for damage or wear (arrows)

6.7 Remove and clean the lost motion assemblies

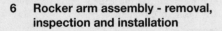

6   Rocker arm assembly - removal, inspection and installation

Removal

Refer to illustration 6.4

1   Remove the valve cover (see Section 4).

2   Rotate the engine to TDC for number 1 piston (see Section 3) and remove the timing belt (see Section 11).

3   Loosen the camshaft bearing cap bolts 1/4-turn at a time, in the reverse of the tightening sequence, until the spring pressure is relieved **(see illustration 6.10)**.

4   Lift the rocker arms and shaft assembly from the cylinder head **(see illustration)**. The camshaft bearing cap bolts will keep the rocker arm assembly components together.

Inspection

Refer to illustrations 6.5, 6.6 and 6.7

5   If you wish to disassemble and inspect the rocker arm assembly, (a good idea as long as you have them off), remove the retaining bolts and slip the rocker arms, springs and bearing caps off the shafts **(see**

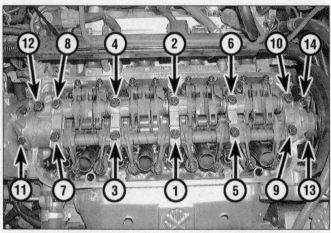

6.10 Rocker arm assembly bolt TIGHTENING sequence

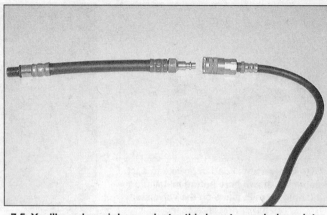

7.5 You'll need an air hose adapter this long to reach down into the spark plug tubes - they're commonly available from auto parts stores

Iillustration). Mark the relationship of the shafts to the bearing caps and keep the parts in order so you can reassemble them in the same positions. **Note:** *On VTEC engines, keep the three intake rockers for each cylinder together by wrapping them with a heavy rubber band.*

6　Thoroughly clean the parts and inspect them for wear and damage. Check the rocker arm faces that contact the camshaft and the rocker arm tips **(see illustration)**. Check the surfaces of the shafts that the rocker arms ride on, as well as the bearing surfaces inside the rocker arms, for scoring and excessive wear. Replace any parts that are damaged or excessively worn. Also, make sure the oil holes in the shafts are not plugged. **Note:** *On VTEC engines, the rocker arms have roller tips; check them for wear and smoothness of operation.*

7　On VTEC engines remove the lost motion assemblies from the cylinder head **(see illustration)**, and clean them. Check for smoothness of plunger operation by pushing down gently with your finger.

Installation

Refer to illustration 6.10

8　Lubricate all components with assembly lube or engine oil and reassemble the shafts. When installing the rocker arms, shafts and springs, note the markings and the difference between the left and right side parts.

9　Coat the cam lobes and journals with camshaft installation lubricant. Apply anaerobic-type sealant to the cylinder head contact surfaces of bearing caps 1 and 6 and install the rocker arm assembly.

10　Tighten the camshaft bearing cap bolts a little at a time, in the proper sequence **(see illustration)** to the torque listed in this Chapter's Specifications.

11　The remainder of installation is the reverse of removal.

12　Check the valve clearance and adjust to Specifications (see Chapter 1).

13　Run the engine and check for oil leaks and proper operation.

7.7a Use a universal, shaft-type valve spring compressor as shown, bolted to valve cover bolt holes in the cylinder head

7.7b Compress the valve spring and remove the keepers from the valve stem with a magnet or small needle-nose pliers

7　Valve springs, retainers and seals - replacement

Refer to illustrations 7.5, 7.7a, 7.7b and 7.15
Note: *Broken valve springs and defective valve stem seals can be replaced without removing the cylinder heads. Two special tools and a compressed air source are normally required to perform this operation, so read through this Section carefully. The universal shaft-type valve spring compressor required for the tight valve spring pockets of this vehicle may not be available at all tool rental yards, so check on the availability before beginning the job.*

1　Remove the valve cover (see Section 4).
2　Remove the spark plug from the cylinder which has the defective component. If all of the valve stem seals are being replaced, all of the spark plugs should be removed.
3　Turn the crankshaft until the piston in the affected cylinder is at Top Dead Center on the compression stroke (refer to Section 3 for instructions). If you're replacing all of the valve stem seals, begin with cylinder number one and work on the valves for one cylinder at a time. Move from cylinder-to-cylinder fol-

lowing the firing order sequence (see this Chapter's Specifications).

4　Remove the rocker arms and shafts (see Section 6).
5　Thread a long adapter into the spark plug hole and connect an air hose from a compressed air source to it **(see illustration)**. Most auto parts stores can supply the air hose adapter. **Note:** *Because of the length of the spark plug tubes, it will be necessary to use a long adapter with a length of hose attached (as used on many cylinder compression gauges) utilizing a quick-disconnect fitting to hook to your air source.*

6　Apply compressed air to the cylinder. **Warning:** *The piston may be forced down by the compressed air, causing the crankshaft to turn suddenly. If the wrench used when positioning the number one piston at TDC is still attached to the bolt in the crankshaft nose, it could cause damage or injury when the crankshaft moves.*

7　Stuff shop rags into the cylinder head holes around the valves to prevent parts and tools from falling into the engine, then use a valve spring compressor to compress the spring **(see illustrations)**. Remove the keep-

7.15 Apply a small dab of grease to each keeper as shown here before installation - it'll hold them in place on the valve stem as the spring is released

ers with small needle-nose pliers or a magnet. **Note:** *The valves should be held in place by the air pressure. If the valve faces or seats are in poor condition, leaks may prevent air pressure from retaining the valves. If the valves cannot hold air, the cylinder head should be removed for a valve job at a machine shop.*

8   Remove the spring retainer, shield and valve spring, then remove the guide seal.

9   Wrap a rubber band or tape around the top of the valve stem so the valve won't fall into the combustion chamber, then release the air pressure.

10   Inspect the valve stem for damage. Rotate the valve in the guide and check the end for eccentric movement, which would indicate that the valve is bent.

11   Move the valve up-and-down in the guide and make sure it doesn't bind. If the valve stem binds, either the valve is bent or the guide is damaged. In either case, the cylinder head will have to be removed for repair.

12   Reapply air pressure to the cylinder to retain the valve in the closed position, then remove the tape or rubber band from the valve stem.

13   Lubricate the valve stem with engine oil and install a new guide seal. **Note:** *Intake valve guide seals have a white spring around the top, while exhaust valve seals have a black spring.*

14   Install the spring(s) in position over the valve, with the more closely wound spring coils toward the cylinder head.

15   Install the valve spring retainer. Compress the valve spring and carefully position the keepers in the groove. Apply a small dab of grease to the inside of each keeper to hold it in place **(see illustration)**.

16   Remove the pressure from the spring tool and make sure the keepers are seated.

17   Disconnect the air hose and remove the adapter from the spark plug hole.

18   Refer to Section 6 and install the rocker arm assembly.

19   Refer to Section 4 and install the valve cover.

20   Install the spark plug(s) and hook up the wire(s).

21   Start and run the engine, then check for

8.4a Disconnect the MAP sensor electrical connector (A) from the throttle body, then tag and remove the hoses (B) from the plenum

8.5 Remove the two bolts (arrows) and position the throttle and cruise control cables aside

oil leaks and unusual sounds coming from the valve cover area.

8   Intake manifold - removal and installation

Warning: *Gasoline is extremely flammable, so take extra precautions when you work on any part of the fuel system. Don't smoke or allow open flames or bare light bulbs near the work area, and don't work in a garage where a natural gas-type appliance (such as a water heater or clothes dryer) with a pilot light is present. Since gasoline is carcinogenic, wear latex gloves when there's a possibility of being exposed to fuel, and, if you spill any fuel on your skin, rinse it off immediately with soap and water. Mop up any spills immediately and do not store fuel-soaked rags where they could ignite. The fuel system is under constant pressure, so, if any fuel lines are to be disconnected, the fuel pressure in the system must be relieved first (see Chapter 4 for more information). When you perform any kind of work on the fuel system, wear safety glasses and have a Class B type fire extinguisher on hand.*

8.4b Disconnect the electrical connector and remove the Idle Air Control valve mounting bolts (arrows)

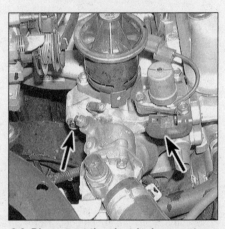

8.6 Disconnect the electrical connectors, then remove the two bolts (arrows) and the thermostat housing

Removal

Refer to illustrations 8.4a, 8.4b, 8.5, 8.6, 8.8 and 8.9

1   Relieve the fuel system pressure (see Chapter 4), then detach the cable from the negative battery terminal. **Caution:** *The radio in your vehicle is equipped with an anti-theft system. Make sure you have the correct activation code before disconnecting the battery.*

2   Drain the cooling system (see Chapter 1).

3   Remove the intake air duct from the air cleaner assembly (see Chapter 4).

4   Clearly label and detach any vacuum lines and electrical connectors which will interfere with removal of the manifold **(see illustrations)**.

5   Disconnect the throttle and cruise control cable (if equipped) from the throttle body (see Chapter 4). Leave the cables in the cable bracket on the intake manifold, but remove the bracket mounting bolts **(see illustration)**.

6   Remove the thermostat housing from the intake manifold **(see illustration)**.

7   Disconnect the fuel feed and return lines at the fuel rail (see Chapter 4).

8.8 Working from underneath the vehicle, remove the intake manifold brace bolts (arrows)

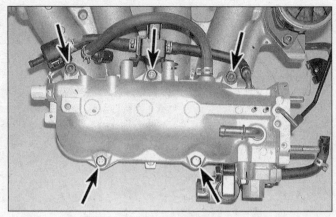

8.9 To separate the plenum from the intake manifold, remove the bolts (arrows)

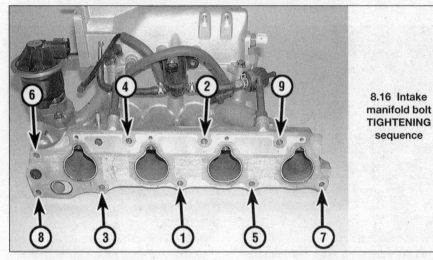

8.16 Intake manifold bolt TIGHTENING sequence

sequence **(see illustration)**, tighten the bolts to the torque listed in this Chapter's Specifications. If the plenum was removed, install it onto the intake manifold with a new gasket.

17   The remainder of the installation procedure is the reverse of removal. Refer to Chapter 1 and refill the cooling system.

---

9   Exhaust manifold - removal and installation

Removal

Refer to illustrations 9.2, 9.3 and 9.4

1   Disconnect the negative battery cable from the battery. **Caution:** *The radio in your vehicle is equipped with an anti-theft system. Make sure you have the correct activation code before disconnecting the battery.*

2   Raise the front of the vehicle and support it securely on jackstands. Detach the exhaust pipe **(see illustration)** from the exhaust manifold. Apply penetrating oil to the fastener threads if they are difficult to remove.

3   Remove the heat shield from the exhaust manifold **(see illustration)**. Be sure to soak the bolts and nuts with penetrating oil

8   Working from underneath the vehicle, remove the intake manifold brace and detach the wiring harness from the brace **(see illustration)**.

9   Remove the intake manifold bolts and remove the manifold from the engine. It is possible to remove the lower intake manifold with the plenum (upper intake manifold) still attached, but it is difficult. The intake mounting bolts are easier to access with the plenum removed **(see illustration)**.

Installation

Refer to illustration 8.16

10   Clean the manifold components with solvent and dry them with compressed air, if available. **Warning:** *Wear eye protection when using compressed air!*

11   Check the mating surfaces of the manifold for flatness with a precision straightedge and feeler gauges. Refer to this Chapter's Specifications for the warpage limit.

12   Before installing the EGR valve, clean out any deposits with solvent and a small wire brush.

13   Inspect the manifold for cracks and distortion. If the manifold is cracked or warped, replace it or see if it can be resurfaced at an automotive machine shop.

14   Check carefully for any stripped or bro-

ken intake manifold bolts/studs. Replace any defective bolts with new parts.

15   Using a scraper, remove all traces of old gasket material from the cylinder head and manifold mating surfaces. Clean the surfaces with lacquer thinner or acetone.

16   Install the intake manifold with a new gasket and tighten the bolts finger tight. Following the recommended tightening

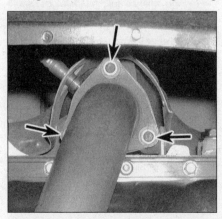

9.2 Remove the flange nuts and lower the exhaust pipe - be sure to spray the nuts with penetrating lubricant before attempting to remove them

9.3 Remove the three heat shield mounting bolts (arrows) and the heat shield

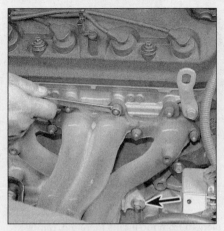

9.4 Remove the exhaust manifold mounting nuts and the lower brace (arrow)

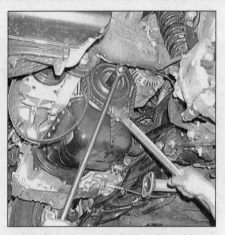

10.5 Hold the crankshaft pulley with a strap wrench while you loosen the crankshaft pulley bolt

10.8a Remove the bolts (arrows) and the upper timing belt cover . . .

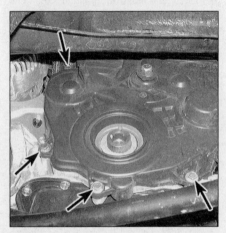

10.8b . . . then remove the bolts (arrows) and the lower belt cover

10.10a Remove the access bolt from the rear side of the engine

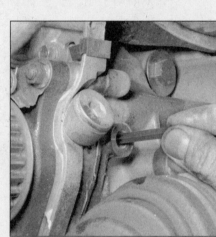

10.10b Use a bolt or Allen wrench (6 x 100 mm) to lock the rear balance shaft into place through the access hole at the rear of the engine block - mark the bolt (or Allen wrench) at 2-29/32 inches and insert it only this far

before attempting to remove them from the manifold.

4   Remove the exhaust manifold nuts **(see illustration)** and detach the exhaust manifold from the cylinder head. **Note:** *Be sure to remove the bolts from the lower brace located near the flange of the exhaust manifold.*

Installation

5   Discard the old gasket and use a scraper to clean the gasket mating surfaces on the manifold and cylinder head, then clean the surfaces with a rag soaked in lacquer thinner or acetone.

6   Place the exhaust manifold in position on the cylinder head and install the nuts. Starting at the center, tighten the nuts in a criss-cross pattern to the torque listed in this Chapter's Specifications.

7   The remainder of installation is the reverse of removal.

8   Start the engine and check for exhaust leaks between the manifold and the cylinder head and between the manifold and the exhaust pipe.

10 Balance shaft belt/sprockets - removal, inspection and installation

Note: *When a loose balance shaft drivebelt is suspected as the cause of excessive noise, the tension must be adjusted. It is possible to do this procedure without removing the timing belt cover (see Step 18). The tensioner simultaneously exerts tension upon the balance shaft belt as well as the timing belt.*

Removal

Refer to illustrations 10.5, 10.8a, 10.8b, 10.10a, 10.10b and 10.11

1   Position the number one cylinder at top dead center on the compression stroke (see Section 3). Disconnect the cable from the negative terminal of the battery. **Caution:** *The radio in your vehicle is equipped with an anti-theft system. Make sure you have the correct activation code before disconnecting the battery.*

2   Remove the power steering belt and disconnect the power steering pump from the mounting bracket (see Chapter 10). Position the power steering pump off to one side.

3   Remove the alternator and brackets from the timing belt cover (see Chapter 5).

4   Raise the vehicle and support it securely on jackstands. Working under the vehicle, remove the splash pan (see Chapter 11) and the left side wheel well cover.

5   Using a strap wrench or equivalent tool to hold the crankshaft pulley, remove the crankshaft pulley bolt **(see illustration)**. Remove the crankshaft pulley, using a puller if necessary.

6   Support the engine with a floor jack and a block of wood under the oil pan. Remove the left side engine mount and bracket (see Section 19).

7   Remove the oil dipstick and the tube from the engine block.

8   Remove the bolts attaching the timing belt covers (upper and lower) to the engine block **(see illustrations)**. Draw a simple diagram showing the location and length of each of the bolts so they can be returned to the same holes from which they were removed.

9   Remove the upper and lower covers.

10.11 Push up on the tensioner and tighten the bolt to release the tension from the belts

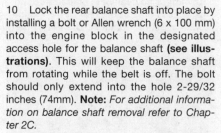

10.16 The front balance shaft has two sets of timing marks; one on the side of the oil pump cover and sprocket and one on the top of the balance shaft and pump cover - the two lower arrows indicate the TDC position of the crankshaft sprocket

10.18 Working under the engine compartment in the wheel well area, it is possible to adjust the belt tension with the timing belt covers assembled

10   Lock the rear balance shaft into place by installing a bolt or Allen wrench (6 x 100 mm) into the engine block in the designated access hole for the balance shaft **(see illustrations)**. This will keep the balance shaft from rotating while the belt is off. The bolt should only extend into the hole 2-29/32 inches (74mm). **Note:** *For additional information on balance shaft removal refer to Chapter 2C.*
11   Temporarily install and tighten one of the timing belt cover bolts through the hole in the left end of the timing belt adjuster arm. This will lock the timing belt adjuster in place when the tensioner nut (which is common to both the balance shaft belt tensioner and the timing belt tensioner) is loosened. Loosen the tensioner nut **(see illustration)** and push the pulley away from the balance shaft belt to release tension on the belt, then tighten the nut. Remove the balance shaft belt. **Note:** *If you intend to reinstall the same balance shaft belt, mark the direction of rotation on the belt so it can be installed correctly.*
12   If the balance shaft sprockets are damaged, remove the bolts that retain the front and rear balance shaft sprockets. While the rear balance shaft is held with a bolt as in **illustration 10.10b**, the front balance shaft can be held with a screwdriver through the service hole in the shaft, just behind the sprocket (see Chapter 2C). Also, remove the crankshaft sprocket from the crankshaft. **Note:** *The rear balance shaft has a set of gears that must be marked correctly before they are removed to ensure proper installation* (see Chapter 2C).

Inspection

13   Check the balance shaft belt, tensioner pulley and sprockets for wear, damage or cracks. Replace parts as necessary.

Installation

Refer to illustrations 10.16 and 10.18
14   Check the condition of the crankshaft

front seal and replace it if necessary (see Section 12). Slide the crankshaft sprocket onto the front of the crankshaft by aligning the keyway in the sprocket with the key on the shaft.
15   Before installing the balance shaft belt and sprockets, make sure the timing belt is properly installed (see Section 11) and the Number One piston is at TDC on the compression stroke (see Section 3). Both balance shafts and the oil pump must also be in place. Make sure the bolt (6 x 100 mm) or equivalent sized shaft is in place in the access hole at the rear side of the engine block **(see illustration 10.10b)**. Retract the balance shaft belt tensioner and hold it in this position following the procedure described in Step 11.
16   Install the balance shaft sprockets, if removed (see Chapter 2C). Double-check the position of the marks on the front balance shaft and sprocket **(see illustration)**. The rear shaft is properly located, due to the pin or bolt inserted into the service hole. Install the balance shaft belt onto the sprockets.
17   Recheck the position of the match marks, then install the balance shaft sprocket bolts and tighten them to the torque listed in this Chapter's Specifications.
18   Adjust the belt tension as follows: Make sure the tensioner adjuster nut is loose and rotate the crankshaft counterclockwise three teeth on the camshaft sprocket to take up any slack in the belt(s), then tighten the tensioner nut to the torque listed in this Chapter's Specifications. **Note 1:** *Check to make sure the belt is properly tensioned by pressing the belt with the tip of your finger near the camshaft sprocket. The belt should be tensioned on both sides of the sprocket.* **Note 2:** *It is possible to adjust the tension of the timing belt and balance shaft belt with the timing covers in place* **(see illustration)**. *However, it is a good idea to make the tensioning adjustments with the cover OFF and then check all the timing marks before reassembling the covers.*

19   If only the balance shaft belt was removed/replaced, remove the bolt that was installed (in Step 11) to secure the timing belt adjuster. Install the timing belt covers onto the engine block and cylinder head **(see illustrations 10.8a and 10.8b)**. Tighten the bolts to the torque listed in this Chapter's Specifications. Make sure the rubber gaskets do not pop out of the gasket rails inside the edge of the timing belt covers.
20   When reinstalling the crankshaft pulley, lubricate the threads and underside of the crankshaft pulley bolt head. Install the bolt and tighten it to the torque listed in this Chapter's Specifications.

11   Timing belt and sprockets - removal, inspection and installation

Note: *When a loose timing belt is suspected as the cause of excessive noise, the tension must be adjusted. It is possible to do this procedure without removing the timing belt cover (see Section 10, Step 18).*

Removal

** CAUTION **
The timing system is complex. Severe engine damage will occur if you make any mistakes. Do not attempt this procedure unless you are highly experienced with this type of repair. If you are at all unsure of your abilities, consult an expert. Double-check all your work and be sure everything is correct before you attempt to start the engine.

Refer to illustration 11.2
1   With the engine at TDC for number 1 cylinder, remove the timing belt covers and the balance shaft belt for access to the timing belt (see Section 10).

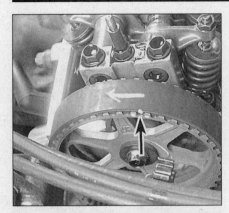

11.2 If you intend on reusing the original belt, make an arrow on the belt indicating the direction of rotation

11.6a Align the mark on the crankshaft sprocket with the mark on the oil pump cover (arrows)

11.6b Alignment marks for the timing belt and the balance shaft belt (arrows). Be sure the word UP is on the upper section of the camshaft sprocket and a bolt (6 X 100mm) or equivalent is placed through the access hole at the rear of the engine block for the rear balance shaft alignment

2   With the balance shaft belt removed (see Section 10) and the tensioner nut loose, push down on the timing belt tensioner pulley then retighten the nut. The timing belt now can be slipped off the sprockets. **Note:** *If you intend to reinstall the original timing belt, mark the direction of rotation on the belt so it can be installed correctly* **(see illustration).** If necessary, the camshaft sprocket can be removed by placing a screwdriver or large punch between the cylinder head and the sprocket casting hole and carefully removing the bolt with a breaker bar and socket. **Caution:** *Do not allow the camshaft to turn.* The sprocket must be removed in order to re-move the belt back cover (two bolts) or the camshaft oil seal.

Inspection

3   Inspect the sprocket teeth for wear and damage. Check the timing belt for any cracks or oil contamination. Also check the camshaft for excessive endplay (see Section 13). Check the timing belt tensioner pulley for smooth operation. Replace any worn parts with new ones. **Note:** *Because of the work involved in getting at the water pump, it is advisable to replace the water pump anytime the timing belt is removed* (see Chapter 3).

Installation
Refer to illustrations 11.6a and 11.6b

** CAUTION **

Before starting the engine, carefully rotate the crankshaft by hand through at least two full revolutions (use a socket and breaker bar on the crankshaft pulley center bolt). If you feel any resistance, STOP! There is something wrong - most likely, valves are contacting the pistons. You must find the problem before proceeding. Check your work and see if any updated repair information is available.

4   If the camshaft sprocket was removed, install it and tighten the bolt to the torque listed in this Chapter's Specifications.

5   Check to make sure the number one piston is still at Top Dead Center (TDC) (see Section 3).
6   Align the timing marks on the crankshaft and camshaft sprockets with the marks on the engine block **(see illustrations). Note:** *The marks on either side of the camshaft pulley must be aligned with the top surface of the cylinder head.* Make sure the bolt (6 x 100mm) or equivalent is in place in the access hole at the rear side of the engine block to align the rear balance shaft **(see illustration 10.10b)**. Install the timing belt onto the sprockets working in a counterclockwise rotation starting with the crank-shaft sprocket, then the tensioner, water pump and finally the camshaft sprocket.
7   Loosen the tensioner nut to allow the timing belt to be tensioned, then tighten the nut. Install the balance shaft belt (see Section 10).
8   After the timing belt and balance shaft belt have been tensioned, rotate the crankshaft two complete revolutions ending back on TDC. Make sure the sprockets return to the original timing marks (use the crankshaft pulley bolt for this test). Re-tension the belts (see Section 10, Step 18).
9   The remainder of installation is the reverse of removal. When reinstalling the crankshaft pulley, lubricate the threads and the underside of the crankshaft pulley bolts head. **Caution:** *Do not use an impact wrench on the crank pulley bolt.*

12   Crankshaft front oil seal - replacement

Refer to illustration 12.5

1   Remove the drivebelts (see Chapter 1).
2   Remove the balance shaft belt and the timing belt (see Sections 10 and 11).
3   Remove the crankshaft pulley (see Section 10).
4   Disconnect the CKP/TDC electrical connector from the main harness. Remove the CKP/TDC sensor mounting bolts and remove the sensor assembly from the oil pump housing.

12.5 Use two screwdrivers and carefully pry the sprocket off the crankshaft

5   Remove the crankshaft sprocket from the crankshaft **(see illustration)**, then remove the concave washer.
6   Carefully pry the seal out of the oil pump housing with a seal removal tool or a screwdriver. Don't scratch the seal bore or damage the crankshaft in the process (if the crankshaft is damaged, the new seal will end up leaking).
7   Clean the bore in the oil pump housing and coat the outer edge of the new seal with engine oil or multi-purpose grease. Using a socket with an outside diameter slightly smaller than the outside diameter of the seal, carefully drive the seal into place squarely with a hammer. If a socket is not available, a short section of a large diameter pipe will work. Check the seal after installation to be sure the spring did not pop out.
8   Install the concave washer and the crankshaft sprocket.
9   The remainder of installation is the reverse of removal.
10   Run the engine and check for leaks.

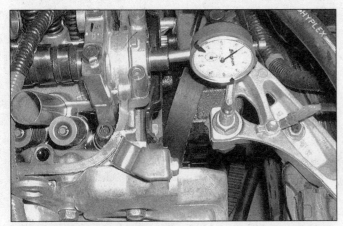

13.7 To check camshaft endplay, mount a dial indicator like this, with the gauge plunger touching the nose of the camshaft

13.8 Remove the camshaft from the cylinder head

13.10a Check the diameter of each camshaft bearing journal, in several locations, to pinpoint excessive wear and out-of-round conditions

13.10b Without expensive measuring tools, Plastigage can be used to measure the camshaft bearing clearance - compare the width of the crushed Plastigage (arrow) with the scale printed on the Plastigage envelope

13.11 Measure the camshaft lobe heights with a micrometer

13 Camshaft - removal, inspection and installation

Removal and inspection

Refer to illustrations 13.7, 13.8, 13.10a, 13.10b and 13.11

1 Remove the valve cover (see Section 4).

2 Position the engine at TDC for cylinder number one (see Section 3).

3 Remove the distributor (see Chapter 5).

4 Remove the balance shaft belt and the timing belt (see Sections 10 and 11).

5 If it is necessary to separate the sprocket from the camshaft, remove the camshaft sprocket bolt. **Note:** *Prevent the camshaft from turning by inserting a screwdriver through one of the holes in the sprocket.*

6 Remove the rocker arm assembly (see Section 6). If the camshaft bearing caps must be removed from the assembly and they don't have numbers on them, number them before removal. Be sure to put the marks on the same ends of all the caps to prevent incorrect orientation of the caps during installation.

7 To check camshaft endplay:

a) *Install the camshaft and secure it with the caps (rocker arm assembly removed).*

b) *Mount a dial indicator on the cylinder head* **(see illustration).**

c) *Using a large screwdriver as a lever at the opposite end, move the camshaft forward-and-backward and note the dial indicator reading.*

d) *Compare the reading with the endplay listed in this Chapter's Specifications.*

e) *If the indicated reading is higher, either the camshaft or the cylinder head is worn. Replace parts as necessary.*

8 Remove the camshaft **(see illustration)**, wipe it off with a clean shop towel and set it aside.

9 To check camshaft runout requires a pair of precision-ground V-blocks and a dial indicator. Only a machine shop would generally have such equipment, so if in doubt about the straightness of a camshaft, have it checked at your local machine shop and compare the runout to this Chapter's Specifications. Replace the camshaft if it is out-of-

specifications.

10 Check the camshaft bearing journals and caps for scoring and signs of wear. If they are worn, replace the cylinder head with a new or rebuilt unit. Measure the journals on the camshaft with a micrometer **(see illustration)**. Check the oil clearance of each camshaft journal with Plastigage, comparing your readings with this Chapter's Specifications **(see illustration)**. If the oil clearance of any of the journals is out-of-specification, replace the camshaft and check the oil clearance again. If it's still out-of-specification replace the cylinder head. **Note:** *For instructions on the use of Plastigage, see Chapter 2, Part C, Sections 24 or 26.*

11 Check the cam lobes for wear:

a) *Check the toe and ramp areas of each cam lobe for score marks and uneven wear. Also check for flaking and pitting.*

b) *If there's wear on the toe or the ramp, replace the camshaft, but first try to find the cause of the wear. Look for abrasive substances in the oil and inspect the oil pump and oil passages for blockage. Lobe wear is usually caused by inadequate lubrication or dirty oil.*

c) *Using a micrometer, measure the cam lobe height* **(see illustration)**. *If the lobe*

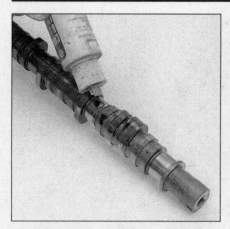

13.15 Be sure to apply camshaft lubricant to the cam lobes and bearing journals before installing the camshaft

14.8 Remove the hose clamp (arrow) and hose connected to the cylinder head under the distributor area

14.10a If the cylinder head sticks to the engine block, pry between the power steering pump bracket and the engine block

wear is greater than listed in this Chapter's Specifications, replace the camshaft.

12   Inspect the rocker arms for wear, galling and pitting of the contact surfaces.

13   If any of the conditions described above are noted, the cylinder head is probably getting insufficient lubrication or dirty oil, so make sure you track down the cause of this problem (low oil level, low oil pump capacity, clogged oil passage, etc.) before installing a new cylinder head, camshaft or rocker arms.

Installation

Refer to illustration 13.15

14   Thoroughly clean the camshaft, the bearing surfaces in the cylinder head and caps and the rocker arms. Remove all sludge and dirt. Wipe off all components with a clean, lint-free cloth.

15   Lubricate the camshaft bearing surfaces in the cylinder head and the bearing journals and lobes on the camshaft with camshaft installation lubricant **(see illustration)**. Carefully lower the camshaft into position with the "**UP** mark" stamped on the camshaft sprocket pointing UP. **Caution:** *Failure to adequately*

lubricate the camshaft and related components can cause serious damage to bearing and friction surfaces during the first few seconds after engine start-up, when the oil pressure is low or nonexistent.

16   Install the rocker arm assembly (see Section 5 or 6). **Note:** *On VTEC models, clean the oil control orifice* **(see illustration 5.22)**.

17   Align the two marks on the camshaft sprocket parallel with the cylinder head top surface. Install the timing belt, balance shaft belt and related components (see Sections 10 and 11).

18   The remainder of installation is the reverse of removal.

---

14   Cylinder head - removal and installation

Caution: *Allow the engine to cool completely before beginning this procedure.*

Removal

Refer to illustrations 14.8, 14.10a, 14.10b, 14.11 and 14.12

1   Position the number one piston at Top

Dead Center (see Section 3).

2   Disconnect the negative cable from the battery. **Caution:** *The radio in your vehicle is equipped with an anti-theft system. Make sure you have the correct activation code before disconnecting the battery.*

3   Drain the cooling system and remove the spark plugs (see Chapter 1).

4   Remove the intake manifold brace and exhaust manifold-to-exhaust pipe flange bolts (see Sections 8 and 9). **Note:** *It isn't necessary to remove the manifolds for cylinder head removal, but the cylinder head will be easier to lift off the engine block if they are removed.*

5   Remove the air intake tube (see Section 8) and the valve cover (see Section 4). Remove the distributor (see Chapter 5), including the cap and wires.

6   Remove the power steering pump (see Chapter 10)

7   Remove the timing belt (see Section 11), rocker arm assembly (see Section 6) and the camshaft (see Section 13).

8   Squeeze the hose clamp and remove the water hose located under the distributor area **(see illustration)**.

14.10b Lift the cylinder head off - this can be done either with or without the intake and exhaust manifolds attached

14.11 Check for cylinder head warpage with a precision straightedge and a feeler gauge - check lengthwise and diagonally across the cylinder head

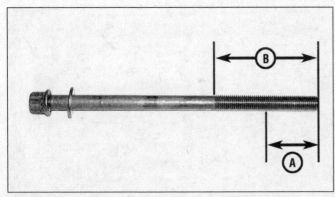

14.12 Measure the thread diameter (peaks, not the valleys) of the cylinder head bolts in two locations - (A) 45 mm from the end and (B) 70 mm from the end - if the diameter is less than 0.480 inches (12.3 mm) in either spot, replace the cylinder head bolt set

14.18 Cylinder head bolt TIGHTENING sequence

9   Loosen the cylinder head bolts in 1/4-turn increments until they can be removed by hand. Work in a pattern that's the reverse of the tightening sequence (see illustration 14.18) to avoid warping the cylinder head. Note where each bolt goes so it can be returned to the same location on installation.

10   Lift the cylinder head off the engine (see illustrations). If resistance is felt, don't pry between the cylinder head and engine block gasket mating surfaces - damage to the mating surfaces will result. Instead, pry between the power steering pump bracket and the engine block. Set the cylinder head on blocks of wood to prevent damage to the gasket sealing surfaces.

11   Cylinder head disassembly and inspection procedures are covered in detail in Chapter 2, Part C. Check the cylinder head for warpage (see illustration).

12   Examine the cylinder head bolts carefully. Use a micrometer or vernier calipers to measure the thread diameter to check for bolt stretch (see illustration). If any bolt fails to meet Specifications, replace the complete set.

Installation

Refer to illustration 14.18

13   The mating surfaces of the cylinder head and engine block must be perfectly clean when the cylinder head is installed.

14   Use a gasket scraper to remove all traces of carbon and old gasket material, then clean the mating surfaces with lacquer thinner or acetone. If there's oil on the mating surfaces when the cylinder head is installed, the gasket may not seal correctly and leaks may develop. When working on the engine block, stuff the cylinders with clean shop rags to keep out debris. Use a vacuum cleaner to remove material that falls into the cylinders. Since the cylinder head and engine block are made of aluminum, aggressive scraping can cause damage. Be extra careful not to nick or gouge the mating surfaces with the scraper.

15   Check the engine block and cylinder head mating surfaces for nicks, deep

15.4 Remove the bolts (arrows) from the engine stiffener plate

scratches and other damage. If damage is slight, it can be removed with a file; if it's excessive, machining may be the only alternative.

16   Use a tap of the correct size to chase the threads in the cylinder head bolt holes in the engine block. Mount each cylinder head bolt in a vise and run a die down the threads to remove corrosion and restore the threads. Dirt, corrosion, sealant and damaged threads will affect torque readings. On F23A5 engines (non-VTEC), remove the oil control orifice from the engine block, clean it and reinstall before replacing the cylinder head.

17   Place a new gasket on the engine block. Check to see if there are any markings (such as "TOP") on the gasket that indicate how it is to be installed. Those identification marks must face UP. Also, apply sealant to the edges of the timing belt cover where it mates with the engine block. Set the cylinder head in position.

18   Lubricate the threads and the seats of the cylinder head bolts, then install them. They must be tightened in a specific sequence (see illustration), in three stages and to the torque listed in this Chapter's Specifications.

19   Attach the camshaft sprocket to the camshaft (see Section 13).

20   Reinstall the remaining parts in the reverse order of removal.

21   Be sure to refill the cooling system and check all fluid levels.

22   Rotate the crankshaft clockwise slowly by hand through two complete revolutions. **Caution:** *If you feel any resistance while turning the engine over, stop and re-check the camshaft timing. The valves may be hitting the pistons.*

23   Start the engine and check the ignition timing (see Chapter 1).

24   Run the engine until normal operating temperature is reached. Check for leaks and proper operation.

15   Oil pan - removal and installation

Removal

Refer to illustrations 15.4 and 15.5

1   Warm up the engine, then drain the oil and replace the oil filter (see Chapter 1). Allow the engine to cool before proceeding.

2   Detach the cable from the negative battery terminal. **Caution:** *The radio in your vehicle is equipped with an anti-theft system. Make sure you have the correct activation code before disconnecting the battery.*

3   Raise the vehicle and support it securely on jackstands.

4   Remove the engine stiffener plate (see illustration).

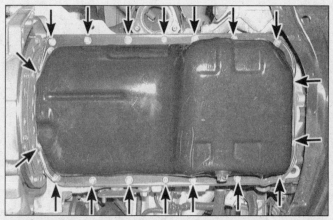

15.5 Remove the oil pan bolts (arrows)

16.3 Remove the oil pick-up tube bolts (arrows) from the oil pump and main bearing cap bridge

16.4a Remove the bolts from the oil pump housing (arrows)

16.4b Lift the oil pump housing from the engine block

5   Remove the bolts securing the oil pan to the engine block (see illustration).
6   Tap on the pan with a soft-face hammer to break the gasket seal, then detach the oil pan from the engine. Don't pry between the engine block and oil pan mating surface.

Installation

7   Using a gasket scraper, remove all traces of old gasket and/or sealant from the engine block and oil pan. Remove the seals from each end of the engine block or oil pan. Clean the mating surfaces with lacquer thinner or acetone. Make sure the threaded bolt holes in the engine block are clean.
8   Clean the oil pan with solvent and dry it thoroughly. Check the gasket flanges for distortion, particularly around the bolt holes. If necessary, place the pan on a block of wood and use a hammer to flatten and restore the gasket surfaces.
9   Apply a small bead of RTV sealant to the mating points of the oil pump-to-block and the rear main seal retainer plate-to-block. Apply RTV sealant to the rear of the one-piece pan gasket at the corners of the semi-circle at the rear.
10   Carefully place the oil pan and gasket in position.
11   Install the two front, two rear and two

center nuts finger tight. Install the remainder of the bolts and tighten them all in small increments to the torque listed in this Chapter's Specifications. Start with the fasteners closest to the center of the pan and work out in a spiral pattern. Don't overtighten them or leakage may occur.
12   Install the engine stiffener plate, tightening the bolts to the torque listed in the Chapter 7A or 7B Specifications.
13   Add oil (see Chapter 1), run the engine and check for oil leaks.

16   Oil pump - removal, inspection and installation

Removal

Refer to illustrations 16.3, 16.4a, 16.4b and 16.5

1   Remove the balance shaft belt and the timing belt (see Sections 10 and 11). Remove the front balance shaft sprocket and the rear balance shaft gear case assembly (see Chapter 2C). Disconnect the CKP/TDC electrical connector from the main harness. Remove the CKP/TDC sensor's four mounting bolts and remove the sensor assembly from the oil pump housing.

2   Remove the oil pan (see Section 15).
3   Remove the oil pick-up tube and screen from the pump housing and the main bearing cap bridge (see illustration).
4   Remove the bolts from the oil pump housing and lift the assembly from the engine (see illustrations).
5   Remove the screws and disassemble the oil pump (see illustration). You may need to use an impact screwdriver to loosen the pump cover screws.

Inspection

Refer to illustrations 16.6a, 16.6b and 16.6c

6   Check the inner-to-outer rotor tip clearance, the rotor-to-pump body clearance and the pump housing-to-rotor axial clearance (see illustrations). Compare your measurements to the figures listed in this Chapter's Specifications. Replace the pump if any of the measurements are outside of the specified limits.
7   Remove the pressure relief valve plug and extract the spring and pressure relief valve plunger from the pump housing. Check the spring for distortion and the relief valve plunger for scoring. Replace parts as necessary.
8   Install the pump rotors. Pack the spaces between the rotors with petroleum jelly (this

16.5 Remove the oil pump cover screws (arrows)

16.6a Using a feeler gauge and straightedge to check the axial clearance

16.6b Using a feeler gauge to check the tooth tip clearance between the inner and outer rotors

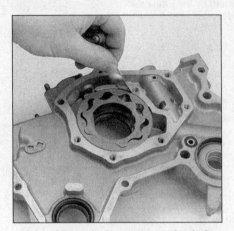

16.6c Using a feeler gauge to check the outer rotor-to-pump body clearance

17.3 Remove the flywheel/driveplate bolts (arrows) from the crankshaft

will prime the pump).

9   Install the pump cover screws and tighten them securely, using thread-locking compound on the screws. Install the oil pressure relief valve, spring and plug, tightening the plug to the torque listed in this Chapter's Specifications.

Installation

10   Apply a thin coat of RTV sealant to the pump housing-to-block sealing surface. Making sure the dowel pin is in place, install the pump housing using new O-rings. Apply RTV sealant to the bolt threads and tighten the bolts to the torque listed in this Chapter's Specifications. **Note:** *Install the oil pump within five minutes of applying the RTV sealant, and make sure the flats on the oil pump rotor are aligned with the flats on the crankshaft as you install it.*

11   Install the rear balance shaft sprocket-and-gear case assembly and the balance shaft belt and timing belt (see Sections 10 and 11).

12   Install the CKP/TDC sensor assembly and the four mounting bolts onto the oil pump housing. Tighten the bolts to the torque listed in this Chapter's Specifications. Connect the

CKP/TDC electrical connector to the main harness.

13   Install the oil pick-up tube and screen, using a new gasket. Tighten the bolts to the torque listed in this Chapter's Specifications.

14   Install the oil pan (see Section 15).

15   The remainder of installation is the reverse of removal. Add the specified type and quantity of oil and coolant (see Chapter 1), run the engine and check for leaks.

17   Flywheel/driveplate - removal and installation

Removal

Refer to illustration 17.3

1   Raise the vehicle and support it securely on jackstands, then refer to Chapter 7 and remove the transaxle.

2   Remove the pressure plate and clutch disc (see Chapter 8) (manual transaxle-equipped models). Now is a good time to check/replace the clutch components.

3   Remove the bolts that secure the flywheel/driveplate to the crankshaft **(see illustration)**. If the crankshaft turns, remove the

starter (see Chapter 5) and wedge a screwdriver in the ring gear teeth (manual transaxle models), or insert a long punch through one of the holes in the driveplate and allow it to rest against a projection on the engine block (automatic transaxle models).

4   Remove the flywheel/driveplate from the crankshaft. Since the flywheel is fairly heavy, be sure to support it while removing the last bolt. **Caution:** *The teeth on the flywheel/driveplate may be sharp; wear gloves or handle the flywheel with rags while removing it.*

5   Clean the flywheel with lacquer thinner or acetone to remove grease and oil. Inspect the surface for cracks, rivet grooves, burned areas and score marks. Light scoring can be removed with emery cloth. Check for cracked and broken ring gear teeth. Lay the flywheel on a flat surface and use a straightedge to check for warpage. If there is any sign of unevenness, heat cracks or scoring, have the flywheel resurfaced at a machine shop.

6   Clean and inspect the mating surfaces of the flywheel/driveplate and the crankshaft. If the rear main oil seal is leaking, replace it before reinstalling the flywheel/driveplate (see Section 18).

18.4a   Carefully pry the oil seal out with a removal tool or a screwdriver - don't nick or scratch the crankshaft or the new seal will be damaged and leaks will develop

18.4b   Because the seal lip is stiff, it won't slide over the end of the crankshaft easily - if you lubricate the journal and the seal lip with multi-purpose grease and carefully work the seal over the journal with a smooth, blunt object, it should go on without damage

Installation

7   Position the flywheel/driveplate against the crankshaft. Note that some engines have an alignment dowel or staggered bolt holes to ensure correct installation. Before installing the bolts, apply a non-hardening thread-locking compound to the threads.

8   Prevent the flywheel/driveplate from turning by using one of the methods described in Step 3. Using a diagonal-crossing pattern, tighten the bolts to the torque listed in this Chapter's Specifications.

9   The remainder of installation is the reverse of the removal procedure.

18   Rear main oil seal - replacement

Refer to illustrations 18.4a and 18.4b

1   The transaxle must be removed from the vehicle for this procedure (see Chapter 7).

2   Remove the flywheel/driveplate (see Section 17).

3   Before removing the seal, it is very important that the clearance between the seal and the outside edge of the retainer is checked. Use a small ruler or caliper and record the distance, which should be between 0.020 to 0.030-inch (approximately 1/64 to 1/32-inch). The new seal must not be driven in past this measurement (refer to Chapter 2C for more details).

4   The seal can be replaced without removing the oil pan or seal retainer. Use a screwdriver and a rag to carefully pry the seal out of the housing **(see illustration)**. Use the rag to be sure no nicks are made in the crankshaft seal surface. Apply a film of clean oil to the crankshaft seal journal and the lip of the new seal and carefully tap the seal into place **(see illustration)**. The lip is stiff so carefully work it onto the seal journal of the crankshaft with a smooth object like the end of a socket extension. Tap the seal into the retainer with a seal driver. If a seal driver isn't available, a large socket or piece of pipe, with an outside

diameter slightly smaller than that of the seal, can be used. Don't rush it or you may damage the seal. **Note:** *Removal of the oil seal retainer and off-engine replacement of the seal are covered in Chapter 2, Part C.*

5   The remaining steps are the reverse of removal.

6   Run the engine and check for oil leaks.

19   Engine mounts - check and replacement

Check

1   During the check, the engine must be raised slightly to remove the weight from the mounts.

2   Raise the vehicle and support it securely on jackstands, then position a jack under the engine oil pan. Place a large block of wood between the jack head and the oil pan, then carefully raise the engine just enough to take the weight off the mounts. **Warning:** *DO NOT place any part of your body under the engine when it's supported only by a jack!*

3   Check the mounts to see if the rubber is cracked, hardened or separated from the casing. Sometimes the rubber will split right down the center.

4   Check for relative movement between the mount plates and the engine or frame (use a large screwdriver or prybar to attempt to move the mounts). If movement is noted, lower the engine and tighten the mount fasteners.

5   Rubber preservative should be applied to the mounts to slow deterioration.

6   Disconnect the negative battery cable from the battery, then set the parking brake, block the rear wheels, raise the front of the vehicle and support it securely on jackstands (if not already done). **Caution:** *The stereo in your vehicle is equipped with an anti-theft system. Make sure you have the correct activation code before disconnecting the battery.*

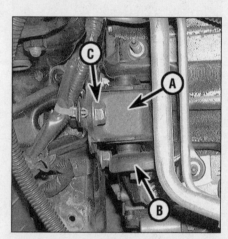

19.8   The passenger-side engine mount (A) is retained by the through-bolt (B) and the mount-to-body bolts (C indicates one of the two)

Replacement

Right (passenger-side) mount

Refer to illustration 19.8

7   The mount supporting the transaxle end of the powertrain is attached to the chassis, and to a bracket mounted at the top of the transaxle. Perform the procedures of Step 6, then use a floor jack under the transaxle to take the weight from the mount.

8   Remove the through-bolt from the mount, then the mount-to-chassis bolts and remove the rubber insulator **(see illustration)**.

9   Installation is the reverse of removal. **Note:** *Tighten the bolts to Specifications only after the powertrain weight is back onto the mounts and the jack is removed. Proceed to Step 19.*

Front mount

Refer to illustration 19.10

10   The front mount is located between the engine and radiator **(see illustration)**.

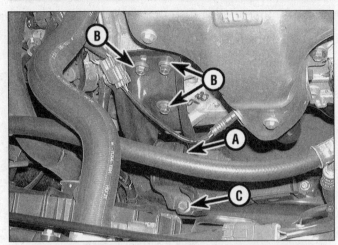

19.10 Front engine mount – (A) indicates location of the through-bolt, (B) indicates bracket-to-block bolts and (C) the bracket-to-chassis bolts (one showing)

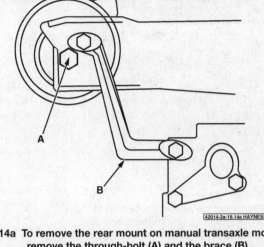

19.14a To remove the rear mount on manual transaxle models, remove the through-bolt (A) and the brace (B)

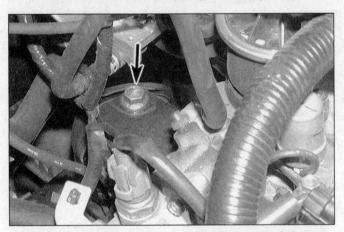

19.14b On automatic transaxle models, Remove the large nut (arrow) at the top of the mount, raise the engine and unbolt the mount from the chassis, disconnecting the vacuum line at the bottom

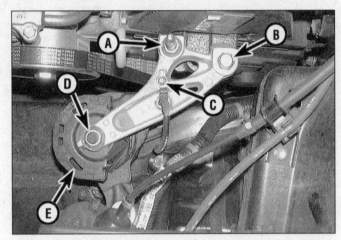

19.16 The driver's-side engine mount - remove the bracket nut (A), bolt (B), ground strap (C), mount nut and bolt (D) and remove the bracket, then remove the mount (E)

11   Perform Steps 7 through 9 to remove the front mount.

12   Installation is the reverse of removal. **Note:** *Tighten the bolts to Specifications only after the powertrain weight is back onto the mounts and the jack is removed. Proceed to Step 19.*

Rear mount

Refer to illustrations 19.14a and 19.14b

13   Unless the intake manifold is removed, access to this mount is tight and only from the bottom. Loosen the through-bolt and raise the engine enough to take the weight off the rear mount.

14   Remove the bolts holding the mount to the chassis, remove the through-bolt, and raise the engine just enough to remove the mount **(see illustration).**

15   Installation is the reverse of removal. **Note:** *Tighten the bolts to Specifications only after the powertrain weight is back onto the mounts and the jack is removed. Proceed to Step 19.*

Left (driver's-side) mount

Refer to illustration 19.16

16   The driver's-side mount is attached to the engine near the timing belt **(see illustration).**

17   With the engine supported, remove the nut and bolts and remove the upper bracket, then remove the through-bolt and remove the mount from the bracket.

18   Installation is the reverse of removal. **Note:** *Tighten the bolts to Specifications only after the powertrain weight is back onto the mounts and the jack is removed. Proceed to Step 19.*

Final tightening, all mounts

19   To ensure maximum bushing life and prevent excessive noise and vibration, the vehicle should be level and the engine weight should be on the mounts during the final tightening stage. **Note:** *Use non-hardening thread locking compound on the nuts/bolts.* Ensure that the bushings are not twisted or offset. If you have replaced more than one

mount, or when you are installing the engine, tighten the mounts in the following order:

a) *Rear mount - bracket-to-block bolts first, then the through-bolt, then the mount-to-chassis bolts.*

b) *Tighten the driver's-side mount bolt/nuts.*

c) *Tighten the through-bolt and nuts on the passenger-side mount.*

d) *Tighten the front engine mount bolts and through-bolt.*

20   Engine Mount Control System - description and check

Description

1   All automatic transaxle models have a special rear engine mount that is computer-controlled to reduce idle speed vibrations from the engine. The interior of the liquid-filled mount has two chambers. When the engine is idling, the Powertrain Control Mod-

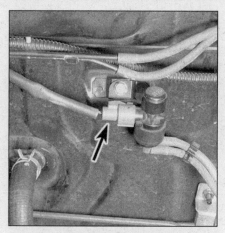

20.4 Disconnect the connector (arrow) at the solenoid and check for battery voltage at the black/yellow wire

ule (PCM) signals a firewall-mounted engine mount control solenoid valve, which allows manifold vacuum to the rear mount. There a

diaphragm changes the flow of liquid between the two chambers, to cancel vibrations at idle speeds. At engine speeds over 1000 rpm, the vacuum is shut off and the motor mount changes to its normal mode.

Check

Refer to illustration 20.4

2   If abnormal vibration is noticed at idle, check the vacuum hoses to the engine mount control solenoid for signs of damage or leakage.

3   With the vehicle idling warm (less than 800 rpm), have an assistant put the car in gear with their foot on the brake and the parking brake on, while you connect and disconnect the connector on the solenoid valve. There should be a noticeable change in smoothness.

4   Put the transmission in PARK or NEUTRAL, disconnect the connector and test the Black/Yellow wire for battery voltage **(see illustration)**. If there is no voltage, check the circuit from the connector to the number 6 fuse in the driver's-side under-dash fuse panel (see Chapter 12).

5   Raise the engine rpm over 1000, and there should **not** be battery voltage at the Black/Yellow wire. If there is, look for a short in the wire to the PCM.

6   Measure between the two wires of the connector at idle speed. Battery voltage should be present, if not, check the circuit between the connector and the PCM.

7   Disconnect the upper vacuum hose from the solenoid and apply 9 inches of vacuum with a hand pump. The vacuum should hold for 20 seconds or more. If not, replace the vacuum hose to the rear engine mount or the engine mount itself.

8   With the engine running, release and reapply vacuum. There should be a noticeable change in engine smoothness.

9   Pull the lower vacuum hose from the solenoid and test for manifold vacuum with a gauge. If vacuum isn't present, check for a bad hose. If vacuum is present, but the engine failed to change in smoothness in Step 8, replace the solenoid.

Chapter 2 Part B
V6 engine

Contents

Specifications

General

Cylinder numbers (timing belt end-to-transaxle end)	
Rear (firewall) side	1-2-3
Front (radiator) side	4-5-6
Direction of crankshaft rotation	clockwise
Firing order	1-4-2-5-3-6
Bore	3.39 inches
Stroke	3.39 inches
Displacement	183 cubic inches (3.0 liters)
Intake/exhaust manifold warpage limit	0.006 inch

0762H

**Cylinder location and
distributor rotation**

*The blackened terminal shown on the
distributor cap indicates the Number
One spark plug wire position*

Camshaft and rocker arms

Camshaft bearing oil clearance
    Standard.. 0.0020 to 0.0035 inch
    Service limit.. 0.006 inch
Camshaft lobe height
    Intake
        Primary.. 1.3628 inches
        Mid... 1.4256 inches
        Secondary... 1.2279 inches
    Exhaust .... 1.4203 inches
Camshaft endplay
    Standard.. 0.002 to 0.008 inch
    Service limit.. 0.008 inch
Camshaft runout limit (total indicator reading) .... 0.002 inch
Rocker arm-to-shaft oil clearance
    Intake
        Standard .... 0.0010 to 0.0026 inch
        Service limit.. 0.0026 inch
    Exhaust
        Standard .... 0.0010 to 0.0030 inch
        Service limit.. 0.0030 inch

Oil pump

Outer rotor-to-body clearance .... 0.006 to 0.008 inch
Outer rotor-to-inner rotor clearance .... 0.002 to 0.008 inch
Housing-to-rotor clearance .... 0.001 to 0.005 inch

Torque specifications

Ft-lbs (unless otherwise indicated)

Note: *One foot-pound (ft-lb) of torque is equivalent to 12 inch-pounds (in-lbs) of torque. Torque values below approximately 15 ft-lbs are expressed in inch-pounds, since most foot-pound torque wrenches are not accurate at these smaller values.*

Camshaft thrust plate bolts 16
Camshaft sprocket bolts 67
Crankshaft pulley bolt.. 181
Cylinder head bolts
    Step 1*... 29
    Step 2*... 51
    Step 3*... 72
Valve cover bolts .... 104 in-lbs
Driveplate bolts.. 54
Exhaust manifold nuts 23
Exhaust heat shield bolts 16
Intake manifold bolts/nuts, upper and lower 16
Oil pan bolts/nuts .... 104 in-lbs
Oil pan drain plug 29
Oil pick-up screen mounting bolts .... 104 in-lbs
Oil pump mounting bolts .... 104 in-lbs
Rocker arm shaft bolts 17
Timing belt tensioner bolts .... 104 in-lbs
Timing belt idler pulley bolt.. 33
Timing belt cover bolts .... 104 in-lbs
Rear main oil seal retainer bolts .... 104 in-lbs
Left-side engine mount engine bracket bolts.......................... 33
Left-side engine mount insulator through-bolt 40
Front engine mount engine bracket bolts............................... 28
Rear engine mount engine bracket bolts................................ 28
Engine mount insulator nut, front and rear 40
Passenger-side engine mount bolts.. 28

*Perform each Step twice

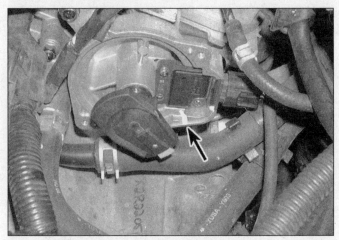

3.6 Mark the distributor below the number one terminal (arrow)

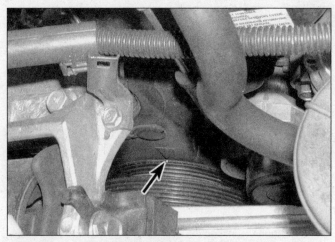

3.8 Align the white TDC mark (arrow) with the pointer - the red mark is used for setting ignition timing only

1   General information

This Part of Chapter 2 is devoted to in-vehicle repair procedures for the V6 engine. All information concerning engine removal and installation and engine block and cylinder head overhaul can be found in Part C of this Chapter.

The following repair procedures are based on the assumption that the engine is installed in the vehicle. If the engine has been removed from the vehicle and mounted on a stand, many of the steps outlined in this Part of Chapter 2 will not apply.

The Specifications included in this Part of Chapter 2 apply only to the procedures contained in this Part. Part C of Chapter 2 contains the Specifications necessary for cylinder head and engine block rebuilding.

2   Repair operations possible with the engine in the vehicle

Many major repair operations can be accomplished without removing the engine from the vehicle.

Clean the engine compartment and the exterior of the engine with some type of degreaser before any work is done. It will make the job easier and help keep dirt out of the internal areas of the engine.

Depending on the components involved, it may be helpful to remove the hood to improve access to the engine as repairs are performed (refer to Chapter 11 if necessary). Cover the fenders to prevent damage to the paint. Special pads are available, but an old bedspread or blanket will also work.

If vacuum, exhaust, oil or coolant leaks develop, indicating a need for gasket or seal replacement, the repairs can generally be made with the engine in the vehicle. The intake and exhaust manifold gaskets, oil pan gasket, crankshaft oil seals and cylinder head gaskets are all accessible with the engine in place.

Exterior engine components, such as the intake and exhaust manifolds, the oil pan, the oil pump, the water pump (see Chapter 3), the starter motor, the alternator, the distributor (see Chapter 5) and the fuel system components (see Chapter 4) can be removed for repair with the engine in place.

Since the cylinder heads can be removed without pulling the engine, valve component servicing can also be accomplished with the engine in the vehicle. Replacement of the camshafts, timing belt and sprockets is also possible with the engine in the vehicle.

In extreme cases caused by a lack of necessary equipment, repair or replacement of piston rings, pistons, connecting rods and rod bearings is possible with the engine in the vehicle. However, this practice is not recommended because of the cleaning and preparation work that must be done to the components involved.

3   Top Dead Center (TDC) for number one piston - locating

Refer to illustrations 3.6, 3.8 and 3.10
Note: *The following procedure is based on the assumption that the distributor is correctly installed. If you are trying to locate TDC to install the distributor correctly, piston position must be determined by feeling for compression at the number one spark plug hole, then aligning the ignition timing marks as described in Step 8.*

1   Top Dead Center (TDC) is the highest point in the cylinder that each piston reaches as it travels up-and-down when the crankshaft turns. Each piston reaches TDC on the compression stroke and again on the exhaust stroke, but TDC generally refers to piston position on the compression stroke.

2   Positioning the piston(s) at TDC is an essential part of several procedures such as camshaft and timing belt/sprocket removal and installation and distributor removal and installation.

3   Before beginning this procedure, be sure to place the transaxle in Neutral and apply the parking brake or block the rear wheels. Also, disable the ignition system by detaching the coil wire from its terminal on the distributor cap and grounding it on the block with a jumper wire. Remove the spark plugs (see Chapter 1).

4   In order to bring any piston to TDC, the crankshaft must be turned using one of the methods outlined below. When looking at the timing belt end of the engine, normal crankshaft rotation is clockwise.

   a) *The preferred method is to remove the lower splash shield on the passenger side and turn the crankshaft with a socket and ratchet attached to the bolt threaded into the front of the crankshaft.*

   b) *A remote starter switch, which may save some time, can also be used. Follow the instructions included with the switch. Once the piston is close to TDC, use a socket and ratchet as described in the previous paragraph.*

   c) *If an assistant is available to turn the ignition switch to the Start position in short bursts, you can get the piston close to TDC without a remote starter switch. Make sure your assistant is out of the vehicle, away from the ignition switch, then use a socket and ratchet as described in Paragraph a) to complete the procedure.*

5   Note the position of the terminal for the number one spark plug wire on the distributor cap. If the plug wire isn't marked, follow the plug wire from the number one cylinder spark plug to the cap.

6   Use a felt-tip pen or chalk to make a mark on the distributor body directly under the terminal **(see illustration)**.

7   Detach the cap from the distributor and set it aside (see Chapter 1 if necessary).

8   Turn the crankshaft (see Step 4) until the TDC mark in the crankshaft pulley is aligned with the pointer on the timing belt cover **(see illustration)**. **Note:** *There are two marks on the pulley. The white mark is for TDC; the red mark is only for setting ignition timing with a timing light.*

3.10 Position the inspection hole cover (A) aside and check the alignment of the camshaft sprocket timing mark (B) with the mark on the rear belt cover (C) (there is an inspection hole on each cylinder bank) - when the marks are aligned, the number 1 piston is at TDC

4.6 Remove the valve cover retaining bolts (arrows)

9   Look at the distributor rotor; the tip should be pointing directly at the mark you made on the distributor body. If the rotor is 180-degrees off, the number one piston is at TDC on the exhaust stroke. Turn the crankshaft one complete turn (360-degrees) clockwise. The rotor tip should now be pointing at the mark on the distributor.

10   Loosen the screw and position the cover aside exposing the camshaft sprocket timing mark on each cylinder bank. Look through the hole in the timing belt cover to check that the camshaft sprocket timing mark is aligned with the mark on the rear cover **(see illustration)**.

11   When the crankshaft pulley timing marks are aligned, and the camshaft sprocket timing marks are aligned, the number one piston is at TDC on the compression stroke.

12   After the number one piston has been positioned at TDC on the compression stroke, TDC for any of the remaining pistons can be located by turning the crankshaft clockwise and following the firing order. Mark the remaining spark plug wire terminal locations on the distributor body just like you did for the number one terminal, then number the marks to correspond with the cylinder num-

bers. As you turn the crankshaft, the rotor will also turn. The crankshaft must be turned 120-degrees to move from one cylinder to the next one in the firing order. When it's pointing directly at one of the marks on the distributor, the piston for that particular cylinder is at TDC on the compression stroke.

4   Valve covers - removal and installation

Removal

Refer to illustration 4.6

1   Disconnect the negative cable from the battery. **Caution:** *The radio in your vehicle is equipped with an anti-theft system. Make sure you have the correct activation code before disconnecting the battery.*

2   Remove the spark plug connectors, wires and brackets from the spark plugs and set them aside. Disconnect the oil temperature sensor located on top of the rear cover, at the timing belt end.

3   Refer to Section 5 and remove the upper intake manifold.

4   At the rear valve cover, pull the PCV hose from the left side and remove the bolt retaining the power steering hose bracket and move the hose aside.

5   At the front valve cover, detach the breather hose from the cover fitting on the left side.

6   Remove the retaining bolts **(see illustration)**, then detach the valve cover. If the cover is stuck to the head, bump the end with a block of wood and a hammer to jar it loose. **Caution:** *Don't pry at the cover-to-head joint or damage to the sealing surfaces may occur, leading to oil leaks after the cover is reinstalled.*

7   Remove the original gasket and seal washers and clean the mating surfaces of the cylinder head and valve cover. Inspect the PCV valve (see Chapter 1) before reattaching it to the rear valve cover.

Installation

8   Position a new gasket in the groove and install new seal washers on the bolts.

9   Install the cover and tighten the bolts to the torque listed in this Chapter's Specifications in three equal steps. The sealing washers, and the areas of the covers they sit on, can be lubricated with soapy water before installation, if necessary.

10   Reinstall the remaining components, run the engine and check for oil leaks.

5   Intake manifold - removal and installation

Warning: *Wait until the engine is completely cool before beginning this procedure.*

Upper intake manifold

Refer to illustrations 5.4a, 5.4b, 5.4c and 5.6

1   Relieve the fuel pressure (see Chapter 4).

2   Disconnect the negative cable from the battery. **Caution:** *The radio in your vehicle is equipped with an anti-theft system. Make sure you have the correct activation code before disconnecting the battery.*

3   Refer to Chapter 4 and remove the air intake duct, then disconnect the throttle linkage, hoses and other connections from the throttle body. Plug the coolant hoses to the throttle body.

4   Remove the intake manifold covers **(see illustrations)**.

5   Following the reverse of the tightening sequence **(see illustration 5.6)**, remove the bolts and nuts and remove the manifold with the throttle body attached.

6   To install the upper manifold, clean the mounting surfaces of the lower manifold with lacquer thinner and remove all traces of the old gasket material or sealant. Install the new gasket over the three studs on the lower manifold, then install the upper intake manifold. Tighten

5.4a Remove the bolts and remove the throttle body cover (arrow) (typical)

5.4b Remove the two screws and the intake manifold end cover (arrow)

the nuts and bolts in sequence **(see illustration)** to the torque listed in this Chapter's Specifications. Check the coolant level and add some, if necessary (see Chapter 1).

Lower intake manifold

Refer to illustrations 5.9 and 5.11

7   Remove the power steering pump and position it aside, without disconnecting the hoses (see Chapter 10).

8   Disconnect the electrical connectors at the fuel injectors (label all connectors first) and remove the fuel rails from the lower intake manifold (see Chapter 4).

9   Remove the mounting nuts and bolts, then detach the two lower intake manifold sections from the cylinder heads **(see illustration)**. If they are stuck, don't pry between the gasket mating surfaces or damage may result. **Note:** *The fuel injectors may be left installed in the lower intake manifolds during removal.*

10   Carefully use a scraper to remove all traces of old gasket material and sealant from the manifold and cylinder heads, then clean the mating surfaces with lacquer thinner or acetone.

11   Install new gaskets **(see illustration)**, then position the lower manifolds on the cylinder heads. Make sure the gaskets and manifolds are aligned over the dowels in the

cylinder heads and install the nuts/bolts.

12   Tighten the fasteners, in three equal steps, to the torque listed in this Chapter's Specifications. Work from the center out towards the ends to avoid warping the manifolds.

13   The remainder of the installation is the reverse of the removal procedure. Check the coolant level and add some, if necessary (see Chapter 1). Run the engine and check for fuel, vacuum and coolant leaks.

6   Exhaust manifolds - removal and installation

Warning: *The engine must be completely cool before beginning this procedure.*

Removal

Refer to illustrations 6.4, 6.5 and 6.6

1   Disconnect the negative cable from the battery. **Caution:** *The radio in your vehicle is equipped with an anti-theft system. Make sure you have the correct activation code before disconnecting the battery.*

5.4c Remove the spark plug wire covers (A) and the spark plug wire holder (B)

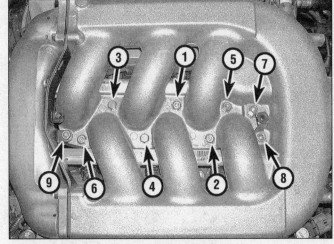

5.6 Upper intake manifold TIGHTENING sequence

5.9 The lower intake manifold is actually two separate sections; remove the fasteners (arrows)

5.11 Position the gasket over the dowels (arrows) in the cylinder head and install the lower intake manifold(s)

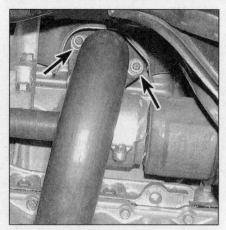

6.4 Remove the exhaust pipe-to-manifold nuts (arrows)

2   Spray penetrating oil on the exhaust manifold fasteners and allow it to soak in.

3   Block the rear wheels to prevent the vehicle from rolling. Set the parking brake and place the transaxle in Park. Raise the front of the vehicle and support it securely on jackstands. Remove the lower splash guard.

4   Disconnect the exhaust pipes from the manifolds and lower the pipes **(see illustration)**.

5   Remove the bolts and the heat shields

from each manifold **(see illustration)**.

6   Remove the self-locking nuts retaining the manifold to the cylinder head and remove the manifold **(see illustration)**. Discard the self-locking nuts and obtain new ones for reassembly.

7   Carefully inspect the manifold and fasteners for cracks and damage. If the manifold is cracked, replace it with a new one.

Installation

7   Use a scraper to remove any traces of old gasket material and carbon deposits from the manifold and cylinder head mating surfaces. If the gasket was leaking, have the manifold checked for warpage at an automotive machine shop and resurfaced if necessary.

8   Position a new gasket over the cylinder head studs.

9   Install the manifold and thread the mounting nuts into place. Working from the center out, tighten the nuts to the torque listed in this Chapter's Specifications in three equal steps. **Note:** *The manifolds are marked with an "F" (front) or an "R" (rear) indicating their location.*

10   Reinstall the remaining parts in the reverse order of removal. Apply engine oil to the studs and install new self-locking nuts.

11   Run the engine and check for exhaust leaks.

7   Timing belt and sprockets - removal, inspection and installation

Removal

** CAUTION **

The timing system is complex. Severe engine damage will occur if you make any mistakes. Do not attempt this procedure unless you are highly experienced with this type of repair. If you are at all unsure of your abilities, consult an expert. Double-check all your work and be sure everything is correct before you attempt to start the engine.

Refer to illustrations 7.10a, 7.10b, 7.11, 7.12a, 7.12b, 7.13, 7.14, 7.15, 7.16, 7.17, 7.18 and 7.19

1   Disconnect the negative cable from the battery. **Caution:** *The radio in your vehicle is equipped with an anti-theft system. Make sure you have the correct activation code before disconnecting the battery.*

2   Place the transaxle in Park or neutral, apply the parking brake and block the rear wheels.

3   Remove the drivebelts (see Chapter 1).

4   Remove the alternator and power steering pump (see Chapters 5 and 10).

5   Remove the spark plugs to make it easier to turn the crankshaft (see Chapter 1), then position the number one piston at TDC (see Section 3).

6   Loosen the lug nuts on the right front wheel. Raise the front of the vehicle and support it securely on jackstands. Remove the right front wheel.

7   Remove the right front inner fender splash guard (see Chapter 11).

8   Support the engine by placing a floor jack under the oil pan (with a block of wood on the jack to protect the pan). Remove the splash shield under the radiator (see Chapter 3).

9   Remove the two bolts (and the wiring harness retainer) holding the passenger-side

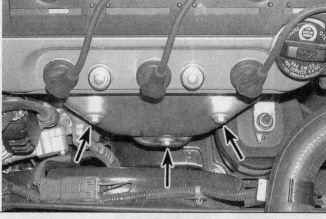

6.6 Remove the heat shield bolts (arrows) and the heat shield (front manifold shown)

6.6 Remove the self-locking nuts (arrows)

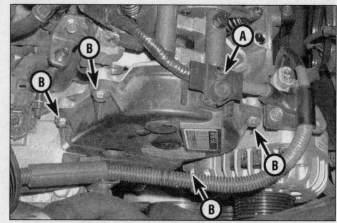

7.10a Detach the wiring harness from the retainer (A) and remove the bolts (B) from the upper timing belt cover (front cylinder bank)

7.10b Remove the upper timing belt cover (arrows indicate two of the four bolts) from the rear cylinder bank

7.11 Mark the direction of rotation on the timing belt

7.12a Camshaft timing marks (arrows) (front cylinder bank) - align the mark on the sprocket with the mark on the rear cover

engine mount to the block, remove the through-bolt, and remove the mount (see Section 18). Remove the engine mount bracket. Remove the engine oil dipstick tube.
10 Remove the upper timing belt covers **(see illustrations)**.
11 If you intend to re-use the belt, mark the belt to indicate the direction of rotation **(see illustration)**.
12 Make sure the timing marks are properly aligned **(see illustrations)**.
13 Using a strap wrench or equivalent tool

to hold the crankshaft, loosen the crankshaft pulley bolt **(see illustration)**. Remove the crankshaft pulley. Note: *When the crankshaft pulley bolt is loosened, the position of the timing marks on the crankshaft pulley and the camshafts may be disturbed. Check and align them again. Temporarily reinstall the crankshaft pulley bolt to turn the crankshaft.*
14 Remove the lower timing belt cover **(see illustration)**.
15 Slip the timing belt guide off the crankshaft sprocket, noting how it's installed. Also note the alignment of the crankshaft

sprocket timing marks **(see illustration)**.
16 Remove one of the long hold-down bolts from the battery tray and bevel the threaded end somewhat with a file or grinder. Thread the bolt into the boss so that it pushes against the timing belt adjuster **(see illustration)**. Do not apply any more than hand pressure in tightening, the bolt is used to hold the adjuster in position.
17 Loosen the idler pulley bolt six turns, then remove the timing belt **(see illustration)**.

7.12b Camshaft sprocket timing marks (arrows) - rear cylinder bank

7.13 Remove the crankshaft pulley bolt (arrow) using a strap wrench to hold the pulley

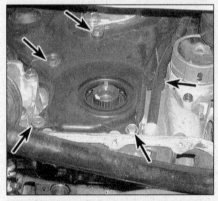

7.14 Remove the bolts (arrows) and the lower timing belt cover

7.15 Crankshaft sprocket timing marks (arrows)

7.16 Thread the long battery hold-down bolt (A) into the boss as shown to hold the timing belt adjuster (B) in position

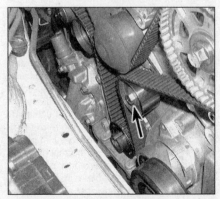

7.17 Loosen the timing belt idler bolt (arrow) about six turns

18   The camshaft sprockets can be removed at this point, if they are damaged or to replace the oil seals **(see illustration)**. Remove the keys from the shafts so they don't fall out and get lost. **Caution:** *Don't allow the camshaft(s) to turn.*

19   If it's worn or damaged, or if you're replacing the crankshaft front oil seal, the crankshaft sprocket can now be removed **(see illustration)**. If it won't come off by hand, carefully pry it off. Also remove the timing belt guide, noting how it's installed.

Inspection

20   Inspect the sprocket teeth for wear and damage. Check the timing belt for any cracks or excessive oil coating. Also check the camshaft for excessive endplay (see Section 11). Check the timing belt tensioner for smooth operation. Replace any worn parts with new ones.

21   Now that the timing belt is removed, inspect the water pump (see Chapter 3). **Note:** *Because of the work involved in getting at the water pump, it is advisable you replace the water pump anytime the timing belt is removed.*

Installation

> ### ** CAUTION **
>
> Before starting the engine, carefully rotate the crankshaft by hand through at least two full revolutions (use a socket and breaker bar on the crankshaft pulley center bolt). If you feel any resistance, STOP! There is something wrong - most likely, valves are contacting the pistons. You must find the problem before proceeding. Check your work and see if any updated repair information is available.

Refer to illustration 7.26

22   Remove all dirt and oil from the timing belt area. Clean the teeth of the sprockets with lacquer thinner.

23   If any of the timing belt sprockets were removed, install them now with their keys and tighten the bolts to the torque listed in this Chapter's Specifications.

24   If removed, install the timing belt guide over the crankshaft sprocket with the chamfered edge facing away from the belt. Also install the crankshaft sprocket.

25   Recheck the position of the timing marks **(see illustrations 7.12a, 7.12b and 7.15)**. Install the timing belt in a clockwise direction, starting at the crankshaft sprocket and tensioner pulley, then rear camshaft sprocket, water pump, front camshaft sprocket, and idler pulley. If you're re-using the original belt, the arrow you made in Step 11 should point in the normal direction of rotation. **Note:** *If the tensioner piston has extended and you're unable to install the timing belt, remove the tensioner and compress the piston as described below.*

26   Install the outer timing belt guide over the crankshaft sprocket with the chamfered

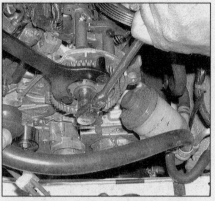

7.18 Prevent the camshaft from turning by inserting a two-pin spanner through the holes in the sprocket while you loosen the bolt

edge facing away from the belt **(see illustration)**.

27   Tighten the idler pulley bolt to the torque listed in this Chapter's Specifications. Remove the battery hold-down bolt that was holding the tensioner pulley in position **(see illustration 7.16)**.

28   Turn the crankshaft slowly six revolutions clockwise using a socket and breaker bar on the crankshaft pulley bolt to seat the belt, then return to TDC. Recheck the alignment of cam and crank timing marks. **Caution:** *If you feel any resistance, back up and recheck the belt timing. Do not force the crankshaft to turn or engine damage will occur!*

29   Install the lower timing belt cover.

30   Install the crankshaft pulley, aligning the pulley keyway with the crankshaft key. Install the bolt and tighten it to the torque listed in this Chapter's Specifications. Use the method described in Step 13 to keep the crankshaft from turning.

31   Recheck the timing marks **(see illustrations 7.12a and 7.12b and 7.15)**. **Caution:** *If the timing marks are not aligned exactly as shown, repeat the timing belt installation procedure. DO NOT start the engine until you're absolutely certain that the timing belt is installed correctly. Serious and costly engine*

7.26 Install the outer timing belt guide (arrow) as shown

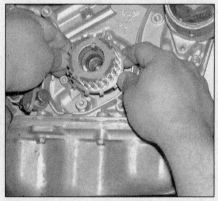

7.19 Remove the belt guide, then carefully remove the crankshaft sprocket

damage could occur if the belt is installed wrong.

32   Reinstall the remaining parts in the reverse order of removal.

Tensioner adjustment

Refer to illustrations 7.36 and 7.37

33   The belt tensioner does not normally need to be removed or adjusted for a timing belt replacement procedure (unless the tensioner piston has extended), but there are other engine procedures (water pump replacement, etc.) that require the tensioner be removed. Once removed, the tensioner piston will extend in length. The following Steps apply only if the tensioner has been removed from the engine.

34   To remove the tensioner, remove the long bolt used in Step 16, and unbolt the tensioner from the block.

35   Clamp the bolt flange of the tensioner in a vise with the service bolt pointing up (do not clamp the body of the tensioner in the vise) and remove the service bolt. Through the service bolt hole, insert a flat-blade screwdriver and turn the piston until it retracts **(see illustration 7.36)**. **Caution:** *Be careful not to tip the tensioner body, spilling the oil inside. If any oil spills or leaks out refill the tensioner with engine oil. Total tensioner oil capacity is 0.22 fluid ounces.*

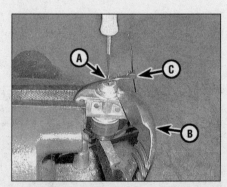

7.36 Remove the bolt from the service hole (A) - retract the piston with a small screwdriver and hold it in with pliers (B) while an assistant tightens the nylon wire-tie (C)

36   The manufacturer uses a special tool to retain the piston in the retracted position. If the tool is not available, hold the piston in the retracted position with a pair of adjustable pliers while an assistant tightens a strong plastic wire-tie around the tensioner body and piston **(see illustration)**. **Note:** *Set-up the tensioner with the wire-tie in position between the jaws of the pliers and the end of the piston before retracting the piston. This is a very delicate procedure and may require several attempts.*

37   Replace the service bolt in the tensioner. Install the tensioner, being careful not to dislodge the wire-tie and tighten the mounting bolts to the torque listed in this Chapter's specifications. After completing the remainder of the timing belt installation procedure, cut the wire-tie and pull it out with pliers **(see illustration)**.

8   Crankshaft front oil seal - replacement

Refer to illustrations 8.2 and 8.4

1   Remove the timing belt and crankshaft sprocket (see Section 7).

2   Carefully pry the seal out of the engine with a screwdriver or seal removal tool **(see illustration)**. If you use a screwdriver, don't scratch the housing bore or damage the crankshaft (if the crankshaft is damaged, the new seal will end up leaking).

3   Clean the oil seal bore and coat the outer edge of the new seal with a small amount of engine oil to ease installation. Apply multi-purpose grease to the seal lip.

4   Using a seal-driver or a socket with an outside diameter slightly smaller than the outside diameter of the seal, carefully drive the new seal into place with a hammer **(see illustration)**. Make sure it's installed squarely and driven in to the same depth as the original. If a socket isn't available, a short section of large-diameter pipe will also work. Check the seal after installation to make sure the garter spring didn't pop out of place.

5   Reinstall the crankshaft sprocket and timing belt (see Section 7).

6   Run the engine and check for oil leaks at the front seal.

9   VTEC system - general description and component checks

General description

1   The VTEC system is Honda's design for Variable Valve Timing and Lift Electronic Control. The VTEC lettering cast into the valve cover identifies models equipped with this system. All V6 engines in the covered models are equipped with the VTEC system.

2   The differences between conventional engines and the VTEC system is strictly in the components and operation of the valve train.

3   The engine management computer has the ability to physically change which

7.37 When timing belt installation is complete, release the tensioner by cutting the wire-tie (arrow) - pull out the wire-tie with pliers

camshaft intake lobes are being used to operate the intake valves. The computer turns the system ON or OFF, depending on sensor input.

4   The following are used to determine VTEC operation:

   a) *Engine speed (rpm)*
   b) *Vehicle speed (mph)*
   c) *Throttle position*
   d) *Engine load measured by Manifold Absolute Pressure (MAP) sensor*
   e) *Coolant temperature*

5   The camshaft has three different intake valve lobe profiles (lift and duration specifications).

6   At low speeds, the secondary intake valve operates on its own camshaft lobe, which has very low lift and duration (compared to the primary valve). The opening is intended to be just enough to keep atomized fuel from puddling at the valve head. This limited valve operation is designed to provide good low end torque and responsiveness, by inducing swirl in the combustion chamber from the primary intake valve, which operates with a normal profile.

7   When performance is needed, the primary and secondary rocker arms are locked together through the use of an electrically controlled hydraulic system. Hydraulically operated synchronizing pistons lock all three

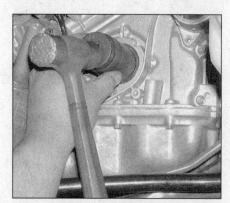

8.4 Lubricate the seal lip and tap the new crankshaft seal into place with a large socket or piece of pipe and a hammer

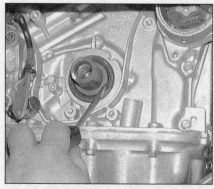

8.2 Carefully pry out the oil seal

rocker arms together. When activated, both intake valves open to the higher lift and duration of the middle rocker arm, which has its own camshaft lobe. **Note:** *The secondary rocker arm no longer contacts its own camshaft lobe, until the system is disengaged.*

Component checks

Note: *Some checks and inspections of the VTEC components requires removal of the rocker arm assembly (see Section 10).*

VTEC lock-up control solenoid valve

Refer to illustrations 9.9, 9.10, 9.13 and 9.14

Note 1: *A problem in the VTEC solenoid valve circuit will set a diagnostic **trouble code** and illuminate the Check Engine light on the dash. Refer to Chapter 6 for accessing trouble codes.*

Note 2: *Most common problems in the VTEC system are associated with the solenoid valve and its filter. Regular engine oil and filter changes are necessary for trouble-free operation of the valve.*

8   The lock-up VTEC solenoid valve and switch are located on the oil filter housing at the right-rear side of the engine, best viewed through the right fenderwell.

9   Disconnect the electrical connector to the VTEC solenoid valve. Check the resistance between the VTEC solenoid valve connector terminal and body ground **(see illustration)**. There should be 14 to 30 ohms; if not, replace the VTEC solenoid valve.

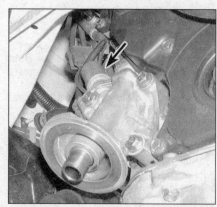

9.9 The VTEC solenoid (arrow) is located on top of the oil filter housing

9.10 Check for continuity between the two terminals of the VTEC oil pressure switch (arrow)

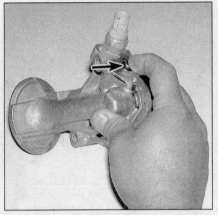

9.13 With your finger, check for free movement of the solenoid plunger (arrow)

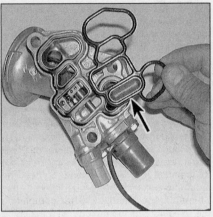

9.14 Whenever problems are suspected in the VTEC system, check the O-ring and filter (arrow) behind the oil filter adapter housing

10 With the ignition off, disconnect the electrical connector from the pressure switch and check for continuity between the two oil pressure switch terminals **(see illustration)**. There should be continuity. If not, replace the oil pressure switch.

11 Turn the ignition on and check for voltage at the blue/black wire of the oil pressure switch connector (harness side). There should be approximately 12 volts. If not, inspect for an open circuit in the blue/black wire between the connector and the PCM.

12 Turn the ignition off and check for continuity between the brown/black wire of the oil pressure switch connector (harness side) and a good chassis ground. If there's no continuity, inspect for an open circuit in the brown/black wire between the connector and ground.

13 Remove the solenoid and push the plunger to check for free movement **(see illustration)**. Use a new O-ring when reinstalling the solenoid.

14 Remove the oil filter adapter housing from the engine and check the filter/O-ring for clogging **(see illustration)**. Clean and reinstall with a new O-ring. A clogged filter screen is often the cause of system problems.

Rocker arms

Refer to illustration 9.16

15 Position the number one piston at Top Dead Center (see Section 3). Remove the valve cover (see Section 4).

16 Press on the mid-intake rocker arm for cylinder number 1 to see that it moves independently of the primary and secondary intake rockers **(see illustration)**. Check the rockers for the other cylinders at their own TDC positions.

Lost motion assembly

Refer to illustration 9.18

17 The lost motion assemblies sit in four pockets in each cylinder head. The rocker arms/shafts must be removed for access to the lost motion assemblies (see Section 10).

18 Test each lost motion assembly by pushing the plunger with your finger **(see**

illustration). A light pressure should move the plunger slightly, and firmer pressure will move it further. If the assembly doesn't move smoothly, replace it.

Synchronizing assembly

Refer to illustration 9.21

19 Once the rocker arm assemblies have been removed and disassembled (see Section 10), separate the rocker arms and synchronizing components.

VTEC components:

   a) *Primary rocker arm*
   b) *Secondary rocker arm*
   c) *Mid rocker arm*
   d) *Synchronizing piston A*
   e) *Synchronizing piston B*
   f) *Timing piston*

20 Inspect the timing spring, making sure it's not broken or collapsed. Replace it if necessary.

21 Inspect all other parts (rocker arms and synchronizing pistons) for wear, galling, scoring or signs of overheating (bluish in color). Use your finger to push on the rocker arm pistons to check for smooth movement **(see illustration)**. Replace any parts necessary.

9.16 Push down on the mid-rocker of cylinder number 1 to check the action of the VTEC rocker assembly - it should move independently of the primary and secondary intake rockers

22 Reassemble each cylinder's components and wrap a rubber band around the rocker arms before trying to assemble them on the rocker shaft (see Section 10).

9.18 Push down on the plunger of each lost motion assembly (arrow) - they should move smoothly

9.21 Check for smooth movement of the piston (arrow) in each VTEC rocker arm

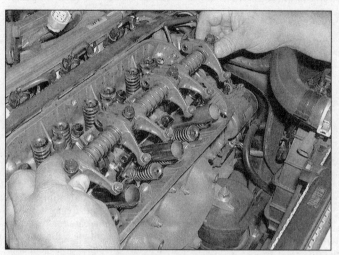

10.4 Leave the rocker assembly mounting bolts in place as you remove the assembly (this will keep the components in order on the shafts)

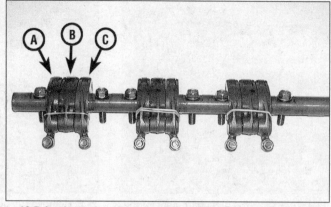

10.5 Intake rocker arm assembly components - rear cylinder bank (on the front cylinder bank A and C are reversed) (note the rubber bands installed to hold the components together)

A   Primary intake rocker arm
B   Mid intake rocker arm
C   Secondary intake rocker arm

10   Rocker arm assembly - removal, inspection and installation

Removal

Refer to illustration 10.4

1   Remove the valve cover (see Section 4).
2   Position the engine at TDC for number 1 piston (see Section 3) and remove the timing belt (see Section 7).
3   Loosen the rocker shaft mounting bolts 1/4-turn at a time, in the reverse of the tightening sequence, until the spring pressure is relieved **(see illustration 10.11)**.
4   Lift the rocker arms and shaft assembly from the cylinder head **(see illustration)**. Do not remove the shaft mounting bolts, they will keep the rocker arm assembly components together.

Inspection

Refer to illustrations 10.5 and 10.6

5   If you wish to disassemble and inspect the rocker arm assembly, (a good idea as long as you have them off), remove the mounting bolts and slip the rocker arms and springs off the shafts **(see illustration)**. Mark the relationship of the shafts to the bearing caps and keep the parts in order so you can reassemble them in the same positions. **Note:** *Keep the three intake rockers for each cylinder together by wrapping them with a heavy rubber band.*
6   Thoroughly clean the parts and inspect them for wear and damage. Check the rocker arm faces that contact the camshaft and the rocker arm tips **(see illustration)**. Check the surfaces of the shafts that the rocker arms ride on, as well as the bearing surfaces inside the rocker arms, for scoring and excessive wear. Replace any parts that are damaged or excessively worn. Also, make sure the oil holes in the shafts are not plugged. Check the roller tips for wear and smoothness of operation.
7   Remove the lost motion assemblies from the cylinder head **(see illustration 9.18)**, and clean them. Check for smoothness of plunger operation by pushing down gently with your finger.

8   Check the smoothness of operation of the VTEC pistons in each intake rocker arm **(see illustration 9.21)**.

Installation

Refer to illustration 10.11

9   Lubricate all components with engine oil and reassemble the shafts. When installing the rocker arms, shafts and springs, note the markings and the difference between the left and right side parts.
10   Coat the wear surfaces of the rocker arms with camshaft installation lubricant and install the rocker arm assembly.
11   Tighten the rocker shaft mounting bolts a little at a time, following the recommended tightening sequence **(see illustration)** to the torque listed in this Chapter's Specifications.
12   The remainder of installation is the reverse of removal.
13   Check the valve clearance and adjust to Specifications (see Chapter 1).
14   Run the engine and check for oil leaks and proper operation.

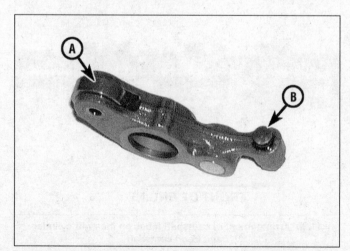

10.6 Inspect the rockers arms for wear and damage at the roller (A) and the valve stem end of the adjusters (B)

10.11 Rocker arm/shaft mounting bolts TIGHTENING sequence

11.4 To access the camshaft plate for the front camshaft, remove the EGR valve (A), then the two bolts on the plate (B)

11 Camshafts - removal, inspection and installation

Removal

Refer to illustrations 11.4, 11.5 and 11.6

1   Remove the valve covers (see Section 4)

11.5 Remove the bolts (A) and set the fuel lines aside, then remove the two bolts (B) and the camshaft retainer plate for the rear camshaft

and the timing belt and sprockets (see Section 7).

2   Remove the distributor (see Chapter 5).

3   Remove the rocker arms/shafts as an assembly (see Section 10).

4   Remove the EGR valve (see Chapter 6)

to access the rear plate for the camshaft **(see illustration)**. **Note:** *Refer to the Inspection procedures below and check camshaft end-play before removing the camshafts.*

5   Remove the camshaft retainer plate for the rear camshaft **(see illustration)**.

6   Carefully slide the camshaft out of the cylinder head, being careful not to nick the lobes or journals as you withdraw it **(see illustration)**.

Inspection

Refer to illustrations 11.8, 11.9a and 11.9b

7   Keeping careful track of the location of the components **(see illustration 10.5)**, remove the rocker arms and springs from the rocker shafts and bolt the bare rocker shafts to the cylinder head, tightening them to the torque listed in this Chapter's Specifications.

8   Mount a dial indicator so that it contacts the nose of the camshaft **(see illustration)**. Pry the camshaft forwards and back with a screwdriver, with the tip taped to prevent damage to the camshaft. Record the movement of the dial indicator and compare it to this Chapter's Specifications. If the endplay is excessive, the camshaft must be replaced.

11.6 Pull the camshaft straight out of the cylinder head, taking care not to nick the journals or bearings

11.8 Check the camshaft endplay with a dial indicator

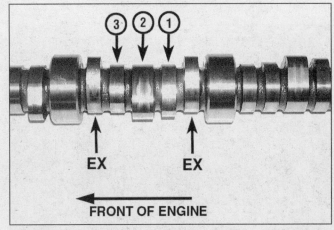

11.9a Arrangement of camshaft lobes on the left cylinder bank (front) camshaft

1   *Primary intake lobe*   3   *Secondary intake lobe*
2   *Mid intake lobe*

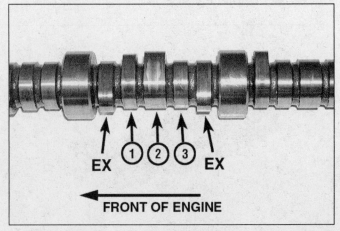

11.9b Arrangement of camshaft lobes on the right cylinder bank (rear) camshaft

1   *Primary intake lobe*   3   *Secondary intake lobe*
2   *Mid intake lobe*

11.10 Remove the two bolts and the timing belt rear cover from each cylinder head

11.11 Pry out the old camshaft oil seal with a screwdriver

17   Run the engine and check for oil leaks at the camshaft seals. Run the engine at low speed for five minutes to allow the air to bleed from the lost motion assemblies, then check for leaks and proper operation. **Note:** *There will be some tappet noise during the first few minutes of operation. If the noise continues, it may indicate a problem with one of the lost motion assemblies.*

9   After the endplay check, remove the rocker shafts and withdraw the camshaft. Measure the journal diameters and lobe heights on each camshaft (see Chapter 2, Part A). Be sure to use the Specifications in this Part of Chapter 2 for the V6 engine. Check also for visual signs of wear, scoring, pitting or overheating. **Note:** *The arrangement of lobes is different between the front and rear camshafts* **(see illustrations)**.

Installation

Refer to illustrations 11.10, 11.11, 11.12 and 11.14

10   Remove the timing belt rear covers from each cylinder head to access the camshaft seals **(see illustration)**.
11   The camshaft oil seal should be replaced whenever the camshaft is removed or replaced. Pry the old seal out with a screwdriver or seal removal tool **(see illustration)**.
12   Lubricate the lips with engine oil, then install a new camshaft oil seal by driving it in squarely with a seal installation tool to the same depth as the original seal **(see illustration)**. A socket of the appropriate size will also work.
13   Clean the camshaft thoroughly with solvent, then lubricate the journals and lobes with camshaft installation lubricant and carefully install the camshaft into the cylinder head.
14   Lubricate and install a new O-ring at the end of the camshaft retainer plate and bolt the retainer plates in place **(see illustration)**.
15   Install the other camshaft in the same manner.
16   Reinstall the remaining components in the reverse order of removal. Refer to Chapter 1 for the valve adjustment procedure.

12   Valve springs, retainers and seals - replacement

Refer to illustrations 12.5, 12.7 and 12.15
Note: *Broken valve springs and defective valve stem seals can be replaced without removing the cylinder heads. Two special tools and a compressed air source are normally required to perform this operation, so read through this Section carefully. The universal-shaft-type valve spring compressor required for the tight valve spring pockets of this vehicle may not be available at all tool rental yards, so check on the availability before beginning the job.*
1   Remove the valve cover(s) (see Section 4).
2   Remove the spark plug from the cylinder that has the defective component. If all of the valve stem seals are being replaced, all of the spark plugs should be removed.
3   Turn the crankshaft until the piston in the affected cylinder is at Top Dead Center on the compression stroke (refer to Section 3). If you're replacing all of the valve stem seals, begin with cylinder number one and work on the valves for one cylinder at a time. Move from cylinder-to-cylinder following the firing order sequence (see this Chapter's Specifications).
4   Remove the rocker arms and shafts (see Section 10).
5   Thread a long adapter into the spark plug hole and connect an air hose from a compressed air source to it **(see illustration)**. Most auto parts stores can supply the air hose adapter. **Note:** *Because of the length of the spark plug tubes, it will be necessary to*

11.12 If a seal driver is not available, use a hammer and a section of pipe or a large socket to drive the new seal into place

11.14 Install a new O-ring (arrow) on each camshaft retainer plate

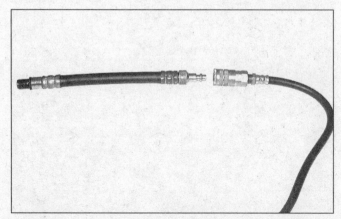

12.5 You'll need an air-hose adapter this long to reach down into the spark plugs tubes - they're commonly available from auto parts stores

use a long spark plug adapter with a length of hose attached (as used on many cylinder compression gauges) utilizing a quick-disconnect fitting to hook to your air source.

6   Apply compressed air to the cylinder. **Warning:** *The piston may be forced down by the compressed air, causing the crankshaft to turn suddenly. If the wrench used when positioning the number one piston at TDC is still attached to the bolt in the crankshaft nose, it could cause damage or injury when the crankshaft moves.*

7   Stuff shop rags into the cylinder head holes around the valves to prevent parts and tools from falling into the engine, then use a valve spring compressor to compress the spring **(see illustration)**. Remove the keepers with small needle-nose pliers or a magnet. **Note:** *The valves should be held in place by the air pressure. If the valve faces or seats are in poor condition, leaks may prevent air pressure from retaining the valves. If the valves cannot hold air, the cylinder head should be removed for a valve job at a machine shop.*

8   Remove the spring retainer, shield and valve spring, then remove the guide seal.

9   Wrap a rubber band or tape around the top of the valve stem so the valve won't fall into the combustion chamber, then release the air pressure.

10   Inspect the valve stem for damage. Rotate the valve in the guide and check the end for eccentric movement, which would indicate that the valve is bent.

11   Move the valve up-and-down in the guide and make sure it doesn't bind. If the valve stem binds, either the valve is bent or the guide is damaged. In either case, the head will have to be removed for repair.

12   Reapply air pressure to the cylinder to retain the valve in the closed position, then remove the tape or rubber band from the valve stem.

13   Lubricate the valve stem with engine oil and install a new guide seal. **Note:** *Intake valve guide seals have a white spring around*

12.7 Use a universal, shaft-type valve spring compressor as shown - lever the spring compressor against the bar and the spring retainer, then remove the keepers from the valve stem with a magnet or small needle-nose pliers

the top, while exhaust valve seals have a black spring.

14   Install the spring(s) in position over the valve, with the more closely wound spring coils toward the head.

15   Install the valve spring retainer. Compress the valve spring and carefully position the keepers in the groove. Apply a small dab of grease to the inside of each keeper to hold it in place **(see illustration)**.

16   Remove the pressure from the spring tool and make sure the keepers are seated.

17   Disconnect the air hose and remove the adapter from the spark plug hole.

18   Refer to Section 10 and install the rocker arm assembly.

19   Refer to Section 4 and install the valve cover.

20   Install the spark plugs and connect the spark plug wires.

21   Start and run the engine, then check for oil leaks and unusual sounds coming from the valve cover area.

12.15 Apply a small dab of grease to each keeper as shown here before installation - it'll hold them in place on the valve stem as the spring is released

13   Cylinder heads - removal and installation

Caution: *Allow the engine to cool completely before beginning this procedure.*

Removal

Refer to illustrations 13.11a, 13.11b and 13.14

1   Disconnect the negative cable from the battery. **Caution:** *The radio in your vehicle is equipped with an anti-theft system. Make sure you have the correct activation code before disconnecting the battery.*

2   Relieve the fuel pressure, disconnect the electrical connectors from the fuel injectors, disconnect the fuel lines, and remove the fuel rails (see Chapter 4).

3   Drain the cooling system, including both block drains (see Chapter 1).

4   Remove the alternator and distributor (see Chapter 5).

5   Disconnect the ground cable at the timing belt end of the engine.

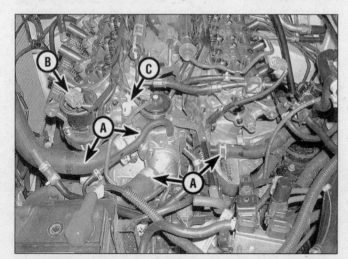

13.11a Disconnect the hoses (A) and electrical connectors (B is the EGR, C is the ECT sensor) at the coolant passage assembly

13.11b At each end of the coolant passage, remove the bolts and nut (arrows) - lightly tap the passage with a soft-faced hammer to break the gasket seal and remove the coolant passage

13.14 Pry up carefully on a casting protrusion

6   Refer to Chapter 10 and remove the power steering pump and set it aside without disconnecting the hoses.
7   Remove the upper intake manifold (see Section 5).
8   Remove the exhaust manifolds (see Section 6).
9   Detach the timing belt and remove the camshaft sprockets (see Section 7).
10   Remove the timing belt rear covers (see Section 11).
11   Detach the coolant passage assembly **(see illustrations)**.
12   Refer to Section 10 and remove the rocker arms/shafts assembly.
13   Using a socket and breaker bar, loosen the cylinder head bolts in 1/4-turn increments until they can be removed by hand. Loosen them in a sequence opposite that of the tightening sequence **(see illustration 13.22)**
14   Lift the cylinder head off the engine block. If the head is stuck, pry against an external casting protrusion **(see illustration)**. **Caution:** *Don't pry between the head and block. The gasket surfaces may be damaged and leaks could result.*
15   Repeat Steps 12 through 14 for the other head. Check the cylinder heads for warpage as shown in Chapter 2C.

Installation

Refer to illustration 13.22

16   The mating surfaces of the cylinder heads and block must be perfectly clean when the heads are installed. Use a gasket scraper to remove all traces of carbon and old gasket material. Be careful not to gouge the delicate aluminum. Clean the mating surfaces with lacquer thinner or acetone. If there's oil on the mating surfaces when the head is installed, the gasket may not seal correctly and leaks could develop. When working on the block, stuff the cylinders with clean shop rags to keep out debris. Use a vacuum cleaner to remove material that falls into the cylinders.
17   Check the block and head mating surfaces for nicks, deep scratches and other damage. If damage is slight, it can be removed with a file; if it's excessive, machining may be the only alternative.
18   Use a tap of the correct size to chase the threads in the head bolt holes, then clean the holes with compressed air – make sure that nothing remains in the holes. **Warning:** *Wear eye protection when using compressed air!*
19   Mount each bolt in a vise and run a die down the threads to remove corrosion and restore the threads. Dirt, corrosion, sealant and damaged threads will affect torque readings.
20   Clean the oil-control jets thoroughly and reinstall them with new O-rings. Position the new gaskets over the oil-control jets and locating dowels in the block.
21   Carefully set the head on the block without disturbing the gasket.
22   Before installing the head bolts, apply a small amount of clean engine oil to the threads and under the bolt heads. Install the bolts and special washers and tighten them finger tight. Following the recommended sequence **(see illustration)**, tighten the bolts to the torque listed in this Chapter's Specifications in three steps. **Note:** *Perform each step twice, i.e., torque all bolts to the Specification for the first step, then again torque all to the same Specification before proceeding to the second step.*
Repeat the entire procedure to install the other cylinder head, if necessary.
23   The remaining installation steps are the reverse of removal.
24   Refill the cooling system, change the oil and filter (see Chapter 1), run the engine and check for leaks. Run the engine at low speed for five minutes to allow the air to bleed from the lost motion assemblies, then check for leaks and proper operation. **Note:** *There will be some tappet noise during the first few minutes of operation. If the noise continues, it may indicate a problem with one of the lost motion assemblies.*

14   Oil pan - removal and installation

Removal

Refer to illustrations 14.6a and 14.6b

1   Disconnect the negative cable from the battery. **Caution:** *The radio in your vehicle is equipped with an anti-theft system. Make sure you have the correct activation code before disconnecting the battery.*
2   Block the rear wheels and set the parking brake. Raise the front of the vehicle and support it securely on jackstands.
3   Remove the lower splash shield.
4   Drain the engine oil and remove the oil filter (see Chapter 1).
5   Unbolt the exhaust pipe from the manifolds (see Section 6) and unbolt the flange at the catalytic converter (see Chapter 4). Remove the pipe.
6   Remove the bolts/nuts **(see illustration)** and lower the oil pan. The bolts at the timing belt end of the engine can be removed with a 1/4-inch drive flex-socket, extension and ratchet. If the pan is stuck, use a dull pry tool at the tabs on the casting corners **(see illustration)**. Don't damage the mating surfaces of the pan and block or oil leaks could develop.

13.22 Cylinder head bolt TIGHTENING sequence

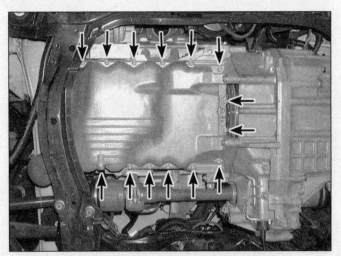

14.6a Remove the bolts from around the perimeter of the oil pan (arrows) and the oil pan-to-transaxle case bolts

14.6b Use a dull screwdriver to pry the pan loose at the cast tabs - DO NOT pry on the gasket surface

15.3 Oil pick-up screen bolt locations (arrows)

Installation

7   Use a scraper to remove all traces of old sealant from the block and oil pan. Be careful not to gouge the delicate aluminum block. Clean the mating surfaces with lacquer thinner or acetone.

8   Make sure the threaded bolt holes in the block are clean.

9   Inspect the oil pump pick-up screen assembly for damage and a blocked strainer (see Section 15).

10   Position a new gasket on the oil pan.

11   Carefully position the oil pan on the engine block and install the bolts/nuts. Working from the center out and alternating from side to side, tighten them to the torque listed in this Chapter's Specifications in three steps.

12   The remainder of installation is the reverse of removal. Be sure to add oil and install a new oil filter. **Note:** *If the oil pump has been replaced, wait 20 minutes (to allow the sealant to cure) before adding oil.*

13   Run the engine and check for oil pressure and leaks.

15 Oil pump - removal, inspection and installation

Removal

Refer to illustrations 15.3 and 15.5

1   Remove the timing belt, crankshaft sprocket and idler pulley (see Section 7). **Note:** *Leave the engine mount on the timing belt end of the engine connected to support the engine.*

2   Refer to Chapter 6 and remove the crankshaft position sensor.

3   Remove the oil pan (see Section 14) and oil pick-up screen **(see illustration)**. If equipped, remove the oil level sensor.

4   Remove the oil filter adapter housing/VTEC solenoid assembly from the front of the oil pump (see Section 9).

5   Remove the bolts and detach the oil pump housing from the engine **(see illustration)**. You may have to pry carefully between the main bearing cap and the pump housing with a screwdriver.

Inspection

Refer to illustrations 15.6 and 15.7

6   Use a large Phillips screwdriver to remove the screws holding the pump cover to the rear of the housing **(see illustration)**.

7   Lift the cover off and inspect the pump rotors **(see illustration)**. If any wear or damage is evident, replace the pump. Check the rotor clearance with a feeler gauge and compare to this Chapter's Specifications.

8   Use a scraper to remove any traces of old sealant from the pump body and engine block, being careful not to damage the delicate aluminum.

Installation

9   Replace the old crankshaft oil seal (see Section 8). Apply multi-purpose grease to the seal lip.

10   Pack the pump cavity with petroleum jelly and install the cover. Apply thread-locking compound to the threads and tighten the screws securely following a criss-cross pattern.

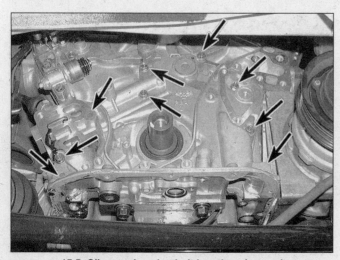

15.5 Oil pump housing bolt locations (arrows)

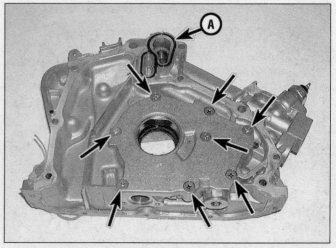

15.6 Remove the screws from the pump cover (arrows) and replace the O-ring seal (A)

15.7 Inspect the condition of the rotors and the inside of the cover - with feeler gauges, measure the clearances at (A) (outer rotor-to-housing) and (B) (inner rotor-to-outer rotor), lay a straightedge across the face of the pump housing and measure the housing-to-rotor axial clearance and compare to Specifications

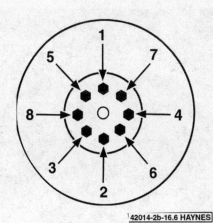

16.6 Driveplate bolt TIGHTENING sequence

11   Use acetone or lacquer thinner and a clean rag to remove all traces of oil from the gasket surfaces.

12   Apply a bead of anaerobic sealant to the oil pump flange and the threads of the mounting bolts. Avoid using an excessive amount of sealant, especially around oil passages and bolt holes. Parts must be assembled within five minutes of sealant application, otherwise the material must be removed and reapplied. Wherever O-rings are employed, use new ones.

13   Engage the flat surfaces on the oil pump drive rotor with the matching flats on the crankshaft and slide the pump into place.

14   Install the pump mounting bolts in their original locations and tighten them to the torque listed in this Chapter's Specifications in a criss-cross pattern.

15   Using a new O-ring, install the oil pick-up screen and tighten the fasteners to the torque listed in this Chapter's Specifications.

16   Reinstall the remaining parts in the reverse order of removal.

17   Wait 20 minutes (to allow the sealant to cure), then add oil, start the engine and check for oil leaks and pressure.

18   Recheck the engine oil level after operating the engine.

16   Driveplate - removal and installation

Refer to illustration 16.2

1   Remove the transaxle (see Chapter 7B). **Warning:** *The engine must be supported from above with an engine hoist or three-bar support cradle before working underneath the vehicle with the transaxle removed.*

2   Remove the bolts that secure the drive-plate to the crankshaft.

3   Clean the driveplate and inspect the surface for cracks. Check for worn, cracked or broken ring-gear teeth. Lay the driveplate on a flat surface and use a straightedge to check for warpage.

4   Clean and inspect the mating surfaces of the driveplate and the crankshaft. If the crankshaft oil seal is leaking, replace it before reinstalling the driveplate (see Section 17).

5   Position the driveplate against the crankshaft. Note that offset bolt holes ensure correct installation.

6   Following the recommended tightening sequence **(see illustration)**, tighten the bolts in several stages to the torque listed in this Chapter's Specifications.

7   The remainder of installation is the reverse of the removal procedure.

17   Rear main oil seal - replacement

Refer to illustrations 17.2 and 17.3

1   The transaxle must be removed from the vehicle for this procedure and the driveplate must be removed from the engine. Refer to Chapter 7 and Section 16 as necessary. **Warning:** *The engine must be supported from above with an engine hoist or three-bar support cradle before working underneath the vehicle with the transaxle removed.*

2   The seal can be replaced without removing the oil pan or removing the seal retainer. However, the lip of the seal is quite stiff and it's possible to cock the seal in the retainer bore or damage it during installation. The preferred method is that described in Chapter 2, Part C, but this requires removal of the oil pan and seal plate. If you want to take the chance and do the installation in-vehicle without

removing the seal retainer plate, pry out the old seal with a screwdriver **(see illustration)**.

3   Apply multi-purpose grease to the crankshaft seal journal and the lip of the new seal and carefully drive the new seal into place **(see illustration)**. Install the seal with the spring side in. Use a socket, section of pipe or seal installation tool. The lip is stiff so carefully work it onto the seal journal of the crankshaft. Don't rush it or you may damage the seal. **Note:** *Drive the seal in squarely and only until it is flush with the back of the seal plate, no further.*

4   The remaining steps are the reverse of removal.

18   Engine mounts - check and replacement

Check

1   There are four engine mounts on V6 models, of which the front and rear are computer-controlled (see Section 19).

2   During the check, the engine must be raised slightly to remove the weight from the mounts.

17.2 Carefully pry the rear main seal out - don't damage the surface of the crankshaft or the new seal will leak

17.3 Drive the new seal in squarely until flush with the housing

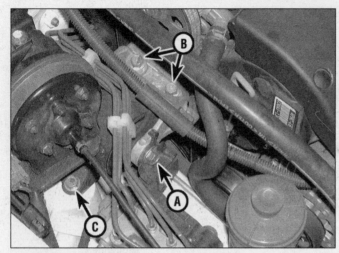

18.9 The passenger-side mount is located at the timing belt end of the engine - Remove the throughbolt (A), then the two mounting bolts on the engine (B), the remove the mount-to-body bolts (C indicates one showing here) to remove the mount

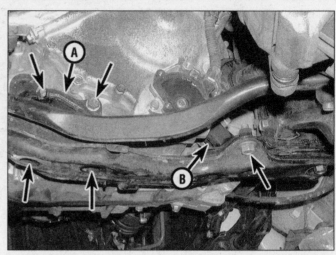

18.11 The driver's-side mounts are located between the transaxle and the subframe - remove the bolts for the front mount (A) and the two lower bolts through the holes in the subframe, then the bolts at the rear mount (B) on the transaxle and subframe

3   Raise the vehicle and support it securely on jackstands, then position a jack under the engine oil pan. Place a large block of wood between the jack head and the oil pan, then carefully raise the engine just enough to take the weight off the mounts. **Warning:** *DO NOT place any part of your body under the engine when it's supported only by a jack!*

4   Check the mounts to see if the rubber is cracked, hardened or separated from the casing.

5   Check for relative movement between the mount plates and the engine or frame (use a large screwdriver or prybar to attempt to move the mounts). If movement is noted, lower the engine and tighten the mount fasteners.

6   Rubber preservative should be applied to the mounts to slow deterioration.

7   Disconnect the negative battery cable from the battery, then apply the parking brake, block the rear wheels, raise the front

of the vehicle and support it securely on jackstands (if not already done). **Caution:** *The stereo in your vehicle is equipped with an anti-theft system. Make sure you have the correct activation code before disconnecting the battery.*

Replacement

Refer to illustrations 18.9, 18.11, 18.14 and 18.20

Right (passenger-side) mount

8   Use a floor jack under the transaxle to take the weight from the mount.

9   Remove the through-bolt from the mount, remove the bolt holding the electrical cable to the engine bracket, then the two bolts holding the engine bracket in place. Remove the three mount-to-chassis bolts and remove the mount **(see illustration)**.

10   Installation is the reverse of removal. **Note:** *Tighten the bolts to Specifications only*

after the powertrain weight is back onto the mounts and the jack is removed. Proceed to Step 24.

Left (driver's-side) mount

11   The driver's-side mount is between the bottom of the transaxle and the subframe **(see illustration)**.

12   With the engine/transaxle supported, remove the two nuts from below the subframe, the two bolts at the transaxle, and remove the mount.

13   Installation is the reverse of removal. **Note:** *Tighten the bolts to Specifications only after the powertrain weight is back onto the mounts and the jack is removed. Proceed to Step 24.*

Front mount

14   The front mount is located between the engine and radiator **(see illustration)**.

15   Remove the large nut where the mount

18.14 The front engine mount is located between the engine and radiator - remove the large nut (A), raise the engine to clear the stud, then remove the four mount-to-chassis bolts (B indicate one see here)

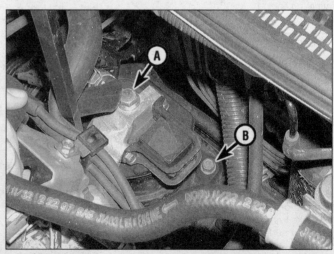

18.20 The rear mount is located between the engine and firewall - remove the nut (A), raise the engine to clear the stud, and remove the mount-to-chassis bolts (arrow B indicates one of the four bolts)

19.1a The control solenoid (arrow) for the front and rear engine mounts on V6 models is located on this bracket at the driver's-side shock tower

19.1b Location of the vacuum line (arrow) to the front engine mount

stud goes through the engine bracket.

16 Remove the four bolts holding the mount to the chassis, then disconnect the vacuum hose from the bottom of the mount.

17 Raise the engine enough for the stud to clear the upper bracket and remove the mount.

18 Installation is the reverse of removal. **Note:** *Tighten the bolts to Specifications only after the powertrain weight is back onto the mounts and the jack is removed. Proceed to Step 24.*

Rear mount

19 The rear mount is between the engine and the firewall, and is computer-controlled, along with the front mount.

20 Remove the large nut where the mount stud goes through the engine bracket **(see illustration)**.

21 Remove the four bolts holding the mount to the chassis, then disconnect the vacuum hose from the bottom of the mount.

22 Raise the engine enough for the stud to clear the upper bracket and remove the mount.

23 Installation is the reverse of removal. **Note:** *Tighten the bolts to Specifications only*

after the powertrain weight is back onto the mounts and the jack is removed. Proceed to Step 24.

Final tightening, all mounts

24 To ensure maximum bushing life and prevent excessive noise and vibration, the vehicle should be level and the engine weight should be on the mounts during the final tightening stage. **Note:** *Use non-hardening thread locking compound on the nuts/bolts. Ensure that the bushings are not twisted or offset.* If you have replaced more than one mount, or when you are installing the engine, tighten the mounts in the following order: front, rear, passenger-side and driver's-side.

---

19 Engine Mount Control System - description and check

Refer to illustrations 19.1a, 19.1b and 19.1c

Both front and rear engine mounts on V6 models are controlled by the engine control computer (PCM), as is the rear mount on four-cylinder models. The system is designed to smooth engine vibrations during idle con-

ditions. Refer to Chapter 2, Part A for a description and check of the system, which operates the same on both models, but refer to the illustrations here for the location of the Engine Mount Control System solenoid and vacuum connections **(see illustrations)**.

19.1c Location of the vacuum line (arrow) to the rear engine mount

Notes

Chapter 2 Part C
General engine overhaul procedures

Contents

Specifications

Four-cylinder engine

General

Bore	3.39 inches
Stroke	3.82 inches
Displacement	138 cu in (2.3 liters)
Cylinder compression pressure	
Standard	178 psi
Minimum	135 psi
Maximum variation between cylinders	28 psi
Oil pressure (engine warm)	
At 3000 rpm	50 psi
At idle	10 psi minimum
Cylinder head warpage service limit	0.002 inch

Valves and related components

Valve margin width	
Intake	
Standard	0.033 to 0.045 inch
Service limit	0.026 inch
Exhaust	
Standard	0.041 to 0.053 inch
Service limit	0.037 inch
Valve stem diameter	
Intake	
Standard	0.2159 to 0.2163 inch
Service limit	0.2148 inch
Exhaust	
Standard	0.2146 to 0.2150 inch
Service limit	0.2134 inch

Valves and related components

Valve stem-to-guide clearance

  Intake

    Standard .... 0.0008 to 0.0018 inch

    Service limit.. 0.0030 inch

  Exhaust

    Standard .... 0.0022 to 0.0031 inch

    Service limit.. 0.0050 inch

Valve spring free length

  VTEC

    Intake .... 2.011 inches

    Exhaust .... 2.188 inches

  Non-VTEC

    Intake .... 2.113 inches

    Exhaust .... 2.188 inches

Valve stem installed height

  Intake

    Standard .... 1.841 to 1.872 inch

    Service limit.. 1.882 inch

  Exhaust

    Standard .... 1.838 to 1.869 inch

    Service limit.. 1.879 inch

Crankshaft and connecting rods

Connecting rod journal

  Diameter.. 1.7707 to 1.7717 inches

  Taper and out-of-round (maximum)...................................... 0.0002 inch

Rod bearing oil clearance

  Standard... 0.0008 to 0.0019 inch

  Service limit.. 0.0024 inch

Connecting rod side clearance (endplay)

  Standard... 0.006 to 0.012 inch

  Service limit.. 0.016 inch

Main bearing journal

  Diameter

    No. 1, 2 and 4 journals.. 2.1646 to 2.1655 inch

    No. 3 journal... 2.1644 to 2.1654 inch

    No. 5 journal... 2.1650 to 2.1660 inch

  Taper and out-of-round (maximum)...................................... 0.0002 inch

  Runout

    Standard .... 0.001 inch

    Service limit.. 0.002 inch

Bearing oil clearance

  No. 1, 2 and 4 journals

    Standard .... 0.0008 to 0.0018 inch

    Service limit.. 0.0020 inch

  No. 3 journal

    Standard .... 0.0010 to 0.0019 inch

    Service limit.. 0.0022 inch

  No. 5 journal

    Standard .... 0.0004 to 0.0013 inch

    Service limit.. 0.0016 inch

Crankshaft endplay

  Standard... 0.004 to 0.014 inch

  Service limit.. 0.018 inch

Crankshaft rear oil seal clearance .... 0.02 to 0.03 inch

Balance shafts

Front shaft

No. 1 journal

  Standard... 1.6820 to 1.6824 inches

  Service limit.. 1.681 inches

  Bearing-to-shaft oil clearance

    Standard .... 0.0026 to 0.0039 inch

    Service limit .... 0.005 inch

No. 2 journal

  Standard... 1.5241 to 1.5246 inches

  Service limit.. 1.524 inches

  Bearing-to-shaft oil clearance

    Standard .... 0.0030 to 0.0043 inch

    Service limit.. 0.005 inch

No. 3 journal
   Standard .... 1.3670 to 1.3675 inches
   Service limit.. 1.367 inches
   Bearing-to-shaft oil clearance
      Standard .... 0.0026 to 0.0039 inch
      Service limit .... 0.005 inch
Journal taper .... 0.0002 inch
Runout... 0.001 inch

Rear shaft
No. 1 journal
   Standard .... 0.8243 to 0.8248 inch
   Service limit.. 0.824 inch
   Bearing-to-shaft oil clearance
      Standard .... 0.002 to 0.003 inch
      Service limit .... 0.004 inch
No. 2 journal
   Standard .... 1.5241 to 1.5246 inches
   Service limit.. 1.524 inches
   Bearing-to-shaft oil clearance
      Standard .... 0.0030 to 0.0043 inch
      Service limit .... 0.005 inch
No. 3 journal
   Standard .... 1.3670 to 1.3675 inches
   Service limit.. 1.367 inches
   Bearing-to-shaft oil clearance
      Standard .... 0.0026 to 0.0039 inch
      Service limit .... 0.005 inch
Journal taper .... 0.0002 inch
Runout... 0.001 inch

Cylinder block
Cylinder block deck warpage
   Standard.. 0.003 inch
   Service limit.. 0.004 inch
Cylinder bore
   Diameter
      Marked A or I (standard) .... 3.3862 to 3.3866 inches
      Marked B or II (standard) .... 3.3858 to 3.3862 inches
         Service limit .... 3.3886 inches
   Taper and out-of-round, service limit................................ 0.002 inch

Pistons and rings
Piston diameter (measured at 0.80-inch from bottom of skirt)
   Letter A or no marking
      Standard .... 3.3850 to 3.3854 inches
      Service limit... 3.3846 inches
   Letter B
      Standard .... 3.3846 to 3.3850 inches
      Service limit... 3.3842 inches
Piston-to-bore clearance
   Standard.. 0.0008 to 0.0016 inch
   Service limit.. 0.002 inch
Piston ring end gap
   Top ring
      Standard .... 0.008 to 0.014 inch
      Service limit... 0.024 inch
   Middle ring
      Standard .... 0.016 to 0.022 inch
      Service limit... 0.028 inch
   Oil ring
      Standard .... 0.008 to 0.028 inch
      Service limit... 0.031 inch
Piston ring side clearance
   Top ring
      Standard .... 0.0014 to 0.0024 inch
      Service limit... 0.005 inch
   Middle ring
      Standard .... 0.0012 to 0.0022 inch
      Service limit... 0.005 inch

Torque specifications* Ft-lbs (unless otherwise indicated)

Note: One foot-pound (ft-lb) of torque is equivalent to 12 inch-pounds (in-lbs) of torque. Torque values below approximately 15 ft-lbs are expressed in inch-pounds, since most foot-pound torque wrenches are not accurate at these smaller values.

Rear balance shaft gear case bolts	18
Main bearing cap/bridge bolts	
Inner (11 mm) bolts	
Step 1	22
Step 2	58
Outer (6 mm) bolts	105 in-lbs
Connecting rod cap nuts	
Step 1	168 in-lbs
Step 2	Tighten an additional 90 degrees
Rear main oil seal retainer bolts	104 in-lbs

Refer to Part A for additional torque specifications.

V6 engine
General

Bore	3.39 inches
Stroke	3.39 inches
Displacement	183 cu in. (3.0 liters)
Cylinder compression pressure at 200 rpm with wide open throttle	
Standard	178 psi
Minimum	135 psi
Maximum variation between cylinders	28 psi
Oil pressure (engine warm)	
At 3000 rpm	71 psi minimum
At idle	10 psi minimum
Cylinder head warpage limit	0.002 inch

Valves and related components

Valve margin width	
Intake	
Standard	0.033 to 0.045 inch
Service limit	0.026 inch
Exhaust	
Standard	0.041 to 0.053 inch
Service limit	0.037 inch
Valve stem diameter	
Intake	
Standard	0.2159 to 0.2163 inch
Service limit	0.2148 inch
Exhaust	
Standard	0.2146 to 0.2150 inch
Service limit	0.2134 inch
Valve stem-to-guide clearance	
Intake	
Standard	0.0008 to 0.0018 inch
Service limit	0.003 inch
Exhaust	
Standard	0.0022 to 0.0031 inch
Service limit	0.005 inch
Valve guide inside diameter	
Standard	0.2171 to 0.2177 inch
Service limit	0.219 inch
Valve spring free length	
Intake	2.009 inches
Exhaust	2.106 inches
Valve stem installed height	
Intake	
Standard	1.841 to 1.872 inch
Service limit	1.882 inch
Exhaust	
Standard	1.838 to 1.869 inch
Service limit	1.879 inch

Crankshaft and connecting rods

Connecting rod journal	
Diameter	2.0857 to 2.0866 inches

Taper and out-of-round
    Standard .... 0.0002 inch
    Service limit... 0.0004 inch
Bearing oil clearance
    Standard .... 0.0008 to 0.0017 inch
    Service limit... 0.002 inch
Connecting rod side clearance (endplay)
    Standard.. 0.006 to 0.012 inch
    Service limit .... 0.016 inch
Main bearing journal
    Diameter.. 2.8337 to 2.8346 inches
    Taper and out-of-round
        Standard .... 0.0002 inch
        Service limit... 0.0004 inch
    Bearing oil clearance
        Standard .... 0.0008 to 0.0017 inch
        Service limit... 0.0020 inch
Crankshaft endplay
    Standard .... 0.004 to 0.014 inch
    Service limit... 0.018 inch
Crankshaft rear oil seal clearance .... 0.008 to 0.020 inch

Cylinder block

Cylinder block warpage
    Standard.. 0.003 inch
    Service limit .... 0.004 inch
Cylinder bore
    Diameter
        Standard .... 3.3858 to 3.3864 inches
        Service limit... 3.3864 inches
    Taper and out-of-round, service limit.. 0.002 inch

Pistons and rings

Piston diameter (measured at 0.70-inch above bottom of skirt)
    Standard .... 3.3848 to 3.3852 inches
    Service limit... 3.3844 inches
Piston-to-bore clearance
    Standard .... 0.0006 to 0.0016 inch
    Service limit... 0.003 inch
Piston ring end gap
    Top ring
        Standard .... 0.008 to 0.014 inch
        Service limit... 0.024 inch
    Middle ring
        Standard .... 0.016 to 0.022 inch
        Service limit... 0.028 inch
    Oil ring
        Standard .... 0.008 to 0.028 inch
        Service limit... 0.031 inch
Piston ring side clearance
    Top ring
        Standard .... 0.0014 to 0.0024 inch
        Service limit... 0.005 inch
    Middle ring
        Standard .... 0.0012 to 0.0022 inch
        Service limit... 0.005 inch

Torque specifications*

Ft-lbs (unless otherwise indicated)

Note: *One foot-pound (ft-lb) of torque is equivalent to 12 inch-pounds (in-lbs) of torque. Torque values below approximately 15 ft-lbs are expressed in inch-pounds, since most foot-pound torque wrenches are not accurate at these smaller values.*

Main bearing bolts
    Cap bolt.. 56
    Side bolt.. 36
Connecting rod cap nuts
    Step 1 .... 168 in-lbs
    Step 2 .... turn an additional 90 degrees
Rear main oil seal retainer bolts .... 104 in-lbs

Refer to Part B for additional torque specifications.

2.2a The oil pressure sending unit (arrow) is located above the oil filter on V6 models - do not confuse it with the VTEC switch and solenoid, the oil sender has a black boot over it

2.2b Four-cylinder oil pressure sending unit location (arrow), directly above the oil filter (oil filter removed for clarity)

1   General information - engine overhaul

Included in this portion of Chapter 2 are the general overhaul procedures for the cylinder head and internal engine components.

The information ranges from advice concerning preparation for an overhaul and the purchase of replacement parts to detailed, step-by-step procedures covering Removal and installation of internal engine components and the inspection of parts.

The following Sections have been written based on the assumption that the engine has been removed from the vehicle. For information concerning in-vehicle engine repair, as well as removal and installation of the external components necessary for the overhaul, see Chapter 2A (four-cylinder models) or 2B (V6 models).

The Specifications included in this Part are only those necessary for the inspection and overhaul procedures which follow. Refer to Chapter 2, Part A or Part B for additional Specifications.

It's not always easy to determine when, or if, an engine should be completely overhauled, as a number of factors must be considered.

High mileage is not necessarily an indication that an overhaul is needed, while low mileage doesn't preclude the need for an overhaul. Frequency of servicing is probably the most important consideration. An engine that's had regular and frequent oil and filter changes, as well as other required maintenance, will most likely give many thousands of miles of reliable service. Conversely, a neglected engine may require an overhaul very early in its life.

Excessive oil consumption is an indication that piston rings, valve seals and/or valve guides are in need of attention. Make sure that oil leaks aren't responsible before deciding that the rings and/or guides are bad. Perform a cylinder compression check to deter-

mine the extent of the work required (see Section 3). Also check the vacuum readings under various conditions (see Section 4).

Loss of power, rough running, knocking or metallic engine noises, excessive valve train noise and high fuel consumption rates may also point to the need for an overhaul, especially if they're all present at the same time. If a complete tune-up doesn't remedy the situation, major mechanical work is the only solution.

An engine overhaul involves restoring the internal parts to the specifications of a new engine. During an overhaul, the piston rings are replaced and the cylinder walls are reconditioned (re-bored and/or honed). If a re-bore is done by an automotive machine shop, new oversize pistons will also be installed. The main bearings, connecting rod bearings and camshaft bearings are generally replaced with new ones and, if necessary, the crankshaft may be reground to restore the journals. Generally, the valves are serviced as well, since they're usually in less-than-perfect condition at this point. While the engine is being overhauled, other components, such as the distributor, starter and alternator, can be rebuilt as well. The end result should be a like new engine that will give many trouble free miles. **Note:** *Critical cooling system components such as the hoses, drivebelts, thermostat and water pump should be replaced with new parts when an engine is overhauled. The radiator should be checked carefully to ensure that it isn't clogged or leaking (see Chapter 3). If you purchase a rebuilt engine or short block, some rebuilders will not warranty their engines unless the radiator has been professionally flushed. Also, we don't recommend overhauling the oil pump - always install a new one when an engine is rebuilt.*

Before beginning the engine overhaul, read through the entire procedure to familiarize yourself with the scope and requirements of the job. Overhauling an engine isn't difficult, but it is time-consuming. Plan on the vehicle being tied up for a minimum of two

weeks, especially if parts must be taken to an automotive machine shop for repair or reconditioning. Check on availability of parts and make sure that any necessary special tools and equipment are obtained in advance. Most work can be done with typical hand tools, although a number of precision measuring tools are required for inspecting parts to determine if they must be replaced. Often an automotive machine shop will handle the inspection of parts and offer advice concerning reconditioning and replacement. **Note:** *Always wait until the engine has been completely disassembled and all components, especially the engine block, have been inspected before deciding what service and repair operations must be performed by an automotive machine shop.* Since the block's condition will be the major factor to consider when determining whether to overhaul the original engine or buy a rebuilt one, never purchase parts or have machine work done on other components until the block has been thoroughly inspected. As a general rule, time is the primary cost of an overhaul, so it doesn't pay to install worn or substandard parts.

As a final note, to ensure maximum life and minimum trouble from a rebuilt engine, everything must be assembled with care in a spotlessly-clean environment.

2   Oil pressure check

Refer to illustrations 2.2a and 2.2b

1   Low engine oil pressure can be a sign of an engine in need of rebuilding. A "low oil pressure" indicator (often called an "idiot light") is not a test of the oiling system. Such indicators only come on when the oil pressure is dangerously low. Even an original pressure gauge in the instrument panel is only a relative indication, although it's much better for driver information than a warning light. An accurate test can only be performed with a mechanical (not electrical) oil pressure gauge. When used in conjunction with an

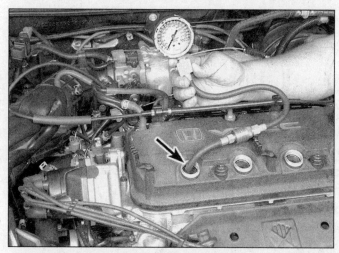

3.6 To use a compression gauge, you must have a gauge with a hose long enough to reach down the spark-plug tubes (arrow) - be sure to open the throttle as far as possible during the compression check

4.4 A simple vacuum gauge can be very handy in diagnosing engine condition and performance

accurate tachometer, the engine's oil pressure performance can be compared to the manufacturer's Specifications for that year and model.

2   Locate the oil pressure indicator sending unit **(see illustrations)**.

3   Remove the oil pressure sending unit and install a fitting which will allow you to directly connect your hand-held, mechanical oil pressure gauge. Use Teflon tape or sealant on the threads of the adapter and the fitting on the end of your gauge's hose.

4   Connect an accurate tachometer to the engine, according to the tachometer manufacturer's instructions.

5   Check the oil pressure with the engine running (full operating temperature) at the specified engine speed, and compare it to this Chapter's Specifications. If it's extremely low, the bearings and/or oil pump are probably worn out.

3   Cylinder compression check

Refer to illustration 3.6

1   A compression check will tell you what mechanical condition the upper end of your engine (pistons, rings, valves, head gaskets) is in. Specifically, it can tell you if the compression is down due to leakage caused by worn piston rings, defective valves and seats or a blown head gasket. **Note:** *The engine must be at normal operating temperature and the battery must be fully charged for this check.*

2   Begin by cleaning the area around the spark plugs before you remove them (compressed air should be used, if available, otherwise a small brush or even a bicycle tire pump will work). The idea is to prevent dirt from getting into the cylinders as the compression check is being done.

3   Remove all of the spark plugs from the engine (see Chapter 1).

4   Block the throttle wide open.

5   Detach the coil wire from the center of the distributor cap and ground it on the engine block. Use a jumper wire with alligator clips on each end to ensure a good ground. The fuel pump circuit should also be disabled (see Chapter 4).

6   Install the compression gauge in the spark plug hole **(see illustration)**.

7   Crank the engine over at least seven compression strokes and watch the gauge. The compression should build up quickly in a healthy engine. Low compression on the first stroke, followed by gradually increasing pressure on successive strokes, indicates worn piston rings. A low compression reading on the first stroke, which doesn't build up during successive strokes, indicates leaking valves or a blown head gasket (a cracked head could also be the cause). Deposits on the undersides of the valve heads can also cause low compression. Record the highest gauge reading obtained.

8   Repeat the procedure for the remaining cylinders and compare the results to this Chapter's Specifications.

9   Add some engine oil (about three squirts from a plunger-type oil can) to each cylinder, through the spark plug hole, and repeat the test on each cylinder.

10   If the compression increases after the oil is added, the piston rings are definitely worn. If the compression doesn't increase significantly, the leakage is occurring at the valves or head gasket. Leakage past the valves may be caused by burned valve seats and/or faces or warped, cracked or bent valves.

11   If two adjacent cylinders have equally low compression, there's a strong possibility that the head gasket between them is blown. The appearance of coolant in the combustion chambers or the crankcase would verify this condition.

12   If one cylinder is slightly lower than the others, and the engine has a slightly rough idle, a worn lobe on the camshaft could be the cause.

13   If the compression is unusually high, the combustion chambers are probably coated with carbon deposits. If that's the case, the cylinder head(s) should be removed and decarbonized.

14   If compression is way down or varies greatly between cylinders, it would be a good idea to have a leak-down test performed by an automotive repair shop. This test will pinpoint exactly where the leakage is occurring and how severe it is.

4   Vacuum gauge diagnostic checks

Refer to illustrations 4.4 and 4.6

A vacuum gauge provides valuable information about what is going on in the engine at a low-cost. You can check for worn rings or cylinder walls, leaking head or intake manifold gaskets, incorrect carburetor adjustments, restricted exhaust, stuck or burned valves, weak valve springs, improper ignition or valve timing and ignition problems.

Unfortunately, vacuum gauge readings are easy to misinterpret, so they should be used in conjunction with other tests to confirm the diagnosis.

Both the absolute readings and the rate of needle movement are important for accurate interpretation. Most gauges measure vacuum in inches of mercury (in-Hg). The following references to vacuum assume the diagnosis is being performed at sea level. As elevation increases (or atmospheric pressure decreases), the reading will decrease. For every 1,000 foot increase in elevation above approximately 2000 feet, the gauge readings will decrease about one inch of mercury.

Connect the vacuum gauge directly to intake manifold vacuum, not to ported (throttle body) vacuum **(see illustration)**. Be sure no hoses are left disconnected during the test or false readings will result.

Before you begin the test, allow the engine to warm up completely. Block the wheels and set the parking brake. With the transmission in Park, start the engine and allow it to run at normal idle speed. **Warning:** *Keep your hands and the vacuum gauge clear of the fans.*

Read the vacuum gauge; an average, healthy engine should normally produce about 17 to 22 inches of vacuum with a fairly steady needle **(see illustration)**. Refer to the following vacuum gauge readings and what they indicate about the engine's condition:

1   A low steady reading usually indicates a leaking gasket between the intake manifold and cylinder head(s) or throttle body, a leaky vacuum hose, late ignition timing or incorrect camshaft timing. Check ignition timing with a timing light and eliminate all other possible causes, utilizing the tests provided in this Chapter before you remove the timing chain cover to check the timing marks.

2   If the reading is three to eight inches below normal and it fluctuates at that low reading, suspect an intake manifold gasket leak at an intake port or a faulty fuel injector.

3   If the needle has regular drops of about two-to-four inches at a steady rate, the valves are probably leaking. Perform a compression check or leak-down test to confirm this.

4   An irregular drop or down-flick of the needle can be caused by a sticking valve or an ignition misfire. Perform a compression check or leak-down test and read the spark plugs.

5   A rapid vibration of about four in.-Hg vibration at idle combined with exhaust smoke indicates worn valve guides. Perform a leak-down test to confirm this. If the rapid vibration occurs with an increase in engine speed, check for a leaking intake manifold gasket or head gasket, weak valve springs, burned valves or ignition misfire.

6   A slight fluctuation, say one inch up and down, may mean ignition problems. Check all the usual tune-up items and, if necessary, run the engine on an ignition analyzer.

7   If there is a large fluctuation, perform a compression or leak-down test to look for a weak or dead cylinder or a blown head gasket.

8   If the needle moves slowly through a wide range, check for a clogged PCV system, incorrect idle fuel mixture, carburetor/throttle body or intake manifold gasket leaks.

9   Check for a slow return after revving the engine by quickly snapping the throttle open until the engine reaches about 2,500 rpm and let it shut. Normally the reading should drop to near zero, rise above normal idle reading (about 5 in.-Hg over) and then return to the previous idle reading. If the vacuum returns slowly and doesn't peak when the throttle is snapped shut, the rings may be worn. If there is a long delay, look for a restricted exhaust system (often the muffler or catalytic converter). An easy way to check this is to temporarily disconnect the exhaust ahead of the suspected part and redo the test.

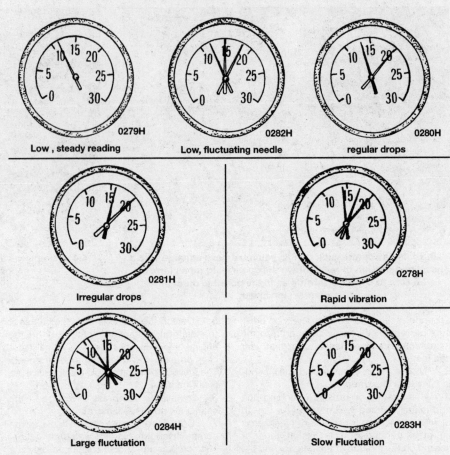

4.6 Typical vacuum gauge readings

5   Engine removal - methods and precautions

If you've decided that an engine must be removed for overhaul or major repair work, several preliminary steps should be taken.

Locating a suitable place to work is extremely important. Adequate work space, along with storage space for the vehicle, will be needed. If a shop or garage isn't available, at the very least a flat, level, clean work surface made of concrete or asphalt is required. Cleaning the engine compartment and engine before beginning the removal procedure will help keep tools clean and organized.

An engine hoist or A-frame will also be necessary. Make sure the equipment is rated in excess of the combined weight of the engine and transaxle. Safety is of primary importance, considering the potential hazards involved in lifting the engine out of the vehicle.

If the engine is being removed by a novice, a helper should be available. Advice and aid from someone more experienced would also be helpful. There are many instances when one person cannot simultaneously perform all of the operations required when lifting the engine out of the vehicle.

Plan the operation ahead of time. Arrange for or obtain all of the tools and equipment you'll need prior to beginning the job. Some of the equipment necessary to perform engine removal and installation safely and with relative ease are (in addition to an engine hoist) a heavy-duty floor jack, complete sets of wrenches and sockets as described in the front of this manual, wooden blocks and plenty of rags and cleaning solvent for mopping up spilled oil, coolant and gasoline. If the hoist must be rented, make sure that you arrange for it in advance and perform all of the operations possible without it beforehand. This will save you money and time.

Plan for the vehicle to be out of use for quite a while. A machine shop will be required to perform some of the work which the do-it-yourselfer can't accomplish without special equipment. These shops often have a busy schedule, so it would be a good idea to consult them before removing the engine in order to accurately estimate the amount of time required to rebuild or repair components that may need work.

Always be extremely careful when removing and installing the engine. Serious injury can result from careless actions. Plan ahead, take your time and a job of this nature, although major, can be accomplished successfully.

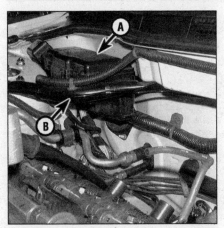

6.2 Disconnect the electrical connectors at the fuse/relay box (A), then remove the mounting bolts and the shock tower brace (B) and set the unit aside

6 Engine - removal and installation

Warning 1: *The air conditioning system is under high pressure. Do not loosen any hose fittings or remove any components until after the system has been discharged. Air conditioning refrigerant should be properly discharged into an EPA-approved recovery/recycling unit at a dealer service department or an automotive air conditioning repair facility. Always wear eye protection when disconnecting air conditioning system fittings.*

Warning 2: *Gasoline is extremely flammable, so take extra precautions when you work on any part of the fuel system. Don't smoke or allow open flames or bare light bulbs near the work area, and don't work in a garage where a natural gas-type appliance (such as a water heater or a clothes dryer) with a pilot light is present. Since gasoline is carcinogenic, wear latex gloves when there's a possibility of being exposed to fuel, and, if you spill any fuel on your skin, rinse it off immediately with soap and water. Mop up any spills immediately and do not store fuel-soaked rags where*

they could ignite. The fuel system is under constant pressure, so, if any fuel lines are to be disconnected, the fuel pressure in the system must be relieved first (see Chapter 4 for more information). When you perform any kind of work on the fuel system, wear safety glasses and have a Class B type fire extinguisher on hand.*

Warning 3: *The models covered by this manual are equipped with Supplemental Restraint systems (SRS), more commonly known as airbags. Always disable the airbag system before working in the vicinity of the impact sensors, steering column or instrument panel to avoid the possibility of accidental deployment of the airbag, which could cause personal injury (see Chapter 12).*

Removal

Refer to illustrations 6.2, 6.6a, 6.6b, 6.6c, 6.14a, 6.14b and 6.14c

Note: *Read through the entire Section before beginning this procedure. The recommended procedure for removing the engine on these models is to remove both engine and transaxle as a unit from below the vehicle. This requires a vehicle hoist or other means of safely raising the vehicle to clear the engine/transaxle.*

1   Relieve the fuel system pressure. Remove the air cleaner assembly and ducts (see Chapter 4).

2   Disconnect the negative cable, then the positive cable from the battery. Disconnect the battery cables from the underhood fuse/relay box, disconnect the electrical connectors at the fuse/relay box, then remove the mounting bolt and the fuse/relay box **(see illustration)**. On V6 models, remove the battery and the battery base and bracket. **Caution:** *The stereo in your vehicle is equipped with an anti-theft system. Make sure you have the correct activation code before disconnecting the battery.*

3   Place protective covers on the fenders and cowl and remove the hood (see Chapter 11).

4   Remove the alternator, distributor and spark plug wires (see Chapter 5).

5   Remove the oil filter, drain the cooling system, transaxle and engine oil and remove the drivebelts (see Chapter 1).

6   Clearly label and disconnect all vacuum lines, coolant and emissions hoses, electrical connectors **(see illustrations)**, ground straps and fuel lines. Masking tape and/or a touch-up paint applicator work well for marking items **(see illustration)**. Take instant photos or sketch the locations of components and brackets as necessary. **Note:** *Refer to Chapter 6 and disconnect the connectors from the PCM, then feed the PCM harness and grommet through the firewall to the engine side.*

7   Remove the cooling fan(s) and radiator (see Chapter 3).

8   Release any residual pressure in the fuel tank by removing the gas cap, then undo the fuel lines connecting the engine to the chassis (see Chapter 4). Plug or cap all open fittings.

9   Disconnect the throttle cable and cruise control cable, if equipped, from the engine (see Chapter 4).

10 Unbolt the power steering pump. If clearance allows, tie the pump aside without disconnecting the hoses. If necessary, remove the pump (see Chapter 10).

11 Remove the splash shields from under the vehicle. On air-conditioned models, unbolt the compressor and set it aside (see Chapter 3). Do not disconnect the refrigerant hoses.

12 Disconnect the electrical connector from the oxygen sensors. Detach the exhaust pipe(s) from the manifold(s) (see Chapter 4). Unbolt the exhaust pipe from the catalytic converter and remove the exhaust pipe.

13 Remove the driveaxles (see Chapter 8). Disconnect the wiring harness, shift linkage and speedometer cable/VSS from the transaxle (see Chapter 7). On manual transaxle models, remove the clutch release cylinder from the transaxle (see Chapter 8). On automatic transaxle models, disconnect the fluid cooler lines from the transaxle (see Chapter 7B).

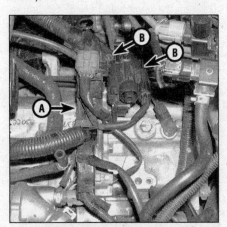

6.6a Disconnect the main electrical harness (arrow) on four-cylinder models and route it out of the way

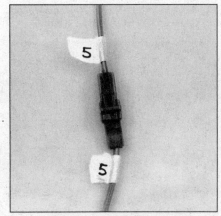

6.6b On V6 models, the main electrical harness (A) must be disconnected in several places (B indicates two connections)

6.6c Label each wire before disconnecting the connector

6.14a Four-cylinder engine - engine lifting eye (arrow)

14   Attach a lifting sling to the brackets on the engine and transaxle **(see illustrations)**. Raise the vehicle several feet off the ground with the vehicle hoist. Position an engine hoist over the engine compartment and connect the lifting sling to it. Take up the slack until there is slight tension on the lifting sling.
15   Recheck to be sure nothing except the mounts are still connecting the engine/transaxle to the vehicle. Disconnect anything still remaining.
16   Remove the nuts/bolts from the engine and transaxle mounts (see the appropriate engine mount procedure in Chapter 2A or 2B). Make paint marks on the chassis and the subframe assembly to insure correct alignment during installation. Remove the subframe mounting bolts and lower the assembly from below the engine compartment (see Chapter 7B).
17   Slowly lower the engine/transaxle a few inches and check to make sure nothing remains connected to it. Continue to lower the hoist until the engine is supported on the floor or preferably, a sturdy dolly. Remove the engine/transaxle assembly from under the vehicle.
18   On automatic transaxle models, remove the torque converter-to-driveplate bolts. Remove the engine-to-transaxle mounting bolts and separate the transaxle from the engine.
19   Remove the flywheel/driveplate and mount the engine on an engine stand.

Installation

20   Check the engine/transaxle mounts. If they're worn or damaged, replace them. Refer to Chapter 2A for testing the Engine Mount Control System used on automatic-transaxle-equipped vehicles.
21   On manual transaxle-equipped models, inspect the clutch components (see Chapter 8) and apply a dab of high temperature grease to the pilot bearing. Install the flywheel and clutch components onto the engine (see Chapter 8).
22   On automatic transaxle-equipped models, inspect the converter seal and bushing, and apply a dab of grease to the nose of the converter and to the seal lips. Install the driveplate.
23   Carefully mate the transaxle with the engine. Refer to Chapter 7 and tighten the transaxle mounting bolts to the specified torque. On automatic transaxle models, install and tighten the torque converter bolts.
24   Raise the vehicle several feet with a vehicle hoist and move the engine/transaxle assembly into position under the engine compartment. Move the engine hoist into position, feed the lifting sling down through the engine compartment and attach it to the engine/transaxle assembly.
25   Raise the engine into position in the engine compartment and install the engine mount brackets. Install the engine mounts and start the insulator throughbolts/nuts, but do not tighten them all the way at this time.
26   Install the subframe, aligning the marks made during removal. Install the bolts/nuts and tighten them to the torque listed in Chapter 7B Specifications.
27   Tighten the engine mount insulator throughbolts/nuts following the proper final tightening procedure (see Chapter 2A or 2B). If the proper tightening sequence is not followed, vibrations may result.
28   Remove the engine hoist and lifting sling.
29   Reinstall the remaining components and fasteners in the reverse order of removal.
30   Add coolant, oil, power steering and transmission fluids and an oil filter as needed (see Chapter 1).
31   Run the engine and check for proper operation and leaks. Shut off the engine and recheck the fluid levels.

7   Engine rebuilding alternatives

The do-it-yourselfer is faced with a number of options when performing an engine overhaul. The decision to replace the engine block, piston/connecting rod assemblies and crankshaft depends on a number of factors, with the number one consideration being the condition of the block. Other considerations are cost, access to machine shop facilities, parts availability, time required to complete the project and the extent of prior mechanical experience on the part of the do-it-yourselfer.

Some of the rebuilding alternatives include:

Individual parts - If the inspection procedures reveal that the engine block and most engine components are in reusable condition, purchasing individual parts may be the most economical alternative. The block, crankshaft and piston/connecting rod assemblies should all be inspected carefully. Even if the block shows little wear, the cylinder bores should be surface-honed.

Crankshaft kit - This rebuild package consists of a reground crankshaft and a matched set of pistons and connecting rods. The pistons will already be installed on the connecting rods. Piston rings and the necessary bearings will be included in the kit. These kits are commonly available for standard cylinder bores, as well as for engine blocks which have been bored to a regular oversize.

Short block - A short block consists of an engine block with renewed crankshaft and piston/connecting rod assemblies already installed. All new bearings are incorporated and all clearances will be correct. The existing cylinder head(s), camshaft, valve train components and external parts can be bolted to the short block with little or no machine shop work necessary.

Long block - A long block consists of a short block plus an oil pump, oil pan, cylinder heads, valve covers, camshaft and valve train components, timing sprockets, timing chain and timing cover. All components are installed with new bearings, seals and gaskets incorporated throughout. The installation of manifolds and external parts is all that is necessary.

Used engine assembly - While overhaul provides the best assurance of a like-new engine, used engines available from wrecking yards and importers are often a very simple and economical solution. Many used engines come with warranties, but always give any engine a thorough diagnostic check-out before purchase. Check compression, vacuum and also for signs of oil leakage. If possible, have the seller run the engine, ether in the vehicle or on a test stand so you can be sure it runs smoothly with no knocking or other noises.

Give careful thought to which alternative is best for you and discuss the situation with local automotive machine shops, auto parts dealers or parts store countermen before ordering or purchasing replacement parts.

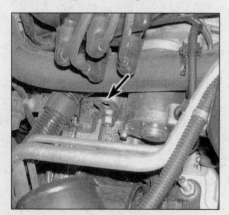

6.14b Four-cylinder engine - transaxle lifting eye (arrow)

6.14c V6 engine - engine lifting eye (arrow)

8 Engine overhaul - disassembly sequence

1   It's much easier to disassemble and work on the engine if it's mounted on a portable engine stand. A stand can often be rented quite cheaply from an equipment rental yard. Before it's mounted on a stand, the flywheel/driveplate should be removed from the engine.

2   If a stand isn't available, it's possible to disassemble the engine with it blocked up on the floor. Be extra careful not to tip or drop the engine when working without a stand.

3   If you're going to obtain a rebuilt engine, all external components must come off first, to be transferred to the replacement engine, just as they will if you're doing a complete engine overhaul yourself. These include:

> Alternator and brackets
> Power steering pump and brackets
> Emissions control components
> Distributor, spark plug wires and spark plugs
> Thermostat and housing cover
> Water pump bypass pipe/hose
> Fuel injection components
> Intake/exhaust manifolds
> Oil filter
> Engine mounts
> Clutch and flywheel or driveplate

Note: *When removing the external components from the engine, pay close attention to details that may be helpful or important during installation. Note the installed position of gaskets, seals, spacers, pins, brackets, washers, bolts, wiring and other small items.*

4   If you're obtaining a short block, which consists of the engine block, crankshaft, pistons and connecting rods all assembled, then the cylinder head(s), oil pan and oil pump will have to be removed as well. See *Engine rebuilding alternatives* for additional information regarding the different possibilities to be considered.

5   If you're planning a complete overhaul, the engine should be disassembled and the internal components removed in the following general order:

> Intake and exhaust manifolds
> Valve cover(s)
> Timing belt covers and bolts
> Timing belt and sprockets
> Rocker arm assembly and camshaft(s)
> Cylinder head(s)
> Water pump
> Oil pan
> Oil pick-up tube
> Front cover/oil pump
> Piston/connecting rod assemblies
> Rear main oil seal retainer
> Crankshaft and main bearings

6   Before beginning the disassembly and overhaul procedures, make sure the following items are available. Also, refer to *Engine overhaul - reassembly sequence* for a list of tools and materials needed for engine reassembly.

> Common hand tools
> Small cardboard boxes or plastic bags for storing parts
> Gasket scraper
> Ridge reamer
> Vibration damper puller
> Micrometers
> Telescoping gauges
> Dial indicator set
> Valve spring compressor
> Cylinder surfacing hone
> Piston ring groove cleaning tool
> Electric drill motor
> Tap and die set
> Wire brushes
> Oil gallery brushes
> Cleaning solvent

9 Cylinder head - disassembly

Refer to illustrations 9.2, 9.3 and 9.4

Note 1: *New and rebuilt cylinder heads are commonly available for most engines at dealerships and auto parts stores. Due to the fact that some specialized tools are necessary for the disassembly and inspection procedures, and some replacement parts may not be readily available, it may be more practical and economical for the home mechanic to purchase replacement head(s) rather than taking the time to disassemble, inspect and recondition the original(s).*

Note 2: *Remove the oil-control-orifice(s) from the block immediately after cylinder head removal. Clean and store them in a plastic bag for reassembly.*

1   Cylinder head disassembly involves removal of the intake and exhaust valves and related components. It's assumed that the rocker arms and camshaft(s) have already been removed (see Chapter 2 Part A or B as needed).

2   Compress the spring on the first valve with a spring compressor and remove the keepers **(see illustration)**. Carefully release the valve spring compressor and remove the

9.2 Use a valve spring compressor to compress the spring, then remove the keepers from the valve stem with a magnet or small pliers

retainer, the spring and the spring seat (if used).

3   After the valves are removed, label and store them, along with their related components, so they can be kept separate and reinstalled in the same valve guides they are removed from **(see illustration)**.

4   Pull the valve out of the head, then remove the oil seal from the guide. If the valve binds in the guide (won't pull through), push it back into the head and deburr the area around the keeper groove with a fine file or whetstone **(see illustration)**.

5   Repeat the procedure for the remaining valves. Remember to keep all the parts for each valve together so they can be reinstalled in the same locations.

6   Once the valves and related components have been removed and stored in an organized manner, the head should be thoroughly cleaned and inspected. If a complete engine overhaul is being done, finish the engine disassembly procedures before beginning the cylinder head cleaning and inspection process.

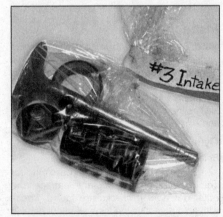

9.3 A small plastic bag, with an appropriate label, can be used to store the valve train components so they can be kept together and reinstalled in the original location

9.4 If the valve won't pull through the guide, deburr the edge of the stem end and the area around the top of the keeper groove with a file or whetstone

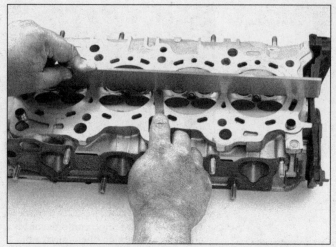

10.13 Check the cylinder head gasket surface for warpage by trying to slip a feeler gauge under the straightedge (see the Specifications for the maximum warpage allowed and use a feeler gauge of that thickness)

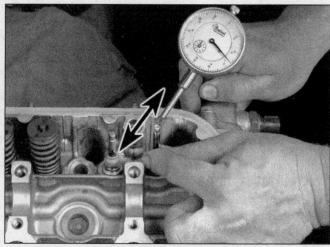

10.15 A dial indicator can be used to measure valve stem-to-guide clearance (move the valve stem back and forth as shown)

10 Cylinder head - cleaning and inspection

Cleaning

1 Thorough cleaning of the cylinder head(s) and related valvetrain components, followed by a detailed inspection, will enable you to decide how much valve service work must be done during the engine overhaul. **Note:** *If the engine was severely overheated, the cylinder head is probably warped (see Steps 12 and 13).*

2 Scrape all traces of old gasket material and sealing compound off the head gasket, intake manifold and exhaust manifold sealing surfaces. Be very careful not to gouge the cylinder head. Special gasket-removal solvents that soften gaskets and make removal much easier are available at auto parts stores.

3 Remove all built up scale from the coolant passages.

4 Run a stiff wire brush through the various holes to remove deposits that may have formed in them.

5 Run an appropriate-size tap into each of the threaded holes to remove corrosion and thread sealant that may be present. If compressed air is available, use it to clear the holes of debris produced by this operation. **Warning:** *Wear eye protection when using compressed air!*

6 Clean the exhaust and intake manifold stud threads with a wire brush.

7 Clean the cylinder head with solvent and dry it thoroughly. Compressed air will speed the drying process and ensure that all holes and recessed areas are clean. **Note:** *Decarbonizing chemicals are available and may prove very useful when cleaning cylinder heads and valvetrain components. These chemicals are very caustic and should be used with caution. Wear rubber gloves, goggles, and be sure to follow the instructions on the container.*

8 Clean the rocker arms with solvent and dry them thoroughly (don't mix them up during the cleaning process). Compressed air will speed the drying process and can be used to clean out the oil passages. **Note:** *On VTEC engines, keep the three intake rockers for each cylinder bundled together with rubber bands.*

9 Clean all the valve springs, spring seats, keepers and retainers with solvent and dry them thoroughly. Work on the components from one valve at a time to avoid mixing up the parts.

10 Scrape off any heavy deposits that may have formed on the valves, then use a motorized wire brush to remove deposits from the valve heads and stems. Again, make sure the valves don't get mixed up.

11 Remove, clean, and store in order the hydraulic tappets or lost-motion assemblies (VTEC models). **Note:** *The oil-control orifice(s) should be removed, cleaned and put away at this time. They are located in the top of the head on four-cylinder engines, and in the block (under the head) on V6 models.*

Inspection

Note: *Be sure to perform all of the following inspection procedures before concluding that machine shop work is required. Make a list of the items that need attention. The inspection procedures for the lifters and rocker arms, as well as the camshafts, can be found in Part A and Part B.*

Cylinder head

Refer to illustrations 10.13 and 10.15

12 Inspect the head very carefully for cracks, evidence of coolant leakage and other damage. If cracks are found, check with an automotive machine shop concerning repair. If repair isn't possible, a new cylinder head should be obtained.

13 Using a straightedge and feeler gauge, check the head-gasket mating surface for warpage **(see illustration)**. If the warpage

exceeds the specified limit, it can be resurfaced at an automotive machine shop.

14 Examine the valve seats in each of the combustion chambers. If they're pitted, cracked or burned, the head will require valve service that's beyond the scope of the home mechanic.

15 Check the valve stem-to-guide clearance with a small hole gauge and micrometer. Also check the valve stem deflection crosswise (parallel to the rocker arm) with a dial indicator attached securely to the head **(see illustration)**. The valve must be in the guide and approximately 1/16-inch off the seat. The total valve stem movement indicated by the gauge needle must be noted and divided in half to obtain the stem-to-guide clearance specification. If it exceeds the stem-to-guide clearance limit listed in this Chapter's specifications, the valve guides should be replaced. After this is done, if there's still some doubt regarding the condition of the valve guides, they should be checked by an automotive machine shop (the cost should be minimal).

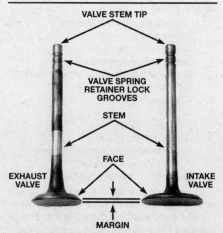

10.16 Check for valve wear at the points shown here

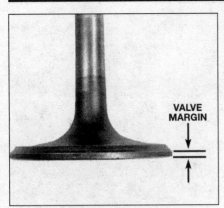

10.17 The margin width on each valve must be as specified (if no margin exists, the valve cannot be reused)

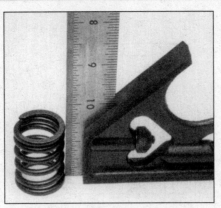

10.18 Check each valve spring for squareness

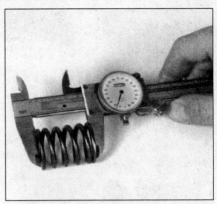

10.19 Measure the free length of each valve spring with a dial or vernier caliper

Valves

Refer to illustrations 10.16 and 10.17

16   Carefully inspect each valve face for uneven wear **(see illustration)**, deformation, cracks, pits and burned areas. Check the valve stem for scuffing and galling and the neck for cracks. Rotate the valve and check for any obvious indication that it's bent. Look for pits and excessive wear on the end of the stem. The presence of any of these conditions indicates the need for valve service by an automotive machine shop.

17   Measure the margin width on each valve **(see illustration)**. Any valve with a margin narrower than that listed in this Chapter's Specifications will have to be replaced with a new one.

Valve components

Refer to illustrations 10.18 and 10.19

18   Check each valve spring for wear (on the ends) and pits. Stand each spring on a flat surface and check it for squareness **(see illustration)**. If any of the springs are distorted or sagged, replace all of them with new parts.

19   Measure the free length of each valve spring with a dial or vernier caliper **(see illustration)**. The tension of all springs should be checked with a special fixture before deciding if they are suitable for use (an automotive

machine shop will perform this service for you). If in doubt, replace all of the valve springs during an overhaul.

20   Check the spring retainers and keepers for obvious wear and cracks. Any questionable parts should be replaced with new ones, as extensive damage will occur if they fail during engine operation.

21   Any damaged or excessively worn parts must be replaced with new ones.

22   If the inspection process indicates that the valve components are in generally poor condition and worn beyond the limits specified, which is usually the case in an engine that's being overhauled, reassemble the valves in the cylinder head and refer to Section 11 for valve servicing recommendations.

11   Valves - servicing

1   Because of the complex nature of the job and the special tools and equipment needed, servicing of the valves, the valve seats and the valve guides, commonly known as a valve job, should be done by a professional.

2   The home mechanic can remove and disassemble the head, do the initial cleaning and inspection, then reassemble and deliver it to a dealer service department or an automotive machine shop for the actual service work. Doing the inspection will enable you to see

what condition the head and valvetrain components are in and will ensure that you know what work and new parts are required when dealing with an automotive machine shop.

3   The dealer service department, or automotive machine shop, will remove the valves and springs, recondition or replace the valves and valve seats, recondition the valve guides, check and replace the valve springs, spring retainers and keepers (as necessary), replace the valve seals with new ones, reassemble the valve components and make sure the installed spring height is correct. The cylinder head gasket surface should also be resurfaced if it's warped. If you're working on a V6 model and one of the heads is warped, have both of them resurfaced.

4   After the valve job has been performed by a professional, the head will be in like new condition. When the head is returned, be sure to clean it again before installation on the engine to remove any metal particles and abrasive grit that may still be present from the valve service or head-resurfacing operations. Use compressed air, if available, to blow out all the oil holes and passages.

12   Cylinder head - reassembly

Refer to illustrations 12.3a, 12.3b, 12.3c, 12.5, 12.6 and 12.7

1   Regardless of whether or not the head was sent to an automotive repair shop for valve servicing, make sure it's clean before beginning reassembly.

2   If the head was sent out for valve servicing, the valves and related components will already be in place. Begin the reassembly procedure with Step 8.

3   Place the spring seats over the guides and install new seals on each of the valve guides **(see illustrations)**. **Note:** *Intake and exhaust valves require different seals - DO NOT mix them up! Exhaust seals have black springs and intake seals have white or silver springs.* Gently tap each valve seal into place with a seal installation tool until it's seated on the guide **(see illustration)**. **Caution:** *Don't hammer on the valve seals once they're seated or you may damage them. Don't twist*

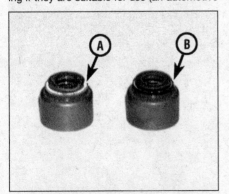

12.3a Intake and exhaust seals must not be interchanged - intake seals (A) have white springs, exhaust seals (B) have black springs

12.3b Place the spring seats over the valve guides

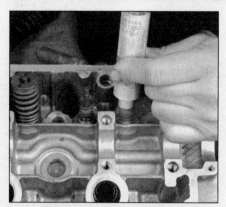

12.3c Gently tap the valve seals into place with a seal installation tool or a deep socket and hammer

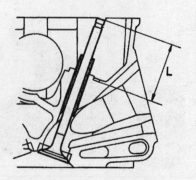

12.5 Check the valve stem installed height (the distance from the spring seat to the top of the valve stem)

12.6 Install the spring (closely-wound coils toward the head) and retainer over the valve stem

or cock the seals during installation or they won't seat properly on the valve stems.

4   Beginning at one end of the head, lubricate and install the first valve. Apply clean engine oil to the valve stem.

5   One at a time, check the valve stem installed height. Pull the valve up against its seat, and measure between the spring seat and the top of the valve stem with a vernier caliper to check the installed height and compare the measurement to Specifications **(see illustration)**. Excessive stem height is usually the result of the valve seat "sinking" into the head due to several valve jobs. If the height is greater than specified, a new valve will be required, or a new valve seat will have to be installed by a machine shop.

6   Set the valve spring and retainer in place **(see illustration)**, with the tightly wound spring coils toward the head.

7   Compress the springs with a valve spring compressor and carefully install the keepers in the upper groove, then slowly release the compressor and make sure the keepers seat properly. Apply a small dab of grease to each keeper to hold it in place if necessary **(see illustration)**.

8   Repeat the procedure for the remaining valves. Be sure to return the components to their original locations - don't mix them up!

9   The camshaft(s) and rocker arm assemblies can be installed after the cylinder head is assembled to the finished short-block.

---

13   Balance shafts (four-cylinder models) - removal and inspection

Removal

Refer to illustrations 13.1 and 13.5

1   Insert a 6 x 100-mm bolt or a suitable-size screwdriver through the access hole in the front balance shaft (just behind the sprocket) and unbolt the front balance shaft sprocket **(see illustration)**.

2   Remove the rear balance shaft gear case.

3   Insert the bolt or screwdriver in the access hole in the rear of the block to secure the rear balance shaft, and unbolt the rear balance shaft gear case (see Chapter 2A for locking the rear balance shaft). With the shaft secured by the bolt or screwdriver, unbolt the rear balance shaft driven gear from the shaft and remove the gear. **Note:** *Make a mark on the bolt 2.9 inches from the tip, and only insert it up to this mark*.

4   Remove the oil pump housing (see Chapter 2A).

5   Remove the two bolts and the thrust plate from the front balance shaft **(see illustration)**. Withdraw the balance shafts carefully to avoid nicking the bearings.

Inspection

6   Clean the balance shafts and inspect the journals for signs of wear, discoloration or scoring. Normally, the wear points exhibit a mirror-like surface.

7   With a micrometer, measure the front and rear edges of each journal. If the difference in measurements (taper) exceeds this Chapter's Specifications, replace the balance shaft.

8   Mount each balance shaft in V-blocks, set-up a dial indicator on the center journal, rotate the shaft and measure the shaft runout. If the runout exceeds this Chapter's Specifications, replace the balance shaft.

9   Measure the journal diameters and compare to this Chapter's Specifications. Measure the inside-diameter of the balance shaft bearings in the block and subtract the journal diameter from each bearing diameter to calculate the shaft-to-bearing oil clearance. Compare these measurements to the Specifications. If the shafts are in good condition, have new balance shaft bearings installed in the engine block at the machine shop.

12.7 Apply a small dab of grease to each keeper before installation to hold them in place on the valve stem until the spring is released

13.1 To remove the front balance shaft sprocket, the shaft must be held with a bolt or screwdriver through this maintenance hole behind the sprocket

13.5 Remove the two bolts (arrows) retaining the front balance shaft thrust plate

14.1 A ridge reamer is required to remove the ridge from the top of each cylinder - do this before removing the pistons!

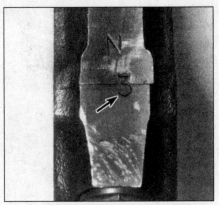

14.5a DO NOT confuse the stamped numbers on the parting surface, such as this 3 (arrow) with cylinder numbers - this number indicates big-end bore size

14.5b Before they're removed, the connecting rods and caps should be marked with a center punch to indicate in which cylinder they're installed

14 Pistons/connecting rods - removal

Refer to illustrations 14.1, 14.5a and 14.5b
Note: *Prior to removing the piston/connecting rod assemblies, remove the cylinder head(s), the oil pan and oil pump pick-up tube by referring to Chapter 2A or 2B.*

1   Use your fingernail to feel if a ridge has formed at the upper limit of ring travel (about 1/4-inch down from the top of each cylinder). If carbon deposits or cylinder wear have produced ridges, they must be completely removed with a special tool **(see illustration)**. Follow the manufacturer's instructions provided with the tool. Failure to remove the ridges before attempting to remove the piston/connecting rod assemblies may result in piston breakage.
2   After the cylinder ridges (if any) have been removed, turn the engine upside-down so the crankshaft is facing up.
3   The oil baffle plate must be removed first to access the connecting rods. **Note:** *On four-cylinder models, the crankshaft main caps are supported by a bridge that attaches to the caps and the block. Check the crankshaft endplay on these models before removing the bridge (see Section 15), and with the baffle plate removed, you can check rod side clearance through holes in the bridge, but remove the bridge to perform rod/piston removal.*
4   Before the connecting rods are removed, check the side clearance (endplay) with feeler gauges. Slide them between the first connecting rod and the crankshaft throw until the play is removed. The endplay is equal to the thickness of the feeler gauge(s). If the endplay exceeds the service limit, new connecting rods will be required. If new rods (or a new crankshaft) are installed, the endplay may fall under the specified minimum (if it does, the rods will have to be machined to restore it (consult an automotive machine shop for advice if necessary). Repeat the procedure for the remaining connecting rods.
5   The existing numbers on the connecting rods indicate the rod bore size, not the posi-

tion in the engine **(see illustration)**. Use a small center punch to make the appropriate number of indentations on each rod and cap (1, 2, 3, etc., depending on the engine type and cylinder they're associated with) **(see illustration)**.
6   Loosen each of the connecting rod cap bolts 1/2-turn at a time until they can be removed by hand. Remove the number one connecting rod cap and bearing insert. Don't drop the bearing insert out of the cap. **Note:** *The main cap bridge must be removed for connecting rod removal on four-cylinder models (see Section 15).*
7   Remove the bearing insert and push the connecting rod/piston assembly out through the top of the engine. Use a wooden hammer handle to push on the end of the rod. If resistance is felt, double-check to make sure that all of the ridge was removed from the cylinder.
8   Repeat the procedure for the remaining cylinders.
9   After removal, reassemble the connecting rod caps and bearing inserts in their respective connecting rods and install the cap bolts finger tight. Leaving the old bearing inserts in place until reassembly will help prevent the connecting rod bearing surfaces from being accidentally nicked or gouged.
10   Don't separate the pistons from the

15.1 Position the dial indicator as shown and move the crankshaft back and forth with a large screwdriver or prybar (typical)

connecting rods (see Section 19 for additional information).

15 Crankshaft - removal

Refer to illustrations 15.1, 15.3, 15.4, 15.5a, 15.5b and 15.6
Note: *The crankshaft can be removed only after the engine has been removed from the vehicle. It's assumed that the flywheel or driveplate, timing belt, oil pan, oil pick-up tube, oil pump and piston/connecting rod assemblies have already been removed. On four-cylinder engines the bridge removal shown below must be performed before the rod removal described in Section 14. The rear main oil seal retainer must be unbolted and separated from the block before proceeding with crankshaft removal (see Chapter 2A or 2B).*

1   Before the crankshaft is removed, check the endplay. Mount a dial indicator with the stem in line with the crankshaft and just touching one of the crank throws **(see illustration)**. **Note:** *The main caps and main-cap bridge (four-cylinder models) should be in place and torqued to Specifications.*
2   Push the crankshaft all the way to the rear and zero the dial indicator. Next, pry the crankshaft to the front as far as possible and check the reading on the dial indicator. The distance that it moves is the endplay. If it's greater than specified, check the crankshaft thrust surfaces for wear. If no wear is evident, new thrust washers should correct the endplay.
3   If a dial indicator isn't available, feeler gauges can be used. Gently pry or push the crankshaft all the way to the front of the engine. Slip feeler gauges between the crankshaft and the back face of the front thrust bearing to determine the clearance **(see illustration)**. The thrust bearing on four-cylinder engines is journal number four, while on the V6 engine it's number three.
4   Check the main bearing caps to see if they're marked to indicate their locations. They should be numbered consecutively

from the front of the engine to the rear **(see illustration)**. If they aren't, mark them with number-stamping dies or a center punch. Main bearing caps generally have a cast-in arrow, which points to the front of the engine.

5   On four-cylinder models, loosen the main bearing bridge/cap bolts 1/4-turn at a time each, working around the engine in sequence, until they can be removed by hand **(see illustrations)**. Remove the main bearing cap bridge. Gently tap the caps with a soft-face hammer and separate them from the engine block. If necessary, use the bolts as levers to remove the caps. Try not to drop the bearing inserts if they come out with the caps.

6   On V6 engines, there are four main cap bolts on each cap, two straight down (looking at the engine bottom-side up) and one on either side of the block going into the sides of the caps **(see illustration)**. Make sure all bolts are removed before trying to remove the caps.

7   Carefully lift the crankshaft out of the engine. It may be a good idea to have an assistant available, since the crankshaft is quite heavy. With the bearing inserts in place in the engine block, return the caps to their respective locations on the engine block, install the main bearing cap bridge on four-cylinder models and tighten the bolts finger tight.

16   Engine block - cleaning

Refer to illustration 16.7

1   Remove the main bearing caps and separate the bearing inserts from the caps and the engine block. Tag the bearings, indicating which cylinder they were removed from and whether they were in the cap or the block, then set them aside.

2   Using a gasket scraper, remove all traces of gasket material from the engine block. Be very careful not to nick or gouge the gasket sealing surfaces.

3   Remove all of the covers and threaded oil gallery plugs from the block. The plugs are usually very tight - they may have to be drilled out and the holes retapped. Use new plugs when the engine is reassembled.

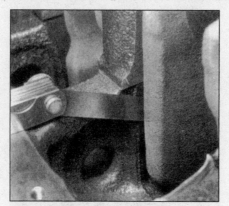

15.3 The endplay can also be checked with a feeler gauge at the thrust bearing journal (typical)

15.4 The main bearing caps should have numbers and arrows - this number indicates it is the second cap and the arrows point toward the timing belt end

4   If the engine is extremely dirty, it should be taken to an automotive machine shop to be cleaned.

5   After the block is returned, clean all oil holes and oil galleries one more time. Brushes specifically designed for this purpose are available at most auto parts stores. Flush the passages with warm water until the water runs clear, dry the block thoroughly and wipe all machined surfaces with a light, rust preventive oil. If you have access to compressed air, use it to speed the drying process and blow out all the oil holes and galleries. **Warning:** *Wear eye protection when using compressed air!*

6   If the block isn't extremely dirty or sludged up, you can do an adequate cleaning job with hot soapy water and a stiff brush. Take plenty of time and do a thorough job. Regardless of the cleaning method used, be sure to clean all oil holes and galleries very thoroughly, dry the block completely and coat all machined surfaces with light oil.

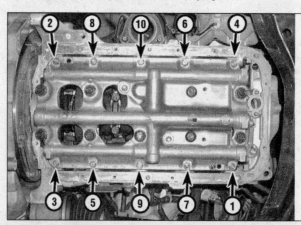

15.5a On four-cylinder models, loosen the outer main cap bridge bolts in this sequence . . .

15.5b . . . then loosen the inner main cap bolts in sequence to avoid warping the bridge

15.6 On V6 engines, first remove the side bolts (upper arrows indicate one side, there are four more on the other side of the block), then remove the main cap bolts (B)

7 The threaded holes in the block must be clean to ensure accurate torque readings during reassembly. Run the proper size tap into each of the holes to remove rust, corrosion, thread sealant or sludge and restore damaged threads **(see illustration)**. If possible, use compressed air to clear the holes of debris produced by this operation. Now is a good time to clean the threads on the head bolts and the main bearing cap bolts as well.

8 Reinstall the main bearing caps and tighten the bolts finger tight.

9 Apply non-hardening sealant (such as Teflon pipe sealant) to the new oil gallery plugs and thread them into the holes in the block. Make sure they're tightened securely.

10 If the engine isn't going to be reassembled right away, cover it with a large plastic trash bag to keep it clean.

17 Engine block - inspection

Refer to illustrations 17.4a, 17.4b, 17.4c and 17.8

1 Before the block is inspected, it should be cleaned as described in Section 16.

2 Visually check the block for cracks, rust and corrosion. Look for stripped threads in the threaded holes. It's also a good idea to have the block checked for hidden cracks by an automotive machine shop that has the special equipment to do this type of work. If defects are found, have the block repaired, if possible, or replaced.

3 Check the cylinder bores for scuffing and scoring.

4 Check the cylinders for taper and out-of-round conditions as follows **(see illustrations)**:

a) *Measure the diameter of each cylinder at the top (just under the ridge area), center and bottom of the cylinder bore, parallel to the crankshaft axis.*

b) *Next measure each cylinder's diameter at the same three locations perpendicular to the crankshaft axis.*

c) *The taper of the cylinder is the difference between the bore diameter at the*

16.7 All bolt holes in the block - particularly the main bearing cap and head bolt holes - should be cleaned and restored with a tap (be sure to remove debris from the holes after this is done)

top of the cylinder and the diameter at the bottom. The out-of-round specification of the cylinder bore is the difference between the parallel and perpendicular readings.

d) *Compare your results to those listed in this Chapter's Specifications.*

5 Repeat the procedure for the remaining pistons and cylinders.

6 If the cylinder walls are badly scuffed or scored, or if they're out-of-round or tapered beyond the limits given in this Chapter's Specifications, have the engine block rebored and honed at an automotive machine shop. If a rebore is done, oversize pistons and rings will be required.

7 If the cylinders are in reasonably good condition and not worn to the outside of the limits, and if the piston-to-cylinder clearances can be maintained properly, then they don't have to be rebored. Honing is all that's necessary (see Section 18).

8 Using a precision straightedge and feeler gauge, check the block deck (the surface that mates with the cylinder head) for distortion **(see illustration)**.

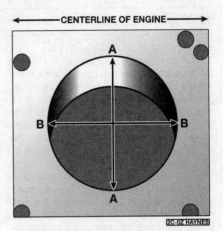

17.4a Measure the diameter of each cylinder at a right angle to the engine centerline (A), and parallel to engine centerline (B) - out-of-round is the difference between A and B, taper is the difference between A and B at the top of the cylinder and A and B at the bottom of the cylinder

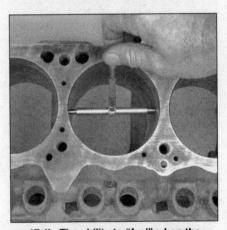

17.4b The ability to "feel" when the telescoping gauge is at the correct point will be developed over time, so work slowly and repeat the check until you're satisfied the bore measurement is accurate

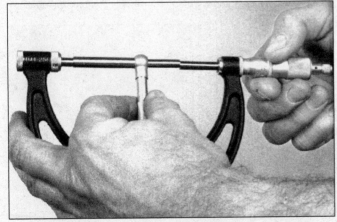

17.4c The gauge is then measured with a micrometer to determine the bore size

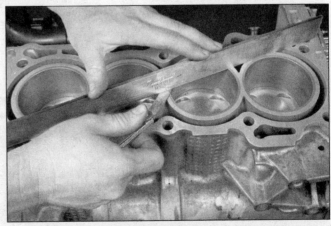

17.8 Check the block deck for distortion with a precision straightedge and feeler gauge - check diagonally and from end-to-end when making the check

18   Cylinder honing

Refer to illustrations 18.3a and 18.3b

1   Prior to engine reassembly, the cylinder bores must be honed so the new piston rings will seat correctly and provide the best possible combustion chamber seal. **Note:** *If you don't have the tools or don't want to tackle the honing operation, most automotive machine shops will do it for a reasonable fee.*

2   Before honing the cylinders, install the main bearing caps or cap assembly (without bearing inserts) and tighten the bolts to the torque listed in this Chapter's Specifications.

3   Two types of cylinder hones are commonly available - the flex hone or "bottle brush" type and the more traditional surfacing hone with spring-loaded stones. Both will do the job, but for the less experienced mechanic the "bottle brush" hone will probably be easier to use. You'll also need some kerosene or honing oil, rags and an electric drill motor. Proceed as follows:

a) *Mount the hone in the drill motor, compress the stones and slip it into the first cylinder* **(see illustration)**. *Be sure to wear safety goggles or a face shield!*

b) *Lubricate the cylinder with plenty of honing oil, turn on the drill and move the hone up-and-down in the cylinder at a pace that will produce a fine crosshatch pattern on the cylinder walls. Ideally, the crosshatch lines should intersect at approximately a 60-degree angle* **(see illustration)**. *Be sure to use plenty of lubricant and don't take off any more material than is absolutely necessary to produce the desired finish.* **Note:** *Piston ring manufacturers may specify a smaller crosshatch angle than the traditional 60-degrees - read and follow any instructions included with the new rings.*

c) *Don't withdraw the hone from the cylinder while it's running. Instead, shut off the drill and continue moving the hone up-and-down in the cylinder until it comes to a complete stop, then compress the stones and withdraw the hone. If you're using a "bottle brush" type hone, stop the drill motor, then turn the chuck in the normal direction of rotation while withdrawing the hone from the cylinder.*

d) *Wipe the oil out of the cylinder and repeat the procedure for the remaining cylinders.*

4   After the honing job is complete, chamfer the top edges of the cylinder bores with a small file so the rings won't catch when the pistons are installed. Be very careful not to nick the cylinder walls with the end of the file.

5   The entire engine block must be washed again very thoroughly with warm, soapy water to remove all traces of the abrasive grit produced during the honing operation. **Note:** *The bores can be considered clean when a lint-free white cloth - dampened with clean engine oil and used to wipe them out - doesn't pick-up any more honing residue, which will show up as gray areas on the cloth.* Be sure to run a brush through all oil holes and galleries and flush them with running water.

6   After rinsing, dry the block and apply a coat of light rust preventive oil to all machined surfaces. Wrap the block in a plastic trash bag to keep it clean and set it aside until reassembly.

19   Pistons/connecting rods - inspection

Refer to illustrations 19.4a, 19,4b, 19.10, 19.11a, 19.11b and 19.16

1   Before the inspection process can be carried out, the piston/connecting rod assemblies must be cleaned and the original piston rings removed from the pistons. **Note:** *Always use new piston rings when the engine is reassembled.*

2   Using a piston ring expander tool, carefully remove the rings from the pistons. Be careful not to nick or gouge the pistons in the process.

3   Scrape all traces of carbon from the top of the piston. A hand held wire brush or a piece of fine emery cloth can be used once the majority of the deposits have been scraped away. Do not, under any circum-

18.3a   A cylinder hone and drill motor are required for cylinder honing

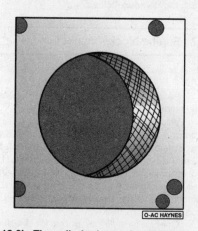

18.3b   The cylinder hone should leave a smooth, crosshatch pattern with the lines intersecting at approximately a 60-degree angle

stances, use a wire brush mounted in a drill motor to remove deposits from the pistons. The piston material is soft and may be eroded away by the wire brush.

4   Use a piston ring groove cleaning tool to remove carbon deposits from the ring grooves. If a tool isn't available, a piece broken off the old ring will do the job. Be very careful to remove only the carbon deposits -

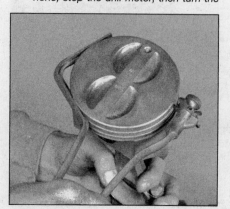

19.4a   The piston ring grooves can be cleaned with a special tool, as shown here . . .

19.4b   . . . or a section of a broken ring

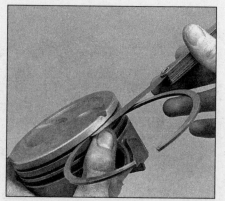

19.10   Check the ring side clearance with a feeler gauge at several points around the groove

19.11a Measure the piston diameter at a 90-degree angle to the piston pin and at the specified distance from the bottom of the skirt

19.11b On four-cylinder engines, match the marks with the letters on the pistons - the marks are located on a pad at the rear of the engine and read from left to right

don't remove any metal and do not nick or scratch the sides of the ring grooves **(see illustrations)**.

5 Once the deposits have been removed, clean the piston/rod assemblies with solvent and dry them with compressed air (if available). **Warning:** *Wear eye protection when using compressed air.* Make sure the oil return holes in the back sides of the ring grooves are clear.

6 If the pistons and cylinder walls aren't damaged or worn excessively, and if the engine block isn't rebored, new pistons won't be necessary. Normal piston wear appears as even vertical wear on the piston thrust surfaces and slight looseness of the top ring in its groove. New piston rings, however, should always be used when an engine is rebuilt.

7 Carefully inspect each piston for cracks around the skirt, at the pin bosses and at the ring lands.

8 Look for scoring and scuffing on the thrust faces of the skirt, holes in the piston crown and burned areas at the edge of the crown. If the skirt is scored or scuffed, the engine may have been suffering from overheating and/or abnormal combustion, which caused excessively high operating temperatures. The cooling and lubrication systems should be checked thoroughly. A hole in the piston crown is an indication that abnormal combustion (pre-ignition) was occurring. Burned areas at the edge of the piston crown are usually evidence of spark knock (detonation). If any of the above problems exist, the causes must be corrected or the damage will occur again. The causes may include intake air leaks, incorrect fuel/air mixture, low octane fuel, ignition timing and EGR system malfunctions.

9 Corrosion of the piston, in the form of small pits, indicates coolant is leaking into the combustion chamber and/or the crankcase. Again, the cause must be corrected or the problem may persist in the rebuilt engine.

10 Measure the piston ring side clearance by laying a new piston ring in each ring groove and slipping a feeler gauge in beside it **(see illustra-**

tion). Check the clearance at three or four locations around each groove. Be sure to use the correct ring for each groove - they are different. If the side clearance is greater than specified in this Chapter's Specifications, new pistons will have to be used.

11 Check the piston-to-bore clearance by measuring the bore (see Section 17) and the piston diameter. Make sure the pistons and bores are correctly matched. Measure the piston across the skirt, at a 90-degree angle to the piston pin **(see illustration)** and the specified distance from the bottom of the skirt. **Note:** *On four-cylinder engines, the pistons are select-fit to the bores in two sizes. The pistons are marked with an A (or no marking) or a B. The block is also marked* **(see illustration)**.

12 Subtract the piston diameter from the bore diameter to obtain the clearance. If it's greater than listed in this Chapter's Specifications, the block will have to be rebored and new pistons and rings installed.

13 Check the piston-to-rod clearance by twisting the piston and rod in opposite directions. Any noticeable play indicates excessive wear, which must be corrected. The piston/connecting rod assemblies should be taken to an

automotive machine shop to have the pistons and rods re-sized and new pins installed.

14 If the pistons must be removed from the connecting rods for any reason, they should be taken to an automotive machine shop. While they are there have the connecting rods checked for bend and twist, since automotive machine shops have special equipment for this purpose. **Note:** *Unless new pistons and/or connecting rods must be installed, do not disassemble the pistons and connecting rods.*

15 Check the connecting rods for cracks and other damage. Temporarily remove the rod caps, lift out the old bearing inserts, wipe the rod and cap bearing surfaces clean and inspect them for nicks, gouges and scratches.

16 Using a micrometer or vernier caliper, measure the connecting rod bolts and compare their thickness in the threaded portion in two locations **(see illustration)**. A variation in thickness larger than 0.004-inch means the rod bolt has stretched and should be replaced with a new set.

17 After checking the rods and rod bolts, replace the old bearings, slip the caps into place and tighten the bolts finger tight. **Note:** *If the engine is being rebuilt because of a connecting rod knock, be sure to install new or remanufactured rods.*

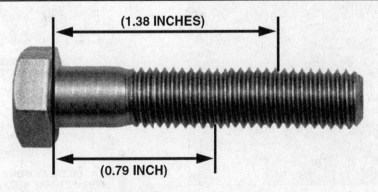

(1.38 INCHES)

(0.79 INCH)

19.16 Compare measurements of the thread diameter of the rod bolts at these two locations - the measuring device should hit the peak of the threads when measuring, not the valleys

20.1 The oil holes should be chamfered so sharp edges don't gouge or scratch the new bearings

20.2 Use a wire or stiff plastic bristle brush to clean the oil passages in the crankshaft

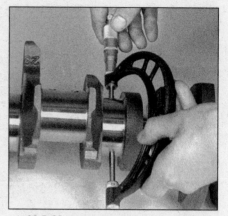

20.5 Measure the diameter of each crankshaft journal at several points to detect taper and out-of-round conditions

20   Crankshaft - inspection

Refer to illustrations 20.1, 20.2, 20.5 and 20.7

1   Remove all burrs from the crankshaft oil holes with a stone, file or scraper **(see illustration)**.
2   Clean the crankshaft with solvent and dry it with compressed air (if available). Be sure to clean the oil holes with a stiff brush **(see illustration)** and flush them with solvent.
3   Check the main and connecting rod bearing journals for uneven wear, scoring, pits and cracks.
4   Check the rest of the crankshaft for cracks and other damage. It should be magnafluxed to reveal hidden cracks - an automotive machine shop will handle the procedure.
5   Using a micrometer, measure the diameter of the main and connecting rod journals and compare the results to this Chapter's Specifications **(see illustration)**. By measuring the diameter at a number of points around each journal's circumference, you'll be able to determine whether or not the journal is out-of-round. Take the measurement at each end of the journal, near the crank throws, to determine if the journal is tapered.

6   If the crankshaft journals are damaged, tapered, out-of-round or worn beyond the limits given in the Specifications, have the crankshaft reground by an automotive machine shop. Be sure to use the correct size bearing inserts if the crankshaft is reconditioned.
7   Check the oil seal journals at each end of the crankshaft for wear and damage. If the seal has worn a groove in the journal, or if it's nicked or scratched **(see illustration)**, the new seal may leak when the engine is reassembled. In some cases, an automotive machine shop may be able to repair the journal by pressing on a thin sleeve. If repair isn't feasible, a new or different crankshaft should be installed.
8   Refer to Section 21 and examine the main and rod bearing inserts.

21   Main and connecting rod bearings - inspection and selection

Inspection

Refer to illustration 21.1

1   Even though the main and connecting rod bearings should be replaced with new ones during the engine overhaul, the old bearings should be retained for close examination, as they may reveal valuable information about the condition of the engine **(see illustration)**.
2   Bearing failure occurs because of lack of lubrication, the presence of dirt or other foreign particles, overloading the engine and corrosion. Regardless of the cause of bearing

20.7 If the seals have worn grooves in the crankshaft journals, or if the seal contact surfaces are nicked or scratched, the new seals will leak

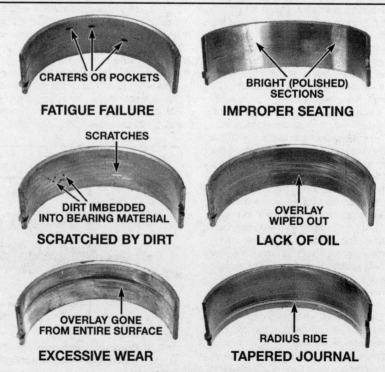

CRATERS OR POCKETS
FATIGUE FAILURE

BRIGHT (POLISHED) SECTIONS
IMPROPER SEATING

SCRATCHES
DIRT IMBEDDED INTO BEARING MATERIAL
SCRATCHED BY DIRT

OVERLAY WIPED OUT
LACK OF OIL

OVERLAY GONE FROM ENTIRE SURFACE
EXCESSIVE WEAR

RADIUS RIDE
TAPERED JOURNAL

21.1 Typical bearing failures

21.10 The main journal bore codes are stamped on the engine block adjacent to the oil pan surface (arrow)

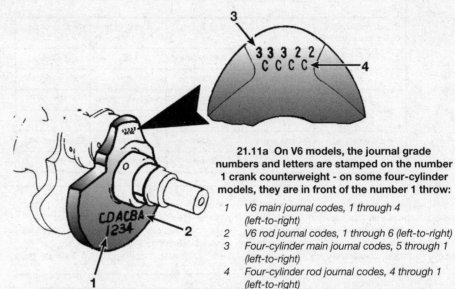

21.11a On V6 models, the journal grade numbers and letters are stamped on the number 1 crank counterweight - on some four-cylinder models, they are in front of the number 1 throw:

1 *V6 main journal codes, 1 through 4 (left-to-right)*
2 *V6 rod journal codes, 1 through 6 (left-to-right)*
3 *Four-cylinder main journal codes, 5 through 1 (left-to-right)*
4 *Four-cylinder rod journal codes, 4 through 1 (left-to-right)*

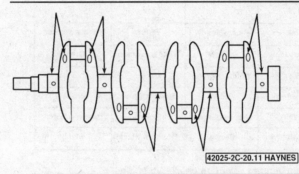

21.11b On other four-cylinder models, the main bearing journal grade numbers may be stamped adjacent to their respective journals

failure, it must be corrected before the engine is reassembled to prevent it from happening again.

3   When examining the bearings, remove them from the engine block, the main bearing caps, the connecting rods and the rod caps and lay them out on a clean surface in the same general position as their location in the engine. This will enable you to match any bearing problems with the corresponding crankshaft journal.

4   Dirt and other foreign particles get into the engine in a variety of ways. It may be left in the engine during assembly, or it may pass through filters or the PCV system. It may get into the oil, and from there into the bearings. Metal chips from machining operations and normal engine wear are often present. Abrasives are sometimes left in engine components after reconditioning, especially when parts are not thoroughly cleaned using the proper cleaning methods. Whatever the source, these foreign objects often end up embedded in the soft bearing material and are easily recognized. Large particles will not embed in the bearing and will score or gouge the bearing and journal. The best prevention for this cause of bearing failure is to clean all parts thoroughly and keep everything spotlessly clean during engine assembly. Frequent and regular engine oil and filter changes are also recommended.

5   Lack of lubrication (or lubrication breakdown) has a number of interrelated causes. Excessive heat (which thins the oil), overloading (which squeezes the oil from the bearing face) and oil leakage or throw off (from excessive bearing clearances, worn oil pump or high engine speeds) all contribute to lubrication breakdown. Blocked oil passages, which usually are the result of misaligned oil holes in a bearing shell, will also oil starve a bearing and destroy it. When lack of lubrication is the cause of bearing failure, the bearing material is wiped or extruded from the steel backing of the bearing. Temperatures may increase to the point where the steel backing turns blue from overheating.

6   Driving habits can have a definite effect on bearing life. low-speed operation in too-high a gear (lugging the engine) puts very high loads on bearings, which tends to squeeze out the oil film. These loads cause the bearings to flex, which produces fine cracks in the bearing face (fatigue failure). Eventually the bearing material will loosen in pieces and tear away from the steel backing. Short-trip driving leads to corrosion of bearings because insufficient engine heat is produced to drive off the condensed water and corrosive gases. These products collect in the engine oil, forming acid and sludge. As the oil is carried to the engine bearings, the acid attacks and corrodes the bearing material.

7   Incorrect bearing installation during engine assembly will lead to bearing failure as well. Tight-fitting bearings leave insufficient bearing oil clearance and will result in oil starvation. Dirt or foreign particles trapped behind a bearing insert result in high spots on the bearing which lead to failure.

Selection

Refer to illustrations 21.10, 21.11a, 21.11b, 21.12a, 21.12b, 21.15, 21.16a and 21.16b

8   If the original bearings are worn or damaged, or if the oil clearances are incorrect (see Section 24 or 26), the following procedures should be used to select the correct new bearings for engine reassembly. However, if the crankshaft has been reground, new undersize bearings must be installed - the following procedure should not be used if undersize bearings are required! The automotive machine shop that reconditions the crankshaft will provide or help you select the correct-size bearings. Regardless of how the bearing sizes are determined, use the oil clearance, measured with Plastigage, as a guide to ensure the bearings are the right size.

Main bearings

9   If you need to use a STANDARD-size main bearing, install one that has the same color code as the original bearing.

10   If the color code on the original main bearing has been obscured, locate the codes stamped into the block for the corresponding cap location (**see illustration**).

11   Locate the main journal grade numbers on the crankshaft as well (**see illustrations**).

12   Use the accompanying charts to determine the correct bearings for each journal (**see illustrations**).

Connecting rod bearings

13   If you need to use a STANDARD-size rod bearing, install one that has the same color code as the original.

14   If the color code has been obscured, locate the number stamped on each connecting rod cap (**see illustration 14.5a**). This code indicates the connecting rod big-end-bearing bore size, **not** the cylinder number it came from.

Block code (right) Crank code (below)	1 or A or I	2 or B or II	3 or C or III	4 or D or IIII
1 or I	Red	Red w/pink	Pink	Yellow
2 or II	Red w/pink	Pink	Yellow	Yellow w/green
3 or III	Pink	Yellow	Yellow w/green	Green
4 or IIII	Yellow	Yellow w/green	Green	Brown
5 or IIIII	Yellow w/green	Green	Brown	Brown w/black
6 or IIIIII	Green	Brown	Brown w/black	Black

21.12a Main bearing selection chart for four-cylinder models - use the number/letter/bars on the block and the number/bars on the crankshaft - example: C3 would require a Yellow-coded bearing half with a Green-coded half - where halves are different colors, it doesn't matter which color is used for the top or bottom bearing

15   Locate the connecting rod journal grade letters stamped on the crank-shaft **(see illustration)**. These denote the size of their respective connecting rod journals. **Note:** Journal grade numbers and letters on four-cylinder models are found on the number 1 crank throw **(see illustration 21.11a)** or they're stamped adjacent to their respective journals **(see illustrations 21.11b and 21.15)**.

16   Use the accompanying charts **(see illustrations)** to determine the correct bearings for each journal.

All bearings

17   Remember, the oil clearance is the final judge when selecting new bearing sizes. If you have any questions or are unsure which bearings to use, get help from your dealer parts or service department.

22   Engine overhaul - reassembly sequence

1   Before beginning engine reassembly, make sure you have all the necessary new parts, gaskets and seals as well as the following items on hand:

Common hand tools
A 1/2-inch drive torque wrench
Piston ring installation tool
Piston ring compressor

Block code (right) Crank code (below)	A or I	B or II	C or III	D or IIII
1 or I	Pink	Pink w/yellow	Yellow	Yellow w/green
2 or II	Pink w/yellow	Yellow	Yellow w/green	Green
3 or III	Yellow	Yellow w/green	Green	Green w/brown
4 or IIII	Yellow w/brown	Green	Green w/brown	Brown
5 or IIIII	Green	Green w/brown	Brown	Brown w/black
6 or IIIIII	Green w/brown	Brown	Brown w/black	Black

21.12b Main bearing selection chart - V6 engine

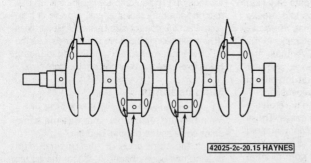

42025-2c-20.15 HAYNES

21.15 On some four-cylinder models, the rod journal code is also found stamped adjacent to their respective journals

Code on rod (right) Code on crank (below)	1 or I	2 or II	3 or III	4 or IIII
A or I	Red	Pink	Yellow	Green
B or II	Pink	Yellow	Green	Brown
C or III	Yellow	Green	Brown	Black
D or IIII	Green	Brown	Black	Blue

21.16a Find the correct connecting rod bearing color code for four-cylinder models by using the letter on each crankshaft throw and the number on the respective connecting rod - example: D4 would be blue

Code on rod (right) Code on crank (below)	1 or I	2 or II	3 or III	4 or IIII
A or I	Pink	Pink w/yellow	Yellow	Yellow w/green
B or II	Pink w/yellow	Yellow	Yellow w/green	Green
C or III	Yellow	Yellow w/green	Green	Green w/brown
D or IIII	Yellow w/green	Green	Green w/brown	Brown
E or IIIII	Green	Green w/brown	Brown	Brown w/black
F or IIIIII	Green w/brown	Brown	Brown w/black	Black

21.16b Find the correct connecting rod bearing color code for V6 models by using the letter on each crankshaft throw and the number on the respective connecting rod - example: D4 would be brown (note that some call for combining halves of two different colors)

Short lengths of rubber or plastic hose
    to fit over "cutoff" connecting rod
    bolts (see text)
Plastigage
Feeler gauges
A fine-tooth file
New engine oil
Engine assembly lubricant
Gasket sealer
Thread-locking compound

2   In order to save time and avoid problems, engine reassembly must be done in the
following general order:

Four-cylinder engine

Piston rings
Crankshaft and main bearings
Piston/connecting rod assemblies
Rear main (crankshaft) oil seal
Main cap bridge
Oil baffle plate
Balance shafts
Oil pump (see Part A)
Oil pick-up (see Part A)
Oil pan (see Part A)
Cylinder head (see Part A)
Camshaft and rockers (see Part A)
Timing belt and sprockets (see Part A)
Timing belt cover (see Part A)
Valve cover (see Part A)
Intake and exhaust manifolds (see Part A)
Flywheel/driveplate (see Part A)

V6 engine

Piston rings
Crankshaft and main bearings
Piston/connecting rod assemblies
Rear main oil seal/retainer
Oil baffle plate
Oil pump (see Part B)
Oil pan (see Part B)
Cylinder heads (see Part B)
Camshafts and valve components (see
    Part B)
Timing belts and sprockets (see Part B)
Timing belt covers (see Part B)
Intake and exhaust manifolds (see Part B)
Valve covers (see Part B)
Flywheel/driveplate (see Part B)

23 Piston rings - installation

Refer to illustrations 23.3, 23.4, 23.9a, 23.9b
and 23.12

1   Before installing the new piston rings,
the ring end gaps must be checked. It's
assumed that the piston ring side clearance
has been checked and verified correct (see
Section 19).
2   Lay out the piston/connecting rod
assemblies and the new ring sets so the ring
sets will be matched with the same piston
and cylinder during the end-gap measurement and engine assembly.
3   Insert the top (number one) ring into the
first cylinder and square it up with the cylinder walls by pushing it in with the top of the
piston (see illustration). The ring should be

**23.3 When checking piston ring end gap,
the ring must be square in the cylinder
bore (this is done by pushing the ring
down with the top of a piston as shown)**

near the bottom of the cylinder, at the lower
limit of ring travel.
4   To measure the end gap, slip feeler
gauges between the ends of the ring until a
gauge equal to the gap width is found (see
illustration). The feeler gauge should slide
between the ring ends with a slight amount of
drag. Compare the measurement to this
Chapter's Specifications. If the gap is larger
or smaller than specified, double-check to
make sure you have the correct rings before
proceeding.
5   If the gap is too small, try another set of
rings - DO NOT file the ends to increase the
clearance.
6   Excess end gap isn't critical unless it's
greater than the service limit listed in this
Chapter's Specifications. Again, double-
check to make sure you have the correct
rings for your engine.
7   Repeat the procedure for each ring that
will be installed in the first cylinder and for
each ring in the remaining cylinders. Remember to keep rings, pistons and cylinders
matched up.
8   Once the ring end gaps have been
checked/corrected, the rings can be installed
on the pistons.

**23.9a Installing the spacer/expander in
the oil control ring groove**

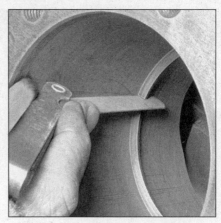

**23.4 With the ring square in the
cylinder, measure the end
gap with a feeler gauge**

9   The oil control ring (lowest one on the
piston) is usually installed first. It's composed
of three separate components. Slip the
spacer/expander into the groove (see illustration). If an anti-rotation tang is used, make
sure it's inserted into the drilled hole in the
ring groove. Next, install the lower side rail.
Do not use a piston-ring installation tool on
the oil ring side rails, as they may be damaged. Instead, place one end of the side rail
into the groove between the spacer/expander
and the ring land, hold it firmly in place and
slide a finger around the piston while pushing
the rail into the groove (see illustration).
Next, install the upper side rail in the same
manner.
10   After the three oil ring components have
been installed, check to make sure that both
the upper and lower side rails can be turned
smoothly in the ring groove.
11   The number two (middle) ring is installed
next. It's usually stamped with a mark which
must face up, toward the top of the piston.
Note: Always follow the instructions printed
on the ring package or box - different manufacturers may require different approaches.
Do not mix up the top and middle rings, as
they have different cross-sections.

**23.9b DO NOT use a piston ring
installation tool when installing the oil ring
side rails**

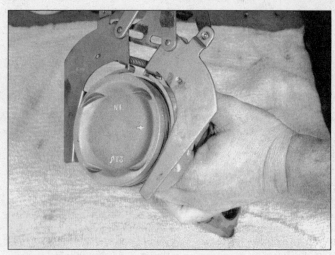

23.12 Installing the compression rings with a ring expander - the mark must face up

24.10 Lay the Plastigage strips (arrow) on the main bearing journals, parallel to the crankshaft centerline

12   Use a piston-ring installation tool and make sure the ring's identification mark is facing the top of the piston, then slip the ring into the middle groove on the piston **(see illustration)**. Don't expand the ring any more than necessary to slide it over the piston.

13   Install the number one (top) ring in the same manner. Make sure the mark is facing up. Be careful not to confuse the number one and number two rings.

14   Repeat the procedure for the remaining pistons and rings.

24 Crankshaft - installation and main bearing oil clearance check

1   Crankshaft installation is the first major step in engine reassembly. It's assumed at this point that the engine block and crankshaft have been cleaned, inspected and repaired or reconditioned.

2   Position the engine with the bottom facing up.

3   Remove the main bearing cap bolts and lift out the caps (and bridge on four-cylinder

models). Lay the caps out in the proper order to ensure correct installation.

4   If they're still in place, remove the old bearing inserts from the block and the main bearing caps. Wipe the main bearing surfaces of the block and caps with a clean, lint free cloth. They must be kept spotlessly clean!

Main bearing oil clearance check

Refer to illustrations 24.10, 24.12a, 24.12b, 24.12c and 24.14

5   Clean the back sides of the new main bearing inserts and lay the bearing half with the oil groove in each main bearing saddle in the block. Lay the other bearing half from each bearing set in the corresponding main bearing cap. Make sure the tab on each bearing insert fits into the recess in the block or cap. Also, the oil holes in the block must line up with the oil holes in the bearing insert.

6   If you're working on a V6 engine, the thrust bearings (washers) must be installed in the number three position. On four-cylinder

models, the thrust bearings (washers) must be installed in the number four position.

7   Clean the faces of the bearings in the block and the crankshaft main bearing journals with a clean, lint free cloth. Check or clean the oil holes in the crankshaft, as any dirt here can go only one way - straight through the new bearings.

8   Once you're certain the crankshaft is clean, carefully lay it in position in the main bearings.

9   Before the crankshaft can be permanently installed, the main bearing oil clearance must be checked.

10   Trim several pieces of the appropriate-size Plastigage (they must be slightly shorter than the width of the main bearings) and place one piece on each crankshaft main bearing journal, parallel with the journal axis **(see illustration)**.

11   Clean the faces of the bearings in the caps and install the caps in their respective positions (don't mix them up) with the arrows pointing toward the front of the engine. Carefully lay the main bearing caps/bridge in place. Don't disturb the Plastigage. Apply a

24.12a On four cylinder models, tighten the inner bridge/cap bolts in sequence first . . .

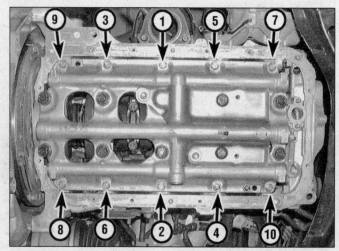

24.12b . . . then tighten the outer bridge bolts in sequence

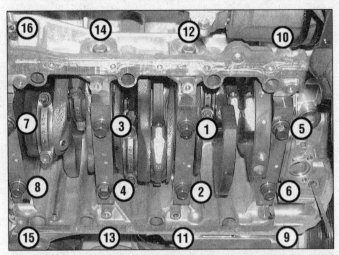

24.12c Bolt tightening sequence for the main bearing caps on V6 models - the main cap bolts are tightened first, then the side bolts (one row of side bolts not visible here)

24.14 Compare the width of the crushed Plastigage to the scale on the envelope to determine the main bearing oil clearance (always take the measurement at the widest point of the Plastigage); be sure to use the correct scale - standard and metric ones are included

light coat of oil to the bolt threads and the under sides of the bolt heads, then install them.

12   Tighten the main bearing cap bolts, in three steps, to the torque listed in this Chapter's Specifications. Don't rotate the crankshaft at any time during this operation! Follow the recommended tightening sequence for each engine type **(see illustrations)**.

13   Remove the bolts and carefully lift off the main bearing caps. Keep them in order. Don't disturb the Plastigage or rotate the crankshaft. If any of the main bearing caps are difficult to remove, tap them gently from side-to-side with a soft-face hammer to loosen them.

14   Compare the width of the crushed Plastigage on each journal to the scale printed on the Plastigage envelope to obtain the main bearing oil clearance **(see illustration)**. Check this Chapter's Specifications to make sure it's correct.

15   If the clearance is not as specified, the bearing inserts may be the wrong size (which means different ones will be required - see Section 21). Before deciding that different inserts are needed, make sure that no dirt or oil was between the bearing inserts and the caps or block when the clearance was measured. If the Plastigage is noticeably wider at one end than the other, the journal may be tapered (see Section 20).

16   Carefully scrape all traces of the Plastigage material off the main bearing journals and/or the bearing faces. Don't nick or scratch the bearing faces.

Final crankshaft installation

17   Carefully lift the crankshaft out of the engine. Clean the bearing faces in the block, then apply a thin, uniform layer of clean moly-based engine assembly lubricant to each of the bearing surfaces. Coat the thrust washers as well.

18   Lubricate the crankshaft surfaces that contact the oil seals with moly-based engine assembly lubricant or clean engine oil.

19   Make sure the journals are clean, then lay the crankshaft back in place in the block. Clean the faces of the bearings in the caps, then apply lubricant to them.

20   With the engine block positioned so the crankshaft is at the top, install the pistons and connecting rods (see Section 26). **Note:** *On four-cylinder models, install the main bearing caps and bolts without the bearing cap bridge. Tighten the main cap bolts approximately 10 to 20 foot pounds (washers may be used if the bolts are to long to secure the bearing caps). This will secure the crankshaft while the piston and connecting rod assemblies are being installed. After the connecting rod final installation procedure has been completed remove the main bearing cap bolts and proceed to Step 21.*

21   Install the caps and bridge in their respective positions with the arrows pointing toward the front of the engine. **Note:** *Be sure to install the thrust washers.*

22   Apply a light coat of oil to the bolt threads and the under sides of the bolt heads, then install them. Start the bolts by hand. Tap the ends of the crankshaft forward and backward with a lead or brass hammer to line up the thrust washer and crankshaft surfaces before the bolts are tightened. Tighten all main bearing cap and bridge bolts to the torque listed in this Chapter's Specifications following the recommended sequence **(see Step 12)**.

23   Rotate the crankshaft a number of times by hand to check for any obvious binding.

24   Check the crankshaft endplay with a feeler gauge or a dial indicator as described in Section 15. The endplay should be correct if the crankshaft thrust faces aren't worn or damaged and new thrust washers have been installed.

25   Install a new rear main oil seal, then bolt the retainer to the block (see Section 25).

25   Rear main oil seal - installation

Refer to illustrations 25.3, 25.4 and 25.5

1   The crankshaft must be installed first and the main bearing caps and bridge bolted in place, then the new seal should be installed in the retainer and the retainer bolted to the block.

2   Check the seal contact surface on the crankshaft very carefully for scratches and nicks that could damage the new seal lip and cause oil leaks. If the crankshaft is damaged, the only alternative is a new or different crankshaft.

3   The old seal can be removed from the retainer by driving it out from the back side with a hammer and punch **(see illustration)**. Be sure to note how far it's recessed into the bore before removing it (measure the clearance with feeler gauges); the new seal will have to be recessed an equal amount. Be very careful not to scratch or otherwise damage the bore in the retainer or oil leaks could develop.

4   Make sure the retainer is clean, then

25.3 Drive the old seal out using a blunt punch and a small hammer

25.4 Drive the new seal into the retainer with a block of wood or a section of pipe - make sure that you don't cock the seal in the retainer bore

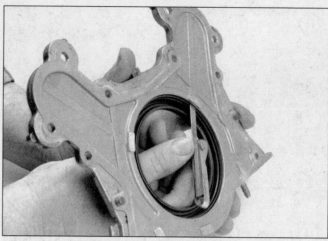

25.5 The depth the oil seal seats in the retainer must be checked as shown with feeler gauges and compared to this Chapter's Specifications

apply a thin coat of engine oil to the outer edge of the new seal. The seal must be pressed squarely into the bore, so hammering it into place isn't recommended. If you don't have access to a press, sandwich the housing and seal between two smooth pieces of wood and press the seal into place with the jaws of a large vise. The pieces of wood must be thick enough to distribute the force evenly around the entire circumference of the seal. Work slowly and make sure the seal enters the bore squarely **(see illustration)**.

5   If a vise in not available, the seal can be tapped into the retainer with a hammer. Use a block of wood to distribute the force evenly and make sure the seal is driven in squarely If the clearance measured with the feeler gauges is the same all around the seal, it is square to the bore **(see illustration)**.

6   The seal lips must be lubricated with clean engine oil before the seal/retainer is slipped over the crankshaft and bolted to the block. No gasket is required. Instead, clean the surface and then apply a 2-mm wide bead of anaerobic sealant to the retainer-to-block surface just prior to installation.

7   Tighten the bolts a little at a time to the torque listed in this Chapter's Specifications.

26 Pistons/connecting rods - installation and rod bearing oil clearance check

1   Before installing the piston/connecting rod assemblies, the cylinder walls must be perfectly clean, the top edge of each cylinder must be chamfered, and the crankshaft must be in place.

2   Remove the cap from the end of the number one connecting rod (check the marks made during removal). Remove the original bearing inserts and wipe the bearing surfaces of the connecting rod and cap with a clean, lint-free cloth. They must be kept spotlessly clean.

Connecting rod bearing oil clearance check

Refer to illustrations 26.5, 26.9, 26.11, 26.13 and 26.17

Note: *Don't touch the faces of the new bearing inserts with your fingers. Oil and acids from your skin can etch the bearings.*

3   Clean the back side of the new upper bearing insert, then lay it in place in the connecting rod. Make sure the tab on the bearing fits into the recess in the rod. Be very careful not to nick or gouge the bearing face. Don't lubricate the bearing at this time.

4   Clean the back side of the other bearing insert and install it in the rod cap. Again, make sure the tab on the bearing fits into the recess in the cap, and don't apply any lubricant. It's critically important that the mating surfaces of the bearing and connecting rod are perfectly clean and oil free when they're assembled.

5   Position the piston ring gaps at intervals around the piston before installing the piston/rod assembly **(see illustration). Caution:** *DO NOT position any ring gap in line with the piston pin or at the piston thrust surfaces (90-degrees to piston pin).*

6   Lubricate the piston and rings with clean engine oil.

7   Attach a piston ring compressor to the piston. Leave the skirt protruding about 1/4-inch to guide the piston into the cylinder. The rings must be compressed until they're flush with the piston.

8   Rotate the crankshaft until the number one connecting rod journal is at BDC (bottom dead center) and apply a coat of engine oil to the cylinder walls.

9   With the mark or notch on top of the piston facing the front of the engine **(see illustration)**, gently insert the piston/connecting rod assembly into the number one cylinder bore and rest the bottom edge of the ring compressor on the engine block.

10   Tap the top edge of the ring compressor to make sure it's contacting the block around its entire circumference.

11   Gently tap on the top of the piston with the end of a wooden or plastic hammer handle **(see illustration)** while guiding the end of the connecting rod into place on the crankshaft journal. The piston rings may try to pop out of the ring compressor just before entering the cylinder bore, so keep some pressure on the ring compressor. Work slowly, and if any resistance is felt as the piston enters the cylinder, stop immediately. Find out what's hanging up and fix it before

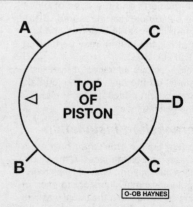

26.5 Piston ring gap positions - align the oil ring spacer gap at (D), the oil ring side rails at (C), the second compression ring at (A) and the top compression ring at (B)

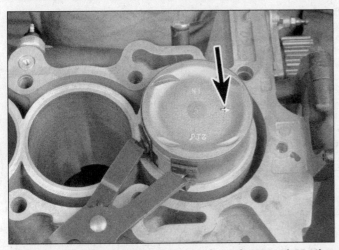

26.9 When installing pistons, the arrow (arrow) must point to the front (timing belt end) of the engine

26.11 The piston can be driven (gently) into the cylinder bore with the end of a wooden or plastic hammer handle

proceeding. Do not, for any reason, force the piston into the cylinder - you might break a ring and/or the piston.

12   Once the piston/connecting rod assembly is installed, the connecting rod bearing oil clearance must be checked before the rod cap is permanently bolted in place.

13   Cut a piece of the appropriate-size Plastigage slightly shorter than the width of the connecting rod bearing and lay it in place on the number one connecting rod journal, parallel with the journal axis **(see illustration)**.

14   Clean the connecting rod cap bearing face and install the rod cap. Make sure the mating mark on the cap is on the same side as the mark on the connecting rod.

15   Install the bolts and tighten them to the torque listed in this Chapter's Specifications. Work up to it in three steps. **Note:** *Use a thin-wall socket to avoid erroneous torque readings that can result if the socket is wedged between the rod cap and bolt. If the socket tends to wedge itself between the bolt and the cap, lift up on it slightly until it no longer contacts the cap. Do not rotate the crankshaft at any time during this operation.*

16   Remove the bolts and detach the rod cap, being very careful not to disturb the Plastigage.

17   Compare the width of the crushed Plastigage to the scale printed on the Plastigage envelope to obtain the oil clearance **(see illustration)**. Compare it to this Chapter's Specifications to make sure the clearance is correct.

18   If the clearance is not as specified, the bearing inserts may be the wrong size (which means different ones will be required). Before deciding different inserts are needed, make sure no dirt or oil was between the bearing inserts and the connecting rod or cap when the clearance was measured. Also, recheck the journal diameter. If the Plastigage was wider at one end than the other, the journal may be tapered.

Final connecting rod installation

19   Carefully scrape all traces of the Plastigage material off the rod journal and/or bearing face. Be very careful not to scratch the

bearing - use your fingernail or the edge of a credit card.

20   Make sure the bearing faces are perfectly clean, then apply a uniform layer of clean moly-based engine assembly lubricant to both of them. You'll have to push the piston into the cylinder to expose the face of the bearing insert in the connecting rod - be sure to slip the protective-sleeved bolts in place first.

21   Slide the connecting rod back into place on the journal, remove the protective-sleeve from the rods, install the rod cap and tighten the bolts to the torque listed in this Chapter's Specifications. Again, work up to the torque in three steps. **Note:** *Again, make sure the mating mark on the cap is on the same side as the mark on the connecting rod.*

22   Repeat the entire procedure for the remaining pistons/connecting rods.

23   The important points to remember are:

a)   *Keep the back sides of the bearing inserts and the insides of the connecting rods and caps perfectly clean when assembling them.*

26.13 Lay the Plastigage strips on each rod bearing journal, parallel to the crankshaft centerline

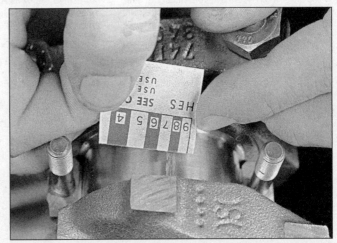

26.17 Measuring the width of the crushed Plastigage to determine the rod bearing oil clearance (be sure to use the correct scale - standard and metric ones are included)

b) *Make sure you have the correct piston/rod assembly for each cylinder.*

c) *The arrow or mark on the piston must face the front of the engine.*

d) *Lubricate the cylinder walls with clean oil.*

e) *Lubricate the bearing faces when installing the rod caps after the oil clearance has been checked.*

24   After all the piston/connecting rod assemblies have been properly installed, rotate the crankshaft a number of times by hand to check for any obvious binding.

25   As a final step, the connecting rod endplay must be checked. Refer to Section 14 for this procedure.

26   Compare the measured endplay to this Chapter's Specifications to make sure it's correct. If it was correct before disassembly and the original crankshaft and rods were reinstalled, it should still be right. If new rods or a new crankshaft were installed, the endplay may be inadequate. If so, the rods will have to be removed and taken to an automotive machine shop for re-sizing.

27   Balance shafts (four-cylinder models) - installation

Refer to illustrations 27.4a and 27.4b

1   Install the cleaned and lubricated balance shafts into the block, guiding them in carefully to avoid nicking the bearings.

2   Secure the front balance shaft in place with its retainer and bolts and install the oil pump (see Chapter 2A).

3   Install the front balance shaft sprocket, and with the rear shaft secured by a bolt or screwdriver (see Section 13), install the rear balance shaft driven gear and bolt.

4   Lubricate the thrust faces of the balance shaft drive and driven gears with clean moly-based engine assembly lubricant. Align the groove on the rear sprocket flange with the pointer on the gear case **(see illustration)**. Install the gear case to the block meshing the drive and driven gears. As you install the gear case and the gears mesh, the sprocket will rotate slightly clockwise. When the gear case

is fully seated against the block, check that the mark on the sprocket is aligned with the pointer on the oil pump cover **(see illustration)**. If the marks are properly aligned, install the bolts and tighten them to the torque listed in this Chapter's Specifications.

5   Refer to Chapter 2A for balance shaft belt installation.

28   Initial start-up and break-in after overhaul

Warning: *Have a fire extinguisher handy when starting the engine for the first time.*

1   Once the engine has been installed in the vehicle, double-check the engine oil and coolant levels.

2   With the spark plugs out of the engine and the ignition system disabled (see Section 3), crank the engine until oil pressure registers on the gauge or the light goes out.

3   Install the spark plugs, connect the plug wires and restore the ignition system functions (see Section 3).

4   Start the engine. It may take a few moments for the fuel system to build up pressure, but the engine should start without a great deal of effort.

5   After the engine starts, allow it to warm up to normal operating temperature. While the engine is warming up, make a thorough check for fuel, oil and coolant leaks. When all new bearings, rings and camshaft(s) are installed, the engine should run for 15 minutes at normal operating temperature on the first start-up to help break in the new components.

6   Shut the engine off and recheck the engine oil and coolant levels.

7   Drive the vehicle to an area with no traffic, accelerate from 30 to 50 mph, then allow the vehicle to slow to 30 mph with the throttle closed. Repeat the procedure 10 or 12 times. This will load the piston rings and cause them to seat properly against the cylinder walls. Check again for oil and coolant leaks.

8   Drive the vehicle gently for the first 500 miles (no sustained high speeds) and keep a constant check on the oil level. It is not

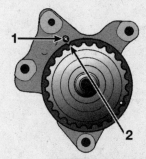

27.4a When installing the rear balance shaft gear case, align the groove in the sprocket flange (2) with the pointer on the gear case (1) and install the gear case to the block

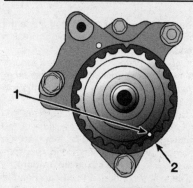

27.4b With the gear case fully seated, the mark on the sprocket (1) should align with the pointer on the oil pump cover (2)

unusual for an engine to use oil during the break-in period.

9   At approximately 500 to 600 miles, change the oil and filter.

10   For the next few hundred miles, drive the vehicle normally. Do not pamper it or abuse it.

11   After 2000 miles, change the oil and filter again and consider the engine broken in.

Chapter 3
Cooling, heating and air conditioning systems

Contents

Specifications

General

Coolant capacity	See Chapter 1
Drivebelt tension	See Chapter 1
Radiator pressure cap rating	14 to 18 psi
Thermostat rating (fully open)	194-degrees F

Torque specifications

Note: *One foot-pound (ft-lb) of torque is equivalent to 12 inch-pounds (in-lbs) of torque. Torque values below approximately 15 ft-lbs are expressed in inch-pounds, since most foot-pound torque wrenches are not accurate at these smaller values.*

Thermostat housing cover bolts	104 in-lbs
Water pump retaining bolts	104 in-lbs

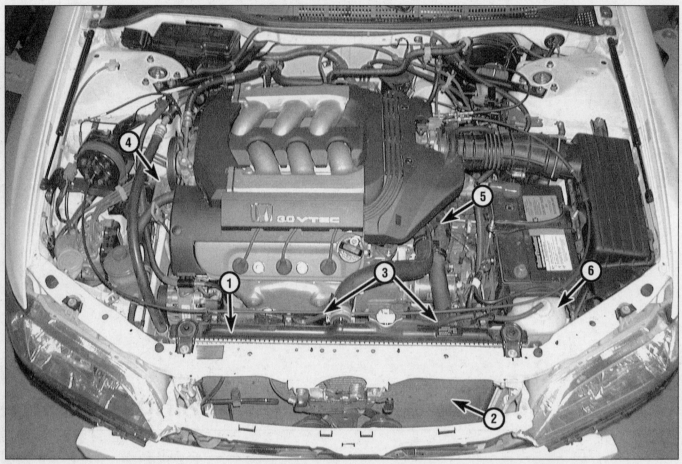

1.1 Cooling, heating and air conditioning components underhood (V6 shown, 4-cylinder similar)

1	Radiator	3	Radiator and condenser fans	5	Thermostat
2	Condenser	4	Water pump	6	Coolant recovery tank

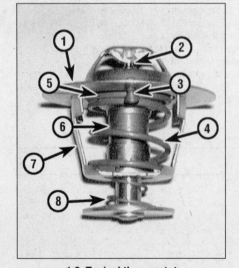

1.2 Typical thermostat

1	Flange	5	Valve seat
2	Piston	6	Valve
3	Jiggle valve	7	Frame
4	Main coil spring	8	Secondary coil spring

1   General information

Refer to illustrations 1.1 and 1.2

Engine cooling system

All vehicles covered by this manual employ a pressurized engine cooling system with thermostatically controlled coolant circulation **(see illustration)**. An impeller-type water pump mounted on the engine block pumps coolant through the engine. The coolant flows around each cylinder and toward the rear of the engine. Cast-in coolant passages direct coolant around the intake and exhaust ports, near the spark plug areas and in close proximity to the exhaust valve guides.

A wax-pellet type thermostat controls engine coolant temperature. During warm up, the closed thermostat prevents coolant from circulating through the radiator. As the engine nears normal operating temperature, the thermostat opens and allows hot coolant to travel through the radiator, where it's cooled before returning to the engine **(see illustration)**.

The cooling system is sealed by a pressure-type radiator cap, which raises the boiling point of the coolant and increases the cooling efficiency of the radiator. If the system pressure exceeds the cap pressure relief value, the excess pressure in the system forces the spring-loaded valve inside the cap off its seat and allows the coolant to escape through the overflow tube into a coolant reservoir. When the system cools the excess coolant is automatically drawn from the reservoir back into the radiator.

The coolant reservoir serves as both the point at which fresh coolant is added to the cooling system to maintain the proper fluid level and as a holding tank for overheated coolant.

This type of cooling system is known as a closed design because coolant that escapes past the pressure cap is saved and reused.

Heating system

The heating system consists of a blower fan and heater core located in the heater box, the hoses connecting the heater core to the engine cooling system and the heater/air conditioning control head on the dashboard. Hot engine coolant is circulated through the heater core. When the heater mode is activated, a flap door opens to expose the heater

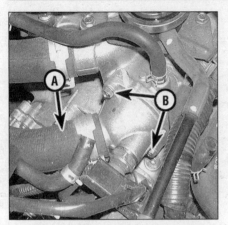

3.10a To replace the V6 thermostat, remove the hose (A), remove the two cover bolts (B), pull off the cover and remove the thermostat from the housing

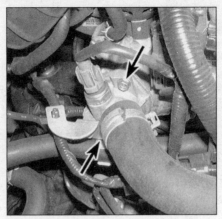

3.10b Four-cylinder thermostat cover bolts (arrows)

3.13 Install a new rubber seal over the thermostat

box to the passenger compartment. A fan switch on the control head activates the blower motor, which forces air through the core, heating the air.

Air conditioning system

The air conditioning system consists of a condenser mounted in front of the radiator, an evaporator mounted adjacent to the heater core, a compressor mounted on the engine, a receiver-drier which contains a high pressure relief valve and the plumbing connecting all of the above components.

A blower fan forces the warmer air of the passenger compartment through the evaporator core (sort of a radiator-in-reverse), transferring the heat from the air to the refrigerant. The liquid refrigerant boils off into low pressure vapor, taking the heat with it when it leaves the evaporator.

2 Antifreeze - general information

Warning: *Do not allow antifreeze to come in contact with your skin or painted surfaces of the vehicle. Rinse off spills immediately with plenty of water. Antifreeze is highly toxic if ingested. Never leave antifreeze lying around in an open container or in puddles on the floor; children and pets are attracted by it's sweet smell and may drink it. Check with local authorities about disposing of used antifreeze. Many communities have collection centers which will see that antifreeze is disposed of safely. Never dump used anti-freeze on the ground or into drains.*
Note: *Non-Toxic coolant is available at local auto parts stores. Although the coolant is non-toxic when fresh, proper disposal is still required.*

The cooling system should be filled with a water/ethylene glycol based antifreeze solution, which will prevent freezing down to at least -20-degrees F, or lower if local climate requires it. It also provides protection against corrosion and increases the coolant

boiling point.

The cooling system should be drained, flushed and refilled at the specified intervals (see Chapter 1). Old or contaminated antifreeze solutions are likely to cause damage and encourage the formation of rust and scale in the system. Use distilled water with the antifreeze.

Before adding antifreeze, check all hose connections, because antifreeze tends to leak through very minute openings. Engines don't normally consume coolant, so if the level goes down, find the cause and correct it.

The exact mixture of antifreeze-to-water which you should use depends on the relative weather conditions. The mixture should contain at least 50-percent antifreeze, but should never contain more than 70-percent antifreeze. Consult the mixture ratio chart on the antifreeze container before adding coolant. Hydrometers are available at most auto parts stores to test the coolant. Use antifreeze which meets the vehicle manufacturer's specifications.

3 Thermostat - check and replacement

Warning: *Do not remove the radiator cap, drain the coolant or replace the thermostat until the engine has cooled completely.*

Check

1   Before assuming the thermostat is to blame for a cooling system problem, check the coolant level, drivebelt tension (see Chapter 1) and temperature gauge operation.
2   If the engine seems to be taking a long time to warm up (based on heater output or temperature gauge operation), the thermostat is probably stuck open. Replace the thermostat with a new one.
3   If the engine runs hot, use your hand to check the temperature of the upper radiator hose. If the hose isn't hot, but the engine is, the thermostat is probably stuck closed, preventing the coolant inside the engine from

escaping to the radiator. Replace the thermostat. **Caution:** *Don't drive the vehicle without a thermostat. The computer may stay in open loop and emissions and fuel economy will suffer.*
4   If the upper radiator hose is hot, it means that the coolant is flowing and the thermostat is open. Consult the *Troubleshooting* section at the front of this manual for cooling system diagnosis.

Replacement

Refer to illustrations 3.10a, 3.10b, 3.13 and 3.14
5   Disconnect the negative battery cable from the battery. **Caution:** *The radio in your vehicle is equipped with an anti-theft system. Make sure you have the correct activation code before disconnecting the battery.*
6   Drain the cooling system (see Chapter 1). If the coolant is relatively new or in good condition (see Chapter 1), save it and reuse it. Read the **Warning** in Section 2.
7   Follow the upper radiator hose to the engine to locate the thermostat housing cover.
8   Loosen the hose clamp, then detach the hose from the fitting. If it's stuck, grasp it near the end with a pair of adjustable pliers and twist it to break the seal, then pull it off. If the hose is old or deteriorated, cut it off and install a new one.
9   If the outer surface of the large fitting that mates with the hose is deteriorated (corroded, pitted, etc.) it may be damaged further by hose removal. If it is, the thermostat housing cover will have to be replaced.
10   Remove the thermostat cover bolts **(see illustrations)** and detach the housing cover. If the cover is stuck, tap it with a soft-face hammer to jar it loose. Be prepared for some coolant to spill as the gasket seal is broken.
11   Note how it's installed - with the jiggle pin up - then remove the thermostat.
12   Remove all traces of old gasket material and/or sealant from the housing and cover.
13   Install a new rubber gasket over the thermostat **(see illustration)**.
14   Install the new thermostat in the housing

3.14 Install the new thermostat in the housing with the spring towards the engine and the jiggle pin (arrow) at the top

4.3b The "A" fan switch (arrow) on V6 models is located on the thermostat housing, near the battery . . .

4.3c . . . while the "B" fan switch (right arrow, V6 models) is located under the timing belt cover at the right end of the front cylinder head - to test either fan switch, disconnect the connector (left arrow), warm up the engine and note the resistance across the terminals as the temperature rises to the range indicated in the text

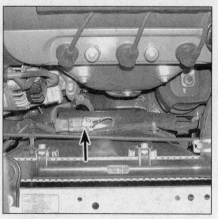

4.1 To test either fan motor, disconnect the electrical connector (arrow) and use jumper wires to connect the fan directly to the battery and ground - if the fan still doesn't work, replace the motor

without using sealant. Make sure the jiggle pin is at the top and the spring end is directed into the engine **(see illustration)**.

15   Install the housing cover and bolts. Tighten the bolts to the torque listed in this Chapter's Specifications.

16   Reattach the hose and tighten the hose clamp securely. Install all components that were removed for access.

17   Refill the cooling system (see Chapter 1).

18   Start the engine and allow it to reach normal operating temperature, then check for leaks and proper thermostat operation (as described in Steps 2 through 4).

4   Engine cooling fans and circuit - check and replacement

Warning: *To avoid possible injury or damage, DO NOT operate the engine with a damaged fan. Do not attempt to repair fan blades - replace a damaged fan with a new one.*
Note: *All air conditioned models have two complete fan circuits - one for the condenser and one for the radiator. The following procedures apply to both.*

4.3a The radiator fan switch (arrow) is located on top of the thermostat housing at the right/rear side of the engine (four-cylinder engine)

Check

Refer to illustrations 4.1a, 4.3a, 4.3b, 4.3c, 4.3d, 4.5a, 4.5b and 4.6

1   To test a fan motor, disconnect the electrical connector at the motor **(see illustration)** and use fused jumper wires to connect the fan directly to the battery. If the fan still doesn't work, replace the motor.

2   If the motor tests OK, check the fuses (located in the fuse box under the driver's side of the dash, check the #3 and #6 fuses on V6 models, the #4 fuse on 4-cylinder models), the coolant temperature switch(es), the radiator fan relay and the condenser fan relay, located in the engine compartment fuse box. Also check the wiring which connects the components. **Note:** *Four-cylinder models have only one cooling fan switch, V6 models have an "A" and a "B" fan switch.*

3   To test either coolant temperature switch, remove the electrical connector at the switch **(see illustrations)**. Start the engine and measure the resistance across the terminals of the switch as the engine warms up. Neither switch should have continuity while the coolant is cold. The radiator fan switch should close between 196 and 203 degrees F. The condenser fan switch should close at about 225 degrees F. If a switch fails to show

Cooling fan switch	Temperature	Continuity
Switch "A"	196 to 203 degrees F	Yes (on)
Switch "A"	5 to 15 degrees F below "ON" temperature	No, (off)
Switch B	217 to 232 degrees F	Yes (on)
Switch B	5 to 23 degrees F below "ON" temperature	No (off)

4.3d Test the continuity of the ECT switches with an ohmmeter on the two terminals - switch "B" is only on V6 models

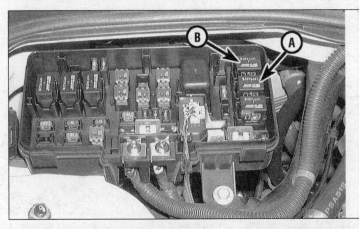

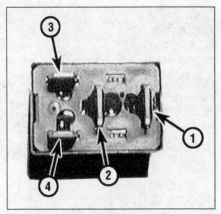

4.5a The radiator fan relay (A) and condenser fan relay (B) (air-conditioned models) are located in the main fuse panel on the right side of the firewall

4.5b Terminal identification for cooling fan relay testing

4.6 To access the radiator fan control module (A), remove the passenger-side knee bolster (see Chapter 11) - backprobe the module connector (B) with the ignition ON and the air conditioning OFF

continuity within this range, replace it. Each switch should open at 5 to 15 degrees F below the temperature it closed at. **Caution:** *Don't run the engine any longer than necessary with the switch disconnected. As soon as you've verified that the switch is good or bad, plug in the connector and let the fan run awhile, then turn off the engine.*

4   On four-cylinder models, there is only one temperature switch, which controls both radiator and condenser fans. On V6 models, there are two switches, one for the radiator fan and one for the condenser fan.

5   To test the cooling fan relays **(see illustrations),** remove the relay and apply battery power to terminal 3 and ground terminal 4. This should close the relay and create continuity between terminals 1 and 2. When the battery power is removed, there should be no continuity between 1 and 2.

Fan control module check

6   V6 models have a radiator fan control module located behind the passenger-side knee bolster (see Chapter 11 for removal). Check each wire with the module connected, the ignition switch ON, and the air conditioning OFF (backprobe the wires with a sharp probe (such as a straight-pin) inserted from the harness side, do not puncture any insula-

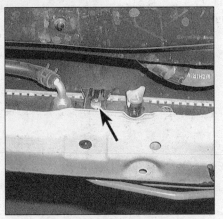

4.15 Remove the lower fan mounting bolt (arrow) (seen from below)

tion) **(see illustration).**

7   Check for continuity to ground at the black wire. If there is no continuity, check for an open to ground.

8   Check for battery voltage at the following wires: white, black/yellow-1, black-yellow-2, yellow/white, and yellow. If you don't get battery voltage, check the fuses in both the underdash fuse panel and the underhood fuse panel.

9   Again with ignition ON and everything connected, connect the green wire to ground. If the fans don't come on, check for opens in the green, yellow and yellow/white circuits.

10   Check the white/green wire for voltage. There should be 11-12 volts when the engine is below 223 degrees F. If not, check for

shorts to body ground, a bad module, or bad temperature switch.

11   Before trying a new module, disconnect both fan relays and check for continuity between the yellow or yellow/white wires and ground (20K ohms scale). There should be no continuity, if these circuits are grounded the new module will be damaged when connected.

Replacement

Refer to illustrations 4.15, 4.16, 4.17, 4.18 and 4.19

Note: *This procedure applies to either fan.*

12   Disconnect the negative battery cable from the battery. **Caution:** *The radio in your vehicle is equipped with an anti-theft system. Make sure you have the correct activation code before disconnecting the battery.*

13   Set the parking brake and block the rear wheels to prevent the vehicle from rolling. Raise the front of the vehicle and support it securely with jackstands. Remove the lower splash pan, if equipped, from under the radiator.

14   Insert a small screwdriver into the connector to lift the lock tab and disconnect the fan wiring connector. **Note:** *On models with cruise control, remove the cruise cable from the plastic clips at the top of the two fan shrouds.*

15   On the condenser fan only, remove the fan lower mounting bolt **(see illustration).**

16   Unbolt the fan from the radiator at the top **(see illustration).**

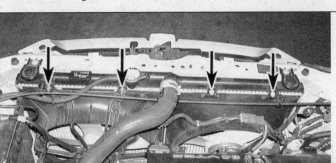

4.16 Remove the upper fan mounting bolts (arrows)

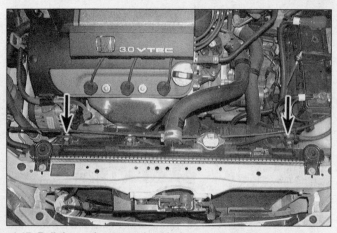

4.17 Pull the cruise control cable from its two clips (arrows) and push it aside to allow fan removal

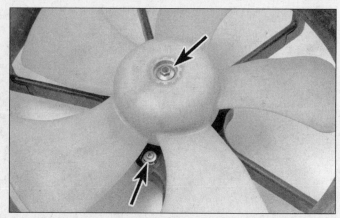

4.18 To remove the fan, unscrew the nut in the center (upper arrow), then pull the fan blade from the motor shaft (the lower arrow points to one of the motor mounting screws)

17   Carefully lift the fan out of the engine compartment. **Note:** *The cruise control cable (if equipped) must be moved from its two clamps to allow fan removal* **(see illustration).**
18   To detach the fan from the motor, remove the motor shaft nut **(see illustration).**
19   To detach the fan motor from the shroud, remove the mounting screws **(see illustration).**
20   Installation is the reverse of removal.

5   Radiator and coolant reservoir- removal and installation

Warning: *Wait until the engine is completely cool before beginning this procedure.*

Coolant reservoir

Refer to illustration 5.2
Warning: *The engine must be completely cool before removing the reservoir. Read the warning at the beginning of Section 2.*
1   The coolant reservoir is mounted adjacent to the radiator in the corner (left corner on V6 models, right corner on four-cylinder models) of the engine compartment, just in front of the battery.
2   Unscrew the cap with the hose still attached. Lift the reservoir straight up out of

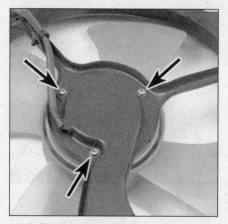

4.19 To detach the condenser fan motor from the shroud, remove these screws (arrows)

the bracket **(see illustration).**
3   Pour the coolant into a container.
4   After washing the reservoir inside and out (use a household "bottle" brush to clean inside), inspect the reservoir for cracks and chafing. If it's damaged or so obscured by age as to make reading the water level difficult, replace it.
5   Installation is the reverse of removal.

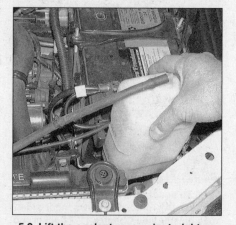

5.2 Lift the coolant reservoir straight up out of its bracket

Radiator

Removal

Refer to illustrations 5.7. 5.9, 5.11 and 5.13
6   Disconnect the negative battery cable from the battery. **Caution:** *The radio in your vehicle is equipped with an anti-theft system. Make sure you have the correct activation code before disconnecting the battery.*
7   Set the parking brake and block the rear wheels. Raise the front of the vehicle and

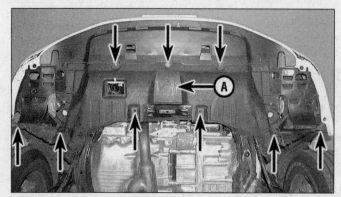

5.7 With the vehicle securely supported, remove the plastic pins (arrows) retaining the large lower splash pan (A)

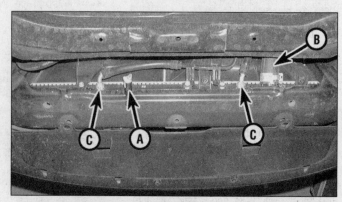

5.9 Drain the coolant at the fitting (A), remove the lower radiator hose (B), and if the vehicle is equipped with an automatic transaxle, disconnect the cooler lines from the radiator (C)

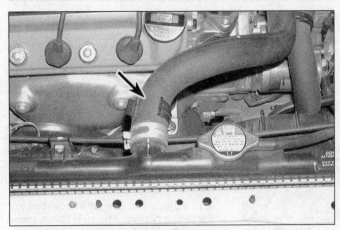

5.11 Loosen the hose clamps and detach the upper and lower radiator hoses - marking one end of each hose with paint makes reassembly easier

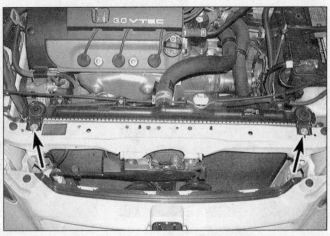

5.13 Remove the two bolts (arrows) that attach the upper radiator mounts to the radiator support

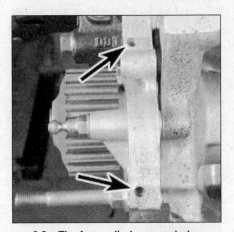

6.3a The four-cylinder weep holes (arrows) are located on the rear side of the water pump

6.3b The weep hole (arrow) on V6 models is on the underside of the pump - you'll need a flashlight and small mirror to inspect it (with the timing belt removed)

support it securely on jackstands. Remove the splash pan beneath the radiator **(see illustration)**.

8   Drain the cooling system (see Chapter 1). If the coolant is relatively new or in good condition, save it and reuse it. Read the **Warning** in Section 2.

9   If the vehicle is equipped with an automatic transaxle, disconnect the cooler lines from the radiator **(see illustration)**. Use a drip pan to catch spilled fluid and plug the lines and fittings.

10   Disconnect the electrical connector for the cooling fan switch (see Section 4).

11   Loosen the hose clamps, then detach the radiator hoses from the fittings **(see illustration)**. If they're stuck, grasp each hose near the end with a pair of slip-joint pliers and twist it to break the seal, then pull it off - be careful not to damage the radiator fittings! If the hoses are old or deteriorated, cut them off and install new ones. Also disconnect the small hose to the coolant reservoir.

12   Remove the engine cooling fans (see Section 4).

13   Unbolt the small brackets that attach the top of the radiator to the radiator support

(see illustration).

14   Carefully lift out the radiator. Don't spill coolant on the vehicle or scratch the paint.

15   Inspect the radiator for leaks and damage. If it needs repair, have a radiator shop or dealer service department perform the work as special techniques are required.

16   Bugs and dirt can be removed from the radiator by spraying with a garden hose nozzle from the back side. The radiator should be flushed out with a garden hose before reinstallation.

17   Check the radiator mounts for deterioration and replace if necessary.

Installation

18   Installation is the reverse of the removal procedure. Guide the radiator into the mounts until they seat properly.

19   After installation, fill the cooling system with the proper mixture of antifreeze and water. Refer to Chapter 1 if necessary, and be sure to use the bleeder screw to bleed air out of the system.

20   Start the engine and check for leaks. Allow the engine to reach normal operating

temperature, indicated by the upper radiator hose becoming hot. Recheck the coolant level and add more if required.

21   If you're working on an automatic-transaxle equipped vehicle, check and add fluid as needed.

6   Water pump - check

Refer to illustrations 6.3a and 6.3b

1   A failure in the water pump can cause serious engine damage due to overheating.

2   There are two ways to check the operation of the water pump while it's installed on the engine. If the pump is defective, it should be replaced with a new or rebuilt unit.

3   Water pumps are equipped with weep (or vent) holes **(see illustrations)**. If a failure occurs in the pump seal, coolant will leak from the hole. With the timing belt cover removed, you'll need a flashlight and small mirror to find the hole on the water pump from underneath to check for leaks.

4   If the water pump shaft bearings fail, there may be a howling sound at the pump while it's running. Shaft wear can be felt with the timing belt removed if the water pump pulley is rocked up and down (with the engine off). Don't mistake drivebelt slippage, which causes a squealing sound, for water pump bearing failure.

5   Even a pump that exhibits no outward signs of a problem, such as noise or leakage, can still be due for replacement. Removal for close examination is the only sure way to tell. Sometimes the fins on the back of the impeller can corrode to the point that cooling efficiency is hampered.

7   Water pump - replacement

Refer to illustrations 7.6a, 7.6b and 7.11
Warning: *Wait until the engine is completely cool before beginning this procedure.*

1   Disconnect the negative battery cable

7.6a Remove the water pump bolts (arrows) and detach the water pump from the engine (four-cylinder models)

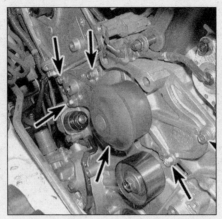

7.6b Water pump mounting bolts (arrows) - V6 engine - one bottom bolt isn't visible in this photo

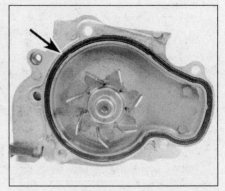

7.11 Apply a thin layer of RTV sealant to the O-ring groove of the new pump, then carefully set a new O-ring in the groove

from the battery. **Caution:** *The radio in your vehicle is equipped with an anti-theft system. Make sure you have the correct activation code before disconnecting the battery.*

2   Drain the cooling system (see Chapter 1). If the coolant is relatively new or in good condition, save it and reuse it. Read the **Warning** in Section 2.

3   Remove the drivebelts (see Chapter 1).

4   Remove the timing belt (see Chapter 2A or 2B), and remove the timing belt tensioner.

5   On four-cylinder models, remove the camshaft sprocket and the timing belt rear cover (see Chapter 2A).

6   Remove the bolts **(see illustrations)** and detach the water pump from the engine. Note the location of the longer bolt(s). Check the impeller on the backside for evidence of corrosion or missing fins.

7   Clean the bolt threads and the threaded holes in the engine to remove corrosion and sealant.

8   Compare the new pump to the old one to make sure they're identical.

9   Remove all traces of old gasket sealant and O-ring from the engine.

10   Clean the engine and new water pump mating surfaces with lacquer thinner or acetone.

11   Apply a thin layer of RTV sealant to the O-ring groove of the new pump, then carefully set a new O-ring in the groove **(see illustration).**

12   Carefully attach the pump to the engine and thread the bolts into the holes finger tight. Use a small amount of RTV sealant on the bolt threads, and make sure that the dowel pins are in their original locations.

13   Install the remaining bolts. Tighten the bolts to the torque listed in this Chapter's Specifications in 1/4-turn increments. Don't overtighten the bolts or the pump may be distorted.

14   Reinstall all parts removed for access to the pump.

15   Refill and bleed the cooling system and check the drivebelt tension (see Chapter 1). Run the engine and check for leaks.

8   Coolant temperature sending unit - check and replacement

Warning: *Wait until the engine is completely cool before beginning this procedure.*

Check

Refer to illustrations 8.1a and 8.1b

1   The coolant temperature indicator system consists of a temperature gauge mounted in the instrument panel and a coolant temperature sending unit mounted in the thermostat housing on the engine **(see illustrations).** Some vehicles have more than one sending unit, but only one is used for the indicator system. 2000 and later models do not have a coolant temperature sending unit. These models utilize the ECT sensor, instead (see Chapter 6, Section 7). **Warning:** *This vehicle is equipped with electric cooling fans. Stay clear of the fan blades, which can come on even when the engine is not running, as long as the ignition is ON.*

2   If an overheating indication occurs even when the engine is cold, check the wiring

between the dash and the sending unit for a short circuit to ground.

3   If the gauge is inoperative, test the circuit by briefly grounding the wire to the sending unit while the ignition is On (engine not running for safety). If the gauge deflects full scale, replace the sending unit.

4   If the gauge doesn't respond in the test outlined in Step 3, check for an open circuit in the gauge wiring.

5   To test the sending unit, disconnect the electrical connector and attach an ohmmeter from the pin on top of the sender to an engine ground. With the engine warm (133 degrees F) resistance should be around 137 ohms. When the engine is hot (185 to 212 degrees F), the resistance should drop to 46 to 30 ohms. If the sender fails the test, replace it.

Replacement

6   If the sending unit must be replaced, simply unscrew it from the engine and quickly install the replacement. Use a conductive sealant on the threads (not Teflon tape). Make sure the engine is cool before removing the defective sending unit. There will be some coolant loss as the unit is removed, so be prepared to catch it. Check the coolant level after the replacement part has been installed.

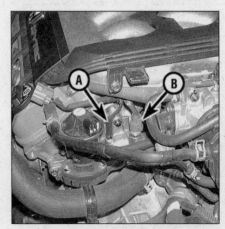

8.1a On 1998 and 1999 V6 models, the temperature sending unit (A) is in the thermostat housing - (B) is the ECT sensor for the computer

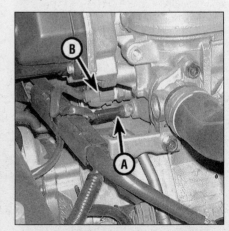

8.1b On 1998 and 1999 four-cylinder models, the gauge sending unit (A) is located under the distributor - (B) is the ECT sensor for the computer

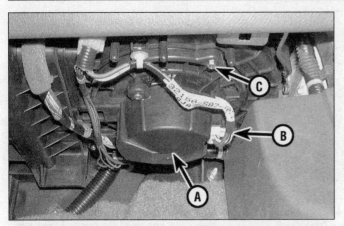

9.4 The blower motor (A) is under the glove box area, (B) is the electrical connector and (C) is one of the mounting screws - two screws aren't visible in this photo

9.8 Blower motor resistor location on the blower housing. Inset identifies connector terminals, and arrows show mounting screw locations

9   Blower motor circuit - check

Refer to illustrations 9.4, 9.8, 9.10a, 9.10b and 9.11

1   If the blower motor doesn't operate, first check all connections in the circuit for looseness and corrosion. Make sure the battery is fully charged. Check fuse 56 in the relay/fuse box in the engine compartment, and fuse 3 in the fuse panel below the driver's side of the dashboard.

2   Locate the blower motor relay in the underhood fuse/relay box. Remove the relay and test it for proper operation (see Chapter 12). If the relay fails the tests, replace it.

3   With the transmission in Park, the parking brake securely set, turn the ignition switch to the ON position. It isn't necessary to start the vehicle.

4   The blower motor is located under the glove compartment area of the dash, near the firewall **(see illustration)**.

5   Switch the heater controls to FLOOR and the blower speed to 4. Listen at the ducts to hear if the blower is operating. If it is, then switch the blower speed to 1 and listen again. Try all the speeds. **Note:** *The blower is switched on the ground side of the circuit.*

6   If the blower didn't operate, and you have checked the fuses and relay, test the blower. Locate the electrical connector at the blower motor. Backprobe the yellow/black wire terminal; there should be at least 10 volts with the mode switch in any position other than Off and the ignition switch On. If not, there is a problem in the circuit from the fuse panel to the heater/air conditioning control panel, or from the control panel to the blower.

7   If there is voltage at the feed wire, but the blower does not operate, backprobe the blue/red wire and connect it to a known good chassis ground with a jumper wire. If it still doesn't operate, replace the blower motor. If the blower now operates there is a problem in the circuit from the blower speed switch to the blower resistor to the blower.

8   If the blower operates, but not at all speeds, check the blower resistor. It's

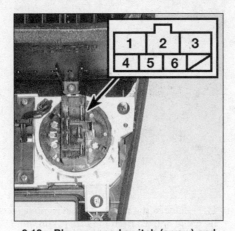

9.10a Blower speed switch (arrow) and terminal identification

located on the blower housing under the right side of the dash **(see illustration)**. There are resistor elements mounted on the resistor board to provide blower speeds 1, 2 and 3 (HI or 4 bypasses the resistor). The blower operates continuously, anytime the ignition switch is On and the mode switch is in any position other than Off.

9   With the resistor removed from the vehicle, visually check the resistor for damage, indicated by the material melting out between

Blower switch position	Continuity between terminals
1	1, 2 and 4
2	1, 2 and 5
3	1,2 and 6
4	1, 2 and 3

9.10b Blower speed switch continuity test

the contacts. Check the resistor block with an ohmmeter between terminals 1 and 5 **(see illustration 9.8)**. If the resistance is not 3 to 3.5 ohms, replace the blower resistor.

10   If the blower operates, but not at all speeds and you have already checked the blower resistor, refer to Section 12 and remove the heater/air conditioning control panel. Disconnect the electrical connector from the back of the blower speed switch and test the terminals for continuity **(see illustrations)**. If the continuity is not as described, replace the blower speed switch.

11   Check the blower relay in the underhood fuse/relay box **(see illustration)**. Remove the relay and test it according to the procedure in Chapter 12. Test the socket for the relay with

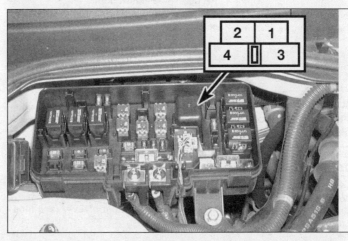

9.11 Blower motor relay location (arrow) and terminal identification

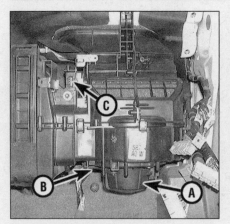

10.2 Blower housing components (shown with dash removed for clarity)

A   *Blower motor*
B   *Blower motor resistor*
C   *Recirculation control motor*

a volt/ohmmeter. There should be battery voltage at terminal 4 at all times, battery voltage at terminal 1 with the key On, and there should be continuity between terminal 2 and ground.

10   Blower motor - removal and installation

Refer to illustrations 10.2 and 10.5
1   Disconnect the negative cable from the battery. **Caution:** *The radio in your vehicle is equipped with an anti-theft system. Make sure you have the correct activation code before disconnecting the battery.*
2   The blower unit is located under the dash, behind the glovebox. The blower motor unit or housing incorporates the blower motor, the blower motor resistor and the recirculation control motor **(see illustration)**.
3   Disconnect the electrical connector from the blower motor and remove the three retaining screws **(see illustration 9.4)**. Remove the blower motor.
4   If you're replacing the blower motor itself, separate the blower motor from the fan wheel and place the fan on the new blower motor.
5   Remove the clip **(see illustration)** to separate the fan wheel from the blower motor.
6   Installation is the reverse of removal. Check for proper operation.

11   Heater/air conditioning control assembly - removal, installation and cable adjustment

Removal and installation

Refer to illustration 11.4
1   Disconnect the negative cable from the battery. **Caution:** *The radio in your vehicle is equipped with an anti-theft system. Make*

10.5 Use pliers to release and remove the clamp, and the blower fan lifts off the motor shaft

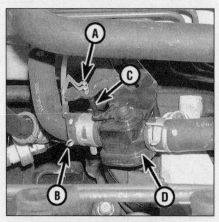

11.7 Release the clamp (A) and remove the cable end (B) from the arm (C) on the heater valve (D)

sure you have the correct activation code before disconnecting the battery.
2   The control panel is mounted to the back of the center instrument panel bezel. Refer to Chapter 11 for removal of bezel.
3   Pull the bezel away far enough to reach and disconnect the two electrical connectors at the heater control panel.
4   Remove the screws from behind the instrument panel bezel and separate the heater/air conditioning control assembly from the bezel **(see illustration)**.
5   Installation is the reverse of the disassembly procedure.

Cable adjustment

Refer to illustrations 11.7 and 11.8
6   The heater valve on the engine side of the firewall controls the passage of hot coolant to the heater core. The valve is operated by a cable that is connected to the air-mix control lever inside the vehicle.
7   In the engine compartment, release the cable from the clamp at the heater valve assembly **(see illustration)**.
8   Inside the vehicle, release the cable clamp and remove the cable eye from the arm on the air-mix control lever **(see illustration)**.

11.4 Remove the screws (arrows) holding the control panel to the back of the bezel

11.8 Heater cable components viewed from under the dash - release the cable from the clamp (A) and from the air-mix control lever at (B)

9   Turn the ignition switch to On and set the heater control to Max Cool to position the arm on the air-mix lever. Attach the cable eye to the arm and reclamp it while the cable's housing is against the stop.
10   At the heater valve end, move the arm back toward the firewall by hand until it stops, then attach the cable eye and clamp the cable housing.

12   Heater core - removal and installation

Warning 1: *The models covered by this manual are equipped with Supplemental Restraint systems (SRS), more commonly known as airbags. Always disconnect the negative battery cable, then the positive battery cable and wait three minutes before working in the vicinity of the impact sensors, steering column or instrument panel to avoid the possibility of accidental deployment of the airbag, which could cause personal injury (see Chapter 12). The yellow wiring harnesses and connectors routed through the console and instrument panel are for this system. Do not*

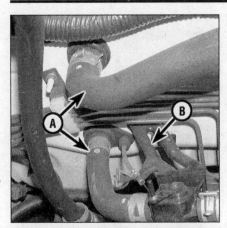

12.4 Loosen the two heater hose clamps and disconnect the heater hoses (A) from the heater core inlet and outlet pipes at the firewall - remove the nut (B) holding the heater valve to the firewall

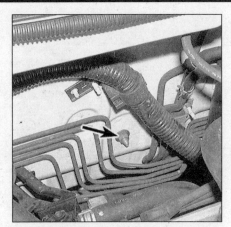

12.5 Remove the heater housing mounting nut (arrow) on the engine side

12.9 Remove the bolts (arrows) holding the heater unit to the firewall

use electrical test equipment on any of the airbag system wiring or tamper with them in any way.

Warning 2: The air conditioning system is under high pressure. Do not loosen any hose fittings or remove any components until after the system has been discharged. Air conditioning refrigerant should be properly discharged into an EPA-approved recovery/recycling unit at a dealer service department or an automotive air conditioning repair facility. Always wear eye protection when disconnecting air conditioning system fittings.

Removal

Refer to illustrations 12.4, 12.5, 12.9, 12.10a and 12.10b

1   Heater core removal on this vehicle is a difficult task for the home mechanic. It can be done with slow, careful attention to detail, but many fasteners and wiring connectors are difficult to get at behind the instrument panel. The air conditioning must be discharged and the entire instrument panel must be removed to allow the heater/air conditioning unit to be removed from the car. The driver and passenger airbags must be disabled, and the steering-column support must be removed.

2   If equipped with air conditioning, have the refrigerant discharged and recovered by an air conditioning technician. Disconnect the negative cable from the battery. **Caution:** The radio in your vehicle is equipped with an anti-theft system. Make sure you have the correct activation code before disconnecting the battery.

3   Drain the cooling system (see Chapter 1). Read the **Warning** in Section 2.

4   Working in the engine compartment, disconnect the heater hoses from the inlet and outlet tubes where they enter the firewall **(see illustration)**. Place a drain pan underneath the hoses to catch any coolant that runs out when the hoses are disconnected. **Note:** Disconnect one hose from the heater core and aim it into a drain pan, then blow through the other hose connection with low

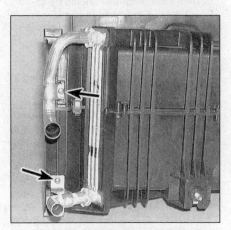

12.10a Remove the screws and clamps (arrows) . . .

pressure compressed air. This will flush the coolant from the heater core and reduce the chance of spilling coolant on the vehicle's interior when removing the heater core.

5   Disconnect the heater valve cable **(see illustration 11.7)** and remove the heater housing mounting nut at the engine side of the firewall **(see illustration)**.

6   Refer to Chapter 11 and remove the console, glove box, and instrument panel.

7   Disconnect the air mix cable (see Section 11) and the blower motor electrical connectors from the heater unit.

8   If the vehicle isn't equipped with air conditioning, remove the heater duct between the heater housing and the blower housing assemblies. If the vehicle is equipped with air conditioning, remove the evaporator (see Section 18).

9   Remove the upper fasteners holding the heater unit to the interior side of the firewall, then remove the heater unit **(see illustra-tion)**.

10   Remove the clamps holding the heater pipes to the housing and remove the heater core from the housing **(see illustrations)**.

Installation

11   Installation is the reverse of removal. Be sure to check the operation of the air control

12.10b . . . and pull the heater core out of the housing

flaps. If any parts bind, correct the problem before installation. Double-check all of your electrical connections.

12   Refill and bleed the cooling system (see Chapter 1), reconnect the battery and run the engine. Check for leaks and proper system operation. If equipped with air conditioning have the system evacuated, charged and leak-tested by an air conditioning technician.

13   Air conditioning and heating system - check and maintenance

Air conditioning system

Refer to illustration 13.1

Warning: The air conditioning system is under high pressure. Do not loosen any hose fittings or remove any components until after the system has been discharged. Air conditioning refrigerant should be properly discharged into an EPA-approved recovery/re-cycling unit at a dealer service department or an automotive air conditioning repair facility. Always wear eye protection when disconnecting air conditioning system fittings.

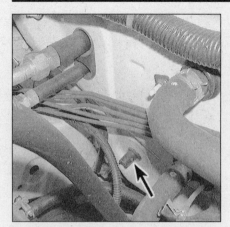

13.1 Check that the evaporator housing drain tube (arrow) at the firewall is clear or any blockage

13.9 Insert a thermometer in the center duct while operating the air conditioning system - the output air should be 35-40 degrees F less than the ambient temperature, depending on humidity (but not lower than 40-degrees F)

13.11 A basic charging kit for R-134a systems is available at most auto parts stores - it must say R-134a (not R-12) and so should the 12-ounce can of refrigerant

Caution: *When replacing entire components, additional refrigerant oil should be added equal to the amount that is removed with the component being replaced. Be sure to read the can before adding any oil to the system, to make sure it is compatible with the R-134a system.*

1   The following maintenance checks should be performed on a regular basis to ensure that the air conditioning continues to operate at peak efficiency.

a) *Inspect the condition of the compressor drivebelt. If it is worn or deteriorated, replace it (see Chapter 1).*

b) *Check the drivebelt tension and, if necessary, adjust it (see Chapter 1).*

c) *Inspect the system hoses. Look for cracks, bubbles, hardening and deterioration. Inspect the hoses and all fittings for oil bubbles or seepage. If there is any evidence of wear, damage or leakage, replace the hose(s).*

d) *Inspect the condenser fins for leaves, bugs and any other foreign material that may have embedded itself in the fins. Use a "fin comb" or compressed air to remove debris from the condenser.*

e) *Make sure the system has the correct refrigerant charge.*

f) *If you hear water sloshing around in the dash area or have water dripping on the carpet, check the evaporator housing drain tube* **(see illustration)** *and insert a piece of wire into the opening to check for blockage.*

2   It's a good idea to operate the system for about ten minutes at least once a month. This is particularly important during the winter months because long term non-use can cause hardening, and subsequent failure, of the seals. Note that using the Defrost function operates the compressor.

3   If the air conditioning system is not working properly, first make sure the compressor clutch is operating (see Section 14).

4   Because of the complexity of the air conditioning system and the special equipment necessary to service it, in-depth trou-

bleshooting and repairs are not included in this manual. However, simple checks and component replacement procedures are provided in this Chapter. For more complete information on the air conditioning system, refer to the *Haynes Automotive Heating and Air Conditioning Manual*. However, simple component replacement procedures are provided in this Chapter.

5   The most common cause of poor cooling is simply a low system refrigerant charge. If a noticeable drop in system cooling ability occurs, one of the following quick checks will help you determine whether the refrigerant level is low. Should the system lose its cooling ability, the following procedure will help you pinpoint the cause.

Check

Refer to illustration 13.9

6   Warm the engine up to normal operating temperature.

7   Place the air conditioning temperature selector at the coldest setting and put the blower at the highest setting. Open the doors (to make sure the air conditioning system doesn't cycle off as soon as it cools the passenger compartment).

8   After the system reaches operating temperature, feel the two pipes connected to the evaporator at the firewall.

9   The pipe (thinner tubing) leading from the condenser outlet to the evaporator should be cold, and the evaporator outlet line (the thicker tubing that leads back to the compressor) should be slightly colder (3 to 10 degrees F). If the evaporator outlet is considerably warmer than the inlet, the system needs a charge. Insert a thermometer in the center air distribution duct **(see illustration)** while operating the air conditioning system - the temperature of the output air should be 35 to 40 degrees F below the ambient air temperature (down to approximately 40 degrees F). If the ambient (outside) air tem-

perature is very high, say 110 degrees F, the duct air temperature may be as high as 60 degrees F, but generally the air conditioning is 35 to 40 degrees F cooler than the ambient air.

10   If the air isn't as cold as it used to be, the system probably needs a charge. Further inspection or testing of the system is beyond the scope of the home mechanic and should be left to a professional. Some on-board diagnostics capability on your vehicle can help point to areas for testing or repair (see subhead below).

Adding refrigerant

Refer to illustrations 13.11, 13.14 and 13.15

Caution: *The vehicles covered by this manual use R-134a refrigerant. Make sure any refrigerant, refrigerant oil or replacement component your purchase is designated as compatible with environmentally-friendly R-134a systems.*

11   Buy an R-134a automotive charging kit at an auto parts store. A charging kit includes a 12-ounce can of refrigerant, a tap valve and a short section of hose that can be attached between the tap valve and the system low side service valve **(see illustration)**. Because one can of refrigerant may not be sufficient to bring the system charge up to the proper level, it's a good idea to buy a couple of additional cans. Make sure that one of the cans contains red refrigerant dye. If the system is leaking, the red dye will leak out with the refrigerant and help you pinpoint the location of the leak. **Warning:** *Never add more than two cans of refrigerant to the system.*

12   Hook up the charging kit by following the manufacturer's instructions. **Warning:** *DO NOT hook the charging kit hose to the system high side!* The fittings on the charging kit are designed to fit **only** on the low side of the system.

13   Back off the valve handle on the charging kit and screw the kit onto the refrigerant

13.14 Attach the refrigerant kit to the low-side charging port (arrow) - it's near the right shock tower on V6 models (shown), and at the right-front of the engine on four-cylinder models - the cap should be marked with an "L"

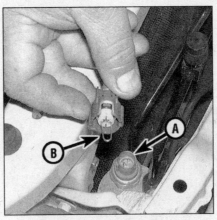

13.15 The air conditioning pressure switch (A) is located on top of the receiver-drier - disconnect the connector and bridge it with a paper clip (B) during the charging procedure

13.23 Some trouble codes can be accessed in standard heating/air-conditioning systems by using a test sequence initiated with the recirculation button (A) and displayed by its indicator light (B)

can, making sure first that the O-ring or rubber seal inside the threaded portion of the kit is in place. **Warning:** *Wear protective eyewear when dealing with pressurized refrigerant cans.*

14   Remove the dust cap from the low-side charging and attach the quick-connect fitting on the kit hose **(see illustration)**.

15   Warm up the engine and turn on the air conditioning. Keep the charging kit hose away from the fan and other moving parts. **Note:** *The charging process requires the compressor to be running. If the clutch cycles off, you can put the air conditioning switch on High and leave the car doors open to keep the clutch on and compressor working.* **Note:** *The compressor can be kept on during the charging by removing the connector from the low-pressure switch (combination high-limit and low-limit switch on some models) and bridging it with a paper clip or jumper wire during the procedure* **(see illustration)**.

16   Turn the valve handle on the kit until the stem pierces the can, then back the handle out to release the refrigerant. You should be able to hear the rush of gas. Add refrigerant to the low side of the system, keeping the can upright at all times, but shaking it occasionally. Allow stabilization time between each addition.

17   If you have an accurate thermometer, you can place it in the center air conditioning duct inside the vehicle and keep track of the output air temperature **(see illustration 13.9)**. A charged system that is working properly should cool down to approximately 40-degrees F. If the ambient (outside) air temperature is very high, say 110 degrees F, the duct air temperature may be as high as 60 degrees F, but generally the air conditioning is 30-40 degrees F cooler than the ambient air.

18   When the can is empty, turn the valve handle to the closed position and release the connection from the low-side port. Replace the dust cap.

19   Remove the charging kit from the can and store the kit for future use with the piercing valve in the UP position, to prevent inadvertently piercing the can on the next use.

Heating systems

20   If the carpet under the heater core is damp, or if antifreeze vapor or steam is coming through the vents, the heater core is leaking. Remove it (see Section 12) and install a new unit (most radiator shops will not repair a leaking heater core).

21   If the air coming out of the heater vents isn't hot, the problem could stem from any of the following causes:

a) *The thermostat is stuck open, preventing the engine coolant from warming up enough to carry heat to the heater core. Replace the thermostat (see Section 3).*

b) *There is a blockage in the system, preventing the flow of coolant through the heater core. Feel both heater hoses at the firewall. They should be hot. If one of them is cold, there is an obstruction in one of the hoses or in the heater core, or the heater control valve is shut. Detach the hoses and back flush the heater core with a water hose. If the heater core is clear but circulation is impeded, remove the two hoses and flush them out with a water hose.*

c) *If flushing fails to remove the blockage from the heater core, the core must be replaced (see Section 12).*

On-board diagnostics

Standard heat/air conditioning system

Refer to illustrations 13.23 and 13.25

22   On these models, you can troubleshoot the electrically-operated controls of the heating/air conditioning system without a scan tool by accessing a self-diagnosis capability.

23   Start with the ignition switch On, and push the recirculation control switch until the indicator light above it comes on **(see illustra-**

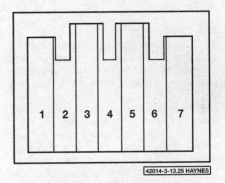

13.25 Terminal numbering for heat/air control motor tests

tion)**. The blower speed switch should be Off.

24   Press the switch again until the light goes out but keep the switch depressed. The light will come on again to indicate the self-test is starting, then begin to blink a simple code sequence. One blink indicates there is a problem in the air mix control motor, either a stuck door, bad motor or a short. Two blinks represents similar conditions, but with the mode control motor. Three blinks indicates an open, short or bad sensor in the evaporator temperature sensor circuit.

Air mix control motor/circuit

25   Remove the electrical connector from the air mix control motor. Attach a jumper wire with battery voltage to the number 1 terminal on the motor, and apply ground to terminal 2 **(see illustration)**. This should run the motor. If it doesn't operate, reverse the two jumper wires and the motor should operate the other direction. If it doesn't operate in either direction, replace the motor. A further test is to check the resistance between terminals 5 and 7 (should be 4.2 to 7.8 K-ohms) and between terminals 3 and 5 (should be 0.58 to 1.09 K-ohms at Max Cool and 3.52 to 6.55 K-ohms at Max Hot).

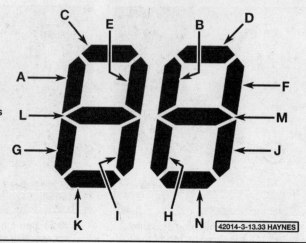

13.33 During the self-test sequence, each portion of the two digits represents a different climate control code when blinking

26   If you suspect the problem may be in the operation of the door, disconnect the control motor's rod from the linkage and perform the jumper wire tests above. If the motor now operates, repair or replace the air mix door or linkage.

Mode control motor

27   Test the mode control motor by attaching a battery power jumper wire to terminal 2 and ground to terminal 1 **(see illustration 13.25)**. It should run in one direction until it stops, but do not leave the power connected once it stops. Reversing the jumper leads should make the motor run the other direction.
28   If you have a digital multimeter (with an output of less than 1 mA at the 20 K-ohm range), check the continuity of the terminals while the test in Step 28 is running. You should see a momentary continuity between terminal 7 and terminals 3, 4, 5 and 6 during the test.
29   If the motor operates slowly or not at all, disconnect it from the door linkage and test again. If it works now, check the door and linkage for binding.

Recirculation control motor

30   Disconnect the electrical connector at the recirculation control motor and test the terminals on the motor itself **(see illustration 13.25)**.
31   Connect a jumper wire with battery power to terminal 1, then ground jumper wires to terminals 5 and 7. The motor should run smoothly and stop at either Fresh or Recirculate when the ground jumpers are removed.
32   If the motor operates slowly or not at all, disconnect it from the door linkage and test again. If it works now, check the door and linkage for binding.

Automatic climate control models

Refer to illustrations 13.33 and 13.35

33   A more elaborate system of self-diagnostics is used on these models, with the LED portion of the control panel allowing display of fourteen codes. When the test procedure is initiated, the number 88 will show up (where the temperature is usually displayed) and each segment of the two numerals represents one trouble code **(see illustration)**.
34   To begin the self-test, turn the ignition key On, and set the controls to Max cool, then back slowly to Max Hot. Wait one minute and press in the Auto button and keep it down. While holding the auto button down,

press and hold the Off button and the number 88 should display.
35   If there are any malfunctions in the system, one or more segments of the two digits will blink. Record the segments that are blinking **(see illustration 13.33)** and look up the codes in the chart to find the portion of the system that needs inspection or repair **(see illustration)**.
36   After any repair work, repeat the self-diagnostics procedure to check your work.

Eliminating air-conditioning odors

37   Unpleasant odors that often develop in air-conditioning systems are caused by the growth of a fungus, usually on the surface of the evaporator core. The warm, humid environment there is a perfect breeding ground for mildew to develop.
38   The evaporator core on most vehicles is difficult to access, and factory dealerships have a lengthy, expensive process for eliminating the fungus by opening up the evaporator case and using a powerful disinfectant and rinse on the core until the fungus is gone. You can service your own system at home, but it takes something much stronger than basic household germ-killers or deodorizers.
39   Aerosol disinfectants for automotive air-conditioning systems are available in most auto parts stores, but remember when shopping for them that the most effective treatments are also the most expensive. The basic procedure for using these sprays is to start by running the system in the RECIRC mode for ten minutes with the blower on its highest speed. Use the highest heat mode to dry out the system and keep the compressor from engaging by disconnecting the wiring connector at the compressor (see Section 16).
40   The disinfectant can usually comes with a long spray hose. Remove the blower motor (see Section 10), point the nozzle inside the hole and to the left towards the evaporator core, and spray according to the manufacturer's recommendations. Try to cover the whole surface of the evaporator core, by aim-

Code segment displayed	Indicated trouble spot	Look for
A	In-vehicle temp sensor	faulty sensor or open circuit
B	In-vehicle temp sensor	short in circuit
C	Outside air temp sensor	faulty sensor or open circuit
D	Outside air temp sensor	short in circuit
E	Sunlight sensor	faulty sensor or open circuit
F	Sunlight sensor	short in circuit
G	Evaporator temp sensor	faulty sensor or open circuit
H	Evaporator temp sensor	short in circuit
I	Air mixture control motor	Open in circuit
J	Air mixture control motor	short in circuit
K	Air mixture control motor	faulty motor or door problem
L	Mode control motor	Open or short in circuit
M	Mode control motor	faulty motor or door problem
N	Heat/air blower motor	faulty motor or open circuit

13.35 Automatic climate control system trouble codes

ing the spray up, down and sideways. Follow the manufacturer's recommendations for the length of spray and waiting time between applications.

41   Once the evaporator has been cleaned, the best way to prevent the mildew from coming back again is to make sure your evaporator housing drain tube is clear **(see illustration 13.1)**.

14   Air conditioning compressor clutch circuit - check

1   Proper operation of the compressor clutch is essential to the function of the air conditioning system. If your system doesn't seem to get cold, first check the clutch operation.

2   With the engine warmed up, set the air conditioning temperature selector on the coldest setting and the fan on high. Open the doors (to make sure the air conditioning system doesn't cycle off as soon as it cools the passenger compartment down).

3   Have an assistant push the A/C button while you observe the front of the compressor. The clutch will make an audible click and the center of the clutch should rotate. If it doesn't, shut the engine off and disconnect the air conditioning system pressure switch **(see illustration 13.15)**. Insert a paper clip as a jumper and try the air conditioning again as in Steps 1 and 2. If it works now, the system pressure is too high or too low. Have your system tested by a dealer service department or air conditioning shop.

4   If the clutch still didn't operate, check the appropriate fuses. Inspect the number 3 fuse in the interior fuse panel under the driver's side of the dash, then the larger number 58 fuse in the large relay/fuse box at the engine side of the firewall.

5   While at the underhood relay/fuse box, remove the compressor clutch relay and test it (see Chapter 12). With the relay out and the ignition Off, check for battery power at the number 1 socket for the compressor clutch relay, which has the same terminals as the fan relay **(see illustration 4.5b)**. There should be battery power. With the key On, there should be battery power at socket 4.

6   With the engine running and the air conditioning on, connect sockets 1 and 2 for the compressor clutch relay with a jumper wire and listen for the clutch to click as you make the connection.

7   If the clutch still doesn't operate, turn off the engine, disconnect the clutch connector at the compressor and attach a jumper wire long enough to allow use of an ohmmeter to check for continuity between the number 2 terminal of the clutch relay socket and the socket in the compressor clutch connector. If there is no continuity, check for a open in the circuit between the relay box and the compressor clutch connector. If it has continuity, check for an open in the circuit from the PCM to the relay box.

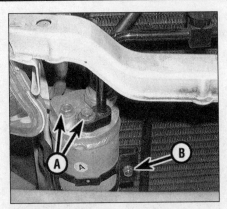

15.3 Remove the bolts (A) to disconnect the refrigerant lines from the receiver-drier - (B) is the receiver-drier clamp bolt

15   Air conditioning receiver-drier - removal and installation

Refer to illustration 15.3

Warning: *The air conditioning system is under high pressure. Do not loosen any hose fittings or remove any components until after the system has been discharged. Air conditioning refrigerant should be properly discharged into an EPA-approved recovery/recycling unit at a dealer service department or an automotive air conditioning repair facility. Always wear eye protection when disconnecting air conditioning system fittings.*

Caution: *When replacing entire components, additional refrigerant oil should be added equal to the amount that is removed with the component being replaced. Be sure to read the can before adding any oil to the system, to make sure it is compatible with the R-134a system.*

1   Have the refrigerant discharged and recovered by an air conditioning technician.

2   Disconnect the battery. **Caution:** *The radio in your vehicle is equipped with an anti-theft system. Make sure you have the correct activation code before disconnecting the battery.*

3   Disconnect the refrigerant lines from the receiver and cap the open fittings to prevent dirt and moisture entry **(see illustration)**. Disconnect the pressure switch connector **(see illustration 13.15)**.

4   Loosen the receiver bracket clamping screw and lift the receiver out of the vehicle.

5   Installation is the reverse of removal, using new O-rings where the lines connect to the receiver-drier.

6   Have the system evacuated, charged and leak tested by an air conditioning technician. If the receiver was replaced, add 1/3 ounce of refrigerant oil.

16   Air conditioning compressor - removal and installation

Refer to illustration 16.7

Warning: *The air conditioning system is*

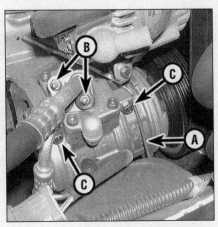

16.7 To remove the compressor, disconnect the electrical connector (A), remove the bolt or nut (B) on each line fitting, and remove the four bolts (C) (two upper bolts indicated here with arrows and two lower bolts are not visible here) (typical)

under high pressure. Do not loosen any hose fittings or remove any components until after the system has been discharged. Air conditioning refrigerant should be properly discharged into an EPA-approved recovery/recycling unit at a dealer service department or an automotive air conditioning repair facility. Always wear eye protection when disconnecting air conditioning system fittings.

Caution: *When replacing entire components, additional refrigerant oil should be added equal to the amount that is removed with the component being replaced. Be sure to read the can before adding any oil to the system, to make sure it is compatible with the R-134a system.*

Note: *The receiver-drier should be replaced whenever the compressor is replaced.*

Removal

1   Have the air conditioning system refrigerant discharged and recovered by an air conditioning technician.

2   Disconnect the negative battery cable from the battery. **Caution:** *The radio in your vehicle is equipped with an anti-theft system. Make sure you have the correct activation code before disconnecting the battery.*

3   Set the parking brake, block the rear wheels and raise the front of the vehicle, supporting it securely on jackstands.

4   Remove the drivebelt (see Chapter 1).

5   On V6 models, remove the alternator (see Chapter 5) and the condenser fan/shroud (see Section 4).

6   Disconnect the compressor clutch wiring harness.

7   Disconnect the refrigerant lines from the compressor. Plug the open fittings to prevent entry of dirt and moisture **(see illustration)**.

8   Unbolt the compressor from the mounting bracket and remove it from the vehicle.

Installation

9   The clutch may have to be transferred

17.5a Disconnect the discharge line (arrow to bolt) at the condenser

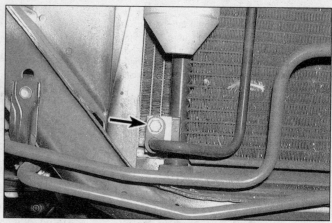

17.5b . . . and the condenser line (arrow) (view is through the front of the grille)

from the old compressor to the new unit.

10   Add the proper amount of refrigerant oil to the new compressor using the following calculations:

  a) *Drain the refrigerant oil from the old compressor through the suction fitting and measure it in ounces.*
  b) *Subtract this number from 5-1/3 ounces.*
  c) *The difference between these two figures is equal to the amount you should drain from the new compressor.*

11   Installation is the reverse of removal, using new O-rings where the line fittings attach to the compressor.

12   Have the system evacuated, recharged and leak tested by an air conditioning technician.

17   Air conditioning condenser - removal and installation

Refer to illustrations 17.5a, 17.5b and 17.6
Warning: *The air conditioning system is under high pressure. Do not loosen any hose fittings or remove any components until after the system has been discharged. Air conditioning refrigerant should be properly discharged into an EPA-approved recovery/recycling unit at a dealer service department or*

an automotive air conditioning repair facility. Always wear eye protection when disconnecting air conditioning system fittings.*
Caution: *When replacing entire components, additional refrigerant oil should be added equal to the amount that is removed with the component being replaced. Be sure to read the can before adding any oil to the system, to make sure it is compatible with the R-134a system.*

Removal

1   Have the refrigerant discharged and recovered by an air conditioning technician.
2   Disconnect the negative cable from the battery. **Caution:** *The radio in your vehicle is equipped with an anti-theft system. Make sure you have the correct activation code before disconnecting the battery.*
3   Remove the coolant reservoir (see Section 5).
4   Disconnect the electrical harness from the engine and condenser cooling fans (see Section 4), and remove the radiator with the fans/shrouds attached (see Section 5).
5   Disconnect the condenser line and discharge line from the condenser **(see illustrations)**. Cap the fittings on the condenser and lines to prevent entry of dirt or moisture.
6   Remove the condenser retaining bolts **(see illustration)**.
7   Remove the condenser.

Installation

8   Installation is the reverse of removal. Assemble all connections with new O-rings, lightly lubricated with R-134a refrigerant oil.
9   Have the system evacuated, charged and leak tested by an air conditioning technician. If a new condenser was installed, add 5/6-ounce of fresh refrigerant oil.

18   Air conditioning evaporator and expansion valve - removal and installation

Refer to illustrations 18.3, 18.7, 18.11a and 18.11b
Warning: *The air conditioning system is under high pressure. Do not loosen any hose fittings or remove any components until after the system has been discharged. Air conditioning refrigerant should be properly discharged into an EPA-approved recovery/recycling unit at a dealer service department or an automotive air conditioning repair facility. Always wear eye protection when disconnecting air conditioning system fittings.*
Caution: *When replacing entire components, additional refrigerant oil should be added equal to the amount that is removed with the component being replaced. Be sure to read the can before adding any oil to the system, to make sure it is compatible with the R-134a system.*

Removal

1   Have the air conditioning system discharged and recovered by an air conditioning technician.
2   Disconnect the cable from the negative battery cable. **Caution:** *The radio in your vehicle is equipped with an anti-theft system. Make sure you have the correct activation code before disconnecting the battery.*
3   Disconnect the receiver line and suction line from the evaporator **(see illustration)**.
4   Plug both lines to prevent contaminants and moisture from entering the air conditioning system.

17.6 Remove the condenser mounting bolts (arrows)

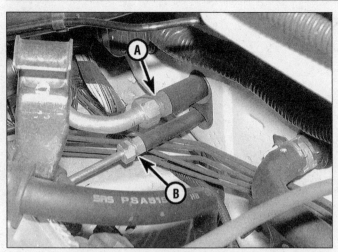

18.3 Disconnect the suction line (A) and the receiver line (B) from the evaporator at the engine side of the firewall - plug both lines to prevent contaminants and moisture from entering the system

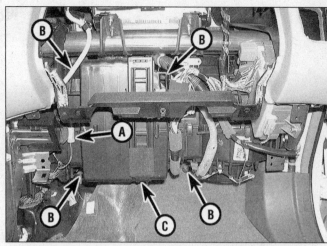

18.7 After removing the glove box and frame, disconnect the electrical connector (A), remove the screws (B) and the nut (C) that retain the evaporator housing to the firewall

5   Remove the passenger knee bolster, the metal brace behind it, the glovebox and the glovebox frame (see Chapter 11).
6   Disconnect the electrical connector from the thermostat.
7   Remove the fasteners retaining the evaporator housing to the firewall and dash structure **(see illustration)**.
8   Disconnect the drain hose and remove the evaporator unit from the vehicle.

9   Remove the thermostat sensor from the evaporator.
10   Remove the air filters/trays (see Chapter 1), then remove the screws, separate the housing and remove the evaporator. If necessary, remove the expansion valve.

Installation

11   Installation is the reverse of removal.

Install new O-rings and coat them with R-134a refrigerant oil. Tape the expansion valve capillary tube to the suction line and install the thermostat sensor in its original location **(see illustrations)**.
12   Have the system evacuated, charged and leak tested by an air conditioning technician. If a new evaporator was installed, add 1-1/3 ounce of new refrigerant oil.

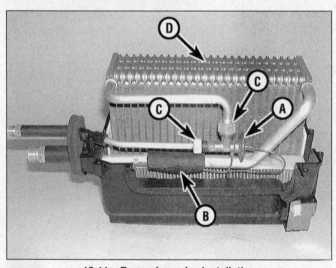

18.11a Expansion valve installation

A   Expansion valve
B   Capillary tube taped in place
C   Pipe connections
D   Evaporator core

18.11b When reinstalling the evaporator core, the temperature sensor (arrow) must be clipped to the core as shown

Notes

Chapter 4
Fuel and exhaust systems

Contents

Specifications

Fuel pressure

Key on, engine off	47 to 54 psi
Fuel system pressure (at idle)	
Four-cylinder engine	
Vacuum hose attached	38 to 46 psi
Vacuum hose detached	47 to 54 psi
V6 engine	
Vacuum hose attached	32 to 40 psi
Vacuum hose detached	41 to 48 psi
Fuel system hold pressure (after five minutes)	30 to 40 psi
Fuel pump pressure (maximum)	65 psi

Injector resistance (approximate)   13.5 to 19 ohms

Torque specifications   Ft-lbs (unless otherwise indicated)

Note: *One foot-pound (ft-lb) of torque is equivalent to 12 inch-pounds (in-lbs) of torque. Torque values below approximately 15 ft-lbs are expressed in inch-pounds, since most foot-pound torque wrenches are not accurate at these smaller values.*

Throttle body mounting nuts	16
Fuel rail mounting bolts (four-cylinder models)	102 in-lbs
Fuel pressure regulator	
Four-cylinder models (bolts)	108 in-lbs
V6 models (threads into fuel rail)	22
Fuel pulsation damper	16

1 General information

Refer to illustrations 1.2a and 1.2b

The fuel system consists of a fuel tank, an electric fuel pump (located in the fuel tank), a fuel pump relay, the fuel rail and fuel injectors, an air cleaner assembly and a throttle body unit. All models are equipped with an electronic fuel injection system.

Programmed Fuel Injection (PGM-FI) system

Programmed Fuel Injection uses timed impulses to inject the fuel directly into the intake port of each cylinder according to its firing order. The injectors are controlled by the Powertrain Control Module (PCM). The PCM monitors various engine parameters and delivers the exact amount of fuel required into the intake ports **(see illustra-** **tions).** The throttle body serves only to control the amount of air passing into the system. Because each cylinder is equipped with its own injector, much better control of the fuel/air mixture ratio is possible.

Fuel pump and lines

Fuel is circulated from the fuel tank to the fuel injection system, and back to the fuel tank, through a pair of metal lines running along the underside of the vehicle. An electric

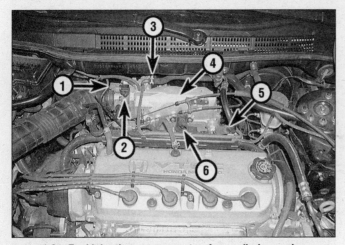

1.2a Fuel injection components - four-cylinder engine

1   Throttle Position Sensor (TPS)
2   Throttle body
3   Idle Air Control (IAC) valve
4   Air intake plenum
5   Fuel pressure regulator
6   Fuel rail (located on intake manifold)

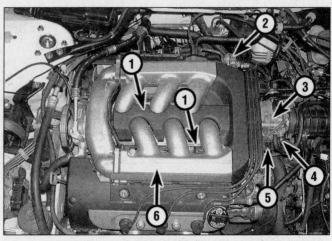

1.2b Fuel injection components - V6 engine

1   Fuel rails (below access cover)
2   Fuel pressure regulator
3   Throttle body
4   Throttle Position Sensor (TPS)
5   Idle Air Control (IAC) valve (below throttle body)
6   Air intake plenum

fuel pump and fuel level sending unit is located inside the fuel tank. A vapor return system routes all vapors back to the fuel tank through a separate return line. The fuel pump/sending unit assembly is accessible through a cover plate in the luggage compartment of the vehicle.

These models are equipped with a fuel injection system main relay located under the dash, fastened to a bracket on the left side of the steering column. The relay is controlled by several different circuits. One circuit is linked directly to battery voltage from the ignition switch. Another circuit is linked to the PCM. The PCM will ground the relay for one second. During cranking, the PCM grounds the relay as long as the cylinder position sensor (CYP) sends its position signal (see Chapter 6). If there are no reference pulses, the fuel pump will shut off after two or three seconds. Another circuit allows the relay to be inoperative unless the clutch pedal is depressed (manual transaxle) or the shift lever is in Park (automatic transaxle). A 7.5 amp fuse protects this circuit in case of overload.

Exhaust system

The exhaust system on V6 engines includes a pair of exhaust manifolds, a diverter (Y) pipe fitted with an upstream (before catalytic converter) and a downstream (after catalytic converter) oxygen sensor, a single catalytic converter, a muffler and a tail pipe. The exhaust system on the four-cylinder engine is simpler. A single exhaust manifold and exhaust pipe connects the catalytic converter to the engine.

The catalytic converter is an emission control device added to the exhaust system to reduce pollutants. A single-bed converter is used in combination with a three-way (reduction) catalyst. Refer to Chapter 6 for more information regarding the catalytic converter.

2   Fuel pressure relief

Refer to illustration 2.3

Warning: *Gasoline is extremely flammable, so take extra precautions when you work on any part of the fuel system. Don't smoke or allow open flames or bare light bulbs near the work area, and don't work in a garage where a natural gas-type appliance (such as a water heater or a clothes dryer) with a pilot light is present. Since gasoline is carcinogenic, wear latex gloves when there's a possibility of being exposed to fuel, and, if you spill any fuel on your skin, rinse it off immediately with soap and water. Mop up any spills immediately and do not store fuel-soaked rags where they could ignite. The fuel system is under constant pressure, so, if any fuel lines are to be disconnected, the fuel pressure in the sys-*

2.3 After the fuel pressure has been relieved, loosen the fuel pulsation damper and allow the fuel to drip into a rag

tem must be relieved first. When you perform any kind of work on the fuel system, wear safety glasses and have a Class B type fire extinguisher on hand.

1   Unscrew the fuel filler cap to relieve any pressure that has built up in the fuel tank. Remove the trunk carpet liner to access the fuel pump/sending unit access cover (see Section 5). Disconnect the electrical connector for the fuel pump.

2   Start the engine and allow it to run until it stops. Disconnect the cable from the negative terminal of the battery before working on the fuel system. **Caution:** *The stereo in your vehicle is equipped with an anti-theft system. Make sure you have the correct activation code before disconnecting the battery.*

3   Using an open-end wrench, loosen the fuel pulsation damper to relieve any residual pressure in the fuel lines **(see illustration)**. Be sure to place a shop rag around the fuel pulsation damper to catch the residual fuel as it bleeds off.

4   The fuel system pressure is now relieved. When you're finished working on the fuel system, tighten the fuel pulsation damper to the torque listed in this Chapter's Specifications, reconnect the fuel pump/sending unit harness connector and connect the negative cable to the battery.

3   Fuel pump/fuel pressure - check

Warning: *Gasoline is extremely flammable, so take extra precautions when you work on any part of the fuel system. See the* **Warning** *in Section 2.*

Note: *In order to perform the fuel pressure test, you will need to obtain a fuel pressure gauge capable of measuring high fuel pressure and an adapter set for the fuel injection system being tested.*

General checks

1   Check that there is adequate fuel in the fuel tank.

2   Verify the fuel pump actually runs. Have an assistant turn the ignition switch to ON - you should hear a brief whirring noise (approximately two seconds) as the pump comes on and pressurizes the system. **Note:** *The fuel pump is easily heard through the gas tank filler neck.* If there is no response from the fuel pump (makes no sound) proceed to Step 9 and check the fuel pump electrical circuit.

Fuel pump output and pressure check

Refer to illustrations 3.3a, 3.3b, 3.5, 3.6 and 3.7

3   Remove the fuel pulsation damper (see Section 2) and install an adapter for a fuel pressure gauge **(see illustrations)**.

4   Turn the ignition switch ON (engine not running) with the air conditioning off. The fuel pump should run for about two seconds - pressure should register on the gauge and should hold steady.

5   Start the engine and let it idle at normal operating temperature. Compare the pressure reading with the value listed in this Chapter's Specifications **(see illustration)**. Now, disconnect the vacuum hose from the fuel pressure regulator - the pressure should increase immediately to the value listed in this Chapter's Specifications. If the pressure readings are correct, the system is operating properly.

6   If the pressure did not increase when the vacuum hose was disconnected, apply 12 to 14 inches of vacuum to the pressure regulator, using a hand-held vacuum pump **(see illustration)**. If the pressure drops, repair the vacuum source to the regulator. If the pressure does not drop, replace the regulator.

7   If the fuel pressure is not within specifications, check the following:

a) *If the pressure is higher than specified, check for vacuum to the fuel pressure regulator* **(see illustration)**. *Vacuum must fluctuate with the increase or decrease in the engine rpm. If vacuum is present, check for a pinched or clogged fuel return hose or pipe. If the return line is OK, replace the regulator.*

b) *If the pressure is lower than specified, change the fuel filter to rule out the possibility of a clogged filter. The fuel filter is an integral component of the fuel pump/sending unit assembly. It must be replaced as a complete assembly (see Section 5). If the pressure is still low, start the engine (if possible) and slowly pinch the return hose shut. If the pressure rises above 47 psi, replace the regulator (see Section 14).* **Warning:** *Don't allow the fuel pressure to exceed 60 psi.*

c) *If the pressure is still low with the fuel return line restricted, an injector (or injectors) may be leaking (see Section 15) or the in-tank fuel pump may be faulty.*

3.3a Install a fuel pressure gauge adapter (arrow) in place of the fuel pulsation damper, then connect the fuel pressure gauge to the hole in the end of the adapter

8   After the testing is done, relieve the fuel pressure (see Section 2) and remove the fuel pressure gauge.

Fuel pump electrical circuit check

Refer to illustrations 3.10 and 3.13

Note: *Refer to Chapter 12 for additional wiring schematics that detail the main relay and circuit.*

9   If the pump does not turn on (makes no sound) with the ignition switch in the ON position, check the Number 1 (15 amp) fuel pump fuse or the ACG S (15 amp) fuse located in the engine compartment fuse center. If the fuse is blown, replace the fuse and see if the pump works. If the pump now works, check for a short in the circuit between the main relay and the fuel pump. **Note:** *These models are equipped with a special starter shut-down circuit that provides power to terminal number 2 on the main relay only if the clutch is pressed down (manual transaxle) or the shift lever is in Park (auto-*

3.6 Connect a vacuum pump to the fuel pressure regulator, apply vacuum and check the fuel pressure - the fuel pressure should decrease as the vacuum increases

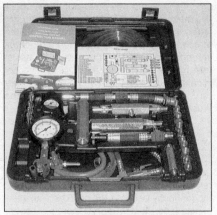

3.3b This aftermarket fuel pressure testing kit contains all the necessary fittings and adapters, along with the fuel pressure gauge, to test most automotive fuel systems

3.5 Check the fuel pressure with the engine at idle

matic transaxle models). A special 7.5 amp fuse protects this circuit in case of overload. Check the Number 13 starter signal fuse (7.5 amp) in the engine compartment fuse center along with the other fuse checks.

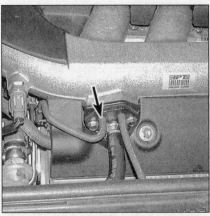

3.7 Disconnect the vacuum hose (arrow) from the air intake plenum and check for vacuum at the port - vacuum must fluctuate with the increase or decrease in engine rpm (V6 model shown)

10   If the pump still does not work, check the main relay circuit. **Note:** *The main relay is located up under the instrument panel, attached to a bracket on the left side of the steering column.* With the help of an assistant, cycle the ignition key ON (engine not running), and OFF, while checking for battery voltage at the relay connector **(see illustration).**

11   If battery voltage does not exist, check the circuit from the PCM to the relay.

12   If battery voltage exists, check the relay.

13   Using a pair of jumper wires, connect battery voltage to the no. 2 terminal of the relay, ground the no. 1 terminal, then check for continuity between the no. 5 and no. 4 terminals **(see illustration).** If there's no continuity, replace the relay.

14   Connect battery voltage to the no. 5 terminal, ground the no. 3 terminal and verify there's continuity between the no. 7 and no. 6 terminals. If there isn't, replace the relay.

15   Connect battery voltage to the no. 6 terminal, ground the no. 1 terminal. Verify there's continuity between the no. 5 and no. 4 terminals. If there is no continuity, replace the relay. If there is continuity, the relay is OK. Check the wiring harness from the fuses to the relay and the pump.

16   If the fuel pump does not activate, check for power to the fuel pump at the fuel tank **(see illustration 5.4).** If voltage is present at the fuel pump connector, replace the fuel pump.

---

4   Fuel lines and fittings - repair and replacement

Warning: *Gasoline is extremely flammable, so take extra precautions when you work on any part of the fuel system. See the* **Warning** *in Section 2.*

1   Always relieve the fuel pressure before servicing fuel lines or fittings (see Section 2).

2   The fuel feed, return and vapor lines extend from the fuel tank to the engine compartment. The lines are secured to the underbody with clip and screw assemblies. These lines must be occasionally inspected for leaks, kinks and dents.

3   If evidence of dirt is found in the system or fuel filter during disassembly, the line should be disconnected and blown out. Check the fuel strainer on the fuel pump pickup unit (see Section 5) for damage and deterioration.

Steel tubing

4   If replacement of a fuel line or emission line is called for, use welded steel tubing meeting the manufacturer's specifications.

5   Don't use copper or aluminum tubing to replace steel tubing. These materials cannot withstand normal vehicle vibration.

6   Because fuel lines used on fuel-injected vehicles are under high pressure, they require special consideration.

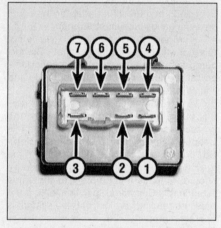

3.10 Check for voltage at the main relay electrical connector terminal 7 with the ignition key OFF. Battery voltage should be present. Terminal 5 will only have battery voltage with the ignition key ON (engine not running) while the starter circuit terminal 2 will only activate when the clutch is depressed or the shift lever in Park

7   Some fuel lines have threaded fittings with O-rings. Any time the fittings are loosened to service or replace components:

  a) *Use a backup wrench while loosening and tightening the fittings.*

  b) *Check all O-rings for cuts, cracks and deterioration. Replace any that appear hardened, worn or damaged.*

  c) *If the lines are replaced, always use original equipment parts, or parts that meet original equipment standards.*

Flexible hose

Warning: *Use only original equipment replacement hoses or their equivalent. Others may fail from the high pressures generated by this system.*

8   Don't route fuel hose within four inches of any part of the exhaust system or within ten inches of the catalytic converter. Metal lines and rubber hoses must never be allowed to chafe against the frame. A minimum of 1/4-inch clearance must be maintained around a line or hose to prevent contact with the frame.

Removal and installation

Refer to illustration 4.10

9   Relieve the fuel pressure (see Section 2).

10   Remove all fasteners attaching the lines to the vehicle body. **Caution:** *The quick-disconnect fittings cannot be serviced separately. Do not attempt to service these types of fuel lines in the event the retainer tabs or the line becomes damaged. Replace the entire fuel line as an assembly. On fuel lines so equipped, detach the clamp(s) that attach the fuel hoses to the metal lines, then pull the hose off the fitting. Twisting the hoses back and forth will allow them to separate more easily. On quick-disconnect fittings, hold the connector with one hand and depress the retaining tabs with the other hand, then separate the connector from the pipe* **(see illustration).**

11   Installation is the reverse of removal. Be sure to use new O-rings at the threaded fittings (if equipped). On quick-disconnect fittings, align the retainer locking pawls with the connector grooves. Push the connector onto the pipe until both retaining pawls lock with a clicking sound.

3.13 Main relay terminal identification

Repair

12   In the event of any fuel line damage (metal or flexible lines) it is necessary to replace the damaged lines with factory replacement parts. Others may fail from the high pressures of this system.

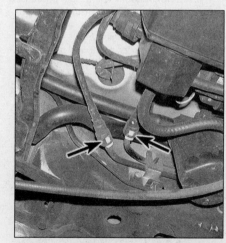

4.10 Some fuel lines can be disconnected by pinching the tabs and separating each connector

5.4 Remove the screws (arrows) from the fuel pump/fuel level sending unit access cover - the inset identifies the fuel pump connector terminals

5.6 Remove the nuts that retain the fuel pump to the fuel tank

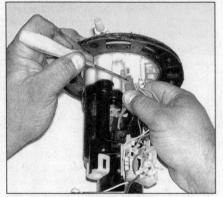

5.8a Disconnect the electrical connector from the mounting flange . . .

5 Fuel pump - removal and installation

Refer to illustrations 5.4, 5.6, 5.8a, 5.8b and 5.10
Warning: *Gasoline is extremely flammable, so take extra precautions when you work on any part of the fuel system. See the* **Warning** *in Section 2.*

1   Detach the cable from the negative battery terminal. **Caution:** *If the stereo in your vehicle is equipped with an anti-theft system, make sure you have the correct activation code before disconnecting the battery.*
2   Relieve the fuel system pressure (see Section 2).
3   Remove the carpet from the trunk.
4   Remove the bolts that retain the fuel pump access cover **(see illustration)**.
5   Unplug the electrical connector from the fuel pump, disconnect the quick-connect fittings on the fuel lines and detach the fuel lines.
6   Remove the fuel pump assembly retaining nuts **(see illustration)**.
7   Remove the fuel pump from the tank.
8   Remove the electrical connector from the fuel pump **(see illustrations)**.
9   Squeeze the hose clamps with a pair of pliers - remove the upper clamp from the hose and slide the lower clamp half-way up the hose, off the fuel pump inlet.
10   Remove the sock filter from the end of the pump **(see illustration)**.
11   Separate the pump from the fuel pump bracket.
12   Installation is the reverse of removal. Be sure to use a new gasket on the pump flange.

6 Fuel level sending unit - check and replacement

Warning: *Gasoline is extremely flammable, so take extra precautions when you work on any part of the fuel system. See the* **Warning** *in Section 2.*

Check

Refer to illustration 6.3
1   Disconnect the negative battery cable.
Caution: *The stereo in your vehicle is equipped with an anti-theft system. Make sure you have the correct activation code before disconnecting the battery.*
2   Remove the fuel pump/fuel level sending unit from the fuel tank (see Section 5).
3   Position the probes of an ohmmeter on the connector terminals and check for resistance **(see illustration)**. Use the 200-ohm scale on the ohmmeter. Check the resistance of the sending unit with the float arm completely down (tank empty) and with the arm up (tank full). The resistance should change steadily from empty to full.
4   When the tank is nearly empty, the resistance of the sending unit should be approximately 105 to 107 ohms.

5.8b . . . and from the fuel pump

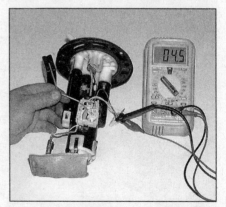

5.10 Pry off the retaining clip with a small screwdriver and detach the filter (sock) from the pump

6.3 Measure the resistance of the fuel level sending unit with the float raised (full tank) and then with the float near the bottom (empty)

5   With the fuel tank completely full, the resistance should be approximately 3 to 5 ohms.

6   If the readings are incorrect, replace the sending unit.

Replacement

Refer to illustrations 6.9 and 6.10

7   Disconnect the negative battery cable. **Caution:** *The stereo in your vehicle is equipped with an anti-theft system. Make sure you have the correct activation code before disconnecting the battery.*

8   Remove the fuel pump/fuel level sending unit from the fuel tank (see Section 5).

9   Disconnect the sending unit electrical connector from the base of the fuel pump/fuel level sending unit **(see illustration)**.

10   Remove the fuel level sending unit retaining screws and separate it from the fuel pump bracket **(see illustration)**.

11   Installation is the reverse of removal. Be sure to use a new gasket under the sealing flange.

7   Fuel tank - removal and installation

Refer to illustrations 7.8, 7.9, 7.13 and 7.15

Warning: *Gasoline is extremely flammable, so take extra precautions when you work on any part of the fuel system. See the* **Warning** *in Section 2.*

Note: *The following procedure is much easier to perform if the fuel tank is empty. Some tanks have a drain plug for this purpose. If the tank does not have a drain plug, the fuel can be siphoned from the tank using a siphoning kit, available at most auto parts stores. NEVER start the siphoning action with your mouth!*

1   Remove the fuel tank filler cap to relieve fuel tank pressure.

2   Relieve the fuel system pressure (see Section 2).

3   Detach the cable from the negative terminal of the battery. **Caution:** *The stereo in*

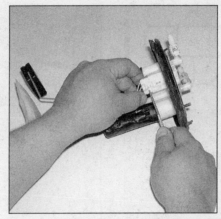

6.9 Disconnect the fuel level sending unit electrical connector

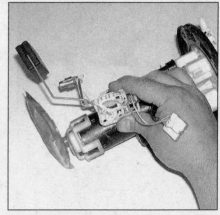

6.10 Push the sending unit down and toward the filter sock to separate it from the fuel pump assembly

your vehicle is equipped with an anti-theft system. Make sure you have the correct activation code before disconnecting the battery.

4   If the tank has a drain plug, remove it and drain the fuel into an approved gasoline container. If it doesn't have a drain plug, siphon the fuel into an approved gasoline container, using a siphoning kit (available at most auto parts stores).

5   Disconnect the fuel level sending unit and fuel pump electrical connectors **(see illustration 5.4)**.

6   Loosen the rear wheel lug nuts, raise the vehicle and support it securely on jackstands. Remove the rear wheels.

7   Remove the catalytic converter (see Chapter 6).

8   Remove the fuel pipe cover mounting bolts **(see illustration)** and separate the cover from the body.

9   Label and disconnect the fuel supply and return hoses from the metal fuel lines. Disconnect the fuel filler hose and vent hose **(see illustration)**.

10   Disconnect the harness connectors from the ABS wheel sensors (if equipped).

11   Remove the stabilizer bar (see Chap-

ter 10), the parking brake cable bracket (see Chapter 9) and the heat shield from the rear suspension.

12   Remove the rear brakes (see Chapter 9).

a) *On rear disc brake systems, remove the parking brake cable, the brake caliper mounting bolts and the calipers. Suspend the calipers using wire. Do not allow the brake lines to stretch, twist or deform in any way once the calipers are removed.*

b) *On rear drum brake systems, remove the brake drum and brake shoes. It will be necessary to detach the brake lines from the wheel cylinders at the rear of the backing plates. Separate the parking brake cable from the backing plate (see Chapter 9). Unbolt the backing plates from the knuckle.*

13   Remove the bolt from the lower end of each shock absorber (see Chapter 10). Place floor jacks under the rear suspension subframe and remove the subframe mounting bolts. Models with four-cylinder engines are equipped with four mounting bolts, while models with V6 engines are equipped with 12

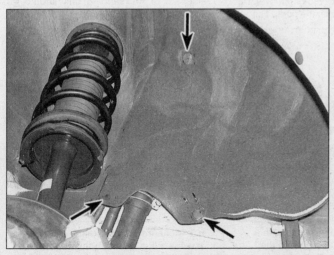

7.8 Remove the retaining screws (arrows) and separate the fuel pipe cover from the inside of the wheel opening

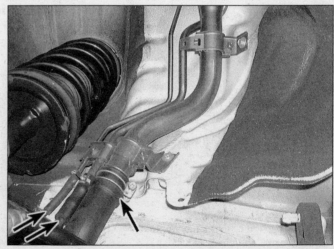

7.9 Remove the clamps that retain the fuel filler hose to the inlet pipe (arrow) and the vent hoses to the metal lines (arrows)

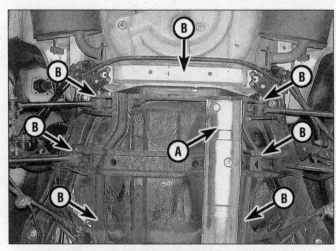

7.13 Fuel tank mounting details (V6 model shown)
a) Heat shield
b) Subframe components

7.15 Disconnect the ORVR and EVAP canister hoses (arrows) before removing the fuel tank

9.2a Remove the clamp from the air intake duct (arrow) (four-cylinder model shown)

9.2b Air intake duct mounting clamp location (arrow) on V6 models

mounting bolts. Lower the subframe from the vehicle (see illustration).

14 Support the fuel tank with a floor jack. Position a wood block between the jack head and the fuel tank to protect the tank.

15 These models are equipped with an ORVR venting system that works in conjunction with the EVAP system. Disconnect the ORVR venting tube clamps and separate the vent tube from the fuel tank and fuel filler pipe (see illustration). Disconnect the hoses from the EVAP canister.

16 Remove the heat shield.

17 Disconnect both fuel tank retaining straps and pivot them down until they are hanging out of the way.

18 Remove the tank from the vehicle.

19 Installation is the reverse of removal.

8 Fuel tank cleaning and repair - general information

1 All repairs to the fuel tank or filler neck should be carried out by a professional who has experience in this critical and potentially dangerous work. Even after cleaning and flushing of the fuel system, explosive fumes can remain and ignite during repair of the tank.

2 If the fuel tank is removed from the vehicle, it should not be placed in an area where sparks or open flames could ignite the fumes coming out of the tank. Be especially careful inside garages where a natural gas-type appliance is located, because the pilot light could cause an explosion.

9 Air cleaner housing - removal and installation

Refer to illustrations 9.2a, 9.2b, 9.4a and 9.4b

1 Detach the cable from the negative terminal of the battery. **Caution:** The stereo in your vehicle is equipped with an anti-theft system. Make sure you have the correct activation code before disconnecting the battery.

2 Detach the air intake duct mounting clamp (see illustrations) from the air cleaner housing.

3 Unlatch the housing cover spring clips, then lift off the air cleaner cover and remove the air filter (see Chapter 1).

4 Remove the air cleaner housing mounting bolts (see illustrations). Carefully lift upward on the air cleaner housing to release the rubber grommets securing the housing to the battery tray. Remove the housing from the vehicle.

5 Installation is the reverse of removal.

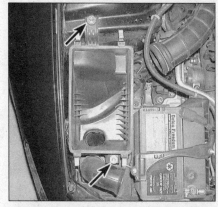

9.4a Remove the bolts (arrows) from the air cleaner housing (four-cylinder models)

9.4b Air cleaner housing bolt locations (arrows) on the V6 models

10 Accelerator cable - removal, installation and adjustment

Refer to illustrations 10.2, 10.3, 10.4 and 10.7

Replacement

1   Detach the cable from the negative battery terminal. **Caution:** *The stereo in your vehicle is equipped with an anti-theft system. Make sure you have the correct activation code before disconnecting the battery.*
2   Loosen the locknut and remove the accelerator cable from its bracket **(see illustration)**.
3   Rotate the throttle shaft bellcrank until the cable is lined up with the slot in the bellcrank, then detach the cable from the bellcrank **(see illustration)**.
4   Working underneath the dash, detach the cable from the accelerator pedal arm **(see illustration)**.
5   Pull the grommet from the firewall and pull the cable through the firewall from the engine compartment side.
6   Installation is the reverse of removal.

Adjustment

7   To adjust the cable **(see illustration)**:

a) *Lift up on the cable to remove any slack.*

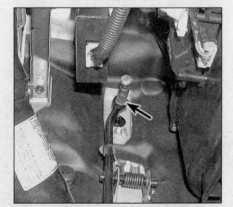

10.4 Working inside the driver's compartment, pull the accelerator cable end (arrow), then pass the cable out of the slot in the pedal arm

10.2 Hold the adjusting nut while loosening the locknut

b) *Turn the adjusting nut until it is 1/8-inch (3 mm) away from the cable bracket.*
c) *Tighten the locknut and check cable deflection at the throttle linkage. Deflection should be 3/8 to 1/2-inch. If deflection is not within specifications, loosen the locknut and turn the adjusting nut until the deflection is as specified.*
d) *After you have adjusted the throttle cable, have an assistant help you verify that the throttle valve opens all the way when you depress the accelerator pedal to the floor and that it returns to the idle position when you release the accelerator. Verify the cable operates smoothly. It must not bind or stick.*

11 Electronic fuel injection system - general information

The Programmed Fuel Injection (PGM-FI) system consists of three sub-systems: air intake, electronic control and fuel delivery. The system uses an Powertrain Control Module (PCM) along with the sensors (coolant temperature sensor, Throttle Position Sensor (TPS), Manifold Absolute Pressure (MAP) sensor etc.) to determine the proper air/fuel

10.7 Lift up the cable to remove the slack, then turn the adjusting nut (B) until it is 1/8-inch from the cable bracket, then tighten the locknut (A)

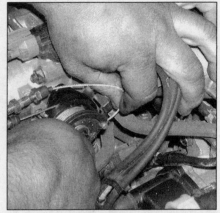

10.3 Detach the cable end from the bellcrank

ratio under all operating conditions.

The fuel injection system and the emissions control system are closely linked in function and design. For additional information, refer to Chapter 6.

Air intake system

The air intake system consists of the air cleaner, the air intake ducts, the throttle body, the idle control system and the intake manifold. Both the four-cylinder and V6 engines are equipped with an intake manifold (lower) and an intake air plenum (upper). Refer to Chapters 2A or 2B for the replacement procedures.

The throttle body is a single barrel, side-draft design. The lower portion of the throttle body is heated by engine coolant to prevent icing in cold weather. The idle adjusting screw is located on top of the throttle body. A throttle position sensor is attached to the throttle shaft to monitor changes in the throttle opening.

When the engine is idling, the air/fuel ratio is controlled by the Idle Air Control (IAC) system, which consists of the Powertrain Control Module (PCM), the Electronic Coolant Temperature (ECT) sensor, the IAC valve and other various sensors (IAT, TPS, MAP, etc.) working in conjunction with the EFI system (see Chapter 6). The IAC valve is controlled by the PCM depending upon the running conditions of the engine (air conditioning system, power steering, cold and warm running etc.). This valve regulates the amount of airflow past the throttle plate and into the intake manifold. The PCM receives information from the sensors (vehicle speed, coolant temperature, air conditioning, power steering load etc.) and adjusts the idle according to the demands of the engine and driver. Finally, to prevent rough running after the engine starts, the IAC valve is opened during cranking and immediately after starting to provide additional air into the intake manifold.

Electronic control system

The electronic control system and the Powertrain Control Module (PCM) are explained in detail in Chapter 6.

12.7 Use a stethoscope or screwdriver to determine if the injectors are working properly - they should make a steady clicking sound that rises and falls with engine speed changes

12.8 Install the "noid" light into each injector electrical connector and confirm that it blinks when the engine is cranking or running

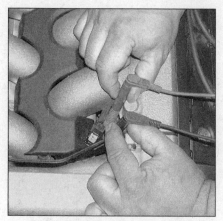

12.9 Disconnect the fuel injector electrical connectors and measure the resistance of each injector

Fuel delivery system

The fuel delivery system consists of these components: The fuel pump, the pressure regulator, the fuel pulsation damper, the fuel injectors and fuel rail, and the main relay.

The fuel pump is an in-line, direct drive type. Fuel is drawn through a filter into the pump, flows past the armature through the one-way valve, passes through another filter and is delivered to the injectors. A relief valve prevents excessive pressure build-up by opening in the event of a blockage in the discharge side and allowing fuel to flow from the high to the low pressure side.

The pressure regulator maintains a constant fuel pressure to the injectors. Excess fuel is routed back to the fuel tank through the return line.

The injectors are solenoid-actuated, constant stroke, pintle types consisting of a solenoid, plunger, needle valve and housing. When current is applied to the solenoid coil, the needle valve raises and pressurized fuel fills the injector housing and squirts out the nozzle. The injection quantity is determined by the length of time the valve is open (the length of time during which current is supplied to the solenoid coils).

Because it determines opening and closing intervals - which in turn determines the air-fuel mixture ratio - injector timing must be quite accurate. To attain the best possible injector response, the current rise time, when voltage is being applied to each injector coil, must be as short as possible. The number of windings in the coil has therefore been reduced to lower the inductance in the coil. However, this creates low coil resistance, which could compromise the durability of the coil. The flow of current in the coil is therefore restricted by a resistor installed in the injector wire harness.

The main relay, located under the dash on the left side of the steering column, is a direct coupler type which contains the relays for the Powertrain Control Module power supply and the fuel pump power supply.

12 Electronic fuel injection (EFI) system - check

Refer to illustrations 12.7, 12.8 and 12.9.
Warning: *Gasoline is extremely flammable, so take extra precautions when you work on any part of the fuel system. See the* **Warning** *in Section 2.*

1   Check all electrical connectors - especially ground connections - for the system. Loose connectors and poor grounds are common causes of engine control system problems.

2   Verify that the battery is fully charged because the Powertrain Control Module (PCM) and sensors cannot operate properly without adequate supply voltage.

3   Refer to Chapter 1 and check the air filter element. A dirty or partially blocked filter will reduce performance and economy.

4   Check fuel pump operation (see Section 3). If the fuel pump fuse is blown, replace it and see if it blows again. If it does, refer to Chapter 12 and the wiring diagrams and look for a grounded wire in the harness to the fuel pump.

5   Inspect the vacuum hoses connected to the intake manifold for damage, deterioration and leakage.

6   Remove the air intake duct from the throttle body and check for dirt, carbon, varnish, or other residue in the throttle body, particularly around the throttle plate. If it's dirty, refer to Chapter 6 and troubleshoot the PCV and EGR systems for the cause of excessive buildup. An extremely dirty throttle body requires replacement.

7   With the engine running, place an automotive stethoscope against each injector, one at a time, and listen for a clicking sound that indicates operation **(see illustration)**. If you don't have a stethoscope, you can place the tip of a long screwdriver against the injector and listen through the handle.

8   If an injector does not seem to be operating electrically (not clicking), purchase a

special injector test light (sometimes called a "noid" light) and install it into the injector wiring harness connector **(see illustration)**. Start the engine and see if the noid light flashes. If it does, the injector is receiving proper voltage. If it doesn't flash, further diagnosis is necessary. You might want to have it checked by a dealership service department or other qualified repair shop.

9   With the engine off and the fuel injector electrical connectors disconnected, measure the resistance of each injector with an ohmmeter **(see illustration)**. Check the specifications at the beginning of this chapter for the correct resistance.

10   Refer to Chapter 6 for other system checks.

13 Throttle body - removal and installation

Refer to illustrations 13.6a and 13.6b
Warning: *Wait until the engine is completely cool before beginning this procedure.*

1   Detach the cable from the negative battery terminal. **Caution:** *The stereo in your vehicle is equipped with an anti-theft system. Make sure you have the correct activation code before disconnecting the battery.*

2   Remove the air intake duct that connects the air cleaner assembly to the throttle body.

3   Disconnect the Throttle Position Sensor (TPS) connector from the throttle body (see Chapter 6). Also label and detach all vacuum hoses from the throttle body.

4   Detach the accelerator cable (see Section 10) and if equipped, the cruise control cable.

5   Detach the coolant hoses from the throttle body. Plug the lines to prevent coolant loss.

6   Remove the four mounting nuts **(see illustrations)** and remove the throttle body and gasket. Remove all traces of old gasket material from the throttle body and air intake plenum.

13.6a Remove the four nuts (arrows) and separate the throttle body from the air intake plenum (four-cylinder models)

13.6b Location of the throttle body mounting nuts (arrows) on V6 models

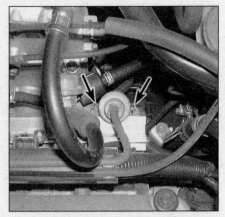

14.5a Remove the fuel pressure regulator mounting bolts (arrows) (four-cylinder models)

7   Installation is the reverse of removal. Be sure to use a new gasket. Adjust the accelerator cable (see Section 10). Check the coolant level and add some, if necessary (see Chapter 1).

14 Fuel pressure regulator - removal and installation

Refer to illustrations 14.5a and 14.5b

Warning: *Gasoline is extremely flammable, so take extra precautions when you work on any part of the fuel system. See the* **Warning** *in Section 2.*

1   Relieve the system fuel pressure (see Section 2).
2   Detach the cable from the negative battery terminal. **Caution:** *The stereo in your vehicle is equipped with an anti-theft system. Make sure you have the correct activation code before disconnecting the battery.*
3   On V6 engines, remove the access covers from the top of the engine (see Chapter 2B).
4   Detach the vacuum hose and fuel hose from the pressure regulator.

5   Remove the fuel pressure regulator from the fuel rail:
  a) *On four-cylinder engines, remove the mounting bolts from the fuel pressure regulator* **(see illustration).**
  b) *On V6 engines, use an open-end wrench and unscrew the fuel pressure regulator from the fuel rail* **(see illustration).**
6   Installation is the reverse of removal. Be sure to use a new O-ring. Lubricate the O-ring with a light coat of clean engine oil before installation. Tighten the fuel pressure regulator mounting bolts (four-cylinder engine) or the regulator itself (V6 engine) to the torque listed in this Chapter's Specifications.
7   Check for fuel leaks after installing the pressure regulator.

15 Fuel rail and injectors - removal and installation

Warning: *Gasoline is extremely flammable, so take extra precautions when you work on any part of the fuel system. See the* **Warning** *in Section 2.*

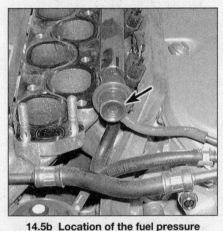

14.5b Location of the fuel pressure regulator (arrow) on V6 models

Note: *The fuel rail on four-cylinder engines can be removed with the air intake plenum attached to the engine. On V6 engines, the air intake plenum must be removed to access the fuel rails (left and right bank). The fuel rails on the V6 engines can be lifted off the engine as a complete assembly along with the fuel injectors attached to the fuel rails.*

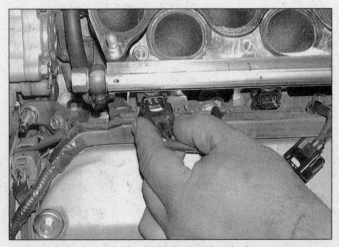

15.5 Disconnect the fuel injector electrical connector from each injector

15.6 Detach the fuel return hose clamp (1) and the fuel feed line (2) from the fuel rail (V6 model shown)

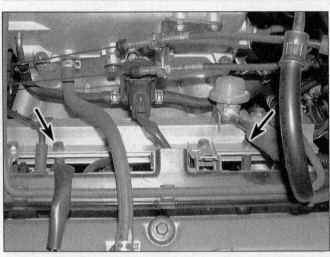

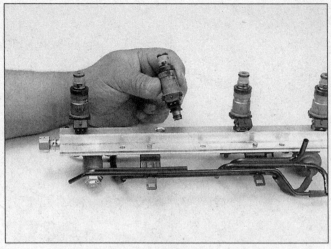

15.9 Location of the fuel rail mounting nuts (four-cylinder model)

15.10a Remove the injectors from the fuel rail

Removal

Refer to illustrations 15.5, 15.6, 15.9, 15.10a, 15.10b and 15.10c

1　Detach the cable from the negative battery terminal. **Caution:** *The stereo in your vehicle is equipped with an anti-theft system. Make sure you have the correct activation code before disconnecting the battery.*

2　Relieve the fuel pressure (see Section 2).

3　On V6 engines, remove the access covers from the top of the engine (see Chapter 2B).

4　On V6 engines, remove the air intake plenum (see Chapter 2B).

5　Disconnect the injector electrical connectors **(see illustration)**.

6　Detach the fuel return hose from the fuel pressure regulator **(see illustration). Note:** *The fuel return line is smaller and is clamped to the fuel pressure regulator using a small spring clamp while the fuel feed hose (pressure line) is bolted to the fuel rail.*

7　Detach any ground cables from the fuel rail.

8　Detach the fuel feed line from the fuel rail.

9　Remove the mounting nuts (four-cylinder engine) or bolts (V6 engine) and lift the fuel rail from the engine **(see illustration)**. On V6 engines, lift the right bank and the left bank fuel rails simultaneously.

10　Remove the injector(s) from the bore(s) in the fuel rail **(see illustration)** and remove and discard the O-ring, cushion ring and seal ring **(see illustrations). Note:** *Whether you're replacing an injector or a leaking O-ring, it's a good idea to remove all the injectors from the fuel rail and replace all the O-rings, seal rings and cushion rings.*

Installation

11　Coat the new cushion rings with clean engine oil and slide them onto the injectors.

12　Coat the new O-rings with clean engine oil and install them on the injector(s), then insert each injector into its corresponding bore in the fuel rail.

13　Coat the new seal rings with clean engine oil and press them into the injector bore(s) in the intake manifold.

14　Install the injectors and fuel rail assembly on the intake manifold. Tighten the fuel rail mounting nuts on four-cylinder models to the torque listed in this Chapter's Specifications. On V6 models, tighten the mounting bolts securely.

15　The remainder of installation is the reverse of removal.

16　After the injector/fuel rail assembly installation is complete, turn the ignition switch to ON, but don't operate the starter (this activates the fuel pump for about two seconds, which builds up fuel pressure in the fuel lines and the fuel rail). Repeat this about two or three times, then check the fuel lines, rail and injectors for fuel leakage.

16 Exhaust system servicing - general information

Refer to illustrations 16.4a, 16.4b and 16.4c
Warning: *Inspection and repair of exhaust system components should be done only after enough time has elapsed after driving the vehicle to allow the system components to cool completely. Also, when working under the vehicle, make sure it is securely supported on jackstands.*
Caution: *All models covered by this manual are equipped with an exhaust system flex tube which is extremely sensitive to sharp bends. Do not allow the flex tube to hang downward during servicing or damage will occur.*

1　The exhaust system consists of the exhaust manifold(s), the catalytic converter, the muffler, the tailpipe and all connecting pipes, brackets, hangers and clamps. The exhaust system is attached to the body with mounting brackets and rubber hangers. If any of the parts are improperly installed, excessive noise and vibration will be transmitted to the body.

2　Conduct regular inspections of the exhaust system to keep it safe and quiet. Look for any damaged or bent parts, open seams, holes, loose connections, excessive corrosion or other defects which could allow exhaust fumes to enter the vehicle. Deteriorated exhaust system components should not be repaired; they should be replaced with new parts.

15.10b Carefully remove the injector O-rings

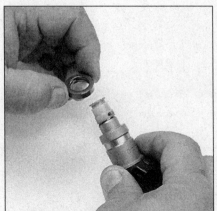

15.10c Remove the seal ring and cushion ring from the injector

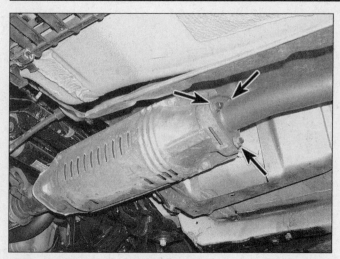

16.4a Location of the catalytic converter mounting nuts (arrows) on V6 models

16.4b Check for any broken or missing rubber hangers (arrow)

3   If the exhaust system components are extremely corroded or rusted together, welding equipment will probably be required to remove them. The convenient way to accomplish this is to have a muffler repair shop remove the corroded sections with a cutting torch. If, however, you want to save money by doing it yourself (and you don't have a welding outfit with a cutting torch), simply cut off the old components with a hacksaw. If you have compressed air, special pneumatic cutting chisels can also be used. If you do decide to tackle the job at home, be sure to wear safety goggles to protect your eyes from metal chips and work gloves to protect your hands.

4   Here are some simple guidelines to follow when repairing the exhaust system:

a) *Work from the back to the front when removing exhaust system components* **(see illustrations).**

b) *Apply penetrating oil to the exhaust system component fasteners to make them easier to remove* **(see illustration).**

c) *Use new gaskets, hangers and clamps when installing exhaust systems components.*

d) *Apply anti-seize compound to the threads of all exhaust system fasteners during reassembly.*

e) *Be sure to allow sufficient clearance between newly installed parts and all points on the underbody to avoid overheating the floor pan and possibly damaging the interior carpet and insulation. Pay particularly close attention to the catalytic converter and heat shield.*

16.4c Use penetrating spray on all exhaust system mounting bolts and fasteners to prevent stripped or damaged threads

Chapter 5
Engine electrical systems

Contents

Specifications

General

Alternator brush length	
New	0.41 inch
Minimum	0.06 inch
Battery voltage	
Engine off	11.5 to 12 volts
Engine running	13.5 to 15 volts
Firing order	
four-cylinder engine	1-3-4-2
V6 engine	1-4-2-5-3-6

Ignition system

Ignition coil resistance	
four-cylinder engine	
VTEC	
Primary resistance	0.45 to 0.55 ohms
Secondary resistance	16.8 to 25.2 K-ohms
Non-VTEC	
Primary resistance	0.63 to 0.77 ohms
Secondary resistance	12.8 to 19.2 K-ohms
1998 and 1999 V6 engine	
Primary resistance	0.34 to 0.42 ohms
Secondary resistance	17.1 to 20.9 K-ohms
Ignition timing	
four-cylinder engine	12 degrees +/- 2 BTDC (red mark B) in Park or Neutral
V6 models	10 degrees +/- 2 BTDC (red mark B) in Park or Neutral
Spark plug wire resistance	
per foot (approximate)	5,000 ohms
maximum	25,000 ohms

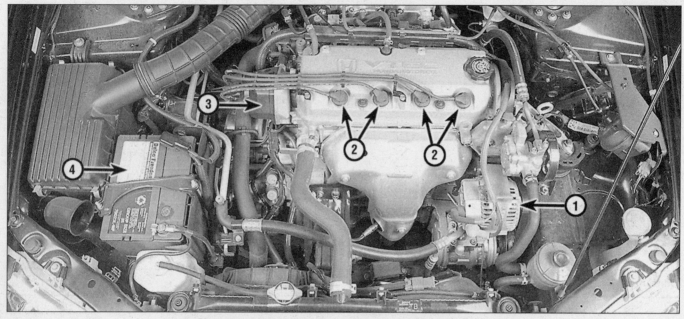

1.1a Charging and ignition system components - four-cylinder engine

1	Alternator	2	Spark plug wires	3	Distributor	4	Battery

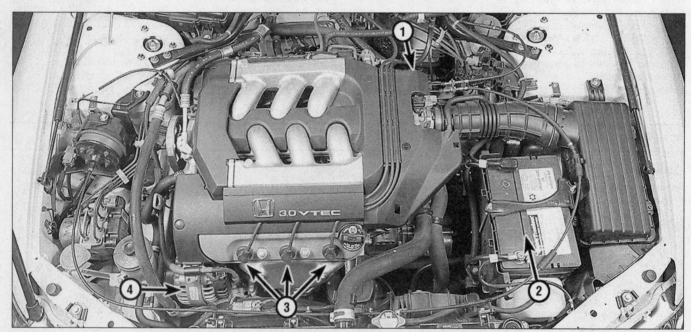

1.1b Charging and ignition system components - 1998 and 1999 V6 engine

1	Distributor	3	Spark plug wires (front cylinder head)	4	Alternator
2	Battery				

1   General information

Refer to illustrations 1.1a and 1.1b

The engine electrical systems include all ignition, charging and starting components **(see illustrations)**. Because of their engine-related functions, these components are considered separately from chassis electrical devices like the lights, instruments, etc.

Be very careful when working on the engine electrical components. They are easily damaged if checked, connected or handled improperly. The alternator is driven by an engine drivebelt which could cause serious injury if your hands, hair or clothes become entangled in it with the engine running. Both the starter and alternator are connected directly to the battery and could arc or even cause a fire if mishandled, overloaded or shorted out.

Never leave the ignition switch on for long periods of time with the engine off. Don't disconnect the battery cables while the engine is running. Correct polarity must be maintained when connecting battery cables from another source, such as another vehicle, during jump starting. Always disconnect the negative cable first and hook it up last or the battery may be shorted by the tool being used to loosen the cable clamps.

Additional safety related information on the engine electrical systems can be found in *Safety first* near the front of this manual. It should be referred to before beginning any operation included in this Chapter.

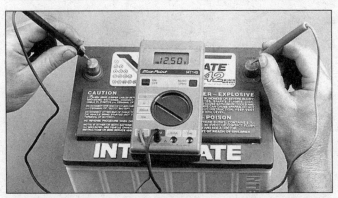

3.2 To test the open circuit voltage of the battery, simply touch the black probe of the voltmeter to the negative terminal and the red probe to the positive terminal of the battery – a fully charged battery should read between 11.5 to 12.5 volts depending on the outside air temperature

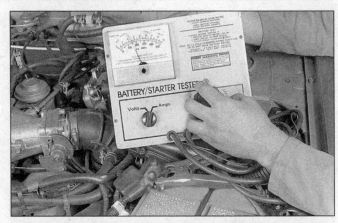

3.3 Some battery load testers are equipped with a ammeter which enables the battery load to be precisely dialed in, as shown – less expensive testers have a load switch and a voltmeter only

2 Battery - emergency jump starting

Refer to the *Booster battery (jump) starting procedure* at the front of this manual.

3 Battery - check and replacement

Caution 1: *Always disconnect the negative cable first and hook it up last or the battery may be shorted by the tool being used to loosen the cable clamps.*
Caution 2: *The radio in your vehicle is equipped with an anti-theft system, make sure you have the correct activation code before disconnecting the battery.*

Check

Refer to illustrations 3.2 and 3.3
1   Disconnect the negative battery cable, then the positive cable from the battery.
2   Check the battery state of charge. Visually inspect the indicator eye on the top of the battery, if the indicator eye is black in color charge the battery as described in Chapter 1. Next perform an open voltage circuit test using a digital voltmeter **(see illustration)**.
Note: *The battery's surface charge must be removed before accurate voltage measurements can be made. Turn On the high beams for ten seconds, then turn them Off, let the vehicle stand for two minutes.* With the engine and all accessories Off, touch the negative probe of the voltmeter to the negative terminal of the battery and the positive probe to the positive terminal of the battery. The battery voltage should be 11.5 to 12.5 volts or slightly above. If the battery is less than the specified voltage, charge the battery before proceeding to the next test. Do not proceed with the battery load test unless the battery charge is correct.
3   Perform a battery load test. An accurate check of the battery condition can only be performed with a load tester (available at most auto parts stores). This test evaluates the ability of the battery to operate the starter

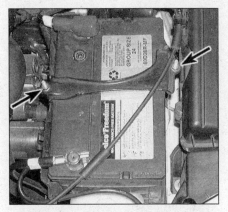

3.5 Remove the two nuts (arrows) and detach the hold-down clamps

and other accessories during periods of heavy amperage draw (load). Install a special battery load testing tool onto the terminals **(see illustration)**. Load test the battery according to the manufacturer's instructions for the particular tool. This tool utilizes a carbon pile to increase the load demand (amperage draw) on the battery. Maintain the load on the battery for 15 seconds or less and observe that the battery voltage does not drop below 9.6 volts. If the battery condition is weak or defective, the tool will indicate this condition immediately. **Note:** *Cold temperatures will cause the minimum voltage requirements to drop slightly. Follow the chart given in the manufacturer's instructions to compensate for cold climates. Minimum load voltage for freezing temperatures (32 degrees F) should be approximately 9.1 volts.*

Replacement

Refer to illustration 3.5
4   Disconnect the negative battery cable, then the positive cable from the battery.
5   Remove the battery hold-down clamp **(see illustration)**.
6   Lift out the battery. Be careful - it's heavy. **Note:** *Battery straps and handlers are available at most auto parts stores for a reasonable price. They make it easier to remove and carry the battery.*

4.2 Check for corrosion or frayed cable strands at the battery cable end (arrow)

7   While the battery is out, inspect the battery tray for corrosion.
8   If corrosion exists on the battery tray, detach the bolts and remove the tray from the engine compartment. Clean the deposits from the metal to prevent the battery tray from further corrosion.
9   If you are replacing the battery, make sure you get one that's identical, with the same dimensions, amperage rating, cold cranking rating, etc.
10   Installation is the reverse of removal.

4 Battery cables - check and replacement

Refer to illustrations 4.2, 4.4a, 4.4b, 4.4c and 4.4d
1   Periodically inspect the entire length of each battery cable for damage, cracked or burned insulation and corrosion. Poor battery cable connections can cause starting problems and decreased engine performance.
2   Check the cable-to-terminal connections at the ends of the cables for cracks, loose wire strands and corrosion **(see illustration)**. The presence of white, fluffy deposits under the insulation at the cable terminal connection is a sign that the cable is

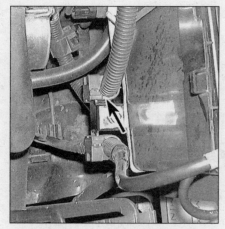

4.4a Detach any battery cable ties or retaining clips (arrows)

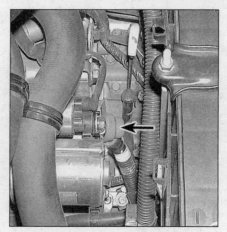

4.4b The positive battery cable is fastened to the starter (arrow)

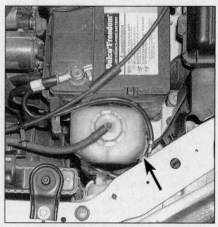

4.4c The negative battery cable is attached to the radiator support (arrow) . . .

4.4d . . . and to the transaxle (arrow)

corroded and should be replaced. Check the terminals for distortion, missing mounting bolts and corrosion.

3   When removing the cables, always disconnect the negative cable first and hook it up last or the battery may be shorted by the tool used to loosen the cable clamps. Even if only the positive cable is being replaced, be sure to disconnect the negative cable from the battery first (see Chapter 1 for further information regarding battery cable removal). **Caution:** *The radio in your vehicle is equipped with an anti-theft system, make sure you have the correct activation code before disconnecting the battery.*

4   Disconnect the old cables from the battery, then trace each of them to their opposite ends and detach them from the starter solenoid and ground terminals. Note the routing of each cable to ensure correct installation **(see illustrations).**

5   If you are replacing either or both of the old cables, take them with you when buying new cables. It is vitally important that you replace the cables with identical parts. Cables have characteristics that make them easy to identify: positive cables are usually red and larger in cross-section; negative cables are usually black and smaller in cross section.

6   Clean the threads of the solenoid or ground connection with a wire brush to remove rust and corrosion. Apply a light coat of battery terminal corrosion inhibitor, or petroleum jelly, to the threads to prevent future corrosion.

7   Attach the cable to the solenoid or ground connection and tighten the mounting nut/bolt securely.

8   Before connecting a new cable to the battery, make sure that it reaches the battery post without having to be stretched.

9   Connect the positive cable first, followed by the negative cable.

5   Ignition system - general information

Warning: *Because of the high voltage generated by the ignition system, extreme care should be taken whenever an operation is performed involving ignition components. This not only includes the igniter, coil, distributor and spark plug wires, but related components such as plug connectors, tachometer and other test equipment.*

1   The Programmed Ignition (PGM-IG) system provides complete control of the ignition timing. The computer (PCM) determines the optimum timing in response to engine speed, coolant temperature, throttle position and vacuum pressure in the intake manifold. These parameters are relayed to the PCM by the CKP/TDC and the CYP sensors, throttle position sensor (TPS), electronic coolant temperature (ECT) sensor and manifold absolute (MAP) sensor. Ignition timing is altered during warm-up, idling and warm running conditions by the PGM-IG system. This electronic ignition system also consists of the ignition switch, battery, coil, distributor, ignition control module, spark plug wires and spark plugs. Refer to the illustrations in Section 1 for component locations. The four-cylinder engines are equipped with an ignition coil mounted inside the distributor while on 1998 and 1999 V6 engines the coil is mounted externally near the distributor. The 2000 through 2002 V6 models utilize a distributorless system which consists of individual coil/ICM units mounted above each spark plug, thereby eliminating the distibutor and spark plug wires.

2   The distributor is driven by the camshaft. The timing is controlled by the Powertrain Control Module. All models employ a crankshaft position sensor (CKP) located inside the lower timing belt cover next to the crankshaft sprocket. The top dead center (TDC) locating sensor is also located near the CKP sensor (opposite) on four-cylinder engines. On V6 engines, the TDC number 1 and the TDC number 2 sensors are mounted behind the camshaft sprocket on the front cylinder head. The cylinder position sensor (CYP), on four-cylinder models, and the ignition control module, on all models, is located inside the distributor. Refer to a dealer parts department or auto parts store for any questions concerning the availability of the distributor parts and assemblies. Testing the TDC, CKP or the CYP sensors are covered in Chapter 6.

6   Ignition system - check

Refer to illustrations 6.2 and 6.8

Warning: *Because of the high voltage generated by the ignition system, extreme care should be taken whenever an operation is performed involving ignition components. This not only includes the igniter, coil, distributor and spark plug wires, but related components such as plug connectors, tachometer and other test equipment.*

1   If a malfunction occurs in the ignition system, do not immediately assume that the distributor is causing the problem. First, check the following items:

a)   *Make sure the battery cable clamps, where they connect to the battery, are clean and tight.*

b)   *Test the condition of the battery (see Section 3). If it does not pass all the tests, replace it with a new battery.*

c)   *Check the external distributor and ignition coil wiring and connections.*

d) Check the fusible links (if equipped) exiting the engine compartment fuse box (see Chapter 12). If they're burned, determine the cause and repair the circuit

2   Check the ignition spark at the plug. If the engine turns over but won't start, disconnect the spark plug wire from any spark plug and attach it to a calibrated tester (available at most auto parts stores) **(see illustration)**. Connect the clip on the tester to a bolt or metal bracket on the engine. If you're unable to obtain a calibrated ignition tester, remove the wire from one of the spark plugs and using an insulated tool, pull back the boot and hold the end of the wire about 1/4-inch from a good ground. Crank the engine and watch the end of the tester or spark plug wire to see if bright blue, well-defined sparks occur.

3   If sparks occur, sufficient voltage is reaching the plug to fire it (repeat the check at the remaining plug wires to verify that the distributor cap and rotor are OK). However, the plugs themselves may be fouled, so remove and check them as described in Chapter 1.

4   If no sparks or intermittent sparks occur, check the cap, rotor and spark plug wires for damage and corrosion as described in Chapter 1. If moisture is present, dry out the cap and rotor, then reinstall the cap and repeat the spark test.

5   If there's still no spark on 1998 and 1999 V6 models, detach the coil secondary wire from the distributor cap and hook it up to the tester (reattach the plug wire to the spark plug), then repeat the spark check. Again, if you don't have a tester, hold the end of the wire about 1/4-inch from a good ground.

6   If there's still no spark on four-cylinder models, check the condition of the spring and carbon button inside the distributor cap for burn marks or damage. Replace the cap if necessary.

7   If sparks now occur, the distributor cap, rotor or plug wire(s) may be defective.

8   If no sparks occur, check the primary wire connections at the coil to make sure they're clean and tight. Check for voltage to

6.2 To use a calibrated ignition tester, simply disconnect a spark plug wire, connect it to the tester, clip the tester to a convenient ground and operate the starter with the ignition On – if there is enough power to fire the plug, sparks will be visible between the electrode tip and the tester body

the coil on the primary circuit from the ignition switch **(see illustration)**. **Note:** *Because the ignition coil is mounted inside the distributor on the four-cylinder models, it is necessary to remove the distributor cap, disconnect the leads from the ignition coil and then check for battery voltage to the ignition coil on the black/yellow terminal* **(see illustration 7.5)**. Make any necessary repairs, then repeat the check again.

9   If voltage exists at the ignition coil and there still are no sparks, check the primary and secondary resistance of the ignition coil (see Section 7). If an open is found (verified by an infinite reading), replace the coil.

10   If the coil is okay, check the Ignition Control Module (ICM) for proper operation (see Section 8).

11   Additional checks on the PGM-IG system should be performed by a dealer service department or other qualified repair shop.

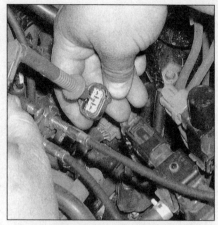

6.8 Check for battery voltage at the ignition coil with the ignition key ON (engine not running) (1998 and 1999 V6 engine)

7   Ignition coil - check and replacement

Four-cylinder engine
Check
Refer to illustrations 7.4a, 7.4b and 7.5

1   Make sure the ignition switch is turned OFF for the following checks.

2   Remove the distributor cap, rotor and the cover.

3   Remove the electrical connectors from the ignition coil primary terminals.

4   Using an ohmmeter, touch the probes to the primary terminals (A and B) of the coil, measure the primary resistance and compare your reading to the value listed in this Chapter's Specifications **(see illustrations)**.

5   Touch the probes to the secondary winding terminal and the positive primary terminal (A), measure the secondary resistance and compare your reading to the resistance value listed in this Chapter's Specifications **(see illustration)**.

6   The figures in the specifications will vary

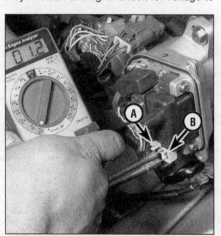

7.4a Ignition coil primary terminal details (non-VTEC four-cylinder engine)

7.4b Ignition coil primary terminal details (VTEC four-cylinder engine)

7.5 Check the resistance between the coil positive terminal (A) and the high-tension (secondary) terminal

7.10 Ignition coil mounting screws (four-cylinder engine)

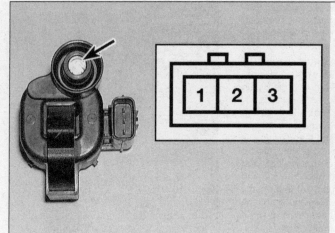

7.15 On 1998 and 1999 V6 engines, check the resistance between the primary terminals (1 and 3), then check the resistance between the secondary winding terminal (arrow) and the middle terminal (2)

somewhat with the temperature of the coil. The specified resistance values are for a coil temperature of about 70-degrees F.

7   If the coil fails either check, replace it with a new part.

Replacement

Refer to illustration 7.10

8   Detach the cable from the negative terminal of the battery. **Caution:** *The radio in your vehicle is equipped with an anti-theft system, make sure you have the correct activation code before disconnecting the battery.*

9   Remove the distributor cap (see Chapter 1) and leak cover (if equipped). Remove the electrical connectors from the ignition coil primary terminals.

10   Remove the coil mounting screws and slide the coil out from the distributor **(see illustration)**.

11   Installation is the reverse of removal.

1998 and 1999 V6 engine

Check

Refer to illustration 7.15

12   Make sure the ignition switch is turned

OFF for the following checks.

13   Detach the high-tension lead from the secondary winding terminal (coil tower).

14   Remove the 3-pin electrical connector from the ignition coil primary terminals.

15   Using an ohmmeter, touch the probes to the primary terminals (1 and 3) of the coil, measure the primary resistance and compare your reading to the value listed in this Chapter's Specifications **(see illustration)**.

16   Touch the probes to the secondary winding terminal and the middle terminal (2), measure the secondary resistance and compare your reading to the resistance value listed in this Chapter's Specifications.

17   The figures in the specifications will vary somewhat with the temperature of the coil. The specified resistance values are for a coil temperature of about 70-degrees F.

18   If the coil fails either check, replace it with a new part.

Replacement

Refer to illustration 7.21

19   Detach the cable from the negative terminal of the battery. **Caution:** *The radio in your vehicle is equipped with an anti-theft system, make sure you have the correct acti-*

vation code before disconnecting the battery.

20   Disconnect all electrical connections from the ignition coil.

21   Remove the bolts that retain the coil **(see illustration)**.

22   Installation is the reverse of removal.

2000 and later V6 engine

Check

23   Because of the complexity of this design and difficulty of testing, it is recommended that these coils be tested by a dealer service department or other qualified shop.

Replacement

24   To access the coils on the front cylinder bank, remove the ignition coil cover.

25   **Note:** *Make sure the ignition switch is turned OFF before detaching any connectors.* After cleaning the area around the coil, push the tab to detach the 3-pin electrical connector at the coil that you are removing.

26   Remove the Allen-head coil mounting screw.

27   Pull the coil straight out, and off of the spark plug.

28   Installation is the reverse of removal.

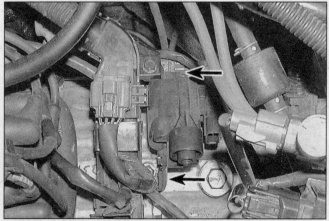

7.21 Ignition coil mounting bolts (arrows) (1998 and 1999 V6 engine)

8.1a Disconnect the distributor harness connector (arrow) and check for battery voltage on terminal number 2 with the ignition key ON (engine not running) (1998 and 1999 V6 engine)

8.1b Disconnect the connectors from the ignition module (arrow) and check for battery voltage on the black/yellow wire with the ignition key ON (engine not running) (four-cylinder engine)

8   Ignition Control Module (ICM) - check and replacement

Note: *For 2000 and later V6 models, see Section 7.*

Check

Refer to illustrations 8.1a and 8.1b

1   Check for battery voltage to the ignition module. Disconnect the harness connector from the ICM unit. With the ignition key turned ON (engine not running), check for voltage:

a) *On 1998 and 1999 V6 engines, install the probes of the voltmeter between the black/yellow wire (terminal number 2) and body ground* **(see illustration)**. *There should be battery voltage.*

b) *On four-cylinder engines, it will be necessary to remove the distributor cap and the rotor and remove the black/yellow wire from the ICM* **(see illustration)**. *Check for battery voltage between the black/yellow wire and body ground with the ignition key ON (engine not running).*

2   Check the ignition circuit and related

8.9a Ignition control module mounting bolts (arrows) (four-cylinder engine)

components. If there is no voltage to the ignition module, check the circuit from the ignition module to the ignition switch. First check the ignition switch fuses number 41 (100 amp) and number 42 (50 amp) in the underhood fuse/relay box. If these fuses are intact check the number 6 (15 amp) fuse in the fuse/relay box under the driver's side dashboard. Follow the circuit carefully and make sure the ignition switch delivers battery voltage to the ICM with the key ON. Refer to the wiring schematics at the end of Chapter 12 for additional information.

3   Check for battery voltage from the ignition coil to the ignition module. With the ignition key turned ON (engine not running), check for voltage between the white/black (VTEC four-cylinder), white/blue wire (non-VTEC four-cylinder) or the blue wire (1998 and 1999 V6 models) and body ground. There should be battery voltage.

4   If there is no voltage, check the circuit between the corresponding wire and the ignition coil. Also check for an open circuit inside the ignition coil by checking for continuity between terminals A and B (four-cylinder models) and 1 and 3 (1998 and 1999 V6 engines) of the ignition coil (see Section 7).

5   If the ignition coil and circuits are good and there is still no spark, replace the ICM.

8.9b Ignition control module mounting screws (arrows) (1998 and 1999 V6 engine)

Replacement

Refer to illustrations 8.9a and 8.9b

6   Disconnect the negative battery cable from the battery terminal. **Caution:** *The radio in your vehicle is equipped with an anti-theft system, make sure you have the correct activation code before disconnecting the battery.*

7   Remove the distributor cap and cover from the distributor (see Chapter 1).

8   Remove all the electrical connectors from the ICM unit.

9   Remove the two mounting screws from the ICM body and pull the ICM unit straight out **(see illustrations)**.

10   Installation is the reverse of removal.

9   Distributor - removal and installation

Removal

Refer to illustrations 9.5a and 9.5b

1   Detach the cable from the negative battery terminal. **Caution:** *The radio in your vehicle is equipped with an anti-theft system, make sure you have the correct activation code before disconnecting the battery.*

2   Detach any clamps and electrical connectors on the distributor. Mark the wires and hoses so they can be returned to their original locations.

3   Look for a raised number or letter on the distributor cap. This marks the location for the number-one cylinder spark plug wire terminal. If the cap does not have a mark for the number-one terminal, locate the number-one spark plug and trace the wire back to the terminal on the cap.

4   Remove the distributor cap (see Chapter 1) and turn the engine over until the rotor is pointing toward the number-one spark plug terminal (see the locating TDC procedure in Chapter 2A or 2B).

5   Make a mark on the edge of the distributor base directly below the rotor tip **(see illustration)** and in line with it. Also, mark the distributor base and the cylinder head to ensure the distributor is installed correctly **(see illustration)**.

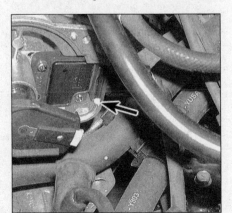

9.5a Make one mark directly underneath the rotor tip and another between the distributor base and the cylinder head

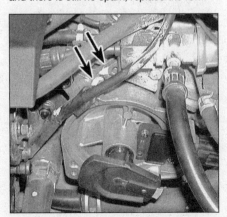

9.5b Mark the position of the distributor body in relation to the cylinder head (arrows) using white paint

6   If not already done, unplug the distributor connector.

7   Remove the distributor hold-down bolt(s) and pull out the distributor. **Caution:** *Do not turn the crankshaft while the distributor is out of the engine, or the alignment marks will be useless.*

Installation

Note: *If the crankshaft has been moved while the distributor is out, the number-one piston must be repositioned at TDC. This can be done by feeling for compression pressure at the number-one plug hole as the crankshaft is turned. Once compression is felt, align the ignition timing mark with the pointer.*

8   Install a new O-ring on the distributor housing.

9   Insert the distributor into the cylinder head in exactly the same relationship to the head that it was when removed. **Note:** *The lugs on the end of the distributor and the corresponding grooves in the camshaft end are offset to eliminate the possibility of installing the distributor 180-degrees out of phase.*

10   Recheck the alignment marks between the distributor base and the cylinder head to verify the distributor is in the same position it was in before removal. Also check the rotor to see if it's aligned with the mark you made on the distributor.

11   Loosely install the hold-down bolt(s).

12   The remainder of installation is the reverse of removal. Check the ignition timing and tighten the distributor hold-down bolt(s) securely.

10   Ignition timing - check

Refer to illustrations 10.3 and 10.6
Note: *This ignition timing procedure only checks the base timing setting specified by the factory. Timing cannot be adjusted, therefore the purpose of this check is to verify that the computer is controlling the ignition timing and that the base setting is correct. In most cases, the ignition system can be checked (see Section 6) but if the base setting remains incorrect, the PCM (computer) is defective. Take the vehicle to the dealer service department to verify and repair the ignition system problem(s).*

1   Start the engine and allow it to reach normal operating temperature.

2   Check and adjust the idle speed if necessary (see Chapter 1).

3   With the ignition off, locate the VECI label under the hood and read through and perform all preliminary instructions concerning ignition timing. Several special tools will be needed for this procedure **(see illustration)**.

4   With the ignition off, hook up an inductive pick-up timing light in accordance with the manufacturer's instructions. Connect the inductive pick-up lead of the timing light to the number-one spark plug wire. Refer to the Specifications in Chapters 2A or 2B for the location of the number 1 cylinder.

5   Refer to Chapter 6 **illustration 2.31** and

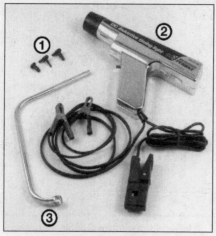

10.3 Tools needed to check and adjust the ignition timing

1   **Vacuum plugs** - *Vacuum hoses will, in most cases, have to be disconnected and plugged. Molded plugs in various shapes and sizes are available for this*

2   **Inductive pick-up timing light** - *Flashes a bright, concentrated beam of light when the number one spark plug fires. Connect the leads according to the instructions supplied with the light*

3   **Distributor wrench** - *On some models, the hold-down bolt for the distributor is difficult to reach and turn with conventional wrenches or sockets. A special wrench like this must be used*

connect terminal numbers 8 and 13 of the Data Link Connector with a jumper wire. This places the PCM in the base timing mode.

6   Locate the timing marks on the front pulley **(see illustration)**.

7   With the engine at normal operating temperature, start the engine and point the timing light at the timing pointer.

8   The red mark on the pulley will appear stationary and be aligned with the pointer if the timing is correct.

9   If the timing is incorrect, have the PCM checked by a dealer service department or other qualified repair facility.

10   Turn off the engine and remove the timing light.

11   Remove the jumper wire from the Data Link Connector.

11   Charging system - general information and precautions

The charging system includes the alternator, an internal voltage regulator, a charge indicator light, the battery, a fusible link and the wiring between all the components. The charging system supplies electrical power for the ignition system, the lights, the radio, etc. The alternator is driven by a drivebelt at the one end of the engine.

The alternator control system changes the voltage generated at the alternator in

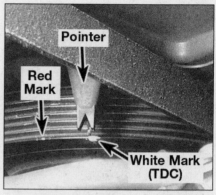

10.6 Be sure when viewing the timing mark on the pulley that you are directly above the pointer aiming the timing light down so as not to create an extreme angle

accordance with driving conditions. Depending upon electric load, vehicle speed, engine coolant temperature, accessories (air conditioning system, radio, cruise control etc.) and the intake air temperature, the system will adjust the amount of voltage generated, creating less load on the engine.

The purpose of the voltage regulator is to limit the alternator's voltage to a preset value. This prevents power surges, circuit overloads, etc., during peak voltage output.

The charging system doesn't ordinarily require periodic maintenance. However, the drivebelt, battery and wires and connections should be inspected at the intervals outlined in Chapter 1.

The dashboard warning light should come on when the ignition key is turned to On, but it should go off immediately after the engine is started. If it remains on, there is a malfunction in the charging system (see Section 12). Some vehicles are also equipped with a voltmeter. If the voltmeter indicates abnormally high or low voltage, check the charging system (see Section 12).

Be very careful when making electrical circuit connections to a vehicle equipped with an alternator and note the following:

a)   *When reconnecting wires to the alternator from the battery, be sure to note the polarity.*

b)   *Before using arc welding equipment to repair any part of the vehicle, disconnect the wires from the alternator and the battery terminals.*

c)   *Never start the engine with a battery charger connected.*

d)   *Always disconnect both battery leads before using a battery charger.*

e)   *The alternator is turned by an engine drivebelt which could cause serious injury it your hands, hair or clothes become entangled in it with the engine running.*

f)   *Because the alternator is connected directly to the battery, it could arc or cause a fire if overloaded or shorted out.*

g)   *Wrap a plastic bag over the alternator and secure it with rubber bands before steam cleaning the engine.*

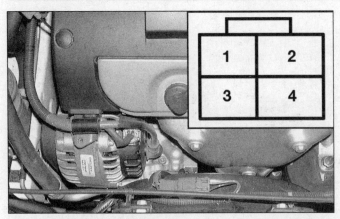

12.1 Disconnect the 4-pin harness connector on the backside of the alternator and ground the correct terminal to activate the charge light

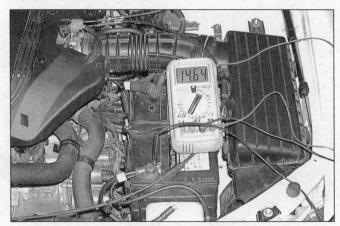

12.3 Install a digital voltmeter onto the battery terminals and observe voltage changes

12 Charging system - check

Refer to illustrations 12.1 and 12.3

1 If a malfunction occurs in the charging circuit, do not immediately assume that the alternator is causing the problem. First, check the following items:

a) *Make sure the battery cable clamps, where they connect to the battery, are clean and tight.*

b) *Test the condition of the battery (see Section 3). If it does not pass all the tests, replace it with a new battery.*

c) *Check the external alternator wiring and connections.*

d) *Check the drivebelt condition and tension (see Chapter 1).*

e) *Check the alternator mounting bolts for tightness.*

f) *Run the engine and check the alternator for abnormal noise.*

g) *Check the fusible links (if equipped) exiting the engine compartment fuse box (see Chapter 12). If they're burned, determine the cause and repair the circuit*

h) *Check the charge light on the dash. It should illuminate when the ignition key is turned ON (engine not running). If it does not, disconnect the 4 terminal connector from the back of the alternator and ground terminal number 3 (V6 engine) or number 4 (four-cylinder engine). The charge light should illuminate* **(see illustration)**. *If it does not, check fuse number 6 (15 amp) and the charge light bulb. If they are blown, replace them.*

i) *Make sure the on board computer has not stored any trouble codes for the Electric Load Detector (ELD) system. Refer to Chapter 6 for the code extraction process and the diagnostic procedures.*

2 With the ignition key off, check the battery voltage at the back of the alternator with no accessories (blower fan, radio, cigarette lighter, cooling fan, etc.) operating. It should be approximately 12.5 volts. It may be slightly higher if the engine had been operating within the last hour.

3 Check the charging voltage with the engine running. Start the engine, raise the engine rpm to 1500 and check the battery voltage again. It should now be approximately 13.8 to 14.8 volts **(see illustration)**.

4 Load the battery and observe the charging voltage. Turn on the high beam headlights, the A/C blower on HIGH, the windshield wipers and the radio. The voltage should drop and then come back up as each accessory is selected. If the charging system is working properly the voltage should stay above 13.5 volts. If the voltage drops below 13 volts, the charging system is weak or defective.

5 Lower the engine rpm back to idle and observe the charging voltage. The charging voltage should not drop below 13 volts with the decrease in engine rpm. Apply the brakes and observe the charging voltage at idle. It should remain above 13 volts. **Note:** *Some smaller amperage alternators may drop below 13 volts but, if they are in good condition, they will regulate the charging voltage to normal.*

6 Turn off all the electrical loads (high beam headlights, the A/C blower on HIGH, the windshield wipers and the radio), run the engine at 1600 rpm and watch the charging voltage rise. It should not rise above 15 volts. **Note:** *Cold temperatures will cause the volt-*

age readings to increase slightly while hot temperatures will lower the charging system voltage readings.

7 If the charging voltage does not exhibit distinct changes when engine rpm increases and accessory loads are added, the voltage regulator is defective. If the charging voltages are low and the drivebelts and battery are all in good condition, the alternator is defective. In this situation, replace the alternator and voltage regulator as a single unit.

13 Alternator - removal and installation

Removal

Refer to illustrations 13.3a, 13.3b and 13.5

1 Detach the cable from the negative terminal of the battery. **Caution:** *The radio in your vehicle is equipped with an anti-theft system, make sure you have the correct activation code before disconnecting the battery.*

2 Mark and detach the electrical connectors and any ground straps from the alternator.

3 On four-cylinder engines, loosen the alternator adjusting bolt and pivot bolt, then detach the drivebelt **(see illustrations)**.

13.3a On four-cylinder engines, loosen the pivot bolt located at the top of the alternator . . .

13.3b . . . then loosen the locknut, located at the bottom of the alternator on the pulley side, and the adusting bolt (arrow)

13.5 After the drivebelt has been removed, remove the alternator mounting bolts (arrows) (V6 engine)

14.2 Remove the three nuts (arrows) and detach the rear cover from the alternator

14.3 Once the rear cover is removed, remove the two screws (arrows) that retain the brush holder

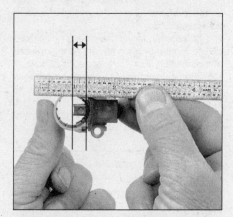

14.5 Measure the exposed length of the brushes and compare your measurements to the specified minimum length to determine if they should be replaced

Note: *The four-cylinder engine uses an adjustment bolt that runs parallel with the drivebelt. This adjustment bolt cannot be adjusted or loosened unless the locknut at the front of the alternator is loosened first. The V6 engine is equipped with an automatic tensioner and serpentine drivebelt. Refer to Chapter 1 for the removal procedure.*

4   On V6 engines, disconnect the electrical connector from the condenser fan, then remove the condenser fan assembly from the engine compartment (see Chapter 3).

5   On four-cylinder engines, remove the adjusting and pivot bolts and separate the alternator from the engine. On V6 engines, simply remove the mounting bolts **(see illustration)** from the upper and lower mounting bracket and maneuver the alternator out and around any wiring or hoses.

6   If you are replacing the alternator, take the old one with you when purchasing a replacement unit. Make sure the new/rebuilt unit looks identical to the old alternator. Look at the terminals - they should be the same in number, size and location as the terminals on the old alternator. Finally, look at the identification numbers - they will be stamped into

the housing or printed on a tag attached to the housing. Make sure the numbers are the same on both alternators.

7   Many new/rebuilt alternators DO NOT have a pulley installed, so you may have to switch the pulley from the old unit to the new/rebuilt one. When buying an alternator, find out the store's policy regarding pulleys; some stores will perform this service free of charge.

Installation

8   Installation is the reverse of removal.

9   After the alternator is installed, adjust the drivebelt tension (see Chapter 1).

10   Check the charging voltage to verify proper operation of the alternator (see Section 12).

---

14   Voltage regulator and alternator brushes - replacement

Note: *This voltage regulator and alternator brush replacement procedure applies only to the Nippondenso alternators equipped on four-cylinder models. The Mitsubishi/Delphi alternators on V6 engines must be replaced as a complete unit.*

1   Remove the alternator (see Section 13) and place it on a clean workbench.

Brushes

Refer to illustrations 14.2, 14.3 and 14.5

2   Remove the three rear cover nuts, the nut and terminal insulator and the rear cover **(see illustration)**.

3   Remove the two brush holder retaining screws **(see illustration)**.

4   Remove the brush holder from the rear end frame.

5   Measure the exposed length of the brush **(see illustration)** and compare it to the specified minimum length. If the length of the brush is less than the minimum listed in this Chapter's Specifications, replace the brush.

6   Make sure that each brush moves smoothly in the brush holder.

14.12 Remove the voltage regulator screws (arrows)

7   Install the brush holder by depressing the brush with a small screwdriver to clear the shaft.

8   Install the brush holder screws into the rear frame.

9   Install the rear cover and tighten the three nuts securely.

10   Install the terminal insulator and tighten it with the nut.

11   Install the alternator (see Section 13).

Voltage regulator

Refer to illustration 14.12

12   Perform steps I through 3 in this section. Remove the retaining screws securing the voltage regulator to the rear frame of the alternator **(see illustration)**.

13   Lift the voltage regulator from the alternator assembly.

14   Installation is the reverse of removal.

---

15   Starting system - general information and precautions

The sole function of the starting system is to turn over the engine quickly enough to

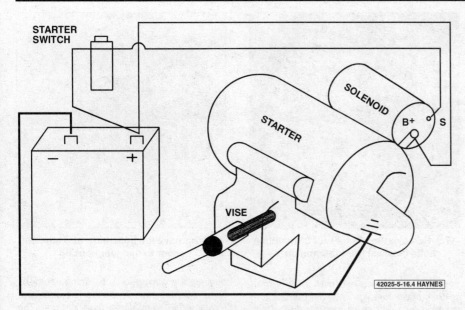

STARTER
SWITCH

SOLENOID

STARTER

B+   S

VISE

42025-5-16.4 HAYNES

16.4 Starter motor bench testing details

allow it to start.

The starting system consists of the battery, the starter motor, the starter solenoid and the wires connecting them. The solenoid is mounted directly on the starter motor.

The solenoid/starter motor assembly is installed on the upper part of the engine, next to the transaxle bellhousing.

When the ignition key is turned to the Start position, the starter solenoid is actuated through the starter control circuit. The starter solenoid then connects the battery to the starter. The battery supplies the electrical energy to the starter motor, which does the actual work of cranking the engine.

The starter motor on vehicles equipped with manual transaxles can only be operated when the clutch pedal is depressed; the starter on vehicles equipped with automatic transaxles can only be operated when the selector lever is in Park or Neutral.

Always observe the following precautions when working on the starting system:

a) *Excessive cranking of the starter motor can overheat it and cause serious damage. Never operate the starter motor for more than 15 seconds at a time without pausing to allow it to cool for at least two minutes.*

b) *The starter is connected directly to the battery and could arc or cause a fire if mishandled, overloaded or shorted out.*

c) *Always detach the cable from the negative terminal of the battery before working on the starting system.*

16 Starter motor and circuit - check

Refer to illustration 16.4

1   If a malfunction occurs in the starting circuit, do not immediately assume that the starter is causing the problem. First, check the following items:

a) *Make sure the battery cable clamps, where they connect to the battery, are clean and tight.*

b) *Check the condition of the battery cables (see Section 4). Replace any defective battery cables with new parts.*

c) *Test the condition of the battery (see Section 3). If it does not pass all the tests, replace it with a new battery.*

d) *Check the starter solenoid wiring and connections. Refer to Chapter 12 wiring diagrams.*

e) *Check the starter mounting bolts for tightness.*

f) *Check the fusible links (if equipped) exiting the engine compartment fuse box (see Chapter 12). If they're burned, determine the cause and repair the circuit. Also, check the ignition switch circuit for correct operation (see Chapter 12).*

g) *Check the operation of the gear position switch (automatic transaxle) or clutch start circuit (manual transaxle). Make sure the shift lever is in PARK or NEUTRAL. (automatic transaxle) or the clutch pedal is pressed (manual transaxle). Refer to Chapter 7 for the gear position switch check and adjustment procedure. Refer to Chapter 12 wiring diagrams for the necessary circuit checks for the clutch activation system. These systems must operate correctly to provide battery voltage to the starter solenoid.*

h) *Check the operation of the starter cut relay. The starter cut relay is located in the fuse/relay box inside the engine compartment. Refer to Chapter 12 for the testing procedure.*

2   If the starter does not activate when the ignition switch is turned to the start position,

check for battery voltage to the solenoid. This will determine if the solenoid is receiving the correct voltage signal from the ignition switch. Install a voltmeter to the starter solenoid "S" terminal while an assistant turns the ignition switch to the start position, observe the voltmeter. It should be approximately battery voltage. If voltage is not available, refer to the wiring diagrams in Chapter 12 and check all the fuses and relays in series with the starting system. Locate the fuse/relay panel in the driver's side dash area and check fuse number 13 (7.5 amp). Also, check the starter cut relay for correct operation. Refer to Chapter 12 for the location of the driver's side relay center along with the relay checks. If voltage is available but there is not movement from the starter motor, remove the starter from the engine (see Section 17) and bench test the starter (see Step 4).

3   If the starter turns over slowly, check the starter cranking voltage and the current draw from the battery. This test must be performed with the starter assembly on the engine. Crank the engine over (for 10 seconds or less) and observe the battery voltage. It should not drop below 8.0 volts on manual transaxle models or 8.5 volts on automatic transaxle models. Also, observe the current draw using an amp meter. It should not exceed 380 amps on automatic transaxle models or 280 amps on manual transaxle models. If the starter motor exceeds these values, replace it with a new unit. There are several conditions that may affect the starter cranking potential. The battery must be in good condition and the battery cold-cranking rating must not be under-rated for the particular application. Be sure to check the battery specifications carefully. The battery terminals and cables must be clean and not corroded. Also, in cases of extreme cold temperatures, make sure the battery and/or engine block is warmed before performing the tests.

4   If the starter is receiving voltage but does not activate, remove and check the starter/solenoid assembly on the bench. Most likely the solenoid is defective. In some rare cases, the engine may be seized so be sure to try and rotate the crankshaft pulley (see Chapter 2A or 2B) before proceeding. With the starter/solenoid assembly mounted in a vise on the bench, install one jumper cable from the negative terminal (—) to the body of the starter **(see illustration)**. Install another jumper cable from the positive terminal (+) on the battery to the B+ terminal on the starter. Install a starter switch and apply battery voltage to the solenoid S terminal (for 10 seconds or less) and observe the solenoid plunger, shift lever and overrunning clutch extend and rotate the pinion drive. If the pinion drive extends but does not rotate, the solenoid is operating but the starter motor is defective. If there is no movement but the solenoid clicks, the solenoid and/or the starter motor is defective. If the solenoid plunger extends and rotates the pinion drive, the starter/solenoid assembly is working properly.

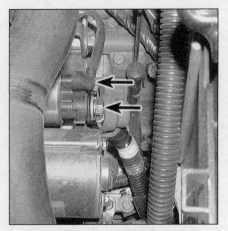

17.4 Disconnect the starter motor electrical connectors (arrows)

17.5 Remove the starter motor mounting bolts (arrows) from the transaxle

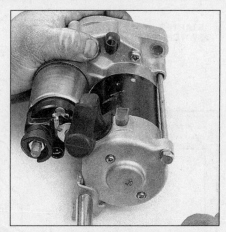

18.4 Remove the bolts that retain the end cover to the gear housing

18.5 Remove the screws (arrows) that retain the gear housing to the gear housing cover

17   Starter motor - removal and installation

Refer to illustrations 17.4 and 17.5

1   Detach the cable from the negative terminal of the battery. **Caution:** *The radio in*

your vehicle is equipped with an anti-theft system, make sure you have the correct activation code before disconnecting the battery.
3   Remove the battery and the battery tray from the engine compartment (see Section 3).
3   Remove the lower radiator hose and the wiring harness from the starter bracket. V6 engines mount the automatic transaxle cooling lines near the starter assembly. Make sure they are positioned out of the way.
4   Clearly label, then disconnect the wires from the terminals on the starter motor solenoid **(see illustration)**. Disconnect any clips securing the wiring to the starter.
5   Remove the mounting bolts **(see illustration)** and detach the starter.
6   Installation is the reverse of removal.

18   Starter solenoid - removal and installation

Refer to illustrations 18.4, 18.5, 18.6 and 18.7
Note: *four-cylinder manual transaxle models are equipped with Nippondenso starters while four-cylinder automatics and V6*

engines are equipped with Mitsuba starters. Nippondenso starters cannot be serviced. Replace the entire starter /solenoid unit. The following procedure applies to only Mitsuba starter assemblies.
1   Disconnect the cable from the negative terminal of the battery. **Caution:** *The radio in your vehicle is equipped with an anti-theft system, make sure you have the correct activation code before disconnecting the battery.*
2   Remove the starter motor (see Section 17).
3   Disconnect the large wire from the solenoid to the starter motor terminal.
4   Remove the long bolts that secure the end cover to the gear housing **(see illustration)** and remove the armature housing from the assembly.
5   Remove the screws from the gear housing **(see illustration)** and separate it from the gear housing cover
6   Remove the screws from the gear housing **(see illustration)** and separate the solenoid.
7   Installation is the reverse of removal. Be sure to apply a slight amount of grease to the solenoid lever and the plunger before installation **(see illustration)**.

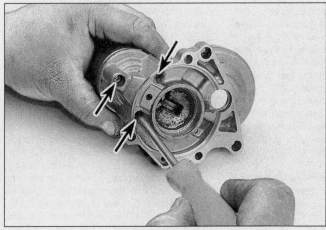

18.6 Remove the screws (arrows) that retain the solenoid to the gear housing

18.7 Apply grease to the lever and plunger (arrow) before reassembly

Chapter 6
Emissions and engine control systems

Contents

Specifications

General

Oxygen sensor voltage	
Open loop	0.1 to 0.2 volts
Closed loop	0.1 to 0.9 volts
CKP/TDC sensor resistance	1,850 to 2,450 ohms
CYP sensor resistance	800 to 1,500 ohms

1   General information

Refer to illustrations 1.1a, 1.1b and 1.5

To prevent pollution of the atmosphere from incompletely burned and evaporating gases, and to maintain good driveability and fuel economy, a number of emission control systems are incorporated **(see illustrations)**. They include the:

On-Board Diagnostic (OBD) system
Electronic engine controls (PGM-FI)
Electronic Load Detector (ELD)
Exhaust Gas Recirculation (EGR) system
Evaporative Emissions Control (EVAP) system
Positive Crankcase Ventilation (PCV) system
Catalytic converter

The Sections in this Chapter include general descriptions, checking procedures within the scope of the home mechanic and component replacement procedures (when possible) for each of the systems listed above.

Before assuming that an emissions control system is malfunctioning, check the fuel and ignition systems carefully. The diagnosis of some emission control devices requires specialized tools, equipment and training. If checking and servicing become too difficult or if a procedure is beyond your ability, consult a dealer service department or other repair shop. Remember, the most frequent cause of emissions problems is simply a loose or broken wire or vacuum hose, so always check the hose and wiring connections first.

This doesn't mean, however, that emissions control systems are particularly difficult to maintain and repair. You can quickly and easily perform many checks and do most of the regular maintenance at home with common tune-up and hand tools. **Note**: *Because of a Federally mandated extended warranty which covers the emissions control system components, check with your dealer about warranty coverage before working on any emissions-related systems. Once the warranty has expired, you may wish to perform some of the component checks and/or replacement procedures in this Chapter to save money.*

Pay close attention to any special precautions outlined in this Chapter. It should be noted that the illustrations of the various systems may not exactly match the system installed on your vehicle because of changes

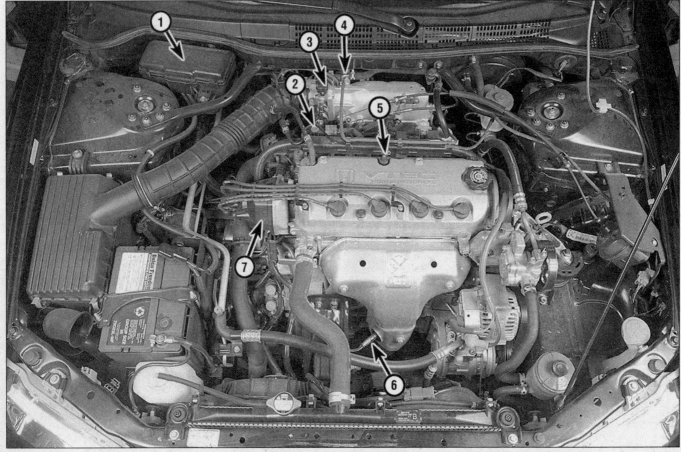

1.1a Typical emission and engine control system components - four-cylinder engine

1 *Electronic Load Detector (part of fuse/relay center)*	5 *Positive Crankcase Ventilation (PCV) valve*
2 *Exhaust Gas Recirculation (EGR) valve*	6 *Oxygen sensor (O2)*
3 *Manifold Absolute Pressure (MAP) sensor*	7 *Cylinder Position sensor (CYP) (part of distributor)*
4 *Idle Air Control (IAC) valve*	

made by the manufacturer during production or from year-to-year.

A Vehicle Emissions Control Information (VECI) label is attached to the underside of the hood **(see illustration)**. This label contains important emissions specifications and adjustment information. Part of this label, the

Vacuum Hose Routing Diagram, provides a vacuum hose schematic with emissions components identified. When servicing the engine or emissions systems, the VECI label and the vacuum hose routing diagram in your particular vehicle should always be checked for up-to-date information.

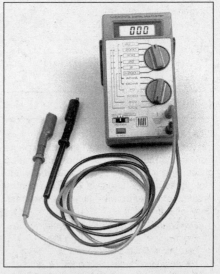

2.1 Digital multimeters can be used for testing all types of circuits; because of their high impedance, they are much more accurate than analog meters for measuring low-voltage computer circuits

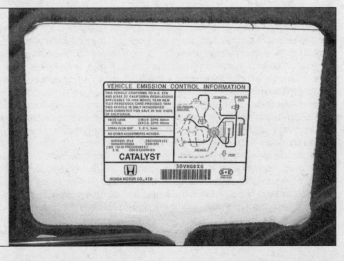

1.5 The Vehicle Emission Control Information (VECI) label is located in the engine compartment and contains information on the emission devices on your vehicle, vacuum line routing, etc. (V6 engine shown)

1.1b Typical emission and engine control system components - 1998 and 1999 V6 engine shown

1   Electric Load Detector (part of fuse/relay center)
2   Positive Crankcase Ventilation (PCV) valve
3   Manifold Absolute Pressure (MAP) sensor
4   Throttle Position Sensor (TPS)
5   Exhaust Gas Recirculation (EGR) valve

2   On Board Diagnosis (OBD) system and trouble codes

Diagnostic tool information

Refer to illustrations 2.1 and 2.2

1   A digital multimeter is necessary for checking fuel injection and emission related components **(see illustration)**. A digital volt-ohmmeter is preferred over the older style analog multimeter for several reasons. The analog multimeter cannot display the volts-ohms or amps measurement in hundredths and thousandths increments. When working with electronic circuits which are often very low voltage, this accurate reading is most important. Another good reason for the digital multimeter is the high impedance circuit. The digital multimeter is equipped with a high resistance internal circuitry (10 million ohms). Because a voltmeter is hooked up in parallel with the circuit when testing, it is vital that none of the voltage being measured should be allowed to travel the parallel path set up by the meter itself. This dilemma does not show itself when measuring larger amounts of voltage (9 to 12 volt circuits) but if you are

measuring a low voltage circuit such as the oxygen sensor signal voltage, a fraction of a volt may be a significant amount when diagnosing a problem.

2   Hand-held scanners are the most powerful and versatile tools for analyzing engine management systems used on later model vehicles **(see illustration)**. Each brand scan tool must be examined carefully to match the year, make and model of the vehicle you are working on. Often, interchangeable cartridges are available to access the particular manufacturer (Ford, GM, Chrysler, etc.). Some manufacturers will specify by continent (Asia, Europe, USA, etc.).

3   With the arrival of the current Federally mandated emission control system (OBD-II), a specially designed scanner must be used. At this time, several manufacturers offer OBD-II scan tools for the home mechanic. Ask the parts salesman at a local auto parts store for additional information concerning availability. It is possible to access the trouble codes on models covered by this manual using a jumper wire positioned on the correct terminal designations on the 16-pin diagnostic connector. Refer to Step 28 for the complete procedure.

2.2 Scanners like the Actron Scantool and the AutoXray XP240 are powerful diagnostic aids - programmed with comprehensive diagnostic information, they can tell you just about anything you want to know about your engine management system

On Board Diagnostic system general description

4   The On Board Diagnostic system incorporates a series of diagnostic monitors that detect and identify emissions systems faults and store the information in the computer memory. The system also tests sensors and output actuators, diagnoses drive cycles, freezes data and clears codes.

5   All engines and powertrain combinations described in this manual are equipped with the On Board Diagnosis II (OBD-II) system. This system consists of an onboard computer, known as the Powertrain Control Module (PCM), and information sensors, which monitor various functions of the engine and send data to the PCM. Based on the data and the information programmed into the computer's memory, the PCM generates output signals to control various engine functions via control relays, solenoids and other output actuators. The diagnostic information can be accessed using an OBD-II compliant SCAN tool through the 16-pin Data Link Connector (DLC) located under the instrument panel on the driver's side. **Note:** *It is possible to access the OBD II trouble codes on models covered by this manual using a jumper wire positioned on the correct terminal designations on the 16-pin OBD II connector. Refer to Step 29 for the complete procedure.*

6   The PCM is the "brain" of the emissions and engine control system. It receives data from a number of sensors and other electronic components (switches, relays, etc.). Based on the information it receives, the PCM generates output signals to control various relays, solenoids and other actuators. The PCM is specifically calibrated to optimize the emissions, fuel economy and driveability of the vehicle. Because of a Federally mandated ex-tended warranty which covers the emissions and engine control system components and because any owner-induced damage to the PCM, the sensors and/or the control devices may void the warranty, it isn't a good idea to attempt diagnosis or replace of the PCM at home while the vehicle is under warranty. Take the vehicle to a dealer service department if the PCM or a system component malfunctions.

Information sensors

7   **Oxygen sensors (O2S)** - The O2S generates a voltage signal that varies with the difference between the oxygen content of the exhaust and the oxygen in the surrounding air.

8   **Crankshaft Position (CKP) sensor -** The CKP sensor provides information on crankshaft position and the engine speed to the PCM. The PCM uses this information to determine fuel injection and ignition timing.

9   **Cylinder Position (CYP) sensor -** The CYP sensor produces a signal in which the PCM uses to identify number 1 cylinder and to time the sequential fuel injection.

10   **Top Dead Center (TDC) sensor -** The TDC sensor determines the ignition timing at start up.

11   **Engine Coolant Temperature (ECT) sensor -** The ECT sensor monitors engine coolant temperature and sends the PCM a voltage signal that affects PCM control of the fuel mixture, ignition timing, and EGR operation.

12   **Intake Air Temperature (IAT) sensor -** The IAT provides the PCM with intake air temperature information. The PCM uses this information to control fuel flow, ignition timing, and EGR system operation.

13   **Throttle Position Sensor (TPS) -** The TPS senses throttle movement and position, then transmits a voltage signal to the PCM. This signal enables the PCM to determine when the throttle is closed, in a cruise position, or wide open.

14   **Manifold Absolute Pressure (MAP) sensor -** The MAP sensor measures the amount (volume) of the intake airflow entering the engine. The MAP sensor, along with the IAT sensor, provide airflow volume and air temperature information for the most precise fuel metering.

15   **Barometric pressure sensor -** the barometric pressure sensor converts atmospheric pressure into a voltage signal for use by the PCM. The PCM uses this information to determine fuel injection duration. The barometric sensor is located inside the PCM and not serviced separately.

16   **Knock sensor -** the knock sensor detects detonation or "spark knock" and signals the PCM accordingly. The PCM will retard the timing until the spark knock is eliminated.

17   **Vehicle Speed Sensor (VSS) -** The vehicle speed sensor provides information to the PCM to indicate vehicle speed.

18   **EGR valve lift sensor -** The EGR valve lift sensor is used to monitor the position of the EGR pintle in relation to the operating conditions of the EGR system.

19   **Fuel tank pressure sensor -** The fuel tank pressure sensor is part of the evaporative emission control system and is used to monitor vapor pressure in the fuel tank. The PCM uses this information to turn on and off the purge valves and solenoids of the evaporative emission system.

20   **Power Steering Pressure (PSP) switch -** The PSP sensor is used to increase transaxle hydraulic line pressure during low-speed vehicle maneuvers.

21   **Transaxle sensors -** In addition to the vehicle speed sensor, the PCM receives input signals from the following sensors inside the transaxle or connected to it: (a) the mainshaft speed sensor and the (b) the countershaft speed sensor.

22   **A/C clutch control switch -** When battery voltage is applied to the air conditioning compressor solenoid, a signal is sent to the PCM, which interprets the signal as an added load created by the compressor and increases engine idle speed accordingly to compensate.

Output actuators

23   **PGM-FI main relay -** The main PCM power relay doubles as a fuel pump relay and main relay. It is activated by the ignition switch and supplies battery power to the PCM and the PGM-FI system when the switch is in the Start or Run position. Refer to Chapter 4 or your owner's manual for more information on relay location.

24   **Fuel injectors -** The PCM opens the fuel injectors individually in firing order sequence. The PCM also controls the time the injector is open, called the "pulse width." The pulse width of the injector (measured in milliseconds) determines the amount of fuel delivered. For more information on the fuel delivery system and the fuel injectors, including injector replacement, refer to Chapter 4.

25   **Ignition Control Module (ICM) -** The ICM triggers the ignition coil and determines proper spark advance based on inputs from the PCM. All models mount the ignition control module within the distributor assembly. Refer to Chapter 5 for more information on the Ignition Control Module.

26   **Idle air control (IAC) valve -** The IAC valve controls the amount of air to bypass the throttle plate when the throttle valve is closed or at idle position. The IAC valve opening and the resulting airflow is controlled by the PCM.

27   **EVAP control canister vent shut valve -** The evaporative emission canister vent shut valve is a solenoid valve, operated by the PCM to purge the fuel vapor canister and route fuel vapor to the intake manifold for combustion.

28   **Canister purge control solenoid -** The evaporative emission canister purge control solenoid is operated by the PCM during the OBD-II evaporative emission monitor and during an emission test of the evaporative system.

Obtaining diagnostic trouble codes

Refer to illustration 2.31

29   The PCM will illuminate the CHECK ENGINE light (also known as the Malfunction Indicator Light) on the dash if it recognizes a component fault for two consecutive drive cycles. It will continue to set the light until the codes are cleared or the PCM does not detect any malfunction for three or more consecutive drive cycles. The diagnostic codes for the OBD-II system can be extracted from the PCM using two methods. The first method requires a jumper wire to bridge terminals number 8 and number 13 on the 16-pin DLC. The second method requires a special SCAN tool that is programmed to interface with the OBD-II system by plugging into the DLC. The following procedure describes the jumper wire method. If necessary, have the codes extracted by a dealer service department or other qualified repair shop.

30   Turn the ignition key On (engine not running) and make sure the CHECK ENGINE light on the instrument panel is on. If the light is off, replace the bulb. After verifying the bulb is good, turn the ignition key Off.

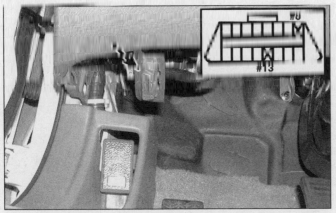

2.31 The Data Link Connector (DLC) (arrow) is located under the instrument panel on the driver's side - Connect terminals 8 and 13 with a jumper wire to obtain the trouble codes

2.33 Location of the CLOCK BACK-UP fuse number 13 (arrow) in the passenger's side fuse/relay panel

31 Locate the Data Link Connector (DLC) (under the instrument panel on the driver's side) and using a small jumper wire, connect terminals 8 and 13 **(see illustration)**. Be careful not to damage the terminals in the DLC.

32 Turn the ignition key On and observe the CHECK ENGINE light on the dash. It will flash the trouble codes in a clear and distinct manner. The first long flash will represent the first digit of the code. The second digit of the code will flash using short flashes. For example, four long flashes will represent the first digit, 4, followed by two short flashes is code 42. Record all the trouble codes onto a notepad and observe the computer codes once again to double-check the accuracy as the PCM repeats the list of trouble codes after all the codes have been displayed one time. If there are no trouble codes stored, the CHECK ENGINE light on the dash will not flash.

Clearing codes

Refer to illustration 2.33

33 After the system has been repaired, the codes can be cleared from the PCM memory. To clear the codes, remove the number 13 fuse (7.5 amp) (CLOCK BACK-UP) **(see illustration)** from the fuse/relay panel located at the end instrument panel on the passenger's side for 10 seconds. Make sure the ignition key is OFF when removing the fuse. If necessary, have the codes cleared by a dealer service department or other qualified repair facility with a scan tool. **Caution:** *Do not disconnect the battery from the vehicle to clear the codes. This will erase stored operating parameters from the memory and cause the engine to run rough for a period of time while the computer relearns the information.*

34 Be sure to clear the codes from the PCM before a new electronic emission control component is installed onto the engine. The PCM will often store trouble codes during sensor malfunctions. The PCM will also record new trouble codes if a new sensor is allowed to operate before the parameters from the old sensor have been erased. Clearing the codes will allow the computer to relearn the new operating parameters relayed by the new component. During the computer relearning process, the engine may experience a rough idle or slight driveability changes. This period of time, however, should last no longer than 15 to 20 minutes.

Trouble Codes

Code	CHECK ENGINE light flash code	Probable cause
P0107	3	Manifold Absolute Pressure (MAP) sensor circuit low input
P0108	3	Manifold Absolute Pressure (MAP) sensor circuit high input
P0112	10	Intake Air Temperature (IAT) sensor circuit low input
P0113	10	Intake Air Temperature (IAT) sensor circuit high input
P0116	86	Electronic Coolant Temperature (ECT) sensor range/performance problem
P0117	6	Electronic Coolant Temperature (ECT) sensor circuit low input
P0118	6	Electronic Coolant Temperature (ECT) sensor circuit high input
P0122	7	Throttle Position Sensor (TPS) circuit low input
P0123	7	Throttle Position Sensor (TPS) circuit high input
P0131	1	Primary heated O2 sensor circuit low voltage
P0132	1	Primary heated O2 sensor circuit high voltage
P0133	61	Primary heated O2 sensor slow response
P0135	41	Primary heated O2 sensor circuit malfunction
P0137	63	Secondary heated O2 sensor circuit low voltage
P0138	63	Secondary heated O2 sensor circuit high voltage
P0139	63	Secondary heated O2 sensor slow response
P0141	65	Secondary heated O2 sensor heater circuit fault
P0171	45	System Adaptive fuel too lean
P0172	45	System Adaptive fuel too rich
P0300	71	Random misfire detected
P0301	71	Cylinder no. 1 misfire detected

Trouble Codes (continued)

Code	CHECK ENGINE light flash code	Probable cause
P0302	72	Cylinder no. 2 misfire detected
P0303	73	Cylinder no. 3 misfire detected
P0304	74	Cylinder no. 4 misfire detected
P0305 (V6)	75	Cylinder no. 5 misfire detected
P0306 (V6)	76	Cylinder no. 6 misfire detected
P0325 (4-cyl)	23	Knock sensor circuit fault
PO335	4	Crankshaft position sensor circuit malfunction
PO336	4	Crankshaft position sensor range performance
P0401	80	EGR insufficient flow detected
P0420	67	Catalyst system efficiency below threshold
P0452	91	EVAP fuel tank pressure sensor low input
P0453	91	EVAP fuel tank pressure sensor high input
P0500 (4-cyl M/T)	17	VSS fault
P0505	14	IAC valve system fault
P0715	70	Automatic transaxle malfunction
P0720	70	Automatic transaxle malfunction
P0725	70	Automatic transaxle malfunction
P0730	70	Automatic transaxle malfunction
P0740	70	Automatic transaxle malfunction
P0753	70	Automatic transaxle malfunction
P0758	70	Automatic transaxle malfunction
P0763	70	Automatic transaxle malfunction
P1106	13	Barometric pressure sensor circuit range performance malfunction
P1107	13	Barometric pressure sensor circuit low voltage
P1108	13	Barometric pressure sensor circuit high voltage
P1121	7	Throttle Position Sensor (TPS) circuit low input
P1122	7	Throttle Position Sensor (TPS) circuit high input
P1128	5	MAP sensor circuit low voltage
P1129	5	MAP sensor circuit high voltage
P1149 (4-cyl)	61	Primary heated O2 sensor circuit range malfunction
P1162 (4-cyl)	48	Primary heated O2 sensor circuit malfunction
P1163 (4-cyl)	61	Primary heated O2 sensor circuit slow response
P1164 (4-cyl)	61	Primary heated O2 sensor circuit range malfunction
P1165 (4-cyl)	61	Primary heated O2 sensor circuit range malfunction
P1166 (4-cyl)	41	Primary heated O2 sensor heater electrical malfunction
P1167 (4-cyl)	41	Primary heated O2 sensor heater system malfunction
P1253 (4-cyl)	21	VTEC system malfunction
P1257 (4-cyl)	22	VTEC system malfunction
P1258 (4-cyl)	22	VTEC system malfunction
P1259	22	VTEC system malfunction
P1297	20	Electric Load Detector (ELD) circuit low voltage
P1298	20	Electric Load Detector (ELD) circuit high voltage
P1359	8	CKP/TDC sensor disconnection
P1361	8	TDC sensor intermittent voltage signal
P1362	8	TDC sensor no voltage signal
P1366 (V6)	58	TDC sensor number 2 intermittent voltage signal
P1367 (V6)	58	TDC sensor number 2 no voltage signal
P1381 (4-cyl)	9	CYP sensor intermittent voltage signal
P1382 (4-cyl)	9	CYP sensor no voltage signal
P1456	90	EVAP control system leak near fuel tank
P1457	90	EVAP control system leak near canister
P1491	12	EGR valve lift insufficient
P1498	12	EGR valve lift sensor high voltage
P1519	14	IAC valve circuit failure

Code	Probable cause

Note: *The following codes do not flash the CHECK ENGINE light. A scan tool is required to read the codes.*

Code	Probable cause
P1607	PCM internal circuit failure
P1705	Automatic transaxle failure
P1706	Automatic transaxle failure
P1738	Automatic transaxle failure
P1739	Automatic transaxle failure
P1753	Automatic transaxle failure
P1768	Automatic transaxle failure
P1773	Automatic transaxle failure
P1791	Automatic transaxle failure

3 Powertrain Control Module (PCM) - removal and installation

Refer to illustration 3.4 and 3.5

Warning: *The models covered by this manual are equipped with Supplemental Restraint systems (SRS), more commonly known as airbags. Always disable the airbag system and wait three minutes before working in the vicinity of the impact sensors, steering column or instrument panel to avoid the possibility of accidental deployment of the airbag, which could cause personal injury (see Chapter 12). The yellow wiring harnesses and connectors routed through the console and instrument panel are for this system. Do not use electrical test equipment on any of the airbag system wiring or tamper with them in any way.*

Caution: *To avoid electrostatic discharge damage to the PCM, handle the PCM only by its case. Do not touch the electrical terminals during removal and installation. If available, ground yourself to the vehicle with a anti-static ground strap, available at computer supply stores.*

Note: *The PCM is a component of the vehicle security system (known as the Immobilizer system). If a new PCM is installed in the vehicle, the immobilizer code must be programmed into the new computer by a dealership service department before the vehicle will start. If it's necessary to install a new PCM, this procedure may be better left to a dealer service department.*

3.5 Remove the PCM mounting bolts (arrows)

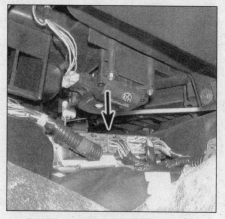

3.4 Disconnect the PCM electrical connectors (arrow)

1 The Powertrain Control Module (PCM) is located inside the passenger compartment under the dashboard near the center console area.

2 Disable the airbag system (see Chapter 12). **Caution:** *If the stereo in your vehicle is equipped with an anti-theft system, make sure you have the correct activation code before disconnecting the battery.*

3 Remove the carpet from the passenger's and driver's side of the center console (see Chapter 11) under the dash. Place the carpet sufficiently out of the way to expose the PCM.

4 Unplug the electrical connectors from the PCM **(see illustration)**. **Caution:** *The ignition switch must be turned OFF when* pulling out or plugging in the electrical connectors to prevent damage to the PCM.

5 Remove the retaining bolts from the PCM bracket **(see illustration)**.

6 Carefully remove the PCM. **Note:** *Avoid any static electricity damage to the computer by grounding yourself to the body before touching the PCM and using a special anti-static pad to store the PCM on once it is removed.*

7 Installation is the reverse of removal. If any PCM other than the original was installed, have the PCM immobilizer code programmed at a dealer service department.

4 Throttle Position Sensor (TPS) - check and replacement

Check

Refer to illustration 4.2

1 The Throttle Position Sensor (TPS) is located on the end of the throttle shaft on the throttle body. By monitoring the output voltage from the TPS, the PCM can determine fuel delivery based on throttle valve angle (driver demand). A broken or loose TPS can cause intermittent bursts of fuel from the injector and an unstable idle because the PCM thinks the throttle is moving. A problem with the TPS will set a Code P0122 or P0123.

2 Check the reference voltage from the PCM to the TPS. Disconnect the TPS harness connector and install the probes of a voltmeter on the REF terminal (+) and the

4.2 The TPS (arrow) is located on the side of the throttle body - backprobe the TPS using straight pins or other suitable probes on the SIG (+) and GND (-) terminals; voltage should be 0.5 to 1.5 volt at closed throttle; open the accelerator completely to wide open throttle, the voltage should increase steadily to 4.5 to 5.0 volts

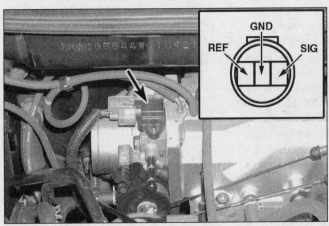

5.2 The MAP sensor (arrow) is located on the throttle body (four-cylinder model shown)

5.8 Remove the MAP sensor mounting screws (arrows)

GND terminal (-). With the ignition key ON (engine not running), it should read approximately 5.0 volts **(see illustration)**. If reference voltage is not available, there is an open circuit to the PCM or a defective PCM.

3   Next, check the TPS signal voltage. With the TPS harness connected to the sensor, using pins, backprobe the electrical connector SIG terminal (+) and the GND terminal (-). Be very careful not to damage the wiring harness. With the ignition key ON (engine not running) and the throttle fully closed, gradually open the throttle valve and observe the TPS signal voltage. With the throttle valve fully closed, the voltage should read approximately 0.5 to 1.5 volts. Slowly move the throttle valve and observe a distinct change in the voltage values as the sensor travels from idle to full throttle. The voltage should increase smoothly to approximately 4.5 volts. If the readings are incorrect, replace the TPS.

Replacement

4   The TPS is permanently attached to the throttle body and not available separately. Replace the throttle body assembly (see Chapter 4).

5   Manifold Absolute Pressure (MAP) sensor - check and replacement

Check

Refer to illustration 5.2

1   The Manifold Absolute Pressure (MAP) sensor monitors the intake manifold pressure changes resulting from changes in engine load and speed and converts the information into a voltage output. The PCM uses the MAP sensor to control fuel delivery and ignition timing. The PCM will receive information as a voltage signal that will vary from 1.0 to 1.5 volts at closed throttle (high vacuum) and 4.0 to 4.5 volts at wide open throttle (low vacuum). The voltage range values will vary slightly according to changes in altitude. The MAP sensor is attached to the throttle body.

A failure in the MAP sensor circuit should set a Code P0107 or P0108.

2   Check the reference voltage from the PCM to the MAP. Disconnect the MAP harness connector and install the probes of a voltmeter on the REF terminal (+) and the GND terminal (-). With the ignition key ON (engine not running), it should read approximately 5.0 volts **(see illustration)**. If reference voltage is not available, there is a short or open circuit to the PCM or a defective PCM.

3   Next, check the MAP signal voltage with the engine not running. Connect the MAP sensor connector and backprobe the connector using pins. Check for voltage on the SIG terminal (+) and GND terminal (–) with the ignition key ON (engine not running). There should be approximately 2.5 to 3.5 volts. This checks signal voltage from the MAP sensor.

4   Check the MAP signal voltage under operating conditions. Start the engine and observe the voltage from the signal wire at idle and as the rpm are raised. Voltage should increase as vacuum decreases. At idle, engine vacuum is high and the MAP sensor should exhibit low voltage readings (0.5 to 1.5). After the engine rpm is raised, manifold vacuum drops and the voltage signal from the MAP sensor should increase. **Note:** *Manifold vacuum can be monitored using a vacuum gauge. Manifold vacuum is high when the engine is idling and decreases as the throttle is opened allowing manifold vacuum to become equal to atmospheric levels. Refer to Chapter 2C for additional information and vacuum testing procedures.*

5   If the readings are incorrect, replace the MAP sensor.

Replacement

Refer to illustration 5.8

6   Disconnect the negative battery terminal. **Caution:** *If the stereo in your vehicle is equipped with an anti-theft system, make sure you have the correct activation code before disconnecting the battery.*

7   Disconnect the electrical connector from the MAP sensor.

8   Remove the bolts that retain the MAP sensor to the throttle body and remove the

MAP sensor **(see illustration)**.

9   Installation is the reverse of removal.

6   Intake Air Temperature (IAT) sensor - check and replacement

Check

Refer to illustrations 6.2a and 6.2b

1   The intake air temperature sensor is a thermistor (a resistor which varies the value of its resistance in accordance with temperature changes). The change in the resistance values will directly affect the voltage signal from the sensor. As the sensor temperature DECREASES, the resistance values will INCREASE. As the sensor temperature INCREASES, the resistance values will DECREASE. A failure in the IAT sensor circuit should set a Code P0112 or P0113.

2   Check the IAT sensor resistance. Disconnect the electrical connector from the IAT sensor which is located on the intake manifold **(see illustrations)**.

3   Using an ohmmeter, measure the resistance between the two terminals on the sensor. It should be approximately 2500 to 3500 ohms at room temperature (68-degrees F).

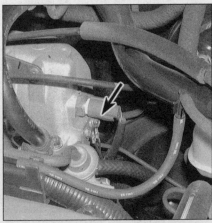

6.2a Location of the IAT sensor (arrow) - four-cylinder engine

6.2b Location of the IAT sensor (arrow) - V6 engine

7.2a Location of the ECT (arrow) - four-cylinder engine

7.2b Location of the ECT (arrow) - V6 engine

Start the engine (or remove the sensor and warm it with a hair dryer or heat gun) and monitor the resistance. The resistance should decrease to approximately 250 to 350 ohms at 180-degrees F. If the test results are incorrect, replace the IAT sensor. Be sure to clear the trouble code if the engine was operated with the sensor connector removed (see Section 2).

Replacement

4   Disconnect the negative battery terminal. **Caution:** *If the stereo in your vehicle is equipped with an anti-theft system, make sure you have the correct activation code before disconnecting the battery.*
5   Disconnect the electrical connector from the IAT sensor.
6   Remove the IAT sensor from the plenum.
7   Installation is the reverse of removal.

7   Engine Coolant Temperature (ECT) sensor - check and replacement

Check

Refer to illustrations 7.2a and 7.2b
1   The engine coolant temperature (ECT) sensor is a thermistor (a resistor which varies the value of its resistance in accordance with

temperature changes). The change in the resistance values will directly affect the voltage signal from the sensor. As the sensor temperature DECREASES, the resistance values will INCREASE. As the sensor temperature INCREASES, the resistance values will DECREASE. A failure in the IAT sensor circuit should set a Code P0116, P0117 and P0118.
2   Check the ECT sensor resistance. Disconnect the electrical connector from the sensor **(see illustrations)**.
3   Using an ohmmeter, measure the resistance between the two terminals on the sensor. It should be approximately 2500 to 3500 ohms at room temperature (68-degrees F). Start the engine (or remove the sensor and warm it in a heated pan of water) and monitor the resistance. The resistance should decrease to approximately 250 to 350 ohms at 180-degrees F. If the test results are incorrect, replace the ETC sensor. Be sure to clear the trouble code if the engine was operated with the sensor connector removed (see Section 2).

Replacement

Warning: *Wait until the engine has cooled completely before beginning this procedure.*
4   Disconnect the negative battery terminal. **Caution:** *If the stereo in your vehicle is equipped with an anti-theft system, make sure you have the correct activation code before disconnecting the battery.*

5   Before installing the new sensor, wrap the threads with Teflon sealing tape to prevent leakage and thread corrosion.
6   To remove the sensor, depress the locking tab, disconnect the electrical connector, then carefully unscrew the sensor. Coolant will leak out when the sensor is removed, so install the new sensor as quickly as possible. **Caution:** *Handle the coolant sensor with care. Damage to this sensor will affect the operation of the entire fuel injection system.*
7   Installation is the reverse of removal.

8   Crankshaft Position/Top Dead Center (CKP/TDC) sensor - check and replacement

Check

1   The crankshaft position sensor (CKP) determines the timing for the fuel injection and ignition on each cylinder. It also detects engine rpm. The TDC sensor determines the ignition timing at start-up (engine cranking). Four-cylinder models are equipped with a TDC sensor and a CKP sensor mounted under the lower timing belt cover. The V6 models are equipped with two TDC sensors mounted behind the front cylinder bank camshaft housing cover and a single CKP sensor mounted, under the lower timing belt cover. On four-cylinder models, a failure in the CKP/TDC sensor circuit should set a Code P0335, P0336, P1361 or P1362. On V6 models, a failure in the TDC sensor circuit should set a Code P1361, P1362, P1366 or P1367. A failure in the CKP sensor circuit should set a Code P0335 or P0336. Refer to the code chart in Section 2 for additional information.

Four-cylinder models

Refer to illustration 8.2
2   To check the CKP/TDC sensor, disconnect the electrical connector at the sensor and probe terminals 1 and 2 with an ohmmeter **(see illustration)**. Refer to the resistance Specifications listed in this Chapter. This test checks the TDC portion of the sensor. Next,

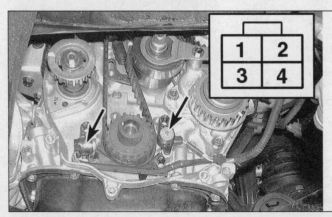

8.2 The CKP/TDC sensors are located under the lower timing belt cover on four-cylinder models but the electrical connector is accessible off to the side of the timing belt cover

8.5 Location of the CKP sensor (right arrow) and electrical connector (left arrow) - V6 models

8.6 Check the TDC sensor number 1 and sensor number 2 resistance at the electrical connector (arrow) (V6 model shown)

8.11 Remove the CKP sensor mounting bolt (arrow)

8.12a To access the TDC sensors on V6 models, remove the rear cover mounting bolts (arrows)

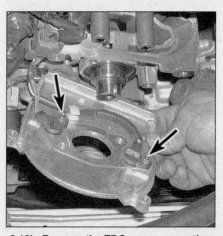

8.12b Remove the TDC sensor mounting bolts (arrows)

probe terminals 3 and 4 to test the CKP portion of the sensor. Compare your measurements with the resistance listed in this Chapter's Specifications.

3   Check for continuity to ground on each terminal. Continuity should NOT exist.

4   If the test results are incorrect, replace the CKP/TDC sensor.

V6 models

Refer to illustrations 8.5 and 8.6

5   To check the CKP sensor, disconnect the electrical connector at the sensor and probe terminals 1 and 2 with an ohmmeter **(see illustration)**. Refer to the resistance Specifications listed in this Chapter. This test checks only the CKP sensor.

6   To check the TDC sensor, disconnect the electrical connector at the sensor(s) and probe terminals 1 and 2 with an ohmmeter **(see illustration)**. This test checks the TDC number 1 sensor portion of the sensor. Next, probe terminals 3 and 4 to test the TDC number 2 sensor portion of the sensor. Compare your measurements with the resistance listed

in this Chapter's Specifications.

7   Check for continuity to ground on each terminal. Continuity should NOT exist.

8   If the test results are incorrect, replace it with a new sensor.

Replacement

Refer to illustrations 8.11, 8.12a and 8.12b

9   Disconnect the cable from the negative battery terminal. **Caution:** *The stereo in your vehicle is equipped with an anti-theft system. Make sure you have the correct activation code before disconnecting the battery.*

10   The timing belt cover must be removed to access the TDC and the CKP sensors on the four-cylinder models. Refer to Chapter 2A for timing belt removal procedures.

11   The timing belt cover must be removed to access the CKP sensor on the V6 engine **(see illustration)**. Refer to Chapter 2B for timing belt cover removal procedures.

12   The timing belt sprocket and rear cover must be removed from the front cylinder head to access the TDC number 1 and TDC number 2 sensors **(see illustrations)**. Refer

to Chapter 2B for the timing belt sprocket and rear cover removal.

---

9   **Cylinder Position (CYP) sensor (four-cylinder models) - check and replacement**

Check

Refer to illustration 9.2

1   The CYP sensor determines the position of the cylinder for sequential fuel injection to each cylinder. The CYP sensor is mounted inside the distributor. A failure in the CYP sensor circuit should set a Code P1381 and P1382.

2   To check the CYP sensor, disconnect the electrical connector at the distributor and probe terminals 3 and 4 with an ohmmeter **(see illustration)**. Compare your measurements with the resistance Specifications listed in this Chapter's Specifications.

3   Check for continuity to ground on each terminal. Continuity should NOT exist.

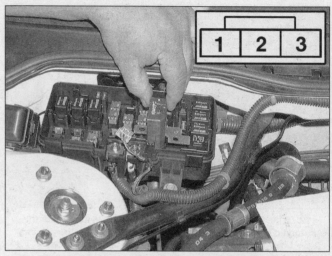

9.2 Disconnect the electrical connector at the distributor and check the CYP sensor resistance at the indicated terminals

10.2 Remove the ELD and disconnect the connector for testing

4   If the test results are incorrect, replace the distributor (see Chapter 5).

Replacement

5   The CYP sensor is permanently mounted in the distributor housing and not available separately. Replace the distributor.

---

10 Electronic Load Detector (ELD) system - check and replacement

Check

Refer to illustration 10.2

1   The ELD system detects excess amperage draw (load) on the electrical circuits that supply the headlights, fuel injection, charging system etc. The prime symptom of an electrical overload is a driveability problem, usually occurring when the engine is idling. A failure in the ELD system should set a Code P1297 or P1298.

2   Remove the ELD (see Step 6) and disconnect the electrical connector. Measure the voltage between the number 1 terminal (+) and body ground (-) on the harness side of the connector with the ignition key ON (engine not running) **(see illustration)**. There should be battery voltage. If no voltage is present, check the wiring harness back to the number 6 fuse (15 amp) and the ELD in the engine compartment.

3   Measure the voltage with the ignition key ON (engine not running) between terminal number 3 (+) and body ground (-) on the harness side of the connector. There should be 4.5 to 5.0 volts. If no voltage is present, check the ELD circuit between the engine and the alternator.

4   Check for continuity between terminal number 2 and body ground. There should be continuity.

5   If the test results are correct, replace the ELD unit.

10.7 To remove the ELD, remove the two screws (arrows) and lift the unit from the fuse/relay center

11.4 Location of the power steering pressure switch (arrow) (four-cylinder model shown)

Replacement

Refer to illustration 10.7

6   The ELD unit is located inside the fuse/relay center in the engine compartment. Disconnect the negative battery terminal. **Caution:** *The stereo in your vehicle is equipped with an anti-theft system. Make sure you have the correct activation code before disconnecting the battery.*

7   Remove the two screws, lift the ELD unit from the fuse/relay center and disconnect the electrical connector from the ELD **(see illustration)**.

8   Installation is the reverse of removal.

---

11 Power Steering Pressure (PSP) switch - check and replacement

Check

Refer to illustration 11.4

1   The power steering pressure (PSP) switch is located in the high-pressure line between the power steering pump and the steering gear. When steering system pressure

reaches a high-pressure setpoint, the PSP switch closes and sends a signal to the PCM that the PCM uses to maintain engine idle speed during parking maneuvers. The On-Board Diagnostic system can detect switch problems and set trouble codes to indicate specific faults.

2   Check the operation of the PSP switch if the engine stalls during parking or if the engine idles continuously at high rpm.

3   Refer to the wiring diagrams at the end of this manual to identify the functions of connector terminals.

4   Disconnect the PSP switch connector and connect an ohmmeter to the terminals on the switch body **(see illustration)**.

5   Start the engine and let it idle.

6   Turn the steering wheel to point the front wheels straight ahead and read the ohmmeter. It should indicate no continuity (infinite resistance).

7   Turn the steering wheel to either side and watch the ohmmeter. The PSP switch should close as the wheel nears the steering stop on either side, and the meter should indicate continuity (zero ohms).

8   If the switch fails either test, replace it.

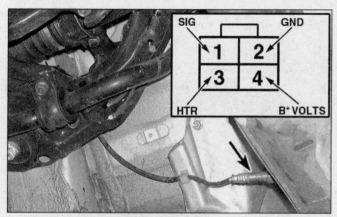

12.7 The secondary oxygen sensor (arrow) is located in the catalytic converter (four-cylinder model shown) - the primary oxygen sensor is located in the exhaust manifold

12.16 Use a slotted socket to remove the oxygen sensor from the exhaust pipe

Replacement

9   Raise the vehicle and support it securely on jackstands.

10.   Disconnect the negative battery terminal. **Caution:** *The stereo in your vehicle is equipped with an anti-theft system. Make sure you have the correct activation code before disconnecting the battery.*

11   Disconnect the electrical connector from the switch and unscrew the switch from the fitting.

12   Install and connect the new switch and lower the vehicle to the ground.

13   Refer to Chapter 10 and bleed air from the power steering system. Add fluid as required (see Chapter 1).

12 Oxygen sensor (O2S) - check and replacement

Check

Refer to illustration 12.7

1   The oxygen sensor monitors the oxygen content of the exhaust gas stream. The oxygen content in the exhaust reacts with the oxygen sensor to produce a voltage output which varies from 0.1-volt (high oxygen, lean mixture) to 0.9-volts (low oxygen, rich mixture). The PCM constantly monitors this variable voltage output to determine the ratio of oxygen to fuel in the mixture. The PCM alters the air/fuel mixture ratio by controlling the pulse width (open time) of the fuel injectors. A mixture ratio of 14.7 parts air to 1 part fuel is the ideal mixture ratio for minimizing exhaust emissions, thus allowing the catalytic converter to operate at maximum efficiency. It is this ratio of 14.7 to 1 which the PCM and the oxygen sensor attempt to maintain at all times. Two oxygen sensor are used; the primary oxygen sensor is located in the exhaust manifold and the secondary oxygen sensor is located after the catalytic converter. By sampling the exhaust gas before and after the catalytic converter, the PCM can also determine the efficiency of the catalytic converter.

2   The oxygen sensor produces no voltage when it is below its normal operating temperature of about 600-degrees F. During this initial period before warm-up, the PCM operates in OPEN LOOP mode.

3   If the engine reaches normal operating temperature and/or has been running for two or more minutes, and if the oxygen sensor is producing a steady signal voltage below 0.45-volts at 1,500 rpm or greater, the PCM will set a Code P0131 or P0132. The PCM will also set other codes if it detects any problem with the heater circuit. Refer to the code chart in Section 2 for additional information.

4   When there is a problem with the oxygen sensor or its circuit, the PCM operates in the open loop mode - that is, it controls fuel delivery in accordance with a programmed default value instead of feedback information from the oxygen sensor.

5   The proper operation of the oxygen sensor depends on four conditions:

a) *Electrical - The low voltages generated by the sensor depend upon good, clean connections which should be checked whenever a malfunction of the sensor is suspected or indicated.*

b) *Outside air supply - The sensor is designed to allow air circulation to the internal portion of the sensor. Whenever the sensor is removed and installed or replaced, make sure the air passages are not restricted.*

c) *Proper operating temperature - The PCM will not react to the sensor signal until the sensor reaches approximately 600-degrees F. This factor must be taken into consideration when evaluating the performance of the sensor.*

d) *Unleaded fuel - The use of unleaded fuel is essential for proper operation of the sensor. Make sure the fuel you are using is of this type.*

6   In addition to observing the above conditions, special care must be taken whenever the sensor is serviced.

a) *The oxygen sensor has a permanently*

attached pigtail and electrical connector which should not be removed from the sensor. Damage or removal of the pigtail or electrical connector can adversely affect operation of the sensor.

b) *Grease, dirt and other contaminants should be kept away from the electrical connector and the louvered end of the sensor.*

c) *Do not use cleaning solvents of any kind on the oxygen sensor.*

d) *Do not drop or roughly handle the sensor.*

e) *The silicone boot must be installed in the correct position to prevent the boot from being melted and to allow the sensor to operate properly.*

7   Locate the oxygen sensor electrical connector and without disconnecting it, insert a long pin into the oxygen sensor connector terminal 1 (+) (SIG) and another pin into terminal 2 (-) (GND) **(see illustrations)**. Install the positive probe of a voltmeter onto terminal 1 pin and the negative probe to terminal 2 pin. Apply the parking brake, shift the transaxle into Park (automatic) or Neutral (manual), raise the front of the vehicle and place it securely on jackstands.

8   Check the signal voltage from the oxygen sensor during operating conditions. Start the engine and monitor the voltage signal as the engine warms up. **Caution:** *Be extremely careful of hot exhaust components when performing this procedure.* **Note:** *Secondary oxygen sensors will produce much slower fluctuating voltage values to reflect the results of the catalyzed exhaust mixture from rich or lean to less presence of CO, HC and Nox molecules. Here the CO_2 and H_2O gaseous forms do not register or react with the oxygen sensors to such a large degree.*

9   The oxygen sensor will produce a steady voltage signal at first (open loop) of approximately 0.1 to 0.2 volts with the engine cold. After a period of approximately two minutes, the engine will reach operating temperature and the oxygen sensor should start to fluctuate between 0.1 to 0.9 volts (closed loop). If the oxygen sensor fails to reach the closed loop mode or there is a very long

13.2 Location of the knock sensor (arrow) on a four-cylinder model

period of time until it does switch into closed loop mode, replace the oxygen sensor.

10   Also inspect the oxygen sensor heater. Disconnect the oxygen sensor electrical connector and connect an ohmmeter between the 3 and 4 terminals. It should measure 10 to 40 ohms.

11   Check for proper supply voltage to the heater. Working on the PCM side of the connector, measure voltage between terminal number 4 and ground (-) oxygen sensor electrical connector. There should be battery voltage with the ignition key ON (engine not running). If there is no voltage, check the circuit between the main relay, the PCM and the sensor.

12   If the oxygen sensor fails any of these tests, replace it with a new part.

Replacement

Refer to illustration 12.16

Note: *Because it is installed in the exhaust manifold or pipe, which contracts when cool, the oxygen sensor may be very difficult to loosen when the engine is cold. Rather than risk damage to the sensor (assuming you are planning to reuse it in another manifold or pipe), start and run the engine for a minute or two, then shut it off. Be careful not to burn yourself during the following procedure.*

13   Disconnect the cable from the negative terminal of the battery. **Caution:** *The stereo in your vehicle is equipped with an anti-theft system. Make sure you have the correct activation code before disconnecting the battery.*

14   Raise the vehicle and place it securely on jackstands.

15   Carefully disconnect the electrical connector from the sensor.

16   Carefully unscrew the sensor from the exhaust manifold (primary) or catalytic converter (secondary) **(see illustration).**

17   Anti-seize compound must be used on the threads of the sensor to facilitate future removal. The threads of new sensors will already be coated with this compound, but if an old sensor is removed and reinstalled, recoat the threads.

18   Install the sensor and tighten it securely.

19   Reconnect the electrical connector of the pigtail lead to the main engine wiring harness.

20   Lower the vehicle, take it on a test drive and check to see that no trouble codes set.

---

13 Knock sensor (four-cylinder models) - check and replacement

Check

Refer to illustration 13.2

1   Knock sensors detect abnormal vibration in the engine. The knock control system is designed to reduce spark knock during periods of heavy detonation. This allows the engine to use maximum spark advance to improve driveability. Knock sensors produce AC output voltage which increases with the severity of the knock. The signal is fed into the PCM and the timing is retarded to compensate for the severe detonation.

2   To check a knock sensor, disconnect the electrical connector **(see illustration)** and drain the engine coolant as described in Chapter 1. Remove the sensor from the engine block, then reconnect the wiring harness to it. These type of sensors must be checked by observing voltage fluctuations with a voltmeter. Simply switch the voltmeter to the lowest voltage scale and connect the negative probe (-) to the sensor body (ground) and the positive probe to the sensor terminal. With the voltmeter connected to the sensor, gently tap on the bottom of the knock sensor with a hammer or similar device (this simulates the knock from the engine) and observe voltage fluctuations on the meter. If no voltage fluctuations can be detected, the sensor is bad and should be replaced with a new part.

Replacement

Warning: *Wait for the engine to cool completely before performing this procedure.*

3   Disconnect the cable from the negative terminal of the battery. **Caution:** *The stereo in your vehicle is equipped with an anti-theft*

14.4a Location of the mainshaft speed sensor (arrow) - automatic transaxle

system. Make sure you have the correct activation code before disconnecting the battery.

4   The knock sensor is threaded into the engine block coolant passage, when it is removed, the coolant will drain from the engine block. Drain the cooling system (see Chapter 1). Place a drain pan under the sensor, disconnect the electrical connector and remove the knock sensor. A new sensor is pre-coated with thread sealant, do not apply any additional sealant or the operation of the sensor may be effected. Install the knock sensor and tighten it securely (approximately 14 ft-lbs). Don't overtighten the sensor or damage may occur. Plug in the electrical connector, refill the cooling system and check for leaks.

---

14 Vehicle Speed Sensor (VSS) - check and replacement

Check

1   The Vehicle Speed Sensor (VSS) is located on the transaxle. This sensor is a permanent magnetic variable reluctance sensor that produces a pulsing voltage whenever vehicle speed is over 3 mph. These pulses are translated by the PCM to vehicle speed and used for speedometer operation and automatic transaxle shift control. Manual transaxle models are equipped with a single VSS. Automatic transaxle models are equipped with a mainshaft and a countershaft speed sensor. On automatic transaxle models, a failure in either sensor will cause a transaxle shifting problem.

Manual transaxle models

2   To check the vehicle speed sensor, disconnect the electrical connector at the sensor. Using a voltmeter, check for voltage at the electrical connector (harness side) black/yellow wire terminal (+) and body ground (-). The circuit should have battery voltage available. If there is no voltage available, check for an open circuit between the VSS and the driver's-side fuse box (be sure to check the fuse). Using an ohmmeter, check the black wire terminal of the connector for continuity to ground.

3   Raise the front of the vehicle and place it securely on jackstands. Block the rear wheels and place the transaxle in Neutral. Connect the electrical connector to the VSS, turn the ignition to ON (engine not running) and backprobe the VSS connector blue/white wire terminal with a voltmeter positive lead. Connect the negative lead of the meter to the black wire terminal. Securely hold or block one of the front wheels, rotate the other wheel by hand. The voltmeter should pulse between zero and 5 volts. If it doesn't, replace the sensor.

Automatic transaxle models

Refer to illustrations 14.4a and 14.4b

4   Disconnect the electrical connector from the mainshaft and countershaft sensors

14.4b Location of the countershaft speed sensor (arrow) - automatic transaxle

15.2a Location of the IAC valve (arrow) - four-cylinder models

15.2b Location of the IAC valve (arrow) - V6 models (typical)

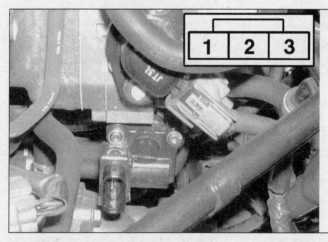

15.5 Disconnect the electrical connector from the IAC valve and check for battery voltage on terminal 2 and continuity to ground on terminal 1 (working on the harness side of connector)

(see illustrations). Using an ohmmeter, measure the resistance across the two terminals of the sensor. The resistance should be approximately 400 to 600 ohms. If the sensor resistance is not correct, replace the sensor.

Replacement

5   To replace the VSS, disconnect the electrical connector from the VSS.
6   Remove the retaining screw and withdraw the VSS from the transaxle.
7   Replace the O-ring with a new part.
8   Installation is the reverse of removal.

---

15 Idle Air Control (IAC) valve - check and replacement

Check

Refer to illustrations 15.2a, 15.2b and 15.5
Warning: *Keep hands, loose clothing, etc. away from any moving engine parts while working on a running engine or personal injury may result.*
1   The engine idle speed is controlled by the IAC valve. The IAC valve controls the amount of air that bypasses the throttle plate into the intake manifold. The IAC valve is activated by the PCM depending upon the running conditions of the engine (air conditioning system, power steering, cold and warm running etc.).
2   Apply the parking brake, block the wheels and place the transaxle in NEUTRAL (manual) or PARK (automatic). Connect a tachometer, according to the manufacturer's instructions, to the engine. Start the engine and hold the accelerator steady at 3,000 rpm until the coolant fan comes on. Allow the engine to idle and note the idle speed (with the cooling fan and all accessories OFF). If the idle speed is 650 to 750 rpm, the system is functioning properly. If the idle speed is less than 650 rpm, disconnect the electrical connector to the IAC valve **(see illustrations)**. The idle speed should fluctuate when the IAC valve is disconnected. If it doesn't, the IAC valve is probably defective.

3   If the idle speed is greater than 750 rpm, stop the engine and disconnect the air intake duct from the throttle body. Start the engine and allow it to idle. Block the lower port in the throttle body with a tool or your finger (the lower port is the one that connects to the IAC valve). If the idle speed is lower with the port blocked, attempt the adjust the idle speed to specifications (see Chapter 1). If the idle speed cannot be adjusted to specifications, the IAC valve is probably defective. If the idle speed did not drop, check the intake system for a vacuum leak.
4   If the IAC valve checks are good and an intermittent idle problem still persists, check the wiring harness from the IAC valve to the PCM for poor connections or damaged wires.
5   Check for battery voltage to the IAC valve. Disconnect the electrical connector from the IAC valve, turn the ignition key ON (engine not running) and measure the voltage between terminal number 2 and body ground **(see illustration)**. There should be battery voltage. If no voltage is present, check for an open circuit in the wire from the IAC valve to the PGM-FI main relay. Refer to the wiring schematics at the end of Chapter 12.
6   Using an ohmmeter, measure the resistance between terminal number 1 on the IAC valve and body ground. It should display continuity. If there is not, repair the ground

circuit wire. Refer to the wiring diagrams at the end of Chapter 12.
7   If the voltage and resistance readings are correct, have the PCM and electrical circuit for the IAC valve diagnosed by a dealer service department or other qualified repair shop.

Replacement

8   Disconnect the electrical connector and hoses from the IAC valve.
9   On V6 models, remove the throttle body from the intake manifold (see Chapter 4).
10   Remove the two mounting screws and remove the valve from the intake manifold (four-cylinder) or throttle body (V6).
11   Installation is the reverse of removal. Be sure to install a new O-ring.

---

16 Fuel Injection Air (FIA) control valve (V6 models) - check and replacement

Check

Refer to illustration 16.3
1   This system supplies filtered air to the fuel injectors when the engine is running. The additional air charge helps lean the mixture

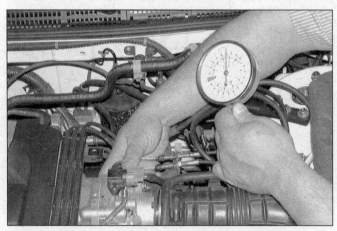

16.3 Connect a vacuum gauge to the FIA valve and monitor the vacuum changes as the throttle is opened

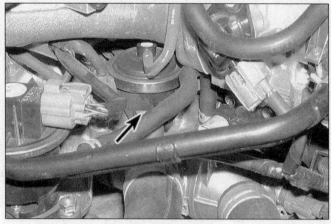

16.6 Remove the bolt (arrow) that retains the FIA valve

and provide complete combustion during acceleration.

2   Start the engine and hold it at 3,000 rpm until the radiator fan activates. Allow the engine to idle.

3   Remove the FIA valve air supply hose from the intake air duct and install a vacuum gauge to the hose **(see illustration)**.

4   Open and close the throttle as you monitor the gauge. The vacuum gauge readings should change as the engine speed changes.

5   If the vacuum does not change, check the vacuum hoses for proper routing, damage or obstructions. If the hoses are good, the valve is probably defective.

Replacement

Refer to illustration 16.6

6   Remove the bolt that retains the valve to the air intake plenum and remove the valve.

7   Installation is the reverse of removal.

17   Positive Crankcase Ventilation (PCV) system

Refer to illustration 17.1

1   The Positive Crankcase Ventilation (PCV) system **(see illustration)** reduces hydrocarbon emissions by scavenging crankcase vapors. It does this by circulating fresh air from the air cleaner through the crankcase, where it mixes with blow-by gases and is then rerouted through a PCV valve to the intake manifold.

2   The main components of the PCV system are the PCV valve, a blow-by filter and the vacuum hoses connecting these two components with the engine.

3   To maintain idle quality, the PCV valve restricts the flow when the intake manifold vacuum is high. If abnormal operating conditions (such as piston ring problems) arise, the system is designed to allow excessive amounts of blow-by gases to flow back through the crankcase vent tube into the air cleaner to be consumed by normal combustion.

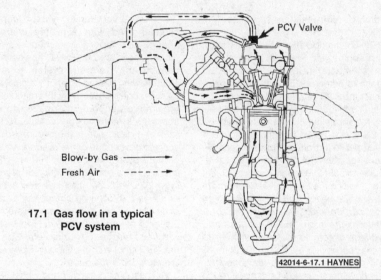

17.1 Gas flow in a typical PCV system

4   Checking and replacement of the PCV valve is covered in Chapter 1.

18   Exhaust Gas Recirculation (EGR) system

General description

1   The EGR system reduces oxides of nitrogen by recirculating exhaust gas through the EGR valve and intake manifold into the combustion chambers.

2   The EGR system consists of the EGR valve, the EGR valve lift sensor, the Powertrain Control Module (PCM) and various sensors. The PCM memory is programmed to produce the ideal EGR valve lift for each operating condition. An EGR valve lift sensor detects the amount of EGR valve lift and sends this information to the PCM. The PCM then compares it with the ideal EGR valve lift, which is determined by data received from the other sensors. If there's any difference between the two, the PCM cuts current to the EGR valve to reduce the amount of exhaust gas recirculation.

Check

Refer to illustration 18.3

3   To check the EGR valve lift sensor, disconnect the electrical connector from the EGR valve and check for continuity between terminals number 1 and 2, then 1 and 3 on the valve. If the sensor circuit is open (no

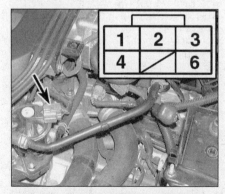

18.3 To check the EGR valve sensor, disconnect the electrical connector (arrow) and check for continuity between terminals no. 1 and 2, and 1 and 3 on the EGR valve

18.8 Remove the two nuts (arrows) from the base of the EGR valve (V6 engine shown)

19.9 Location of the EVAP control canister hose (1) and the EVAP two-way valve (2)

continuity, or high resistance), replace the EGR valve.

4   To check the operation of the EGR valve, start the engine and warm it to its normal operating temperature (wait for the electric cooling fan to come on). Stop the engine and disconnect the EGR valve electrical connector.

5   Install a fused jumper wire from the battery positive terminal (+) to terminal number 4 on the EGR valve. Start the engine and connect a jumper lead from the battery negative terminal (-) to terminal 6 on the EGR valve. The engine should idle rough and/or stall. If it does not, replace the EGR valve. **Caution:** *Be careful when applying battery voltage to an electrical component. Disconnect the component from the main wiring harness and apply voltage directly to the component or to the harness connector leading to the component. Do not apply voltage to the connector on the vehicle harness-side or damage to the Powertrain Control Module may result.*

6   Further checking of the EGR control system requires special tools and equipment.

EGR valve replacement

Refer to illustrations 18.8

7   Disconnect the electrical connector for the EGR valve lift sensor.

8   Remove the two nuts that secure the EGR valve and detach the EGR valve **(see illustration)**.

9   Clean the mating surfaces of the EGR valve and adapter.

10   Install the EGR valve, using a new gasket. Tighten the nuts securely.

11   Plug in the electrical connector.

---

19 Evaporative emissions control (EVAP) system

General description

1   The fuel evaporative emissions control (EVAP) system absorbs fuel vapors and, during engine operation, releases them into the engine intake where they mix with the incoming air-fuel mixture.

2   Every evaporative system employs a canister filled with activated charcoal to absorb fuel vapors. The means by which these vapors are controlled, however, varies considerably from one system to another. The following descriptions of a typical system for the models covered by this manual should provide you enough information to understand the system on your vehicle. **Note:** *The following descriptions are not intended as a specific description of the evaporative system on your particular vehicle. Rather, they are intended as a general description of a typical system used on fuel-injected vehicles. Although the following components are most likely all used on your particular system, there may also be other devices, not included here, which are unique to your system. Check with the VECI label and the Vacuum Hose Routing Diagram under the hood.*

3   The fuel filler cap is fitted with a two-way valve as a safety device. The valve vents fuel vapors to the atmosphere if the evaporative control system fails.

4   The On Board Refueling Vapor Recovery (ORVR) vent shut valve is mounted near the fuel tank to recirculate the fuel vapors from the filler neck during fill-up. The vapor is sent through the ORVR valve into the EVAP canister.

5   Fuel vapors travel through the two-way valve to get to the canister. After passing through the two-way valve, fuel vapor is carried by vent hoses to the charcoal canister in the engine compartment. The activated charcoal in the canister absorbs and stores these vapors.

6   When the engine is running and warmed to a pre-set temperature, a purge cut-off solenoid valve near the canister closes, allowing a purge control diaphragm valve in the charcoal canister to be opened by intake manifold vacuum. Fuel vapors from the canister are then drawn through the purge control diaphragm valve by intake manifold vacuum.

7   A fuel tank pressure sensor is mounted on the tank to monitor pressure changes within the tank during operating and non-operating conditions.

Check

Refer to illustrations 19.9, 19.11, 19.14 and 19.16

Note: *Complete checking of the evaporative emissions control system is beyond the scope of the average home mechanic. Fortunately, the evaporative control system, like all emission control systems, is protected by a Federally-mandated warranty (see your owners manual for more information). The EVAP system probably won't fail during the service life of the vehicle; however, if it does, the hoses or charcoal canister are usually to blame.*

8   Always check the hoses first. A disconnected, damaged or missing hose is the most likely cause of a malfunctioning EVAP system. Refer to the Vacuum Hose Routing Diagram (attached to the underside of the hood) to determine whether the hoses are correctly routed and attached. Repair any damaged hoses or replace any missing hoses as necessary.

9   Disconnect the vacuum line from the EVAP control canister **(see illustration)** and connect a vacuum gauge to the hose. With the engine cool (below 149 degrees F) and idling, there should be no vacuum present. If vacuum is present, there is most likely a problem with the purge control solenoid (see Step 14). If no vacuum is present, raise the engine rpm to 3,000 and allow the engine to reach normal operating temperature with the cooling fan activated. Vacuum should be present. Check the purge control solenoid if there is no vacuum present (see Step 14).

10   Disconnect the vacuum hose from the EVAP two-way valve (located near the charcoal canister) and connect a vacuum pump to the hose. Make sure the vacuum pump is linked directly to the two-way valve. With the ignition switch ON (engine not running), apply vacuum and observe that the valve holds vacuum (pressure) steadily. Replace the two-way valve if it leaks.

11   With the ignition ON (engine not running), disconnect the EVAP control canister vent shut valve **(see illustration)** and observe that the EVAP two-way valve holds vacuum.

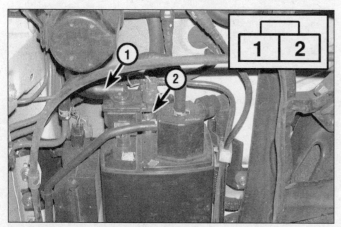

19.11 Location of the vent shut-off valve harness connector (2) and the vent shut-off valve vacuum hose (1)

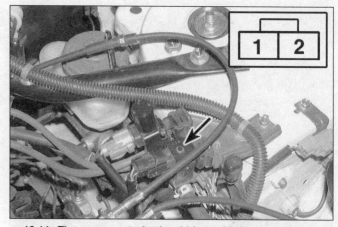

19.14 The purge control solenoid (arrow) is located near the shock tower on the V6 models

If it holds vacuum, replace the EVAP control canister vent shut valve and O-ring. If it does not hold vacuum, check the harness between the vent shut valve and the PCM.

12 Disconnect the vacuum hose from the canister vent shut valve, install a vacuum pump and with the ignition key ON (engine not running), make sure the valve does not leak. If it does, check the circuit.

13 Disconnect the harness connector from the canister vent shut valve and with the ignition ON (engine not running), check for battery voltage terminal number 1 and ground. Battery voltage should be present. If no battery voltage is present, check the harness between the canister vent shut valve and fuse number 6 (15 amp).

14 Disconnect the two-pin connector from the purge control solenoid (see illustration), with the ignition key ON (engine not running), battery voltage should be present on the number 1 terminal. If battery voltage is not available, check the harness from the purge control solenoid to the number 6 fuse (15 amp). Note: *The purge control solenoid valve is located on the left side firewall on V6 models and on the intake manifold on four-cylinder models.*

15 Warm the engine up to normal operating temperature (cooling fan must come on). Check for vacuum back to the intake manifold from the purge control solenoid. If there is still no vacuum present from the purge control solenoid, disconnect the two-pin connector and check for manifold vacuum now. If there is no vacuum, check to make sure the vacuum hoses are routed correctly. If there is vacuum, check for a short in the wiring harness between the two-pin connector and the PCM.

16 Disconnect the two-pin connector from the EVAP bypass solenoid valve (see illustration), with the ignition key ON (engine not running), battery voltage should be present on the number 1 terminal. If battery voltage is not available, check the harness from the EVAP bypass solenoid valve and the number 6 fuse (15 amp).

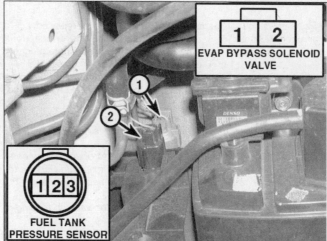

19.16 The fuel tank pressure sensor (1) is located on top of the EVAP bypass solenoid valve (2)

17 Disconnect the three-pin connector from the fuel tank pressure sensor with the ignition key ON (engine not running), measure the voltage between terminals number 1 and 2, then between terminal number 2 and 3. There should be approximately 5 volts. If the voltage values are correct but the fuel tank pressure sensor codes are set once again, then the sensor is defective.

18 Check the charcoal canister for leaks. Remove the charcoal canister and plug all the vent lines with plugs. Install a vacuum pump to the canister vent shut valve, apply vacuum (pressure) and make sure there are no leaks. Replace the charcoal canister if necessary.

Replacement

Charcoal canister

19 Disconnect all the vent hoses to the charcoal canister, remove the bolts and separate the canister from the underside of the vehicle. Be sure to mark all the hoses to insure correct reassembly.

20 Installation is the reverse of removal.

EVAP two-way valve, vent shut-off valve, fuel tank pressure sensor and EVAP bypass solenoid valve

21 To access these valves and sensors, remove the charcoal canister and separate each component individually.

22 Installation is the reverse of removal.

Purge control solenoid valve

23 Disconnect the vacuum hoses from the purge control solenoid.

24 Remove the mounting bolt and separate the solenoid from the engine compartment.

25 Installation is the reverse of removal.

20 Catalytic converter

Note: *Because of a Federally mandated warranty which covers emissions-related components such as the catalytic converter, check with a dealer service department before replacing the converter at your own expense.*

General description

1 The catalytic converter is an emission control device added to the exhaust system to reduce pollutants from the exhaust gas stream. There are two types of converters. The conventional oxidation catalyst reduces the levels of hydrocarbon (HC) and carbon

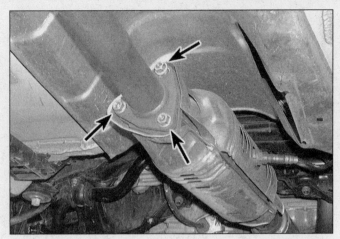

20.5a Spray penetrating lubricant onto the threads of the rear mounted studs (arrows) of the catalytic converter (four-cylinder models shown)

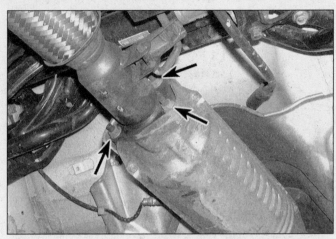

20.5b Forward mounted catalytic converter flange nuts (arrows) (V6 models)

monoxide (CO). The three-way catalyst lowers the levels of oxides of nitrogen (NOx) as well as hydrocarbons (HC) and carbon monoxide (CO).

Check

2   The test equipment for a catalytic converter is expensive and highly sophisticated. If you suspect that the converter on your vehicle is malfunctioning, take it to a dealer or authorized emissions inspection facility for diagnosis and repair.

3   Whenever the vehicle is raised for servicing of underbody components, check the converter for leaks, corrosion, dents and other damage. Check the welds/flange bolts that attach the front and rear ends of the converter to the exhaust system. If damage is discov-ered, the converter should be replaced.

4   Although catalytic converters don't break too often, they can become plugged. The easiest way to check for a restricted converter is to use a vacuum gauge to diagnose the effect of a blocked exhaust on intake vacuum.

a) Connect a vacuum gauge to an intake manifold vacuum source (see Chapter 2C).
b) Warm the engine to operating temperature, place the transaxle in Park (automatic) or Neutral (manual) and apply the parking brake.
c) Note and record the vacuum reading at idle.
d) Quickly open the throttle to near full throttle and release it shut. Note and record the vacuum reading.
e) Perform the test three more times, recording the reading after each test.
f) If the reading after the fourth test is more than one in-Hg lower than the reading recorded at idle, the exhaust system may be restricted (the catalytic converter could be plugged or an exhaust pipe or muffler could be restricted).

Component replacement

Refer to illustrations 20.5a and 20.5b

5   Be sure to spray the exhaust nuts on the flange studs before removing them from the catalytic converter **(see illustrations)**.

6   Remove the nuts and separate the catalytic converter from the exhaust system.

7   Installation is the reverse of removal.

Chapter 7 Part A
Manual transaxle

Contents

Specifications

Torque specifications

	Ft-lbs
Engine stiffener	
10 mm bolts	33
12 mm bolt	47
Subframe mounting bolts	
12 mm bolts	47
14 mm bolts	75
Transaxle-to-engine bolts	47
Rear engine mount bracket bolts	40

1 General information

All V6 models are equipped with an automatic transaxle only. Information on the manual transaxle is included in this Part of Chapter 7. Information on the automatic transaxle can be found in Chapter 7 Part B. You'll also find certain procedures common to both transaxles - such as oil seal replacement - in this chapter.

The manual transaxle is a synchronized, 5-speed design, designated P2A8. The transaxle model number is stamped onto a plate on the transaxle. Refer to *Vehicle identification numbers* at the front of this manual for the location of the plate.

Depending on the expense involved in having a transaxle overhauled, it might be a better idea to consider replacing it with either a new or rebuilt unit. Your local auto parts store, dealer or transaxle shop should be able to supply information concerning cost, availability and exchange policy. Regardless of how you decide to remedy a transaxle problem, you can still save a lot of money by removing and installing the unit yourself.

2 Driveaxle oil seals - replacement

Refer to illustrations 2.4 and 2.6

1   Oil leaks frequently occur due to wear of the driveaxle oil seals. Replacement of these seals is relatively easy, since the repair can usually be performed without removing the transaxle from the vehicle.
2   The driveaxle oil seals are located at the sides of the transaxle, where the driveaxles are attached. If leakage at the seal is suspected, raise the vehicle and support it securely on jackstands. If the seal is leaking, lubricant will be found on the sides of the transaxle, below the seals.
3   Refer to Chapter 8 and remove the driveaxle(s).
4   Using a screwdriver or prybar, carefully pry the oil seal out of the transaxle bore **(see illustration)**.

5   If the oil seal cannot be removed with a screwdriver or prybar, a special oil seal removal tool (available at auto parts stores) will be required.

2.4 Insert the tip of a large screwdriver or prybar behind the oil seal and very carefully pry it out

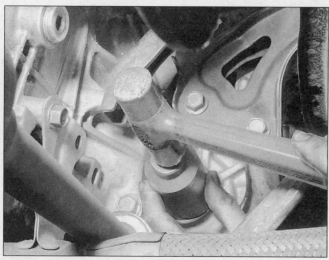

2.6 Using a large socket or a section of pipe, drive the new seal squarely into the bore

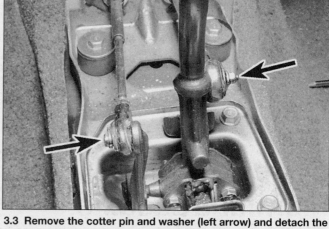

3.3 Remove the cotter pin and washer (left arrow) and detach the select cable from the change lever linkage, then remove the self-locking nut and washer (right arrow) and detach the shift cable from the shift lever

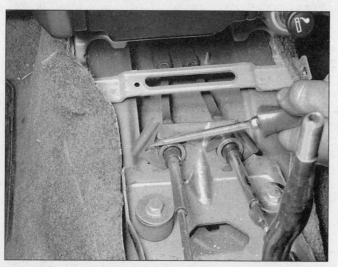

3.4 Pry off the retaining clips and detach the select and shift cables from the shift lever base plate

3.5 Remove the cotter pins, steel washers and plastic washers and disconnect the select cable from the select lever (lower right arrow) and the shift lever from the shift arm lever (upper right arrow), then pry off the retaining clip (left arrows) from the cable brackets

6   Using a large section of pipe or a large deep socket (slightly smaller than the outside diameter of the seal) as a drift, install the new oil seal **(see illustration)**. Drive it into the bore squarely and make sure it's completely seated. Coat the seal lip with transaxle lubricant.

7   Install the driveaxle(s). Be careful not to damage the lip of the new seal.

3   Shift cables and lever - removal and installation

Warning: *The models covered by this manual are equipped with Supplemental Restraint systems (SRS), more commonly known as airbags. Always disable the airbag system before working in the vicinity of the impact sensors, steering column, console or instrument panel to avoid the possibility of accidental deployment of the airbag, which could cause personal injury (see Chapter 12). The*

yellow wiring harnesses and connectors routed through the console and instrument panel are for this system. Do not use electrical test equipment on any of the airbag system wiring or tamper with them in any way.

Shift cables

Refer to illustrations 3.3, 3.4 and 3.5
Note: *Even if only one cable is broken, you must replace the select and shift cables as an assembly - they're not available separately.*

1   Unscrew and remove the shift lever knob.

2   Remove the console (see Chapter 11).

3   Remove the cotter pin and washer and detach the select cable from the change lever linkage **(see illustration)**. Remove the self-locking nut and washer and detach the shift cable from the shift lever.

4   Remove the retaining clips and detach the cables from the shift lever base plate **(see illustration)**.

5   Open the hood and locate the forward

ends of the cables **(see illustration)**. Disconnect the select cable from the select lever (the one on the top of the shift arm cover) and the shift cable from the shift arm lever (the one on the side). Remove the retaining clips from the cable bracket.

6   Follow the cables back to the firewall and remove the cable grommet.

7   Pull the cables out.

8   Installation is the reverse of removal. At the shift arm cover, make sure the plastic washer is between the steel washer and the cable; at the shift lever, make sure it's between the steel washer and the cotter pin.

Shift lever

Refer to illustration 3.12

9   Unscrew and remove the shift lever knob.

10   Remove the console (see Chapter 11).

11   Disconnect the select and shift cables from the shift lever (see Steps 1 through 7).

12   Remove the shift lever base mounting

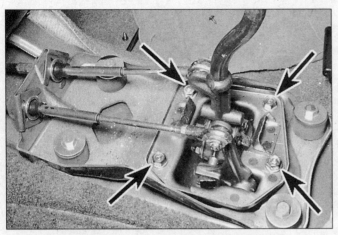

3.12 Shift lever base mounting bolts (arrows)

4.4 The back-up light switch (arrow) is threaded into the transaxle housing

bolts **(see illustration)**.
13   Remove the shift lever assembly.
14   Installation is the reverse of removal.

4   Back-up light switch - check and replacement

Check

Refer to illustration 4.4
1   Before testing the back-up light switch, check the fuse in the under-dash fuse box. Check the number 9 (10 amp) fuse. If the fuse is defective, replace it with a new one. If the fuse blows immediately (without the shift lever in reverse), check the circuit from the back-up light switch to the fuse box. If the fuse blows when the shift lever is placed in reverse, check the circuit between the back-up light switch and the back-up lights. Refer to the wiring diagrams at the end of Chapter 12.
2   Place the shift lever in REVERSE and turn the ignition switch to On. The back-up lights should go on. Turn off the ignition switch.
3   If the back-up lights didn't go on, check the back-up light bulbs in the tail light assembly.
4   If the fuse and bulbs are both okay, disconnect the electrical connector from the back-up light switch **(see illustration)** and connect an ohmmeter or continuity tester across the two switch terminals.
5   With the shift lever in REVERSE, there should be continuity; there should be no continuity with the shifter in any other gear.
6   If the switch fails the above tests, replace the switch (see below).
7   If the switch is OK, check for a poor ground in the circuit; if the grounds are good, look for an open circuit condition in the wires.

Replacement

8   Disconnect the back-up light switch electrical connector.
9   Unscrew and remove the back-up light switch.

5.7 Disconnect the VSS harness connector (arrow)

10   Discard the old washer.
11   Using a new washer, install the new switch.
12   Plug in the connector.

5   Manual transaxle - removal and installation

Removal

Refer to illustrations 5.7 and 5.10
1   Disconnect the negative cable and then the positive cable from the battery. Remove the battery and the battery tray (see Chapter 5). **Caution:** *The stereo in your vehicle is equipped with an anti-theft system. Make sure you have the correct activation code before disconnecting the battery.*
2   Remove the air intake duct and the air cleaner housing (see Chapter 4).
3   Disconnect the starter motor cables and remove the starter motor (see Chapter 5).
4   Disconnect the transaxle ground cable, disconnect the back-up light switch connectors (see Section 4) and detach the wiring harness clamp from the transaxle.
5   Shift the transaxle into reverse gear.

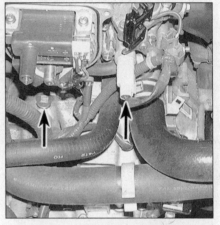

5.10 Remove the two upper transaxle mounting bolts (arrows) before raising the vehicle

6   Disconnect the shift and select cables from the transaxle (see Section 3). It's not necessary to disconnect the cables from the cable bracket assembly, simply disconnect the bracket itself from the transaxle and leave the cables attached to the bracket.
7   Disconnect the electrical connector for the vehicle speed sensor (VSS) **(see illustration)**.
8   Remove the clutch fluid hose-to-clutch fluid pressure line junction, the clutch fluid pressure line, the release cylinder and the release cylinder pushrod as a single assembly (see Chapter 8). **Caution:** *Be careful not to bend or kink the clutch fluid pressure line. And do NOT depress the clutch pedal while the clutch release cylinder is removed. Remove the clutch damper assembly, but don't disconnect the lines. Support it with a piece of wire.*
9   Refer to Chapter 2A and remove the front engine mount bracket-to-block bolts and the rear engine mount brace.
10   Detach the wiring harness from the retainers and remove the two upper transaxle mounting bolts **(see illustration)**.
11   Loosen the front wheel lug nuts, raise the vehicle and support it securely on jack-

stands. Secure the engine using a engine support fixture that is installed above the engine compartment. If an engine support fixture is not available, use an engine hoist and a lifting chain assembly. This will keep the engine stable during the transaxle removal procedure.

12 Remove the front wheels.

13 Remove the splash shield from under the front of the vehicle.

14 Drain the transaxle lubricant (see Chapter 1).

15 Disconnect the lower control arms from the steering knuckles, then disconnect the damper forks from the lower control arms (see Chapter 10).

16 Pry the left driveaxle out of the intermediate shaft and the right driveaxle out of the transaxle (see Chapter 8). Support the driveaxles with pieces of wire so they don't hang by the outer CV joints. Tie plastic bags over the inner CV joints to keep them clean.

17 Unbolt the bearing support and detach the intermediate shaft from the transaxle (see Chapter 8).

18 Remove the right damper fork pinch bolt and separate the damper fork from the shock absorber (see Chapter 10).

19 Remove the mounting bolts from both radius rods (see Chapter 10).

20 Detach the power steering fluid line from the retainers on the subframe.

21 Remove the subframe assembly (see Chapter 7B). Be sure to apply reference marks on the subframe and chassis joints to insure correct alignment when the subframe is reinstalled.

22 Remove the clutch access cover or engine stiffener assembly.

23 Remove the intake manifold bracket.

24 Swivel the right driveaxle inner CV joint forward so that it's out of the way.

25 Place a floor jack under the transaxle and raise the transaxle just enough to take the weight off the mounts. Secure the transaxle to the jack with a chain.

26 Remove the transaxle mount and mount bracket. Refer to the *Engine mounts - check and replacement* Section in Chapter 2A for additional information. Remove the stud bolt from the transaxle housing.

27 Remove the transaxle mounting bolt above the intermediate shaft and the transaxle mounting bolt near the clutch release cylinder. Remove the two rear engine mount bracket bolts.

28 Make a final check that all wires and hoses have been disconnected from the transaxle, then carefully pull the transaxle and jack away from the engine. Once the input shaft is clear, lower the transaxle and remove it from under the vehicle.

29 With the transaxle removed, the clutch components are now accessible and can be inspected. In most cases, new clutch components should be routinely installed when the transaxle is removed (see Chapter 8).

Installation

30 If removed, install the clutch components (see Chapter 8.)

31 With the transaxle secured to the jack by a chain, raise it into position behind the engine, then carefully slide it forward, engaging the four dowel pins on the transaxle with the corresponding holes in the block and the input shaft with the clutch plate hub splines. Do not use excessive force to install the transaxle - if the input shaft does not slide into place, readjust the angle of the transaxle so it is level and/or turn the input shaft so the splines engage properly with the clutch plate hub.

32 Install the lower transaxle mounting bolts and the rear engine mount bracket bolts. Tighten the bolts to the torque listed in this Chapter's Specifications.

33 Install the transaxle mount stud bolt and install the transaxle mount and mount bracket. Tighten the mount-to-body bolts, install the through-bolt, but not too tight; then tighten the three bracket-to-transaxle nuts; and finally, tighten the through-bolt (refer to Chapter 2A for the torque specifications).

34 Install the subframe, aligning the marks made during removal and tighten the bolts to the torque listed in this Chapter's Specifications. Clamp the power steering fluid line in the retainers.

35 Install the engine stiffener and the intake manifold brace.

36 Install the intermediate shaft and driveaxles. Be sure to use new retaining clips on the driveaxles (see Chapter 8)

37 Connect the radius rods to the lower control arms, install the damper forks and connect the lower control arms to the steering knuckles (see Chapter 10).

38 Install the splash shield and front wheels and lower the vehicle. Tighten the lug nuts to the torque listed in the Chapter 1 Specifications.

39 Install the two upper transaxle mounting bolts, the front engine mount bracket bolts and the rear engine mount bracket brace.

40 The remainder of installation is the reverse of removal.

41 Refill the transaxle with the specified amount of lubricant (see Chapter 1).

42 Check the clutch operation and bleed the hydraulic system, if necessary (see Chapter 8).

43 Road test the vehicle for proper operation and check for leaks.

44 Loosen and retighten the engine mounts in sequence (see Chapter 2A) if vibration is evident.

45 Have the front end aligned.

6 Manual transaxle overhaul - general information

Overhauling a manual transaxle is difficult for the do-it-yourselfer. Not only must you disassemble and reassemble many small parts, but you must also measure numerous clearances and, if necessary, change them with select-fit shims, thrust washers and spacer collars.

If transaxle problems arise, you can save a lot of money by removing and installing the transaxle yourself. Then buy a rebuilt transaxle (check with your dealer parts department and auto parts stores). The cost for an overhaul almost always exceeds the cost of a rebuilt unit. If rebuilt units aren't available, have the transaxle rebuilt by a dealer or a shop that specializes in rebuilding these units.

Chapter 7 Part B
Automatic transaxle

Contents

Specifications

General
Fluid type and capacity	See Chapter 1

Transaxle control solenoids
Lock-up control/shift solenoid A	12 to 25 ohms
Shift control solenoids B and C	12 to 25 ohms
Clutch control solenoids	5 ohms

Torque specifications
Ft-lbs (unless otherwise indicated)

Note: *One foot-pound (ft-lb) of torque is equivalent to 12 inch-pounds (in-lbs) of torque. Torque values below approximately 15 ft-lbs are expressed in inch-pounds, since most foot-pound torque wrenches are not accurate at these smaller values.*

Engine stiffener bolts	
Four-cylinder models	
10 mm bolts	33
12 mm bolt	47
V6 models	28
Gear position switch-to-case bolts	108 in-lbs
Shift cable locking nut	16
Shift cable holder bolts	108 in-lbs
Shift cable cover bolts	16
Speed sensor bolt	108 in-lbs
Subframe mounting bolts	
10 mm bolts	47
12 mm bolts	75
Torque converter-to-driveplate bolts	108 in-lbs
Torque converter cover bolts	108 in-lbs
Transaxle-to-engine bolts	47
Transaxle control solenoid bolts	107 in-lbs

1   General information

Refer to illustration 1.2

Four-cylinder models covered by this manual are equipped with either a manual transaxle or an automatic transaxle. All V6 models are equipped with an automatic transaxle. Information on the automatic is included in this Part of Chapter 7. Information on the manual transaxle can be found in Chapter 7 Part A. You'll also find certain procedures common to both transaxles - such as oil seal replacement - in Chapter 7A.

The automatic transaxle is an electronically controlled, 4-speed model. The automatic transaxles are designated B7XA (V6 models) and BAXA (four-cylinder models) **(see illustration)**. The transaxle model number is stamped onto a plate on the transaxle. Refer to *Vehicle identification numbers* at the front of this manual for the location of the plate.

Due to the complexity of the clutches and the hydraulic control system, and because of the special tools and expertise required to perform an automatic transaxle overhaul, it should not be undertaken by the home mechanic. Therefore, the procedures in this Chapter are limited to general diagnosis, routine maintenance, adjustment and transaxle removal and installation.

If the transaxle requires major repair work, it should be left to a dealer service department or an automotive or transmission repair shop. You can, however, remove and install the transaxle yourself and save the expense, even if the repair work is done by a transmission shop (but be sure a proper diagnosis has been made before removing the transaxle).

2   Diagnosis - general

Note: *Automatic transaxle malfunctions may be caused by five general conditions: poor engine performance, improper adjustments, hydraulic malfunctions, mechanical malfunctions or malfunctions in the computer or its signal network. Diagnosis of these problems should always begin with a check of the easily repaired items: fluid level and condition (see Chapter 1), shift control cable adjustment and gear position switch adjustment. Next, perform a road test to determine if the problem has been corrected or if more diagnosis is necessary. If the problem persists after the preliminary tests and corrections are completed, additional diagnosis should be done by a dealer service department or transmission repair shop. Refer to the Troubleshooting section at the front of this manual for information on symptoms of transaxle problems.*

Preliminary checks

1   Drive the vehicle to warm the transaxle to normal operating temperature.
2   Check the fluid level as described in Chapter 1:

a) *If the fluid level is unusually low, add enough fluid to bring the level within the designated area of the dipstick, then check for external leaks (see below).*

b) *If the fluid level is abnormally high, drain off the excess, then check the drained fluid for contamination by coolant. The presence of engine coolant in the automatic transmission fluid indicates that a failure has occurred in the internal radiator walls that separate the coolant from the transmission fluid (see Chapter 3).*

c) *If the fluid is foaming, drain it and refill the transaxle, then check for coolant in the fluid, or a high fluid level.*

3   Check the engine idle speed. **Note:** *If the engine is malfunctioning, do not proceed with the preliminary checks until it has been repaired and runs normally.*
4   Check the throttle control cable for freedom of movement (see Chapter 4).
5   Inspect the shift control linkage (see Section 4). Make sure that it's properly adjusted and that the linkage operates smoothly.

1.2 An underside view of the automatic transaxle and related components

1	Engine stiffener	3	Shift cable	5	Shift control cable cover
2	Subframe	4	Shift control cable holder		

3.2 Remove the locking nut from the shift cable (1) and then rotate the grommet (2) slightly to separate the cable assembly

Fluid leak diagnosis

6   Most fluid leaks are easy to locate visually. Repair usually consists of replacing a seal or gasket. If a leak is difficult to find, the following procedure may help.

7   Identify the fluid. Make sure it's transmission fluid and not engine oil or brake fluid (automatic transmission fluid is a deep red color).

8   Try to pinpoint the source of the leak. Drive the vehicle several miles, then park it over a large sheet of cardboard. After a minute or two, you should be able to locate the leak by determining the source of the fluid dripping onto the cardboard.

9   Make a careful visual inspection of the suspected component and the area immediately around it. Pay particular attention to gasket mating surfaces. A mirror is often helpful for finding leaks in areas that are hard to see.

10   If the leak still cannot be found, clean the suspected area thoroughly with a degreaser or solvent, then dry the area.

11   Drive the vehicle for several miles at normal operating temperature and varying speeds. After driving the vehicle, visually inspect the suspected component again.

12   Once the leak has been located, the cause must be determined before it can be properly repaired. If a gasket is replaced but the sealing flange is bent, the new gasket will not stop the leak. The bent flange must be straightened.

13   Before attempting to repair a leak, check to make sure that the following conditions are corrected or they may cause another leak. **Note:** *Some of the following conditions cannot be fixed without highly specialized tools and expertise. Such problems must be referred to a transmission shop or a dealer service department.*

Gasket leaks

14   Check the right side cover periodically. Make sure the bolts are tight, no bolts are missing, the gasket is in good condition and the cover is not damaged.

15   If the leak is from the right side cover area, the bolts may be too tight, the sealing surface of the transaxle housing may be damaged, the gasket may be damaged or the transaxle casting may be cracked or porous. If sealant instead of gasket material has been used to form a seal between the cover and the transaxle housing, it may be the wrong sealant.

Seal leaks

16   If a transaxle seal is leaking, the fluid level or pressure may be too high, the vent may be plugged, the seal bore may be damaged, the seal itself may be damaged or improperly installed, the surface of the shaft protruding through the seal may be damaged or a loose bearing may be causing excessive shaft movement.

17   Make sure the dipstick tube seal is in good condition and the tube is properly seated. Periodically check the area around the speedometer gear or sensor for leakage. If transmission fluid is evident, check the O-ring for damage.

Case leaks

18   If the case itself appears to be leaking, the casting is porous and will have to be repaired or replaced.

19   Make sure the oil cooler hose fittings are tight and in good condition.

Fluid comes out vent pipe or fill tube

20   If this condition occurs, the transaxle is overfilled, there is coolant in the fluid, the case is porous, the dipstick is incorrect, the vent is plugged or the drain-back holes are plugged.

3   Shift cable - removal, installation and adjustment

Warning: *The models covered by this manual are equipped with Supplemental Restraint systems (SRS), more commonly known as airbags. Always disable the airbag system before working in the vicinity of the impact sensors, steering column or instrument panel to avoid the possibility of accidental deployment of the airbag, which could cause personal injury (see Chapter 12). The yellow wiring harnesses and connectors routed through the console and instrument panel are for this system. Do not use electrical test equipment on any of the airbag system wiring or tamper with it in any way.*

Removal

Refer to illustrations 3.2, 3.6, 3.7 and 3.9

1   Remove the center console (see Chapter 11).

2   Remove the locking nut from the cable adjuster **(see illustration)**.

3   Rotate the grommet counterclockwise a quarter turn and slide the grommet along with the cable from the bracket.

4   Raise the vehicle and secure it on jackstands.

5   Working under the vehicle, remove the exhaust pipe (see Chapter 4) and the heat shield.

6   Working under the vehicle near the console, remove the shift cable guide bracket and grommet from the body **(see illustration)**.

7   Remove the bolts from the shift control cable holder **(see illustration)**. **Note:** *To prevent damage to the control lever joint, remove the shift cable holder first, and then the shift cable cover.*

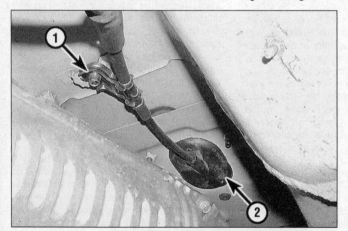

3.6 Remove the guide bracket mounting bolt (1) and pry the cable body grommet (2) from the body to separate the shift cable from the underside

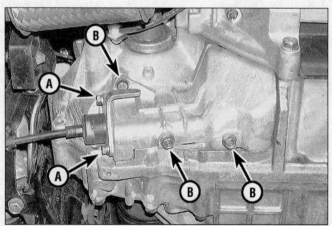

3.7 First, remove the shift control cable holder mounting bolts (A) and then the shift control cable cover mounting bolts (B)

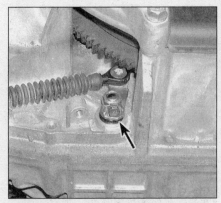

3.9 Remove the lock bolt (arrow) and slide the control lever off the transaxle

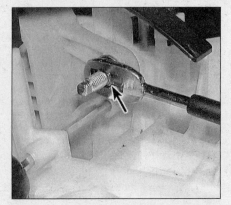

3.18 Align the shift cable with the square tabs on the mounting bolt (arrow)

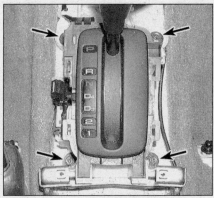

4.7 Remove the mounting screws (arrows) from the shift lever bracket base

8   Remove the bolts from the shift control cover and separate it from the transaxle.
9   Working on the transaxle linkage, remove the lock bolt, the control lever and shift cable from the assembly **(see illustration)**.

Installation

Refer to illustration 3.18

10   Working under the vehicle, insert the new shift cable through the access hole. Install the cable guide bracket.
11   Position the shift lever in REVERSE position.
12   Working on the transaxle, install the control lever with the shift cable onto the control shaft.
13   Install a new lock bolt and washer onto the control lever and bend the lock washer tab against the bolt.
14   Install the shift cable holder onto the cover and then install the cover assembly to the transaxle.
15   Working inside the passenger compartment, rotate the grommet clockwise a quarter turn and slide the assembly onto the bracket.
16   Turn the ignition ON (engine not running) and make sure the REVERSE position light activates.
17   If the cable is out of position, push the shift cable until it stops and then back one click into the reverse position.
18   Install the shift cable end to the shift lever mounting bolt and align the square surface with the alignment casting on the mounting bolt **(see illustration)**.
19   Move the shift lever to each gear to verify the correct shifting position.
20   The remainder of installation is the reverse of removal. Be sure to adjust the shift cable if necessary.

Adjustment

21   Start the engine. Shift into reverse and note whether the reverse gear engages and the reverse gear activates. If it doesn't, adjust the cable. Turn off the engine.
22   Remove the console (see Chapter 11).
23   Shift to the Neutral position, then remove the lock nut from the cable.
24   Push the shift cable until it stops and release your hand. This is the PARK position.

Pull back one click until the cable stops (locks-in) in position. This is the REVERSE position.
25   Insert a 0.24 inch pin into the positioning hole on the shift lever bracket base. The positioning hole is located on the driver's side of the shift lever housing. The diameter of the positioning hole is the same diameter as the hole located on the shifter. Once the pin is slid through the positioning hole on the shift lever bracket base, align the shift lever and slide the pin into the shift lever positioning hole to lock the assembly into place.
26   Install the shift cable end to the shift lever mounting bolt and align the square surface with the alignment casting on the mounting bolt.
27   Install the lock nut on the cable and tighten the cable in this position.
28   Remove the alignment pin from the shift lever bracket base.
29   Start the engine and check the shift lever in all gears. If any gear doesn't work properly, refer to Section 2.

4   Shift lever - removal and installation

Refer to illustration 4.7

Warning: *The models covered by this manual are equipped with Supplemental Restraint systems (SRS), more commonly known as airbags. Always disable the airbag system before working in the vicinity of the impact sensors, steering column or instrument panel to avoid the possibility of accidental deployment of the airbag, which could cause personal injury (see Chapter 12). The yellow wiring harnesses and connectors routed through the console and instrument panel are for this system. Do not use electrical test equipment on any of the airbag system wiring or tamper with it in any way.*

1   Remove the center console (see Chapter 11).
2   Disconnect the shift cable from the shift lever assembly (see Section 3).
3   Remove the shift lever knob screws and the knob. There are two mounting screws, one on each side of the shift lever knob.
4   Remove the gear position indicator

panel.
5   Disconnect the gear position light.
6   Disconnect the shift lock solenoid.
7   Remove the four mounting bolts from the shift lever bracket base **(see illustration)**.
8   Installation is the reverse of removal.

5   Shift Interlock system - description, check and component replacement

Warning: *The models covered by this manual are equipped with Supplemental Restraint systems (SRS), more commonly known as airbags. Always disable the airbag system before working in the vicinity of the impact sensors, steering column or instrument panel to avoid the possibility of accidental deployment of the airbag, which could cause personal injury (see Chapter 12). The yellow wiring harnesses and connectors routed through the console and instrument panel are for this system. Do not use electrical test equipment on any of the airbag system wiring or tamper with it in any way.*

Description

1   Vehicles equipped with an automatic transaxle have an interlock system to prevent unintentional shifting. The shift interlock system consists of two subsystems: a shift lock system and a key interlock system.
2   The key interlock system prevents the ignition key from being removed from the ignition switch unless the shift lever is in the PARK position. If you insert the key when the shift lever is in any position other than PARK, a solenoid is activated, making it impossible for you to remove the key until the shift lever is moved to the PARK position.
3   The shift lock system prevents the shift lever from moving from the PARK position into the REVERSE or DRIVE positions unless the brake pedal is depressed. Nor can the shift lever be shifted when the brake pedal and the accelerator pedal are depressed at the same time. In the event of a system malfunction, you can release the shift lever by inserting a key into the release slot near the shift lever.

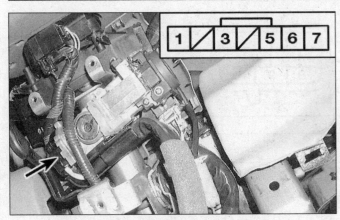

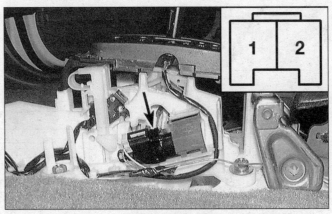

5.6 Remove the harness connector (arrow) from the key interlock solenoid

5.11 Disconnect the harness connector from the shift lock solenoid

Check

4   The following checks are simple tests of the key interlock solenoid and the shift lock solenoid.

Key interlock solenoid

Refer to illustration 5.6

5   Remove the lower instrument panel and knee bolster (see Chapter 11).

6   Disconnect the 7-pin electrical connector from the main wire harness **(see illustration)**.

7   Check for continuity between the terminals in each switch position. With the key pushed in, there should be continuity between terminals 5 and 7; with the key released, there should be no continuity between terminals 5 and 7.

8   Verify that the key can't be removed when the battery is connected to the 7 (+) and 3 (-) terminals.

9   If the key can't be removed, the key interlock solenoid is okay; if the key can be removed, the steering lock assembly needs to be replaced (see Chapter 12). The key interlock solenoid isn't available separately.

Shift lock solenoid

Refer to illustration 5.11

10   Remove the console (see Chapter 11).

11   Disconnect the two-pin electrical connector for the shift lock solenoid from the

wiring harness **(see illustration)**.

12   Using a pair of jumper wires, momentarily touch a positive battery lead to the no. 1 terminal of the two-pin connector and a negative lead to the no. 2 terminal and make sure the shift lever can be moved from the PARK position. If it doesn't, replace it. **Caution 1:** *Be careful when applying battery voltage to an electrical component. Disconnect the component from the main wiring harness and apply voltage directly to the component or to the harness connector leading to the component. Do not apply voltage to the connector on the vehicle harness-side or damage to the Powertrain Control Module may result.* **Caution 2:** *Make sure you don't connect the battery voltage leads to the wrong connector terminals. Reversing the polarity can damage or destroy the diode inside the solenoid.*

13   Remove the jumper leads from the battery terminals and the two pin connector and move the shift lever and lock it back in position in PARK.

14   Make sure the shift lock releases when the lever is pushed and locks when the lever is released.

Shift lever position switch

Refer to illustration 5.16

15   Remove the center console (see Chapter 11).

16   Disconnect the four-pin electrical connector for the shift lever position switch from the center console area **(see illustration)**.

17   Position the shift lever in PARK and check for continuity between terminals 3 and 4. There should be continuity.

18   Position the shift lever in NEUTRAL and check for continuity on terminals 3 and 4. There should be continuity.

19   If the shift lever position switch fails these tests, replace it with a new part.

Shift lock solenoid replacement

Refer to illustration 5.22

Note: *The following procedure pertains only to the shift lock solenoid. The key interlock solenoid is an integral component of the lock cylinder assembly and is not sold separately. For information on how to replace the key interlock solenoid, refer to the "Ignition switch and key lock cylinder - check and replacement" Section in Chapter 12.*

20   Remove the center console (see Chapter 11).

21   Disconnect the two-pin harness connector from the solenoid.

22   Pry off the solenoid clamp **(see illustration)**.

23   Remove the shift lock solenoid along

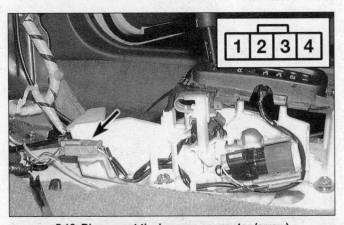

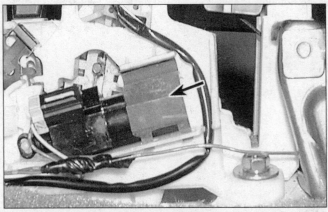

5.16 Disconnect the harness connector (arrow) from the shift lever position switch

5.22 Pry the clamp from the shift lever position switch

6.2 Disconnect the gear position switch harness connector (arrow)

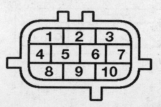

6.3 Gear position switch terminal guide and continuity table

Gear Position	Continuity between
PARK	1,3 and 10
REVERSE	3 and 9
NEUTRAL	1,3 and 8
DRIVE-4	2,3 and 7
DRIVE-3	2,3 and 6
SECOND	2,3 and 5
FIRST	3 and 4

with the plunger and plunger spring.

24 Installation is the reverse of removal.

6 Gear position switch - check, adjustment and replacement

Check

Refer to illustrations 6.2 and 6.3

1 Access to the switch connector for testing can be obtained from the engine compartment.

2 Disconnect the 10-pin electrical connector for the gear position switch **(see illustration)**.

3 Move the shift lever into each position and check for continuity between the indicated terminals in accordance with the accompanying table **(see illustration)**.

4 If the continuity isn't as designated in the table, attempt to adjust the switch. If the switch can't be adjusted to obtain the proper continuity, replace the switch.

Adjustment

5 Place the shift lever in the Neutral position.

6 Disconnect the 10-pin connector and connect an ohmmeter to terminals 1 and 3 **(see illustration 6.3)**.

7 Remove the cover and loosen the switch mounting bolts slightly. Rotate the

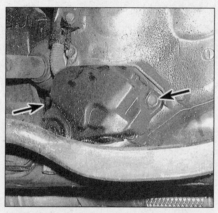

6.12a First, remove the gear position switch cover (arrows) and . . .

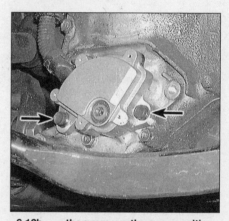

6.12b . . . then remove the gear position switch mounting bolts (arrows)

switch to the Neutral position. The switch will "click" in the Neutral position and continuity should be indicated on the meter.

8 Tighten the mounting bolts, install the cover and connect the connector.

Replacement

Refer to illustrations 6.12a, 6.12b, 6.13a and 6.13b

9 Raise the vehicle and support it securely on jackstands.

10 Disconnect the 10-pin connector **(see illustration 6.2)**. Remove the wiring harness

retainer bolt.

11 Position the shift lever in Neutral position.

12 Remove the gear position switch cover and the gear position switch mounting bolts **(see illustrations)**.

13 Position the switch and the transaxle control shaft in the Neutral position **(see illustrations)**. Install the new switch onto the control shaft. Make sure the switch remains in the Neutral position when you tighten the bolts.

14 Reconnect the connector, clamp the harness and install the cover.

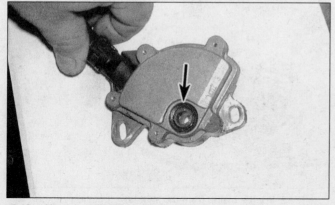

6.13a Align the NEUTRAL position tab (arrow) in the UP position

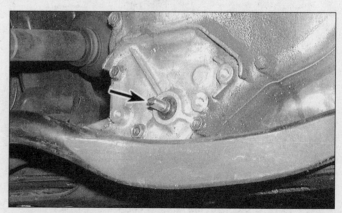

6.13b Slide the gear position switch over the control shaft

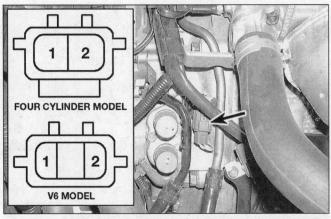

7.2 Disconnect the lock-up control/shift control solenoid A harness connector (arrow)

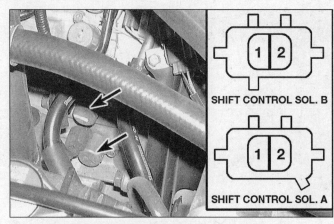

7.4 Disconnect the shift control solenoid B and C harness connectors (arrows)

15   Make sure the engine starts only when the shift lever is in the Neutral or Park position.

7   Transaxle control solenoids - check and replacement

Check

Refer to illustrations 7.2, 7.4 and 7.6
1   There are three pairs of transaxle control solenoids that can be checked; the lock-up control solenoid/shift solenoid A, the shift control solenoids B and C and the clutch pressure control solenoids. **Caution:** *Be careful when applying battery voltage to an electrical component. Disconnect the component from the main wiring harness and apply voltage directly to the component or to the harness connector leading to the component. Do not apply voltage to the connector on the vehicle harness-side or damage to the Powertrain Control Module may result.*

Lock-up control solenoid/shift control solenoid A
2   Disconnect the lock-up control sole-

noid/shift solenoid A two pin connector and measure the resistance between the connector terminal 1 and ground and then terminal 2 and ground (solenoid side) **(see illustration)**. Compare your measurements to the resistance listed in this Chapter's Specifications. If the resistance is out of specification for either terminal, replace the solenoid assembly.
3   Using a fused jumper wire, connect the battery positive terminal to terminal 1 and then alternate the same jumper wire to terminal 2. You should hear a clicking sound as each solenoid valve is energized. If you don't hear a distinct "click", replace the solenoid assembly.

Shift control solenoids B and C
4   Disconnect the shift control solenoid connectors and measure the resistance between terminals 1 and 2 of the connector (solenoid side) **(see illustration)**. Compare your measurements to the resistance listed in this Chapter's Specifications. If the resistance is out of specification for either solenoid, replace the solenoid.
5   Using a fused jumper wire, connect the battery positive terminal to terminal 2 and connect terminal 1 to ground. You should hear a clicking sound as each solenoid valve

is energized. If you don't hear a distinct "click", replace the solenoid.

Clutch pressure control solenoids
6   Disconnect the clutch pressure control solenoid connectors and measure the resistance between terminals 1 and 2 of the connector (solenoid side) **(see illustration)**. Compare your measurements to the resistance listed in this Chapter's Specifications. If the resistance is out of specification for either terminal, replace the solenoid assembly.
7   Using a fused jumper wire, connect the battery positive terminal to terminal 1 and connect terminal 2 to ground. You should hear a clicking sound as each solenoid valve is energized. If you don't, replace the solenoid assembly.

Replacement
Refer to illustrations 7.8a, 7.8b and 7.8c
Note: *The lock-up control solenoid/shift solenoid A and the clutch pressure control solenoids are replaced as an assembly, while the shift control solenoids B and C may be replaced individually.*
8   Remove the mounting bolts and remove the transaxle control solenoid valve assembly **(see illustrations)**.

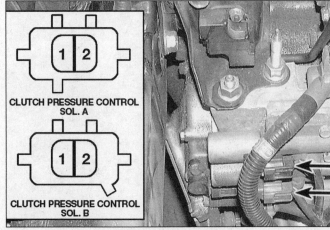

7.6 Disconnect the harness connectors from the clutch pressure control solenoids (arrows)

7.8a Remove the lock-up control/shift control solenoid A mounting bolts (arrows)

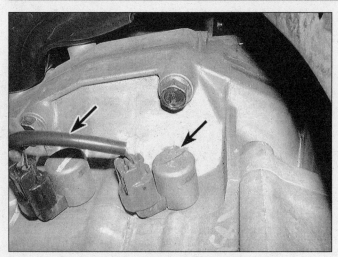

7.8b Remove the shift control solenoid B and C mounting bolts (arrows)

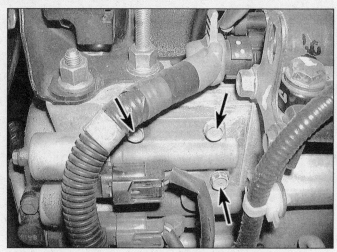

7.8c Remove the clutch pressure control solenoids mounting bolts (arrows) (not all bolts shown)

9   Clean the mounting surface and oil passages; make sure all dirt and dust is removed.

10   Install a new base gasket or O-ring, as required, and install the new solenoid valve assembly. Tighten the solenoid valve bolts to the torque listed in this Chapter's Specifications.

11   Check the electrical connector for dirt, corrosion and oil; clean it thoroughly if necessary.

12   Check the solenoid valves as described above and make sure the new unit is functioning properly.

8   Automatic transaxle - removal and installation

Removal

Refer to illustrations 8.11, 8.18, 8.19, 8.20, 8.23a, 8.23b, 8.26 and 8.30

1   Disconnect the negative cable from the battery. **Caution:** *The stereo in your vehicle is equipped with an anti-theft system. Make sure you have the correct activation code*

before disconnecting the battery.

2   Remove the air intake hose and the air cleaner housing (see Chapter 4).

3   Remove the battery and the battery tray (see Chapter 5). Disconnect the ground cable from the transaxle.

4   Disconnect the starter motor cables, remove the starter motor mounting bolts and remove the starter motor (see Chapter 5).

5   Disconnect the vehicle speed sensor electrical connector. Disconnect the electrical connectors from the transaxle control solenoids and gear position switch (see Sections 6 and 7).

6   Raise the vehicle and support it securely on jackstands. Remove the front wheels.

7   Secure the engine using an engine support fixture that is installed above the engine compartment. If an engine support fixture is not available, connect an engine hoist and a lifting chain assembly. This will keep the engine stable during the transaxle removal procedure. The engine must be supported in this manner the entire time the transaxle is out of the vehicle.

8   On four-cylinder models, remove the front engine mount bracket-to-transaxle

bolts. On V6 models, remove the front engine mount insulator-to-bracket nut.

9   Remove the splash shield underneath the front of the vehicle.

10   Drain the transaxle fluid (see Chapter 1). Reinstall the drain plug. Be sure to use a new washer.

11   Disconnect the transmission fluid cooler hoses **(see illustration)**.

12   Disconnect the electrical connector for the oxygen sensor (see Chapter 6).

13   Remove the exhaust pipe (see Chapter 4).

14   Separate the damper forks from the control arms (see Chapter 10).

15   Remove the balljoint castle nut and disconnect the lower arms from the steering knuckles (see Chapter 10).

16   Separate the driveaxles from the transaxle (see Chapter 8). Cover the inner CV joints with plastic bags to keep them clean. Support the driveaxles with wire so they don't hang from the outer CV joints. Remove the intermediate shaft.

17   Remove the right and left radius rod bolts and separate the radius rods from the control arms (see Chapter 10).

8.11 Disconnect the automatic transaxle cooler lines (arrows) (four-cylinder shown)

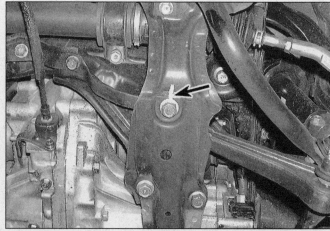

8.18 Paint a reference mark on the subframe and chassis to insure correct alignment (do this on both sides)

8.19 Subframe mounting bolts (arrows)

8.20 Engine stiffener plate bolts (arrows)

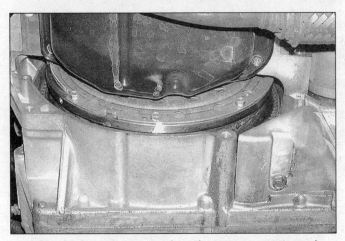

8.23a Apply a reference mark on the torque converter and driveplate to maintain the static balance on installation

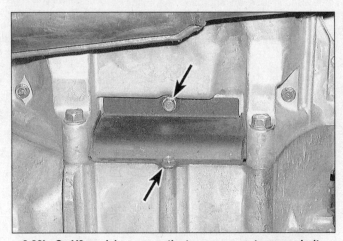

8.23b On V6 models, remove the torque converter cover bolts (arrows) and remove the cover to access the torque converter

18   Make paint marks on the chassis and the subframe assembly to insure correct alignment **(see illustration)**. Detach the power steering fluid lines from the clamps on the subframe.
19   On V6 models, remove the nuts securing the lower mounts to the subframe. Remove the subframe mounting bolts and lower the assembly from below the engine compartment **(see illustration)**
20   On V6 models remove the engine stiffener bolts. On four-cylinder models, remove the engine stiffener assembly **(see illustration)**.
21   Remove the shift cable holder (see Section 3).
22   Remove the shift cable (see Section 3).
23   Mark the relationship of the torque converter to the driveplate so they can be installed in the same position **(see illustrations)**.
24   Remove the torque converter-to-driveplate bolts. Turn the crankshaft pulley bolt for access to each bolt.
25   Remove the two rear transaxle housing bolts on the engine side.
26   Remove the bolts from the rear engine mounting bracket on four-cylinder models **(see illustration)**.

27   Remove the intake manifold bracket on four-cylinder models. The intake manifold bracket is mounted adjacent to the rear engine mounting bracket.
28   Remove the engine mounts from the transaxle. Refer to Chapter 2A or 2B for engine mount replacement procedures. On V6 models, remove the front mount bracket.

29   Place a transmission jack or a floor jack under the transaxle. Secure the transaxle to the jack with a safety chain. Raise the transaxle assembly just enough to take the load off the transaxle mount.
30   Remove the mounting bracket nuts and remove the transaxle housing mounting bolts **(see illustration)**.

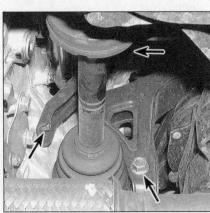

8.26 On four-cylinder models, remove the rear engine mount bracket bolts and the intake manifold bracket bolts (arrows)

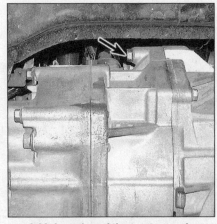

8.30 Location of the top transaxle mounting bolt (arrow)

31 Remove any other chassis or suspension components which might interfere with transaxle removal.

32 Move the transaxle back to disengage it from the engine block dowel pins and make sure the torque converter is detached from the driveplate. Secure the torque converter to the transaxle so it will not fall out during removal. Lower the transaxle from the vehicle. **Note:** *It may be necessary to slowly lower the hoist supporting the engine while the jack supporting the transaxle is being lowered. This will provide more clearance between the transaxle and the body.*

Installation

33 The manufacturer recommends flushing the transmission cooler and cooler hoses/lines with solvent whenever the transmission is removed from the vehicle for repair or overhaul. Use an approved automatic transmission flushing solvent. Flush the lines and fluid cooler thoroughly and make sure no solvent remains in the lines or cooler after flushing.

34 Prior to installation, make sure that the torque converter hub is securely engaged in the pump.

35 With the transaxle secured to the jack, raise it into position. Be sure to keep it level so the torque converter does not slide out.

36 Turn the torque converter to line it up with the driveplate. The white paint mark on the torque converter and the driveplate in Step 23 must align.

37 Make sure the two dowel pins are still installed, then move the transaxle forward carefully until the dowel pins and the torque converter are engaged.

38 Install the four transaxle housing-to-engine bolts. Tighten them to the torque listed in this Chapter's Specifications. **Caution:** *Don't use the bolts to force the transaxle and engine together. If the transaxle doesn't slide easily up against the engine, find out why before you tighten the bolts.*

39 The remainder of installation is the reverse of removal. When installing the subframe, align the marks made during removal. Tighten the subframe and suspension fasten-

ers to the torque listed in this Chapter's Specifications and Chapter 10 Specifications. Refer to Chapter 2A or 2B for the correct sequence when tightening the engine mount bolts.

40 Refill the transaxle with the recommended fluid to the specified level (see Chapter 1). Note that the transaxle may require more fluid than in a normal fluid and filter change, since the torque converter may be empty (the converter is not drained during a fluid change).

41 Start the engine, set the parking brake and shift the transaxle through all gears three times. Make sure the shift control cable is working properly (see Section 4).

42 Allow the engine to reach its proper operating temperature with the transaxle in Park or Neutral, then turn it off and check the fluid level.

43 Road test the vehicle and check for fluid leaks.

44 Loosen and retighten the engine mounts in sequence (see Chapter 2A or 2B) if vibration is experienced during the road test.

45 Have the front end aligned.

Chapter 8
Clutch and driveaxles

Contents

Specifications

General

Clutch pedal disengagement height	3 to 3-1/2 inches
Clutch pedal freeplay	3/8 to 5/8 inch
Clutch pedal standard height	7-1/2 inches
Clutch pedal stroke	5-3/4 inches

Driveaxles

Driveaxle length	
Four-cylinder engine	
Manual transaxle	
Left axle	20-13/32 to 20-19/32 inches
Right axle	19-19/32 to 19-13/16 inches
Automatic transaxle	
Left	34-3/16 to 34-13/32 inches
Right	19-19/32 to 19-13/16 inches
V6 engine	
Left	20-29/32 to 21-3/32 inches
Right	21-5/16 to 21-1/2 inches

Torque specifications

Ft-lbs (unless otherwise indicated)

Note: *One foot-pound (ft-lb) of torque is equivalent to 12 inch-pounds (in-lbs) of torque. Torque values below approximately 15 ft-lbs are expressed in inch-pounds, since most foot-pound torque wrenches are not accurate at these smaller values.*

Clutch master cylinder mounting nuts	110 in-lbs
Clutch release cylinder mounting bolts	17
Clutch pressure plate bolts	19
Driveaxle/hub nut	181
Intermediate shaft bearing support bolts	29

1   General information

The information in this Chapter deals with the components from the rear of the engine to the front wheels, except for the transaxle, which is dealt with in the previous Chapter. For the purposes of this Chapter, these components are grouped into two cat-egories - clutch and driveaxles. Separate Sections within this Chapter offer general descriptions and checking procedures for components in each of the two groups.

Since nearly all the procedures covered in this Chapter involve working under the vehicle, make sure it's securely supported on sturdy jackstands or on a hoist where the vehicle can be easily raised and lowered.

2   Clutch - description and check

1   All vehicles with a manual transaxle use a single dry-plate, diaphragm-spring type clutch. The clutch disc has a splined hub which allows it to slide along the splines of the transmission input shaft. The clutch and pressure plate are held in contact by spring

pressure exerted by the diaphragm in the pressure plate.

2   The clutch release system is operated by hydraulic pressure. The hydraulic release system consists of the clutch pedal, a master cylinder and fluid reservoir, the hydraulic line, a release (or slave) cylinder which actuates the clutch release lever and the clutch release (or throwout) bearing.

3   When pressure is applied to the clutch pedal to release the clutch, hydraulic pressure is exerted against the outer end of the clutch release lever. As the lever pivots the shaft fingers push against the release bearing. The bearing pushes against the fingers of the diaphragm spring of the pressure plate assembly, which in turn releases the clutch plate.

4   Terminology can be a problem when discussing the clutch components because common names are in some cases different from those used by the manufacturer. For example, the driven plate is also called the clutch plate or disc, the clutch release bearing is sometimes called a throwout bearing, the release cylinder is sometimes called the operating or slave cylinder.

5   Other than to replace components with obvious damage, some preliminary checks should be performed to diagnose clutch problems. These checks assume that the transaxle is in good working condition.

a) *The first check should be of the fluid level in the clutch master cylinder (see Chapter 1). If the fluid level is low, add fluid as necessary and inspect the hydraulic system for leaks. If the master cylinder reservoir has run dry, bleed the system as described in Section 5 and retest the clutch operation.*

b) *To check "clutch spin-down time," run the engine at normal idle speed with the transmission in Neutral (clutch pedal up - engaged). Disengage the clutch (pedal down), wait several seconds and shift the transmission into Reverse. No grinding noise should be heard. A grinding noise would most likely indicate a problem in the pressure plate or the clutch disc.*

c) *To check for complete clutch release, run the engine (with the parking brake applied to prevent movement) and hold the clutch pedal approximately 1/2-inch from the floor. Shift the transmission between 1st gear and Reverse several times. If the shift is rough, component failure is indicated. Check the release cylinder pushrod travel. With the clutch pedal depressed completely, the release cylinder pushrod should extend substantially. If it doesn't, check the fluid level in the clutch master cylinder.*

d) *Visually inspect the pivot bushing at the top of the clutch pedal to make sure there is no binding or excessive play.*

e) *Crawl under the vehicle and make sure the clutch release lever is solidly mounted on the ball stud.*

3.3 Pinch off the fluid feed hose with a pair of locking pliers to prevent the fluid from running out of the end of the hose when you disconnect it from the clutch master cylinder

3   Clutch master cylinder - removal and installation

Removal

Refer to illustrations 3.3 and 3.6

1   Disconnect the cable from the negative battery terminal. **Caution:** *If the radio in your vehicle is equipped with an anti-theft system, make sure you have the correct activation code before disconnecting the battery.*

2   Working under the dashboard, remove the cotter pin from the master cylinder pushrod clevis. Pull out the clevis pin to disconnect the pushrod from the pedal.

3   Detach the clutch master cylinder reservoir. Clamp a pair of locking pliers onto the clutch fluid feed hose, a couple of inches downstream of the reservoir **(see illustration)**. The pliers should be just tight enough to prevent fluid flow when the hose is disconnected. Detach the feed hose from the reservoir, remove the reservoir mounting bolt and separate the reservoir from the engine compartment.

4   Remove the retaining clip and disconnect the hydraulic line at the cylinder. Have rags handy, as some fluid will be lost as the line is removed. Cap or plug the ends of the lines (and/or hose) to prevent fluid leakage and the entry of contaminants. **Caution:** *Don't allow brake fluid to come into contact with the paint, as it will damage the finish.*

5   Remove the power relay and bracket from the fenderwell.

6   Working under the dash, unscrew the two clutch master cylinder retaining nuts **(see illustration)** and remove the cylinder.

Installation

7   Place the master cylinder in position and install the mounting bolts finger tight.

8   Using a new O-ring, connect the hydraulic line to the clutch master cylinder, then install the retaining clip. Attach the fluid feed hose to the cylinder and tighten the

3.6 To disconnect the clutch master cylinder from the clutch pedal, remove the cotter pin and clevis pin that attach it to the top of the pedal; to detach the master cylinder from the firewall, remove the two mounting nuts (arrows)

hose clamp.

9   Tighten the mounting bolts securely, then tighten the hydraulic line fitting securely. Tighten the clutch master cylinder mounting nuts to the torque listed in this Chapter's Specifications.

10   Connect the pushrod to the clutch pedal. Use a new cotter pin to secure the clevis pin.

11   Install the power relay and bracket.

12   Remove the locking pliers from the feed hose. Fill the clutch master cylinder reservoir with brake fluid conforming to DOT 3 specifications and bleed the clutch system as outlined in Section 5.

4   Clutch release cylinder - removal and installation

Removal

1   Disconnect the negative cable from the battery. **Caution:** *The stereo in your vehicle is equipped with an anti-theft system. Make sure you have the correct activation code before disconnecting the battery.*

2   Raise the vehicle and support it securely on jackstands.

3   Disconnect the hydraulic line at the release cylinder. Using a hammer and punch, drive out the roll pin from the cylinder, then detach the fitting from the cylinder. Have a small can and rags handy, as some fluid will be spilled as the line is removed.

4   Remove the two release cylinder mounting bolts.

5   Remove the release cylinder.

Installation

6   Install the release cylinder on the clutch housing, tightening the bolts to the torque listed in this Chapter's Specifications. Make sure the pushrod is seated in the release fork pocket.

5.5 When bleeding the clutch hydraulic system, a hose is connected to the bleeder valve at the release cylinder and then submerged in brake fluid. When the pedal is depressed and the valve is opened, air will be seen as bubbles in the hose and container

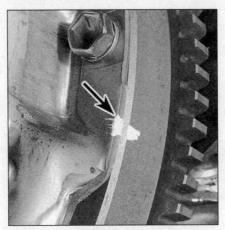

6.5 Mark the relationship of the pressure plate to the flywheel (just in case you're going to re-use the old pressure plate)

6.6 Remove the pressure plate bolts (arrows) gradually and evenly in a criss-cross pattern

7   Install a new O-ring on the hydraulic line fitting, push the fitting into the release cylinder and install the roll pin.
8   Fill the clutch master cylinder with brake fluid conforming to DOT 3 specifications.
9   Bleed the system as described in Section 5.
10   Lower the vehicle and connect the negative battery cable.

5   Clutch hydraulic system - bleeding

Refer to illustration 5.5
1   Bleed the hydraulic system whenever any part of the system has been removed or the fluid level has fallen so low that air has been drawn into the master cylinder. The bleeding procedure is very similar to bleeding a brake system.
2   Fill the master cylinder with new brake fluid conforming to DOT 3 specifications. **Caution:** *Do not re-use any of the fluid coming from the system during the bleeding operation or use fluid which has been inside an open container for an extended period of time.*
3   Raise the vehicle and place it securely on jackstands to gain access to the release cylinder, which is located on the front of the transaxle.
4   Remove the dust cap which fits over the bleeder valve and push a length of plastic hose over the valve. Place the other end of the hose into a clear container with about two inches of brake fluid. The hose end must be in the fluid at the bottom of the container.
5   Have an assistant depress the clutch pedal and hold it. Open the bleeder valve on the release cylinder, allowing fluid to flow through the hose **(see illustration)**. Close the bleeder valve when the flow of fluid (and bubbles) ceases. Once closed, have your assis-

tant release the pedal.
6   Continue this process until all air is evacuated from the system, indicated by a solid stream of fluid being ejected from the bleeder valve each time with no air bubbles in the hose or container. Keep a close watch on the fluid level inside the clutch master cylinder reservoir - if the level drops too far, air will get into the system and you'll have to start all over again.
7   Install the dust cap and lower the vehicle. Check carefully for proper operation before placing the vehicle into normal service.

6   Clutch components - removal, inspection and installation

Warning: *Dust produced by clutch wear and deposited on clutch components may contain asbestos, which is hazardous to your health. DO NOT blow it out with compressed air and DO NOT inhale it. DO NOT use gasoline or petroleum-based solvents to remove the dust. Brake system cleaner should be used to flush the dust into a drain pan. After the clutch components are wiped clean with a rag, dispose of the contaminated rags and cleaner in a covered, marked container.*

Removal

Refer to illustrations 6.5 and 6.6
1   Access to the clutch components is normally accomplished by removing the transaxle, leaving the engine in the vehicle. If the engine is being removed for major overhaul, check the clutch for wear and replace worn components as necessary. However, the relatively low cost of the clutch components compared to the time and trouble spent gaining access to them warrants their replacement anytime the engine or transaxle is removed, unless they are new or in near-perfect condition. The following procedures are based on the assumption the engine will stay in place.

2   Remove the transaxle from the vehicle (see Chapter 7, Part A). Support the engine while the transaxle is out. Preferably, an engine hoist should be used to support it from above. However, if a jack is used underneath the engine, make sure a piece of wood is positioned between the jack and oil pan to spread the load. **Caution:** *The pick-up for the oil pump is very close to the bottom of the oil pan. If the pan is bent or distorted in any way, engine oil starvation could occur.*
3   The clutch fork and release bearing can remain attached to the transaxle housing for the time being.
4   To support the clutch disc during removal, install a clutch alignment tool through the clutch disc hub.
5   Carefully inspect the flywheel and pressure plate for indexing marks. The marks are usually an X, an O or a white letter. If they cannot be found, scribe or paint marks yourself so the pressure plate and the flywheel will be in the same alignment during installation **(see illustration)**.
6   Turning each bolt a little at a time, loosen the pressure plate-to-flywheel bolts **(see illustration)**. Work in a criss-cross pattern until all spring pressure is relieved. Then hold the pressure plate securely and completely remove the bolts, followed by the pressure plate and clutch disc.

Inspection

Refer to illustrations 6.9, 6.11a and 6.11b
7   Ordinarily, when a problem occurs in the clutch, it can be attributed to wear of the clutch driven plate assembly (clutch disc). However, all components should be inspected at this time.
8   Inspect the flywheel for cracks, heat checking, grooves and other obvious defects. If the imperfections are slight, a machine shop can machine the surface flat and smooth, which is highly recommended regardless of the surface appearance. Refer to Chapter 2 for the flywheel removal and installation procedure.
9   Inspect the lining on the clutch disc.

6.9 The clutch disc

1   *Lining* - this will wear down in use
2   *Springs or dampers* - check for cracking and deformation
3   *Splined hub* - the splines must not be worn and should slide smoothly on the transaxle input shaft splines
4   *Rivets* - these secure the lining and will damage the flywheel or pressure plate if allowed to contact the surfaces

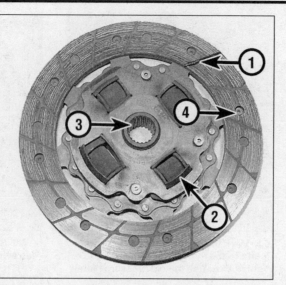

There should be at least 1/16-inch of lining above the rivet heads. Check for loose rivets, distortion, cracks, broken springs and other obvious damage **(see illustration)**. As mentioned above, ordinarily the clutch disc is routinely replaced, so if in doubt about the condition, replace it with a new one.

10   The release bearing should also be replaced along with the clutch disc (see Section 7).

11   Check the machined surfaces and the diaphragm spring fingers of the pressure plate **(see illustrations)**. If the surface is grooved or otherwise damaged, replace the pressure plate. Also check for obvious damage, distortion, cracking, etc. Light glazing can be removed with emery cloth or sandpaper. If a new pressure plate is required, new and factory-rebuilt units are available.

Installation

Refer to illustration 6.13

12   Before installation, clean the flywheel and pressure plate machined surfaces with brake cleaner, lacquer thinner or acetone. It's important that no oil or grease is on these surfaces or the lining of the clutch disc. Handle the parts only with clean hands.

13   Position the clutch disc and pressure plate against the flywheel with the clutch held in place with an alignment tool **(see illustration)**. Make sure the disc is installed properly (most replacement clutch discs will be marked "flywheel side" or something similar - if not marked, install the clutch disc with the damper springs toward the transaxle).

14   Tighten the pressure plate-to-flywheel bolts only finger tight, working around the pressure plate.

15   Center the clutch disc by ensuring the alignment tool extends through the splined hub and into the pocket in the crankshaft. Wiggle the tool up, down or side-to-side as needed to center the disc. Tighten the pressure plate-to-flywheel bolts a little at a time, working in a criss-cross pattern to prevent distorting the cover. After all of the bolts are snug, tighten them to the torque listed in this Chapter's Specifications. Remove the alignment tool.

16   Using high-temperature grease, lubricate the inner groove of the release bearing (see Section 7). Also place grease on the release lever contact areas and the transaxle input shaft bearing retainer.

17   Install the clutch release bearing (see Section 7).

NORMAL FINGER WEAR

EXCESSIVE WEAR

EXCESSIVE FINGER WEAR

BROKEN OR BENT FINGERS

6.11a Replace the pressure plate if any of these conditions are noted

6.11b Inspect the pressure plate surface for excessive score marks, cracks and signs of overheating

6.13 Center the clutch disc in the pressure plate with a clutch alignment tool

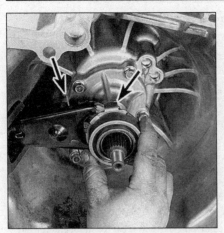

7.3 Reach behind the release lever and disengage the lever from the ball stud by pulling on the retention spring (left arrow), then remove the lever and slide the bearing tangs (right arrow) off the lever

7.4 To check the bearing, hold it by the outer race and rotate the inner race while applying pressure; if the bearing doesn't turn smoothly or if it is noisy, replace the bearing

7.6 Apply a light coat of high-temperature grease to the bearing surface of the retainer (before installing the transaxle, apply the same grease to the input shaft splines and the ball stud to help the shaft slide through the clutch hub)

18   Install the transaxle and all components removed previously.

---

7   Clutch release bearing and fork - removal, inspection and installation

---

Warning: *Dust produced by clutch wear and deposited on clutch components may contain asbestos, which is hazardous to your health. DO NOT blow it out with compressed air and DO NOT inhale it. DO NOT use gasoline or petroleum-based solvents to remove the dust. Brake system cleaner should be used to flush the dust into a drain pan. After the clutch components are wiped clean with a rag, dispose of the contaminated rags and cleaner in a covered, marked container.*

Removal

Refer to illustration 7.3

1   Unbolt the clutch release cylinder (see Section 4), but don't disconnect the fluid line

between the master cylinder and the release cylinder. Suspend the release cylinder out of the way with a piece of wire.
2   Remove the transaxle (see Chapter 7, Part A).
3   Slide the release bearing off the input shaft. Pull the clutch release fork off the ball stud and remove the fork **(see illustration)**.

Inspection

Refer to illustration 7.4

4   Hold the bearing by the outer race and rotate the inner race while applying pressure **(see illustration)**. If the bearing doesn't turn smoothly or if it's noisy, replace it with a new one. Wipe the bearing with a clean rag and inspect it for damage, wear and cracks. It's common practice to replace the bearing with a new one whenever a clutch job is performed, to decrease the possibility of a bearing failure in the future. Don't immerse the bearing in solvent - it's sealed for life and to do so would ruin it.
5   Check the release lever for cracks and bends.

Installation

Refer to illustrations 7.6, 7.7a and 7.7b

6   Fill the inner groove of the release bearing with high temperature grease. Also apply a light coat of the same grease to the transaxle input shaft splines, ball stud and the front bearing retainer **(see illustration)**.
7   Lubricate the release fork ball socket, fork ends and release cylinder pushrod socket with high temperature grease **(see illustrations)**.
8   Attach the release bearing to the release fork.
9   Slide the release bearing onto the transaxle input shaft front bearing retainer while passing the end of the release fork through the opening in the clutch housing. Push the clutch release fork onto the ball stud until it's firmly seated.
10   Apply a light coat of high temperature grease to the face of the release bearing where it contacts the pressure plate diaphragm fingers.
11   The remainder of installation is the reverse of the removal procedure.

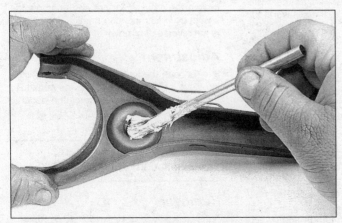

7.7a Using high temperature grease, lubricate the ball stud socket in the back of the release lever . . .

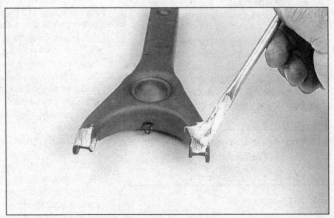

7.7b . . . the lever ends and the depression for the release cylinder pushrod

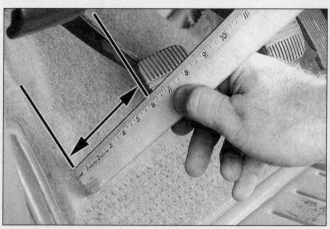

8.1 Clutch pedal height is the distance between the pedal pad and the floor

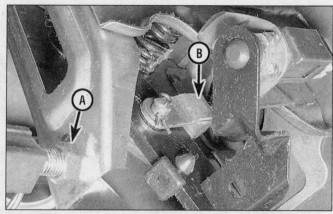

8.2 Back-out the stopper bolt or switch (A) for clearance, then loosen the locknut on the pushrod (B). Turn the pushrod to adjust the pedal height

8   Clutch pedal adjustment

Pedal height

Refer to illustrations 8.1 and 8.2

1   The height of the clutch pedal is the distance the pedal sits off the floor **(see illustration)**. If the pedal height is not within the specified range, it must be adjusted.

2   To adjust the clutch pedal, loosen the locknut on the clutch switch or adjusting bolt and back the switch out until it no longer touches the pedal, then loosen the locknut on the clutch pushrod **(see illustration)**. **Note:** *The clutch switch is the lower of the two switches (the upper one is the starter/clutch interlock switch).* Turn the pushrod to adjust the pedal height, then tighten the locknut.

3   Turn the switch or bolt clockwise until it just contacts the pedal arm, then turn it in an additional 3/4 to 1 turn. Tighten the locknut.

4   Adjust the starter/clutch interlock switch as described in Section 9.

Pedal freeplay

Refer to illustration 8.5

5   The freeplay is the pedal slack, or the distance the pedal can be depressed before it begins to have any effect on the clutch system **(see illustration)**. If the pedal freeplay is not within the specified range, it must be adjusted.

6   To adjust the pedal freeplay, loosen the locknut on the clutch pushrod. Then back off the pushrod to adjust the pedal freeplay to the specified range and retighten the locknut.

7   Check and, if necessary, adjust the starter/interlock switch (see Section 9).

9   Starter/clutch interlock switch - check, replacement and adjustment

Refer to illustration 9.4

Check

1   The starter/clutch interlock switch is

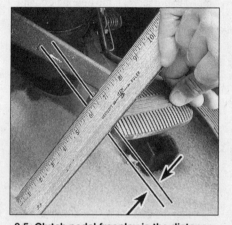

8.5 Clutch pedal freeplay is the distance from the natural resting point of the pedal to the point at which resistance is felt

located near the upper end of the clutch pedal. It has two wires - one coming from the starter relay and one going to ground. When the ignition switch key is turned to the Start position and the clutch pedal is depressed, the starter relay's path to ground is closed by the starter/clutch interlock switch and the starter motor is activated.

2   If the engine won't crank when the clutch pedal is depressed, adjust the switch (see Step 6) and try again. If it still won't turn over, check the switch (see Step 3) and, if necessary, replace it (see Step 5). If the engine starts when the clutch pedal isn't depressed, adjust the switch and try again.

3   If the engine won't start when the clutch pedal is depressed, either there's no voltage from the starter relay to the switch, or there's no continuity between the two terminals on the switch.

4   Check the voltage to the switch using a voltmeter or test light. When you turn the ignition key to the START position and depress the clutch pedal, there should be voltage in the wire from the starter relay **(see illustration)**. If there isn't, look for an open or short circuit condition somewhere between the starter relay and the switch. If there is voltage in this wire, check the other

9.4 Location of the starter clutch interlock switch (arrow) (dash disassembled for clarity)

side of the switch for voltage (with the pedal depressed). If there's voltage on both sides of the switch, the switch should be operating correctly. Try adjusting it (see Step 6). If voltage isn't present on both sides, the switch is bad.

Replacement

5   Disconnect the electrical connector, loosen the adjustment nut and unscrew the switch from its mounting bracket. Installation is the reverse of removal.

Adjustment

6   Loosen the locknut and turn the switch in or out, as necessary, to provide continuity through the switch when the clutch pedal is depressed.

10   Driveaxle - removal and installation

Removal

Refer to illustrations 10.1, 10.2, 10.6, 10.7a and 10.7b

1   Remove the wheel cover or hub cap.

10.1 If the driveaxle nut is "staked," use a center punch to unstake it (wheel removed for clarity)

10.2 Loosen the driveaxle/hub nut with a long breaker bar

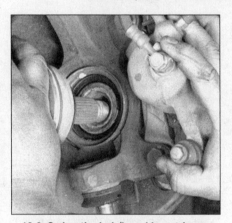

10.6 Swing the hub/knuckle out (away from the vehicle) and pull the driveaxle from the hub

10.7a Use a large screwdriver or a prybar to pop the inner end of the driveaxle from the transaxle, or . . .

10.7b . . . if you're removing the left driveaxle, insert the prybar between the intermediate shaft bearing and the driveaxle to pop it loose

Caution: *On some models the lug nuts retain the wheel cover. If this is the case on your vehicle, loosen the lug nuts, raise the vehicle, remove the lug nuts and wheel cover, then install the lug nuts and lower the vehicle. If the driveaxle/hub nut is staked, unstake it with a punch or chisel* **(see illustration)***; if it's secured by locking tabs, bend the tabs out.*

2   Break the hub nut loose with a socket and large breaker bar **(see illustration)**.

3   Loosen the wheel lug nuts, raise the vehicle and support it securely on jackstands. Remove the wheel. Drain the transaxle lubricant (see Chapter 1).

4   Disconnect the damper fork from the shock absorber assembly and the lower control arm (see Chapter 10).

5   Separate the lower control arm from the steering knuckle (see Chapter 10). Now remove the driveaxle/hub nut.

6   Swing the knuckle/hub assembly out (away from the vehicle) until the end of the driveaxle is free of the hub **(see illustration)**. **Note:** *If the driveaxle splines stick in the hub, tap on the end of the driveaxle with a plastic hammer.* Support the outer end of the driveaxle with a piece of wire to avoid unnecessary strain on the inner CV joint.

7   Carefully pry the inner end of the driveaxle from the transaxle or intermediate shaft using a large screwdriver or prybar positioned between the transaxle or bearing support and the CV joint housing **(see illustrations)**. Support the CV joints and carefully remove the driveaxle from the vehicle. To prevent damage to the intermediate shaft seal or the differential seal, hold the inner CV joint horizontal until the driveaxle is clear of the intermediate shaft or transaxle.

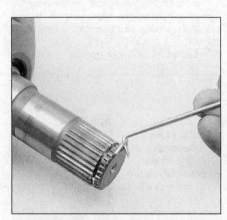

10.8a Pry the old spring clip from the inner end of the driveaxle with a small screwdriver or awl

Installation

Refer to illustrations 10.8a and 10.8b

8   Pry the old spring clip from the inner end of the driveaxle and install a new one **(see illustrations)**. Lubricate the differential or intermediate shaft seal with multi-purpose grease and raise the driveaxle into position while supporting the CV joints.

10.8b To install the new spring clip, start one end in the groove and work the clip over the shaft end, into the groove

11.5 The intermediate shaft bearing support is retained by three bolts - two are shown here (arrows)

12.3a Cut off the boot clamps and discard them - don't try to reuse old clamps

12.3b Slide the boot down the driveaxle, out of the way

9   Insert the splined end of the inner CV joint into the differential side gear or intermediate shaft and make sure the spring clip locks in its groove.

10   Apply a light coat of multi-purpose grease to the outer CV joint splines, pull out on the strut/steering knuckle assembly and install the stub axle into the hub.

11   Insert the stud of the steering knuckle balljoint into the lower control arm and tighten the nut (see the torque specifications in Chapter 10). Be sure to use a new cotter pin. Install the damper fork (see Chapter 10).

12   Install the driveaxle/hub nut (and, if applicable, a new locking tab washer). Tighten the hub nut securely, but don't try to tighten it to the actual torque specification until you've lowered the vehicle to the ground.

13   Grasp the inner CV joint housing (not the driveaxle) and pull out to make sure the driveaxle has seated securely in the transaxle.

14   Install the wheel and lug nuts, then lower the vehicle.

15   Tighten the lug nuts to the torque listed in the Chapter 1 Specifications. Tighten the driveaxle/hub nut to the torque listed in this Chapter's Specifications. Using a hammer and punch, stake the nut to the groove in the driveaxle. If the hub nut uses a locking tab, be sure to bend the tabs up against the nut. Install the wheel cover (if applicable).

16   Refill the transaxle with the recommended type and amount of lubricant (see Chapter 1).

11   Intermediate shaft - removal and installation

Removal

Refer to illustration 11.5

1   Loosen the left (driver's side) front wheel lug nuts, raise the front of the vehicle and support it securely on jackstands. Remove the wheel.

2   Drain the transaxle lubricant (see Chapter 1).

3   Remove the damper fork and separate the left lower control arm from the steering knuckle (see Chapter 10).

4   Pry the inner CV joint housing from the intermediate shaft. Position the driveaxle out of the way and hang it with a piece of wire. Do not allow it to hang unsupported, as the outer CV joint may be damaged.

5   Remove the three bearing support-to-engine block bolts **(see illustration)** and slide the intermediate shaft out of the transaxle. Be careful not to damage the differential seal when pulling the shaft out.

6   Check the support bearing for smooth operation by turning the shaft while holding the bearing. If you feel any roughness, take the bearing support to a dealer service department or other repair shop to have a new bearing installed. To do the job at home, you'd need specialized tools.

Installation

7   Lubricate the lips of the differential seal with multi-purpose grease. Carefully guide the intermediate shaft into the differential side gear then install the mounting bolts through the bearing support. Tighten the bolts to the torque listed in this Chapter's Specifications.

8   Install a new spring clip on the inner CV joint **(see illustrations 10.8a and 10.8b)** and seat the driveaxle into the intermediate shaft splines.

9   Connect the lower control arm to the steering knuckle and tighten the balljoint stud nut to the torque listed in the Chapter 10 Specifications. Install the damper fork, tightening its fasteners to the torque listed in the Chapter 10 Specifications.

10   Install the wheel and lug nuts, lower the vehicle and tighten the lug nuts to the torque listed in the Chapter 1 Specifications.

11   Refill the transaxle with the proper type and amount of lubricant (see Chapter 1).

12   Driveaxle boot - replacement

Note 1: *If the CV joints are worn, indicating the need for an overhaul (usually due to torn boots), explore all options before beginning the job. Complete rebuilt driveaxles are available on an exchange basis, which eliminates much time and work.*

Note 2: *Some auto parts stores carry "split" type replacement boots, which can be installed without removing the driveaxle from the vehicle. This is a convenient alternative; however, the driveaxle should be removed and the CV joint disassembled and cleaned to ensure the joint is free from contaminants such as moisture and dirt which will accelerate CV joint wear.*

1   Remove the driveaxle from the vehicle (see Section 10).

2   Mount the driveaxle in a vise. The jaws of the vise should be lined with wood or rags to prevent damage to the driveaxle.

12.4 Mark the relationship of the tri-pot assembly to the outer race

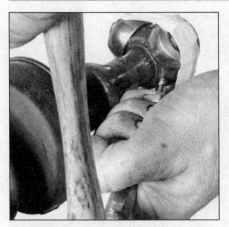

12.6 Secure the bearing rollers with tape and drive the tri-pot off the shaft with a hammer and brass drift, then remove the stop-ring

12.10a Wrap the splined area of the axleshaft with tape to prevent damage to the boot when installing it

12.10b Remove the tape and install the stop-ring on the axleshaft, making sure it seats in its groove

Inner CV joint and boot

Disassembly

Refer to illustrations 12.3a, 12.3b, 12.4 and 12.6

3   Cut off both boot clamps and slide the boot towards the center of the driveaxle **(see illustrations)**.

4   Remove the outer race from the tri-pot assembly, but keep them in the same relationship to each other. Clean off the grease, then scribe or paint alignment marks on the outer race and the tri-pot bearing assembly so they can be returned to their original position **(see illustration)**.

5   Remove the snap-ring from the end of the axleshaft.

6   Secure the bearing rollers with tape, then remove the tri-pot bearing assembly from the axleshaft with a brass drift and a hammer **(see illustration)**. Remove the tape, but don't let the rollers fall off and get mixed up.

7   Remove the stop-ring, slide the old boot off the driveaxle and discard it.

Inspection

8   Clean the old grease from the outer race

and the tri-pot bearing assembly. Carefully disassemble each section of the tri-pot assembly, one at a time so as not to mix up the parts, and clean the needle bearings with solvent.

9   Inspect the rollers, tri-pot, bearings and outer race for scoring, pitting or other signs of abnormal wear, which will warrant the replacement of the inner CV joint.

Reassembly

Refer to illustrations 12.10a, 12.10b, 12.12, 12.13, 12.14, 12.15, 12.16, 12.17a, 12.17b, 12.17c, 12.17d and 12.17e

10   Wrap the splines of the axleshaft with tape to avoid damaging the new boot, then slide the boot onto the axleshaft **(see illustration)**. Remove the tape and slide the inner stop-ring into place **(see illustration)**.

11   Slide the tri-pot assembly onto the axleshaft.

12   Install the outer snap-ring **(see illustration)**.

13   Apply a coat of CV joint grease to the inner bearing surfaces to hold the needle bearings in place when reassembling the tri-pot assembly **(see illustration)**. Make sure each roller is installed on the same post as

12.12 Install the tri-pot assembly on the axleshaft, then install the snap-ring

before. **Note:** *If the rollers are equipped with a flat, rectangular shaped surface, make sure the flat sides are positioned closest to the driveaxle.*

14   Pack the outer race with half of the grease furnished with the new boot and place the remainder in the boot. Install the outer race **(see illustration)**. Make sure the marks

12.13 Use plenty of CV joint grease to hold the needle bearings in place when you install the roller assemblies on the tri-pot, and make sure you put each roller in its original position

12.14 Pack the outer race with grease and slide it over the tri-pot assembly - make sure the match marks on the outer race and tri-pot line up

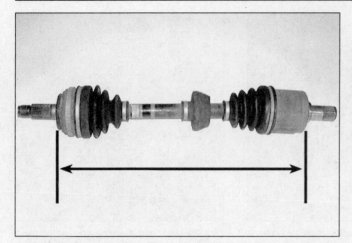

12.15 Before tightening the boot clamps, adjust the driveaxle length to the dimension listed in this Chapter's Specifications

12.16 Equalize the pressure inside the boot by inserting a small, dull screwdriver between the boot and the outer race

you made on the tri-pot assembly and the outer race are aligned.

15   Seat the boot in the grooves in the outer race and the axleshaft, then adjust the driveaxle to the proper length **(see illustration)**.

16   With the driveaxle set to the proper length, equalize the pressure in the boot by inserting a blunt screwdriver between the boot and the outer race **(see illustration)**. Don't damage the boot with the tool.

17   Install and tighten the new boot clamps **(see illustrations)**.

18   Install the driveaxle assembly (see Section 10).

Outer CV joint and boot

Disassembly

19   Following Steps 3 through 7, remove the inner CV joint from the driveaxle and disassemble it.

20   If the driveaxle is equipped with a dynamic damper, scribe or paint a location mark on the axleshaft along the outer edge of the damper (the side facing the outer CV

12.17a To install new fold-over type clamps, bend the tang down . . .

joint), cut the retaining clamp and slide the damper off. **Note:** *If you're planning to replace the axleshaft and outer CV joint assembly, measure the distance between the outer CV joint boot and the dynamic damper.*

12.17b . . . and flatten the tabs to hold it in place

Record this measurement.

21   Cut the boot clamps from the outer CV joint. Slide the boot off the shaft. **Note:** *The outer CV joint can't be disassembled or removed from the shaft.*

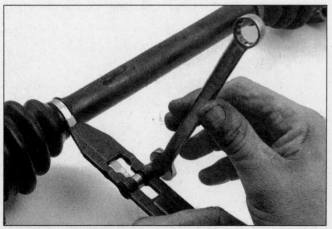

12.17c To install band-type clamps you'll need a special tool; install the band with its end pointing in the direction of axle rotation and tighten it securely, then pivot the tool up 90-degrees and tap the center of the clip with a center punch . . .

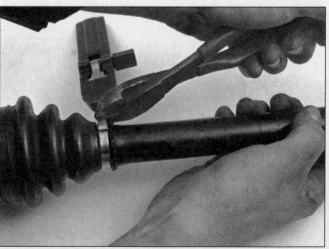

12.17d . . . then bend the end of the clamp back over the clip and cut off the excess

12.17e If you're installing crimp-type boot clamps, you'll need a pair of special crimping pliers (available at most auto parts stores)

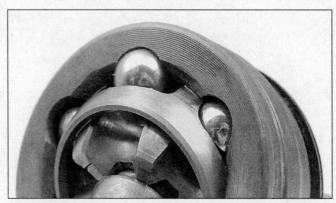

12.23 After the old grease has been rinsed away and the solvent has been blown out with compressed air, rotate the outer joint assembly through its full range of motion and inspect the bearing surfaces for wear and damage - if any of the ball bearings, the race or the cage look damaged, replace the driveaxle and outer joint assembly

Inspection

Refer to illustration 12.23

22 Thoroughly wash the inner and outer CV joints in clean solvent and blow them dry with compressed air, if available. **Warning:** *Wear eye protection when using compressed air.* **Note:** *Because the outer joint can't be disassembled, it is difficult to wash away all the old grease and to rid the bearing of solvent once it's clean. But it is imperative that the job be done thoroughly, so take your time and do it right.*

23 Bend the outer CV joint housing at an angle to the axleshaft to expose the bearings, inner race and cage **(see illustration).**

Inspect the bearing surfaces for signs of wear. If the bearings are damaged or worn, replace the driveaxle.

Reassembly

24 Slide the new outer boot onto the axleshaft. It's a good idea to wrap tape around the splines of the shaft to prevent damage to the boot **(see illustration 12.10a)**. When the boot is in position, add the specified amount of grease (included in the boot replacement kit) to the outer joint and the boot (pack the joint with as much grease as it will hold and put the rest into the boot). Slide the boot on

the rest of the way and install the new clamps **(see illustrations 12.17a through 12.17e)**.

25 Slide the dynamic damper, if equipped, onto the shaft. Make sure its outer edge is aligned with the previously applied mark. **Note:** *If you're using a new axleshaft and outer CV joint assembly, return the damper to the same relative position to the outer boot that it was on the old shaft (as measured in Step 20). Install a new retaining clamp.*

26 Clean and reassemble the inner CV joint by following Steps 8 through 17, then install the driveaxle as outlined in Section 10.

Notes

Chapter 9 Brakes

Contents

Specifications

General

Brake pedal
Height (with carpet removed)

Manual transaxle	6-1/2 inches
Automatic transaxle	6-5/8 inches
Freeplay	1/16 to 3/16 inch

Parking brake lever travel

Disc	6 to 9 clicks
Drum	4 to 7 clicks

Power brake booster pushrod-to-master cylinder piston clearance
(with a vacuum of 20 in-Hg applied to booster) .... 0.0 to 0.020 inch

Disc brakes

Brake pad minimum thickness	See Chapter 1
Disc minimum thickness	Refer to minimum thickness cast into disc
Thickness variation (parallelism)	No more than 0.0006 inch
Runout limit	0.004 inch

Drum brakes

Brake lining minimum thickness	See Chapter 1
Drum diameter (maximum)	Refer to maximum diameter cast into drum

Torque specifications Ft-lbs (unless otherwise indicated)

Note: *One foot-pound (ft-lb) of torque is equivalent to 12 inch-pounds (in-lbs) of torque. Torque values below approximately 15 ft-lbs are expressed in inch-pounds, since most foot-pound torque wrenches are not accurate at these smaller values.*

General

Brake hose-to-caliper banjo bolt (front or rear)	25
Master cylinder mounting nuts	132 in-lbs
Strut brace mounting nuts	16
Brake booster mounting nuts	110 in-lbs
Wheel sensor mounting bolts	88 in-lbs

Front disc brake

Caliper mounting bolts

Four cylinder models	54
V6 models	36
Caliper mounting bracket bolts	80

Rear disc brake

Caliper mounting bolts	19
Caliper mounting bracket bolts	28
Disc-to-hub screws	84 in-lbs

Rear drum brake

Wheel cylinder nuts	80 in-lbs

1   General information

General

All vehicles covered by this manual are equipped with hydraulically operated, power-assisted brake systems. All front brake systems are disc type. Some models use drum type brakes at the rear, others are equipped with rear disc brakes.

All brakes are self-adjusting. The front and rear disc brakes automatically compensate for pad wear, while the rear drum brakes incorporate an adjustment mechanism which is activated as the brakes are applied, either through the pedal or the parking brake lever.

The hydraulic system is a split design, meaning there are two separate circuits that control the brakes. If one circuit fails, the other circuit will remain functional and a warning indicator will light up on the dashboard when a substantial amount of brake fluid is lost, showing that a failure has occurred.

Master cylinder

The master cylinder is bolted to the power brake booster, which is mounted on the driver's side of the firewall. To locate the master cylinder, look for the large fluid reservoir on top. The fluid reservoir is plastic, secured to the master cylinder by grommets and a roll pin.

The master cylinder is designed for the "split system" mentioned earlier and has separate piston assemblies for each circuit.

Proportioning valve

The proportioning valve assembly is located on the firewall, near the master cylinder. It regulates the hydraulic pressure to the rear brakes during heavy braking to eliminate rear wheel lock-up. Under normal braking conditions, it allows full pressure to the rear brake system until a predetermined pedal pressure is reached. Above that point, the pressure to the rear brakes is limited.

The proportioning valve is not serviceable. If a problem develops with the valve, it must be replaced as an assembly.

Power brake booster

The power brake booster, which uses engine manifold vacuum and atmospheric pressure to provide assistance to the hydraulically operated brakes, is mounted on the firewall in the engine compartment.

Parking brake

A parking brake lever inside the vehicle operates a rod attached to a pair of rear cables, each of which is connected to its respective rear brake. When the parking-brake lever is pulled up on drum brake models, each rear cable pulls on a lever attached to the brake shoe assembly, causing the shoes to expand against the drum. When the lever is pulled on models with rear disc brakes, the rear cables pull on levers that are attached to screw-type actuators in the caliper housings, which apply force to the caliper pistons, clamping the brake pads against the brake disc.

Precautions

There are some general cautions and warnings involving the brake system on these vehicles:

a) *Use only brake fluid conforming to DOT 3 specifications.*

b) *The brake pads and linings may contain asbestos fibers, which are hazardous to your health if inhaled. Whenever you work on brake system components, clean all parts with brake system cleaner. Do not allow the fine dust to become airborne, and wear a filter/mask over your nose and mouth when cleaning or servicing brakes, regardless of the material the pads are made of.*

c) *Safety should be paramount whenever any servicing of the brake components is performed. Do not use parts or fasteners which are not in perfect condition, and be sure that all clearances and torque specifications are adhered to. If you are at all unsure about a certain procedure, seek professional advice. Upon completion of any brake system work, test the brakes carefully in a controlled area before putting the vehicle into normal service.*

d) *If a problem is suspected in the brake system, don't drive the vehicle until it's fixed.*

2   Anti-lock Brake System (ABS) (and Traction Control System on 2001 and later V6 models) - general information and trouble codes

General information

In a conventional braking system, if you press the brake pedal too hard, the wheels can "lock up" (stop turning) and the vehicle can go into a skid. If the wheels lock up, you can lose control of the vehicle. The Anti-lock Brake System (ABS) prevents the wheels from locking up by modulating (pulsing on and off) the pressure of the brake fluid at each caliper. On 2001 and later V6 models, a Traction Control System (TCS) works in conjunction with the ABS. The TCS helps to maintain wheel traction during low-speed driving on loose or slippery surfaces.

The Anti-lock Brake System has two basic subsystems: One is an electrical system and the other is hydraulic. The electrical half has four "gear pulsers," four wheel sensors, a computer and an electrical circuit connecting all the components. The hydraulic part of the system consists of a solenoid/modulator, the disc brake calipers and the hydraulic fluid lines between the solenoid/modulator and the calipers.

In principle, the system is pretty simple: Each wheel has a wheel sensor monitoring a gear pulser (a ring with evenly spaced raised ridges cast into its circumference). The wheel sensor "counts" the ridges of the gear pulser as they pass by, converts this information into an electrical output and transmits it back to the computer. The computer constantly "samples" the voltage inputs from all four wheel sensors and compares them to each other. As long as the gear pulsers at all four wheels are rotating at the same speed, the Anti-lock Brake System is inactive. But when a wheel locks up, the voltage signal from that wheel sensor deviates from the signals coming from the other wheels. So the computer "knows" the wheel is locking up. It sends an electrical signal to the solenoid/modulator assembly, which releases the brake fluid pressure to the brake caliper at that wheel. As soon as the wheel unlocks and resumes turning at the same rate of speed as the other wheels, its wheel sensor voltage output once again matches the output of the other wheels and the computer deactivates the signal to the solenoid/modulator.

The TCS operates by utilizing the ABS/TCS Control Unit, a switch, a relay and other ABS components. The TCS is designed to operate up to speeds of approximately 18 mph to improve traction during acceleration and on slippery surfaces. The system operates by simultaneously applying braking to the front wheel that is losing traction, and retarding the engine.

In reality, the Anti-lock Brake System and Traction Control System are far more complex than they sound, so we don't recommend that you attempt to diagnose or service them. If the Anti-lock Brake System or TCS on your vehicle develops problems, take it to a dealer service department or other qualified shop.

ABS and TCS trouble codes

Normally, the ABS indicator light should come on when the engine is started, then go off immediately. Under certain conditions, however, the indicator light may remain on. If this occurs, the ABS computer has stored a diagnostic trouble code because it has detected a problem in the ABS system. To access the ABS codes, it will be necessary to connect a special SCAN tool to the 16 pin Test Connector located under the driver's side kick panel. If the special SCAN tool is not available, have the diagnostic codes extracted from the Powertrain Control Module (PCM) by a dealer service department or other qualified repair facility.

The following code chart lists the ABS and TCS codes for the most common Anti-lock Brake System and Traction Control System problems. Most ABS and TCS repairs must be performed by a dealer service department or other qualified automotive repair facility.

The diagnostic codes must be cleared from the computer memory after the repairs have been performed. The diagnostic codes can only be erased using the special SCAN tool. If the SCAN tool is not available, have the code clearing procedure performed by a dealership service department or other qualified repair facility. Refer to Chapter 6 for additional information on SCAN tools and accessing diagnostic trouble codes.

ABS Trouble Codes

Code	Probable cause
11	Right front wheel sensor (open/short to body ground or short to power)
12	Right front wheel sensor (electrical noise or intermittent interruption)
13	Left front wheel sensor (open/short to body ground or short to power)
14	Left front wheel sensor (electrical noise or intermittent interruption)
15	Right rear wheel sensor (open/short to body ground or short to power)
16	Right rear wheel sensor (electrical noise or intermittent interruption)
17	Left rear wheel sensor (open/short to body ground or short to power)
18	Left rear wheel sensor (electrical noise or intermittent interruption)
21	Right front pulser
22	Left front pulser
23	Right rear pulser
24	Left rear pulser
31	Right front inlet solenoid
32	Right front outlet solenoid
33	Left front inlet solenoid
34	Left front outlet solenoid
35	Right rear inlet solenoid
36	Right rear outlet solenoid
37	Left rear inlet solenoid
38	Left rear outlet solenoid
41	Right front wheel lock
42	Left front wheel lock
43	Right rear wheel lock
44	Left rear wheel lock
51	Motor lock
52	Motor remains OFF
53	Motor remains ON
54	Fail safe relay
61	Low ignition voltage
62	High ignition voltage
71	Different diameter tire
81	Central Processing Unit and ROM/RAM diagnostics

TCS Trouble Codes

Code	Probable cause
24	Right front normally-open solenoid
25	Right front normally-closed solenoid
26	Left front normally-open solenoid
27	Left front normally-closed solenoid
28	TCS relay
31	Engine retard command
32	Engine speed
34	Reference voltage
36	Throttle position sensor
61	Automatic Transmission shift position
81	Continuous TCS operation

3 Disc brake pads - replacement

Warning: *Disc brake pads must be replaced on both front wheels at the same time - never replace the pads on only one wheel. Also, the dust created by the brake system may contain asbestos, which is harmful to your health. Never blow it out with compressed air and don't inhale any of it. An approved filtering mask should be worn when working on the brakes. Do not, under any circumstances, use petroleum-based solvents to clean brake parts. Use brake system cleaner only!*

Note: *This procedure applies to front and rear disc brakes.*

1   Remove the cap from the brake fluid reservoir.

2   Loosen the wheel lug nuts, raise the front, or rear, of the vehicle and support it securely on jackstands.

3   Remove the front, or rear, wheels. Work on one brake assembly at a time, using the assembled brake for reference if necessary.

4   Inspect the brake disc carefully as outlined in Section 5. If machining is necessary, follow the information in that Section to remove the disc, at which time the calipers and pads can be removed as well.

3.5 Using a large C-clamp, push the piston back into the caliper - note that one end of the clamp is on the back side of the caliper and the other end (screw end) is pressing on the outer brake pad

3.6a Before removing anything, spray the disc, caliper and brake pads with brake system cleaner to remove the dust produced by brake pad wear - DO NOT blow the dust off with compressed air!

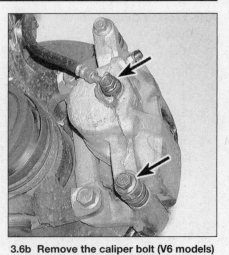

3.6b Remove the caliper bolt (V6 models) or pin (four-cylinder models) (lower arrow; upper arrow points to banjo fitting for the brake hose, which should not be disconnected unless you are removing the caliper from the vehicle for replacement)

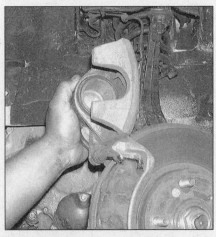

3.6c Swing the caliper up . . .

3.6d . . . and secure the caliper in this position with a piece of wire

3.6e Remove the outer brake pad and shim

3.6f Remove the inner brake pad and shim(s)

3.6g Remove and inspect the upper and lower pad retainer clips

3.6h The pad retainer clips should fit snugly in the caliper mounting bracket; if they don't, replace them. Apply a thin film of high-temperature grease to the retainer

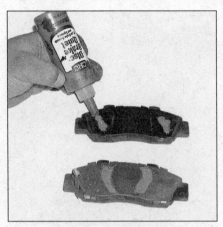

3.6i Apply anti-squeal compound to the back of the pads

Front pads

Refer to illustrations 3.5 and 3.6a through 3.6o

5   Push the piston back into the bore to provide room for the new brake pads. A C-clamp can be used to accomplish this **(see illustration)**. As the piston is depressed to the bottom

3.6j Install the new inner pad and shim(s); make sure the "ears" on the upper and lower ends of the pad are fully engaged with their respective grooves and the pad retainer clips

of the caliper bore, the fluid in the master cylinder will rise. Make sure it doesn't overflow. If necessary, drain off some of the fluid.

6   Follow the accompanying photos, beginning with **illustration 3.6a**, for the

3.6k Install the new outer pad and shim (if the new pad has no shim, take the old shim off the old pad and install it on the new outer pad)

actual pad replacement procedure. Be sure to stay in order and read the caption under each illustration. When you have completed the Steps described in the accompanying photos, proceed to Step 13.

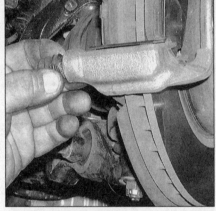

3.6l Before installing the caliper, remove the caliper pin dust boots and inspect them for tears and cracks; if they're damaged, replace them

3.6m Clean off the caliper pin (V6 models) and coat it with high-temperature grease

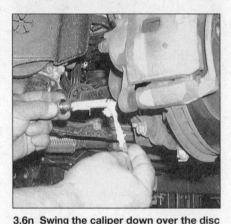

3.6n Swing the caliper down over the disc and new pads (if the piston hits the inner pad, depress the piston further into the caliper bore with your C-clamp) - on four-cylinder models, lubricate the sliding surface of the bolt with high-temperature grease

3.6o Install the lower bolt and tighten it to the torque listed in this Chapter's Specifications

3.7a Remove the brake hose retaining bolt (arrow) and detach the brake hose from the bracket

3.7b Remove the two caliper mounting bolts (arrows) . . .

3.7c . . . and lift the caliper from its mounting bracket; hang the caliper out of the way with a piece of wire - don't let it hang by the brake hose

3.7d Remove the outer pad and shim

3.7e Remove the inner pad and shim

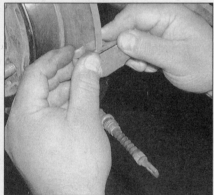

3.7f Remove the brake pad retainers from the mounting bracket

3.8 Before installing the brake pads, apply a coat of disc brake anti-squeal compound to the backing plates of the pads - follow the manufacturer's instructions on the label

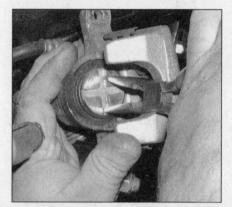

3.12a To provide clearance for the new brake pads, back the piston into the caliper bore by rotating it with a pair of needle-nose pliers

Rear pads

Refer to illustrations 3.7a through 3.7f, 3.8, 3.12a and 3.12b

7   Wash the brake assembly with brake system cleaner **(see illustration 3.6a)**, then follow the accompanying photos, beginning with **illustration 3.7a**, for the actual pad replacement procedure. Be sure to stay in order and read the caption under each illustration. When you have completed the Steps described in the accompanying photos, proceed to Step 8.

8   Apply a thin coat of disc brake anti-squeal compound, in accordance with the manufacturer's recommendations, on the backing plates of the new pads **(see illustration)**.
9   Install the shims onto their pads.
10   Install the pad retainers in the caliper mounting bracket. Lubricate the retainers with a thin film of high-temperature grease.
11   Install the new pads and shims to the

caliper mounting bracket.
12   Retract the caliper piston by engaging the tips of a pair of needle-nose pliers with two of the grooves in the top of the piston and turning it clockwise until it bottoms out **(see illustration)**. Now, rotate the piston out until one of its grooves is aligned with the tab on the inner brake pad when you install the caliper **(see illustration)**. You may have to adjust the piston position by turning it back and forth until the tab fits. If the piston dust boot becomes distorted when the piston is turned, turn the piston in the opposite direction to restore the shape of the boot, but make sure the cut-out still lines up.

Front or rear pads

13   Install the wheel and lug nuts, lower the vehicle and tighten the lug nuts to the torque specified in Chapter 1.
14   Check the brake fluid level and add fluid, if necessary (see Chapter 1).
15   Apply and release the brake pedal several times to bring the pads into contact with the brake discs. Check the operation of the brakes in an isolated area before driving the vehicle in traffic.

3.12b Align the tab on the inner pad with the slot in the caliper piston

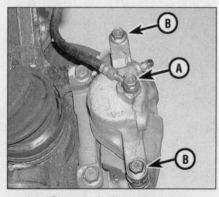

4.2a Remove the brake hose banjo bolt (A), then unscrew the caliper mounting bolts (B)

4.2b Using a short piece of rubber hose of the appropriate diameter, plug the brake line banjo fitting

4.9 Remove the clip and separate the parking brake cable from the bracket

4.10 Detach the parking brake cable end from the caliper lever

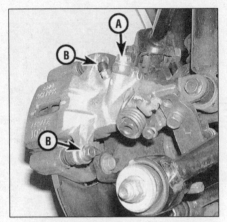

4.12 Remove the brake hose banjo bolt (A) and the caliper mounting bolts (B)

5.3 The brake pads on this vehicle were obviously neglected, as they wore down to the rivets; the rivets then cut deep grooves into the disc, and now the disc must be replaced

4   Brake caliper - removal and installation

Warning: *Dust created by the brake system may contain asbestos, which is harmful to your health. Never blow it out with compressed air and don't inhale any of it. An approved filtering mask should be worn when working on the brakes. Do not, under any circumstances, use petroleum-based solvents to clean brake parts. Use brake system cleaner only!*
Note: *Always replace the calipers in pairs - never replace just one of them.*

Front
Removal
Refer to illustrations 4.2a and 4.2b

1   Loosen - but don't remove - the lug nuts on the front wheels. Raise the front of the vehicle and place it securely on jackstands. Remove the front wheels.
2   Disconnect the brake line from the caliper and plug it to keep contaminants out of the brake system and to prevent losing any more brake fluid than is necessary **(see illustration)**.
3   Remove the caliper mounting bolts.
4   Detach the caliper from its mounting bracket.

Installation
5   Install the caliper by reversing the removal procedure. Remember to replace the sealing washers on either side of the brake line fitting with new ones. Tighten the caliper mounting bolts and the banjo bolt to the torque listed in this Chapter's Specifications.
6   Bleed the brake system (see Section 10).
7   Install the wheels and lug nuts and lower the vehicle. Tighten the wheel lug nuts to the torque listed in the Chapter 1 Specifications.

Rear
Removal
Refer to illustrations 4.9, 4.10 and 4.12

8   Loosen - but don't remove - the lug nuts on the rear wheels. Raise the rear of the vehicle and place it securely on jackstands. Remove the rear wheels.
9   Release the parking brake handle and remove the clip from the parking brake cable **(see illustration)** located on the back side of the caliper assembly.
10   Separate the parking brake cable from the lever on the caliper **(see illustration)**.
11   Unscrew the banjo bolt and detach the brake line from the caliper. Plug the fitting to prevent fluid loss and contamination **(see illustration 4.2b)**
12   Remove the caliper mounting bolts **(see illustration)**.
13   Detach the caliper from its mounting bracket.

Installation
14   Install the caliper by reversing the removal procedure. Remember to replace the sealing washers on either side of the brake line fitting with new ones.
15   Bleed the brake system (see Section 10).
16   Install the wheels and lug nuts. Lower the vehicle and tighten the lug nuts to the torque listed in the Chapter 1 Specifications.

5   Brake disc - inspection, removal and installation

Note: *This procedure applies to both the front and (on vehicles so equipped) rear brake discs.*

Inspection
Refer to illustrations 5.3, 5.4a, 5.4b, 5.5a and 5.5b

1   Loosen the wheel lug nuts, raise the vehicle and support it securely on jackstands. Remove the wheel and install the lug nuts with 3 mm thick washers under them to hold the disc in place (if the two disc retaining screws are still in place, this will be unnecessary). If you're checking the rear disc, release the parking brake.
2   Remove the brake caliper (see Section 4), but don't disconnect the brake hose. After removing the caliper bolts, suspend the caliper out of the way with a piece of wire.
3   Visually inspect the disc surface for scoring or damage **(see illustration)**. Light scratches and shallow grooves are normal after use and may not always be detrimental to brake operation, but deep scoring (over 0.015 inch) requires refinishing by an automotive machine shop. Be sure to check both sides of the disc.

5.4a Make sure the disc retaining screws or lug nuts are tight, then rotate the disc and check the runout with a dial indicator - if the reading exceeds the maximum allowable runout limit, the disc will have to be machined or replaced

5.4b Using a swirling motion, remove the glaze from the disc with emery cloth or sandpaper

5.5a The minimum allowable thickness is stamped into the disc (typical)

5.5b A micrometer is used to measure disc thickness

5.6a Before you can remove the front disc, you'll have to remove these caliper mounting bracket-to-steering knuckle bolts (arrows) and the bracket

5.6b To remove the rear disc, remove the caliper mounting bracket-to-knuckle bolts (arrows), then remove the caliper mounting bracket

5.7a If the disc retaining screws are stuck, use an impact screwdriver to loosen them

5.7b If the disc is stuck, thread two bolts into the disc and tighten them to force the disc off the hub

4   If you've noted pulsation during braking, suspect disc runout. To check disc runout, place a dial indicator at a point about 1/2-inch from the outer edge of the disc **(see illustration)**. Set the indicator to zero and turn the disc. The indicator reading should not exceed the specified allowable runout limit. If it does, have the disc refinished by an automotive machine shop. **Note:** *Professionals recommend that the discs be resurfaced regardless of the dial indicator reading, as this will impart a smooth finish and ensure a perfectly flat surface, eliminating any brake pedal pulsation or other undesirable symptoms related to questionable discs. At the very least, if you elect not to have the discs resurfaced, remove the glazing from the surface with emery cloth or sandpaper using a swirling motion* **(see illustration)**.

5   It is absolutely critical that the disc not be machined to a thickness less than the minimum allowable thickness. The minimum wear (or discard) thickness is stamped on the disc **(see illustration)**. The disc thickness can be checked with a micrometer **(see illustration)**. Check the thickness at several points.

Removal

Refer to illustrations 5.6a, 5.6b, 5.7a and 5.7b

6   Remove the two caliper mounting bracket-to-steering knuckle bolts **(see illustration)** or, on rear calipers, the bracket-to-knuckle bolts **(see illustration)**, and remove the mounting bracket.

7   Remove the two lug nuts which were put on to hold the disc in place, or the two disc retaining screws, if present **(see illustration)** and remove the disc from the hub. If the disc is stuck to the hub and won't come off, thread two bolts into the holes provided **(see illustration)** and tighten them. Alternate between the bolts, turning them a couple of turns at a time, until the disc is free.

6.2 If the drum is hard to pull off, thread a pair of 8 mm bolts into the holes provided to force the drum off

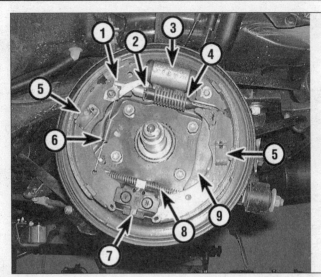

6.4a Details of the rear drum brake assembly

1   Self adjuster lever
2   Adjuster assembly
3   Wheel cylinder
4   Upper return spring
5   Retainer spring
6   Self adjuster spring
7   Lower return spring
8   Parking brake cable
9   Parking brake lever

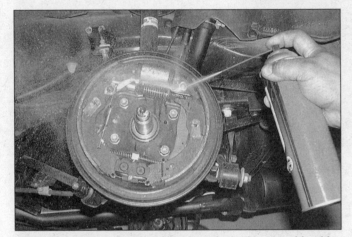

6.4b Before removing anything, clean the brake assembly with brake cleaner and allow it to dry – position a drain pan under the brake assembly to catch the residue – DO NOT USE COMPRESSED AIR TO BLOW BRAKE DUST OFF THE PARTS!

6.4c Push down on the retainer spring with a screwdriver, then turn the pin to align its blade with the slot (repeat this on the other spring)

Installation

8   Place the disc in position over the threaded studs. Install the disc retaining screws and tighten them securely.

9   Install the caliper mounting bracket, brake pads and caliper over the disc. Tighten the mounting bracket and caliper bolts to the torque listed in this Chapter's Specifications.

10   Install the wheel, then lower the vehicle to the ground. Depress the brake pedal a few times to bring the brake pads into contact with the disc. Bleeding of the system will not be necessary unless the fluid hose was disconnected from the caliper. Check the operation of the brakes carefully before placing the vehicle into normal service.

6   Drum brake shoes - replacement

Refer to illustrations 6.2, 6.4a through 6.4p and 6.5

Warning: *Drum brake shoes must be replaced on both wheels at the same time - never*

replace the shoes on only one wheel. Also, the dust created by the brake system may contain asbestos, which is harmful to your health. Never blow it out with compressed air and don't inhale any of it. An approved filtering mask should be worn when working on the brakes. Do not, under any circumstances, use petroleum-based solvents to clean brake parts. Use brake system cleaner only!

Caution: *Whenever the brake shoes are replaced, the return and hold-down springs should also be replaced. Due to the continuous heating/cooling cycle that the springs are subjected to, they lose their tension over a period of time and may allow the shoes to drag on the drum and wear at a much faster rate than normal.*

1   Loosen the wheel lug nuts, raise the rear of the vehicle and support it securely on jackstands. Block the front wheels to keep the vehicle from rolling. Remove the rear wheels. Release the parking brake.

2   Remove the brake drum. It should simply pull straight off the hub. If the drum won't come off, tap it carefully with a soft-faced

mallet, or screw a couple of 8.0 mm bolts into the tapped holes **(see illustration)**. If it still won't budge, the shoes have probably carved wear grooves into the drum. To get the drum off, you'll have to retract them. Remove the rubber plug in the backing plate. Use one screwdriver inserted through the hole in the backing plate to hold the self-adjuster lever away from the adjuster star wheel, then use another screwdriver to rotate the star wheel until the drum can be removed.

3   Replacing the shoes is a lot easier if you remove the rear wheel bearing cap, spindle nut and washer, and slide off the hub unit (see Chapter 10).

4   Follow **illustrations 6.4a through 6.4p** for the inspection and replacement of the brake shoes. Be sure to stay in order and read the caption under each illustration. All four rear brake shoes must be replaced at the same time, but to avoid mixing up parts, work on only one brake assembly at a time.

5   Before reinstalling the drum it should be checked for cracks, score marks, deep

6.4d Pull the upper return spring back while supporting the brake shoe and unhook the spring from the shoe (a pair of diagonal cutting pliers are being used here because they grip the spring well, but care must be taken so as not to damage the spring)

6.4e Remove the adjuster/spring assembly from the leading brake shoe

6.4f Detach the lower return spring . . .

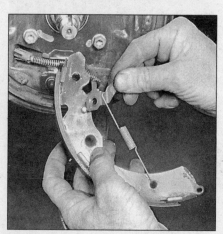

6.4g . . . and remove the self adjuster lever and spring

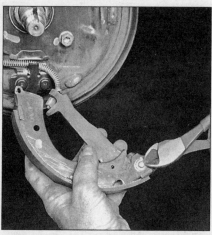

6.4h Remove the parking brake lever retaining clip; be careful not to lose the wave washer that is under the clip

6.4i Lubricate the brake shoe contact areas on the backing plate with high-temperature grease

6.4j Clean the adjuster bolt and clevis, then lubricate the threads and ends with high-temperature grease

6.4k Put the new trailing shoe on the lever, place the wave washer over the pin, then install the retaining clip; crimp the ends of the clip together with a pair of needle-nose pliers

scratches and hard spots, which will appear as small discolored areas. If the hard spots cannot be removed with fine emery cloth or if any of the other conditions listed above exist, the drum must be taken to an automotive machine shop to have it machined. **Note:** *Professionals recommend resurfacing the drums whenever a brake job is done. Resurfacing will eliminate the possibility of out-of-round drums.* If the drums are worn so much that they can't be resurfaced without exceeding the maximum allowable diameter (stamped into the drum) **(see illustration)**, then new ones will be required. At the very least, if you elect not to have the drums resurfaced, remove the glazing from the surface with sandpaper or emery cloth using a swirling motion.

6   Install the hub and bearing unit, the washer and a *new* spindle nut if removed previously (see Chapter 10). Tighten the nut to the torque listed in the Chapter 10 Specifications.

6.4l Install the adjusting lever and spring on the new leading shoe

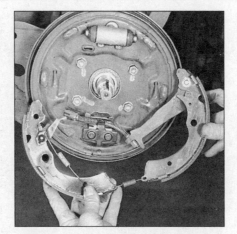

6.4m Install the lower return spring

6.4n Install the adjuster assembly . . .

6.4o . . . and connect the upper return spring

6.4p Install both retainer springs

6.5 The maximum allowable diameter is cast into the drum (typical)

7   Install the brake drum. Insert a screwdriver through the hole in the backing plate and turn the star wheel on the adjuster until the brake shoes drag on the drum, then turn the adjuster in the opposite direction until they don't drag as the drum is turned (this is a preliminary adjustment).

8   Mount the wheel, install the lug nuts, then lower the vehicle. Tighten the lug nuts to the torque listed in the Chapter 1 Specifications.

9   Depress the brake pedal several times, which will bring the shoes into the proper adjustment.

10   Check brake operation before driving the vehicle in traffic. **Warning:** *Do not operate the vehicle if you are in doubt about the effectiveness of the brake system.*

---

7   Wheel cylinder - removal and installation

Refer to illustration 7.4
Note: *If the wheel cylinders leak, they must be replaced with new ones - the manufacturer does not recommend rebuilding them.*

Removal

1   Raise the rear of the vehicle and support it securely on jackstands. Block the front wheels to keep the vehicle from rolling.

2   Remove the brake shoe assembly (see Section 6).

3   Remove all dirt and foreign material from around the wheel cylinder.

4   Unscrew the brake line fitting **(see illustration)**. **Note:** *If available, use a flare-nut wrench to avoid rounding off the corners of the fittings.* Don't pull the brake line away from the wheel cylinder.

5   Remove the wheel cylinder mounting bolts.

6   Detach the wheel cylinder from the brake backing plate. Immediately plug the brake line to prevent fluid loss and contamination. Golf tees or rubber vacuum caps work well for plugging or capping flared metal lines. **Note:** *If the brake shoe linings are contaminated with brake fluid, install new brake shoes and clean the drums with brake system cleaner.*

Installation

7   Apply RTV sealant to the mating surface of the wheel cylinder and the brake backing plate, place the cylinder in position and connect the brake line. Don't tighten the fitting completely yet.

8   Install the mounting bolts, tightening them to the torque listed in this Chapter's Specifications. Tighten the brake line fitting. Install the brake shoe assembly.

9   Bleed the brakes (see Section 10).

7.4 Unscrew the brake line fitting (arrow), then remove the two wheel cylinder bolts

8.4 Use a flare-nut wrench to unscrew the threaded fittings at the master cylinder - a regular wrench can round off the corners

8.6 To detach the master cylinder from the brake booster, remove the two nuts (arrows)

8.8 The best way to bleed air from the master cylinder before installing it on the vehicle is with a pair of bleed tubes that direct brake fluid into the reservoir during bleeding

10   Check brake operation before driving the vehicle in traffic. **Warning:** *Do not operate the vehicle if you are in doubt about the effectiveness of the brake system.*

8   Master cylinder - removal and installation

Note: *If the master cylinder is defective, it must be replaced with a new one - the manufacturer does not recommend rebuilding it.*

Removal

Refer to illustrations 8.4 and 8.6
1   The master cylinder is located in the engine compartment, mounted to the power brake booster.
2   Remove as much fluid as you can from the reservoir with a syringe, such as an old turkey baster. **Warning:** *If a baster is used, never again use it for the preparation of food.*
3   Place rags under the fluid fittings and prepare caps or plastic bags to cover the ends of the lines once they are disconnected. **Caution:** *Brake fluid will damage paint. Cover all body parts and be careful not to spill fluid during this procedure.*
4   Loosen the fittings at the ends of the brake lines where they enter the master cylinder **(see illustration).** To prevent rounding off the corners on these nuts, the use of a flare-nut wrench, which wraps around the nut, is preferred. Pull the brake lines slightly away from the master cylinder and plug the ends to prevent contamination.
5   Remove the strut brace from the engine compartment.
6   Disconnect the electrical connector at the brake fluid level switch on the master cylinder reservoir, then remove the nuts attaching the master cylinder to the power booster **(see illustration).** Pull the master cylinder off the studs and out of the engine compartment. Again, be careful not to spill the fluid as this is done.

Installation

Refer to illustration 8.8
7   Bench bleed the new master cylinder before installing it. Mount the master cylinder in a vise, with the jaws of the vise clamping on the mounting flange.
8   Attach a pair of master cylinder bleeder tubes to the outlet ports of the master cylinder **(see illustration).**
9   Fill the reservoir with brake fluid of the recommended type (see Chapter 1).
10   Slowly push the pistons into the master cylinder (a large Phillips screwdriver can be used for this) - air will be expelled from the pressure chambers and into the reservoir. Because the tubes are submerged in fluid, air can't be drawn back into the master cylinder when you release the pistons.
11   Repeat the procedure until nor more air bubbles are present.
12   Remove the bleed tubes, one at a time, and install plugs in the open ports to prevent fluid leakage and air from entering. Install the reservoir cap.
13   Install the master cylinder over the studs on the power brake booster and tighten the attaching nuts only finger tight at this time.
14   Thread the brake line fittings into the master cylinder. Since the master cylinder is still a bit loose, it can be moved slightly in order for the fittings to thread in easily. Do not strip the threads as the fittings are tightened.
15   Fully tighten the mounting nuts, then the brake line fittings.
16   Install the strut brace and tighten the nuts to the torque listed in this Chapter's Specifications.
17   Fill the master cylinder reservoir with fluid, then bleed the master cylinder and the brake system as described in Section 10. To bleed the cylinder on the vehicle, have an assistant depress the brake pedal and hold the pedal to the floor. Loosen the fitting nut to allow air and fluid to escape. Repeat this procedure on both fittings until the fluid is clear of air bubbles. **Caution:** *Have plenty of rags*

on hand to catch the fluid - brake fluid will ruin painted surfaces. After the bleeding procedure is completed, rinse the area under the master cylinder with clean water.
18   Test the operation of the brake system carefully before placing the vehicle into normal service. **Warning:** *Do not operate the vehicle if you are in doubt about the effectiveness of the brake system.*

9   Brake hoses and lines - inspection and replacement

Refer to illustrations 9.4a, 9.4b and 9.5
1   About every six months the flexible hoses which connect the steel brake lines with the rear brakes and front calipers should be inspected for cracks, chafing of the outer cover, leaks, blisters, and other damage.
2   Replacement steel and flexible brake lines are commonly available from dealer parts departments and auto parts stores. Do not, under any circumstances, use anything other than genuine steel brake lines or approved flexible brake hoses as replacement items.
3   When installing the brake line, leave at least 3/4-inch clearance between the line and any moving or vibrating parts.
4   To disconnect a hose and line, use a flare-nut wrench **(see illustration).** Then remove the clip and slide the hose out of the bracket **(see illustration).**
5   To disconnect a hose from a caliper, unscrew the banjo bolt and discard the sealing washers. Always install new sealing washers when reconnecting the hose fitting **(see illustration).**
6   When disconnecting two hoses, use normal wrenches on the hose fittings. When connecting two hoses, make sure they are not twisted or strained.
7   Steel brake lines are usually retained along their span with clips. Always remove

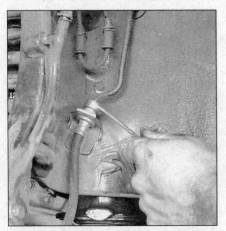

9.4a Use a flare-nut wrench to loosen the brake line-to-hose fitting . . .

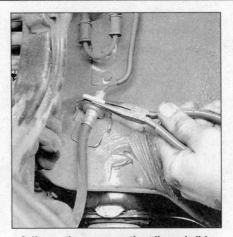

9.4b . . . then remove the clip and slide the hose out of the bracket

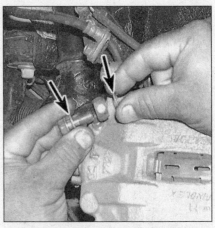

9.5 Always install new sealing washers on either side of the banjo fitting

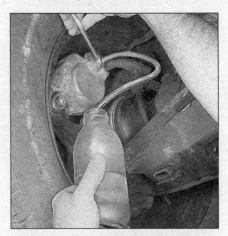

10.8 When bleeding the brakes, a hose is connected to the bleed screw at the caliper or wheel cylinder and then submerged in brake fluid - air will be seen as bubbles in the tube and container (all air must be expelled before moving to the next wheel)

these clips completely before removing a rigid brake line. Always reinstall these clips, or new ones if the old ones are damaged, when replacing a brake line, as they provide support and keep the lines from vibrating, which can eventually break them.

8   When replacing brake lines, be sure to use the correct parts. NEVER use copper tubing! Purchase genuine steel brake lines from a dealer or auto parts store.

9   When installing a steel line, make sure it's securely supported in the brackets and has plenty of clearance between moving or hot components.

10   After installation, check the fluid level in the master cylinder and add fluid as necessary. Bleed the brake system as described in Section 10 and test the brakes carefully before driving the vehicle in traffic. **Warning:** *Do not operate the vehicle if you are in doubt about the effectiveness of the brake system.*

10   Brake hydraulic system - bleeding

Refer to illustration 10.8

Warning: *Wear eye protection when bleeding the brake system. If the fluid comes in contact with your eyes, immediately rinse them with water and seek medical attention.*

1   Bleeding the hydraulic system is necessary to remove any air that manages to find its way into the system when it's been opened during removal and installation of a hose, line, caliper or master cylinder. It will probably be necessary to bleed the system at all four brakes if air has entered the system due to low fluid level, or if the brake lines have been disconnected at the master cylinder.

2   If a brake line was disconnected only at a wheel, then only that caliper or wheel cylinder must be bled.

3   If a brake line is disconnected at a fitting located between the master cylinder and any of the brakes, that part of the system served by the disconnected line must be bled.

4   Remove any residual vacuum from the power brake booster by applying the brake several times with the engine off.

5   Remove the master cylinder reservoir cover and fill the reservoir with brake fluid. Reinstall the cover. **Note:** *Check the fluid level often during the bleeding operation and add fluid as necessary to prevent the fluid level from falling low enough to allow air bubbles into the master cylinder.*

6   Have an assistant on hand, as well as a supply of new brake fluid, a clear container partially filled with clean brake fluid, a length of clear tubing to fit over the bleed screw and a wrench to open and close the bleed screw.

7   Beginning at the left front wheel, loosen the bleed screw slightly, then tighten it to a point where it is snug but can still be loosened quickly and easily.

8   Place one end of the tubing over the bleed screw and submerge the other end in brake fluid in the container **(see illustration)**.

9   Have the assistant push the brake pedal to the floor and hold the pedal firmly depressed.

10   While the pedal is held depressed, open the bleed screw just enough to allow a flow of fluid to leave the screw. Watch for air bubbles to exit the submerged end of the tube. When the fluid flow slows after a couple of seconds, close the screw and have your assistant release the pedal.

11   Repeat Steps 9 and 10 until no more air is seen leaving the tube, then tighten the bleed screw and proceed to the right front wheel, the right rear wheel and the left rear wheel, in that order, and perform the same procedure. Be sure to check the fluid in the master cylinder reservoir frequently.

12   Never use old brake fluid. It contains moisture which can boil, rendering the brakes inoperative.

13   Refill the master cylinder with fluid at the end of the operation.

14   Check the operation of the brakes. The pedal should feel solid when depressed, with no sponginess. If necessary, repeat the entire process. **Warning:** *Do not operate the vehicle if you are in doubt about the effectiveness of the brake system.*

11   Power brake booster - check, removal and installation

Operating check

1   Depress the brake pedal several times with the engine off and make sure there is no change in the pedal reserve distance (the distance between the pedal and the floor).

2   Depress the pedal and start the engine. If the pedal goes down slightly, operation is normal.

Airtightness check

3   Start the engine and turn it off after one or two minutes. Depress the brake pedal several times slowly. If the pedal goes down farther the first time but gradually rises after the second or third depression, the booster is airtight.

4   Depress the brake pedal while the engine is running, then stop the engine with the pedal depressed. If there is no change in

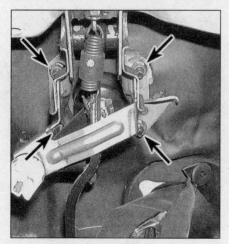

11.12 The power brake booster is secured to the firewall with four nuts (arrows)

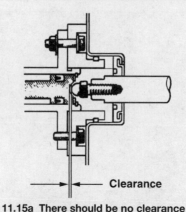

← **Clearance**

11.15a There should be no clearance between the booster pushrod and the master cylinder piston, but no interference either – if there is interference between the two, the brakes may drag; if there is clearance, there will be excessive brake pedal travel

11.15b Measure the distance that the pushrod protrudes from the brake booster at the master cylinder mounting surface (including the gasket, if equipped)

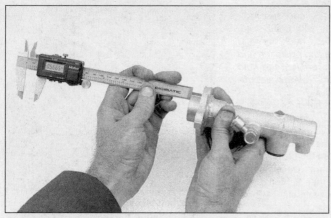

11.15c Measure the distance from the mounting flange to the end of the master cylinder

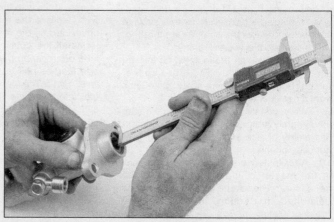

11.15d Measure the distance from the piston pocket to the end of the master cylinder

the pedal reserve travel after holding the pedal for 30 seconds, the booster is airtight.

Removal

Refer to illustration 11.12

5   Power brake booster units should not be disassembled. They require special tools not normally found in most automotive repair stations or shops. They are fairly complex and because of their critical relationship to brake performance it is best to replace a defective booster unit with a new or rebuilt one.

6   To remove the booster, first remove the brake master cylinder as described in Section 8.

7   On manual transaxles, remove the clutch master cylinder (see Chapter 8).

8   Disconnect the vacuum hose leading from the engine to the booster. Be careful not to damage the hose when removing it from the booster fitting.

9   If you're working on a four-cylinder model, remove the Intake Air Temperature (IAT) sensor (see Chapter 6).

10   Locate the pushrod clevis pin connecting the booster to the brake pedal.

11   Remove the cotter pin with pliers and pull out the clevis pin.

12   Remove the four mounting nuts holding the brake booster to the firewall **(see illustration)**. You may need a light to see them, because they're up under the dash area.

13   Slide the booster straight out from the firewall until the studs clear the holes, turn the booster to the right (towards the center of the vehicle) so the clevis clears the firewall, then remove the booster from the engine compartment.

Installation

Refer to illustrations 11.15a 11.15b, 11.15c, 11.15d and 11.16

14   Installation procedures are basically the reverse of those for removal. Tighten the booster mounting nuts to the torque listed in this Chapter's Specifications. Also, be sure to use a new cotter pin on the clevis pin.

15   If a new power brake booster unit is being installed, check the pushrod clearance **(see illustration)** as follows:

a) *Using a hand-held vacuum pump, apply a vacuum of 20 in-Hg to the booster.*

Measure the distance that the pushrod protrudes from the master cylinder mounting surface on the front of the power brake booster, including the gasket (if used). Write down this measurement **(see illustration)**. *This is "dimension A."*

b) *Measure the distance from the mounting flange to the end of the master cylinder* **(see illustration)**. *Write down this measurement. This is "dimension B."*

c) *Measure the distance from the end of the master cylinder to the bottom of the pocket in the piston* **(see illustration)**. *Write down this measurement. This is "dimension C."*

d) *Subtract measurement B from measurement C, then subtract measurement A from the difference between B and C. This the pushrod clearance.*

e) *Compare your calculated pushrod clearance to the pushrod clearance listed in this Chapter's Specifications. If necessary, adjust the pushrod length to achieve the correct clearance (see the next Step).*

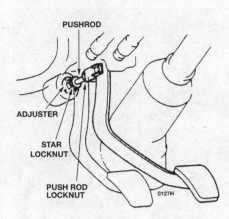

11.16 To adjust the length of the booster pushrod, loosen the star locknut and turn the adjuster in or out, as necessary, to achieve the desired setting

12.4 Location of the parking brake cable adjusting nut (arrow)

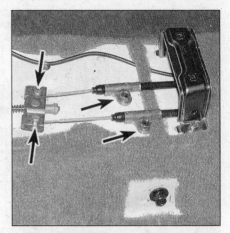

13.3a When removing a cable, unscrew the clamp bolts (right arrows) and lift off the clamps, then detach the cable ends from the equalizer (left arrows)

13.3b Remove the bolts (arrows) and separate the parking brake cable housing from the body

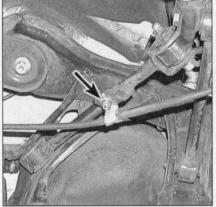

13.3c The parking brake cable is attached to the rear suspension on the lower arm with a bolt (arrow)

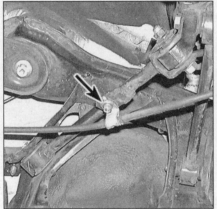

13.4a To detach the parking brake cable from a drum brake, compress the spring with a pair of pliers and pass the cable through its slot in the parking brake lever

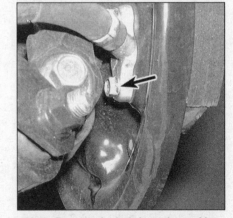

13.4b Remove the bolt from the parking brake cable housing at the backing plate and pull the cable out of the backing plate

16   If the clearance is more or less than specified, loosen the star locknut and turn the adjuster on the power booster pushrod until the clearance is within the specified limit **(see illustration)**. After adjustment, tighten the locknut. Recheck the clearance. Repeat this step as often as necessary until the clearance is correct.

17   After the final installation of the master cylinder and brake hoses and lines, bleed the brakes as described in Section 10.

12 Parking brake - adjustment

Refer to illustration 12.4

1   Refer to Chapter 11 and remove the console trim around the parking brake lever.

2   Remove the center console.

3   Block the front wheels, raise the rear of the vehicle and support it securely on jackstands. Apply the parking brake lever until you hear one click.

4   Turn the adjusting nut on the equalizer **(see illustration)** clockwise while rotating the rear wheels. Stop turning the nut when the

brakes just start to drag on the rear wheels.

5   Release the parking brake lever and check to see that the brakes don't drag when the rear wheels are turned. When properly adjusted, the travel on the parking brake lever should be as listed in this Chapter's Specifications.

6   Lower the vehicle and reinstall the console or cover.

13 Parking brake cable(s) - replacement

Refer to illustrations 13.3a, 13.3b, 13.3c, 13.4a and 13.4b

1   Block the front wheels and loosen the rear wheel lug nuts. Raise the rear of the vehicle and support it securely on jackstands.

2   On vehicles with rear drum brakes, remove the brake drum(s) (see Section 6).

3   Following the procedure in the previous Section, loosen the cable adjusting nut. Unhook the cable from the equalizer **(see illustration)**. Remove the cable clamp from the cable housing **(see illustrations)**.

4   On models with rear drum brakes, remove the brake shoes (see Section 6) and disconnect the cable end from the lever on the trailing brake shoe **(see illustrations)**. Depress the tangs on the cable housing

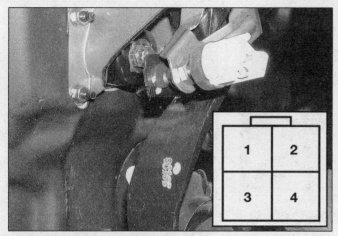

14.3 The brake light switch is mounted on a bracket near the top of the brake pedal

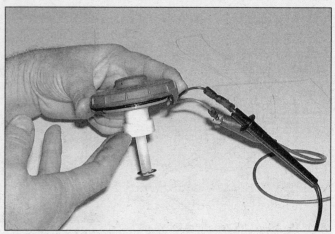

15.2 Use an ohmmeter to check the brake fluid level switch - with the float in the UP position, there should be no continuity

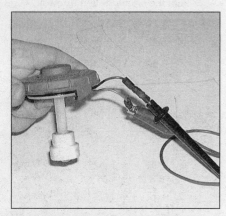

15.3 The ohmmeter should indicate continuity when the float is at the bottom of its travel

retainer and pass the cable through the backing plate using needle-nose pliers or a 12 mm off-set wrench. This compresses all the tangs simultaneously. **Note:** *If you do not have this wrench, you can also use a small screw-type hose clamp. Tighten the clamp around the tangs, start the cable through the hole and remove the hose clamp.*

5   On models with rear disc brakes, remove the clip and clevis to disconnect the cable end from the actuator lever on the caliper (see Section 6), then remove the spring clip to free the cable housing from the support bracket.

6   Unbolt the cable housing clamps from the underbody, noting how the cable is routed, then remove the cable from the vehicle. It may be necessary to remove the exhaust pipe heat shield bolts at the rear to allow cable removal.

7   If both cables are to be removed, repeat the above steps to remove the remaining cable.

8   Installation is the reverse of the removal procedure. After the cable(s) are installed, be sure to adjust them according to the procedure described in Section 13.

14 Brake light switch - check, replacement and adjustment

Check

Refer to illustration 14.3

1   To check the brake light switch, push on the brake pedal and verify that the brake lights come on.

2   If they don't, check the brake light fuse (see Chapter 12 or check your owner's manual for fuse locations). Also check the brake light bulbs in both tail light assemblies (don't forget to check the high-mount brake light).

3   Locate the brake light switch at the top of the brake pedal **(see illustration)**.

4   Unplug the switch connector.

5   Check for continuity across switch terminals 2 and 3 with an ohmmeter. When the brake pedal is depressed, there should be continuity; when it's released, there should be no continuity.

6   Check for continuity across switch terminals 1 and 4 with an ohmmeter. When the brake pedal is depressed, there should be no continuity; when it's released, there should be continuity. If the switch doesn't operate as described, replace it.

Replacement

7   Disconnect the electrical connector from the switch, if you haven't already done so.

8   Remove the locknut on the pedal side of the switch and unscrew the switch from the bracket.

9   Installation of the brake light switch is the reverse of the removal procedure.

Adjustment

10   Loosen the brake light switch locknut and back off the brake light switch until it's not touching the brake pedal.

11   Loosen the master cylinder pushrod locknut and screw the pushrod in or out with pliers until the pedal height from the floor is correct (as listed in this Chapter's Specifications). **Note:** *Measure from the top face of the pedal pad to the floor (not the carpet).*

12   Tighten the locknut securely.

13   Screw in the brake light switch until its plunger is fully depressed (threaded end touching the pad on the pedal arm), then back off the switch 1/2-turn and tighten the locknut securely.

14   Depress the pedal with your hand and measure the pedal freeplay. It should be within the dimensions listed in this Chapter's Specifications. Make sure the brake lights operate when the pedal is depressed and go off when the pedal is released.

15 Brake fluid level switch - check and replacement

Check

Refer to illustrations 15.2 and 15.3

1   To check the brake fluid level switch, disconnect the harness connector and remove the cap from the brake fluid reservoir on top of the master cylinder.

2   Check the switch continuity with the float in the UP position **(see illustration)**. There should be no continuity.

3   Check the switch continuity with the float in the DOWN position **(see illustration)**. There should be continuity.

4   If the switch doesn't operate as described, replace it.

Replacement

5   Disconnect the electrical connector from the switch, if you haven't already done so.

6   Remove the cap from the brake fluid reservoir. Replace the cap as a complete unit.

7   Installation of the brake fluid level switch and cap is the reverse of the removal procedure.

Chapter 10
Suspension and steering systems

Contents

Specifications

General

Power steering fluid type	See Chapter 1

Torque specifications

Ft-lbs (unless otherwise indicated)

Note: *One foot-pound (ft-lb) of torque is equivalent to 12 inch-pounds (in-lbs) of torque. Torque values below approximately 15 ft-lbs are expressed in inch-pounds, since most foot-pound torque wrenches are not accurate at these smaller values.*

Front suspension

Damper fork pinch bolt	32
Damper fork-to-lower control arm through-bolt/nut	47
Lower control arm inner pivot bolt	47
Radius rod-to-crossmember nut	32
Radius rod-to-lower control arm bolts	119
Shock absorber-to-body mounting nuts	
8 X 1.25	144 in-lbs
10 X 1.25	37
Damper shaft nut	22
Stabilizer bar link nut	29
Stabilizer bar bracket bolts	22
Lower balljoint nut	36 to 43
Upper balljoint nut	29 to 35
Upper control arm pivot bolts	47
Wheel speed sensor bracket nut	84 in-lbs

Rear suspension

Lower arm inner pivot bolt	43
Lower arm-to-knuckle bolt/nut	43
Control arm inner pivot bolt/nut	40
Control arm-to-knuckle nut	43
Trailing arm-to-chassis bolt	43
Trailing arm-to-knuckle bolt	43
Leading arm inner pivot bolt	43
Leading arm-to-knuckle bolt	43
Upper arm inner pivot bolt	43
Upper arm-to-knuckle castle nut	36 to 43
Hub nut	139
Damper shaft nut	22
Stabilizer bar link nut	29
Stabilizer bar bracket bolts	22
Shock absorber-to-knuckle bolt	43
Shock absorber upper mounting nuts	37

Airbag system

Airbag module Torx bolts	86 in-lbs

Steering system

Intermediate shaft pinch bolt	16
Power steering pump mounting bolts	16
Power steering line bolts	96 in-lbs
Steering wheel nut	29
Steering gear mounting bolts	28
Stiffener plate bolts	
Small bolts	28
Large bolts	32
Tie-rod end-to-steering knuckle nut	32

1.1 Front suspension and steering components

1	Radius rod	4	Lower control arm	6	Stabilizer bar
2	Shock absorber/coil spring assembly	5	Tie-rod end	7	Steering gear
3	Lower balljoint				

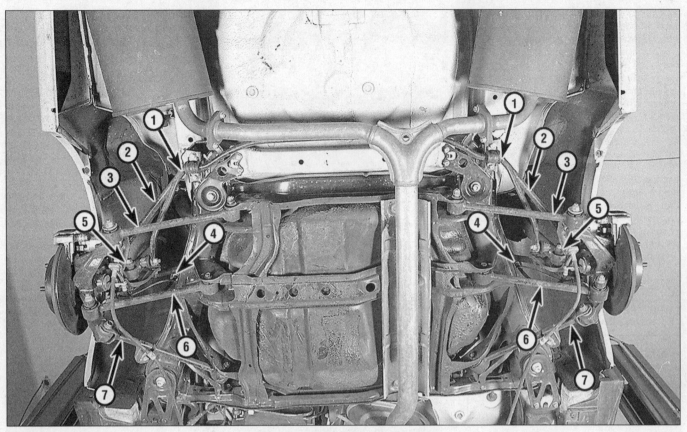

1.2a Rear suspension components

1   Stabilizer bar
2   Leading arm
3   Control arm

4   Upper arm
5   Shock absorber/coil spring assembly

6   Lower arm
7   Trailing arm

1   General information

Refer to illustrations 1.1, 1.2a and 1.2b

The front suspension is a fully independent design with upper and lower control arms, shock absorber/coil spring assemblies and a stabilizer bar **(see illustration)**.

Each side of the rear suspension uses a trailing arm, a leading arm, two unequal length lower control arms (one is called a lower arm, the other is called the control arm), an upper control arm and a shock absorber/coil spring unit **(see illustrations)**. A stabilizer bar connects the suspension on each side, to reduce body roll.

All models use a power-assisted rack-and-pinion steering gear. The power steering system employs an engine-driven pump connected by hoses to the steering gear.

Frequently, when working on the suspension or steering system components, you may come across fasteners which seem impossible to loosen. These fasteners on the underside of the vehicle are continually subjected to water, road grime, mud, etc., and can become rusted or "frozen," making them extremely difficult to remove. In order to unscrew these stubborn fasteners without damaging them (or other components), be sure to use lots of penetrating oil and allow it to soak in for a while. Using

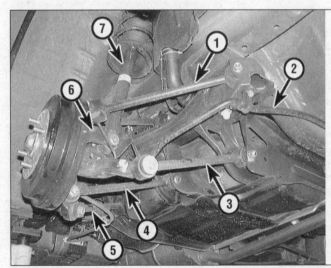

1.2b Rear suspension arms components (view from rear of vehicle)

1   Leading arm
2   Stabilizer bar
3   Control arm
4   Lower arm
5   Trailing arm
6   Rear knuckle
7   Shock absorber/coil spring assembly

a wire brush to clean exposed threads will also ease removal of the nut or bolt and prevent damage to the threads. Sometimes a sharp blow with a hammer and punch is effective in breaking the bond between a nut and bolt threads, but care must be taken to prevent the punch from slipping off the fastener and ruining the threads. Heating the stuck fastener and surrounding area with a torch sometimes helps too, but isn't recommended because of

the obvious dangers associated with fire. Long breaker bars and extension, or "cheater," pipes will increase leverage, but never use an extension pipe on a ratchet - the ratcheting mechanism could be damaged. Sometimes, turning the nut or bolt in the tightening (clockwise) direction first will help to break it loose. Fasteners that require drastic measures to unscrew should always be replaced with new ones.

Since most of the procedures that are dealt with in this Chapter involve jacking up the vehicle and working underneath it, a good pair of jackstands will be needed. A hydraulic floor jack is the preferred type of jack to lift the vehicle, and it can also be used to support certain components during various operations. **Warning:** *Never, under any circumstances, rely on a jack to support the vehicle while working on it. Whenever any of the suspension or steering fasteners are loosened or removed they must be inspected and, if necessary, be replaced with new ones of the same part number or of original equipment quality and design. Torque specifications must be followed for proper reassembly and component retention. Never attempt to heat or straighten any suspension or steering component. Instead, replace any bent or damaged part with a new one.*

2 Shock absorber/coil spring assembly (front) - removal and installation

Removal

Refer to illustrations 2.4, 2.5a, 2.5b and 2.6

1   Loosen the wheel lug nuts, raise the vehicle and support it securely on jackstands. Remove the wheel.
2   Unbolt the brake hose from the shock absorber assembly.
3   Disconnect the stabilizer bar from the lower control arm (see Section 6).
4   Place a floor jack under the lower control arm to support it when the shock absorber assembly is removed. Remove the damper fork pinch bolt **(see illustration)**.
5   Remove the damper fork-to-lower control arm bolt and remove the fork **(see illustrations)**. It may be necessary to tap the fork from the shock absorber.
6   Support the shock absorber and coil spring assembly and remove the five upper mounting nuts **(see illustration)**. Remove the unit from the fenderwell.

Installation

7   Guide the shock absorber assembly up into the fenderwell and insert the five upper mounting studs through the holes in the body. Once the studs protrude from the holes, install the nuts so the assembly won't fall back through, but don't tighten the nuts completely yet. The shock absorber is heavy and awkward, so get an assistant to help you, if possible.
8   Insert the lower end of the shock absorber into the damper fork. Make sure the aligning tab on the back of the shock body enters the slot in the damper fork.
9   Connect the damper fork to the lower control arm, tightening the nut to the torque listed in this Chapter's Specifications. Now tighten the damper fork pinch bolt to the torque listed in this Chapter's Specifications.
10   Attach the brake hose to its bracket and tighten the bolt securely.

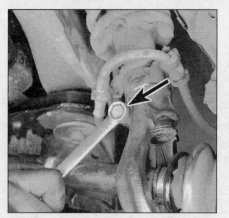

2.4   Remove the damper fork pinch bolt

11   Install the wheel and lug nuts, lower the vehicle and tighten the lug nuts to the torque listed in the Chapter 1 Specifications.
12   Tighten the upper mounting nuts to the torque listed in this Chapter's Specifications.

3 Shock absorber or coil spring - replacement

Refer to illustrations 3.5, 3.6a and 3.6b

1   Remove the shock absorber/coil spring assembly (see Section 2 or 11).
2   Check the shock absorber for leaking fluid, dents, cracks or other obvious damage. Check the coil spring for chips or cracks which could cause premature failure and inspect the spring seats for hardness or general deterioration. The shock absorber assemblies, complete with the coil springs, are available on an exchange basis which eliminates much time and work. So, before disassembling your shock to replace individual components, check on the availability of parts and the price of a complete rebuilt unit. **Warning:** *Disassembling a shock absorber/coil spring assembly is potentially dangerous and utmost attention must be*

2.6   Remove these nuts (arrows) from the shock absorber mounting studs

1   10 X 1.25 mounting nuts
2   8 X 1.25 mounting nuts

2.5a   Remove the through-bolt that connects the damper fork to the lower control arm

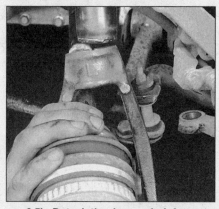

2.5b   Detach the damper fork from the shock absorber

directed to the job, or serious injury may result. Use only a high-quality spring compressor and carefully follow the manufacturer's instructions furnished with the tool.
3   Mount the shock absorber assembly in a vise. Line the vise jaws with wood or rags to prevent damage to the unit and don't tighten the vise excessively.

3.5   Install the spring compressor according to the tool manufacturer's instructions and compress the spring until all pressure is relieved from the mounting base

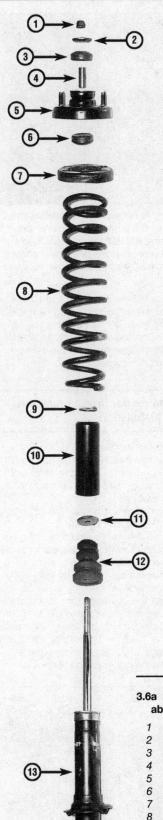

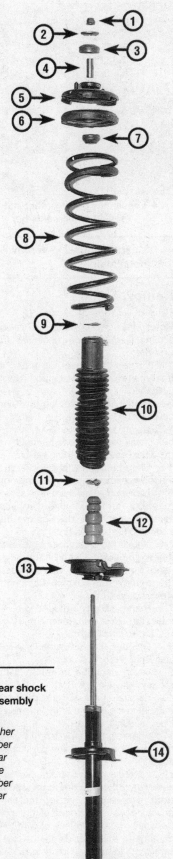

4   Mark the relationship of the damper mounting base to the spring (or if the spring is being replaced, put the mark on the damper unit). This will ensure correct positioning of the mounting base when the unit is reassembled.

5   Following the tool manufacturer's instructions, install the spring compressor (which can be obtained at most auto parts stores or equipment yards on a daily rental basis) on the spring and compress it sufficiently to relieve all pressure from the damper mounting base **(see illustration)**.

6   Remove the damper cap **(see illustrations)**. Unscrew the self-locking nut while holding the damper shaft with an Allen wrench to prevent it from turning. Remove the parts from the upper part of the shock and lay them out in the exact order in which they're removed.

7   Carefully lift the compressed spring from the assembly and set it in a safe place. **Warning:** *Keep the ends of the spring facing away from your body!*

8   Slide the rest of the parts off of the damper shaft and lay them out in the exact order in which they're removed.

9   Install the bump stop, bump stop plate (if equipped), dust cover and dust cover plate onto the new damper unit. Extend the damper shaft as far as it will go and slide the components down to the damper body.

10   Carefully place the coil spring onto the shock absorber body, with the end of the spring resting in the lowest part of the seat.

11   Install the spring mounting rubber, lower mounting rubber, damper mounting collar, damper mounting base, seal, upper mounting rubber, damper mounting washer and a new self-locking nut. Before tightening the nut, align the previously applied marks on the mounting base and the spring (or damper body).

12   Tighten the self-locking nut securely, again using the Allen wrench to prevent the shaft from turning. Remove the spring compressor. Install the damper cap.

13   Install the shock absorber/coil spring assembly (see Section 2 or 11).

3.6a Exploded view of a front shock absorber/coil spring assembly

1	Self-locking nut
2	Damper mounting washer
3	Damper mounting rubber
4	Damper mounting collar
5	Damper mounting base
6	Damper mounting rubber
7	Spring mounting rubber
8	Spring
9	Dust cover plate
10	Dust cover
11	Bump stop plate
12	Bump stop
13	Damper unit

3.6b Exploded view of a rear shock absorber/coil spring assembly

1	Self-locking nut
2	Damper mounting washer
3	Damper mounting rubber
4	Damper mounting collar
5	Damper mounting base
6	Damper mounting rubber
7	Spring mounting rubber
8	Spring
9	Dust cover plate
10	Dust cover
11	Bump stop plate
12	Bump stop
13	Spring seat cushion
14	Damper unit

4.4 Loosen the driveaxle/hub nut with a socket and breaker bar

4.12 Lift the knuckle out (away from the vehicle) and pull the driveaxle from the hub

6.2 If you're removing the stabilizer bar, remove the upper link nut; if you're replacing the link, remove both nuts (and if you're removing the lower control arm, just remove the lower nut)

4 Steering knuckle - removal and installation

Removal

Refer to illustrations 4.4 and 4.12
Note: *If the wheel cover on your vehicle is not secured by the lug nuts, begin this procedure with Step 4.*
1 Loosen the wheel lug nuts, raise the front of the vehicle and support it securely on jackstands.
2 Remove the wheel lug nuts and wheel cover.
3 Using a punch, unstake the front axle nut. Install the wheel and lug nuts, excluding the wheel cover. Lower the vehicle.
4 Use a breaker bar and socket and loosen the driveaxle/hub nut **(see illustration)**.
5 Loosen the wheel lug nuts slightly, raise the front of the vehicle and support it securely on jackstands. Remove the wheel and the driveaxle/hub nut.
6 Unbolt the brake hose bracket from the steering knuckle. Unbolt the brake caliper, hang it out of the way with a piece of wire, then remove the caliper mounting bracket (see Chapter 9).
7 Remove the two mounting screws that retain the brake disc to the hub. Remove the brake disc (see Chapter 9).
8 Remove the ABS wheel speed sensor (see Chapter 9).
9 Disconnect the tie-rod end from the steering knuckle (see Section 17).
10 Separate the lower control arm from the balljoint in the bottom of the steering knuckle (see Section 8).
11 Separate the upper end of the knuckle from the upper control arm balljoint (see Section 9).
12 Carefully pull the knuckle and hub assembly off of the driveaxle **(see illustration)**. If necessary, tap on the end of the driveaxle with a soft-face hammer. Support the driveaxle with a piece of wire to prevent damage to the inner CV joint. **Caution:** *Be careful not to overextend the inner CV joint.*
13 If the wheel bearing is in need of replacement, take the steering knuckle/hub assembly to an automotive machine shop or

other qualified repair facility to have the old wheel bearing pressed out and a new one pressed in.

Installation

14 If removed, install the hub assembly to the steering knuckle (this must be performed by an automotive machine shop if the necessary tools are not available).
15 Apply a light coat of wheel bearing grease to the driveaxle splines. Insert the driveaxle through the splined bore of the hub while guiding the steering knuckle into position.
16 Connect the upper end of the knuckle to the upper control arm balljoint (see Section 9). Tighten the balljoint stud nut to the torque listed in this Chapter's Specifications. Install a new cotter pin. **Note:** *Tighten the nut to the lower torque value given in the Specifications, then, if necessary, tighten it an additional amount to line up the slots in the nut with the hole in the balljoint stud to allow cotter pin insertion.*
17 Connect the balljoint on the bottom of the knuckle to the lower control arm (see Section 8). Tighten the nut to the torque listed in this Chapter's Specifications. Install a new cotter pin (see the Note in the previous Step).
18 Attach the brake disc to the hub, install the disc retaining screws and tighten them securely.
19 Install the caliper mount and caliper, tightening the bolts to the proper torque (see Chapter 9). Attach the brake hose bracket to the knuckle, tightening the bolts securely.
20 Install the driveaxle/hub nut and tighten it securely.
21 Install the wheel and lug nuts, lower the vehicle and tighten the lug nuts to the torque listed in the Chapter 1 Specifications.
22 Tighten the driveaxle/hub nut to the torque listed in the Chapter 8 Specifications.

5 Hub and wheel bearing assembly (front) - removal and installation

1 Remove the steering knuckle and hub assembly from the vehicle (see Section 4).

2 Due to the special tools and expertise required to press the hub and bearing from the steering knuckle, the assembly should be taken to an automotive machine shop or other qualified repair facility to have the bearing replaced if it is worn.

6 Stabilizer bar (front) - removal and installation

Refer to illustrations 6.2 and 6.3
1 Apply the parking brake. Loosen the front wheel lug nuts, raise the front of the vehicle and support it securely on jackstands. Remove the wheels.
2 Detach the stabilizer bar links from the stabilizer bar **(see illustration)**.
3 Remove the bolts which attach the stabilizer bar brackets to the underside of the vehicle **(see illustration)**.
4 Remove the bar from under the vehicle.
5 Pull the brackets off the stabilizer bar and inspect the bushings for cracks, chips and other signs of deterioration. If the bushings are damaged, replace them. Also check the stabilizer bar links for loose balljoints and other damage, replacing them if necessary.
6 Installation is the reverse of removal.

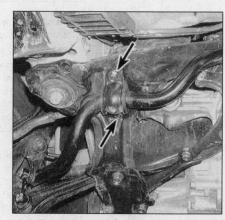

6.3 Stabilizer bar bracket bolts (arrows)

7.3 To detach the front end of the radius rod, remove the plug in the plastic splash shield, then remove this nut from the rod

7.4 To detach the rear end of the radius rod, remove the two bolts (arrows) that attach the radius rod to the lower control arm

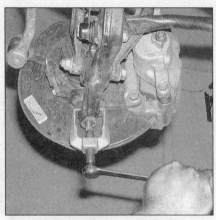

8.5 Separate the lower control arm from the steering knuckle balljoint with a two-jaw puller

7 Radius rod - removal and installation

Refer to illustrations 7.3 and 7.4

1   Loosen the wheel lug nuts, raise the front of the vehicle and place it securely on jackstands. Remove the wheel.

2   Remove the plug from the plastic splash shield.

3   Remove the nut from the front end of the radius rod in the front crossmember **(see illustration)**.

4   Remove the bolts that attach the rear end of the radius rod to the lower control arm **(see illustration)** and remove the rod.

5   Installation is the reverse of removal. Be sure to tighten all fasteners to the torque values listed in this Chapter's Specifications.

6   Drive the vehicle to an alignment shop and have the front end alignment checked and, if necessary, adjusted.

8 Lower control arm (front) - removal and installation

Refer to illustrations 8.5 and 8.6

1   Loosen the front wheel lug nuts, raise the vehicle, place it securely on jackstands and remove the wheel.

2   Remove the through-bolt and detach the damper fork from the lower control arm (see Section 2).

3   Detach the radius rod from the lower control arm (see Section 7).

4   Detach the stabilizer bar link from the lower control arm (see Section 6).

5   Remove the cotter pin from the castle nut on the lower balljoint stud. Loosen the nut, but don't remove it yet (this will prevent the components from separating violently. Using a two-jaw puller, separate the lower control arm from the balljoint in the steering knuckle **(see illustration)**. Remove the nut.

6   Remove the pivot bolt from the inner end of the lower control arm **(see illustration)** and remove the arm.

7   Installation is the reverse of removal. Be

sure to install a new cotter pin (and read the Note in Section 4, Step 16).

9 Upper control arm (front) - removal and installation

Refer to illustration 9.3

1   Loosen the front wheel lug nuts, raise the vehicle, place it securely on jackstands and remove the wheel. Support the lower control arm with a floor jack.

2   Remove the shock absorber/coil spring assembly (see Section 2). Remove the ABS wheel speed sensor bracket from the upper control arm.

3   Remove the cotter pin, then loosen, but do not remove, the castle nut from the upper balljoint stud **(see illustration)**. The nut will prevent the upper control arm and the steering knuckle from separating violently in the next step.

4   Separate the upper control arm from the steering knuckle with a two-jaw puller, then remove the nut. Don't let the top of the steering knuckle fall out. If necessary, secure it with a piece of wire.

5   Remove the upper control arm pivot bolts **(see illustration 9.3)** and the upper control arm.

6   Installation is the reverse of removal. Be sure to tighten all of the fasteners to the torque values listed in this Chapter's Specifications. Install a new cotter pin (and read the Note in Section 4, Step 16).

10 Balljoints - replacement

The front suspension uses two balljoints; the upper balljoint is mounted in the upper control arm, and the lower balljoint is mounted in the steering knuckle. The rear suspension uses one balljoint, on the outer end of the upper arm. At the time of writing, these components were not available separately, requiring replacement of the upper control arm or the steering knuckle in the event of balljoint failure. Check with your

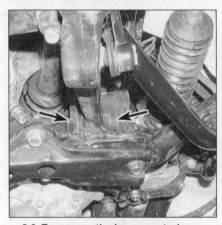

8.6 To remove the lower control arm, remove the pivot bolt from the inner end of the arm

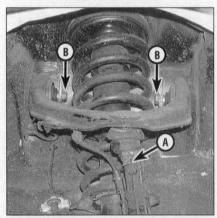

9.3 To remove the upper control arm, remove the balljoint castle nut (A) and separate the knuckle from the upper control arm, then remove the two pivot bolts (B)

local auto parts store or a dealer parts department on the availability of parts before disassembling your vehicle.

The balljoint boots, however, are replaceable. They are secured by a wire set ring and are easily replaced after the components have been separated.

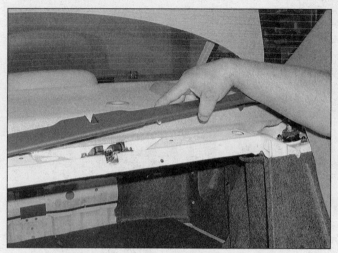

11.2 Remove the rear seat trim panel (package tray) for access to the shock absorber upper mount

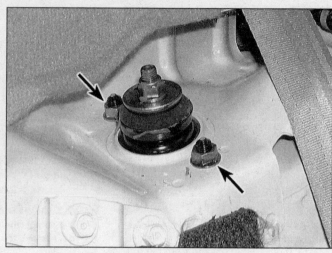

11.3 Remove the rear shock absorber upper mounting nuts (arrows)

11   Shock absorber/coil spring assembly (rear) - removal and installation

Refer to illustrations 11.2, 11.3 and 11.5

1   Loosen the rear wheel lug nuts, raise the vehicle, place it securely on jackstands and remove the rear wheels.

2   Remove the rear package shelf (trim panel) covering the upper mount of the shock absorber **(see illustration)**. Refer to Chapter 11 for additional information.

3   Remove the shock absorber upper mounting nuts **(see illustration)**.

4   Remove the nut from the upper end of the stabilizer link and separate the link from its mount for additional clearance.

5   Remove the shock absorber lower mounting bolt **(see illustration)**.

6   Pull the rear knuckle down and remove the shock absorber/coil spring assembly.

7   To inspect or replace the shock absorber or coil spring, see Section 3.

8   Installation is the reverse of removal. Be sure to tighten all fasteners to the torque val-

ues listed in this Chapter's Specifications. Tighten the wheel lug nuts to the torque listed in the Chapter 1 Specifications.

12   Rear knuckle - removal and installation

Removal

1   Loosen the rear wheel lug nuts, raise the rear of the vehicle and support it securely on jackstands. Remove the wheel.

Disc brake models

2   Unbolt the brake hose bracket from the knuckle. Unbolt the brake caliper, hang it out of the way with a piece of wire, then remove the caliper mounting bracket (see Chapter 9).

3   Remove the two mounting screws that retain the brake disc to the hub. Remove the brake disc (see Chapter 9).

Drum brake models

4   Disconnect the brake line from the wheel cylinder (see Chapter 9).

5   Remove the brake drum and brake shoes (see Chapter 9).

All models

6   Remove the hub and bearing assembly from the knuckle (see Section 13).

7   Remove the nut and detach the upper end of the stabilizer bar link from its mount (see Section 14).

8   Detach the lower end of the shock absorber assembly from the knuckle (see Section 11).

9   Unbolt the suspension arms from the knuckle (see Section 15).

10   Remove the knuckle from the suspension arms.

11   If the wheel bearing is in need of replacement, replace the hub and bearing assembly as a single unit.

Installation

12   Connect the suspension arms to the knuckle (see Section 15). Tighten the nuts to the torque listed in this Chapter's Specifications.

13   Connect the lower end of the shock absorber to the knuckle, tightening the nut/bolt to the torque listed in this Chapter's Specifications.

14   Attach the stabilizer bar link to its bracket on the knuckle, tightening the nut to the torque listed in this Chapter's Specifications.

15   Install the hub and bearing assembly (see Section 13).

16   Install the brake components (see Chapter 9). If you're working on a model with drum brakes, be sure to bleed the brake system.

17   Install the wheel and lug nuts, lower the vehicle and tighten the lug nuts to the torque listed in the Chapter 1 Specifications.

13   Hub and wheel bearing assembly (rear) - removal and installation

Refer to illustrations 13.3a, 13.3b, 13.5 and 13.6

Note: *The rear hub and bearing assembly is sealed for life and requires no lubrication or attention. If the bearing is worn or damaged, replace the entire hub and bearing assembly.*

1   Loosen the rear wheel lug nuts, raise the rear of the vehicle and support it securely on jackstands. Remove the wheel.

2   If you're working on a model with rear disc brakes, remove the brake caliper, mounting bracket and disc. If you're working on a model with rear drum brakes, remove the brake drum (see Chapter 9).

3   Remove the dust cover. Using a punch or chisel, unstake the rear hub nut **(see illustrations)**.

4   Using a breaker bar and socket, remove the hub nut.

11.5 Remove the lower mounting bolt from the rear shock absorber assembly

13.3a Using a hammer and chisel, remove the dust cover

13.3b Unstake the hub nut

13.5 Remove the hub and bearing assembly from the knuckle

5   Remove the hub and bearing assembly from the knuckle **(see illustration)**. If the hub assembly is stuck, strike it carefully with a brass hammer to jar it loose.

6   Install the new hub and bearing assembly, tighten the new nut to the torque listed in this Chapter's Specifications, then stake its edge into the groove in the spindle **(see illustration)**.

7   Install the dust cover by tapping lightly around the edge until it is seated.

8   The remainder of installation is the reverse of removal. Be sure to tighten the caliper mount bolts and caliper bolts to the torque listed in the Chapter 9 Specifications. Tighten the wheel lug nuts to the torque listed in the Chapter 1 Specifications.

14   Stabilizer bar (rear) - removal and installation

Refer to illustrations 14.2 and 14.3

1   Loosen the rear wheel lug nuts, raise the rear of the vehicle, place it securely on jackstands and remove the rear wheels.

2   Remove the stabilizer bar-to-link nuts **(see illustration)**.

3   Remove the stabilizer-to-body clamp bolts **(see illustration)** and remove the stabilizer bar.

4   Pull the brackets off the stabilizer bar and inspect the bushings for cracks, breaks and other signs of deterioration. If the bushings are damaged, replace them. Also check the stabilizer bar links for loose balljoints and other damage, replacing them if necessary.

5   Installation is the reverse of removal.

15   Rear suspension arms - removal and installation

1   Loosen the rear wheel lug nuts, raise the vehicle, place it securely on jackstands and remove the wheel.

Upper arm

Refer to illustration 15.5

2   To disconnect the outer end of the upper arm from the knuckle, remove the nut from the balljoint stud at the knuckle, install a

13.6 Stake the hub nut back into place

small two-jaw puller and separate the arm from the knuckle.

3   Remove the brake hose bracket bolts and swing the hose/hydraulic line to the side.

4   If the vehicle is equipped with ABS, remove the wheel speed sensor to prevent damage to the wiring harness.

14.2 If you're removing the stabilizer bar, remove the lower link nut; if you're removing the knuckle or shock absorber, remove the upper link nut

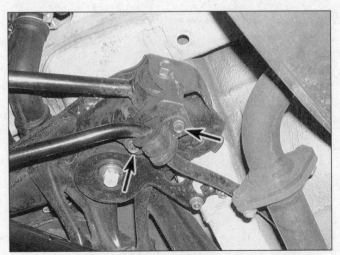

14.3 To detach the stabilizer bar from the body, remove these bolts (arrows) from each bracket

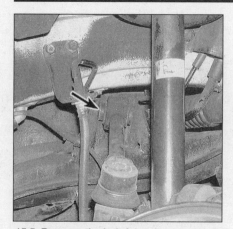

15.5 Remove the bolt from the upper arm at the chassis (arrow)

5   Remove the mounting bolt that attaches the inner end of the upper arm to the chassis **(see illustration)**.
6   Remove the upper arm. Inspect the bushing for cracks and deterioration and the balljoint for looseness and other signs of wear. If any undesirable conditions exist, replace the arm.

7   Installation is the reverse of removal. Be sure to tighten all fasteners to the torque values listed in this Chapter's Specifications. Install a new cotter pin (and read the Note in Section 4, Step 16).

Lower arm

Refer to illustration 15.8

8   Remove the nut and bolt that attaches the lower arm to the knuckle **(see illustration)**.
9   Remove the pivot bolt that attaches the inner end of the lower arm to the chassis.
10   Remove the lower arm.
11   Inspect the lower arm bushings for cracks and deterioration. If either of them are worn, replace the arm.
12   Installation is the reverse of removal. Be sure to tighten all fasteners to the torque values listed in this Chapter's Specifications.

Trailing arm

Refer to illustration 15.14

13   Disconnect the parking brake cable bracket from the trailing arm.
14   Remove the bolt that attaches the trailing arm to the knuckle **(see illustration)**.
15   Remove the bolt that attaches the trail-

ing arm to the chassis.
16   Remove the trailing arm.
17   Inspect the bushing at the forward end of the arm. If it's cracked or deteriorated, replace the arm.
18   Installation is the reverse of removal. Be sure to tighten all fasteners to the torque listed in this Chapter's Specifications.

Leading arm

Refer to illustration 15.19

19   Remove the bolt that attaches the leading arm to the knuckle **(see illustration)**.
20   Remove the bolt that attaches the leading arm to the chassis.
21   Remove the leading arm.
22   Inspect the bushing at the inner end of the arm. If it's cracked or deteriorated, replace the arm.
23   Installation is the reverse of removal. Be sure to tighten all fasteners to the torque listed in this Chapter's Specifications.

Control arm

Refer to illustration 15.24

24   Remove the nut that attaches the control arm to the knuckle **(see illustration)**.
25   Mark the relationship of the adjustment

15.8 Remove the nut and bolt from the lower arm at the knuckle (left arrow) and the bolt at the inner end of the arm (right arrow)

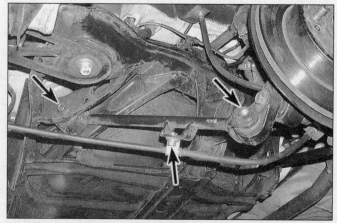

15.14 Detach the parking brake cable bracket, then remove the bolts from each end of the trailing arm

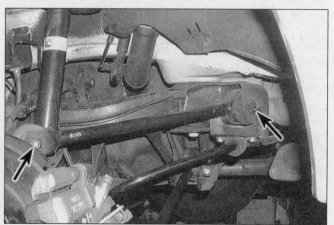

15.19 Remove the bolts (arrows) from each end of the leading arm

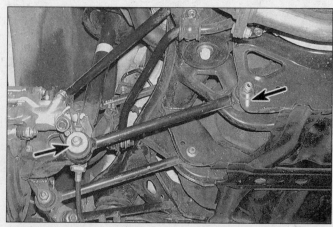

15.24 Remove the nut (left arrow) from the control arm at the knuckle - also mark the position of the adjustment cam at the inner end of the arm, then remove the nut and pivot bolt (right arrow)

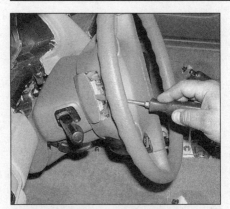

16.2 Remove the access plate from the steering wheel

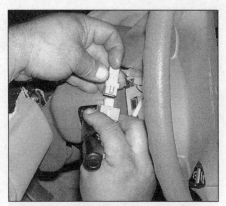

16.3 Disconnect the airbag module-to-cable reel 2-pin harness connector (yellow)

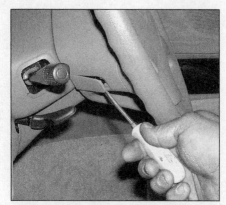

16.4a Remove the access covers for the airbag module bolts (one on each side of steering column)

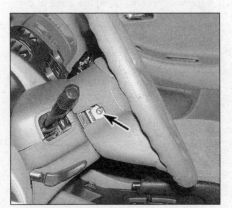

16.4b Remove the Torx bolts (arrow) that attach the airbag module to the steering wheel

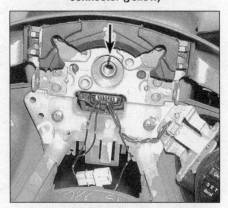

16.7 After removing the steering wheel bolt, mark the relationship of the steering wheel to the shaft (arrow)

16.10 Before installing the steering wheel, make sure the front wheels are pointed straight ahead and the "TOP" mark points straight up on the cable reel for the airbag system

cam to the mounting bracket at the inner end of the arm **(see illustration 15.24)**. Remove the nut and bolt that attaches the inner end of the control arm to the chassis.

26   Remove the control arm.

27   Inspect the control arm bushings for cracks and deterioration. If either of them are worn, replace the arm.

28   Installation is the reverse of removal. Be sure to align the mark on the adjustment cam with the mark on the chassis bracket, and tighten all fasteners to the torque values listed in this Chapter's Specifications.

16   Steering wheel - removal and installation

Warning 1: *The models covered by this manual are equipped with Supplemental Restraint systems (SRS), more commonly known as airbags. Always disconnect the negative battery cable, then the positive battery cable and wait three minutes before working in the vicinity of the impact sensors, steering column or instrument panel to avoid the possibility of accidental deployment of the airbag, which could cause personal injury (see Chapter 12). The yellow wiring harnesses and connectors routed through the steering column, console and instrument panel are for this system. Do not use electrical test equipment on the airbag*

system wiring or tamper with it in any way.
Warning 2: *Make sure the steering shaft is not turned while the steering wheel is removed or you could damage the airbag system. To prevent the shaft from turning, position the wheels straight ahead, turn the ignition key to the lock position and remove the key before beginning work. Due to the possible damage to the airbag system, we recommend only experienced mechanics attempt this procedure.*

Removal

Refer to illustrations 16.2, 16.3, 16.4a, 6.4b, and 16.7

1   Disconnect the cable from the negative battery terminal, then disconnect the positive battery cable. **Caution:** *The stereo in your vehicle is equipped with an anti-theft system. Make sure you have the correct activation code before disconnecting the battery.* Wait at least three minutes before proceeding to the next step to allow the airbag's back-up power supply to be depleted.

2   Remove the access plate from the steering wheel **(see illustration)**.

3   Unplug the airbag module-to-cable reel 2-pin connector to disable the airbag module **(see illustration)**.

4   Remove the access panels from each side of the steering wheel. Remove both Torx bolts retaining the airbag module to the steering wheel **(see illustrations)**.

5   Pull off the airbag module and carefully set it in a safe location. **Warning:** *Carry the airbag module with the trim side facing away from your body, and set it down with the trim side facing up.*

6   Unplug the electrical connectors for the horn and, if equipped, the cruise control system.

7   Remove the steering wheel retaining bolt. Make a mark indicating the relationship of the steering wheel hub to the steering shaft **(see illustration)**.

8   Remove the steering wheel using a steering wheel puller. **Caution 1:** *Don't thread the bolts of the puller into the steering wheel more than five turns, as they could contact the airbag cable reel and damage it.* **Caution 2:** *While the steering wheel is removed, DO NOT turn the steering shaft. If you do so, the airbag cable reel could be damaged.*

Installation

Refer to illustration 16.10 and 16.12

9   Make sure the front wheels are pointed straight ahead.

10   Make absolutely sure that the cable reel is centered with the arrow on the cable reel pointing up **(see illustration)**. This shouldn't

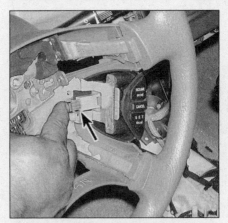

16.12 Make sure the cruise control connector is plugged in (arrow)

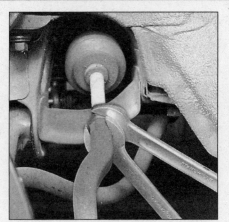

17.2a Using a back-up wrench to prevent the tie-rod end from turning, loosen the jam nut

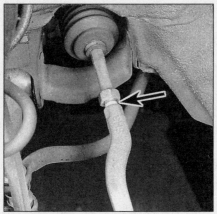

17.2b Make an alignment mark on the exposed threads, along the edge of the tie-rod end, so the new tie-rod end will be installed in the exact same position

be a problem as long as you have not turned the steering shaft while the wheel was removed. If for some reason the shaft was turned, center the cable reel as follows:

a) *Rotate the cable reel clockwise until it stops.*

b) *Rotate the cable reel counterclockwise about 2-1/2 turns until the arrow on the cable reel points straight up.*

11   Be sure to align the index mark on the steering wheel hub with the mark on the shaft when you slip the wheel onto the shaft. Make sure the locating pins on the cable reel engage the holes in the backside of the steering wheel, and the notches in the steering wheel hub engage the tabs on the turn signal canceling cam. Install the steering wheel bolt and tighten it to the torque listed in this Chapter's Specifications.

12   Plug in the horn connector and, if equipped, the cruise control connector **(see illustration)**.

13   Reattach the airbag module with NEW Torx bolts and tighten the bolts to the torque listed in this Chapter's Specifications. Install the Torx bolt access panels.

14   Plug the airbag and cable reel connector halves together.

15   Install the access plate.

17   Tie-rod ends - removal and installation

Removal

Refer to illustrations 17.2a, 17.2b and 17.4

1   Loosen the wheel lug nuts. Raise the front of the vehicle, support it securely on jackstands and remove the wheel.

2   Hold the tie-rod end with a back-up wrench and loosen the jam nut enough to mark the position of the tie-rod end in relation to the threads **(see illustrations)**.

3   Remove the cotter pin and loosen the nut on the tie-rod end stud. Don't completely remove the nut.

4   Separate the tie-rod from the steering knuckle arm with a puller **(see illustration)**. Remove the nut and detach the tie-rod end.

5   Unscrew the tie-rod end from the tie-rod.

Installation

6   Thread the tie-rod end on to the marked position and insert the tie-rod stud into the steering knuckle arm. Don't tighten the jam nut yet.

7   Install the nut on the stud and tighten it to the torque listed in this Chapter's Specifications. Install a new cotter pin.

8   Tighten the jam nut securely.

9   Install the wheel and lug nuts. Lower the vehicle and tighten the lug nuts to the torque listed in the Chapter 1 Specifications.

10   Have the wheel alignment checked and, if necessary, adjusted.

18   Steering gear boots - replacement

Refer to illustration 18.3

1   Loosen the lug nuts, raise the front of the vehicle and support it securely on jackstands. Remove the wheel.

2   Remove the tie-rod end and jam nut (see Section 17).

3   Remove the steering gear boot clamps **(see illustration)** and slide off the boot.

4   Before installing the new boot, wrap the threads and serrations on the end of the tie-rod with a layer of tape so the small end of the new boot isn't damaged.

5   Slide the new boot into position on the

17.4 Use a two-jaw puller to separate the tie-rod end from the steering knuckle arm

18.3 Remove the clamps from the steering gear boot (arrows)

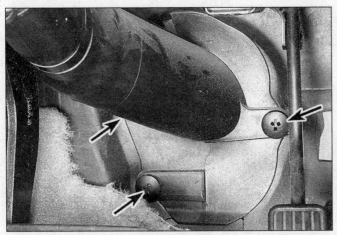

19.1 Pop off the upper and lower clamps (left arrow points to lower clamp; upper clamp not visible in this photo) and slide off the cover - when you put it back on, make sure the two retainers (arrows) on the flange at the lower end are pushed into the holes in the floor

19.2 Mark the relationship of the intermediate shaft to the steering gear input shaft and remove the pinch bolt (arrow)

steering gear until each end seats in its groove, then install and tighten the new clamps.

6   Remove the tape and install the tie-rod end (see Section 17).

7   Install the wheel and lug nuts. Lower the vehicle and tighten the lug nuts to the torque listed in the Chapter 1 Specifications.

19 Steering gear - removal and installation

Warning 1: *The models covered by this manual are equipped with Supplemental Restraint systems (SRS), more commonly known as airbags. Always disconnect the negative battery cable, then the positive battery cable and wait three minutes before working in the vicinity of the impact sensors, steering column or instrument panel to avoid the possibility of accidental deployment of the airbag, which could cause personal injury (see Chapter 12).*
Warning 2: *Make sure the steering shaft is not turned while the steering gear is removed or you could damage the airbag system. To prevent the shaft from turning, position the wheels straight ahead, turn the ignition key to the lock position and remove the key before beginning work or run the seat belt through the steering wheel and clip the seat belt into place. Due to the possible damage to the airbag system, we recommend only experienced mechanics attempt this procedure.*
Caution: *The stereo in your vehicle is equipped with an anti-theft system. Make sure you have the correct activation code before disconnecting the battery.*

Removal

Refer to illustrations 19.1, 19.2, 19.4, 19.9 and 19.10

1   Disconnect the cable from the negative terminal of the battery, then disconnect the cable from the positive terminal and wait three minutes before proceeding. Working under the dash, remove the steering joint cover **(see illustration)**.

2   Mark the relationship of the intermediate shaft universal joint to the steering gear input shaft **(see illustration)** and remove the pinch bolt.

3   Apply the parking brake. Loosen the front wheel lug nuts, raise the front of the vehicle and support it securely on jackstands. Remove the wheels.

4   Drain the power steering fluid. Place a drain pan under the steering gear. Disconnect the power steering fluid pressure and return lines **(see illustration)**. **Note:** *Don't disconnect the fittings on the lines that lead to the steering gear pressure cylinder.*

5   Install caps into the ends of the power steering lines to prevent fluid loss.

6   Separate the tie-rod ends from the steering knuckle arms (see Section 17).

7   Unplug the oxygen sensor electrical connector (see Chapter 6) and remove the catalytic converter from the exhaust system.

8   Disconnect the shift cable(s) (see Chapter 7A or 7B).

9   Remove the stiffener plates from the chassis and steering gear **(see illustration)**.

19.4 To drain the fluid from the power steering system, disconnect the power steering lines (arrows) from the steering gear and let the fluid drain into a pan

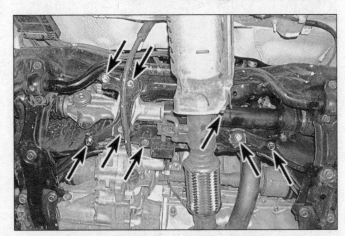

19.9 Remove the bolts (arrows) from the stiffener plates

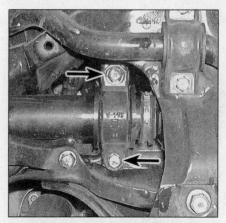

19.10 Remove the steering gear mounting bolts (arrows) - left side shown

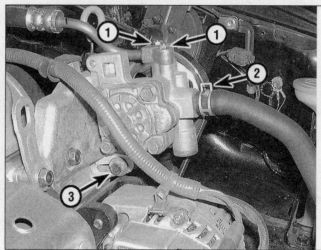

20.3a Power steering pump details - four-cylinder model

1 *Pressure hose mounting bolts*
2 *Feed hose and clamp*
3 *Adjustment bolt*

10   Support the steering gear and remove the mounting bolts **(see illustration)**. Lower the unit, separate the intermediate shaft from the steering gear input shaft and remove the steering gear from the vehicle. It will be necessary to angle the steering gear slightly to clear the rear beam.

Installation

11   Raise the steering gear into position and connect the intermediate shaft, aligning the marks.

12   Install the steering gear mounting bolts and washers and tighten them to the torque listed in this Chapter's Specifications.

13   Install the stiffener plates, tightening the bolts to the torque listed in this Chapter's Specifications.

14   Connect the tie-rod ends to the steering knuckle arms (see Section 16).

15   Install the intermediate shaft pinch bolt and tighten it to the torque listed in this Chapter's Specifications.

16   Install the steering joint cover and clamps. Make sure the two retainers on the flange at the lower end of the shield are aligned with (and pushed into) the holes in the floor.

17   Connect the power steering lines to the steering gear and fill the power steering pump reservoir with the recommended fluid (see Chapter 1).

18   Install the wheels and lug nuts. Lower the vehicle and tighten the lug nuts to the torque listed in the Chapter 1 Specifications.

19   Bleed the steering system (see Section 21).

20   Power steering pump - removal and installation

Refer to illustrations 20.3a, 20.3b and 20.4

1   Clamp the power steering feed hose shut so fluid loss will be minimized when the hose is disconnected.

2   On V6 models, remove the intake manifold cover (see Chapter 2B).

3   Disconnect the feed hose and pressure line at the pump **(see illustrations)**. Note the difference between the pressure and the feed hoses; the feed hose is held to the pump with a spring type clamp, and the pressure line has two bolts holding it to the pump body. Cap or plug the line and hose to prevent leakage or contamination.

4   Remove the pump mounting bolt and adjuster bolt **(see illustration)**. Remove the pump.

5   Installation is the reverse of removal. Install a new O-ring on the end of the pressure line. Be sure to adjust the drivebelt tension (see Chapter 1), check the power steering fluid level and add some, if necessary (see Chapter 1), then bleed the power steering system (see Section 21).

21   Power steering system - bleeding

1   Following any operation in which the power steering fluid lines have been disconnected, the power steering system must be bled to remove all air and obtain proper steering performance.

2   With the front wheels in the straight ahead position, check the power steering

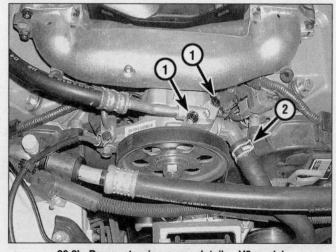

20.3b Power steering pump details - V6 model

1 *Pressure hose mounting bolts*
2 *Feed hose and clamp*

20.4 Location of the upper mounting bolt on a four cylinder model – refer to illustration 20.3a for the location of the adjustment bolt

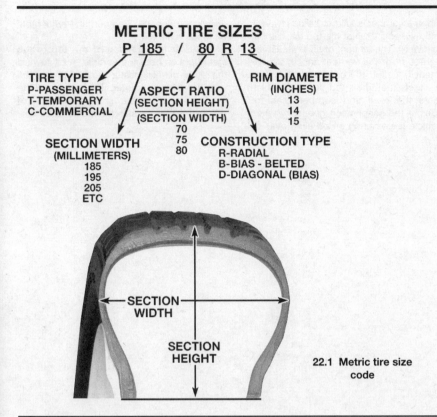

METRIC TIRE SIZES

P 185 / 80 R 13

TIRE TYPE
P-PASSENGER
T-TEMPORARY
C-COMMERCIAL

ASPECT RATIO
(SECTION HEIGHT)
───────────────
(SECTION WIDTH)
70
75
80

SECTION WIDTH
(MILLIMETERS)
185
195
205
ETC

CONSTRUCTION TYPE
R-RADIAL
B-BIAS - BELTED
D-DIAGONAL (BIAS)

RIM DIAMETER
(INCHES)
13
14
15

SECTION
WIDTH

SECTION
HEIGHT

22.1 Metric tire size code

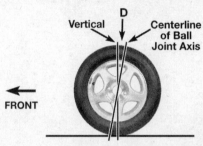

CAMBER ANGLE (FRONT VIEW)

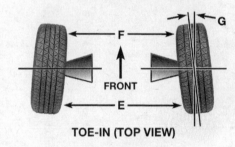

CASTER ANGLE (SIDE VIEW)

TOE-IN (TOP VIEW)

23.1 Wheel alignment details

A minus B = C (degrees camber)
D = caster (expressed in degrees)
E minus F = toe-in (measured in inches)
G = toe-in (expressed in degrees)

fluid level (see Chapter 1). If it's low, add fluid until it reaches the lower mark on the reservoir.

3   Start the engine and allow it to run at fast idle. Recheck the fluid level and add more if necessary to reach the Cold mark on the dipstick.

4   Bleed the system by turning the wheels from side-to-side, without hitting the stops. This will work the air out of the system. Keep the reservoir full of fluid as this is done.

5   When the air is worked out of the system, return the wheels to the straight ahead position and leave the vehicle running for several more minutes before shutting it off.

6   Road test the vehicle to be sure the steering system is functioning normally and noise free.

7   Recheck the fluid level to be sure it is up to the Hot mark on the reservoir while the engine is at normal operating temperature. Add fluid if necessary (see Chapter 1).

22 Wheels and tires - general information

Refer to illustration 22.1

1   All vehicles covered by this manual are equipped with metric-sized fiberglass or steel belted radial tires **(see illustration)**. Use of other size or type of tires may affect the ride and handling of the vehicle. Don't mix different types of tires, such as radials and bias belted, on the same vehicle as handling may be seriously affected. It's recommended that tires be replaced in pairs on the same axle,

but if only one tire is being replaced, be sure it's the same size, structure and tread design as the other.

2   Because tire pressure has a substantial effect on handling and wear, the pressure on all tires should be checked at least once a month or before any extended trips (see Chapter 1).

3   Wheels must be replaced if they are bent, dented, leak air, have elongated bolt holes, are heavily rusted, out of vertical symmetry or if the lug nuts won't stay tight. Wheel repairs that use welding or peening are not recommended.

4   Tire and wheel balance is important to the overall handling, braking and performance of the vehicle. Unbalanced wheels can adversely affect handling and ride characteristics as well as tire life. Whenever a tire is installed on a wheel, the tire and wheel should be balanced by a shop with the proper equipment.

23 Wheel alignment - general information

Refer to illustration 23.1

1   A wheel alignment refers to the adjustments made to the wheels so they are in proper angular relationship to the suspension and the ground. Wheels that are out of proper alignment not only affect steering control, but also increase tire wear. Toe-in and caster can be adjusted on the front wheels, and the rear toe-in can also be adjusted. The front and rear camber angle, and rear caster, should be

checked to determine if any of the suspension components are worn out or bent **(see illustration)**.

2   Getting the proper wheel alignment is a very exacting process, one in which complicated and expensive machines are necessary to perform the job properly. Because of this, you should have a technician with the proper equipment perform these tasks. We will, however, use this space to give you a basic idea of what is involved with wheel alignment so you can better understand the process and deal intelligently with the shop that does the work.

3   Toe-in is the turning in of the wheels. The purpose of a toe specification is to ensure parallel rolling of the wheels. In a vehicle with zero toe-in, the distance between the front edges of the wheels will be the same as the distance between the rear edges of the wheels. The actual amount of toe-in is normally only a fraction of an inch. At the front end, toe-in is controlled by the tie-rod end

position on the tie-rod. At the rear it is adjusted by turning an adjusting cam bolt on the inner end of the rear control arm. Incorrect toe-in will cause the tires to wear improperly by making them scrub against the road surface.

4   Camber is the tilting of the wheels from the vertical when viewed from the front or rear of the vehicle. When the wheels tilt out at the top, the camber is said to be positive (+). When the wheels tilt in at the top the camber is negative (-). The amount of tilt is measured in degrees from the vertical and this measurement is called the camber angle. This angle affects the amount of tire tread which contacts the road and compensates for changes in the suspension geometry when the vehicle is cornering or traveling over an undulating surface. Camber isn't adjustable on these vehicles.

5   Caster is the tilting of the top of the steering axis from the vertical. A tilt toward the rear is positive caster and a tilt toward the front is negative caster. The caster on the front end is adjustable by installing shims of different thicknesses on the radius rod.

Study

Chapter 11 Body

Contents

1 General information

These models feature a "unibody" layout, using a floor pan with front and rear frame side rails which support the body components, front and rear suspension systems and other mechanical components.

Certain components are particularly vulnerable to accident damage and can be unbolted and repaired or replaced. Among these parts are the body moldings, bumpers, the hood and trunk lid, doors and all glass.

Only general body maintenance practices and body panel repair procedures within the scope of the do-it-yourselfer are included in this Chapter.

2 Body - maintenance

1   The condition of your vehicle's body is very important, because the resale value depends a great deal on it. It's much more difficult to repair a neglected or damaged body than it is to repair mechanical compo-nents. The hidden areas of the body, such as the wheel wells, the frame and the engine compartment, are equally important, although they don't require as frequent attention as the rest of the body.

2   Once a year, or every 12,000 miles, it's a good idea to have the underside of the body steam cleaned. All traces of dirt and oil will be removed and the area can then be inspected carefully for rust, damaged brake lines, frayed electrical wires, damaged cables and other problems.

3   At the same time, clean the engine and the engine compartment with a steam cleaner or water-soluble degreaser.

4   The wheel wells should be given close attention, since undercoating can peel away and stones and dirt thrown up by the tires can cause the paint to chip and flake, allowing rust to set in. If rust is found, clean down to the bare metal and apply an anti-rust paint.

5   The body should be washed about once a week. Wet the vehicle thoroughly to soften the dirt, then wash it down with a soft sponge and plenty of clean soapy water. If the surplus dirt is not washed off very carefully, it can wear down the paint.

6   Spots of tar or asphalt thrown up from the road should be removed with a cloth soaked in kerosene. Scented lamp oil is available in most hardware stores and the smell is easier to work with than straight kerosene.

7   Once every six months, wax the body and chrome trim. If a chrome cleaner is used to remove rust from any of the vehicle's plated parts, remember that the cleaner also removes part of the chrome, so use it sparingly. On any plated parts where chrome cleaner is used, use a good paste wax over the plating for extra protection.

3 Vinyl trim - maintenance

Don't clean vinyl trim with detergents, caustic soap or petroleum-based cleaners. Plain soap and water works just fine, with a soft brush to clean dirt that may be ingrained. Wash the vinyl as frequently as the rest of the vehicle.

After cleaning, application of a high quality rubber and vinyl protectant will help prevent oxidation and cracks. The protectant can also be applied to weather stripping, vacuum lines and rubber hoses, which often fail as a result of chemical degradation, and to the tires.

4   Upholstery and carpets - maintenance

1   Every three months remove the floormats and clean the interior of the vehicle (more frequently if necessary). Use a stiff whisk broom to brush the carpeting and loosen dirt and dust, then vacuum the upholstery and carpets thoroughly, especially along seams and crevices.

2   Dirt and stains can be removed from carpeting with basic household or automotive carpet shampoos available in spray cans. Follow the directions and vacuum again, then use a stiff brush to bring back the "nap" of the carpet.

3   Most interiors have cloth or vinyl upholstery, either of which can be cleaned and maintained with a number of material-specific cleaners or shampoos available in auto supply stores. Follow the directions on the product for usage, and always spot-test any upholstery cleaner on an inconspicuous area (bottom edge of a backseat cushion) to ensure that it doesn't cause a color shift in the material.

4   After cleaning, vinyl upholstery should be treated with a protectant. **Note:** *Make sure the protectant container indicates the product can be used on seats - some products may make a seat too slippery.* **Caution:** *Do not use protectant on vinyl-covered steering wheels.*

5   Leather upholstery requires special care. It should be cleaned regularly with saddlesoap or leather cleaner. Never use alcohol, gasoline, nail polish remover or thinner to clean leather upholstery.

6   After cleaning, regularly treat leather upholstery with a leather conditioner, rubbed in with a soft cotton cloth. Never use car wax on leather upholstery.

7   In areas where the interior of the vehicle is subject to bright sunlight, cover leather seating areas of the seats with a sheet if the vehicle is to be left out for any length of time.

5   Body repair - minor damage

Plastic body panels

The following repair procedures are for minor scratches and gouges. Repair of more serious damage should be left to a dealer service department or qualified auto body shop. Below is a list of the equipment and materials necessary to perform the following repair procedures on plastic body panels. Although a specific brand of material may be mentioned, it should be noted that equivalent products from other manufacturers may be used instead.

Wax, grease and silicone removing solvent

Cloth-backed body tape
Sanding discs
Drill motor with three-inch disc holder
Hand sanding block
Rubber squeegees
Sandpaper
Non-porous mixing palette
Wood paddle or putty knife
Curved-tooth body file
Flexible parts repair material

Flexible panels (front and rear bumper fascia)

1   Remove the damaged panel, if necessary or desirable. In most cases, repairs can be carried out with the panel installed.

2   Clean the area(s) to be repaired with a wax, grease and silicone removing solvent applied with a water-dampened cloth.

3   If the damage is structural, that is, if it extends through the panel, clean the backside of the panel area to be repaired as well. Wipe dry.

4   Sand the rear surface about 1-1/2 inches beyond the break.

5   Cut two pieces of fiberglass cloth large enough to overlap the break by about 1-1/2 inches. Cut only to the required length.

6   Mix the adhesive from the repair kit according to the instructions included with the kit, and apply a layer of the mixture approximately 1/8-inch thick on the backside of the panel. Overlap the break by at least 1-1/2 inches.

7   Apply one piece of fiberglass cloth to the adhesive and cover the cloth with additional adhesive. Apply a second piece of fiberglass cloth to the adhesive and immediately cover the cloth with additional adhesive in sufficient quantity to fill the weave.

8   Allow the repair to cure for 20 to 30 minutes at 60-degrees to 80-degrees F.

9   If necessary, trim the excess repair material at the edge.

10   Remove all of the paint film over and around the area(s) to be repaired. The repair material should not overlap the painted surface.

11   With a drill motor and a sanding disc (or a rotary file), cut a "V" along the break line approximately 1/2-inch wide. Remove all dust and loose particles from the repair area.

12   Mix and apply the repair material. Apply a light coat first over the damaged area; then continue applying material until it reaches a level slightly higher than the surrounding finish.

13   Cure the mixture for 20 to 30 minutes at 60-degrees to 80-degrees F.

14   Roughly establish the contour of the area being repaired with a body file. If low areas or pits remain, mix and apply additional adhesive.

15   Block sand the damaged area with sandpaper to establish the actual contour of the surrounding surface.

16   If desired, the repaired area can be temporarily protected with several light coats of primer. Because of the special paints and techniques required for flexible body panels,

it is recommended that the vehicle be taken to a paint shop for completion of the body repair.

Steel body panels

See photo sequence

Repair of minor scratches

17   If the scratch is superficial and does not penetrate to the metal of the body, repair is very simple. Lightly rub the scratched area with a fine rubbing compound to remove loose paint and built up wax. Rinse the area with clean water.

18   Apply touch-up paint to the scratch, using a small brush. Continue to apply thin layers of paint until the surface of the paint in the scratch is level with the surrounding paint. Allow the new paint at least two weeks to harden, then blend it into the surrounding paint by rubbing with a very fine rubbing compound. Finally, apply a coat of wax to the scratch area.

19   If the scratch has penetrated the paint and exposed the metal of the body, causing the metal to rust, a different repair technique is required. Remove all loose rust from the bottom of the scratch with a pocket knife, then apply rust inhibiting paint to prevent the formation of rust in the future. Using a rubber or nylon applicator, coat the scratched area with glaze-type filler. If required, the filler can be mixed with thinner to provide a very thin paste, which is ideal for filling narrow scratches. Before the glaze filler in the scratch hardens, wrap a piece of smooth cotton cloth around the tip of a finger. Dip the cloth in thinner and then quickly wipe it along the surface of the scratch. This will ensure that the surface of the filler is slightly hollow. The scratch can now be painted over as described earlier in this Section.

Repair of dents

20   When repairing dents, the first job is to pull the dent out until the affected area is as close as possible to its original shape. There is no point in trying to restore the original shape completely as the metal in the damaged area will have stretched on impact and cannot be restored to its original contours. It is better to bring the level of the dent up to a point which is about 1/8-inch below the level of the surrounding metal. In cases where the dent is very shallow, it is not worth trying to pull it out at all.

21   If the back side of the dent is accessible, it can be hammered out gently from behind using a soft-face hammer. While doing this, hold a block of wood firmly against the opposite side of the metal to absorb the hammer blows and prevent the metal from being stretched.

22   If the dent is in a section of the body which has double layers, or some other factor makes it inaccessible from behind, a different technique is required. Drill several small holes through the metal inside the damaged area, particularly in the deeper sections. Screw

long, self tapping screws into the holes just enough for them to get a good grip in the metal. Now the dent can be pulled out by pulling on the protruding heads of the screws with locking pliers.

23   The next stage of repair is the removal of paint from the damaged area and from an inch or so of the surrounding metal. This is easily done with a wire brush or sanding disk in a drill motor, although it can be done just as effectively by hand with sandpaper. To complete the preparation for filling, score the surface of the bare metal with a screwdriver or the tang of a file or drill small holes in the affected area. This will provide a good grip for the filler material. To complete the repair, see the Section on filling and painting.

Repair of rust holes or gashes

24   Remove all paint from the affected area and from an inch or so of the surrounding metal using a sanding disk or wire brush mounted in a drill motor. If these are not available, a few sheets of sandpaper will do the job just as effectively.

25   With the paint removed, you will be able to determine the severity of the corrosion and decide whether to replace the whole panel, if possible, or repair the affected area. New body panels are not as expensive as most people think and it is often quicker to install a new panel than to repair large areas of rust.

26   Remove all trim pieces from the affected area except those which will act as a guide to the original shape of the damaged body, such as headlight shells, etc. Using metal snips or a hacksaw blade, remove all loose metal and any other metal that is badly affected by rust. Hammer the edges of the hole in to create a slight depression for the filler material.

27   Wire brush the affected area to remove the powdery rust from the surface of the metal. If the back of the rusted area is accessible, treat it with rust inhibiting paint.

28   Before filling is done, block the hole in some way. This can be done with sheet metal riveted or screwed into place, or by stuffing the hole with wire mesh.

29   Once the hole is blocked off, the affected area can be filled and painted. See the following subsection on filling and painting.

Filling and painting

30   Many types of body fillers are available, but generally speaking, body repair kits which contain filler paste and a tube of resin hardener are best for this type of repair work. A wide, flexible plastic or nylon applicator will be necessary for imparting a smooth and contoured finish to the surface of the filler material. Mix up a small amount of filler on a clean piece of wood or cardboard (use the hardener sparingly). Follow the manufacturer's instructions on the package, otherwise the filler will set incorrectly.

31   Using the applicator, apply the filler paste to the prepared area. Draw the applicator across the surface of the filler to achieve the desired contour and to level the filler surface. As soon as a contour that approximates the original one is achieved, stop working the paste. If you continue, the paste will begin to stick to the applicator. Continue to add thin layers of paste at 20-minute intervals until the level of the filler is just above the surrounding metal.

32   Once the filler has hardened, the excess can be removed with a body file. From then on, progressively finer grades of sandpaper should be used, starting with a 180-grit paper and finishing with 600-grit wet-or-dry paper. Always wrap the sandpaper around a flat rubber or wooden block, otherwise the surface of the filler will not be completely flat. During the sanding of the filler surface, the wet-or-dry paper should be periodically rinsed in water. This will ensure that a very smooth finish is produced in the final stage.

33   At this point, the repair area should be surrounded by a ring of bare metal, which in turn should be encircled by the finely feathered edge of good paint. Rinse the repair area with clean water until all of the dust produced by the sanding operation is gone.

34   Spray the entire area with a light coat of primer. This will reveal any imperfections in the surface of the filler. Repair the imperfections with fresh filler paste or glaze filler and once more smooth the surface with sandpaper. Repeat this spray-and-repair procedure until you are satisfied that the surface of the filler and the feathered edge of the paint are perfect. Rinse the area with clean water and allow it to dry completely.

35   The repair area is now ready for painting. Spray painting must be carried out in a warm, dry, windless and dust free atmosphere. These conditions can be created if you have access to a large indoor work area, but if you are forced to work in the open, you will have to pick the day very carefully. If you are working indoors, dousing the floor in the work area with water will help settle the dust which would otherwise be in the air. If the repair area is confined to one body panel, mask off the surrounding panels. This will help minimize the effects of a slight mismatch in paint color. Trim pieces such as chrome strips, door handles, etc., will also need to be masked off or removed. Use masking tape and several thickness of newspaper for the masking operations.

36   Before spraying, shake the paint can thoroughly, then spray a test area until the spray painting technique is mastered. Cover the repair area with a thick coat of primer. The thickness should be built up using several thin layers of primer rather than one thick one. Using 600-grit wet-or-dry sandpaper, rub down the surface of the primer until it is very smooth. While doing this, the work area should be thoroughly rinsed with water and the wet-or-dry sandpaper periodically rinsed as well. Allow the primer to dry before spraying additional coats.

37   Spray on the top coat, again building up the thickness by using several thin layers of paint. Begin spraying in the center of the repair area and then, using a circular motion, work out until the whole repair area and about two inches of the surrounding original paint is covered. Remove all masking material 10 to 15 minutes after spraying on the final coat of paint. Allow the new paint at least two weeks to harden, then use a very fine rubbing compound to blend the edges of the new paint into the existing paint. Finally, apply a coat of wax.

6   Body repair - major damage

1   Major damage must be repaired by an auto body shop specifically equipped to perform unibody repairs. These shops have the specialized equipment required to do the job properly.

2   If the damage is extensive, the body must be checked for proper alignment or the vehicle's handling characteristics may be adversely affected and other components may wear at an accelerated rate.

3   Due to the fact that some of the major body components (hood, fenders, doors, etc.) are separate and replaceable units, any seriously-damaged components should be replaced rather than repaired. Sometimes the components can be found in a wrecking yard that specializes in used vehicle components, often at considerable savings over the cost of new parts.

7   Hinges and locks - maintenance

Once every 3000 miles, or every three months, the hinges and latch assemblies on the doors, hood and trunk (or liftgate) should be given a few drops of light oil or lock lubricant. The door latch strikers should also be lubricated with a thin coat of grease to reduce wear and ensure free movement. Lubricate the door and trunk (or liftgate) locks with spray-on graphite lubricant.

8   Windshield and fixed glass - replacement

Replacement of the windshield and fixed glass requires the use of special fast-setting adhesive/caulk materials and some specialized tools and techniques. These operations should be left to a dealer service department or a shop specializing in glass work.

9   Hood - removal, installation and adjustment

Note: *The hood is somewhat awkward to remove and install, at least two people should perform this procedure.*

These photos illustrate a method of repairing simple dents. They are intended to supplement *Body repair - minor damage* in this Chapter and should not be used as the sole instructions for body repair on these vehicles.

1 If you can't access the backside of the body panel to hammer out the dent, pull it out with a slide-hammer-type dent puller. In the deepest portion of the dent or along the crease line, drill or punch hole(s) at least one inch apart . . .

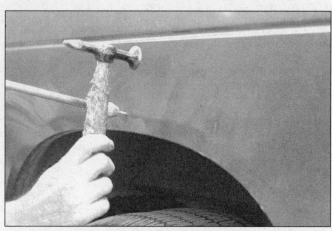

2 . . . then screw the slide-hammer into the hole and operate it. Tap with a hammer near the edge of the dent to help 'pop' the metal back to its original shape. When you're finished, the dent area should be close to its original contour and about 1/8-inch below the surface of the surrounding metal

3 Using coarse-grit sandpaper, remove the paint down to the bare metal. Hand sanding works fine, but the disc sander shown here makes the job faster. Use finer (about 320-grit) sandpaper to feather-edge the paint at least one inch around the dent area

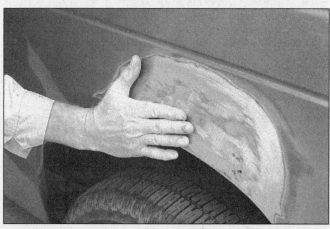

4 When the paint is removed, touch will probably be more helpful than sight for telling if the metal is straight. Hammer down the high spots or raise the low spots as necessary. Clean the repair area with wax/silicone remover

5 Following label instructions, mix up a batch of plastic filler and hardener. The ratio of filler to hardener is critical, and, if you mix it incorrectly, it will either not cure properly or cure too quickly (you won't have time to file and sand it into shape)

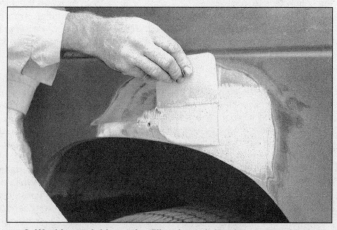

6 Working quickly so the filler doesn't harden, use a plastic applicator to press the body filler firmly into the metal, assuring it bonds completely. Work the filler until it matches the original contour and is slightly above the surrounding metal

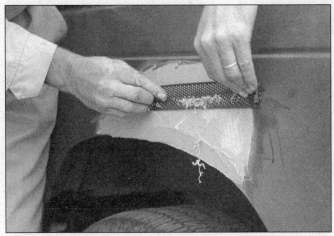

7 Let the filler harden until you can just dent it with your fingernail. Use a body file or Surform tool (shown here) to rough-shape the filler

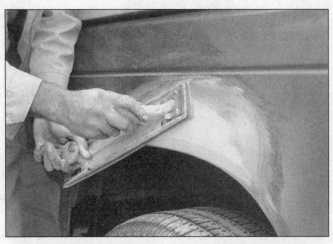

8 Use coarse-grit sandpaper and a sanding board or block to work the filler down until it's smooth and even. Work down to finer grits of sandpaper - always using a board or block - ending up with 360 or 400 grit

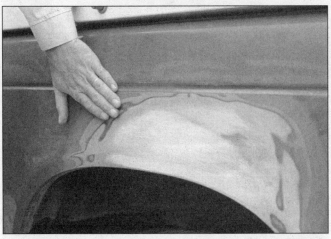

9 You shouldn't be able to feel any ridge at the transition from the filler to the bare metal or from the bare metal to the old paint. As soon as the repair is flat and uniform, remove the dust and mask off the adjacent panels or trim pieces

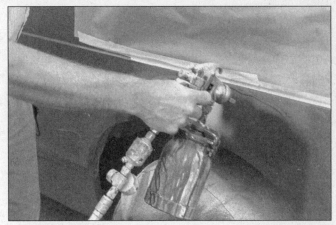

10 Apply several layers of primer to the area. Don't spray the primer on too heavy, so it sags or runs, and make sure each coat is dry before you spray on the next one. A professional-type spray gun is being used here, but aerosol spray primer is available inexpensively from auto parts stores

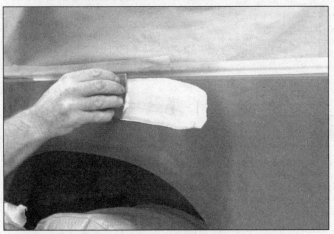

11 The primer will help reveal imperfections or scratches. Fill these with glazing compound. Follow the label instructions and sand it with 360 or 400-grit sandpaper until it's smooth. Repeat the glazing, sanding and respraying until the primer reveals a perfectly smooth surface

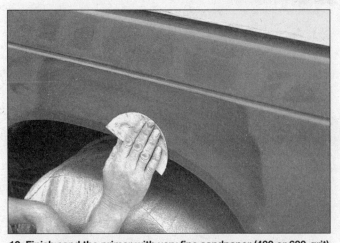

12 Finish sand the primer with very fine sandpaper (400 or 600-grit) to remove the primer overspray. Clean the area with water and allow it to dry. Use a tack rag to remove any dust, then apply the finish coat. Don't attempt to rub out or wax the repair area until the paint has dried completely (at least two weeks)

9.3 Scribe or draw alignment marks around the hood hinges to ensure proper alignment of the hood when it's reinstalled

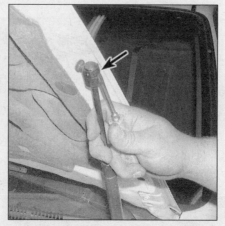

9.4 On V6 models, detach the hood support rods by prying out the clip (arrow) and pulling the strut from the stud

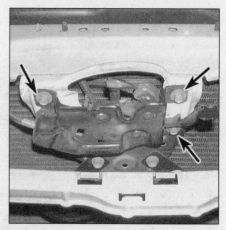

9.10 To adjust the hood latch horizontally or vertically, loosen these bolts (arrows)

Removal and installation

Refer to illustrations 9.3 and 9.4

1   Open the hood, then place blankets or pads over the fenders and cowl area of the body. This will protect the body and paint as the hood is lifted off.

2   Disconnect any cables or wires that will interfere with removal. Disconnect the windshield washer tubing from the nozzles on the hood.

3   Make marks or scribe a line around the hood hinge to ensure proper alignment during installation **(see illustration)**.

4   Have an assistant support the weight of the hood and, on V6 models, detach the support struts by prying out the clips at the top **(see illustration)**.

5   Remove the hinge-to-hood bolts and lift off the hood.

6   Installation is the reverse of removal. Align the hinge bolts with the marks made in step 3.

Adjustment

Refer to illustrations 9.10 and 9.11

7   Fore-and-aft and side-to-side adjustment of the hood is done by moving the hinge plate slot after loosening the bolts or nuts.

8   Scribe a line around the entire hinge plate so you can determine the amount of movement.

9   Loosen the bolts or nuts and move the hood into correct alignment. Move it only a little at a time. Tighten the hinge bolts and carefully lower the hood to check the position.

10   If necessary after installation, the entire hood latch assembly can be adjusted up-and-down as well as from side-to-side on the radiator support so the hood closes securely and flush with the fenders. Scribe a line or mark around the hood latch mounting bolts to provide a reference point, then loosen them and reposition the latch assembly, as necessary **(see illustration)**. Following adjustment, retighten the mounting bolts.

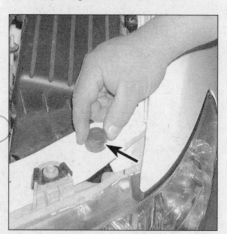

9.11 To adjust the vertical height of the front edge of the hood so that it's flush with the fenders, turn each edge cushion (arrow indicates one) clockwise (to lower the hood) or counterclockwise (to raise the hood)

11   Finally, adjust the hood bumpers on the radiator support so the hood, when closed, is flush with the fenders **(see illustration)**.

12   The hood latch assembly, as well as the hinges, should be periodically lubricated with white, lithium-base grease to prevent binding and wear.

10   Hood latch and release cable - removal and installation

Warning: *The models covered by this manual are equipped with Supplemental Restraint systems (SRS), more commonly known as airbags. Always disconnect the negative battery cable, then the positive battery cable and wait three minutes before working in the vicinity of the impact sensors, steering column or instrument panel to avoid the possibility of accidental deployment of the airbag, which could cause personal injury (see Chapter 12). The yellow wiring harnesses and con-*

10.2 Pry out the cable retainer (arrow) from the backside of the hood latch assembly, then disengage the cable

nectors routed through the console and instrument panel are for this system. Do not use electrical test equipment on any of the airbag system wiring or tamper with them in any way.

Caution: *The stereo in your vehicle is equipped with an anti-theft system. Make sure you have the correct activation code before disconnecting the battery.*

Latch

Refer to illustration 10.2

1   Scribe a line around the latch to aid alignment when installing, then remove the plastic cover over the latch, retained by plastic pins. Remove the retaining bolts securing the hood latch to the radiator support **(see illustration 9.10)**. Remove the latch.

2   Disconnect the hood release cable by disengaging the cable from the latch assembly **(see illustration)**.

3   Installation is the reverse of removal.

Note: *Adjust the latch so the hood engages securely when closed and the hood bumpers are slightly compressed.*

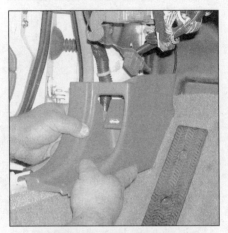

10.7 Pry up the door sill cover, then remove the driver's side kick panel

10.8 Remove the two bolts (arrows) retaining the hood release lever to the body

11.3a Remove the bolts, screws and plastic pins (arrows) on each side retaining the bumper cover to the splash shields (right shown, left side similar)

Cable

Refer to illustrations 10.7 and 10.8

4   Disconnect the hood release cable from the latch assembly as described in step 1.

5   Attach a piece of thin wire or string to the end of the cable and unclip all remaining cable retaining clips. at the radiator support.

6   Refer to Section 12 and remove the plastic inner fenderwell.

7   Working in the passenger compartment, remove the driver's side door sill cover and kick panel **(see illustration)**.

8   Remove the two hood release lever mounting bolts and detach the hood release lever **(see illustration)**.

9   Pull the cable and grommet rearward into the passenger compartment until you can see the wire or string. Ensure that the new cable has a grommet attached then remove the wire or string from the old cable and fasten it to the new cable.

10   With the new cable attached to the wire or string, pull the wire or string back through the firewall until the new cable reaches the latch assembly.

11   Working in the passenger compart-ment, reinstall the new cable into the hood

release lever, making sure the cable hous-ing fits snugly into the notch in the handle bracket.

12   The remainder of the installation is the reverse of removal. **Note:** *Push on the grom-met with your fingers from the passenger compartment to seat the grommet in the fire-wall correctly.*

11 Bumper covers - removal and installation

Warning: *The models covered by this manual are equipped with Supplemental Restraint systems (SRS), more commonly known as airbags. Always disconnect the negative bat-tery cable, then the positive battery cable and wait three minutes before working in the vicinity of the impact sensors, steering col-umn or instrument panel to avoid the possibil-ity of accidental deployment of the airbag, which could cause personal injury (see Chap-ter 12). The yellow wiring harnesses and con-nectors routed through the console and instrument panel are for this system. Do not use electrical test equipment on any of the airbag system wiring or tamper with them in any way.*

Caution: *The stereo in your vehicle is equipped with an anti-theft system. Make sure you have the correct activation code before disconnecting the battery.*

Front bumper

Refer to illustrations 11.3a, 11.3b and 11.4

1   Apply the parking brake, raise the vehi-cle and support it securely on jackstands.

2   Disconnect the negative battery cable. then the positive battery cable and wait two minutes before proceeding any further.

3   Working under the vehicle, detach the screws securing the lower edges of the bumper cover **(see illustrations)**. **Note:** *Use a small screwdriver to pop the center button up on the plastic fasteners, but do not try to remove the center buttons. They stay in the ferrules.*

4   Working at the top, detach the retaining bolts securing the bumper cover to the hood latch support **(see illustration)**. Remove the cover.

5   Installation is the reverse of removal. Make sure the tabs on the top edge of the bumper cover fit into the corresponding clips on the body before attaching the bolts and screws. An assistant is helpful.

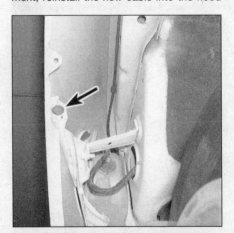

11.3b Remove the bolt on each side (arrow indicates bolt on driver's side) where the bumper cover attaches to the fender

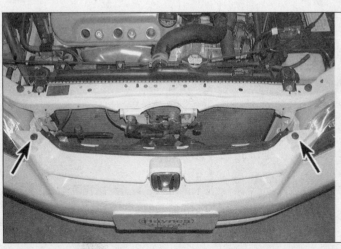

11.4 Remove the two bolts (arrows) holding the top of the bumper cover to the hood latch support

Rear bumper

Refer to illustrations 11.7, 11.8 and 11.9

6   If necessary for working clearance, raise the rear of the vehicle and support it securely on jackstands.

7   Working under the vehicle, detach the plastic clips securing the lower edge of the bumper cover **(see illustration)**.

8   Remove the bolt and clip securing the bumper cover in each rear wheel opening **(see illustration)**.

9   Open the trunk lid and remove the clips securing the upper edge of the bumper cover **(see illustration)**. Pull the bumper cover assembly out and away from the vehicle. **Note:** *Use a small screwdriver to pop the center button up on the plastic fasteners, but do not try to remove the center buttons. They stay in the ferrules.*

10   Installation is the reverse of removal.

---

12   Front fender - removal and installation

Refer to illustrations 12.3, 12.4, 12.5a, 12.5b, 12.6a and 12.6b

1   Raise the vehicle, support it securely on

11.7 Remove the two plastic clips (arrows) at the bottom of the rear bumper cover

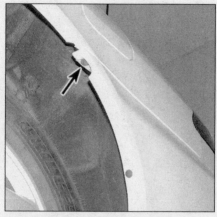

11.8 In each rear fenderwell, remove the bolt (arrow) and the clip securing the front edges of the rear bumper cover

jackstands and remove the front wheel.

2   Remove the front bumper cover (see Section 11).

3   Detach the inner fenderwell screws and clips, then remove the inner fenderwell and mud shield **(see illustration)**.

4   Open the front door, and remove the upper fender-to-body bolt **(see illustration)**.

5   Remove the screws along the bottom of the body and pull away the plastic rocker panel cover to access the lower fender-to-body bolt **(see illustrations)**.

6   Remove the remaining fender mounting bolts **(see illustrations)**.

7   Detach the fender. It's a good idea to have an assistant support the fender while

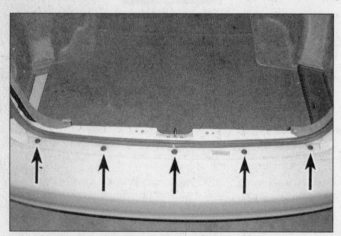

11.9 Disengage the clips (arrows) securing the top edge of the rear bumper cover to the trunk opening

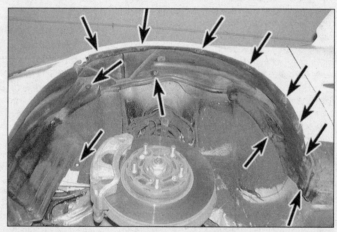

12.3 Detach the inner fenderwell, secured by bolts, screws and plastic clips (arrows)

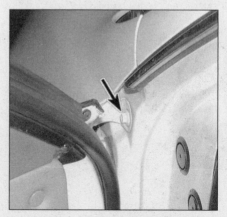

12.4 Remove the upper fender bolt (arrow) with the door open

12.5a Remove the bolts (arrows) and pull the rocker panel away to access the lower bolt for the front fender

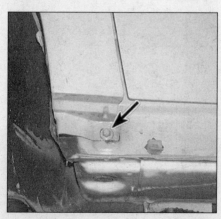

12.5b With the plastic rocker panel pulled away, remove the lower fender-to-body bolt (arrow)

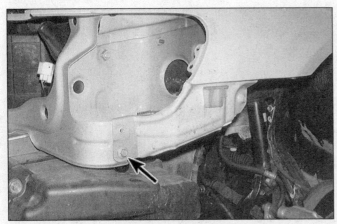

12.6a Remove the one bolt (arrow) at the lower front of the fender

12.6b Remove the three bolts (arrows) along the top of the fender

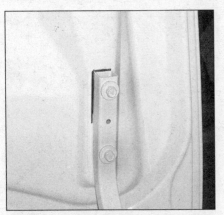

13.3 Draw around the trunk hinges with a marking pen before loosening the bolts to ensure proper alignment of the trunk lid when it's reinstalled

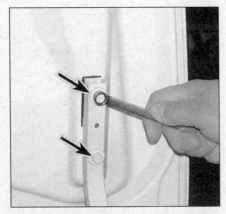

13.4 With an assistant holding the trunk lid, remove the four hinge bolts (arrows indicate two) and lift off the trunk lid

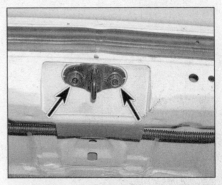

13.7 Loosen the bolts (arrows) and move the striker as necessary to adjust the trunk lid flush with the body in the closed position

it's being moved away from the vehicle to prevent damage to the surrounding body panels.

8   Installation is the reverse of removal.

13 Trunk lid - removal, installation and adjustment

Note: *The trunk lid is heavy and somewhat awkward to remove and install - at least two people should perform this procedure.*

Removal and installation

Refer to illustrations 13.3 and 13.4

1   Open the trunk lid and cover the edges of the trunk compartment with pads or cloths to protect the painted surfaces when the lid is removed.

2   Unplug the electrical connectors for the license plate lights, brake lights, and trunk lock actuator, and remove the wire harness and actuator cable from the trunk lid (see Sections 14 and 15). Tie string or wire to the cables before withdrawing them from the trunk lid so they can be pulled back into the trunk lid when its reinstalled.

3   Scribe or draw alignment marks around

the trunk hinges **(see illustration)**.

4   Remove the hinge-to-trunk lid bolts from both sides and lift off the trunk lid **(see illustration)**.

5   Installation is the reverse of removal. Be sure to align the hinge flanges with the marks made on the trunk lid during removal.

Adjustment

Refer to illustration 13.7

6   After installation, close the lid and see if it's in proper alignment with the adjacent body surfaces. Fore-and-aft and side-to-side adjustments of the lid are controlled by the position of the hinge bolts in the slots. To adjust it, loosen the hinge bolts, reposition the lid and retighten the bolts.

7   The height of the rear of the lid in relation to the surrounding body panels when closed can be adjusted by loosening the lock striker bolts, moving the striker up/down or left/right, then re-tightening the bolts **(see illustration)**. **Note:** *Make a reference mark around the striker before making adjustments.*

8   Finally, you can fine-tune the height of the trailing edge of the trunk lid by turning the trunk lid edge cushions (round rubber bumpers, one on each side) in or out to lower or raise the trunk as necessary.

14 Trunk lid latch and lock cylinder - removal and installation

Trunk lid latch

Refer to illustrations 14.3 and 14.4

1   Open the trunk and scribe a line around the trunk lid latch assembly for a reference point to aid the installation procedure.

2   Disconnect the electrical connector.

3   Detach the two retaining bolts and remove the latch **(see illustration)**.

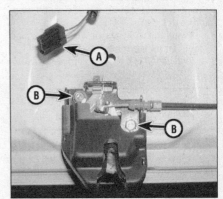

14.3 Disconnect the electrical connector (A) and remove the two latch mounting bolts (B)

14.4 Pry the release cable (arrow) out of the latch assembly

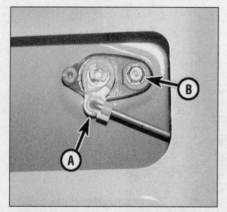

14.6 Pry the rod from its clip (A) and remove the lock cylinder mounting bolt (B)

15.2 Twist the fuel door cable end (arrow) one quarter-turn to remove it from the fuel door housing

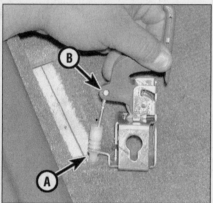

15.8 Remove the cable from the clip (A) and the cable eye from the slot in the lever (B)

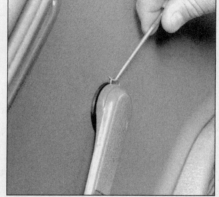

16.1 On models equipped with a manual window regulator, remove the window crank handle by pulling this clip off with a wire hook

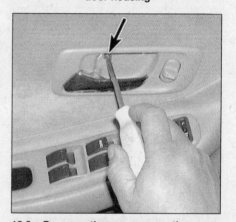

16.3a Pry open the cap, remove the screw (arrow) and pull the inner handle away from the door panel

4   Remove the end of the latch release cable from the latch **(see illustration)**.
5   Installation is the reverse of removal.

Trunk lock cylinder

Refer to illustration 14.6
6   Open the trunk and look upward through the trunk lid access hole behind the right taillight. Remove the lock cylinder rod from its clip and remove the lock's mounting bolt **(see illustration)**. On models so equipped, disconnect the electrical connector from the lock.
7   Twist the lock about 45 degrees and remove it from the trunk.
8   Installation is the reverse of removal.

15 Trunk release and fuel door cable - removal and installation

Refer to illustrations 15.2 and 15.8
1   Refer to Section 14 for removal of the trunk latch and disengagement of the cable from the latch.
2   Inside the trunk, remove the spare tire cover, left-side panel and side storage pocket for access to the fuel door cable end. Twist the fuel door latch cable end one one

quarter turn and pull it from the fuel door housing **(see illustration)**.
3   Remove the rear seat bottom as described in Section 27. On coupe models, both seat back and bottom must be removed.
4   Pry up the driver's side door sill covers (only one cover on coupe models). On four-door models, remove the center door pillar's lower trim panel.
5   Peel back the carpeting to access the release cable. Open all of the clips holding the cable to the body.
6   Pry open the upper lid around the lock cylinder in the cable release lever housing next to the driver's seat. Insert your key and rotate the lock cylinder hard counterclockwise until the cylinder can be withdrawn with the key.
7   At the side of the release lever housing that faces the seat, remove the small plastic cover and loosen the bolt, using a socket and extension through the hole where the lock cylinder was. Push the release lever housing rearward to free it from the bolt.
8   Turn the housing over and remove the cable housing from the clip and the eye from the lever **(see illustration)**.

9   Attach a piece of thin wire to the end of the cable.
10   Working in the trunk compartment, pull the cable assembly towards the rear of the vehicle until you can see the wire.
11   Attach the wire to the front of the new cable and fish it back through the body until it can be attached to the lever. The remainder of the installation is the reverse of removal.

16 Door trim panels - removal and installation

Caution: *Wear gloves when working inside the door openings to protect against cuts from sharp metal edges.*
Refer to illustrations 16.1, 16.3a, 16.3b, 16.4, 16.5a, 16.5b, 16.5c, 16.6a, 16.6b and 16.7

Removal

1   On manual window regulator equipped models, remove the window crank handle **(see illustration)**.
2   Remove the door lock knob.
3   Remove the inside door handle by prying out the small cap, revealing the single mounting screw. Pull the handle away from the door panel enough to disconnect the link-

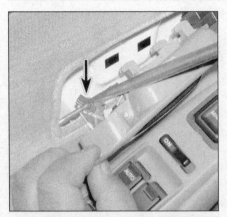

16.3b With the handle pulled out a little, you can disconnect the linkage rod (arrow)

16.4 Pry off the trim cover from the outside mirror

16.5a Remove the screw from inside the door pull/switch assembly - power window model shown; on non-power models, simply remove the screw and pull-pocket

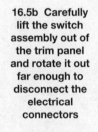

16.5b Carefully lift the switch assembly out of the trim panel and rotate it out far enough to disconnect the electrical connectors

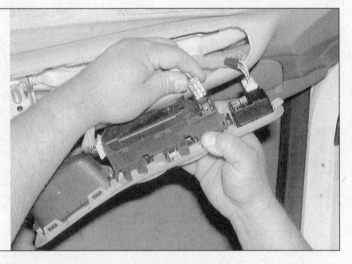

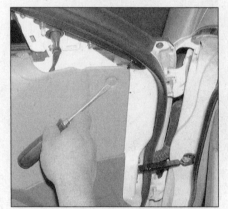

16.5c Pry off the protective cap and remove the front upper trim panel retaining screw

age rod and, if equipped, the power door lock electrical connector **(see illustrations)**.

4   Pry out the outside mirror cover **(see illustration)**.

5   Remove the door trim panel retaining screws and the screw in the door arm rest **(see illustrations)**, then carefully pull the panel out until the clips disengage. Work slowly and carefully around the outer edge of the trim panel until it's free. **Note:** *The clips are too far in from the edge of the panel to use a standard trim-panel pry tool.*

6   Once all of the clips are disengaged, pull the trim panel up, unplug any wiring harness connectors and remove the panel **(see illustrations)**.

7   For access to the door outside handle or the door window regulator inside the door, raise the window fully, remove the power window control unit (if equipped), the door panel bracket and the speaker assembly (see

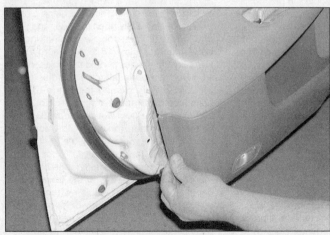

16.6a Carefully pull the panel away from the door until the retaining clips release, then grasp the front and rear of the panel and lift it straight up

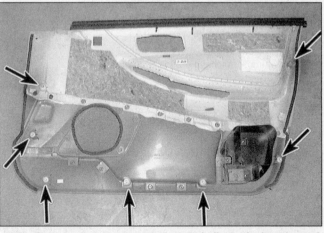

16.6b The trim panel is removed here to indicate the locations of the clips (arrows)

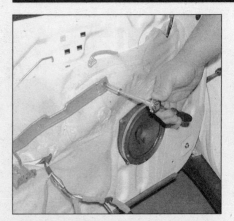

16.7 Remove the armrest support bracket and carefully peel back the plastic watershield

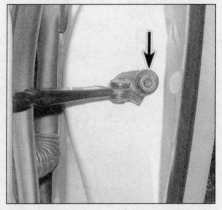

17.6 Remove the bolt (arrow) retaining the door stop strut

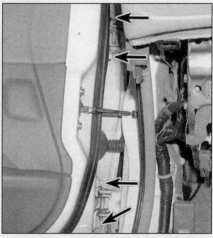

17.8a Remove the four door hinge bolts (arrows) with the door supported

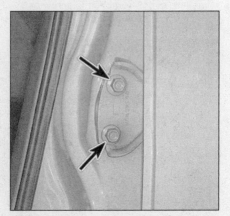

17.8b Open the front door to access the rear door hinge-to-body bolts (arrows)

17.11 Loosen the hinge-to-body bolts using a ratchet with a swivel socket to adjust the doors

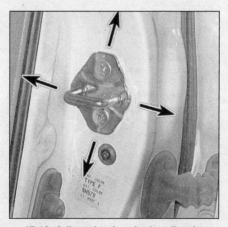

17.13 Adjust the door lock striker by loosening the mounting screws and gently tapping the striker in the desired direction (arrows)

Chapter 12), then carefully peel back the plastic watershield **(see illustration)**.

Installation

8   Prior to installation of the door trim panel, be sure to reinstall any clips in the panel which may have come out when you removed the panel.

9   Plug in the wire harness connectors for the power door lock switch and the power window switch, if equipped, and place the panel in position in the door. Press the door panel into place until the clips are seated. Install the inner door handle and its screw. Install the power door lock switch assembly, if equipped, or the pull-pocket and its screw. Install the manual-regulator crank handle or power window switch assembly.

17   Door - removal, installation and adjustment

Note: *The door is heavy and somewhat awkward to remove and install - at least two people should perform this procedure.*
Caution: *Wear gloves when working inside the door openings to protect against cuts from sharp metal edges.*

Removal and installation

Refer to illustrations 17.6, 17.8a and 17.8b
1   Lower the window completely in the door and then disconnect the negative cable from the battery.
2   Open the door all the way and support it from the ground on jacks or blocks covered with rags to prevent damaging the paint.
3   Remove the door trim panel and water deflector as described in Section 16.
4   Disconnect all electrical connections, ground wires and harness retaining clips from the door. **Note:** *It is a good idea to label all connections to aid the reassembly process.*
5   From the door side, detach the rubber conduit between the body and the door. Then pull the wiring harness through conduit hole and remove from the door.
6   Remove the door stop strut bolt **(see illustration)**.
7   Mark around the door hinges with a pen or a scribe to facilitate realignment during reassembly.
8   With an assistant holding the door, remove the hinge to door bolts **(see illustrations)** and lift the door off. **Note:** *Draw a reference line around the hinges before removing the bolts.*
9   Installation is the reverse of removal.

Adjustment

Refer to illustrations 17.11, and 17.13
10   Having proper door to body alignment is a critical part of a well-functioning door assembly. First check the door hinge pins for excessive play. Fully open the door and lift up and down on the door without lifting the body. If a door has 1/16-inch or more excessive play, the hinges should be replaced.
11   Door-to-body alignment adjustments are made by loosening the hinge-to-body bolts **(see illustration)** or hinge-to-door bolts and moving the door. Proper body alignment is achieved when the top of the doors are parallel with the roof section, the front door is flush with the fender, the rear door is flush with the rear quarter panel and the bottom of the doors are aligned with the lower rocker panel. If these goals can't be reached by adjusting the hinge-to-body or hinge-to-door bolts, body alignment shims may have to be purchased and inserted behind the hinges to achieve correct alignment.
12   To adjust the door closed position, scribe a line or mark around the striker plate

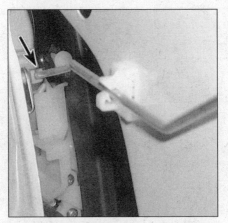

18.2 Detach the plastic clips on the actuating rod (arrow) leading to the latch

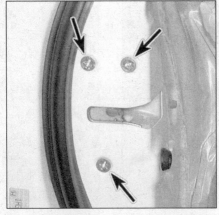

18.4 Remove the latch screws (arrows) from the end of the door and withdraw the latch assembly through the access hole

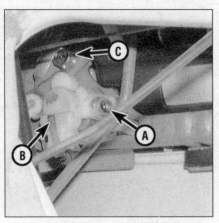

18.7 Detach the actuating rods, then remove the screw (A) and the lock switch (B) – C indicates one of the two bolts retaining the outer handle protector

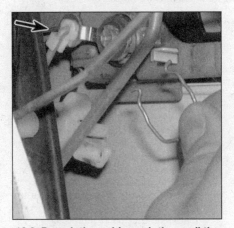

18.9 Detach the rod (arrow), then pull the clip and the lock cylinder can be removed

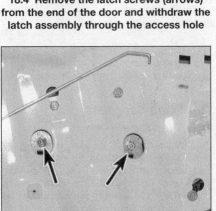

19.3 Raise the window just enough to access the glass-retaining bolts (arrows) through the holes in the door frame

8   Remove the access plug in the door and remove the outside handle retaining bolts **(see illustration 18.7)**.
9   Remove the handle and lock cylinder assembly from the vehicle. The lock cylinder can be removed from the handle assembly by removing a clip, or the electrical connector can be unbolted and the cylinder left on the handle assembly **(see illustration)**.
10   Installation is the reverse of removal.

19 Door window glass - removal and installation

Caution: *Wear gloves when working inside the door openings to protect against cuts from sharp metal edges.*

Front door glass

Refer to illustration 19.3

1   Remove the door trim panel and the plastic watershield (see Section 16).
2   Lower the window glass all the way down into the door.
3   Raise the window just enough to access the window retaining bolts through the hole in the door frame **(see illustration)**. On some models, the window is retained by a glass guide bar, similar to the one described below for the rear window glass (see Step 8).
4   Place a rag over the glass to help prevent scratching the glass and remove the two glass mounting bolts.
5   Remove the glass by pulling it up and out.
6   Installation is the reverse of removal.

Rear door and quarter-window glass (four-door models)

Refer to illustration 19.9

7   Remove the door panel and waterseal (see Section 16).
8   Lower the window enough to see the bolts on the glass guide bar. Loosen the bolts and push the guide bar to the rear while hold-

---

to provide a reference point, then check that the door latch is contacting the center of the latch striker. If not adjust the up and down position first.
13   Finally adjust the latch striker sideways position, so that the door panel is flush with the center pillar or rear quarter panel and provides positive engagement with the latch mechanism **(see illustration)**.

18 Door latch, lock cylinder and handle - removal and installation

Caution: *Wear gloves when working inside the door openings to protect against cuts from sharp metal edges.*

Door latch

Refer to illustrations 18.2 and 18.4

1   Raise the window, then remove the door trim panel and watershield (see Section 16).
2   Working through the large access hole, disengage the outside door handle-to-latch rod, outside door lock-to-latch rod, the inside handle-to-latch rod, and the lock solenoid-to-latch rod **(see illustration)**.
3   All door lock rods are attached by plastic clips. The plastic clips can be removed by

---

unsnapping the portion engaging the connecting rod and then pulling the rod out of its locating hole. On models with power door locks, disconnect the electrical connectors at the latch.
4   Remove the screws securing the latch to the door **(see illustration)**. Remove the latch assembly from the door.
5   Installation is the reverse of removal.

Outside handle and door lock cylinder

Refer to illustrations 18.7 and 18.9

6   To remove the outside handle and lock cylinder assembly, raise the window and remove the door trim panel and watershield (see Section 16). **Caution:** *Take care not to scratch the paint on the outside of the door. Wide masking tape applied around the handle opening before beginning the procedure can help avoid scratches.*
7   Working through the access hole, disengage the plastic clips that secure the outside handle-to-latch rod, the outside door lock-to-latch rod, and the screw holding the lock cylinder switch to the lock cylinder **(see illustration)**.

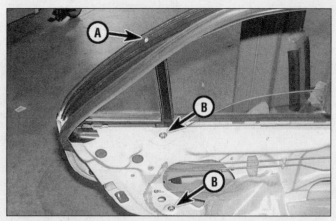

19.9 Pull away the interior weatherstripping from the rear door and channel, then pull a portion of the exterior weatherstripping to expose the upper channel screw (A), then remove the two bolts (B)

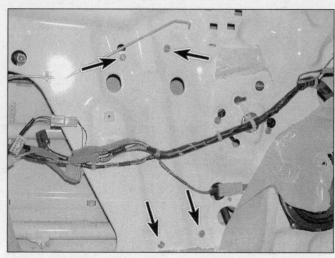

20.4a Remove the equalizer bolts (arrows) . . .

ing up the glass. Push the glass from the guide bar and lower the glass carefully to the bottom of the door.

9   Pull the inner weatherstripping away from the door and rear channel to allow enough slack to extract the channel. Pull the outer weatherstripping away from the door until the upper channel screw can be removed **(see illustration)**.

10   Pull the glass channel forward, away from the quarter-glass, and pull it up out of the door, letting it hang by the weatherstripping. Protect the exterior paint of the door with a towel taped in place.

11   The main door glass can now be removed through the window opening.

12   The quarter-window glass can be pulled out of the door. Work carefully when pulling the glass. The rubber seal around the quarter-glass may be stiff and hinder easy removal.

13   Installation is the reverse of the removal procedure. If the weatherstripping won't stay tightly in the door or channel, apply a little weatherstripping cement under it and press it in place. Masking tape can be used to hold it in place until the cement sets up. **Note:** *When reinstalling the main glass in the rear door,*

push the glass forward against the front channel before tightening the glass-mounting bolts.

Rear quarter glass (coupe models)

14   Replacement of the fixed quarter-glass requires the use of special fast-setting adhesive/caulk materials and some specialized tools and techniques. These operations should be left to a dealer service department or a shop specializing in glass work.

20   Door window glass regulator - removal and installation

Caution: *Wear gloves when working inside the door openings to protect against cuts from sharp metal edges.*

Front

Refer to illustrations 20.4a and 20.4b

1   Remove the door trim panel and the plastic watershield (see Section 16).

2   Remove the window glass assembly (see Section 19).

3   On power operated windows, disconnect the electrical connector from the window regulator motor.

4   Remove the regulator/motor assembly mounting bolts **(see illustrations)**.

5   On coupe models, the regulator assembly is a scissors-type. Before removing the bolts, mark the position of the rear bolt of the upper roller guide. Remove the bolts for the upper and lower roller guides, then the four bolts holding the motor (crank assembly on non-power window models) to the door.

6   Pull the equalizer arm and regulator assemblies through the service hole in the door frame to remove it.

7   Installation is the reverse of removal. Lubricate the rollers and wear points on the regulator with white grease before installation.

Rear

Refer to illustration 20.11

8   Remove the door trim panel and the plastic watershield (see Section 16).

9   Remove the window glass assembly (see Section 19).

10   On power operated windows, disconnect the electrical connector from the window regulator motor.

11   Remove the regulator/motor assembly mounting bolts **(see illustration)**.

12   Pull the equalizer arm and regulator assemblies through the service hole in the door frame to remove it.

13   Installation is the reverse of removal. Lubricate the rollers and wear points on the regulator with white grease before installation.

21   Mirrors - removal and installation

Outside mirrors

Refer to illustration 21.4

1   On power-mirror-equipped models, remove the door trim panel and the plastic watershield (see Section 16).

20.4b . . . then the regulator/motor bolts (arrows)

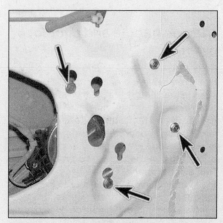

20.11 On rear doors, remove these mounting bolts (arrows)

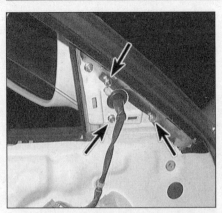

21.4 Disconnect the electrical connector (A), if equipped, then remove the three mirror mounting bolts (arrows)

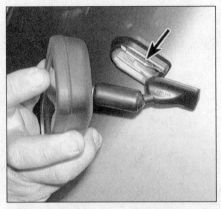

21.6 Push the inside mirror downward and pry it out of the clip (arrow) in the base

21.7 To reinstall the inside mirror, turn it 90 degrees and push the bottom of the stalk up into the base, then rotate the mirror to its normal position

2   Pry off the mirror trim cover **(see illustration 16.4)**.
3   Disconnect the electrical connector from the mirror (if equipped).
4   Remove the three mirror retaining bolts and detach the mirror from the vehicle **(see illustration)**.
5   Installation is the reverse of removal.

Inside mirror

Refer to illustrations 21.6 and 21.7
6   Slide the mirror downward in its mount toward the dashboard, then pry between the mirror mount and the base of the mirror stalk with a screwdriver tip covered with tape **(see illustration)**. There is a hairpin-type spring holding the mirror stalk in the base. If necessary, pry the spring out to remove the mirror.
7   To install the mirror, reinsert the spring if it was removed earlier. Turn the mirror at right angles to its normal position and insert the mirror stalk's lug into the mount **(see illustration)**. Push upward and twist the mirror one-quarter turn to its normal position. Make sure the mirror is secure in the base.

22   Center console - removal and installation

Refer to illustrations 22.2, 22.3, 22.5, 22.6, 22.7a, 22.7b and 22.7c
Warning: *The models covered by this manual are equipped with Supplemental Restraint systems (SRS), more commonly known as airbags. Always disconnect the negative battery cable, then the positive battery cable and wait three minutes before working in the vicinity of the impact sensors, steering column or instrument panel to avoid the possibility of accidental deployment of the airbag, which could cause personal injury (see Chapter 12). The yellow wiring harnesses and connectors routed through the console and instrument panel are for this system. Do not use electrical test equipment on any of the airbag system wiring or tamper with them in any way.*
Caution: *The stereo in your vehicle is equipped with an anti-theft system. Make*

sure you have the correct activation code before disconnecting the battery.
1   Disconnect the battery cables, see the **Warning** above.
2   Use a screwdriver with the tip taped to prevent scratching panels, pry the console front cover off **(see illustration)**.
3   Pry out the gear selector trim bezel from the console **(see illustration)**. On manual-transaxle models, refer to Chapter 7 and

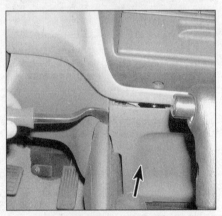

22.2 Pry off the console front cover (arrow)

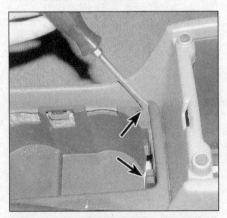

22.5 Pry up the shift indicator trim panel (arrows indicate tangs at the rear of the panel)

remove the shift knob.
4   Pry the beverage holder out of the console, prying only at the front of the beverage holder. Do not pull it out by the lid.
5   Carefully pry and pull the shift indicator trim panel from the console **(see illustration)**.
6   Lift up the armrest and pull up the console glove compartment trim panel **(see illustration)**.

22.3 Pry or pull the plastic trim ring from around the shifter (automatic transaxle models shown)

22.6 Pull the glove compartment trim panel (arrow) from the rear of the console

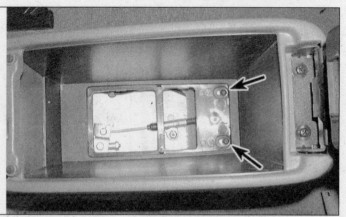

22.7a Remove the two screws (arrows) under the armrest area . . .

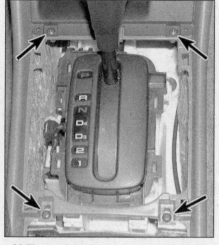

22.7b . . . then the four screws (arrows) under the shifter area . . .

22.7c . . . and the four screws (arrows indicate two at right side) at the front of the console

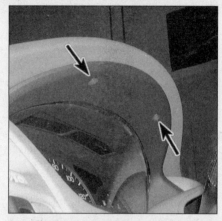

23.3 Detach the retaining screws (arrows) at the top of the bezel, then pull the bezel outward to disengage the clips at the bottom

7   Remove the screws holding the console to the floor **(see illustrations)**.

8   Remove the front console screws and lift the console up and over the shift lever. Disconnect any electrical connections and remove the console from the vehicle.

9   Installation is the reverse of removal.

23   Dashboard trim panels - removal and installation

Warning: *The models covered by this manual are equipped with Supplemental Restraint systems (SRS), more commonly known as airbags. Always disconnect the negative battery cable, then the positive battery cable and wait three minutes before working in the vicinity of the impact sensors, steering column or instrument panel to avoid the possibility of accidental deployment of the airbag, which could cause personal injury (see Chapter 12). The yellow wiring harnesses and connectors routed through the console and instrument panel are for this system. Do not use electrical test equipment on any of the airbag system wiring or tamper with them in any way.*

Caution: *The stereo in your vehicle is equipped with an anti-theft system. Make sure you have the correct activation code*

before disconnecting the battery.

1   Disconnect the negative battery cable, see **Warning** and **Caution** above.

Instrument cluster bezel

Refer to illustration 23.3

2   If equipped with a tilt steering column, tilt the column all the way down.

3   Remove the two screws at the top of the

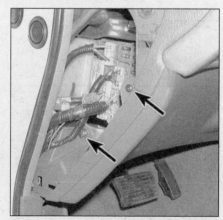

23.7 Remove the plastic fusebox cover at the left of the dashboard, then remove these bolster screws (arrows)

instrument cluster bezel **(see illustration)**.

4   Using as screwdriver with the tip taped with masking tape, carefully pry the lower portion of the bezel away from the instrument panel until the clips are released. Take care not to scratch the surrounding trim on the instrument panel.

5   Installation is the reverse of the removal procedure. Make sure the clips are engaged properly before pushing the bezel firmly into place.

Knee bolster

Refer to illustrations 23.7 and 23.8

6   Refer to Section 22 and remove the console front cover.

7   Pry the plastic cover from the fusebox at the left end of the dashboard **(see illustration)**. Remove the two knee bolster screws accessible there.

8   Remove the one screw at the upper right corner of the knee bolster and pry the bolster away to release the remaining clips **(see illustration)**.

9   Remove the retaining bolts securing the knee bolster reinforcement, if needed for access to components under the dashboard.

23.8 One bolster screw (arrow) is accessed when the console front cover is removed

23.11 With a taped screwdriver, pry the clock bezel outward

23.13 Center instrument panel retaining screw locations (arrows)

23.14 Disconnect the two electrical connectors (arrows) at the heater controls, then remove the panel with the controls attached

Pull outward on the lower edge of the knee bolster reinforcement panel and detach it from the vehicle.

10   Installation is the reverse of removal.

Center trim panel

Refer to illustrations 23.11, 23.13 and 23.14

11   Pry the clock bezel carefully from the center instrument panel bezel **(see illustration)**.

12   Pull the clock bezel out enough to disconnect the electrical connector from the clock and the hazard warning switch.

13   Detach the retaining screws from the trim panel **(see illustration)**. There is one at the top in the clock bezel cavity and two at the bottom. The remainder of the panel fasteners are clips. Pry carefully on the panel until the clips are disengaged.

14   The air conditioning and heater control panel is attached to the center instrument panel by screws on the back. Pull the panel away from the dashboard enough to disconnect the two electrical connectors at the heater controls and remove the panel **(see illustration)**.

15   Installation is the reverse of removal.

Passenger's side lower trim panel and glove box

Refer to illustration 23.16, 23.18 and 23.19

16   The passenger's side lower cover is removed in much the same manner as the driver's knee bolster (see above). Pry off the plastic dashboard endcap on the right side of the dashboard (with the passenger door open for access). Remove the two trim panel screws there and the one screw at the top left of the panel **(see illustration)**.

17   Pry the bottom of the panel out until the clips are disengaged and remove the panel.

18   Remove the screws along the bottom edge of the glove box assembly **(see illustration)**.

19   Open the glovebox door and use a small, taped screwdriver to pry out the screw covers, then remove the screw at each top side and the two in the center **(see illustration)**.

20   Push the two glovebox door hinges toward each other to disengage the clips in the dashboard, then pull the glovebox assembly down and out. **Note:** *Once the glovebox is partway out of the dashboard,*

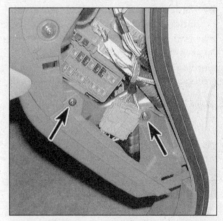

23.16 Remove the passenger's side lower trim panel retaining screws (arrows) (revealed when the dashboard end panel is removed)

disconnect the electrical connector for the glovebox light.

21   Installation is the reverse of removal.

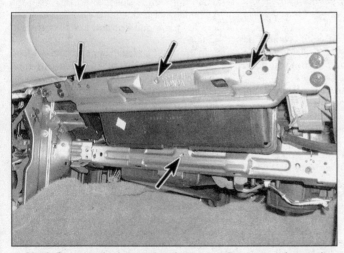

23.18 Remove the lower glovebox mounting screws (arrows)

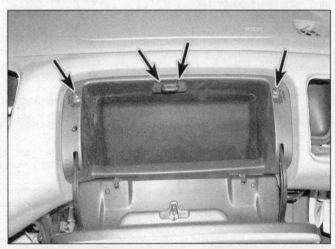

23.19 Pry out the small plastic covers, then remove the upper glovebox screws (arrows)

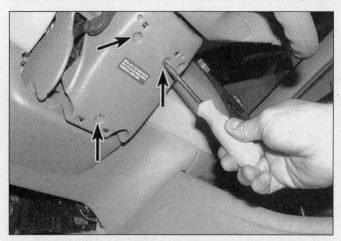

24.2 Remove the screws (arrows) at the lower column cover, then remove the upper and lower covers

25.6 Remove the steering column retaining bolts (arrows indicate the top two) and lower it away from the instrument panel

24 Steering column cover - removal and installation

Refer to illustration 24.2

Warning: *The models covered by this manual are equipped with Supplemental Restraint systems (SRS), more commonly known as airbags. Always disconnect the negative battery cable, then the positive battery cable and wait three minutes before working in the vicinity of the impact sensors, steering column or instrument panel to avoid the possibility of accidental deployment of the airbag, which could cause personal injury (see Chapter 12). The yellow wiring harnesses and connectors routed through the console and instrument panel are for this system. Do not use electrical test equipment on any of the airbag system wiring or tamper with them in any way.*

Caution: *The stereo in your vehicle is equipped with an anti-theft system. Make sure you have the correct activation code before disconnecting the battery.*

1   On tilt steering columns, move the column to the lowest position.

2   Remove the screws, then separate the halves and remove the upper and lower steering column covers **(see illustration)**.

3   Installation is the reverse of the removal procedure.

25 Instrument panel - removal and installation

Refer to illustrations 25.6, 25.7, 25.8, 25.9a, 25.9b, 25.9c and 25.10

Warning: *The models covered by this manual are equipped with Supplemental Restraint systems (SRS), more commonly known as airbags. Always disconnect the negative battery cable, then the positive battery cable and wait three minutes before working in the vicinity of the impact sensors, steering column or instrument panel to avoid the possibil-*

25.7 With the coin tray removed, remove the screws (arrows) and pry out the driver's side air vent

ity of accidental deployment of the airbag, which could cause personal injury (see Chapter 12). The yellow wiring harnesses and connectors routed through the console and instrument panel are for this system. Do not use electrical test equipment on any of the airbag system wiring or tamper with them in any way.

Caution: *The stereo in your vehicle is equipped with an anti-theft system. Make sure you have the correct activation code before disconnecting the battery.*

1   Disconnect the negative battery cable see the **Warning** and **Caution** above.

2   Remove the dashboard trim panels (see Section 23) and the center floor console (see Section 22).

3   Remove the instrument cluster (see Chapter 12) and the glove box (see Section 23).

4   Disconnect the passenger side air bag (if equipped) and remove it (see Chapter 12).

5   Remove the audio unit from the center of the dashboard (see Chapter 12).

6   Remove the driver's knee bolster and reinforcement panel (see Section 23). Then detach the bolts securing the steering col-

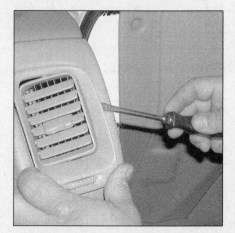

25.8 Pry out the passenger's side air vent

umn and lower it away from the instrument panel **(see illustration)**.

7   Remove the coin tray from the bottom of the driver's side air vent, then remove the vent mounting screws **(see illustration)**. Pry the upper and center portion of the vent assembly from the clips in the dashboard. When the vent is pulled out away from the dashboard, disconnect the electrical connectors for the moonroof and cruise control (if equipped).

8   Pry out the passenger side air vent **(see illustration)**. **Caution:** *Use masking tape around the grille to protect the dashboard covering.*

9   A number of electrical connectors must be disconnected in order to remove the instrument panel. Most are designed so that they will only fit on one matching connector (male or female), but if there is any doubt, mark the connectors with masking tape and a marking pen before disconnecting them **(see illustrations)**.

10   Remove all of the bolts holding the instrument panel to the body **(see illustration)**. Once all are removed, lift the panel up (it is held to the body by three plastic pins behind it) then pull it away from the windshield and take it out through the driver's

25.9a Disconnect the electrical connectors (arrows) at the driver's side fusebox

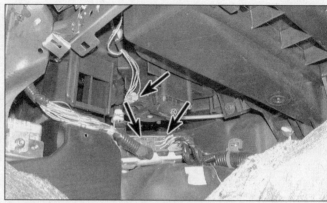

25.9b Under the center of the dashboard, disconnect the PCM connector, the airbag harness connector, the connectors to the airmix control motor and evaporator temperature sensor (arrows) - also disconnect the ground strap and radio antenna cable (not seen here)

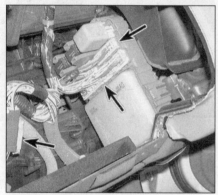

25.9c Disconnect the electrical connectors (arrows) at the passenger's side fusebox

door opening.
11   Installation is the reverse of removal.

26   Cowl cover - removal and installation

Refer to illustrations 26.2
1   Remove the wiper arms (see Chapter 12).

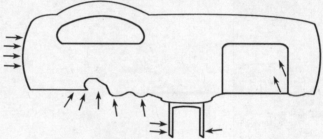

25.10 Remove the 14 bolts (arrows) holding the instrument panel to the body - four are at the left end, five at the steering column area (four are up inside the steering column cavity), three at the console, and two inside the glovebox cavity

2   Carefully pry out the three clips securing the cowl cover from the vehicle (see illustration). The rubber hood seal can stay attached to the cowl cover during removal.
3   Installation is the reverse of removal. If the cowl panel rubber seal is being replaced, pry the old one out and press the new one into the holes provided in the cowl cover.

27   Seats - removal and installation

Front seat

Refer to illustration 27.2
1   Position the seat all the way forward or all the way to the rear to access the front seat retaining bolts.
2   Detach any bolt trim covers and remove the retaining bolts (see illustration).
3   Tilt the seat upward to access the underside, then disconnect any electrical connectors and lift the seat from the vehicle.
4   Installation is the reverse of removal.

Rear seat

Refer to illustrations 27.5a, 27.5b, 27.6a and 27.6b
5   Flip the rear seat back panel down, then pull up four of the plastic clips holding the trunk mat to the center-rear of the seat back,

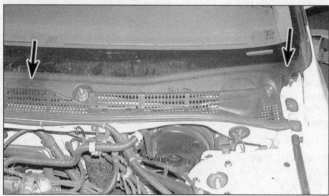

26.2 Pry up the plastic fastener clips (arrows indicate one end clip and the center clip) and remove the cowl cover

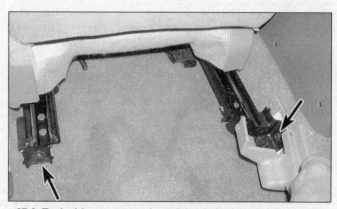

27.2 Typical front seat track retaining bolts (arrows) (rear bolts shown, front bolts similar)

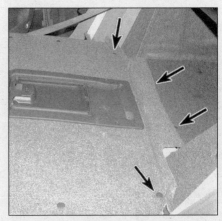

27.5a With the seat back folded down, pry up the plastic clips (arrows) and fold back the carpet . . .

27.5b . . . to expose the pivot brackets, then remove the bolts (arrow indicates driver's side bolt)

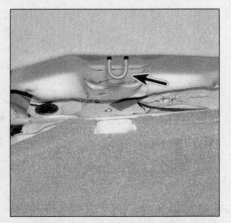

27.6a Pull up the rear seat bottom cushion from the clips (arrow indicates one) . . .

27.6b . . . and remove the bolt at the rear center (arrow)

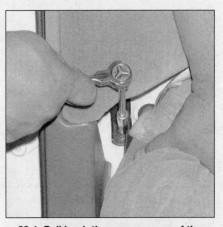

28.1 Pull back the rear corners of the lower cushion to remove the bolts holding the seat back side trim panels

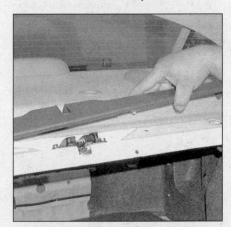

28.2 Pull up the bulkhead trim panel

exposing the corner bolts to remove **(see illustrations)**.

6   Lift up on the front edge of the rear seat bottom cushion, remove the rear mounting bolt and remove the cushion from the vehicle **(see illustrations)**. **Note:** *Work the seat belts out of the slits at the back of the cushion.*

7   Installation is the reverse of removal.

28 Rear package shelf - removal and installation

Refer to illustrations 28.1

1   To remove the package shelf, first unlock and flip forward the seat back, then pull back the corners of the seat bottom to expose the bolts holding the seat back side trim panels **(see illustration)**. Pull the side trim panels out.

2   Carefully pull up the rear bulkhead cover (plastic trim panel at the front of the package shelf) to release it from the four clips **(see illustration)**.

3   From inside the trunk, release the clips and remove the high-mount brake light **(see illustration)**.

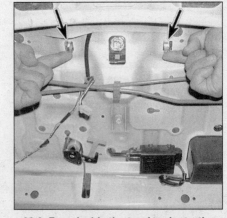

28.3 From inside the trunk, release the two plastic catches (arrows), then pull the high-mount brake light unit from the package shelf

4   The package shelf can now be lifted up from the body and pulled forward **(see illustration)**. **Note:** *If the package shelf is to be replaced, the center shoulder belt mount must be unbolted from the body, since the seat belt goes through the package shelf. If*

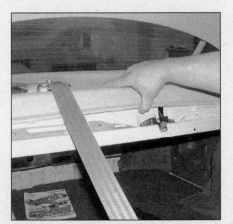

28.4 The package shelf can now be pulled forward - the shoulder belt needs to be unbolted only if the package shelf is to be replaced

the package shelf is being pulled forward for access to the screws mounting the radio antenna amplifier, the belt doesn't have to be removed.

5   The installation is the reverse of the removal procedure.

Chapter 12
Chassis electrical system

Contents

1 General information

The electrical system is a 12-volt, negative ground type. Power for the lights and all electrical accessories is supplied by a lead/acid-type battery which is charged by the alternator.

This Chapter covers repair and service procedures for the various electrical components not associated with the engine. Information on the battery, alternator, distributor and starter motor can be found in Chapter 5. It should be noted that when portions of the electrical system are serviced, the negative battery cable should be disconnected from the battery to prevent electrical shorts and/or fires. **Caution:** *The stereo in your vehicle may be equipped with an anti-theft system. Refer to the information at the front of this manual before detaching the battery cables.*

2 Electrical troubleshooting - general information

Refer to illustration 2.15

A typical electrical circuit consists of an electrical component, any switches, relays, motors, fuses, fusible links or circuit breakers related to that component and the wiring and connectors that link the component to both the battery and the chassis. To help you pinpoint an electrical circuit problem, wiring diagrams are included at the end of this Chapter.

Before tackling any troublesome electrical circuit, first study the appropriate wiring diagrams to get a complete understanding of what makes up that individual circuit. Trouble spots, for instance, can often be narrowed down by noting if other components related to the circuit are operating properly. If several components or circuits fail at one time, chances are the problem is in a fuse or ground connection, because several circuits are often routed through the same fuse and ground connections.

Electrical problems usually stem from simple causes, such as loose or corroded connections, a blown fuse, a melted fusible link or a failed relay. Visually inspect the condition of all fuses, wires and connections in a problem circuit before troubleshooting the circuit.

If test equipment and instruments are going to be utilized, use the diagrams to plan ahead of time where you will make the necessary connections in order to accurately pinpoint the trouble spot.

The basic tools needed for electrical troubleshooting include a circuit tester or voltmeter (a 12-volt bulb with a set of test leads can also be used), a continuity tester, which includes a bulb, battery and set of test leads, and a jumper wire, preferably with a circuit breaker incorporated, which can be used to bypass electrical components. Before attempting to locate a problem with test instruments, use the wiring diagram(s) to decide where to make the connections.

Voltage checks

Voltage checks should be performed if a circuit is not functioning properly. Connect one lead of a circuit tester to either the negative battery terminal or a known good ground. Connect the other lead to a connector in the circuit being tested, preferably nearest to the battery or fuse. If the bulb of the tester lights, voltage is present, which means that the part of the circuit between the connector and the battery is problem free. Continue checking the rest of the circuit in the same fashion. When you reach a point at which no voltage is present, the problem lies between that point and the last test point with voltage. Most of the time the problem can be traced to a loose connection. **Note:** *Keep in mind that some circuits receive voltage only when the ignition key is in the Accessory or Run position.*

Finding a short

One method of finding shorts in a circuit is to remove the fuse and connect a test light or voltmeter in place of the fuse terminals. There should be no voltage present in the circuit. Move the wiring harness from side-to-side while watching the test light. If the bulb goes on, there is a short to ground somewhere in that area, probably where the insulation has rubbed through. The same test can be performed on each component in the circuit, even a switch.

Ground check

Perform a ground test to check whether a component is properly grounded. Disconnect the battery and connect one lead of a self-powered test light, known as a continuity tester, to a known good ground. Connect the other lead to the wire or ground connection being tested. If the bulb goes on, the ground is good. If the bulb does not go on, the ground is not good.

Continuity check

A continuity check is done to determine if there are any breaks in a circuit - if it is passing electricity properly. With the circuit off (no power in the circuit), a self-powered continuity tester can be used to check the circuit. Connect the test leads to both ends of the circuit (or to the "power" end and a good ground), and if the test light comes on the circuit is passing current properly. If the light doesn't come on, there is a break somewhere in the circuit. The same procedure can be used to test a switch, by connecting the continuity tester to the switch terminals. With the switch turned On, the test light should come on.

2.15 To backprobe a connector, insert a small, sharp probe (such as a straight-pin) into the back of the connector alongside the desired wire until it contacts the metal terminal inside; connect your meter leads to the probes - this allows you to test a functioning circuit

Finding an open circuit

When diagnosing for possible open circuits, it is often difficult to locate them by sight because oxidation or terminal misalignment are hidden by the connectors. Merely wiggling a connector on a sensor or in the wiring harness may correct the open circuit condition. Remember this when an open circuit is indicated when troubleshooting a circuit. Intermittent problems may also be caused by oxidized or loose connections.

Electrical troubleshooting is simple if you keep in mind that all electrical circuits are basically electricity running from the battery, through the wires, switches, relays, fuses and fusible links to each electrical component (light bulb, motor, etc.) and to ground, from which it is passed back to the battery. Any electrical problem is an interruption in the flow of electricity to and from the battery.

Connectors

Most electrical connections on these vehicles are made with multiwire plastic connectors. The mating halves of many connec-

3.1c The power distribution box is located in the engine compartment adjacent to the battery - it contains cartridge type fusible links, miniaturized fuses, and relays

3.1a One interior fuse block is located at the end of the driver's side of the instrument panel - It contains 13 miniaturized fuses

tors are secured with locking clips molded into the plastic connector shells. The mating halves of large connectors, such as some of those under the instrument panel, are held together by a bolt through the center of the connector.

To separate a connector with locking clips, use a small screwdriver to pry the clips apart carefully, then separate the connector halves. Pull only on the shell, never pull on the wiring harness as you may damage the individual wires and terminals inside the connectors. Look at the connector closely before trying to separate the halves. Often the locking clips are engaged in a way that is not immediately clear. Additionally, many connectors have more than one set of clips.

Each pair of connector terminals has a male half and a female half. When you look at the end view of a connector in a diagram, be sure to understand whether the view shows the harness side or the component side of the connector. Connector halves are mirror images of each other, and a terminal shown on the right side end view of one half will be on the left side end view of the other half.

It is often necessary to take circuit voltage measurements with a connector connected. Whenever possible, carefully insert the test probes of your meter into the rear of the connector shell to contact the terminal inside. This kind of connection is called "backprobing" **(see illustration)**. When inserting a test probe into a male terminal, be careful not to distort the terminal opening.

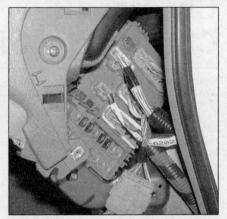

3.1b There is another fuse panel on the passenger's side, under a plastic cover at the right end of the dashboard (cover shown removed)

Doing so can lead to a poor connection and corrosion at that terminal later.

3 Fuses - general information

Refer to illustrations 3.1a, 3.1b, 3.1c and 3.3

1   The electrical circuits of the vehicle are protected by a combination of fuses and circuit breakers. The two fuse blocks are located under the instrument panel and on the right side of the engine compartment **(see illustrations)**.
2   Each of the fuses is designed to protect a specific circuit (or circuits), and the various circuits are identified on the fuse panel itself.
3   Miniaturized fuses are employed in the fuse block. These compact fuses, with blade terminal design, allow fingertip removal and replacement. If an electrical component fails, always check the fuse first. To check the fuses, turn the ignition key to the On position and, using a test light, probe each exposed terminal of each fuse. If the test light glows on both terminals of a fuse, the fuse is good. If power is available on one side of the fuse but not the other, the fuse is blown. When removed, a blown fuse is easily identified through the clear plastic body. Visually inspect the element for evidence of damage **(see illustration)**.
4   Be sure to replace blown fuses with the correct type. Fuses of different ratings are physically interchangeable, but only fuses of

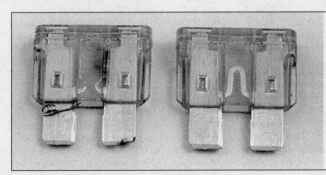

3.3 The fuses can easily be checked visually to see if they are blown (the fuse on the left is blown)

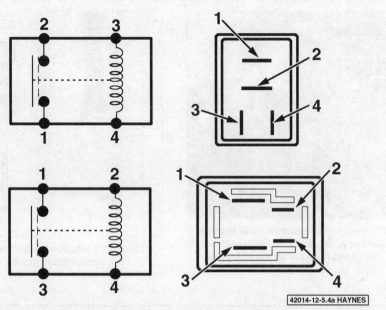

5.4a Typical four-terminal relay designs, terminal numbering and circuit connections

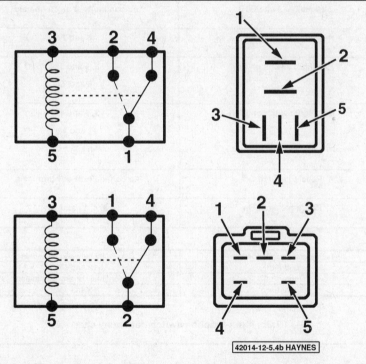

5.4b Typical five-terminal relay designs, terminal numbering and circuit connections

ment fuse box. It's very similar in appearance to standard fuses and is replaced in the same way. If you have to replace a main fuse, make sure you install a replacement unit that's equivalent to the old fuse. In other words, if the old main fuse is an 80A unit, replace it with an 80A fuse; if it's a 100A unit, replace it with a 100A fuse. Don't switch amperage ratings on the main fuse!

4 Circuit breakers - general information

Circuit breakers protect components such as sunroof motors, power window motors and airbag inflator resistors.

On some models the circuit breaker resets itself automatically, so an electrical overload in a circuit-breaker-protected system will cause the circuit to fail momentarily, then come back on. If the circuit does not come back on, check it immediately. Once the condition is corrected, the circuit breaker will resume its normal function. Some circuit breakers must be reset manually.

5 Relays - general information and testing

General information

1   Several electrical accessories in the vehicle, such as the fuel injection system, horns, starter, and fog lamps use relays to transmit the electrical signal to the component. Relays use a low-current circuit (the control circuit) to open and close a high-current circuit (the power circuit). If the relay is defective, that component will not operate properly. The various relays are mounted in engine compartment **(see illustration 3.1c)** and several locations throughout the vehicle. If a faulty relay is suspected, it can be removed and tested using the procedure below or by a dealer service department or a repair shop. Defective relays must be replaced as a unit.

Testing

Refer to illustrations 5.4a and 5.4b

2   It's best to refer to the wiring diagram for the circuit to determine the proper hook-ups for the relay you're testing. However, if you're not able to determine the correct hook-up from the wiring diagrams, you may be able to determine the test hook-ups from the information that follows.

3   On most relays, two of the terminals are the relay's control circuit (they connect to the relay coil which, when energized, closes the large contacts to complete the circuit). The other terminals are the power circuit (they are connected together within the relay when the control-circuit coil is energized).

4   Most relays are marked as an aid to help you determine which terminals are the control circuit and which are the power circuit **(see illustrations)**.

the proper rating should be used. Replacing a fuse with one of a higher or lower value than specified is not recommended. Each electrical circuit needs a specific amount of protection. The amperage value of each fuse is molded into the fuse body.

5   If the replacement fuse immediately fails, don't replace it again until the cause of the problem is isolated and corrected. In most cases, the cause will be a short circuit in the wiring caused by a broken or deteriorated wire.

6   All models are equipped with a main

fuse (either an 80A or 100A) which protects all the circuits coming from the battery. If these circuits are overloaded, the main fuse blows, preventing damage to the main wiring harness. The main fuse consists of a metal strip which will be visibly melted when overloaded. Always disconnect the battery before replacing a main fuse (available from your dealer). **Caution:** *The stereo in your vehicle is equipped with an anti-theft system. Refer to the information at the front of this manual before detaching the battery cables.* The main fuse is located in the engine compart-

5   Connect a fused jumper wire between one of the two control circuit terminals and the positive battery terminal. Connect another jumper wire between the other control circuit terminal and ground. When the connections are made, the relay should click. On some relays, polarity may be critical, so, if the relay doesn't click, try swapping the jumper wires on the control circuit terminals.

6   With the jumper wires connected, check for continuity between the power circuit terminals as indicated by the markings on the relay.

7   If the relay fails any of the above tests, replace it.

6   Turn signal/hazard flasher - check and replacement

Refer to illustration 6.1
Warning: *The models covered by this manual are equipped with Supplemental Restraint systems (SRS), more commonly known as airbags. Always disconnect the negative battery cable, then the positive battery cable and wait three minutes before working in the vicinity of the impact sensors, steering column or instrument panel to avoid the possibility of accidental deployment of the airbag, which could cause personal injury (see Section 26). The yellow wiring harnesses and connectors routed through the console and instrument panel are for this system. Do not use electrical test equipment on any of the airbag system wiring or tamper with them in any way.*

1   The turn signal and hazard flashers are controlled from a single electronic flasher unit which is mounted to the side of the interior fuse block **(see illustration)**.

2   When the flasher unit is functioning properly, an audible click can be heard during its operation. If the turn signals fail on one side or the other and the flasher unit does not make its characteristic clicking sound, a faulty turn signal bulb is indicated.

3   If both turn signals fail to blink, the problem may be due to a blown fuse, a faulty flasher unit, a broken switch or a loose or open connection. If a quick check of the fuse box indicates that the turn signal fuse has blown, check the wiring for a short before installing a new fuse.

4   To replace the flasher, simply unplug it from the instrument panel fuse block (driver's side).

5   Make sure that the replacement unit is identical to the original. Compare the old one to the new one before installing it.

6   Installation is the reverse of removal.

7   Steering column switches - check and replacement

Warning: *The models covered by this manual are equipped with Supplemental Restraint systems (SRS), more commonly known as*

6.1 Turn signal/hazard flasher location (arrow) in the driver's side fuse panel, accessed from below the left end of the dashboard

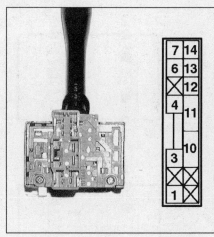

7.3a Multi-function switch terminal identification guide

Switch position	Continuity between terminals
Headlight switch Off	no continuity at any terminals
Headlight switch on Park	6 and 7
Headlight switch on Low	3, 4 and 11
	6 and 7
Headlight switch on High	3, 4 and 11
	11 and 10
	6 and 7
Passing switch Off	no continuity at any terminals
Passing switch On	3, 4, 11 and 10

Turn signal switch position	Continuity between terminals
Left turn	12 and 13
Center (off)	no continuity at any terminals
Right turn	13 and 14

7.3b Multi-function switch continuity chart

airbags. Always disconnect the negative battery cable, then the positive battery cable and wait three minutes before working in the vicinity of the impact sensors, steering column or instrument panel to avoid the possibility of accidental deployment of the airbag, which could cause personal injury (see Section 26). The yellow wiring harnesses and connectors routed through the console and instrument panel are for this system. Do not use electrical test equipment on any of the airbag system wiring or tamper with them in any way.
Caution: *The stereo in your vehicle is equipped with an anti-theft system. Make sure you have the correct activation code before disconnecting the battery.*

Multi-function switch

Check

Refer to illustrations 7.3a and 7.3b

1   The multi-function switch is located on the left side of the steering column. It incorporates the turn signal, hazard and headlight dimmer functions into one switch.

2   Remove the multi-function switch (see Step 4).

3   Using an ohmmeter or self-powered test light and the accompanying diagrams, check for continuity between the indicated switch terminals with the switch in each of the indicated positions **(see illustrations)**. If the continuity isn't as specified, replace the switch.

7.6a To remove the multi-function switch, remove the two screws (arrows) - steering wheel removed for clarity

7.6b Pull the multi-function switch out for access, then unplug the connector (arrow) (steering wheel removed for clarity)

Replacement

Refer to illustrations 7.6a and 7.6b

4   Disconnect the negative battery cable, then the positive battery cable and wait three minutes before proceeding any further.

5   Remove driver's knee bolster and the steering column covers (see Chapter 11).

6   Remove the switch retaining screws, disconnect the electrical connectors, then detach the switch from the steering column **(see illustrations)**.

7   Installation is the reverse of removal.

Wiper switch

Check

Refer to illustrations 7.10a and 7.10b

8   The wiper/washer switch is located on the right side of the steering column.

9   Remove the wiper/washer switch (see Step 11).

10   Using an ohmmeter or self-powered test light and the accompanying diagrams, check for continuity between the indicated switch terminals with the switch in each of the indicated positions **(see illustrations)**. If the continuity isn't as specified, replace the switch.

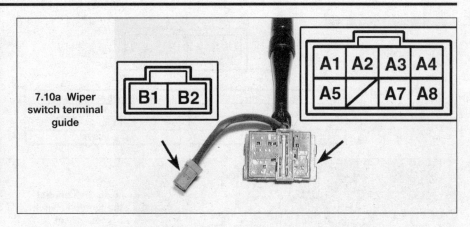

7.10a Wiper switch terminal guide

Wiper/washer switch position	Continuity between terminals
Off	A3 and A5
Intermittent	A2 and A7
	A3 and A5
Low	A3 and A8
High	A4 and A8
Mist switch On	A4 and A8
Washer switch On	A1 and A7
Intermittent dwell controller On	0 to 30k-ohms resistance
	B1 to B2

7.10b Windshield wiper switch continuity chart

7.13a Remove the two wiper/washer switch screws (arrows) (steering wheel removed for clarity) . . .

7.13b . . . use a small screwdriver to gently pry the switch free as you guide it out of the housing . . .

Replacement

Refer to illustrations 7.13a, 7.13b and 7.13c

11   Disconnect the negative battery cable, then the positive battery cable and wait three minutes before proceeding any further.

12   Remove driver's knee bolster and the steering column covers (see Chapter 11).

13   Remove the switch retaining screws, disconnect the electrical connectors, then detach the switch from the steering column **(see illustrations)**.

14   Installation is the reverse of removal.

Cruise control set/resume switch

Check

Refer to illustration 7.17

15   On these models, the set/resume switch is in the steering wheel, but the main On/Off

7.13c . . . then pull the switch out of the way and unplug the electrical connector

7.17 Continuity chart for terminals on the steering-wheel-mounted Set/Resume/Cancel switches

Switch position	Continuity between terminals
Set (on)	1 and 3
Resume (on)	1 and 2
Cancel (on)	1, 2 and 3

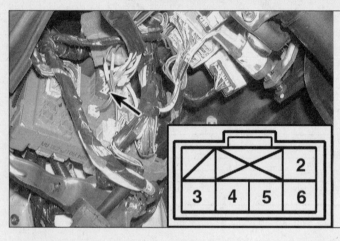

8.4a Disconnect the ignition switch electrical connector (arrow) from the fuse-relay box (inset shows terminal identification)

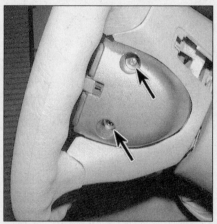

7.20 Remove the cruise control actuator switch retaining screws (arrows) at the right side of the steering column

8.4b Check the ignition switch terminals for continuity in each of the indicated positions

Ignition switch position	Continuity between terminals
Lock	no continuity at any terminals
Accessory	2 and 3
On	2, 3, 4 and 5
Start	2, 5 and 6

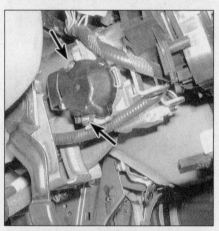

8.10 Remove the ignition switch by turning the key to the Lock position, then remove the screws (arrows)

switch is on the instrument panel, to the left of the steering wheel. For testing and replacement of the On/Off switch, see Section 9.

16   Refer to the Steps below for switch removal.

17   Using an ohmmeter and the accompanying diagram, check for continuity in each of the switch positions indicated **(see illustration)**. If the resistance isn't as specified, replace the switch. If the switches check OK, but the functions aren't correct when the switches are installed, check the harness from the switch to the control unit under the dash.

Replacement

Refer to illustration 7.20

18   Refer to the Warning at the beginning of this Section and disconnect the battery.

19   Remove the driver's side airbag module from the steering wheel (see Chapter 10).

20   Detach the switch retaining screws **(see illustration)**. Then disconnect the electrical connections and remove the switches from the steering wheel.

21   Installation is the reverse of removal.

---

8   Ignition switch and key lock cylinder - check and replacement

---

Warning: *The models covered by this manual*

are equipped with Supplemental Restraint systems (SRS), more commonly known as airbags. Always disconnect the negative battery cable, then the positive battery cable and wait three minutes before working in the vicinity of the impact sensors, steering column or instrument panel to avoid the possibility of accidental deployment of the airbag, which could cause personal injury (see Section 26). The yellow wiring harnesses and connectors routed through the console and instrument panel are for this system. Do not use electrical test equipment on any of the airbag system wiring or tamper with them in any way.

Caution: *The stereo in your vehicle is equipped with an anti-theft system. Make sure you have the correct activation code before disconnecting the battery.*

1   Remove the steering column covers, instrument panel lower cover and knee bolster (see Chapter 11).

Check

Refer to illustrations 8.4a and 8.4b

2   Disconnect the negative battery cable, then the positive battery cable (see **Caution** and **Warning** above).

3   Refer to Chapter 11 and remove the dashboard lower panel on the driver's side. Trace the wire harness for the ignition

switch/key lock cylinder assembly to the fuse box under the left side of the dash, then unplug the connector from the fuse box.

4   Check the connector for continuity between the indicated terminals with the key in each position **(see illustrations)**.

5   If the continuity is not as specified, replace the switch.

6   Check the lock cylinder in each position to make sure it isn't worn or loose and that the key position corresponds to the markings on the housing. If the lock cylinder is faulty, the entire steering column lock assembly will have to be replaced.

Replacement

Switch

Refer to illustration 8.10

7   Disconnect the negative battery cable, then the positive battery cable (see **Caution** and **Warning** above).

8   Refer to Chapter 11 and remove the upper and lower steering column covers.

9   Turn the ignition key to the Lock position.

8.13 Drill out the heads of these two bolts (arrows) then separate the clamp halves

10   Remove the screws retaining the switch to the steering column **(see illustration)**.

Lock Cylinder

Refer to illustration 8.13

11   Remove the steering column covers and lower instrument panel (see Chapter 11).

12   Remove the retaining nuts and lower the steering column. Disconnect the electrical connectors from the immobilizer unit if equipped.

13   The lock assembly is clamped to the steering column by two shear-head bolts **(see illustration)**. Use a center punch to make a dimple in the head of each bolt, then drill them out with a 3/16-inch bit.

14   Separate the clamp and remove the assembly from the steering column. Remove the immobilizer unit (if equipped) from the old lock cylinder and install it onto the new lock cylinder. **Note:** *If the original immobilizer unit installed by the factory is replaced for any reason, the PCM must be reprogrammed by a dealer service department.*

15   Place the new cylinder in position without the key inserted and tighten the bolts until they are snug.

16   Insert the key and check the lock cylinder for proper operation.

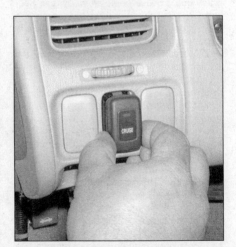

9.3 Pry the cruise control On/Off switch from the left side of the dashboard

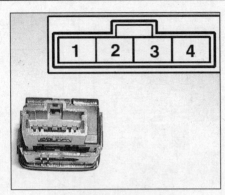

9.2a Cruise control On/Off switch terminals

17   Tighten the bolts until their hex-heads break off. Reconnect the immobilizer connectors (if equipped).

18   The remainder of installation is the reverse of removal.

19   Connect the positive battery cable, followed by the negative cable.

---

9   Instrument panel switches - check and replacement

Warning: *The models covered by this manual are equipped with Supplemental Restraint systems (SRS), more commonly known as airbags. Always disconnect the negative battery cable, then the positive battery cable and wait three minutes before working in the vicinity of the impact sensors, steering column or instrument panel to avoid the possibility of accidental deployment of the airbag, which could cause personal injury (see Section 26). The yellow wiring harnesses and connectors routed through the console and instrument panel are for this system. Do not use electrical test equipment on any of the airbag system wiring or tamper with them in any way.*
Caution: *The stereo in your vehicle is equipped with an anti-theft system. Make sure you have the correct activation code before disconnecting the battery.*

Cruise control switch positions	Continuity between terminals
On	1, 2 and 3 4 and 5
Off	1 and 2 4 and 5

9.2b Cruise control On/Off switch continuity chart

Cruise control On/Off switch

Check

Refer to illustrations 9.2a and 9.2b

1   To check the switch it must first be removed (see below).

2   Using an ohmmeter or self-powered test light and the accompanying diagrams, check for continuity between the indicated switch terminals with the switch in each of the indicated positions **(see illustrations)**. If the continuity isn't as specified, replace the switch.

Replacement

Refer to illustration 9.3

3   To remove the cruise control On/Off switch, pry it from the instrument panel with a screwdriver **(see illustration)**. **Note:** *Tape the tip of the screwdriver to avoid damaging the instrument panel covering.*

4   Unplug the electrical connector and remove the switch from the vehicle.

5   Installation is the reverse of removal.

Hazard warning switch

Check

Refer to illustration 9.7

6   To check the switch it must first be removed from the clock housing (see below).

7   Test for continuity between the terminals of the switch **(see illustration)**. If the switch fails, replace it.

Replacement

Refer to illustration 9.9

8   Carefully pry the clock housing and clock from the upper center of the instrument panel.

Hazard Warning switch positions	Continuity between terminals
On	6 and 7 1, 2 and 3 5 and 9
Off	6 and 7 5 and 10

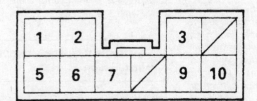

9.7 Continuity test for the Hazard Warning switch

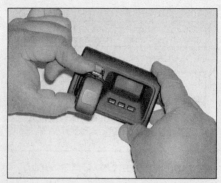

9.9 To remove the Hazard Warning switch from the clock bezel, push down the tab with a screwdriver and withdraw the switch from the bezel

9   Disconnect the 10-pin electrical connector at the rear of the switch. Depress the tab and remove the switch from the clock housing **(see illustration)**.

Rear window defogger

Check

Refer to illustration 9.11

10   The rear window defogger switch is part of the heating/air conditioning control panel. Refer to Chapter 3 for removal of the control panel.

11   Using an ohmmeter or self-powered test light and the diagram of the 22-terminal connection at the back of the heating/air conditioning control panel, check for continuity between terminals B4 and B9 **(see illustration)**. There should be continuity between these two terminals only when the defogger switch is depressed. If the continuity isn't as specified, replace the switch.

Replacement

12   Remove the screws holding the front and rear sections of the control panel together. Keep the panel face-up while removing the front panel. **Note:** *Make sure you have a new switch before disassembling the control panel. A new switch will probably be a special-order part from your dealer.*

13   Remove the defogger switch and install the new one, clamp the two halves of the control panel together by hand, then flip it over and reinstall the screws.

14   Installation of the control panel is the reverse of the removal procedure (see Chapter 3).

10   Instrument panel gauges - check

Warning: *The models covered by this manual are equipped with Supplemental Restraint systems (SRS), more commonly known as airbags. Always disconnect the negative battery cable, then the positive battery cable and wait three minutes before working in the vicinity of the impact sensors, steering column or instrument panel to avoid the possibility of accidental deployment of the airbag, which*

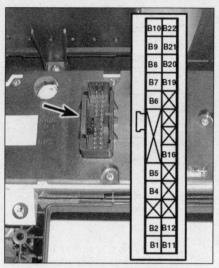

9.11 Terminal location and identification of the 22-pin connector (arrow) at the heater control panel

could cause personal injury (see Section 26). The yellow wiring harnesses and connectors routed through the console and instrument panel are for this system. Do not use electrical test equipment on any of the airbag system wiring or tamper with them in any way.
Note: *This procedure applies to conventional analog type gauges (NON-digital) only.*

Fuel and temperature gauges

1   All tests below require the ignition switch to be turned to Off position before testing.

2   If the gauge pointer does not move from the empty or cold positions, check the fuse. If the fuse is OK, locate the particular sending unit for the circuit you're working on (see Chapter 4 for fuel sending unit location or Chapter 3 for the temperature gauge sending unit location). Connect the sending unit connector to ground with a jumper wire.

3   Turn the ignition key to On momentarily. If the pointer goes to the full or hot position replace the sending unit. **Note:** *Turn the key Off right away, grounding the sending unit for too long could damage the gauge*. If the pointer stays in same position, use a jumper wire to ground the sending unit terminal on the back of the gauge. If necessary, refer to the wiring diagrams at the end of this Chapter. If the pointer moves, the problem lies in the wiring between the gauge and the sending unit. If the pointer does not move with the sending unit terminal on the back of the gauge grounded, check for voltage at the other terminal of the gauge. There should not be voltage.

11   Instrument cluster - removal and installation

Refer to illustrations 11.3a and 11.3b
Warning: *The models covered by this manual*

11.3a Remove the instrument cluster screws (arrows)

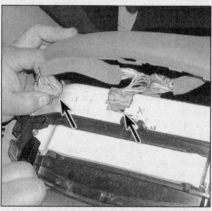

11.3b Pull the instrument cluster out and unplug the three electrical connectors (arrows indicate two)

are equipped with Supplemental Restraint systems (SRS), more commonly known as airbags. Always disconnect the negative battery cable, then the positive battery cable and wait three minutes before working in the vicinity of the impact sensors, steering column or instrument panel to avoid the possibility of accidental deployment of the airbag, which could cause personal injury (see Section 26). The yellow wiring harnesses and connectors routed through the console and instrument panel are for this system. Do not use electrical test equipment on any of the airbag system wiring or tamper with them in any way.
Caution: *The stereo in your vehicle is equipped with an anti-theft system. Make sure you have the correct activation code before disconnecting the battery.*

1   Disconnect the negative cable from the battery, followed by the positive cable. Review the **Warning** and **Caution** above.

2   Remove the instrument cluster bezel (see Chapter 11).

3   Remove the instrument cluster screws, pull out the cluster and unplug the electrical connectors **(see illustrations)**.

4   Installation is the reverse of removal. Be sure to connect the positive cable to the battery first, then the negative cable.

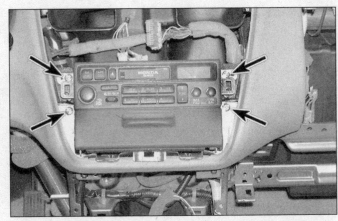

12.3a Remove the screws (arrows) securing the radio to the instrument panel

12.3b Pull the radio out and disconnect the antenna lead (A) and the electrical connector (B)

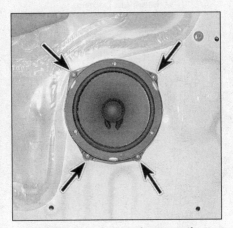

12.6 Remove the speaker mounting screws (arrows), pull the speaker away from the door and disconnect the electrical connector

12.8 Remove the speaker grille mounting screws (arrows) from inside the trunk

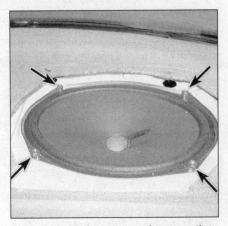

12.9 Remove the rear speaker mounting screws (arrows)

12 Radio and speakers - removal and installation

Radio

Refer to illustrations 12.3a and 12.3b

2   Remove the radio trim bezel (see Chapter 11).

3   Remove the retaining screws and pull the radio outward to access the backside, then disconnect the electrical connectors and the antenna lead and lift the radio out of the vehicle **(see illustrations)**.

4   Installation is the reverse of removal.

Front speakers

Refer to illustration 12.6

5   Remove the front door trim panel (see Chapter 11).

6   Remove the speaker retaining bolts. Disconnect the electrical connector and remove the speaker from the vehicle **(see illustration)**.

7   Installation is the reverse of removal.

Rear speakers

Refer to illustrations 12.8 and 12.9

8   From inside the trunk, remove the two

screws retaining each speaker cover **(see illustration)**.

9   Remove the grille for access to the speaker retaining screws **(see illustration)**. Disconnect the electrical connector and remove the speaker from the vehicle.

10   Installation is the reverse of removal.

Tweeters

11   In addition to the standard door and rear speakers, these models are equipped with tweeters for improved high-range sound. Mounted in the top of the instrument panel, they can be removed by simply prying under the edge of the tweeter with a screwdriver tip covered with tape. Pull the tweeter out and disconnect the electrical connector.

12   Installation is the reverse of removal.

13 Antenna - general information and check

Refer to illustrations 13.3, 13.5 and 13.7

1   Your vehicle is equipped with a wire-grid-type antenna attached to the rear window glass. It's signal is boosted by a coil mounted in the trunk, under the rear interior shelf.

2   If there is a problem with radio reception, examine the antenna wires by checking for continuity with an ohmmeter.

3   Wrap small pieces of aluminum foil around the tips of your ohmmeter probes and touch them to the wires of the antenna grid. With one probe at one of the antenna terminals, move the other probe along the wire, checking for continuity until a break is found **(see illustration)**.

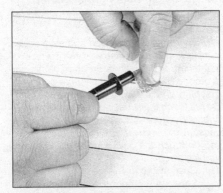

13.3 When checking the continuity of the rear window antenna grid, wrap a small piece of aluminum foil around each meter test probe to make better contact with the antenna grid

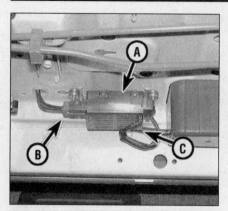

13.5 The antenna coil unit (A) is mounted in the trunk, under the back seat package shelf - connector (B) has two terminals, connector (C) has one

13.7 Antenna coil mounting bolts (arrows) on the rear package shelf

14.3 Twist the headlight bulb holder counterclockwise and remove it from the headlight housing

4   If a break is found, the wire can be repaired in the same manner as rear window defogger wire (see Section 21).

5   If the antenna wire is intact all the way, check the antenna's coil unit. Disconnect the two electrical connectors from the coil unit **(see illustration)**. On the coil side of the single-wire connection, check for continuity with an ohmmeter from the single terminal to ground. If there's continuity, replace the coil unit. **Note:** *Pry down the small clips holding the cover on the bottom of the unit to make removal of the connectors easier. Also, allow your meter to register for a few moments before checking the reading. The reading may show continuity at first, but should drop to zero after 20 seconds or so. This applies to both continuity tests of the coil unit.*

6   Check for continuity between the two terminals on the other side of the coil unit. If there is continuity, replace the coil unit. See the **Note** in Step 5.

7   To replace the coil unit, refer to Chapter 11 and remove the rear seat package shelf. Remove the two bolts holding the antenna coil **(see illustration)**.

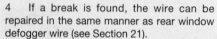

14   Headlight bulb - replacement

Refer to illustration 14.3
Warning: *Halogen gas filled bulbs are under pressure and may shatter if the surface is scratched or the bulb is dropped. Wear eye protection and handle the bulbs carefully, grasping only the base whenever possible. Do not touch the surface of the bulb with your fingers because the oil from your skin could cause it to overheat and fail prematurely. If you do touch the bulb surface, clean it with rubbing alcohol.*

1   Open the hood.

2   Squeeze the connector at the back of the bulb assembly to release it.

3   Rotate the headlight bulb holder counterclockwise as viewed from the rear **(see illustration)**. **Note:** *The coolant recovery tank may have to be pulled up and out (see Chap-*

ter 3) when replacing one of the headlight bulbs (on passenger side on four-cylinder models, on the driver's side on V6 models).

4   Withdraw the bulb assembly from the headlight housing.

5   Remove the bulb from the bulb holder by pulling it straight out.

6   If its necessary to replace the bulb holder, simply unplug the electrical connector and replace it with a new one.

7   Without touching the glass with your bare fingers, insert the new bulb into the socket assembly and then lock the bulb holder into the place by aligning the tabs with the headlight housing and rotating the bulb holder clockwise until stops.

8   Reinstall the electrical connector and test the headlight operation, then close the hood.

15   Headlights - adjustment

Refer to illustrations 15.1 and 15.3
Note: *The headlights must be aimed correctly. If adjusted incorrectly they could blind the driver of an oncoming vehicle and cause a serious accident or seriously reduce your ability to see the road. The headlights should be checked for proper aim every 12 months*

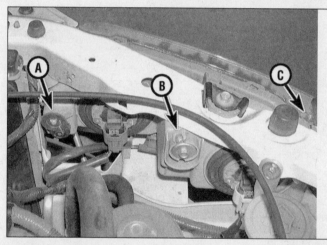

15.1 Headlight adjustment is made with a Phillips screwdriver at the horizontal adjuster (A) and the vertical adjuster (B) - (C) is the bubble level

and any time a new headlight is installed or front end body work is performed. It should be emphasized that the following procedure is only an interim step which will provide temporary adjustment until the headlights can be adjusted by a properly equipped shop.*

1   The headlights have two adjusting screws each, one inboard and one outboard. Both adjusters are accessible from the rear of the headlight assembly and are turned using a Phillips screwdriver **(see illustration)**.

2   These models are equipped with bubble-level gauges for headlight aiming **(see illustration 15.1)**. If the headlights still don't aim properly after adjusting the vertical and horizontal adjusters until the indicators show level, there may be body damage in the headlight area. Proceed to the following Steps for adjustment.

3   Position masking tape vertically on the wall in reference to the vehicle centerline and the centerlines of both headlights **(see illustration)**.

4   Position a horizontal tape line in reference to the centerline of all the headlights. **Note:** *It may be easier to position the tape on the wall with the vehicle parked only a few inches away.*

5   Adjustment should be made with the vehicle parked 25 feet from the wall, sitting

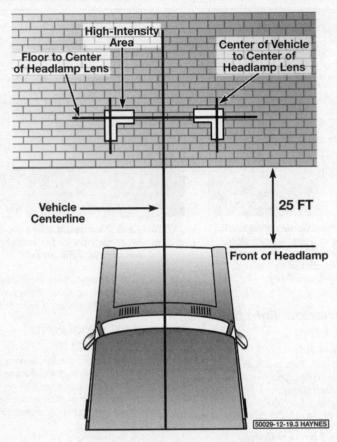

15.3 Headlight adjustment details

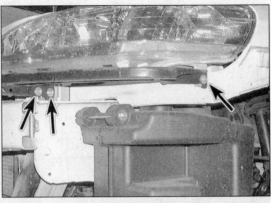

16.3a Remove the three lower headlight housing mounting bolts (arrows)

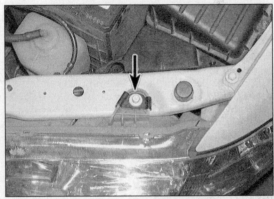

16.3b Remove the upper headlight housing mounting bolt (arrow)

level, the gas tank half-full and no unusually heavy load in the vehicle.

6   Starting with the low beam adjustment, position the high intensity zone so it is two inches below the horizontal line and two inches to the right of the headlight vertical line. Adjustment is made by turning the top adjusting screw clockwise to raise the beam and counterclockwise to lower the beam. The adjusting screw on the side should be used in the same manner to move the beam left or right.

7   With the high beams on, the high intensity zone should be vertically centered with the exact center just below the horizontal line. **Note:** *It may not be possible to position the headlight aim exactly for both high and low beams. If a compromise must be made, keep in mind that the low beams are the most used and have the greatest effect on safety.*

8   Have the headlights adjusted by a dealer service department or service station at the earliest opportunity.

16   Headlight housing - replacement

Refer to illustrations 16.3a and 16.3b

Warning : *The models covered by this manual are equipped with Supplemental Restraint systems (SRS), more commonly known as airbags. Always disconnect the negative bat-* *tery cable, then the positive battery cable and wait three minutes before working in the vicinity of the impact sensors, steering column or instrument panel to avoid the possibility of accidental deployment of the airbag, which could cause personal injury (see Section 26). The yellow wiring harnesses and connectors routed through the console and instrument panel are for this system. Do not use electrical test equipment on any of the airbag system wiring or tamper with them in any way.*

Caution: *The stereo in your vehicle is equipped with an anti-theft system. Make sure you have the correct activation code before disconnecting the battery.*

1   Unplug the electrical connectors, and remove the halogen bulbs (see Section 14).

2   Remove the front bumper cover (see Chapter 11).

3   Remove the headlight housing mounting bolts and remove the housing **(see illustrations).**

4   Installation is the reverse of removal. After you're done, adjust the headlights (see Section 14).

17   Bulb replacement

Warning: *Bulbs remain hot for up to twenty minutes after they're turned off. Be sure bulbs are off and cool before you touch them.*

Front turn signal/side marker light

Refer to illustration 17.2

1   Remove one of the plastic pushbutton fasteners on the inner fender liner and pull back the plastic liner to access the turn signal-side marker light from the rear. **Note:** *Depending on which side you are accessing, turn the front wheels left or right for better access.*

2   Turn the bulb holder counterclockwise and pull it out of the housing **(see illustration)**.

3   Pull the bulb out of the holder.

4   Installation is the reverse of removal.

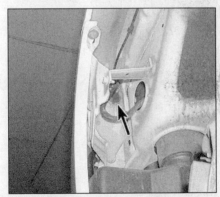

17.2 With the fender liner pulled back for access, twist and remove the front turn signal/side marker light (arrow)

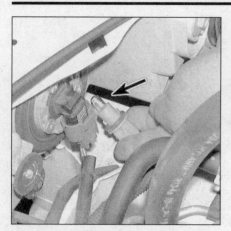

17.5 Front parking light bulb holder location (arrow)

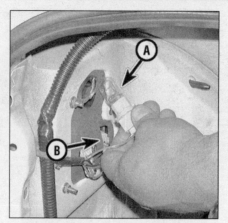

17.8 With the trunk panel pulled back, there is access to both the turn signal bulb (A) and the stoplight/taillight bulb (B) in the body-mounted half of the taillight assembly

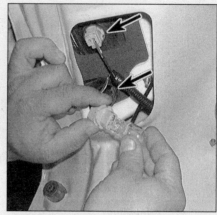

17.10 Inside the trunklid, there are bulb holders on either side for the taillight and the backup light (arrows)

Front parking light

Refer to illustration 17.5

5   Open the hood and twist the parking light bulb holder (below the headlight bulb holder) one-quarter turn counterclockwise and pull it out **(see illustration)**.
6   Pull the bulb straight out.
7   Installation is the reverse of removal.

Rear turn signal and stoplight/taillight bulbs (body mounted)

Refer to illustration 17.8

Note: *On these models, there is a taillight housing on both the quarter panel of the body and on the trunk lid. The body-mounted half houses a turn signal bulb and a stoplight/tail-light bulb. The trunk mounted section houses a backup light bulb and a taillight bulb.*

8   Open the trunk. Twist the fastener of the trunk carpet panel with a screwdriver or coin, then pull back the panel to expose the two bulbs **(see illustration)**.
9   Rotate either bulb holder 1/8-turn counterclockwise and pull it out of the housing, then pull the bulb out.

Taillight and backup light bulb (trunklid mounted)

Refer to illustration 17.10

10   Open the trunklid. Turn the bulb holder 1/8-turn counterclockwise and pull it out of the housing **(see illustration)**.
11   Pull the bulb straight out of the holder.
12   Installation is the reverse of removal.

High-mounted brake light

Refer to illustration 17.14

13   Open the trunk to access the bulb holder for the high-mount brake light, under the rear seat package shelf.
14   Twist the bulb holder counterclockwise to remove it, then pull the bulb straight out of the holder **(see illustration)**.
15   Installation is the reverse of removal.

License plate lights

Refer to illustration 17.16

16   Pull the license plate light assembly out from the body.
17   Remove the bulb holder by releasing the

clips on the lens housing **(see illustration)**.
18   Pull the bulb straight out of the holder.
19   Installation is the reverse of removal.

Instrument panel lights

Refer to illustration 17.21

20   To gain access to the instrument panel lights, the instrument cluster will have to be removed first (see Section 11).
21   Rotate the bulb counterclockwise and remove it from the instrument cluster **(see illustration)**.
22   Pull the bulb straight out of the holder.
23   Installation is the reverse of removal.
Note: *Make sure you replace the bulb with the same wattage as the original bulb. The gauge bulbs have higher wattage than the indicator bulbs.*

Dome/door/vanity/trunk lights

Refer to illustrations 17.24 and 17.25

24   All of the dome light, door light trunk light and vanity (right sunvisor) lights are replaced in the same manner. Carefully pry the lens off **(see illustration)**.
25   Remove the bulb from the terminals. It may be necessary to pry the bulb out - if this is the case, pry on the ends of the glass (other-

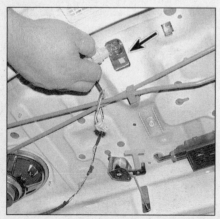

17.14 From inside the trunk, twist out the bulb holder (arrow) for the high-mount brake light

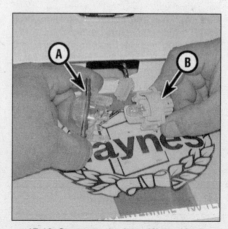

17.16 Separate the lens (A) from the license plate bulb holder (B) by releasing the clips

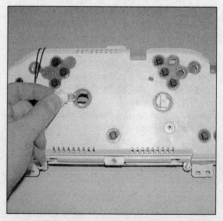

17.21 To remove an instrument cluster bulb, depress it and turn it counterclockwise

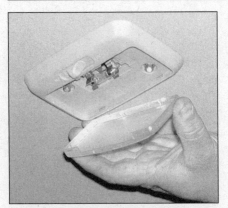

17.24 Pry the lens gently downward with a tape-wrapped screwdriver, then remove it (dome light shown, others similar)

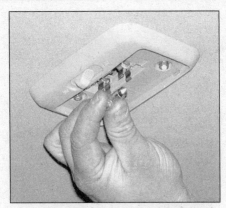

17.25 Remove the bulb from its clips (dome light shown, others also pull straight out of their sockets)

wise the glass may shatter) **(see illustration)**.

26   Installation is the reverse of removal.

18   Daytime Running Lights (DRL) - general information

The Daytime Running Lights (DRL) system used on Canadian models illuminates the headlights whenever the engine is running. The only exception is with the engine running and the parking brake engaged. Once the parking brake is released, the lights will remain on as long as the ignition switch is on, even if the parking brake is later applied.

The DRL system supplies reduced power to the headlights so they won't be too bright for daytime use, while prolonging headlight life.

19   Wiper motor - check and replacement

Wiper motor circuit check

Refer to illustrations 19.2a and 19.2b
Note: *Refer to the wiring diagrams for wire colors and locations in the following checks. When checking for voltage, probe a grounded 12-volt test light to each terminal at a connector until it lights; this verifies voltage (power) at the terminal. If the following checks fail to locate the problem, have the system diagnosed by a dealer service department or other properly equipped repair facility. The multiplex control unit is capable of storing trouble codes that can be retrieved with the proper equipment.*

1   If the wipers work slowly, make sure the battery is in good condition and has a strong charge (see Chapter 1). If the battery is in good condition, remove the wiper motor (see below) and operate the wiper arms by hand. Check for binding linkage and pivots. Lubricate or repair the linkage or pivots as necessary. Reinstall the wiper motor. If the wipers still operate slowly, check for loose or corroded connections, especially the ground connection. If all connections look OK, replace the motor.

2   If the wipers fail to operate when activated, check the fuse. If the fuse is OK, connect a jumper wire between the wiper motor and ground, then retest. If the motor works now, repair the ground connection. If the motor still doesn't work, turn the wiper switch to the HI position and check for voltage at the motor **(see illustrations)**. **Note:** *The cowl cover will have to be removed (see Chapter 11) and the motor removed to access the electrical connector underneath it (see **Replacement** below). If there's voltage at the connector, remove the motor and check it off the vehicle with fused jumper wires from the battery. If the motor now works, check for binding linkage (see Step 1 above). If the motor still doesn't work, replace it. If there's no voltage to the motor, check for voltage at the wiper control relays. If there's voltage at the wiper control relays and no voltage at the wiper motor, check the switch for continuity (see Section 7). If the switch is OK, the wiper control relays or the multiplex control unit are probably bad. Have the multiplex control unit diagnosed by a dealer service department or other properly-equipped repair facility.

3   If the interval (delay) function is inoperative, check the continuity of all the wiring between the switch and wiper control module. If the wiring is OK, check the resistance of the delay control knob of the multi-function switch (see Section 7). If the delay control knob is within the specified resistance, have the multiplex control unit diagnosed by a dealer service department or other properly equipped repair facility.

4   If the wipers stop at the position they're in when the switch is turned off (fail to park), check for voltage at the park feed wire of the wiper motor connector when the wiper switch is OFF but the ignition is ON. If no voltage is present, check for an open circuit between the wiper motor and the fuse panel.

5   If the wipers won't shut off unless the ignition is OFF, disconnect the wiring from the wiper control switch. If the wipers stop, replace the switch. If the wipers keep running, there's a defective limit switch in the motor; replace the motor.

6   If the wipers won't retract below the hood line, check for mechanical obstructions in the wiper linkage or on the vehicle's body which would prevent the wipers from parking.

19.2a Wiper motor connector (arrow) terminal identification - with the motor running, check voltage between terminals 5 and 3; there should be 4 volts or less in an on-off-on-off repeating pattern

SWITCH POSITIONS	VOLTAGE READING
Low speed	battery power to 4 ground to 2
High speed	battery power to 4 ground to 1

19.2b Windshield wiper motor tests

19.7 Remove the wiper arm nut, then pull the arm off carefully to avoid scratching the hood

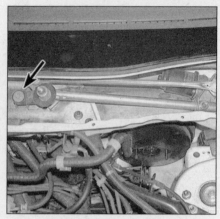

19.9 Remove the single wiper linkage-to-body bolt (arrows) - the assembly sits on two pins at the motor end

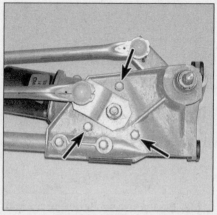

19.10 Mark the position of the wiper link to the linkage assembly, then remove the motor-to-linkage assembly bolts (arrows)

If there are no obstructions, check the wiring between the switch and motor for continuity. If the wiring is OK, replace the wiper motor.

Wiper motor replacement

Refer to illustrations 19.7, 19.9 and 19.10

7   Remove the windshield wiper arms **(see illustration)**.
8   Remove the cowl cover (see Chapter 11).
9   Detach the wiper motor/linkage assembly from the cowl **(see illustration)**.
10   Remove the wiper motor retaining bolts **(see illustration)**.
11   Remove the wiper motor from the wiper linkage assembly.
12   Disconnect the electrical connector from the wiper motor.
13   Installation is the reverse of removal.

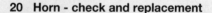

20   Horn - check and replacement

Check

Refer to illustration 20.3
Note: *Check the fuses before beginning electrical diagnosis.*
1   Disconnect the electrical connector from the horns.
2   To test the horns, connect battery voltage to the horn terminal with a pair of jumper wires. If either horn doesn't sound, replace it.
3   If the horn does sound, check for voltage at the horn connector when the horn switch is depressed **(see illustration)**. If there's voltage at the connector, check for a bad ground at the horn.
4   If there's no voltage at the horn, check the relay (see Section 5).
5   If the relay is OK, check for voltage to the relay power and control circuits. If either of the circuits is not receiving voltage, inspect the wiring between the relay and the fuse panel.
6   If both relay circuits are receiving voltage, depress the horn switch and check the circuit from the relay to the horn switch for continuity to ground. If there's no continuity, check the circuit for an open. If there's no open circuit, replace the horn switch.

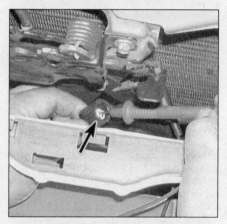

20.3 Connect a voltmeter to the horn terminal (arrow) and ground - test for voltage while the switch is depressed

7   If there's continuity to ground through the horn switch, check for an open or short in the circuit from the relay to the switch.

Replacement

Refer to illustration 20.9
8   To access the horns, the left front inner fenderwell must first be removed (see Chapter 11).
9   Disconnect the electrical connectors and remove the bracket bolts **(see illustration)**.
10   Installation is the reverse of removal.

21   Rear window defogger - check and repair

1   The rear window defogger consists of a number of horizontal heating elements baked onto the inside surface of the glass. Power is supplied through a large fuse from the power distribution box in the engine compartment. The heater is controlled by the instrument panel switch.
2   Small breaks in the element can be repaired without removing the rear window.

20.9 Disconnect the electrical connector, remove the bolts (arrows) and detach the horns

Check

Refer to illustrations 21.5, 21.6 and 21.8
3   Turn the ignition switch and defogger switches to the ON position.
4   Using a voltmeter, place the positive probe against the defogger grid positive terminal and the negative probe against the ground terminal. If battery voltage is not indicated, check the fuse, defogger switch and related wiring. If voltage is indicated, but all or part of the defogger doesn't heat, proceed with the following tests.
5   When measuring voltage during the next two tests, wrap a piece of aluminum foil around the tip of the voltmeter positive probe and press the foil against the heating element with your finger **(see illustration)**. Place the negative probe on the defogger grid ground terminal.
6   Check the voltage at the center of each heating element **(see illustration)**. If the voltage is 5 to 6 volts, the element is okay (there is no break). If the voltage is 0 volts, the element is broken between the center of the element and the positive end. If the voltage is 10 to 12 volts the element is broken between the center of the element and the ground side. Check each heating element.

21.5 When measuring the voltage at the rear window defogger grid, wrap a piece of aluminum foil around the positive probe of the voltmeter and press the foil against the wire with your finger

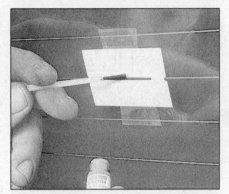

21.14 To use a defogger repair kit, apply masking to the inside of the window at the damaged area, then brush on the special conductive coating

7   If none of the elements are broken, connect the negative probe to a good chassis ground. The voltage reading should stay the same, if it doesn't the ground connection is bad.
8   To find the break, place the voltmeter negative probe against the defogger ground terminal. Place the voltmeter positive probe with the foil strip against the heating element at the positive side and slide it toward the negative side. The point at which the voltmeter deflects from several volts to zero is the point where the heating element is broken **(see illustration)**.

Repair

Refer to illustration 21.14

9   Repair the break in the element using a repair kit specifically for this purpose, such as Dupont paste No. 4817 (or equivalent). The kit includes conductive plastic epoxy.
10   Before repairing a break, turn off the system and allow it to cool for a few minutes.
11   Lightly buff the element area with fine steel wool; then clean it thoroughly with rubbing alcohol.
12   Use masking tape to mask off the area being repaired.
13   Thoroughly mix the epoxy, following the kit instructions.

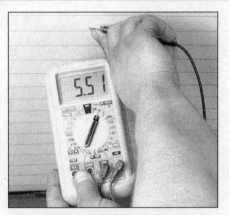

21.6 To determine if a wire has broken, check the voltage at the center of each wire. If the voltage is 5 to 6 volts, the wire is unbroken; if the voltage is 10 to 12 volts, the wire is broken between the center of the wire and the ground side; if the voltage is 0 volts, the wire is broken between the center of the wire and the power side

14   Apply the epoxy material to the slit in the masking tape, overlapping the undamaged area about 3/4-inch on either end **(see illustration)**.
15   Allow the repair to cure for 24 hours before removing the tape and using the system.

---

22   Cruise control system – description, check and cable adjustment

---

Refer to illustrations 22.5a, 22.5b, 22.5c and 22.5d

1   The cruise control system maintains vehicle speed with a servo motor located in the engine compartment on the driver's side fenderwell (passenger fenderwell on V6 models), which is connected to the throttle linkage by a cable. The system consists of the

22.5a Make sure the cruise control and accelerator linkage mounted on the throttle body are not damaged and that they operate smoothly together when the throttle is opened

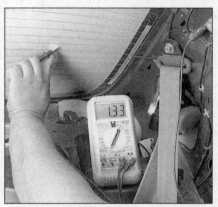

21.8 To find the break, place the voltmeter negative lead against the defogger ground terminal, place the voltmeter positive lead with the foil strip against the heat wire at the positive terminal end and slide it toward the negative terminal end - the point at which the voltmeter deflects from several volts to zero volts is the point at which the wire is broken

servo motor, brake switch (clutch switch on manual transmission models), control switches, speed sensors and relays. Some features of the system require special testers and diagnostic procedures which are beyond the scope of this manual. Listed below are some general procedures that may be used to locate common problems.
2   Locate and check the fuse (see Section 3).
3   The brake pedal position (BPP) switch (or stop lamp switch) deactivates the cruise control system. Have an assistant press the brake pedal while you check the stop lamp operation.
4   If the brake lights do not operate properly, correct the problem and retest the cruise control.
5   Check the control cable between the cruise control servo/amplifier and the throttle

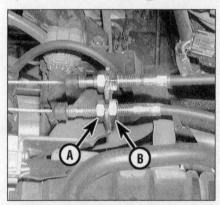

22.5b If the freeplay in the cruise control linkage is greater or less than 0.150 inches, pull the cable by hand until the engine speed just begins to go up, then lock both the adjuster nut (A) and the locknut (B) . . .

linkage and adjust/replace as necessary **(see illustrations)**.

6   The cruise control system uses a speed sensing device. The speed sensor is located in the transmission. To test the speed sensor, see Chapter 6.

7   Test drive the vehicle to determine if the cruise control is now working. If it isn't, take it to a dealer service department or an automotive electrical specialist for further diagnosis.

23   Power window system - description and check

Refer to illustrations 23.12a and 23.12b

1   The power window system operates electric motors, mounted in the doors, which lower and raise the windows. The system consists of the control switches, the motors, regulators, glass mechanisms and associated wiring.

2   The power windows can be lowered and raised from the master control switch by the driver or by remote switches located at the individual windows. Each window has a separate motor which is reversible. The position of the control switch determines the polarity and therefore the direction of operation.

3   The circuit is protected by a fuse and a circuit breaker. Each motor is also equipped with an internal circuit breaker; this prevents one stuck window from disabling the whole system.

4   The power window system will only operate when the ignition switch is ON. In addition, many models have a window lockout switch at the master control switch which, when activated, disables the switches at the rear windows and, sometimes, the switch at the passenger's window also. Always check these items before troubleshooting a window problem.

5   These procedures are general in nature, so if you can't find the problem using them, take the vehicle to a dealer service department or other properly equipped repair facility.

6   If the power windows won't operate, always check the fuse and circuit breaker first.

7   If only the rear windows are inoperative, or if the windows only operate from the master control switch, check the rear window lockout switch for continuity in the unlocked position. Replace it if it doesn't have continuity.

8   Check the wiring between the switches and fuse panel for continuity. Repair the wiring, if necessary.

9   If only one window is inoperative from the master control switch, try the other control switch at the window. **Note:** *This doesn't apply to the drivers door window.*

10   If the same window works from one switch, but not the other, check the switch for continuity.

11   If the switch tests OK, check for a short or open in the circuit between the affected switch and the window motor.

22.5c . . . now back off the adjusting nut until it is 0.150-inches from the cable bracket (arrow) . . .

22.5d . . . and pull the cable toward the bracket, then tighten the adjuster nut (arrow) to establish the proper freeplay

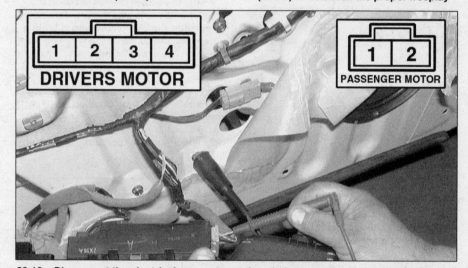

23.12a Disconnect the electrical connector at the window motor and check for proper operation - male side of terminals shown

SWITCH POSITION	VOLTAGE READING
Down	battery power to 2 ground to 1
Up	battery power to 1 ground to 2

23.12b Power window motor tests

12   If one window is inoperative from both switches, remove the trim panel from the affected door and check for voltage at the switch **(see illustrations)** and at the motor while the switch is operated.

13   If voltage is reaching the motor, disconnect the glass from the regulator (see Chapter 11). Move the window up and down by hand while checking for binding and damage. Also check for binding and damage to the regulator. If the regulator is not damaged and the window moves up and down smoothly,

replace the motor. If there's binding or damage, lubricate, repair or replace parts, as necessary.

14   If voltage isn't reaching the motor, check the wiring in the circuit for continuity between the switches and motors. You'll need to consult the wiring diagram for the vehicle. If the circuit is equipped with a relay, check that the relay is grounded properly and receiving voltage.

15   Test the windows after you are done to confirm proper repairs.

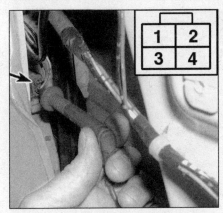

24.9a Check lock actuator operation by applying battery power and ground to the terminals

SWITCH POSITION	VOLTAGE READING
Unlock	battery power to 2 ground to 1
Lock	battery power to 1 ground to 2

24.9b Door lock actuator tests

24 Power door lock and keyless entry system - description and check

Power door lock system

Refer to illustrations 24.9a and 24.9b

1   The power door lock system operates the door lock actuators mounted in each door. The system consists of the switches, actuators, and associated wiring. Diagnosis can usually be limited to simple checks of the wiring connections and actuators for minor faults which can be easily repaired.

2   Power door lock systems are operated by bi-directional solenoids or motors located in the doors. The lock switches have two operating positions: Lock and Unlock. On later models with keyless entry the switches activate a module which in turn connects voltage to the door lock solenoids or motors. Depending on which way the switch is activated, it reverses polarity, allowing the two sides of the circuit to be used alternately as the feed (positive) and ground side. On earlier models without keyless entry, the switches directly activate the door lock solenoids or motors.

3   If you are unable to locate the trouble using the following general steps, consult your dealer service department.

4   Always check the circuit protection first. On these models the battery voltage passes through fuses 6 and 13 in the passenger's side fuse block, and fuse 9 in the drivers side fuse block.

5   Operate the door lock switches in both directions (Lock and Unlock) with the engine off. Listen for the faint click of the door lock relay operating.

6   If there's no click, check for voltage at the switches. If no voltage is present, check the wiring between the fuse block and the switches for shorts and opens.

7   If voltage is present but no click is heard, test the switch for continuity. Replace it if there's no continuity in both switch positions.

8   If the switch has continuity but the solenoid or motor doesn't click, check the wiring between the switch and solenoid for continuity. Repair the wiring if there's not continuity.

9   If all but one lock solenoids operate, remove the trim panel from the affected door (see Chapter 11) and check for voltage at the solenoid while the lock switch is operated **(see illustrations)**. One of the wires should have voltage in the Lock position; the other should have voltage in the unlock position.

10   If the inoperative solenoid is receiving voltage, replace the solenoid. **Note:** *It's common for wires to break in the portion of the harness between the body and door (opening*

and closing the door fatigues and eventually breaks the wires).

Keyless entry system

11   The keyless entry system consists of a remote control transmitter that sends a coded infrared signal to a receiver which then operates the door lock system.

12   Replace the transmitter batteries when the red LED light on the side of the case doesn't light when the button is pushed.

13   Use a small screwdriver to carefully separate the case halves.

14   Replace the CR2025 lithium battery.

15   Snap the case halves together.

25 Electric side view mirrors - description and check

Refer to illustrations 25.6, 25.7a and 25.7b

1   Most electric rear view mirrors use two motors to move the glass; one for up-and-down adjustments and one for left-to-right adjustments. In addition, some mirrors have electrically heated glass defroster circuits, which are usually powered through the rear window defogger relay.

2   The control switch usually has a selector portion which sends voltage to the left or right side mirror. With the ignition ON but the engine OFF, roll down the windows and operate the mirror control switch through all functions (left-right and up-down) for both the left and right side mirrors.

3   Listen carefully for the sound of the electric motors running in the mirrors.

4   If the motors can be heard but the mirror glass doesn't move, there's probably a problem with the drive mechanism inside the mirror. Remove and disassemble the mirror to locate the problem.

5   If the mirrors don't operate and no sound comes from the mirrors, check the fuse (see Chapter 1).

6   If the fuse is OK, remove the mirror control switch from its mounting without disconnecting the wires attached to it **(see illustration)**. Turn the ignition ON and check for voltage at the switch. There should be voltage at one terminal. If there's no voltage at the switch, check for an open or short in the wiring between the fuse panel and the switch.

7   If there's voltage at the switch, disconnect it. Check the switch for continuity in all its operating positions **(see illustrations)**. If

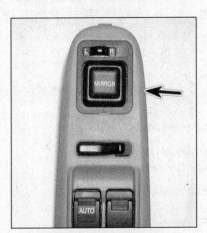

25.6 Use a small screwdriver to carefully pry the window switch (arrow) from the door panel

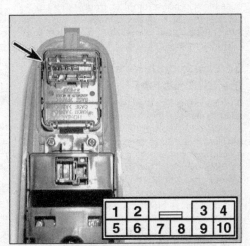

25.7a Power mirror switch (arrow) connector identification

Mirror switch positions	Continuity between terminals
Right mirror, Up	1 and 4 2 and 7
Right mirror, Down	1 and 8 2 and 4
Right mirror, Left	1 and 8 2 and 10
Right mirror, Right	1 and 10 2 and 8
Left mirror, Up	1 and 4 2 and 7
Left mirror, Down	1 and 7 2 and 4
Left mirror, Left	1 and 7 2 and 9
Left mirror, Right	1 and 9 2 and 7

25.7b Power mirror continuity tests

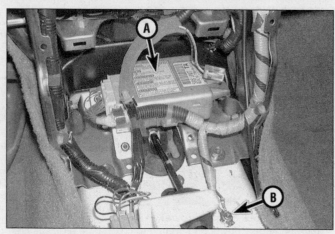

26.2 The airbag diagnostic module (A) is mounted on top of the transmission tunnel ahead of the console front cover; (B) is the airbag module ground cable mounting bolt

the switch does not have the designated continuity, replace it.

8   Re-connect the switch. Locate the wire going from the switch to ground. Leaving the switch connected, connect a jumper wire between this wire and ground. If the mirror works normally with this wire in place, repair the faulty ground connection.

9   If the mirror still doesn't work, remove the cover and check the wires at the mirror for voltage with a test light. Check with ignition ON and the mirror selector switch on the appropriate side. Operate the mirror switch in all its positions. There should be voltage at one of the switch-to-mirror wires in each switch position (except the neutral "off" position).

10   If there's no voltage in any switch position, check the wiring between the mirror and control switch for opens and shorts.

11   If there's voltage, remove the mirror and test it off the vehicle with jumper wires. Replace the mirror if it fails this test (see Chapter 11).

26   Airbag system - general information, removal and installation

Description

Refer to illustration 26.2

1   All models are equipped with a Supplemental Restraint System (SRS), more commonly known as an airbag. There are two airbags, one for the driver and one for the front seat passenger. The SRS system is designed to protect the driver (and on later models, the passenger as well) from serious injury in the event of a head-on or frontal collision.

2   The SRS system consists of an SRS unit - which contains a safing sensor, self-diagnosis circuit and a back-up power circuit - located under the dash, right in front of the floor console **(see illustration)**, two impact

sensors, an airbag assembly in the center of the steering wheel and a second airbag assembly for the front seat passenger, located in the top of the dashboard right above the glove box.

Operation

3   For the airbag(s) to deploy, one or both impact sensors and the safing sensor must be activated. When this condition occurs, the circuit to the airbag inflator is closed and the airbag inflates. If the battery is destroyed by the impact, or is too low to power the inflator, a back-up power unit inside the SRS unit provides power.

Self-diagnosis system

4   A self-diagnosis circuit in the SRS unit displays a light when the ignition switch is turned to the On position. If the system is operating normally, the light should go out after about six seconds. If the light doesn't come on, or doesn't go out after six seconds, or if it comes on while you're driving the vehicle, there's a malfunction in the SRS system. Have it inspected and repaired as soon as possible. Do not attempt to troubleshoot or service the SRS system yourself. Even a small mistake could cause the SRS system to malfunction when you need it.

Servicing components near the SRS system

5   Nevertheless, there are times when you need to remove the steering wheel, radio or service other components on or near the dashboard. At these times, you'll be working around components and wire harnesses for the SRS system. The SRS wiring harnesses are easy to identify: They're all bright yellow. Do not unplug the connectors for these wires. And do not use electrical test equipment on yellow wires; it could cause the airbag(s) to deploy. ***ALWAYS DISABLE THE SRS SYSTEM BEFORE WORKING NEAR THE SRS SYSTEM COMPONENTS OR RELATED WIRING.***

Disabling the SRS system

Refer to illustration 26.9

Warning: *Any time you are working in the vicinity of airbag wiring or components, DISABLE THE SRS SYSTEM.*

6   Disconnect the battery negative cable, then disconnect the positive cable and wait three minutes. **Caution:** *The stereo in your vehicle is equipped with an anti-theft system. Make sure you have the correct activation code before disconnecting the battery.*

Driver's side airbag

7   Remove the access panel below the airbag and unplug the two-pin connector between the airbag and the cable reel (see Chapter 10).

Passenger's side airbag

8   Remove the glove box (see Chapter 11).

9   Unplug the two-pin electrical connector between the passenger side airbag and the SRS main wiring harness **(see illustration)**.

Enabling the system

10   After you've disabled the airbag and performed the necessary service, reconnect the two-pin airbag connector into the two-pin cable reel connector (driver's side) or the SRS main harness (passenger's side). Reinstall the lid to the underside of the steering wheel or reinstall the glove box.

11   Turn the ignition switch to the Off position.

12   Reattach the positive battery cable first and then the negative cable.

Removal and installation

Refer to illustration 26.16

Driver's side airbag

13   Refer to Chapter 10 for removal and installation of the driver's side airbag.

Passenger side airbag

14   Disconnect the battery cables, see the **Warning** above.

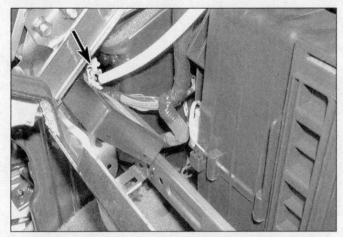

26.9 With the glovebox removed, disconnect the two-pin connector (arrow) for the passenger airbag

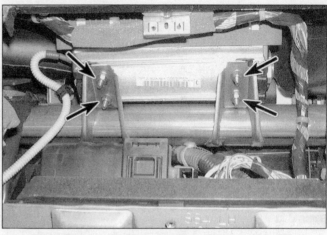

26.16 Remove the four mounting nuts (arrows) for the passenger airbag

15   Refer to Chapter 11 and remove the glove box.

16   Disconnect the two-pin connector **(see illustration 26.9)**. Remove the four nuts and gently pry the airbag unit from the dashboard with a screwdriver **(see illustration)**. **Note:** *The airbag has snap-tabs that hold it in the dashboard, use tape on the screwdriver tip to protect the surface of the dashboard.* **Warning:** *Be extremely careful when prying under the airbag. Too much force could cause the airbag to deploy.*

17   Installation is the reverse of the removal procedure.

27   Wiring diagrams - general information

Since it isn't possible to include all wiring diagrams for every year and model covered by this manual, the following diagrams are those that are typical and most commonly needed.

Prior to troubleshooting any circuits, check the fuse and circuit breakers (if equipped) to make sure they're in good condition. Make sure the battery is properly charged and check the cable connections (see Chapter 1).

When checking a circuit, make sure that all connectors are clean, with no broken or loose terminals. When unplugging a connector, do not pull on the wires. Pull only on the connector housings themselves.

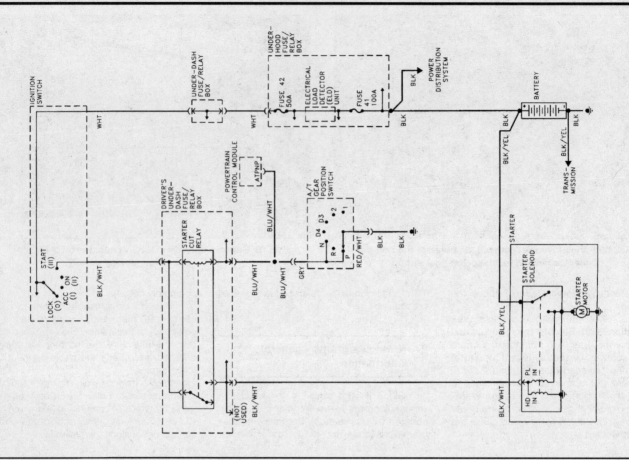

Starting system - V6 engine

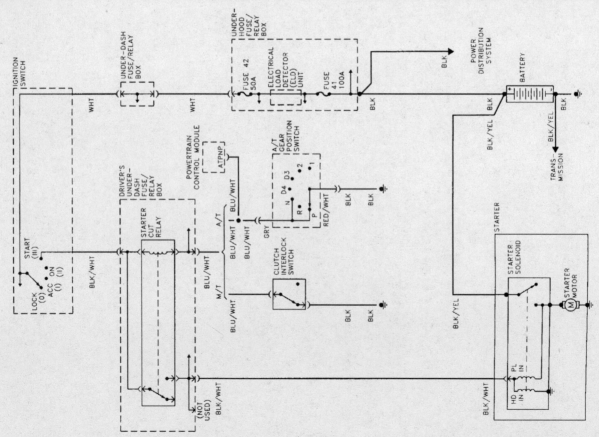

Starting system - four-cylinder engine

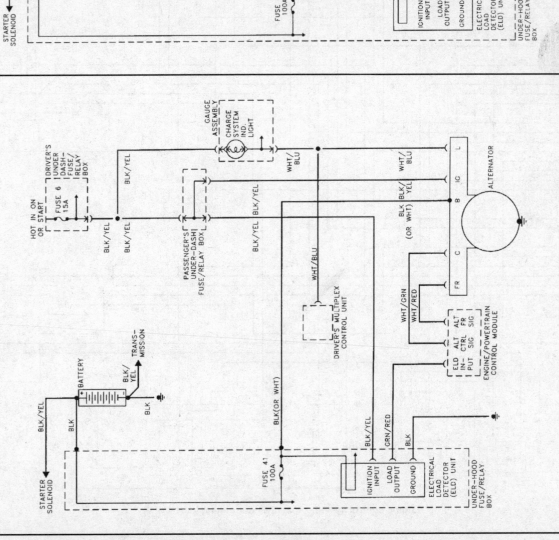

Charging system - V6 engine

Charging system - four-cylinder engine

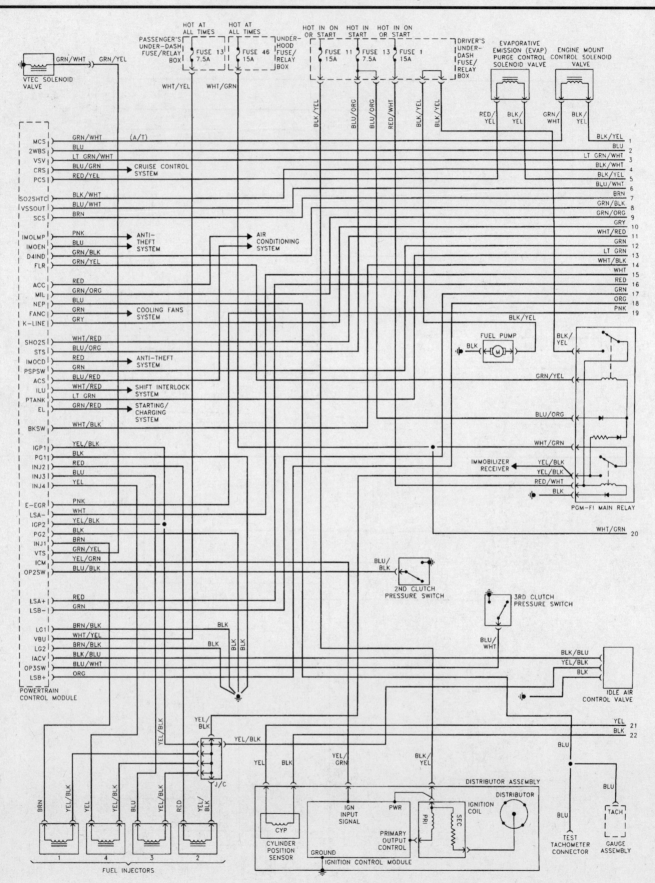

Engine control system - four-cylinder engine (part 1 of 3)

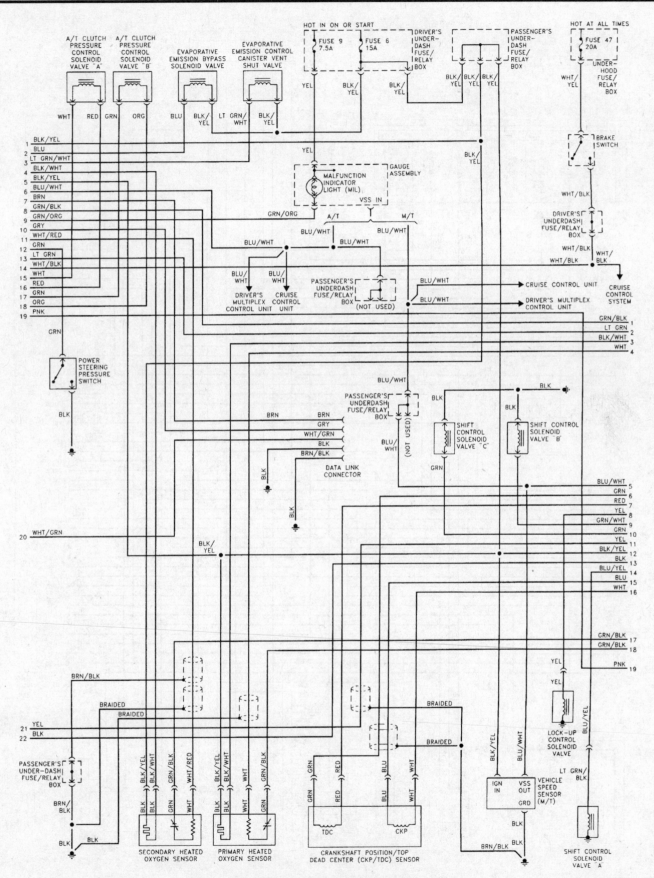

Engine control system - four-cylinder engine (part 2 of 3)

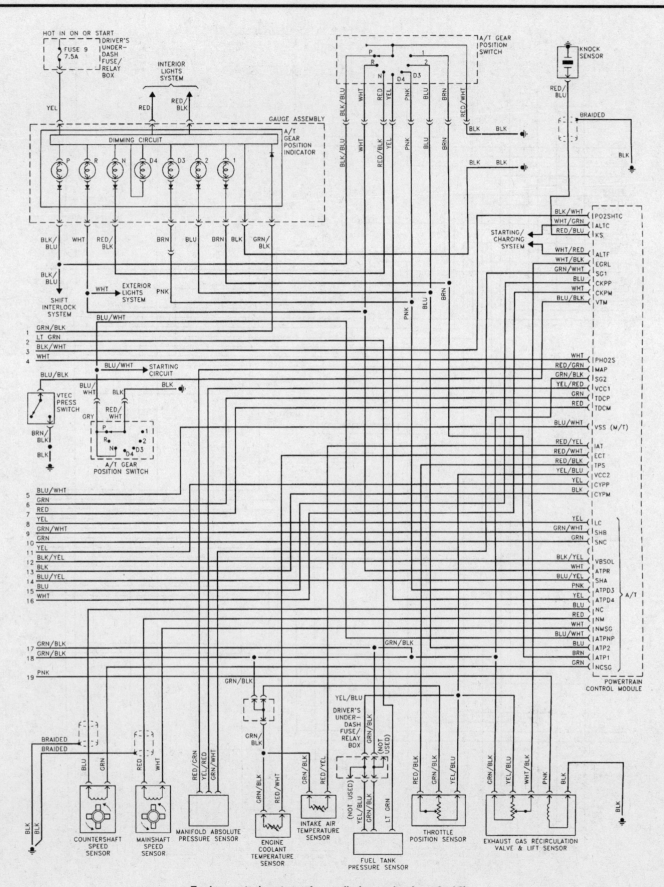

Engine control system - four-cylinder engine (part 3 of 3)

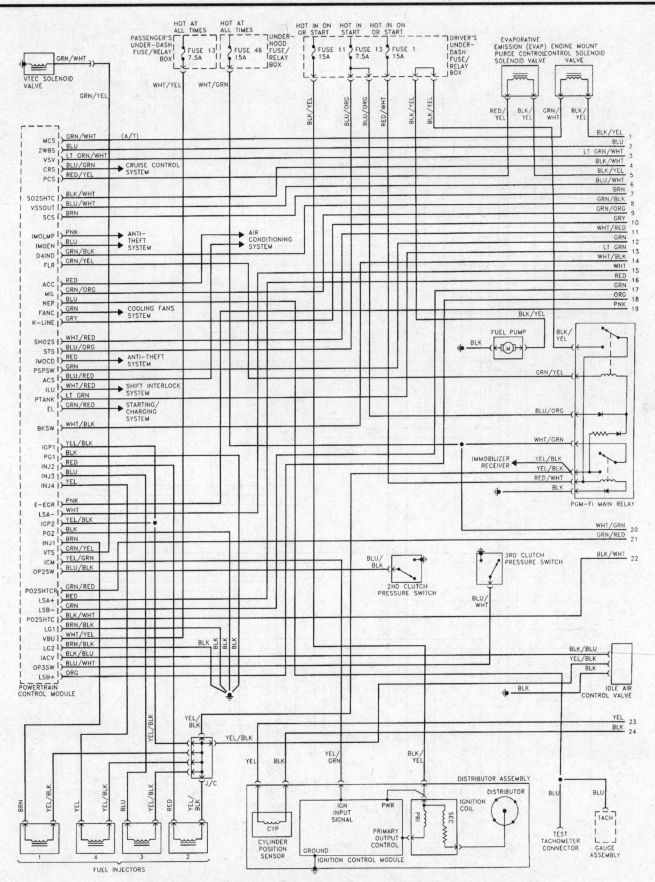

Engine control system - four-cylinder engine with Ultra-Low Emissions (part 1 of 3)

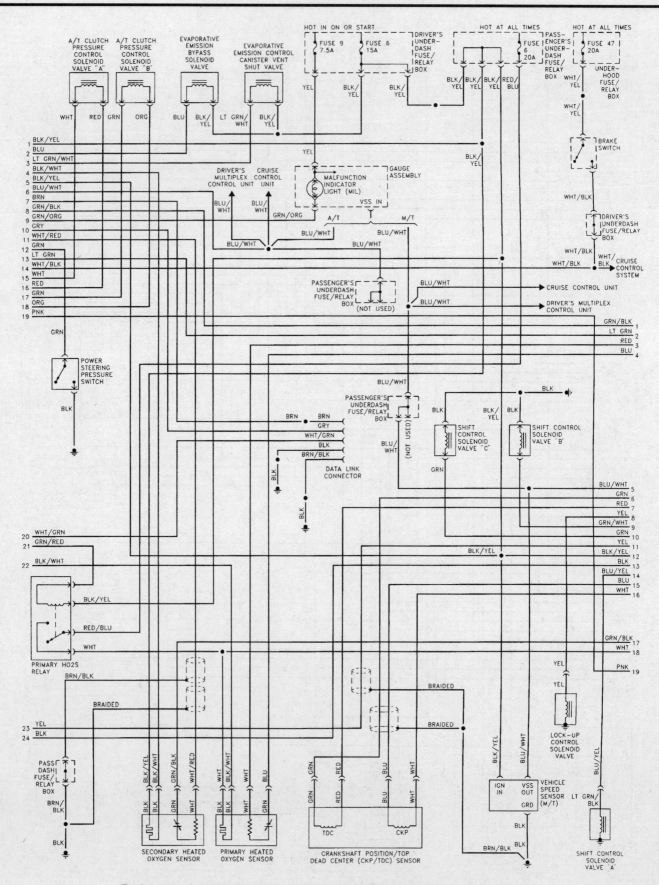

Engine control system - four-cylinder engine with Ultra-Low Emissions (part 2 of 3)

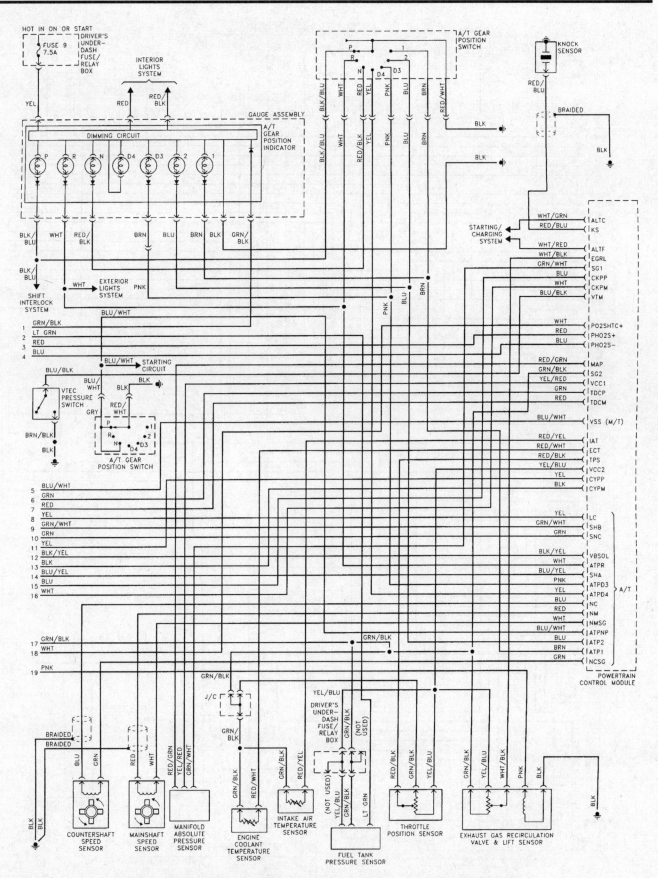

Engine control system - four-cylinder engine with Ultra-Low Emissions (part 3 of 3)

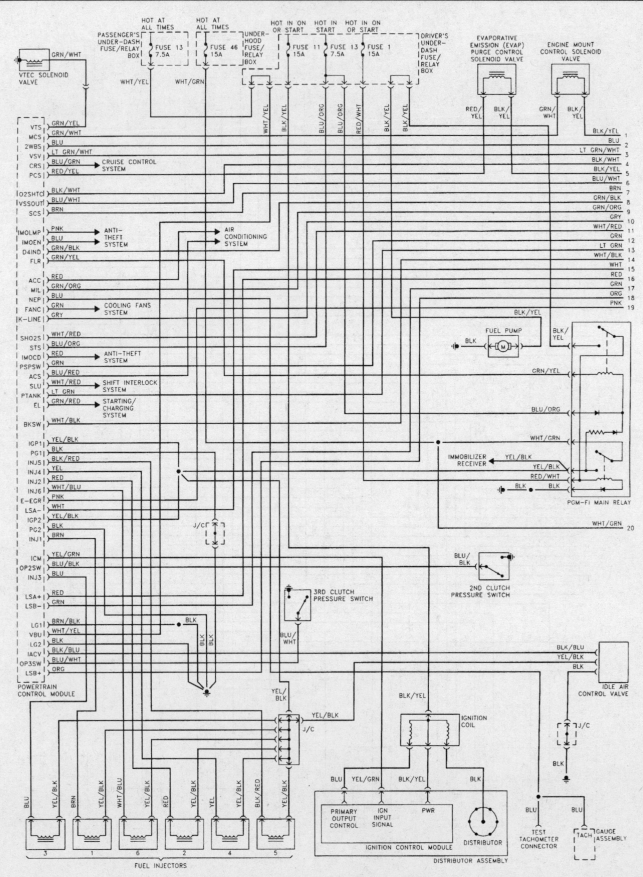

Engine control system - V6 engine (part 1 of 3)

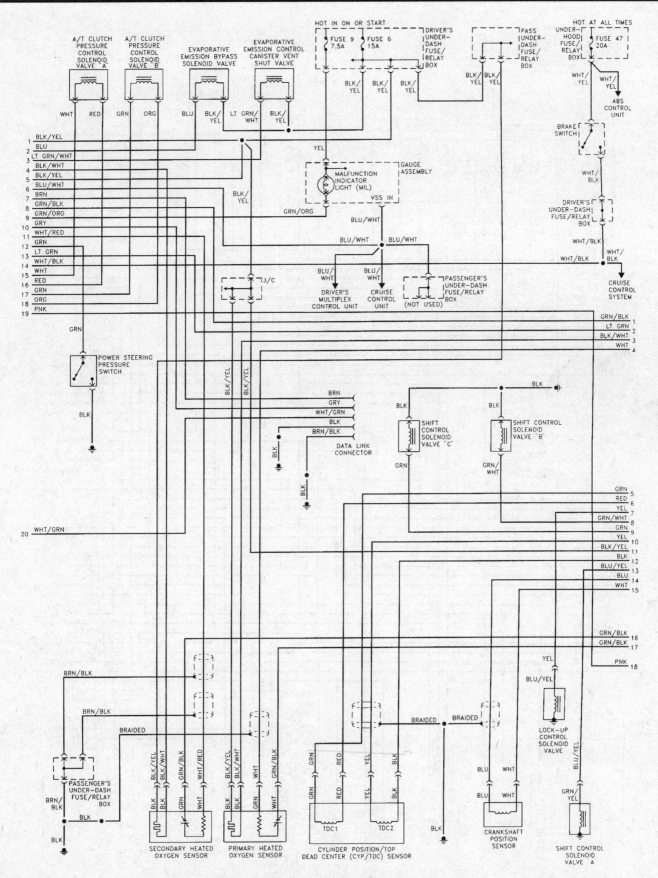

Engine control system - V6 engine (part 2 of 3)

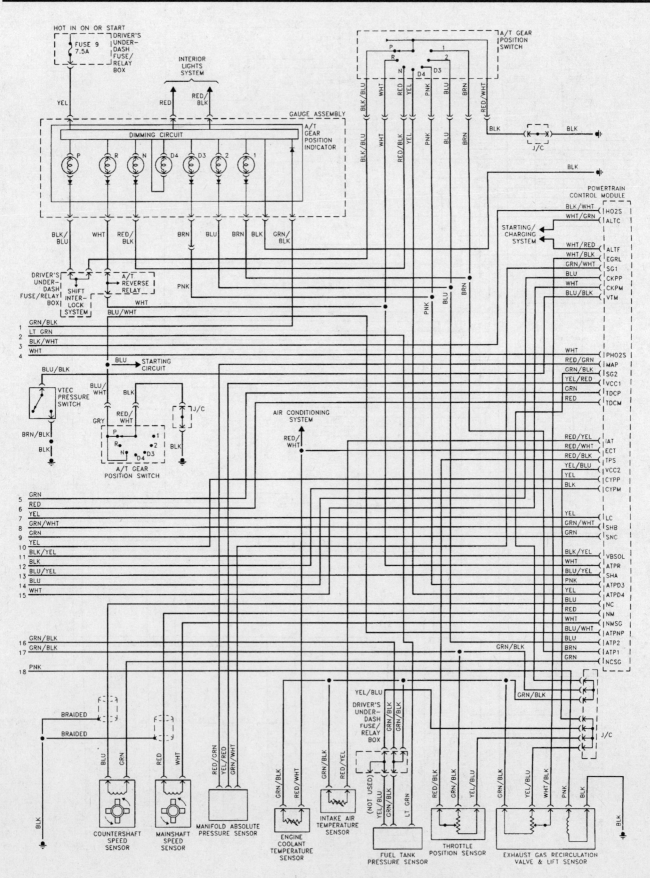

Engine control system - V6 engine (part 3 of 3)

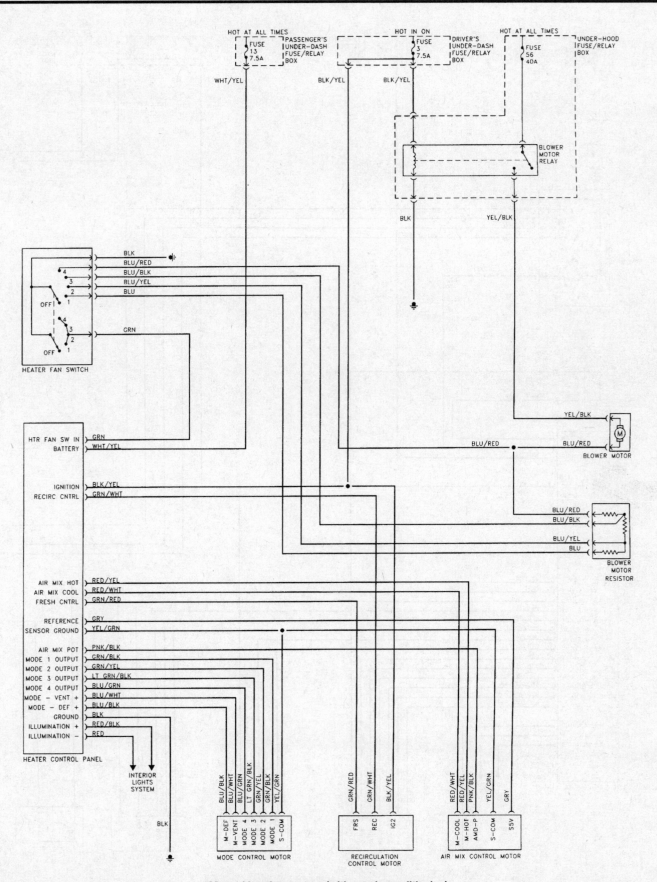

Manual heating system (without air conditioning)

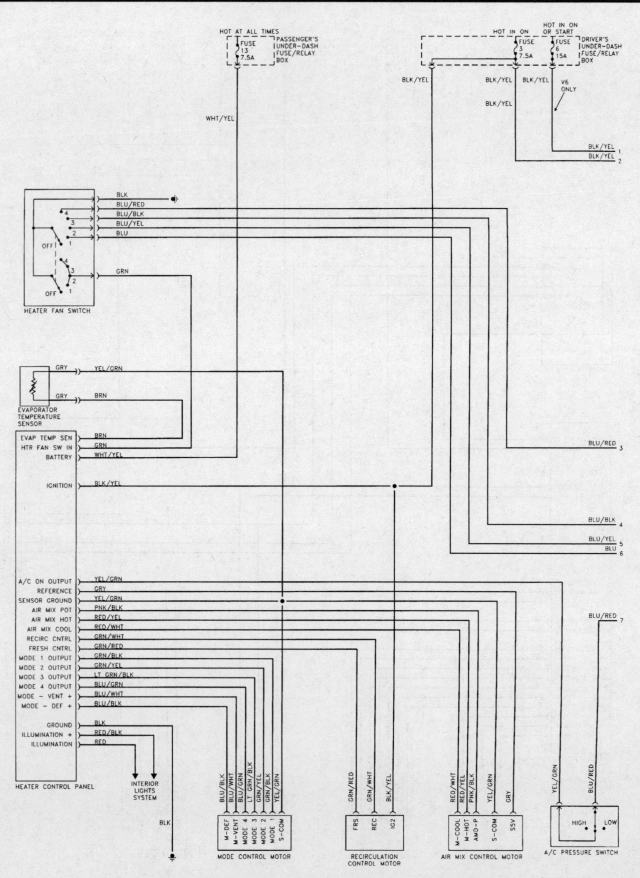

Manual heating and air conditioning system (includes engine cooling) (part 1 of 2)

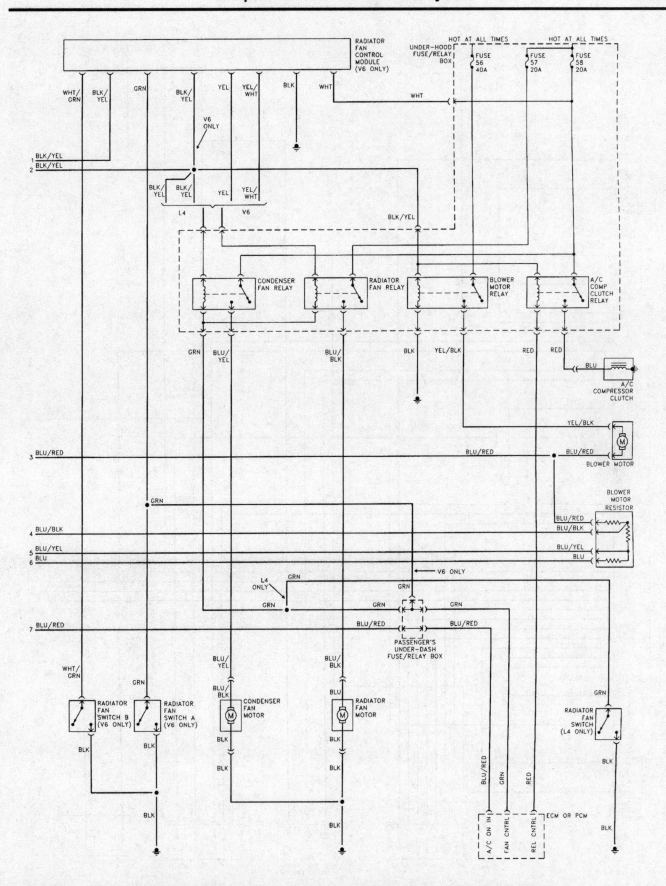

Manual heating and air conditioning system (includes engine cooling) (part 2 of 2)

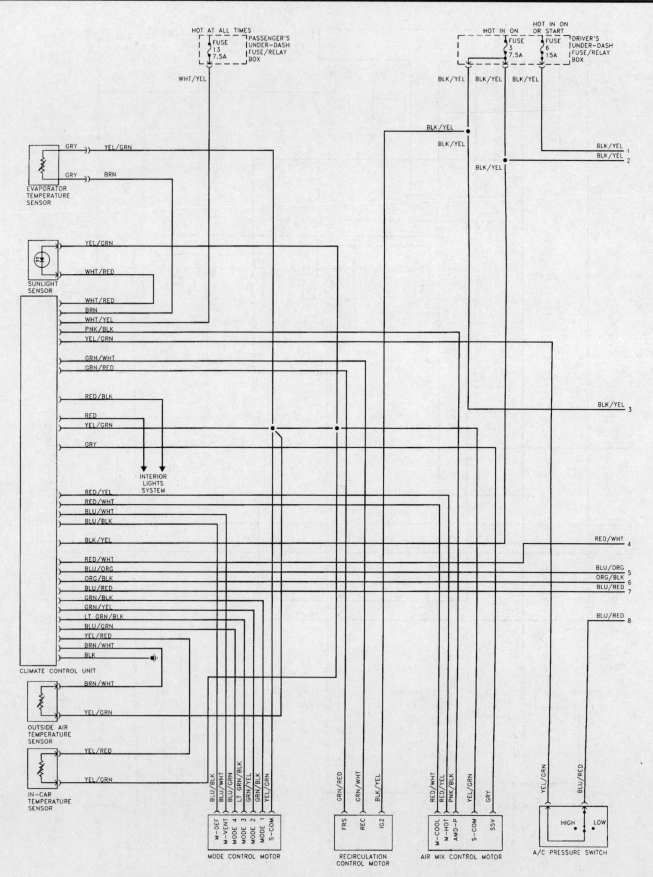

Automatic heating and air conditioning system (includes engine cooling) (part 1 of 2)

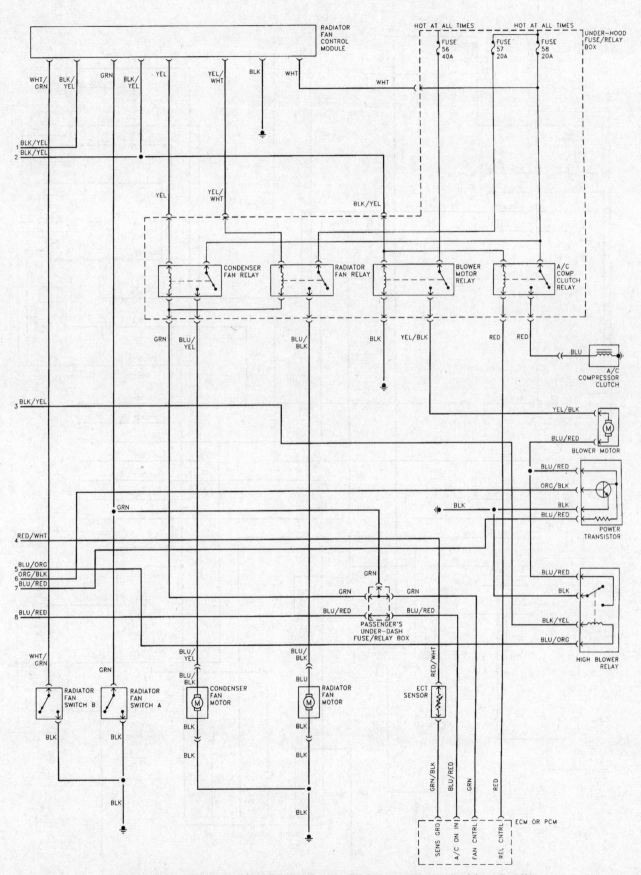

Automatic heating and air conditioning system (includes engine cooling) (part 2 of 2)

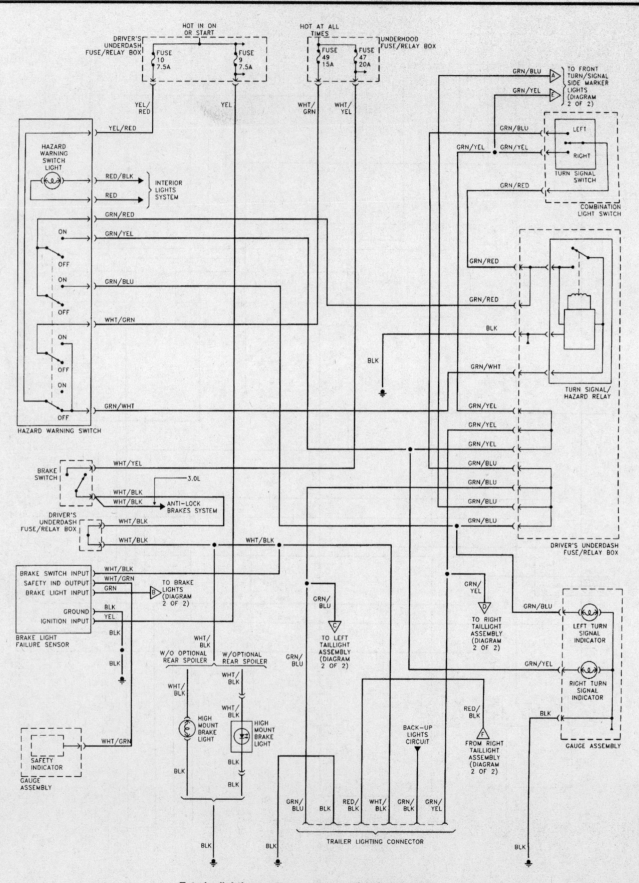

Exterior lighting system - coupe models (part 1 of 2)

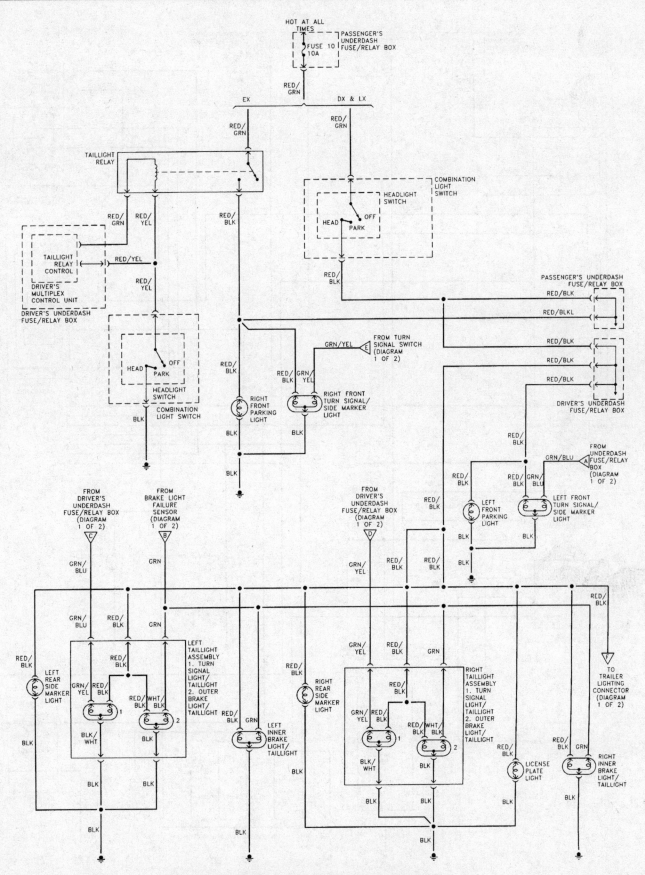

Exterior lighting system - coupe models (part 2 of 2)

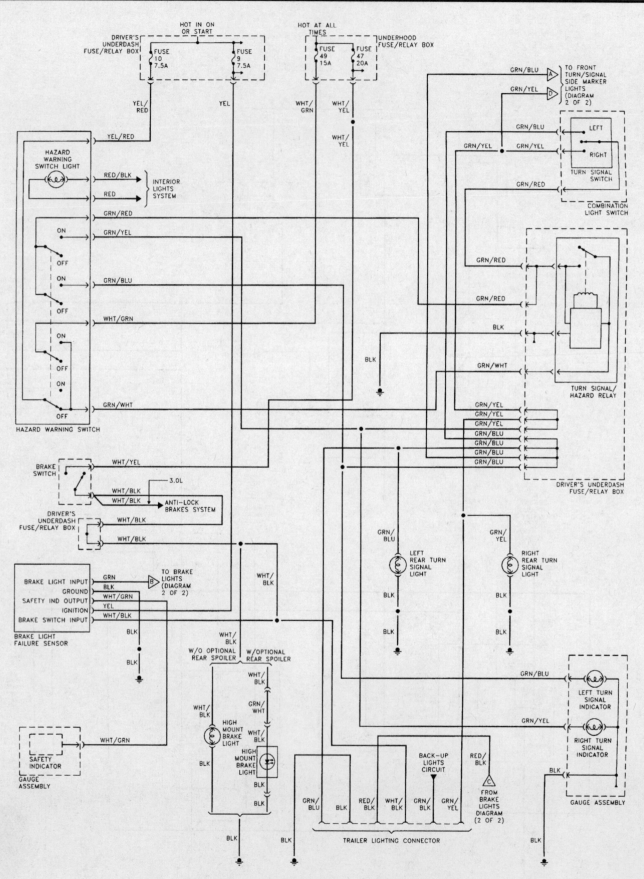

Exterior lighting system - sedan models (part 1 of 2)

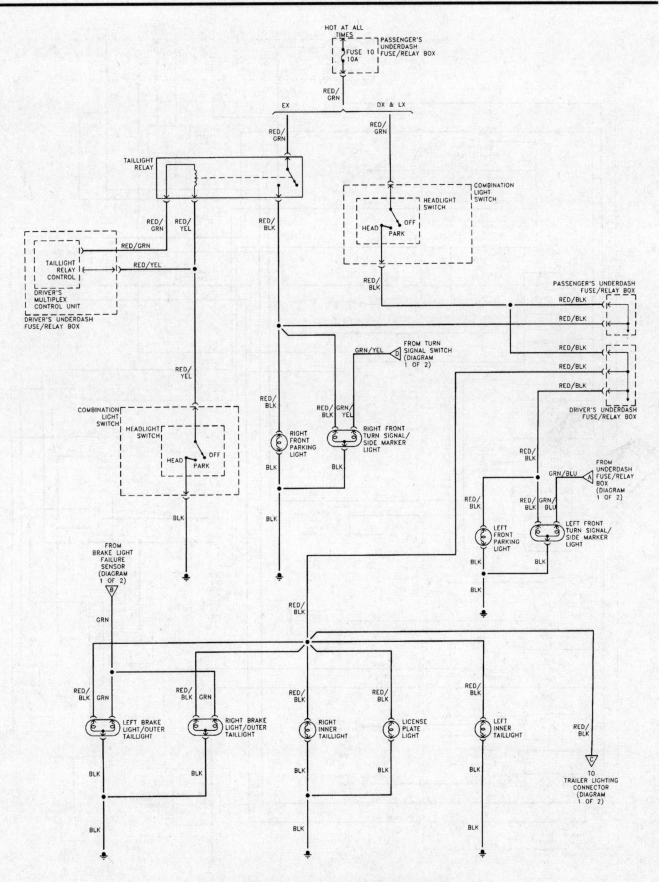

Exterior lighting system - sedan models (part 2 of 2)

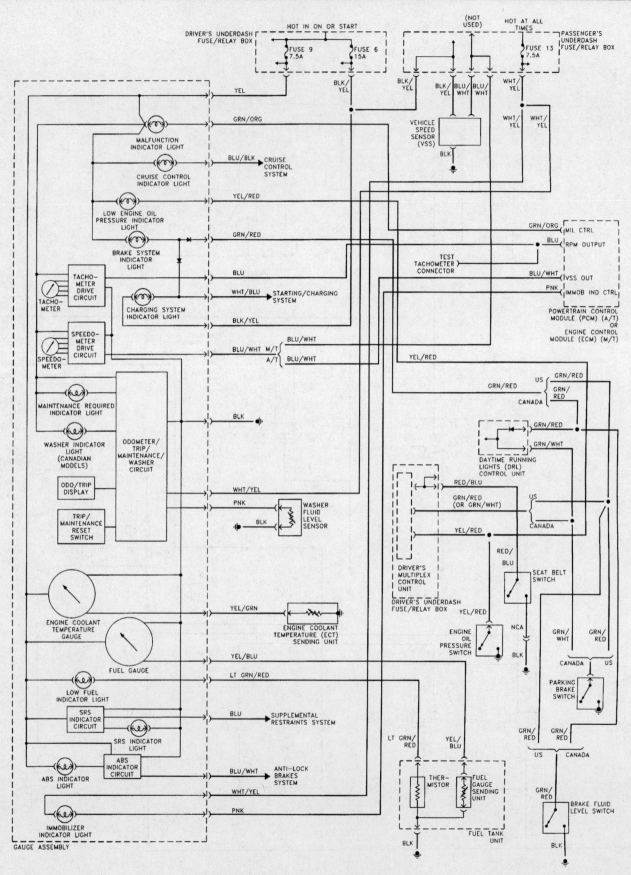

Typical instrument panel warning system

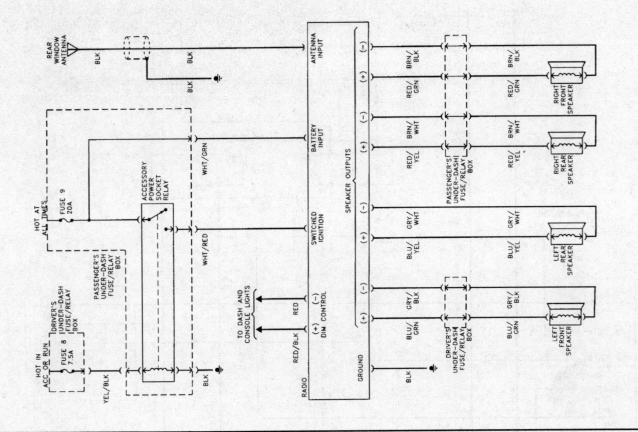

Typical audio system

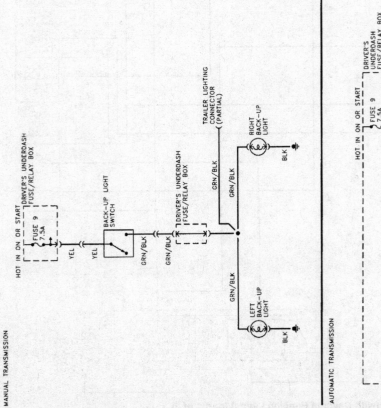

MANUAL TRANSMISSION

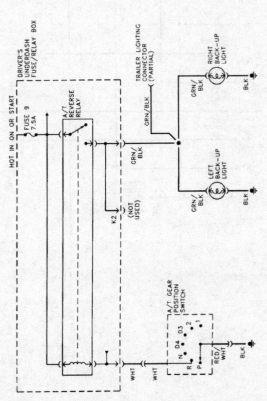

AUTOMATIC TRANSMISSION

Typical backup.light system

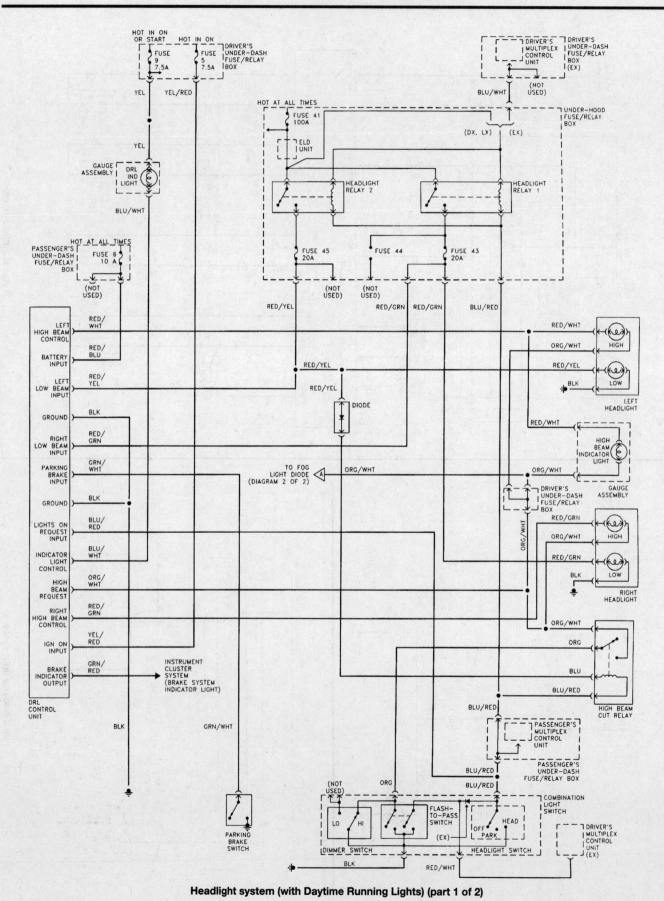

Headlight system (with Daytime Running Lights) (part 1 of 2)

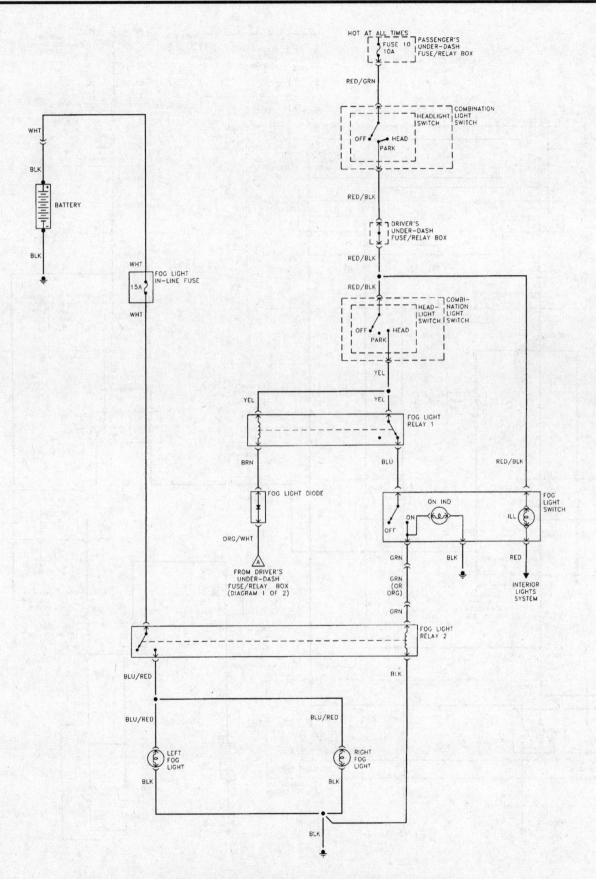

Headlight system (with Daytime Running Lights) (part 2 of 2)

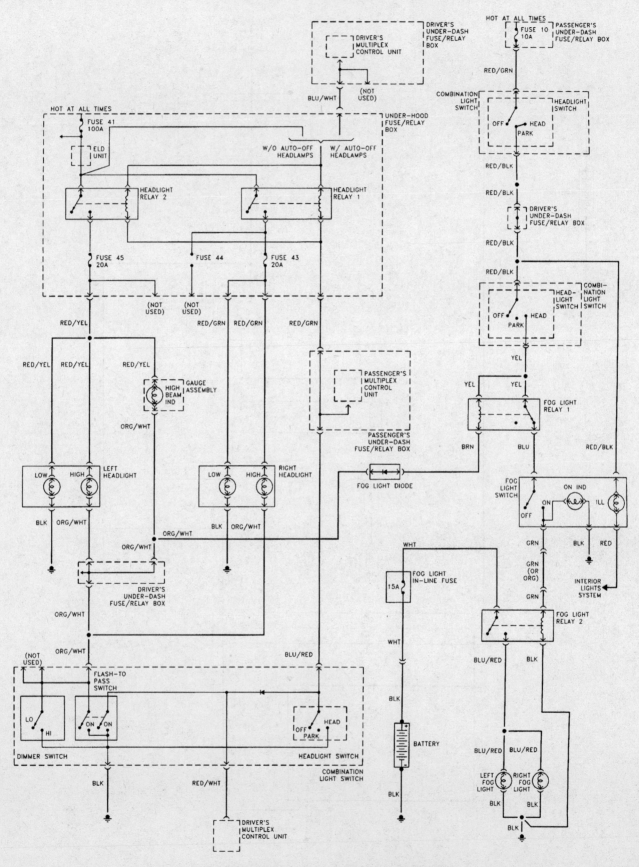

Headlight system (without Daytime Running Lights)

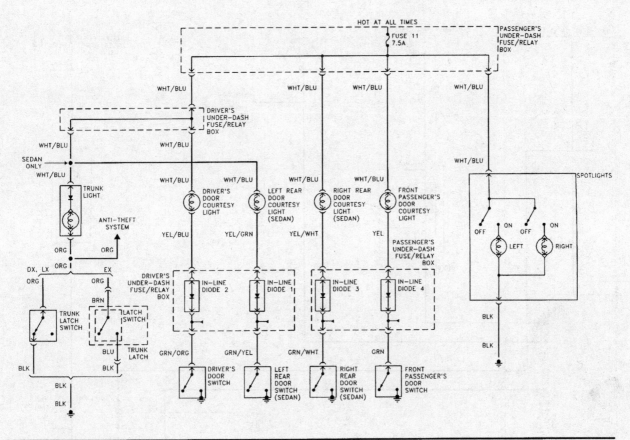

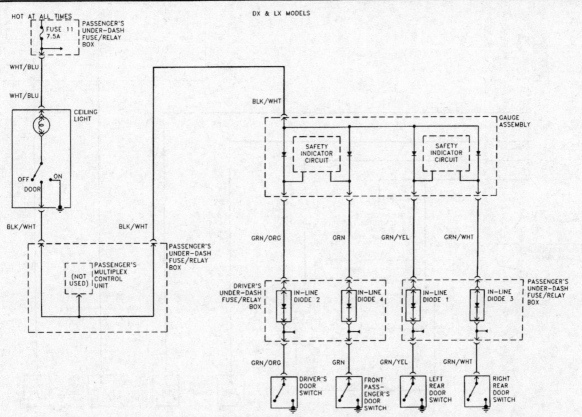

Interior lighting system (part 1 of 3)

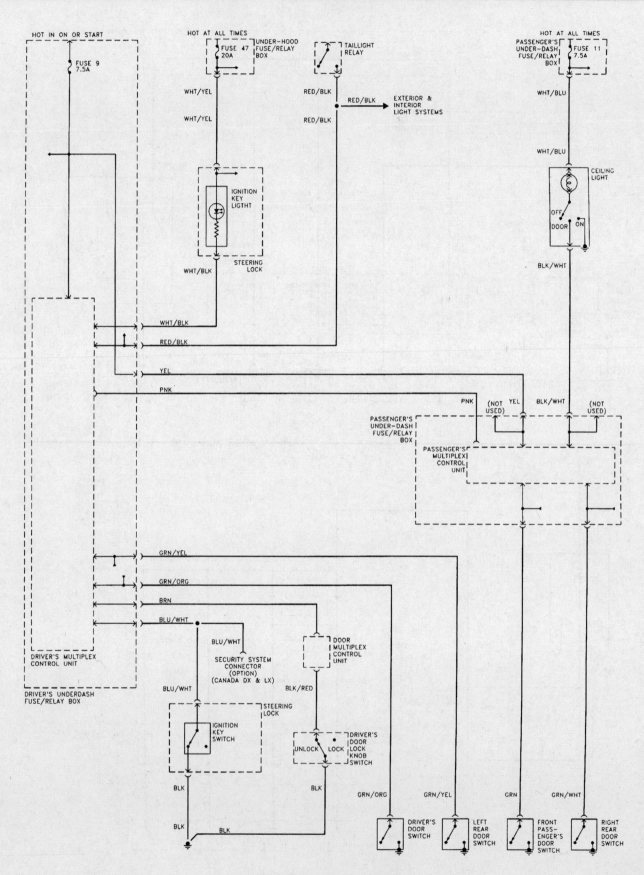

Interior lighting system (part 2 of 3)

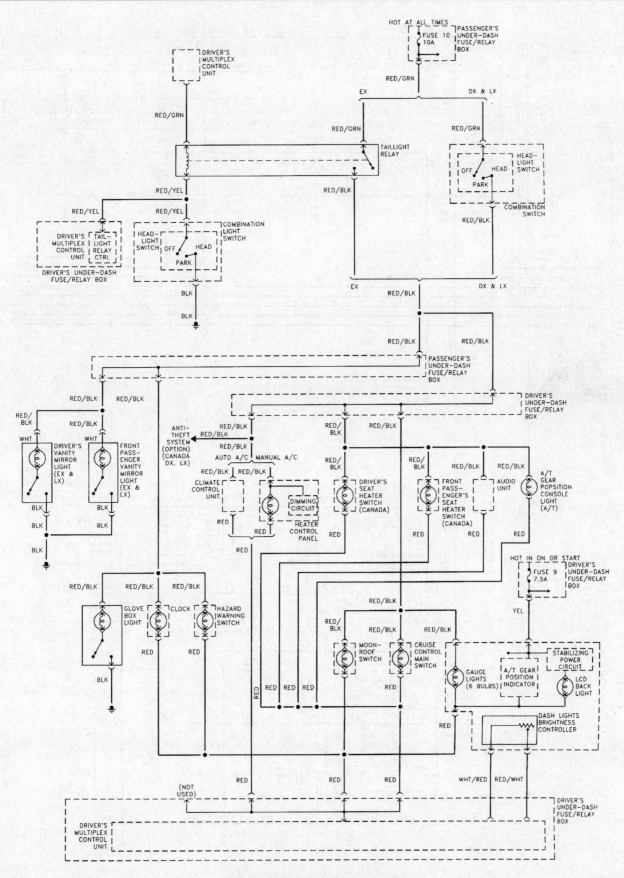

Interior lighting system (part 3 of 3)

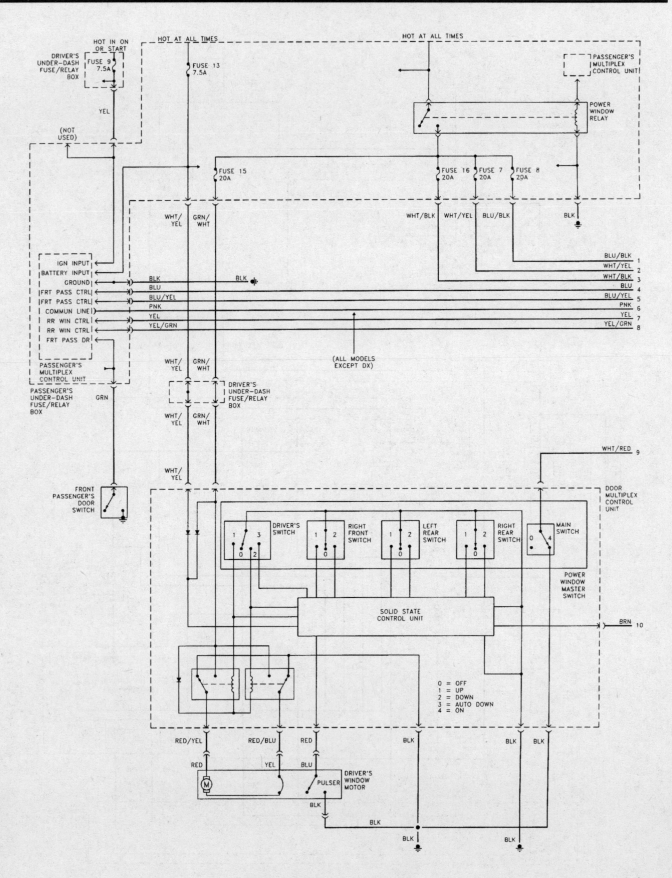

Power window system (part 1 of 2)

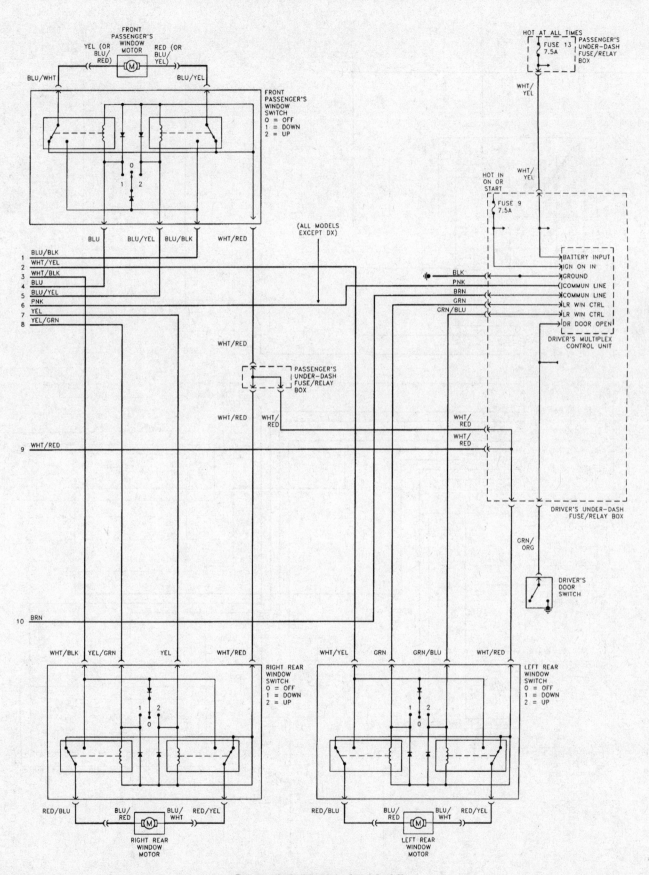

Power window system (part 2 of 2)

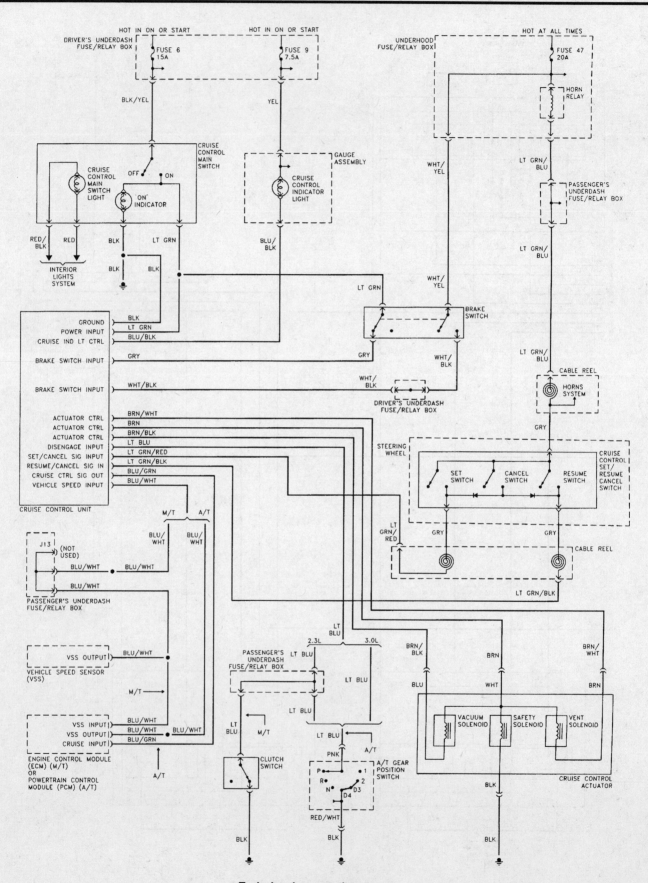

Typical cruise control system

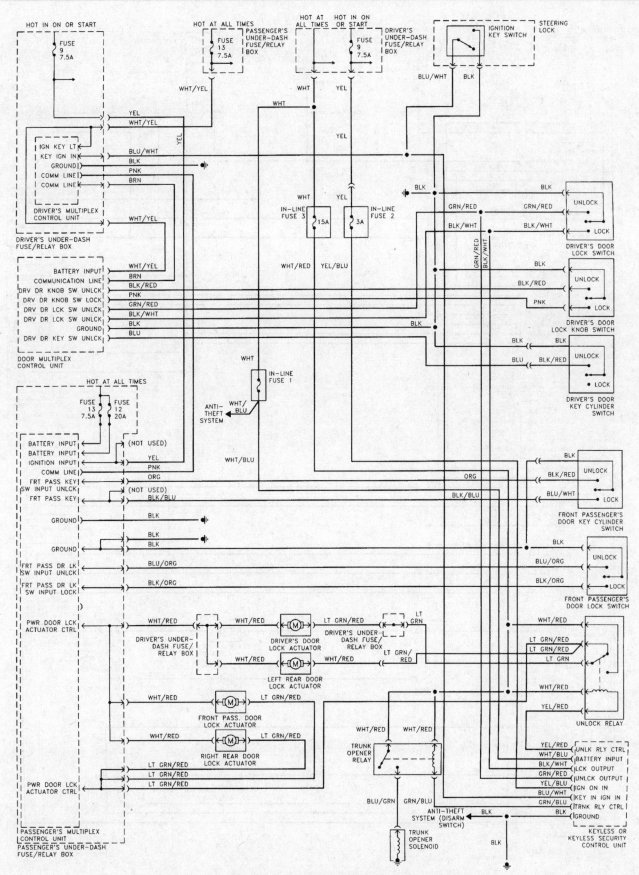

Power door lock system - LX model (with keyless entry system)

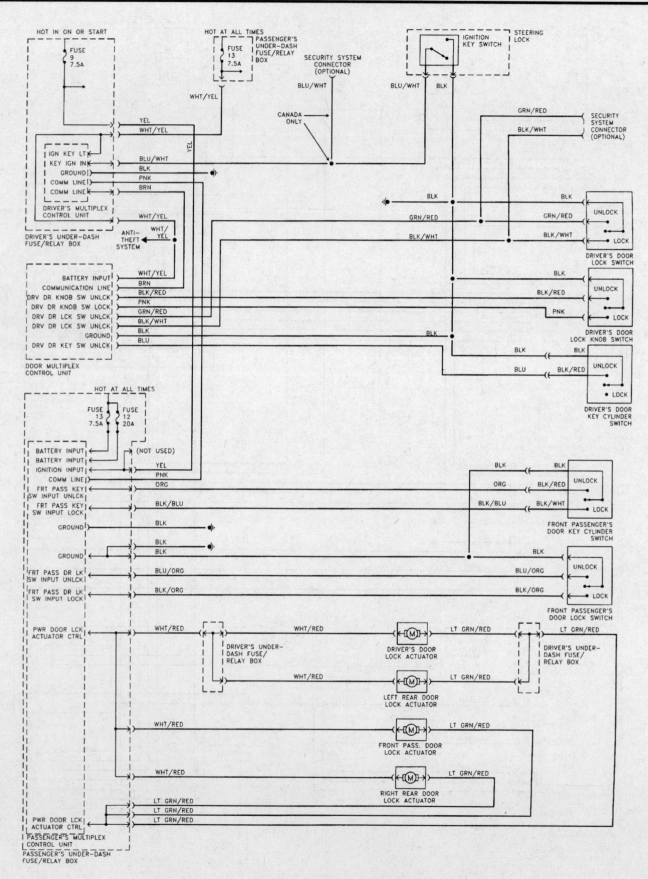

Power door lock system - LX model (without keyless entry system)

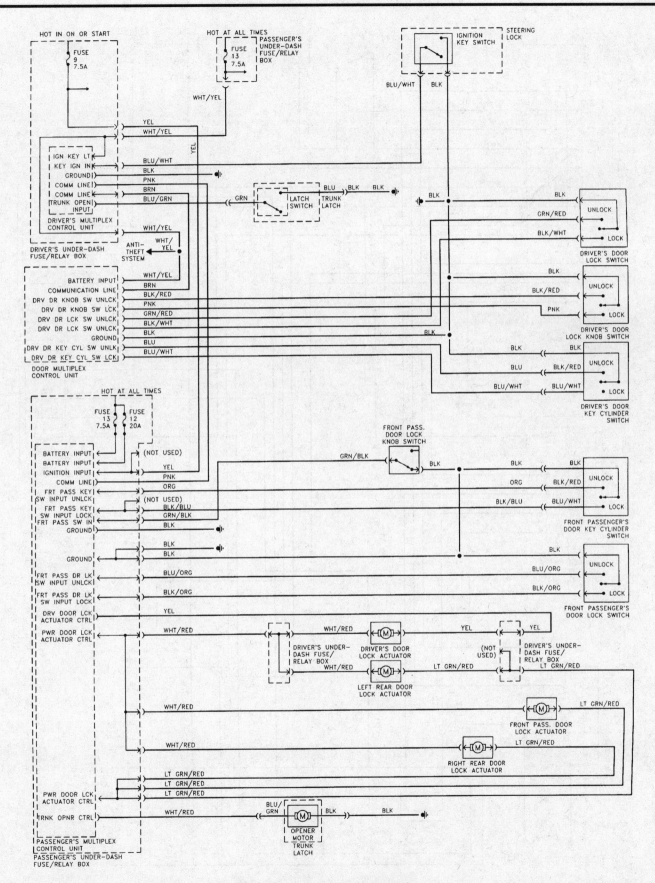

Power door lock system - EX model

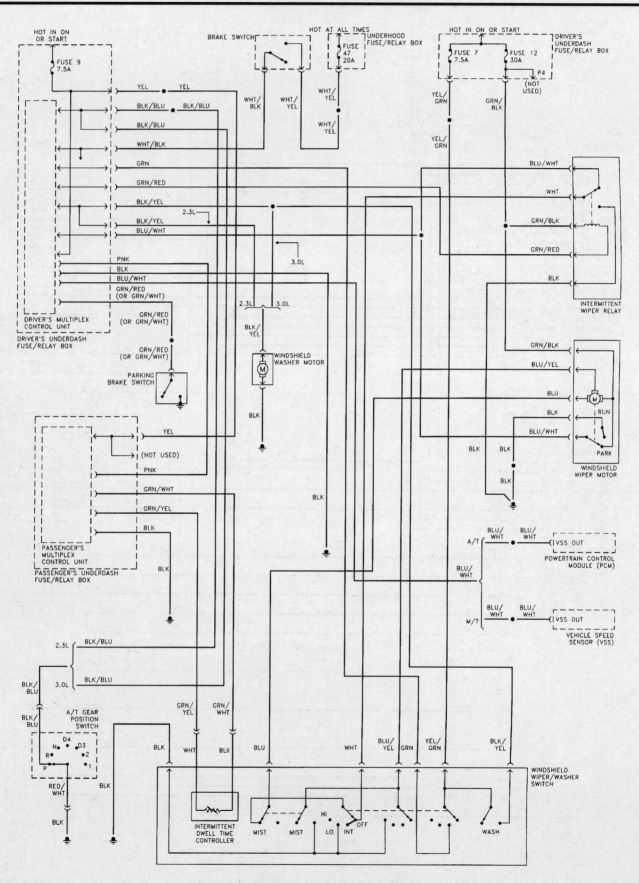

Typical windshield wiper and washer system

Index

Haynes Automotive Manuals

ACURA
- **12020 Integra** '86 thru '89 & **Legend** '86 thru '90
- **12021 Integra** '90 thru '93 & **Legend** '91 thru '95
- **Integra** '94 thru '00 - see HONDA Civic (42025)
- **MDX** '01 thru '07 - see HONDA Pilot (42037)
- **12050 Acura TL** all models '99 thru '08

AMC
- **Jeep CJ** - see JEEP (50020)
- **14020 Mid-size models** '70 thru '83
- **14025 (Renault) Alliance & Encore** '83 thru '87

AUDI
- **15020 4000** all models '80 thru '87
- **15025 5000** all models '77 thru '83
- **15026 5000** all models '84 thru '88
- **Audi A4** '96 thru '01 - see VW Passat (96023)
- **15030 Audi A4** '02 thru '08

AUSTIN-HEALEY
- **Sprite** - see MG Midget (66015)

BMW
- **18020 3/5 Series** '82 thru '92
- **18021 3-Series** incl. Z3 models '92 thru '98
- **18022 3-Series** incl. Z4 models '99 thru '05
- **18023 3-Series** '06 thru '10
- **18025 320i** all 4 cyl models '75 thru '83
- **18050 1500 thru 2002** except Turbo '59 thru '77

BUICK
- **19010 Buick Century** '97 thru '05
- **Century** (front-wheel drive) - see GM (38005)
- **19020 Buick, Oldsmobile & Pontiac Full-size (Front-wheel drive)** '85 thru '05
- **Buick** Electra, LeSabre and Park Avenue; **Oldsmobile** Delta 88 Royale, Ninety Eight and Regency; **Pontiac** Bonneville
- **19025 Buick, Oldsmobile & Pontiac Full-size (Rear wheel drive)** '70 thru '90
- **Buick** Estate, Electra, LeSabre, Limited, **Oldsmobile** Custom Cruiser, Delta 88, Ninety-eight, **Pontiac** Bonneville, Catalina, Grandville, Parisienne
- **19030 Mid-size Regal & Century** all rear-drive models with V6, V8 and Turbo '74 thru '87
- **Regal** - see GENERAL MOTORS (38010)
- **Riviera** - see GENERAL MOTORS (38030)
- **Roadmaster** - see CHEVROLET (24046)
- **Skyhawk** - see GENERAL MOTORS (38015)
- **Skylark** - see GM (38020, 38025)
- **Somerset** - see GENERAL MOTORS (38025)

CADILLAC
- **21015 CTS & CTS-V** '03 thru '12
- **21030 Cadillac Rear Wheel Drive** '70 thru '93
- **Cimarron** - see GENERAL MOTORS (38015)
- **DeVille** - see GM (38031 & 38032)
- **Eldorado** - see GM (38030 & 38031)
- **Fleetwood** - see GM (38031)
- **Seville** - see GM (38030, 38031 & 38032)

CHEVROLET
- **10305 Chevrolet Engine Overhaul Manual**
- **24010 Astro & GMC Safari Mini-vans** '85 thru '05
- **24015 Camaro V8** all models '70 thru '81
- **24016 Camaro** all models '82 thru '92
- **24017 Camaro & Firebird** '93 thru '02
- **Cavalier** - see GENERAL MOTORS (38016)
- **Celebrity** - see GENERAL MOTORS (38005)
- **24020 Chevelle, Malibu & El Camino** '69 thru '87
- **24024 Chevette & Pontiac T1000** '76 thru '87
- **Citation** - see GENERAL MOTORS (38020)
- **24027 Colorado & GMC Canyon** '04 thru '10
- **24032 Corsica/Beretta** all models '87 thru '96
- **24040 Corvette** all V8 models '68 thru '82
- **24041 Corvette** all models '84 thru '96
- **24045 Full-size Sedans** Caprice, Impala, Biscayne, Bel Air & Wagons '69 thru '90
- **24046 Impala SS & Caprice and Buick Roadmaster** '91 thru '96
- **Impala** '00 thru '05 - see LUMINA (24048)
- **24047 Impala & Monte Carlo** all models '06 thru '11
- **Lumina** '90 thru '94 - see GM (38010)
- **24048 Lumina & Monte Carlo** '95 thru '05
- **Lumina APV** - see GM (38035)
- **24050 Luv Pick-up** all 2WD & 4WD '72 thru '82
- **Malibu** '97 thru '00 - see GM (38026)
- **24055 Monte Carlo** all models '70 thru '88
- **Monte Carlo** '95 thru '01 - see LUMINA (24048)
- **24059 Nova** all V8 models '69 thru '79
- **24060 Nova and Geo Prizm** '85 thru '92
- **24064 Pick-ups** '67 thru '87 - Chevrolet & GMC
- **24065 Pick-ups** '88 thru '98 - Chevrolet & GMC

- **24066 Pick-ups** '99 thru '06 - Chevrolet & GMC
- **24067 Chevrolet Silverado & GMC Sierra** '07 thru '12
- **24070 S-10 & S-15 Pick-ups** '82 thru '93, Blazer & Jimmy '83 thru '94,
- **24071 S-10 & Sonoma Pick-ups** '94 thru '04, including Blazer, Jimmy & Hombre
- **24072 Chevrolet TrailBlazer, GMC Envoy & Oldsmobile Bravada** '02 thru '09
- **24075 Sprint** '85 thru '88 & Geo Metro '89 thru '01
- **24080 Vans - Chevrolet & GMC** '68 thru '96
- **24081 Chevrolet Express & GMC Savana** Full-size Vans '96 thru '10

CHRYSLER
- **10310 Chrysler Engine Overhaul Manual**
- **25015 Chrysler Cirrus, Dodge Stratus, Plymouth Breeze** '95 thru '00
- **25020 Full-size Front-Wheel Drive** '88 thru '93
- **K-Cars** - see DODGE Aries (30008)
- **Laser** - see DODGE Daytona (30030)
- **25025 Chrysler LHS, Concorde, New Yorker, Dodge** Intrepid, **Eagle** Vision, '93 thru '97
- **25026 Chrysler LHS, Concorde, 300M, Dodge** Intrepid, '98 thru '04
- **25027 Chrysler 300, Dodge Charger & Magnum** '05 thru '09
- **25030 Chrysler & Plymouth Mid-size** front wheel drive '82 thru '95
- **Rear-wheel Drive** - see Dodge (30050)
- **25035 PT Cruiser** all models '01 thru '10
- **25040 Chrysler Sebring** '95 thru '06, **Dodge** Stratus '01 thru '06, **Dodge Avenger** '95 thru '00

DATSUN
- **28005 200SX** all models '80 thru '83
- **28007 B-210** all models '73 thru '78
- **28009 210** all models '79 thru '82
- **28012 240Z, 260Z & 280Z** Coupe '70 thru '78
- **28014 280ZX** Coupe & 2+2 '79 thru '83
- **300ZX** - see NISSAN (72010)
- **28018 510 & PL521 Pick-up** '68 thru '73
- **28020 510** all models '78 thru '81
- **28022 620 Series Pick-up** all models '73 thru '79
- **720 Series Pick-up** - see NISSAN (72030)
- **28025 810/Maxima** all gasoline models '77 thru '84

DODGE
- **400 & 600** - see CHRYSLER (25030)
- **30008 Aries & Plymouth Reliant** '81 thru '89
- **30010 Caravan & Plymouth Voyager** '84 thru '95
- **30011 Caravan & Plymouth Voyager** '96 thru '02
- **30012 Challenger/Plymouth Saporro** '78 thru '83
- **30013 Caravan, Chrysler Voyager, Town & Country** '03 thru '07
- **30016 Colt & Plymouth Champ** '78 thru '87
- **30020 Dakota Pick-ups** all models '87 thru '96
- **30021 Durango** '98 & '99, **Dakota** '97 thru '99
- **30022 Durango** '00 thru '03 **Dakota** '00 thru '04
- **30023 Durango** '04 thru '09, **Dakota** '05 thru '11
- **30025 Dart, Demon, Plymouth Barracuda, Duster & Valiant** 6 cyl models '67 thru '76
- **30030 Daytona & Chrysler Laser** '84 thru '89
- **Intrepid** - see CHRYSLER (25025, 25026)
- **30034 Neon** all models '95 thru '99
- **30035 Omni & Plymouth Horizon** '78 thru '90
- **30036 Dodge and Plymouth Neon** '00 thru '05
- **30040 Pick-ups** all full-size models '74 thru '93
- **30041 Pick-ups** all full-size models '94 thru '01
- **30042 Pick-ups** full-size models '02 thru '08
- **30045 Ram 50/D50 Pick-ups & Raider and Plymouth Arrow Pick-ups** '79 thru '93
- **30050 Dodge/Plymouth/Chrysler RWD** '71 thru '89
- **30055 Shadow & Plymouth Sundance** '87 thru '94
- **30060 Spirit & Plymouth Acclaim** '89 thru '95
- **30065 Vans - Dodge & Plymouth** '71 thru '03

EAGLE
- **Talon** - see MITSUBISHI (68030, 68031)
- **Vision** - see CHRYSLER (25025)

FIAT
- **34010 124 Sport Coupe & Spider** '68 thru '78
- **34025 X1/9** all models '74 thru '80

FORD
- **10320 Ford Engine Overhaul Manual**
- **10355 Ford Automatic Transmission Overhaul**
- **11500 Mustang '64-1/2 thru '70 Restoration Guide**
- **36004 Aerostar Mini-vans** all models '86 thru '97
- **36006 Contour & Mercury Mystique** '95 thru '00
- **36008 Courier Pick-up** all models '72 thru '82
- **36012 Crown Victoria & Mercury Grand Marquis** '88 thru '10
- **36016 Escort/Mercury Lynx** all models '81 thru '90
- **36020 Escort/Mercury Tracer** '91 thru '02

- **36022 Escape & Mazda Tribute** '01 thru '11
- **36024 Explorer & Mazda Navajo** '91 thru '01
- **36025 Explorer/Mercury Mountaineer** '02 thru '10
- **36028 Fairmont & Mercury Zephyr** '78 thru '83
- **36030 Festiva & Aspire** '88 thru '97
- **36032 Fiesta** all models '77 thru '80
- **36034 Focus** all models '00 thru '11
- **36036 Ford & Mercury Full-size** '75 thru '87
- **36044 Ford & Mercury Mid-size** '75 thru '86
- **36045 Fusion & Mercury Milan** '06 thru '10
- **36048 Mustang V8** all models '64-1/2 thru '73
- **36049 Mustang II** 4 cyl, V6 & V8 models '74 thru '78
- **36050 Mustang & Mercury Capri** '79 thru '93
- **36051 Mustang** all models '94 thru '04
- **36052 Mustang** '05 thru '10
- **36054 Pick-ups & Bronco** '73 thru '79
- **36058 Pick-ups & Bronco** '80 thru '96
- **36059 F-150 & Expedition** '97 thru '09, **F-250** '97 thru '99 & **Lincoln Navigator** '98 thru '09
- **36060 Super Duty Pick-ups, Excursion** '99 thru '10
- **36061 F-150 full-size** '04 thru '10
- **36062 Pinto & Mercury Bobcat** '75 thru '80
- **36066 Probe** all models '89 thru '92
- **Probe** '93 thru '97 - see MAZDA 626 (61042)
- **36070 Ranger/Bronco II** gasoline models '83 thru '92
- **36071 Ranger** '93 thru '10 & Mazda Pick-ups '94 thru '09
- **36074 Taurus & Mercury Sable** '86 thru '95
- **36075 Taurus & Mercury Sable** '96 thru '05
- **36078 Tempo & Mercury Topaz** '84 thru '94
- **36082 Thunderbird/Mercury Cougar** '83 thru '88
- **36086 Thunderbird/Mercury Cougar** '89 thru '97
- **36090 Vans** all V8 Econoline models '69 thru '91
- **36094 Vans** full size '92 thru '10
- **36097 Windstar Mini-van** '95 thru '07

GENERAL MOTORS
- **10360 GM Automatic Transmission Overhaul**
- **38005 Buick Century, Chevrolet Celebrity, Oldsmobile Cutlass Ciera & Pontiac 6000** all models '82 thru '96
- **38010 Buick Regal, Chevrolet Lumina, Oldsmobile Cutlass Supreme & Pontiac Grand Prix (FWD)** '88 thru '07
- **38015 Buick Skyhawk, Cadillac Cimarron, Chevrolet Cavalier, Oldsmobile Firenza & Pontiac J-2000 & Sunbird** '82 thru '94
- **38016 Chevrolet Cavalier & Pontiac Sunfire** '95 thru '05
- **38017 Chevrolet Cobalt & Pontiac G5** '05 thru '11
- **38020 Buick Skylark, Chevrolet Citation, Olds Omega, Pontiac Phoenix** '80 thru '85
- **38025 Buick Skylark & Somerset, Oldsmobile Achieva & Calais and Pontiac Grand Am** all models '85 thru '98
- **38026 Chevrolet Malibu, Olds Alero & Cutlass, Pontiac Grand Am** '97 thru '03
- **38027 Chevrolet Malibu** '04 thru '10
- **38030 Cadillac Eldorado, Seville, Oldsmobile Toronado, Buick Riviera** '71 thru '85
- **38031 Cadillac Eldorado & Seville, DeVille, Fleetwood & Olds Toronado, Buick Riviera** '86 thru '93
- **38032 Cadillac DeVille** '94 thru '05 & **Seville** '92 thru '04 **Cadillac DTS** '06 thru '10
- **38035 Chevrolet Lumina APV, Olds Silhouette & Pontiac Trans Sport** all models '90 thru '96
- **38036 Chevrolet Venture, Olds Silhouette, Pontiac Trans Sport & Montana** '97 thru '05
- **General Motors Full-size Rear-wheel Drive** - see BUICK (19025)
- **38040 Chevrolet Equinox** '05 thru '09 **Pontiac Torrent** '06 thru '09
- **38070 Chevrolet HHR** '06 thru '11

GEO
- **Metro** - see CHEVROLET Sprint (24075)
- **Prizm** - '85 thru '92 see CHEVY (24060), '93 thru '02 see TOYOTA Corolla (92036)
- **40030 Storm** all models '90 thru '93
- **Tracker** - see SUZUKI Samurai (90010)

GMC
- **Vans & Pick-ups** - see CHEVROLET

HONDA
- **42010 Accord CVCC** all models '76 thru '83
- **42011 Accord** all models '84 thru '89
- **42012 Accord** all models '90 thru '93
- **42013 Accord** all models '94 thru '97
- **42014 Accord** all models '98 thru '02
- **42015 Accord** '03 thru '07
- **42020 Civic 1200** all models '73 thru '79
- **42021 Civic 1300 & 1500 CVCC** '80 thru '83
- **42022 Civic 1500 CVCC** all models '75 thru '79

(Continued on other side)

Haynes North America, Inc., 859 Lawrence Drive, Newbury Park, CA 91320-1514 • (805) 498-6703 • http://www.haynes.com

Haynes Automotive Manuals (continued)

NOTE: If you do not see a listing for your vehicle, consult your local Haynes dealer for the latest product information.

42023 Civic all models '84 thru '91
42024 Civic & del Sol '92 thru '95
42025 Civic '96 thru '00, CR-V '97 thru '01, Acura Integra '94 thru '00
42026 Civic '01 thru '10, CR-V '02 thru '09
42035 Odyssey all models '99 thru '10
Passport - see ISUZU Rodeo (47017)
42037 Honda Pilot '03 thru '07, Acura MDX '01 thru '07
42040 Prelude CVCC all models '79 thru '89

HYUNDAI
43010 Elantra all models '96 thru '10
43015 Excel & Accent all models '86 thru '09
43050 Santa Fe all models '01 thru '06
43055 Sonata all models '99 thru '08

INFINITI
G35 '03 thru '08 - see NISSAN 350Z (72011)

ISUZU
Hombre - see CHEVROLET S-10 (24071)
47017 Rodeo, Amigo & Honda Passport '89 thru '02
47020 Trooper & Pick-up '81 thru '93

JAGUAR
49010 XJ6 all 6 cyl models '68 thru '86
49011 XJ6 all models '88 thru '94
49015 XJ12 & XJS all 12 cyl models '72 thru '85

JEEP
50010 Cherokee, Comanche & Wagoneer Limited all models '84 thru '01
50020 CJ all models '49 thru '86
50025 Grand Cherokee all models '93 thru '04
50026 Grand Cherokee '05 thru '09
50029 Grand Wagoneer & Pick-up '72 thru '91
Grand Wagoneer '84 thru '91, Cherokee & Wagoneer '72 thru '83, Pick-up '72 thru '88
50030 Wrangler all models '87 thru '11
50035 Liberty '02 thru '07

KIA
54050 Optima '01 thru '10
54070 Sephia '94 thru '01, Spectra '00 thru '09, Sportage '05 thru '10

LEXUS
ES 300/330 - see TOYOTA Camry (92007) (92008)
RX 330 - see TOYOTA Highlander (92095)

LINCOLN
Navigator - see FORD Pick-up (36059)
59010 Rear-Wheel Drive all models '70 thru '10

MAZDA
61010 GLC Hatchback (rear-wheel drive) '77 thru '83
61011 GLC (front-wheel drive) '81 thru '85
61012 Mazda3 '04 thru '11
61015 323 & Protegé '90 thru '03
61016 MX-5 Miata '90 thru '09
61020 MPV all models '89 thru '98
Navajo - see Ford Explorer (36024)
61030 Pick-ups '72 thru '93
Pick-ups '94 thru '00 - see Ford Ranger (36071)
61035 RX-7 all models '79 thru '85
61036 RX-7 all models '86 thru '91
61040 626 (rear-wheel drive) all models '79 thru '82
61041 626/MX-6 (front-wheel drive) '83 thru '92
61042 626, MX-6/Ford Probe '93 thru '02
61043 Mazda6 '03 thru '11

MERCEDES-BENZ
63012 123 Series Diesel '76 thru '85
63015 190 Series four-cyl gas models, '84 thru '88
63020 230/250/280 6 cyl sohc models '68 thru '72
63025 280 123 Series gasoline models '77 thru '81
63030 350 & 450 all models '71 thru '80
63040 C-Class: C230/C240/C280/C320/C350 '01 thru '07

MERCURY
64200 Villager & Nissan Quest '93 thru '01
All other titles, see FORD Listing.

MG
66010 MGB Roadster & GT Coupe '62 thru '80
66015 MG Midget, Austin Healey Sprite '58 thru '80

MINI
67020 Mini '02 thru '11

MITSUBISHI
68020 Cordia, Tredia, Galant, Precis & Mirage '83 thru '93
68030 Eclipse, Eagle Talon & Ply. Laser '90 thru '94
68031 Eclipse '95 thru '05, Eagle Talon '95 thru '98
68035 Galant '94 thru '12
68040 Pick-up '83 thru '96 & Montero '83 thru '93

NISSAN
72010 300ZX all models including Turbo '84 thru '89
72011 350Z & Infiniti G35 '03 thru '08
72015 Altima all models '93 thru '06
72016 Altima '07 thru '10
72020 Maxima all models '85 thru '92
72021 Maxima all models '93 thru '04
72025 Murano '03 thru '10
72030 Pick-ups '80 thru '97 Pathfinder '87 thru '95
72031 Frontier Pick-up, Xterra, Pathfinder '96 thru '04
72032 Frontier & Xterra '05 thru '11
72040 Pulsar all models '83 thru '86
Quest - see MERCURY Villager (64200)
72050 Sentra all models '82 thru '94
72051 Sentra & 200SX all models '95 thru '06
72060 Stanza all models '82 thru '90
72070 Titan pick-ups '04 thru '10 Armada '05 thru '10

OLDSMOBILE
73015 Cutlass V6 & V8 gas models '74 thru '88
For other OLDSMOBILE titles, see BUICK, CHEVROLET or GENERAL MOTORS listing.

PLYMOUTH
For PLYMOUTH titles, see DODGE listing.

PONTIAC
79008 Fiero all models '84 thru '88
79018 Firebird V8 models except Turbo '70 thru '81
79019 Firebird all models '82 thru '92
79025 G6 all models '05 thru '09
79040 Mid-size Rear-wheel Drive '70 thru '87
Vibe '03 thru '11 - see TOYOTA Matrix (92060)
For other PONTIAC titles, see BUICK, CHEVROLET or GENERAL MOTORS listing.

PORSCHE
80020 911 except Turbo & Carrera 4 '65 thru '89
80025 914 all 4 cyl models '69 thru '76
80030 924 all models including Turbo '76 thru '82
80035 944 all models including Turbo '83 thru '89

RENAULT
Alliance & Encore - see AMC (14020)

SAAB
84010 900 all models including Turbo '79 thru '88

SATURN
87010 Saturn all S-series models '91 thru '02
87011 Saturn Ion '03 thru '07
87020 Saturn all L-series models '00 thru '04
87040 Saturn VUE '02 thru '07

SUBARU
89002 1100, 1300, 1400 & 1600 '71 thru '79
89003 1600 & 1800 2WD & 4WD '80 thru '94
89100 Legacy all models '90 thru '99
89101 Legacy & Forester '00 thru '06

SUZUKI
90010 Samurai/Sidekick & Geo Tracker '86 thru '01

TOYOTA
92005 Camry all models '83 thru '91
92006 Camry all models '92 thru '96
92007 Camry, Avalon, Solara, Lexus ES 300 '97 thru '01
92008 Toyota Camry, Avalon and Solara and Lexus ES 300/330 all models '02 thru '06
92009 Camry '07 thru '11
92015 Celica Rear Wheel Drive '71 thru '85
92020 Celica Front Wheel Drive '86 thru '99
92025 Celica Supra all models '79 thru '92
92030 Corolla all models '75 thru '79
92032 Corolla all rear wheel drive models '80 thru '87
92035 Corolla all front wheel drive models '84 thru '92
92036 Corolla & Geo Prizm '93 thru '02
92037 Corolla models '03 thru '11
92040 Corolla Tercel all models '80 thru '82
92045 Corona all models '74 thru '82
92050 Cressida all models '78 thru '82
92055 Land Cruiser FJ40, 43, 45, 55 '68 thru '82
92056 Land Cruiser FJ60, 62, 80, FZJ80 '80 thru '96
92060 Matrix & Pontiac Vibe '03 thru '11
92065 MR2 all models '85 thru '87
92070 Pick-up all models '69 thru '78
92075 Pick-up all models '79 thru '95
92076 Tacoma, 4Runner, & T100 '93 thru '04
92077 Tacoma all models '05 thru '09
92078 Tundra '00 thru '06 & Sequoia '01 thru '07
92079 4Runner all models '03 thru '09
92080 Previa all models '91 thru '95
92081 Prius all models '01 thru '08
92082 RAV4 all models '96 thru '10
92085 Tercel all models '87 thru '94
92090 Sienna all models '98 thru '09
92095 Highlander & Lexus RX-330 '99 thru '07

TRIUMPH
94007 Spitfire all models '62 thru '81
94010 TR7 all models '75 thru '81

VW
96008 Beetle & Karmann Ghia '54 thru '79
96009 New Beetle '98 thru '11
96016 Rabbit, Jetta, Scirocco & Pick-up gas models '75 thru '92 & Convertible '80 thru '92
96017 Golf, GTI & Jetta '93 thru '98, Cabrio '95 thru '02
96018 Golf, GTI, Jetta '99 thru '05
96019 Jetta, Rabbit, GTI & Golf '05 thru '11
96020 Rabbit, Jetta & Pick-up diesel '77 thru '84
96023 Passat '98 thru '05, Audi A4 '96 thru '01
96030 Transporter 1600 all models '68 thru '79
96035 Transporter 1700, 1800 & 2000 '72 thru '79
96040 Type 3 1500 & 1600 all models '63 thru '73
96045 Vanagon all air-cooled models '80 thru '83

VOLVO
97010 120, 130 Series & 1800 Sports '61 thru '73
97015 140 Series all models '66 thru '74
97020 240 Series all models '76 thru '93
97040 740 & 760 Series all models '82 thru '88
97050 850 Series all models '93 thru '97

TECHBOOK MANUALS
10205 Automotive Computer Codes
10206 OBD-II & Electronic Engine Management
10210 Automotive Emissions Control Manual
10215 Fuel Injection Manual '78 thru '85
10220 Fuel Injection Manual '86 thru '99
10225 Holley Carburetor Manual
10230 Rochester Carburetor Manual
10240 Weber/Zenith/Stromberg/SU Carburetors
10305 Chevrolet Engine Overhaul Manual
10310 Chrysler Engine Overhaul Manual
10320 Ford Engine Overhaul Manual
10330 GM and Ford Diesel Engine Repair Manual
10333 Engine Performance Manual
10340 Small Engine Repair Manual, 5 HP & Less
10341 Small Engine Repair Manual, 5.5 - 20 HP
10345 Suspension, Steering & Driveline Manual
10355 Ford Automatic Transmission Overhaul
10360 GM Automatic Transmission Overhaul
10405 Automotive Body Repair & Painting
10410 Automotive Brake Manual
10411 Automotive Anti-lock Brake (ABS) Systems
10415 Automotive Detailing Manual
10420 Automotive Electrical Manual
10425 Automotive Heating & Air Conditioning
10430 Automotive Reference Manual & Dictionary
10435 Automotive Tools Manual
10440 Used Car Buying Guide
10445 Welding Manual
10450 ATV Basics
10452 Scooters 50cc to 250cc

SPANISH MANUALS
98903 Reparación de Carrocería & Pintura
98904 Manual de Carburador Modelos Holley & Rochester
98905 Códigos Automotrices de la Computadora
98906 OBD-II & Sistemas de Control Electrónico del Motor
98910 Frenos Automotriz
98913 Electricidad Automotriz
98915 Inyección de Combustible '86 al '99
99040 Chevrolet & GMC Camionetas '67 al '87
99041 Chevrolet & GMC Camionetas '88 al '98
99042 Chevrolet & GMC Camionetas Cerradas '68 al '95
99043 Chevrolet/GMC Camionetas '94 al '04
99048 Chevrolet/GMC Camionetas '98 al '09
99055 Dodge Caravan & Plymouth Voyager '84 al '95
99075 Ford Camionetas y Bronco '80 al '94
99076 Ford F-150 '97 al '09
99077 Ford Camionetas Cerradas '69 al '91
99088 Ford Modelos de Tamaño Mediano '75 al '86
99089 Ford Camionetas Ranger '93 al '10
99091 Ford Taurus & Mercury Sable '86 al '95
99095 GM Modelos de Tamaño Grande '70 al '90
99100 GM Modelos de Tamaño Mediano '70 al '88
99106 Jeep Cherokee, Wagoneer & Comanche '84 al '00
99110 Nissan Camioneta '80 al '96, Pathfinder '87 al '95
99118 Nissan Sentra '82 al '94
99125 Toyota Camionetas y 4Runner '79 al '95

Over 100 Haynes motorcycle manuals also available

7-12

Haynes North America, Inc., 859 Lawrence Drive, Newbury Park, CA 91320-1514 • (805) 498-6703 • http://www.haynes.com